THE BUILDINGS OF ENGLAND

BE I I

ESSEX

NIKOLAUS PEVSNER AND
ENID RADCLIFFE

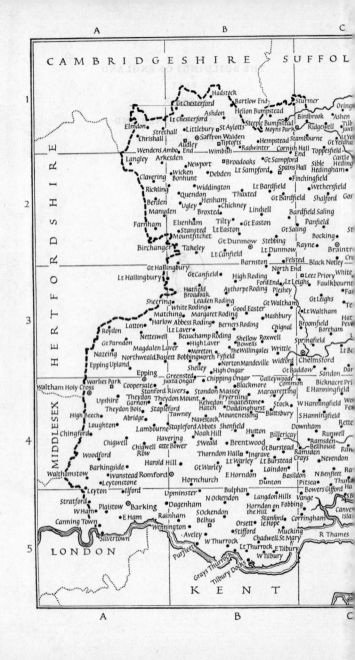

Scale of Miles
0   10

SUFFOLK

N
W E
S

C   D   E

W
rth   Liston
hamp St Paul   Borley
Belchamp Otton
lmer   Belchamp Walter
gthorpe   Middleton
am   Gt Henny
Lamarsh
Twinstead   Alphamstone   R. Stour   Longham   Dedham
Maplestead   Pebmarsh   Boxted   Manningtree
plestead   Mount Bures   Wormingford   Gt Horkesley   Lawford   Mistley   Wrabness   Harwich
ead Colne   Lt Horkesley   Bradfield   Ramsey   Dovercourt
Engaine   White Colne   Ardleigh   Lt Bromley   Wix   Lt Oakley
Earls   Wakes Colne   Chappel   Fordham   W Bergholt   Gt Bromley   Gt Oakley
Colne   R. Colne   Colchester   Elmstead   Beaumont
reshall   Gt Tey   Aldham   Lexden   Greenstead   Lt Bentley   cum Moze
Pattiswick   Lt Tey   Marks   Stanway   Hythe   Frating   Gt Bentley   Tendring
geshall   Tey   Copford   Berechurch   Wivenhoe   Weeley   Thorpe   Kirby
well   Lt Coggeshall   Easthorpe   E Donyland   Alresford   le Soken   le Soken   Walton on
hall   Feering   Birch   Layer   Fingringhoe   Thorrington   Lt Clacton   the Naze
Kelvedon   Messing   de la   Abberton   Brightlingsea   Gt Clacton   Frinton on Sea
Rivenhall   Inworth   Haye   Langenhoe   Gt Holland
am   Gt Braxted   Layer Marney   Peldon   St Osyth
Lt Braxted   Tollesbury Knights   Gt Wigborough   E Mersea   Clacton on Sea
Gt Totham   Salcott   Virley   Lt Wigborough
Wickham Bishops   Tolleshunt D'Arcy   W Mersea
Lt Totham   Goldhanger   Tollesbury
am   Langford   Heybridge
Maldon   R. Blackwater   Bradwell juxta Mare
Beeleigh Abbey
mer   Mundon   Steeple   Tillingham
Purleigh   Dengie
Latchingdon   Mayland   Asheldham
ries   Cold Norton   Althorne   Southminster
abridge   Creeksea   Burnham on Crouch
S Fambridge   Canewdon   R. Crouch
Ashingdon   Paglesham
y Hawkwell   Lt Stambridge   Foulness
ochford   Gt Stambridge
Sutton   Burling
Eastwood   Shopland   Lt Wakering
eigh   N Shoebury   Gt Wakering
Southend   Southchurch
on Sea   S Shoebury

ESSEX

C   D   E

See note at foot of Contents page

THE BUILDINGS OF ENGLAND

Essex

BY

NIKOLAUS PEVSNER

★

REVISED BY

ENID RADCLIFFE

PENGUIN BOOKS

Penguin Books Ltd, Harmondsworth, Middlesex
U.S.A.: Penguin Books Inc., 3300 Clipper Mill Road, Baltimore 11, Md
AUSTRALIA: Penguin Books Pty Ltd, Ringwood, Victoria

—

First published 1954
Second edition 1965

Copyright © Nikolaus Pevsner, 1954

—

Made and printed in Great Britain
by William Clowes and Sons, Limited, London and Beccles
Gravure plates by Harrison & Sons Ltd
Set in Monotype Plantin

TO THE
MOUATS OF SHENFIELD

*

CONTENTS

*

*

The map on pages 2–3 shows all those places, whether towns, villages or isolated buildings, which are the subject of separate entries in the text. The index on pages 471 ff. gives references to the map square in which each place mentioned will be found.

FOREWORD

Essex has proved a difficult county to deal with. For one thing, though it is large, its character and the quality and number of its works of architecture did not seem to justify devoting to it two volumes of this series. That meant – for reasons purely dependent on the organization of work on the series – longer journeys than should be undertaken. There are limits to one's receptivity to the charms and the little problems of village churches and farmhouses, and if they are exceeded, concentration and indeed enthusiasm become an effort. I hope that the effort has been successful.

There was however an additional complication. The Royal Commission on Historical Monuments has published its inventory of all monuments prior to 1714. The inventory is in four volumes and is naturally far more detailed than this book of mine can be, which, moreover, had to go up to the present day in its registering and discussing of buildings and works of art. That meant a great deal of picking and choosing from the Royal Commission volumes – choosing what to see and what to include. For even the seeing of all that the Royal Commission mentions was utterly impossible, at least as far as farmhouses and cottages go. There are about 750 houses of dates earlier than the Reformation. And as regards everything earlier than 1714, individual parishes exist with over a hundred houses noted by the Commission (e.g. Felsted). So I had to try to gather from the descriptions of the Commission what would be specially interesting to me and the users of this book. In the course of the work, however, I found that I had perhaps been too restrictive, and so Mrs Michaelson, who had already helped so much in previous volumes, had to come to the rescue and add more. These additions, indicating houses not personally known to me, are given in brackets with an RC. With their help this volume certainly contains far more on farmhouses than I could, in the blissful ignorance caused by the absence of Royal Commission inventories, put into the volumes on, say, Nottinghamshire or Derbyshire.

The preparation of this book otherwise, that is all the reading and extracting of literature other than the Royal Commission volumes, has been done by Miss G. Bondi as carefully and intelligently as her preparation of earlier volumes. The entries on prehistoric and Roman antiquities are by Mr Jon Manchip White. I owe Dr Bondi and Mr Jon Manchip White a great deal of gratitude. I am very grateful also to Mr H. de C. Hastings for the generous loan of a caravan to make work and life comfortable, to my wife for coping with the propelling of an object of such magnitude, and for planning the day-to-day programmes of our researches, to Mary Mouat for creating and keeping all the files connected with the travelling and the ensuing correspondence, to all those rectors and vicars who have taken trouble in answering my questions on their churches, and to all owners or tenants of houses who have either had the kindness to show me round or answer what enquiries I had. I owe it to them to make it quite clear here that inclusion of a house in this volume does not mean that it is open to the public. Especially, many questions had to be directed to libraries. Here I wish to thank in particular Mr F. G. Emmison, the County Archivist, Mr A. C. Edwards and Mr Robin Hull who have taken the trouble to check proofs, Mr K. J. Lace, the County Librarian, Mr A. T. Austing, Mr John O'Leary, Mr W. Pollitt, and Mr E. R. Gamester, the Librarians of Colchester, Dagenham, Southend-on-Sea, and West Ham respectively, and also the Librarians of Chelmsford, Romford, and Saffron Walden and Mr Alec Hunter of Thaxted. Mr Cecil Farthing and Mrs Parry of the National Buildings Record have been as helpful as ever – what would a topographical writer be without that admirable organization? Also as helpful as ever has been the Ministry of Housing and Local Government which has a statutory duty to compile lists of buildings of architectural or historical interest. They have once more given me access to unpublished lists and much other information selected by the Chief Investigator and his staff. Wherever I have relied entirely on these lists, I have inserted MHLG. To continue with the pleasant subject of help received, Mr Rex Wailes provided me with information on windmills in Essex and photographs of plates 3 and 23. Then there is the list of Victorian churches by Mr H. S. Goodhart-Rendel (here quoted as GR) and the list of Victorian stained glass by Sir Thomas Kendrick (here quoted as TK). Mr Goodhart-Rendel and Sir Thomas Kendrick have once more allowed me to make full use of these. As a newcomer amongst indispensable tools for the topographer, Mr Rupert Gunnis's 'Dictionary of British Sculptors' must be most warmly welcomed. It is a prodigiously full catalogue of the work of sculptors between 1660 and 1851. I could for the first time make full use of it for this volume although only after I had completed my travels. Mr Gunnis therefore kindly answered a number of supplementary questions which I took the liberty of putting to him. My gratitude to them for the tedious and extensive work involved is greater than I can say.

For information on Hatfield Broad Oak and for the photograph appearing on plate 20b, I have to thank Mr H. J. Melliss; for permission to use the photographs on plates 24b and 32, the Reynolds-Stephens's Trustees (Mr Allan Howes and Mr John Durham); for permission to use the photograph of the Harvey monument (plate 38), Mr Geoffrey Keynes and Mr Percy Hennell; for the photograph on plate 64, Mr Frederick Gibberd.

As in the preceding volumes of this series I have made a point of seeing everything myself. One exception has already been referred to. Another is the interiors of many minor Georgian houses. Major houses I have seen save one or two. The principle of inclusion is the same as in counties already published: all churches prior to 1800, selected nineteenth- and twentieth-century churches (selected as a rule for reasons of what seemed to me their architectural value), selected secular buildings from the beginning to the present day, all church furnishings worth recording, but few house furnishings, all pictures and sculpture in churches but not in houses, hardly any moats, of which there are so many in Essex, no church bells, not all worthwhile church doors and church chests, few coffin-lids with crosses or foliated crosses, all church plate before 1714, and a selection from the eighteenth century.

It is easy to explain these principles, but hard to make them work. A book of this kind is bound to remain inadequate and faulty however much trouble one may take over checking. I shall therefore be most grateful to all users for drawing my attention to errors and omissions.

Winter, 1953–4

FOREWORD TO THE SECOND EDITION

This second edition is an improvement on the first in that many mistakes have been eliminated and that steps have been taken to include buildings erected since 1954, the date of the first edition. The mistakes were corrected, to a small degree thanks to my own second thoughts, but to a very large degree thanks to letters received from users. Among the most comprehensive were those of John Bensusan Butt, P. G. M. Dickinson, V. Howlett, Ian Lowe, H. V. Molesworth Roberts, David Morgan, N. C. S. Motley, D. M. Palliser, E. S. Phillips, H. Richman, G. Spain, Alec Clifton-Taylor, and J. Elsden Tuffs. I am infinitely grateful to them all. As for new buildings, I had collected as much evidence as I could, but I also wrote to the librarians of Barking and Barkingside, Brentwood, Chelmsford, Chigwell, Chingford, Clacton-on-Sea, Colchester, Dagenham, Harwich, East Ham, Epping, Hornchurch, Ilford, Leyton, Loughton, Maldon, Romford, Saffron Walden, Southend-on-Sea, Tilbury, Upminster, Waltham Holy Cross, Wanstead, and Woodford, and in their answers they not only told me of buildings newly erected, but also of old buildings demolished, and they put right many further errors. Special thanks must go to Mr L. Helliwell and his staff for their contributions to the revision of the section dealing with Southend-on-Sea. I must also thank Miss Nancy Briggs, Arthur C. Edwards, and F. G. Emmison of the Essex Record Office, D. T.-D. Clarke, Curator of the Colchester Museum, M. Maybury, Barking Borough Architect, F. G. Southgate, Walthamstow Borough Architect, J. T. Smith, Dr H. M. Taylor, and Miss M. E. Weaver. In addition Mr Frederick Gibberd and his staff rewrote Harlow New Town nearly completely and Mr A. B. Davies Basildon New Town. Mr Derek Simpson comprehensively revised the introduction and gazetteer referring to prehistoric and Roman remains.

What with all this help and with our own corrections, changes between the first and this edition amount to several hundred. Even so, the changes cannot be of the same standard as the information packed into the first edition. The reasons are practical and personal, and it may be just as well to admit them. Had I treated all the new data as they would be treated in a completely new volume, this would have meant an extra long journey and more extra work than I could spare without endangering the work on future volumes. I do think that the publication of these future volumes is worth more than perfection for a second edition.

The shortcomings are, as far as I can see, these. Essex is still treated according to its boundaries before the creation of the Greater London Council. Re-assessments are not undertaken (except in the one case of Audley End). Few actual omissions are remedied, because I could not, merely on the strength of letters received, make up my mind, while not on the spot, whether they were serious or not. Thus e.g. I would include now in a new volume more Victorian churches than I did twelve or fifteen years ago. New buildings are as a rule just listed and not evaluated. The most important exceptions are Harlow and Basildon New Towns, as just mentioned.

The intricate and thankless job of all the necessary correspondence and re-editing was done by Mrs Enid Radcliffe, and I can assure readers that she has done it extremely well, and would have done it yet better if I had been able to widen her terms of reference. As it is, she has not really had a fair chance.

However, in spite of all these limitations, the new edition should serve its purpose. It will have few errors and many new facts, and as long as users are ready not to ask for more, they will, I hope, be satisfied.

Christmas 1964   NIKOLAUS PEVSNER

INTRODUCTION

ESSEX is not as popular a touring and sight-seeing county as it deserves to be. People say that is due to the squalor of Liverpool Street Station. Looking round the suicidal waiting-room on platform 9 and the cavernous left luggage counters behind platforms 9 and 10, I am inclined to agree. But there are other more palpable reasons militating against a just appreciation of Essex. The county is too big and varied to be taken in as one. With its 978,000 acres it is the eighth in England, ranking behind Yorkshire, Lincolnshire, Devon, Norfolk, Northumberland, Lancashire, and Somerset. In variety of character it must be given precedence over most of them. It comprises first of all an area of solidly built-over East London large enough to house over one million people, then the loosely built outer suburbs of London towards Epping Forest and the new housing estates towards Southend, the mud flats of the estuary of the Thames, with their cement and other works, the coast with more estuaries (Crouch to Burnham, Blackwater to Maldon, Stour to Harwich and Manningtree), with large, flat islands (Canvey, Foulness, Mersea), fishing and sailing harbours (Wivenhoe, Brightlingsea, etc.), and seaside resorts ranging in character from uproariously popular Southend to select Frinton. The landscape behind the coasts is not specially attractive. It is a little like Holland, but less peaceful, because everywhere affected by suburban-looking housing. But it is in fact still genuinely rural, and it can be said that farmers in Essex will be found occupied with farming more often than in most other counties. This applies to the plain as well as to the rolling country round Dunmow and up north towards the Stour and the Suffolk border. Here there are more trees and patches of wood, and the scenery has a great deal of pretty charm. Grand it is nowhere. The large forests of the past have all gone, except for the 5,500 acres to which Epping Forest is now reduced. With its spreading old hornbeams it is still a blessing so near London. But one must not try to impress the foreigner from the United States or indeed Germany by taking him to a Forest which one can cross on foot in one direction in an hour and in the other in three and a bit.

Villages vary just as much as scenery. Spectacular village

greens are rare. The largest is that of Great Bentley, the prettiest perhaps that of Writtle; except of course for Finchingfield I which, with its pond and bridge and little ascending street leading to the church, is justly celebrated. The less concentrated centre of Wethersfield can compete in village charm with Finchingfield.

Big towns do not exist in Essex, save for what Dickens calls London-over-the-Border. The river Lea is no longer a boundary between the East End of London, of the county of London, and Stratford, Leyton, Leytonstone, Walthamstow, West Ham, East Ham, and so on. These boroughs are not on the whole slummy, but they are mostly inhabited by the poorer classes, and to the eye they are exceedingly drab. Yet neither parks nor open spaces are lacking, and the green belt on their E border towards Woodford and Wanstead is indeed a great blessing. In the Middle Ages all these places had been villages. They became London only in the C19, at the time of the worst, wholly unplanned housing development. Their population now has begun to decrease – the process familiar from the London East End. Walthamstow, Leyton, West Ham, and East Ham had a population of 696,000 in 1931; they have now (1961) 466,000. Equally familiar is the parallel process of a sudden alarming growth further out, drawing villages and rural districts into the suburban net of London: to the E Ilford in the last thirty years has gone up from 131,000 to 178,000, Romford from 38,000 to 115,000, Hornchurch from 39,000 to 131,000. To the NE Chingford had 22,000 inhabitants in 1931, it has over 46,000 now. The corresponding figures for Chigwell are 16,000 and 61,000. Yet Chigwell is still – no doubt not for long – the first real village one reaches in leaving London in that direction. The first real towns with lives of their own are Epping and Chipping Ongar to the NE, Romford to the E. But far beyond Ilford the L.C.C. had begun, after the First World War, to stretch out its housing estates. Becontree, a dormitory, not a town, houses more than 100,000 Londoners, and Harold Hill, begun after the Second World War, seems in danger of growing to a similar size under similar conditions.

Southend, to most people's surprise, is the largest town of Essex outside the orbit of London. Yet with its 166,000 inhabitants it is not a big town, and so one can say that one of the characteristic features of Essex is the absence of any really big industrial city. Chelmsford, the county town, has some important industrial enterprises, but remains in its centre surprisingly quiet and human, a Georgian more than a Victorian town. The seaside places of Essex on the other hand are decidedly C19 in their character, though remarkably varied, Walton of 1820–30, Clacton mid-Victorian, Frinton late Victorian and later. Colchester is without doubt the town of the greatest architectural importance, as a whole as well as in its individual buildings.

What is most impressive at Colchester, more impressive than in any other town in England, is the continuity of its architectural interest. It began before the time of the Romans and lasted through to the C18. But to understand this continuity it will now be necessary first to go back to the beginnings of human history in Essex and follow the districts of the present county from the Old Stone Age to the departure of the Romans. On the whole – with the exception of Colchester – the PREHISTORY of Essex is visually disappointing. Its situation at the SE corner of Britain was favourable to cultural influence and settlement from the adjacent areas of the continent, but its heavy clay soils and the dense oak woods these must have supported produced an uninviting environment for primitive agriculturalists. More favourable were the coastal regions and the lands bordering the Thames. The lightly forested gravels in the latter area appear to have attracted numerous settlers, although subsequent cultivation has obliterated almost all surface indications of their presence. In recent years intensified gravel digging, in conjunction with the increasing use of aerial reconnaissance, have greatly augmented the number of known sites and finds.

The earliest human settlement of the region is represented by a series of edged and pointed flake tools of flint forming an industry which takes its name from the type site at Clacton. The makers of these tools, which may be dated c. 400,000 B.C., were followed at a later stage in the glacial period by groups manufacturing Acheulean hand axes. These tools have been found in a number of gravel deposits in the county, the most recent being a fine series from a quarry at Purfleet.

Among the Mesolithic groups who crossed to Britain by the land bridge which still linked it with the main continental land mass at the end of the last glaciation, two distinct strains can be recognized: the Maglemoseans, with their barbed bone and antler points and heavy flint industry, including axes, and the Sauveterrians, characterized by small geometric flint blades or microliths. The development of the axe by the first group is a reflection of the gradual spread of forest conditions as the climate became warmer after the retreat of the ice. Evidence of the activities of the Sauveterrians has been found in the Colne valley, and of a mixed group of Sauveterrians and Maglemoseans in the Essex greensands.

The first farming communities settled in Britain in the middle of the fourth millennium B.C., and their pottery has been found associated with a circular, ditched enclosure at Rainham (excavated in 1963 and since destroyed by gravel quarrying), but in a context which suggests that the area was among the last in s Britain to be colonized by these peoples. Numerically more important are finds of later Neolithic cultures – the coarse bowls of the Peterborough culture richly ornamented with cord, bone, and other impressions, and the bucket-shaped vessels of the Rinyo-Clacton culture with its associated flint equipment which appears to owe much to Mesolithic traditions. Essex has again produced the type site for the s form of this latter culture. The ground stone axes, manufactured from rock outcrops at Graig Llwyd in North Wales, occurring generally as surface finds in the county, may be attributed to the trading activities of these later Neolithic groups. Secondary Neolithic pottery and artefacts have been found on the 'Lyonesse surface' off the Essex coast, which has been examined in the area of Clacton, Dovercourt, and elsewhere. Before this Lyonesse surface disappeared beneath the sea in a subsidence c.1800 B.C., groups of Beaker folk had settled on it. The comparative rarity of Beaker material is surprising in view of the county's proximity to the Low Countries from which these people migrated to Britain.

Evidence of settlement in the Bronze Age (1600–500 B.C.) is again marked by little in the way of surviving structural remains. A continuance of Secondary Neolithic potting tradition is reflected in the form and decoration of the Early Bronze Age collared urns, and this Neolithic element can also be traced in the later bucket urns decorated with applied cordons and finger-tip impressions. A more exotic form is represented by the contemporary vessels of globular form, in some cases with perforated lugs, which have no parallel among earlier native wares, and must represent fresh incursions from the continent. These urns are generally found grouped in flat cremation cemeteries on the coastal belt and on the gravel areas of river valleys (e.g. Ardleigh; Bocking; Colchester). The latter part of the Bronze Age is also marked by an increasing abundance of metal objects and by a reorganizing of the distributive side of the industry. To this period belong the great hoards of scrap metal such as that from the parish of Hatfield Broad Oak. Among the fragmentary objects from this hoard were the ring handles of a bronze cauldron, evidence of the increasing continental links which are an aspect of the period.

The first iron-using peoples appear to have settled in the county in the C4. Their Iron Age A (Hallstatt) culture is associated with small isolated farmsteads (e.g. Linford). The pottery at Linford suggests some influence from Iron Age B (La Tene) settlers, but the next major movement of peoples took place c.100 B.C., when Belgic (Iron Age C) groups began to settle the region. In the fifty years preceding this settlement there must have been small-scale landings of Belgae, judging by the distribution of gold coins of this period minted on the continent and found in the lands bordering the Thames Estuary. At the beginning of the C1, however, these coins began to be struck in Britain, and contemporaneously with them other aspects of Belgic culture, notably cremation burials, appear. At the time of Julius Caesar's campaigns in 55 and 54 B.C., Essex lay within the tribal territory of the Trinovantes, the most powerful tribe in southern Britain. Caesar established friendly relations with this tribe and undertook to provide protection from their neighbours in the W, the Catuvellauni. Once this protection was removed, however, the Trinovantes were soon overwhelmed by the Catuvellauni, who, under their great leader, Cunobelin, annexed the whole of south-east England. Cunobelin established his new capital at Colchester, which he named Camulodunum, after Camulos, the war god of the Catuvellauni. This tribal capital in no way resembled the later towns of Roman Britain in appearance. Within the twelve square miles of territory enclosed by the great defensive earthworks of the Lexden Dykes there was room not only for the many circular and rectangular timber-framed huts of the tribesmen, but also for their cattle and local industries such as potting. If it did not resemble a town in form, however, Camulodunum did share many of the functions of a town in that it was an administrative centre for the tribal area, had coin mints, and served as the commercial focus of the area. The choice of site appears to have been conditioned by both strategic and economic reasons. The rivers Colne and Roman provided a readily defensible area large enough to contain the court of a Belgic king and his followers, and also provided suitable water and grazing land for their cattle. It was ideally situated for communication with other areas of East Anglia to the N, W, and S, and the later Roman roads which radiate from Colchester must in part have followed earlier prehistoric trackways. Finally the Colne provided a port for trade with the continent. The exports of slaves, hunting dogs, corn, and hides could all be provided in the surrounding territory, and much of this trade with the continent must have been by the Colne. In return came wine, pottery, and glass, and the princely tombs of the period, notably that beneath the great barrow at Lexden which may be the burial of Cunobelin himself, mark the increasing Romanization of the Catuvellauni in the years preceding the Roman occupation.

The first ROMAN action in the county appears to have been the occupation of Camulodunum, which Claudius entered to receive the submission of eleven native kings. The existence of a fort at this period before the foundation of the *colonia* in A.D. 49 has not yet been proved by excavation, although the tombstones clearly attest military occupation. Supplies for this force were probably unloaded at Fingringhoe, where traces of a Claudian port have been found. The foundation of the *colonia* was followed by a wave of unrest and complaints against dispossessions and the heavy cost of the new imperial cult, whose most outstanding monument was the Temple of Claudius. These are the reasons given by Tacitus for the participation of the Trinovantes in the great revolt of the Iceni in A.D. 61, when Boudicca's followers destroyed Camulodunum and massacred its inhabitants. The new *colonia* which rose from the ashes of the town sacked by Boudicca appears to have occupied the same area as its predecessor. It was among the first of the towns of Roman Britain to be provided with walled defences in the second half of the C2. The rigid adherence to a geometric arrangement of streets and houses is more apparent here than in many other Romano-British towns, and the hundred or more mosaic pavements which have been found attest the wealth and sophistication of its inhabitants.

The degree of Romanization of the countryside varied with the varying geological and geographical conditions in the county. The coastal belt in the E and SE appears to have been little altered from prehistoric times. The most notable features in this area are the Red Hills, low mounds varying from ½ to 30 acres in area, composed of burnt earth and containing fragments of large, coarsely made, trough-shaped vessels. The domestic pottery also found in these mounds varies from Early Iron Age to C4 Roman wares. The remains are thought to represent the debris of salt panning. The small round huts of these coastal dwellers, little altered from prehistoric times, have been found at several sites along the coast and estuary (e.g. Tilbury). The majority of villas in the county lie within ten miles of Colchester, although there is a small but important concentration in the valley of the Stort. As there was no suitable building stone in the county, many of the villas would be constructed largely of wood, and in some cases what were thought in the C19 to be small stone-built villas are in fact probably the bath suites of much larger establishments of timber. Other aspects of the Romanization of the county are pottery kilns, again concentrated in the Colchester area (e.g. Billericay; Halstead), and tile kilns at Alphamstone and Theydon Garnon.

In the C3 the activities of Saxon pirates again made military action necessary and a series of Saxon Shore forts were established in East and South-East England. The fort at Bradwell is the only example of this category of defensive work in Essex. Finds from it suggest that occupation continued into the C5.

On the departure of the Eagles in the C5 the cultural history of Essex remained substantially the same as it had been from time immemorial.

The incoming East Saxons gravitated naturally towards the districts which had been successfully farmed by the Romano-British agriculturalists. They could hardly be blamed for leaving central and southern Essex severely alone. There is nevertheless some slight evidence of pagan Saxon occupation of those pockets of land along the coast which had been inhabited from the earliest times. The occupation is most marked in the vicinity of Southend and Shoeburyness. The Saxon inhabitants of Essex, unenvied possessors of an unattractive domain, seem to have been awarded the inferior social status of their Iron Age forebears, the Trinovantes. It was in Saxon times that great Camulodunum was allowed to decay, to become a dead city. The natives of Britain had never taken kindly to the civic regime imposed on them by the urban-minded Romans, and as soon as the Legions sailed away, they reverted to a predominantly rural and loosely organized pattern of social life. Camulodunum, which the Saxons called Colchester, disappears from the stage of history, and is not even so much as mentioned in any Saxon source until the C10.

Meanwhile, the earliest SAXON building which survives in Essex can be dated considerably earlier. It is the church of St Peter's at Bradwell, built, we can say with every probability, 4b c.654. It consists almost entirely of Roman brick and other Roman materials. In type it belongs to the Kentish or South-East English group. It had originally an apse and a tripartite chancel arch or screen, and also probably *porticus* or side chambers on the l. and r. But most Saxon churches were no doubt of timber. Essex was in the Middle Ages widely wooded, and if any one feature is characteristic of the county as against all others right through to the time of the Reformation, it is the importance of timber in church architecture. So it is happily fitting that the only surviving medieval English timber church is in Essex, Greensted. It is built of oak-logs split vertically in halves and set vertically. Its date is 1013.* The other Saxon churches of Essex also belong to the last fifty years before the Conquest, and so at this point a few general remarks on medieval church architecture in the county may be useful.

In accordance with the size and variety of the county is the variety of BUILDING MATERIALS. In the south-east walls are most often of Kentish rag, in the east of brown septaria and that curious conglomerate puddingstone, in the north-west of flint and pebble rubble. Knapped flint and flushwork decoration belong of course to the East Anglian border, but go as far s as for instance St Osyth. The making of bricks in England seems to have started in Essex, and earlier than many people realize. Little Coggeshall has c 13 home-made bricks, 1¾ to 2 in. thick, Copford, c.1300 at the latest, a brick pier inside, and c 14 brick appears at and near Colchester. At Dengie (c 14) the colour of the brickwork is so pale that one can speak of an example of yellow bricks. In the late Middle Ages brick became the favourite material in ecclesiastical as well as secular architecture, wherever a rich man wanted to make a display. Timber however was not wholly displaced in the county until long after the end of the Middle Ages. Timber roofs, it is true, are not as spectacular as in Suffolk and Norfolk, but the timber towers of Essex fully deserve more detailed comment, and this will be provided later. Timber church porches are also a feature of some importance, and as for domestic building, timber-framing remained the accepted local technique, in spite of the inroads made by brick.

Now to return to the historical survey of building in Essex, Saxon stone churches of the c 11 or fragments of such are far
13a from common. Hadstock is the most interesting case, where the nave as well as the transepts with their arches towards the nave are preserved, and a doorway complete with door. Otherwise there are Inworth, Chickney, and Strethall (with a mid c 11 chancel arch), the w towers of Holy Trinity Colchester (with a
5a triangular head to its doorway) and of Little Bardfield, and odd windows in a few other places. Harold's abbey church of Waltham does not survive. Sculptured stones are extremely rare.

* Possibly much earlier, in the light of recent investigations. See note on p. 215.

The only one of some merit is the fragment of a cross-shaft at Barking.

The NORMANS must have inherited from the Romans in some obscure way the respect for Colchester. For here William erected a keep larger than any other in Europe. It belongs to the type known as hall-keeps, i.e. the type of the White Tower in London, and had, likewise, a chapel with an apse projecting beyond the square walls and subdivisions of the main inner area into divers chambers. Of the more familiar type of the tower-keep Castle Hedingham of c.1135, the stronghold of the de Veres, Earls of Oxford, is perhaps the most impressive example in the whole of England. The other castles of Essex are small (Saffron Walden for example) and mostly only surviving by their mounds or mottes (Pleshey, Chipping Ongar, Great Canfield, Great Easton, Rayleigh, Stansted Mountfitchet). The largest medieval churches of Essex were monastic churches. The county had not possessed a cathedral until in 1913 Chelmsford was raised to cathedral status. The grandest surviving monastic fragments are the complete nave of Waltham, dating from the early C12, and the magnificent ruin of the nave of St Botolph, Colchester, of the end of the C11. Both have massive circular piers, but Waltham is much more richly decorated, while St Botolph still has the grim bareness of the Early Norman style. The w front of St Botolph is specially English in that its twin towers are placed outside the aisles. The same was done at Colne Priory, which was begun about 1100–5. Of the original E ends of Waltham and St Botolph nothing is known. At Colne it had five staggered apses, and the same ending has been excavated at the Benedictine nunnery church of Barking, a church 300 ft long. The nave of Waltham is 90 ft, that of St Botolph 108.

Barking Abbey was one of the most famous of nunnery churches of England. Altogether Essex was a county abounding in MONASTIC FOUNDATIONS. Benedictine nuns were also at Castle Hedingham (no remains) and Wix, Benedictine monks at St John's Colchester (only the gatehouse survives), Earls Colne, Hatfield Peverel, Hatfield Broad Oak, and Takeley, Cluniac Benedictines at Prittlewell (founded c.1110), Stanesgate, and Little Horkesley (early C12). But the most powerful order in the county were the Augustinians, canons not monks. St Botolph Colchester was their first house in England. It was followed by Little Dunmow (founded 1106), St Osyth (c.1120), and, smaller, Berden, Bicknacre, Blackmore, Latton, Thoby (Mountnessing), Thremhall, Tiptree, and (from 1177) Waltham. The newcomers amongst orders of the C12 were the Cistercian monks and the Premonstratensian canons, of the C13 the friars. Cistercian houses in Essex were Stratford Langthorne (1134–5), Little Coggeshall (c.1140), and Tilty (1153); the Premonstratensians are represented by Beeleigh (c.1180, which moved here from Great Parndon). Of Little Coggeshall and Tilty the *capellae extra muros* remain, of Beeleigh the chapter house and dormitory, of Prittlewell the refectory, of St Osyth one corridor apart from the early C16 abbot's mansion and the large gatehouse. No friars' architecture survives, though it is known that the Franciscans had a settlement at Colchester, the Carmelites at Maldon, the Crutched Friars at Colchester.

Compared with monastic churches other Norman remains in Essex are all minor – with one exception: the parish church of Castle Hedingham which was under the special patronage of the de Veres up at the castle. It is 125 ft in length and belongs to the 15a transitional style of the second half of the C12. The nave is provided with aisles separated by alternatingly circular and octagonal piers; the chancel has a straight E end with a fine group of windows including a wheel-window (which is a rarity in England). The tower stood at the W, but has been replaced by a later tower. The most impressive Norman W tower is now at Corringham, broad and massive in shape. Others survive at Stambourne, Finchingfield, Felsted, and so on. A speciality of the county are 7 round towers. Lamarsh, Great Leighs, and Broomfield are C12 examples, Bardfield Saling and Pentlow are as late as the C14. The existence of former round towers has also been proved at Arkesden, Birchanger, South Ockendon, and West Thurrock. Textbooks explain their introduction by the absence of good local building stone for corner-pieces, and that may well be true; for if Norman builders used Roman bricks so extensively for quoins and door and window surrounds, the reason was certainly that they had nothing equally hard available.

The majority of surviving Norman churches in Essex are of very simple plan, just a nave and chancel (Chipping Ongar and South Shoebury, Southend-on-Sea), or a nave and apse (Easthorpe), or a nave, narrower chancel, and apse (Copford, East 5b Ham, Great and Little Braxted, Hadleigh, Pentlow, etc.). Langford is unique in England for having a W apse, a German custom. Copford and Great Clacton are almost unique for having had tunnel-vaulted naves (but cf. Chepstow, Monmouthshire). All these churches are small, and for parish churches with aisles there seems to have been as yet little demand. Arcades or indications of arcades remain at Blackmore, Great Tey, and Rainham. In other cases where more space was desired, naves were made remarkably wide. Such is the case at Great Clacton, Great Waltham, High Easter, St Mary Maldon, and Southminster. The usual plan for a larger Norman parish church however was cruciform: nave, crossing, transepts, and chancel. In these cases the tower would be placed above the crossing. A specially big example is Great Tey. Others are or were Boreham, Fyfield, Great Easton, Hatfield Peverel, Mount Bures, and Wakes Colne. The W walls of Norman churches, where they are not hidden by W towers, have occasionally a nice grouping of windows, including circular ones (Blackmore, Copford, Faulkbourne).

Of Norman details not much need be said. There are no specially spectacular doorways. What there is has occasionally prettily carved columns with zigzag, spiral, or similar motifs (Belchamp Otton, Elsenham, Great Clacton, Margaret Roding, Middleton, South Ockendon). Lintels are often curved (Chadwell, Chigwell, High Ongar, Margaret Roding, Orsett, Stansted 6 Mountfitchet) and tympana often decorated with geometrical all-over patterns such as diapers (Chigwell, Elsenham, Great Canfield, High Ongar, Margaret Roding, South Weald, Stansted Mountfitchet). There is only one Norman tympanum in the whole county which has figure carving, at Birchanger, and that has no more than one humble and incompetently rendered little lamb.

For the later C12 Castle Hedingham church has already been mentioned. By far the most important work, the huge E extension of Waltham, begun, it seems, in 1177, has disappeared entirely. The same alternation of circular and octagonal piers as at Hedingham exists at East Tilbury and Felsted* (which has also some ornamental details in common with Hedingham).

The C13 was not an age of great activity in Essex, except for the completion of the *novum opus* at Waltham. The church was consecrated in 1242. But no major work in the EARLY ENGLISH style survives in the county. Transepts exist or have existed at Berden, Great Chesterford, Great Sampford, and Newport. At St Osyth and Leez Priory they are provided with E aisles. Good Easter has a chancel of c.1230–40 with much enrichment inside, Berden an even richer chancel of c.1260. Windows at first were lancets, but by 1260 (Berden etc.) lancets are coupled, and pierced 16a

---

* Continued in the C13 at Braintree. The remaining piers of Little Dunmow Priory make one regret the destruction of the rest of the late C12 work 15b there.

circles or cusped circles placed above them. Bar tracery does not occur so early. But by the early C14 it had developed into forms heralding in their wilfulness and illogicality the Decorated style to come (Gestingthorpe, Great Dunmow, Great Sampford). Clerestories occasionally have quatrefoil windows (Horndon-on-the-Hill).* Piers are usually circular and have moulded capitals, but stiff-leaf foliage occurs quite often and is occasionally of excellent quality (Berden, Stisted, etc.). Other pier shapes are rare (quatrefoil Saffron Walden, Wimbish; quatrefoil with four shafts in the diagonals Radwinter; circular with four attached shafts St Osyth; circular with eight attached shafts St Osyth). The double piscina at Barnston may in addition be noted. It is of the type of Jesus and St John's Chapels at Cambridge, i.e. with two intersected round arches. Finally towers. Here the only references necessary are to Maldon, which has that unique conceit, a triangular tower, and to Grays Thurrock with a C13 tower in transeptal position. That disposes of the Early English style.

As to the DECORATED, it can be seen in all its somewhat un-
17 healthy luxuriance in the chancel of Lawford, with its highly unusual tracery and its delicious foliage growing up inside the
16b window surrounds, in the S aisle of Maldon, and the chancel of
8 Tilty. The surviving S chapel of Waltham Abbey is earlier and less *outré*, but has lovely double tracery in its straight-headed W windows. The surviving S chapel of Little Dunmow is later, hardly before 1360, and shows the deliberate mixing in of some Perp motifs in the window tracery.‡ That circumscribes the extent in time of the Decorated in Essex. Now for details. Piers are usually octagonal and capitals moulded. Sometimes the octagonal shape is continued upward above the capital so that the arches die into it. Frequent also are piers of quatrefoil section, with or without fillets on the shafts (Blackmore, Burnham, Danbury, Elmstead, Henham, Hythe, Lindsell, Maldon, Rickling, Upminster). Sometimes between the foils of the quatrefoil there is a hollow (Hempstead consecrated 1365, Orsett) or a keeled shaft (Long Melford in Suffolk, Bardfield Saling, Little Maplestead, Shalford) or a filleted shaft (Finchingfield, Great Sampford,
19 Thaxted). Sometimes the main attached shafts are polygonal instead of semicircular (Stebbing), sometimes the quatrefoil is replaced by a square with four attached semicircular shafts (Halstead, Witham, Feering). Quatrefoil windows, as they occurred

---

* The refectory at Prittlewell has pointed trefoil windows.
‡ The introduction of such highly ornamental S chapels is incidentally a speciality worth studying in other counties as well.

already in the C13, are found in the C14 clerestories of Little Sampford and Sible Hedingham and the C14 porches of Great Bardfield and Stebbing. These two churches also possess what must be called the most spectacular pieces of interior stone decoration, rood screens filling with shafts, arches, and tracery the whole height of the chancel arch. Stebbing is earlier, c.1340, 28 Great Bardfield on the verge of Perp. As the same motif occurs at Trondheim in Norway, it must be assumed that it comes from some lost major work.*

We now approach the PERPENDICULAR style, the style corresponding to the period of greatest prosperity in East Anglia. As in Suffolk and Norfolk the wool and cloth trades were the chief source of wealth. An Elizabethan statute speaks of the 'fair large towns of Essex inhabited of a long time with clothmakers'. Yet there are only three churches in the county which can stand up to a comparison with Long Melford and Lavenham in Suffolk or the best and grandest in Norfolk: Saffron Walden, nearly 200 ft 9a long, Thaxted 183 ft long, and Dedham c.170 ft long. The re- 19 building of Thaxted began first (c.1340), and it remained the richest of all. Saffron Walden was begun c.1450 and has its nearest parallels at Cambridge. Dedham of c.1500 is wholly Suffolk in character. Similarly a church like Stansted Mountfitchet is of a Hertfordshire kind (see the 'spike' here and in other churches of the neighbourhood). East Anglian again are Brightlingsea and Great Bromley. Great Bromley like Dedham has the very effective motif of twice as many clerestory as aisle windows. Window tracery of the Perp style is on the whole not rewarding. Dec motifs occasionally remain in use. Of this an exceedingly interesting example is the font of Little Totham. A specially good group of Early Perp windows, straight-headed with varying tracery, belongs to the area of Great Bardfield, with Finchingfield, Wethersfield, and Shalford. The proudest steeples are those of Thaxted, 181 ft high, and Saffron Walden (rebuilt). Thaxted employs a curious system to strengthen its buttressing. The buttresses are of the set-back type, but the angle of the tower is not visible, because the buttresses are connected diagonally by a canting of the angle itself. The same system, but with a straight diagonal, is to be found at Bocking, Chelmsford, Great Bromley, Great Dunmow, and Little Sampford, i.e. nearly all churches

---

* As a postscript the much restored church of Little Maplestead must be mentioned. It belonged to the Hospitallers and had therefore a circular nave, in imitation of the church of the Holy Sepulchre at Jerusalem. It is one of five churches with circular naves in England.

with sizeable towers. Flushwork, that typically East Anglian type
of decoration, i.e. patterns formed by knapped flint and ashlar
stone, has already been noted. The most elaborate examples are
48 the gatehouses of St Osyth and of St John Colchester. On churches
9b it is to be found at Dedham, Ardleigh, Brightlingsea, and Chelmsford. Fingringhoe church makes use of alternating bands of flint
and stone, and its doorway and the doorways of Ardleigh, Brightlingsea, and Great Bromley have figures of St George and the
Dragon in the spandrels, Thaxted, Brightlingsea, Great Bromley, and others employ other means to enrich doorways. The
richest porches are those of Saffron Walden (one with a tier-
ceron- and one with a fan-vault) and Dedham (panel-vaulted
tower hall; cf. the N chapel at Pentlow). In the porches of Littlebury the projected fan-vaults were never completed, or if they
were, only fragments remain. Inside, the finest ensembles are
without doubt again Saffron Walden and Thaxted. The greatest
variety within the Perp style is met in the forms of piers. Generally speaking they tend to complexity and slenderness. The rela-
tive size of arches grows and of supports decreases so as to allow
for the freest flow of space across, through nave and aisles.
Slenderness of piers is often achieved by using a basic lozenge
shape which appears at its thinnest when seen straight on from
the nave. Fine mouldings of the sides add to the effect of slim
verticality. Both elements are found to perfection at Saffron
Walden. The lozenge shape at its simplest appears at Chelmsford, with four attached shafts and no capitals at all at Little
Sampford, with four attached shafts and concave sides at Dedham
and St James Colchester, and so on. The octagon with concave
sides is particularly characteristic of the desire for interpenetra-
tion of space. It can be seen at Prittlewell (Southend), Terling,
etc. Another characteristic variety of piers is that in which semicircular shafts towards the nave are replaced by elongated
semi-octagonal ones. This is the fashion adopted at St Peter
Colchester, Great Waltham, Broxted, etc. To end this account a
few piers must be recorded which are of other materials than
22 stone. Shenfield has a Perp arcade of timber,* St Osyth parish
church, Blackmore, and St Nicholas Chignal have Perp arcades
completely of brick.‡

So we have reached the two most characteristic building
materials of the late Middle Ages in Essex, timber and brick.
Timber of course had been the universal material in most parts

---

* To this Theydon Garnon is to be added; but the arcade here is of 1644.
‡ Cf. also the arcade to the chancel chapel at Ingatestone.

of England in early days. It is no accident that the carpenter was called the wright, i.e. the worker in general. But in Essex timber was not finally replaced in church work until brick arrived and in domestic work until after the Restoration. One church, Marks Tey, even has an oak font. Considering this faith and skill in timber-craft, it seems odd that in CHURCH ROOFS the county only rarely achieved the highest distinction. One must not think of Norfolk and Suffolk when looking at even the most ambitious roofs, the double hammerbeam roofs of Castle Hedingham, Gestingthorpe (by *Thomas Loveday*), Great Bromley, and Stur- 29 mer, and the single hammerbeams of Hythe, and Berechurch near Colchester, Little Bentley, Peldon, St Osyth, and Wrabness. But one hammerbeam roof in Essex deserves a place in any book on English roofs in general: Tendring. Here only one truss survives, ingeniously linked up with a wooden door surround. But that surround in all its details makes it clear beyond doubt that the roof must be earlier than 1350. Since usually the hammerbeams of Westminster Hall are called the earliest in England and since they date from the 1390s, Tendring is indeed a document of great importance. Otherwise Essex roofs are in the south mostly of the tie-beam kind with king-posts and four-way struts (specially good St Martin Colchester; alternating tie-beam and hammerbeam Great Waltham), in the N they are flat-pitched, as for example at Thaxted.

Secondly there are TIMBER PORCHES. These are of course not confined to Essex. Hertfordshire, Middlesex, and other counties near by have them. Of Essex ones the remarkable porch at Radwinter may be singled out for the C14, Margaretting for the 10a C15. But the glory of Essex timber construction is the BELFRIES and W TOWERS. We call belfry a W turret which seems to stand on or near the W end of the church roof but in fact stands on posts visible inside. The basic arrangement is four posts connected from N to S and sometimes also from E to W by tie-beams. These often rest on arched braces, and in addition there is, more usually from E to W than from N to S, diagonal cross-bracing in a trellis of slighter straight braces. Instead of four posts, six or even eight may be used, forming as it were a nave and aisles. The ultimate elaboration is to make a W tower proper of the belfry, i.e. set it up outside the W wall of the nave. It is in such cases occasionally provided with a W aisle as well (Blackmore, Margaretting, and 23 Navestock are perhaps the best). The result may be a whole little centrally planned building with four main posts carrying the tower and an ambulatory all round. That sounds like a type

of central church of venerable antiquity, the type of S. Satiro
in Milan (879) and Hosios Lukas, but whether there are connexions, as Mr Braun has recently suggested, or whether the
Essex type is rather Early Medieval-Germanic in its origin, it is
not possible to say. The many examples which we possess cannot
with certainty be dated, but recent radiocarbon tests at Navestock
indicate that the timber is over seven hundred years old. This
could possibly mean a C13 date of construction, which is much
earlier than most scholars had assumed, and may well apply to
many of these Essex belfries. They are rough work, they lack decorative refinements, mouldings, or ornament, and must be compared to the splendid barns of Essex rather than to screens or
domestic interiors. But they are in their sturdy directness extremely impressive, and they are wholly out of the ordinary.

Now for BRICK. It has already been said that locally made brick
appears in Essex as early as the C13. But not before the C15 did
the material become accepted for work of any ambition. Its
popularity then grew rapidly until in the early decades of the
Tudor dynasty it was clearly the most fashionable of all materials.
Otherwise Wolsey would never have used it for Hampton Court.
Its rise in secular building will be considered later. Here attention must be drawn only to the occurrence of brick in churches.
No attempt has yet been made to date the various brick porches
and brick towers, so as to trace a development. Porches, often
10b with stepped gables, appear in at least fifteen churches. It is im-
11a possible to single out one or two as specially worth while. Of
towers there are about thirty. The most magnificent, tall, often
adorned with trefoiled corbel friezes and stepped battlements,
are probably those of Ingatestone, Rochford, and Layer Marney.
Dated towers are at Gestingthorpe c.1498, Theydon Garnon
1520, and Castle Hedingham 1616. The lower parts at Hedingham
are no doubt earlier, but it is illuminating to realize that, except
for the changing shape of bricks, the appearance of an early C17
tower in Essex is in no way different from one of the early C16.
The long survival of Perp towers in brick is altogether a remarkable fact. The Early Tudor church builders for example
liked to make their windows of brick as well, instead of dressing
them with stone. A specially fine example is the clerestory of
Great Baddow. Brick mullions, brick arches to the individual
lights of mullioned windows, and even brick tracery, most usually
intersected under depressed, four-centred heads, occur often,
and again as late as c.1550 (West Ham), and later. In a chapel
added to the church of Stapleford Abbots the windows are for

the first time of an arched Renaissance type. The date here is 1638. Other brick chapels added late and still in the Perp style can be seen at Ingatestone, C16 and early C17. Whole brick arcades have already been mentioned. How far the craze for brick went can best be realized by looking at the brick font of Chignal St Nicholas.

That brings us to Essex CHURCH FURNISHINGS. First FONTS. The raw decoration of the font at Little Maplestead suggests an C11 date. A good C12 example, circular with scrolls, etc., is at Belchamp Walter. But the most usual late C12 and C13 type is that provided in so many places and counties by the Purbeck quarries: a square bowl, rather flat, like a table top, and the sides decorated by shallow blank arcades, first with round then with pointed heads. A variety of this type adds interest by motifs of fleurs-de-lis, sun and moon, and a curious unexplained whorl. Not all these fonts come necessarily from Purbeck. Once the type was established it was imitated in the stones of other regions as well. Norton Mandeville for example has a font of Barnack stone of a design similar to a Purbeck type. The best C13 fonts in Essex are at Newport with gabled arches in bold relief and at Springfield with rich stiff-leaf foliage. Of *c.*1300 is the handsome octagonal font of Roydon with four heads at the corners, men wearing hats with rolled-up brims. Perp fonts are more than can be counted, and most of them are dull: octagonal with the standard decoration by quatrefoils framing shields or rosettes. One group at and near Dedham has figures or symbols of the evangelists instead, but the standard of carving is low.

FONT COVERS and font cases are effective pieces of decoration in a few churches. Takeley is perhaps the most sumptuous 30a (though much restored). Others are at Thaxted and Littlebury, and also at Pentlow and at Fingringhoe and Great Horkesley (much repaired).

Essex SCREENS cannot compare with the screens of Suffolk and Norfolk. A few (Foxearth, Great Yeldham, Stambourne) have painted figures on the dado as in East Anglia. At North Weald Bassett the ribbed coving under the rood-loft is preserved. But as far as the design of the screens themselves is concerned, one is hardly tempted to analyse it in detail. The richest screens are probably those of Finchingfield, Castle Hedingham, Henham, and Manuden, the oldest those with thin columns with shaft-rings instead of moulded mullions (Corringham, Magdalen Laver). They may belong to the earlier C14; of the late C14 is the screen of Bardfield Saling. The magnificent C14 stone

28 screens of Stebbing and Great Bardfield have already been
mentioned.

PULPITS are on the whole disappointing. There are only seven
of pre-Reformation date in the county, and not one of them is
anything special. BENCHES and BENCH ENDS and STALLS and
STALL ENDS also do not deserve much comment here. Several
complete sets of benches are preserved, but they are plain (e.g. in
the Bardfield area; also Hadstock, Stanford Rivers, Takeley,
Wendens Ambo). Some have figures on the top of the ends
(Belchamp St Paul, Danbury, Writtle), and a few stalls have
misericords of no particular interest (Belchamp St Paul, Castle
Hedingham). An item of historical as well as architectural interest is the Dunmow Flitch Chair at Little Dunmow; it has been
established as part of a C13 chancel stall. In North Essex is a
small group of oak LECTERNS of the C15: Hadstock, Littlebury,
Newport, and Ridgewell. Oak COFFERS are frequent in Essex
churches, both of the dugout and the iron-bound type. Of the
former fourteen have been counted, usually undateable, of the
latter eleven. By far the most interesting example is the later C13
coffer at Newport, with external arcading and paintings inside
the lid. Also of the C13 is the coffer at Little Canfield with prettily ornamented short legs. Two specially good chests of c.1500
are at Thaxted. Not much need be said of other timberwork in
churches. The Saxon DOOR at Hadstock has been referred to;
C12 and C13 doors with ornamental ironwork are not infrequent
(C12 Black Notley, Castle Hedingham, Elmstead, Navestock,
Willingale Spain; C13 Aldham, Bocking, Colchester St Peter,
High Roding, Little Leighs, Little Totham, Margaret Roding).
Typical of the C14 are doors with blank arched and traceried
panels such as occur at Colchester St Giles, Finchingfield, Great
Bardfield, and White Notley.

CHURCH PLATE earlier than the Reformation is very rare. At
Radwinter is the base and stem of a C15 cup, from Holy
Trinity Colchester a C15 mazer, at Earls Colne a paten of the late
C15, at Hythe a mazer of 1521, at Great Waltham a paten of 1521,
and at North Benfleet a cup of 1506. That is all.

STAINED GLASS also is on the whole not rewarding. By far the
26 best is the C12 and C13 glass at Rivenhall, and that is French and
was bought only in the C19. Then there are small C13 and early
C14 figures at Harlow, Lindsell, North Ockendon, White Notley,
Newport, and Stapleford Abbots, and late C14 figures at Great
Bardfield and Thaxted. At Sheering in the tracery lights is a
complete little late C14 Coronation of the Virgin with angels. Of

later glass the most noteworthy are the complete, if restored, Jesse window at Margaretting, the stories from Genesis at Thaxted, the panels of the story of St Katherine of the Norwich school at Clavering, and the kneeling members of the Macwilliam family in the chancel of Stambourne which that family had given.

WALL PAINTING has much more to give in Essex than stained glass. Here any history of the art of England would be incomplete without at least two or three of the works in Essex village churches. First and foremost is Copford of c.1150, once with cycles all over the walls and no doubt also the vault, and even now with fragments in the apse and a story of the healing of Jairus's daughter and Virtues and Vices on the nave walls. The one seated prophet preserved at Little Easton also deserves mention as a contemporary piece of a similar style, a style derived from Bury St Edmunds and St Albans. The mid C13 is represented by the exquisite seated Virgin at Great Canfield, near in style to Matthew Paris. It is painted above the altar against the E wall of the church, between two windows – a rare and delightful composition. Interesting also are the stories of the Passion of Christ in four tiers, of c.1275, at Fairstead church. The C14 is not well represented (St Christopher Lambourne, remains of a cycle at Wendens Ambo, c.1330, remains at Bradwell-juxta-Coggeshall, Virgin at Belchamp Walter), the C15 by the iconographically remarkable cycle at Little Easton and the Doom at Waltham Abbey.

SCULPTURE other than monuments need not be mentioned, except for the scanty remains of two alabaster altars at Great Hallingbury and Saffron Walden, and such small decorative figure work as the numerous head stops of hood-moulds or the delightful climbing and dancing jugglers and musicians in the window surrounds at Lawford or the Virgin and Child at Henham.

Of MONUMENTS a little more must be said, although here also Essex has none of national importance. The earliest monuments are of knights and belong to the C13. That at Toppesfield is covered over and cannot be seen; others, a little later, are at Clavering and Faulkbourne. There follows the interesting group of oaken effigies at Danbury, Elmstead, Little Baddow, and Little Leighs. The dates go from the late C13 to the middle of the C14. Good cross-legged knights of c.1300 to 1310 are at Thorpe-le-Soken and Stansted Mountfitchet. Brasses and the technically similar incised stone slabs begin with the C14. The earliest stone slab is probably the demi-figure of a priest at Barking. Flemish in style is the mid C14 incised stone, 7 ft long, of a priest at Middle-

ton, and of Flemish style also are some of the best brasses in the
county. The earliest Essex brass is that of Sir William Fitzralph
at Pebmarsh (c.1323). The best C14 brasses are the splendid,
6 ft long figure of c.1350 at Bowers Gifford, the elegant small
figures of c.1347 in the head of a foliated cross at Wimbish, and
the figures in architectural surrounds of 1370 at Aveley and 1380
at Chrishall. The best of the later brasses is at Wivenhoe. The
whole plate here is as large as 9 ft. Of alabaster monuments the
33a finest by far is that of the Fitzwalters of Little Dunmow, a piece
of sculpture of really high quality, a thing not frequent amongst
English C15 funeral monuments. Of canopies over monuments
the most sumptuous belong to the Dec style. They are at Shalford and Belchamp Walter (1324). Of the many tomb-chests under Perp canopies only the following can here be noted: the
wrongly so-called cenotaph of John Hawkwood at Sible Hedingham (1394?), the Bourchier tomb at Halstead (1400), and the
34 Webbe monument at Dedham. The type remains the same when
Renaissance ornament appears. The appearance of this can be
dated almost precisely in Essex. It is connected with Lord
Marney's rebuilding of his mansion at Layer Marney about 1520
and the monuments erected to him and his son after their deaths
in 1523 and 1525.

It is significant that the coming of the Renaissance is seen in
domestic architecture at the same moment as, or even earlier
than, in church architecture. From now onwards secular building
takes precedence over ecclesiastical. So it is time now to retrace
our steps and turn to the history of the house in Essex. So far
only the castles of the earlier Middle Ages have been mentioned.
Of LATE MEDIEVAL CASTLES only one stands, an impressive
ruin: Hadleigh, which was rebuilt about 1365 by Edward III.
Strictly DOMESTIC ARCHITECTURE, though on a much more
modest scale, takes us back a good deal further. Essex indeed possesses substantial remains of one hall of the C13. It is at Little
Chesterford Farm, and still shows clear evidence of one of its
two aisles, with the quatrefoil timber columns and a tie-beam
roof with crown-posts* and two-way struts. Rather later, mid
C14, are the impressive remains of the aisled hall of Tiptofts near
Wimbish, also with quatrefoil piers, tie-beams, and crown-posts,
but with four-way struts. Also of the C14 is the aisled hall of St
Clair's Hall near St Osyth which has octagonal piers. With the

---

* As far as is known at present all roofs of secular buildings of this type in
Essex are without ridge-pieces. The term crown-post is used to distinguish
this construction from a king-post carrying a ridge-piece.

C15 and especially the Early Tudor decades examples multiply rapidly. Only a few notes can here be given. Halls are now no longer provided with aisles, since means of constructing timber roofs had been found to allow larger spans. Hammerbeam roofs for instance are partly preserved at Panfield Hall and the Chantry House Halstead, a big tie-beam roof with arched braces, collar-beam, and wind-braces at St Aylotts near Saffron Walden, where an oriel window and the remains of a bay window also survive. The development of the farmhouse or smaller manor house under the influence of this change in the shape of the hall has been described and illustrated in vol. 4 of the Royal Commission Inventory. From the beginning the hall lay in the middle and was flanked on one side by the offices and kitchen, on the other by the solar and what lies below it. These two wings usually have cross gables. In the C15 and after the gables have as a rule oversailing upper storeys. Continuous eaves along the whole front without cross gables are typical of some houses of c.1500 and after. With the late C16 and early C17 halls cease to go through to the roof. They are now built only to ground-floor height with another major room above, and where earlier halls existed, a ceiling was as a rule now put in. With few exceptions Essex houses before the C15 are timber-framed. The thickness of the studs and their narrow distance from one another is an indication of early date. How far timber-framed houses were originally plastered or how far the studding was allowed to remain visible can now no longer be decided. We prefer the visible timbers so much that we are inclined to forget that they were by no means universal. That they did exist is proved by many pictures in illuminated manuscripts, and also by a wall painting of the C15 in an Essex church: at Tilbury-juxta-Clare. Here the infilling between the studs is by means of bricks, i.e. the technique known as brick-nogging.

Side by side with timber-framed farmhouses their BARNS must find mention. Here again Essex has got much of impressive size and design to offer. It is hard to point out just three or four. But amongst them will certainly have to be the magnificent barley barn and wheat barn of Cressing Temple Farm, thought, until 46b recently, to date from c.1450 and c.1530 but now regarded as of the early C14 or even earlier. (*See* p. 153.) The wheat barn is 140 ft long. 159 ft is the length of the barn at Leighs Lodge near Felsted, 130 ft of that at Grange Farm, Little Coggeshall, 120 ft of that at Clees Hall, Alphamstone. These barns are all timber-framed and have splendidly sturdy timbers inside forming a nave and aisles. Many are weatherboarded. A specially impressive one at New Hall, High Roding, of the early C16 has brick infilling. Similar are the fine stables of Colville Hall, White Roding.

Of timber-framed TOWN HOUSES also Essex has got a number of outstanding examples. The most attractive ones visually are 46a probably Paycocke's House at Great Coggeshall and the Monk's Barn at Newport with its carving of the Virgin below an oriel window. What is now the Marquess of Granby Inn at Colchester 45 possesses the richest carving inside, also with figures below the corbels of the main beam. The Red Lion at Colchester was converted into an inn as early as c.1500, and from that time dates its richly panelled and traceried façade. Saffron Walden has the present Youth Hostel as an example of a fairly extensive merchant's house with store-rooms of c.1500, and former shop windows in two houses in King Street. Southfields near Dedham, to go on to buildings of a less usual purpose, appears to be a master-weaver's private house with the dwellings of the workmen arranged round a courtyard of which the master's house also forms part. Another courtyard house is preserved at Rickling, but that is of brick, c.1500. The Guildhall of Lavenham in Suffolk is well enough known. Its open ground floor is a feature characteristic of such 44 buildings as guildhalls and town halls. It recurs in the so-called Guildhall at Steeple Bumpstead, and here the upper floor was taken by the school founded in 1592.* Finally, near Great Horkesley and at North End are priest's houses attached immediately to chapels. The former of these two however is of brick and not of timber.

BRICK IN SECULAR ARCHITECTURE is specially characteris-49a tic of buildings after 1500, but Faulkbourne with its mighty angle tower, its other towers, and its bay window with two little brick vaults on the two floors is as good an example of C15 brickwork as any. The use of brickwork began indeed at Faulkbourne shortly after 1439, so that the house must range with Caister and the admittedly grander Tattershall and Herstmonceaux of the 1440s as one of the early examples of brick on a grand scale. In Essex 49b Faulkbourne is followed immediately by Horham Hall of c.1502–c.1525. Although here only the hall range survives, this, with its spectacular bay window and a gateway with a stair-turret, makes a splendid show. As for the C16 it is hard to choose; there is so much to enjoy and admire, minor things such as the charming garden-wall with its angle turrets at Killigrews, Margaretting of c.1500, or the stair-turret with its crocketed pyramid roof at

* The Moot Hall at Maldon should have been mentioned earlier. It was originally a fortified town tower.

Jacobes, Brightlingsea, as well as major things. Belhus was called 'newly builded' in 1520.* It has an inner courtyard and no symmetrical layout. As at Horham the gateway has an attached stair-turret. The chief decorative motif of the house is stepped gables. After 1536 Leez Priory was converted to become Lord Rich's mansion. Its tall gatehouse is famous. The ranges were grouped round an outer and an inner courtyard, again, it seems, without regard for symmetry. Leez Priory is a typical case of the ruthless despoliation of monastic property by the *nouveaux riches* of Henry VIII's court. They used the existing buildings as quarries without any sentimentality, or any romantic delight in ruins, and it is difficult now to visualize how they put up with new houses set amidst decaying old ones. Such certainly must have been the impression around the large, proud new ranges set up by Lord Darcy at St Osyth. They are not of brick, but of septaria and limestone and date from after 1558. Yet no Renaissance detail appears anywhere. The foremost brick mansions of the mid c16 in Essex are Boreham New Hall, a courtyard house built by Henry VIII (of his time however chiefly the spectacular coat of arms inside remains; the rest is Elizabethan), Ingatestone Hall with its two courtyards and stepped gables, not yet symmetrically composed nor provided with Renaissance decoration, Rochford Hall of *c.*1545 with two or even four courtyards, straight gables with graceful pinnacles, large transomed windows in the upper storey, and a main front almost completely symmetrical, and Gosfield Hall with one courtyard and a façade made wholly symmetrical to the l. and the r. of the central gateway.

Of all the gatehouses of Essex, and indeed of England, the most ambitious, a showpiece of crazy height, is at Layer Marney. This was begun by Lord Marney *c.*1520, and it is here, as has already been said, that the RENAISSANCE first appears in the county. The Renaissance motifs are of terracotta, no doubt the work of Italians; for the Florentine Pietro Torrigiani had apparently introduced terracotta into England some ten years before. The motifs are window mullions transformed into shafts with Renaissance candelabra in their sunk panels, ogee-arched window tops transformed into Renaissance scrolls and double-scrolls, and cresting transformed into Renaissance shell-shapes. Immediately after, some bits of Renaissance ornament appeared in Abbot Vintoner's big oriel window at St Osyth (*c.*1527). A little later the fashion began to affect domestic panelling, which had, until then, been chiefly of the linenfold kind. Now roundels with heads

* Now demolished.

or busts, foliage scrolls, candelabra, etc. appear, first in two Essex sets now at the Victoria and Albert Museum of which the one from Beckingham Hall is dated 1546; the other comes from Waltham Cross. Still *in situ* is coarser Early Renaissance panelling at Tolleshunt d'Arcy Hall. The full ELIZABETHAN style appears on a large scale at Hill Hall, Theydon Mount, chiefly of 1568–c.1580, and Boreham New Hall of 1573. Both are still of the courtyard type, Hill Hall characterized by the unusual motif of attached colonnades in two orders above each other all round the courtyard, Boreham New Hall by the amazing show of seven identical bay windows all along the façade of what was then the inner side of the N range. Audley End also, by far the grandest JACOBEAN building of Essex and one of the biggest Jacobean mansions in England, still adhered to the courtyard plan – a late example, since it was built only in 1603–16. Like Hampton Court, it had an outer courtyard with lower buildings and a broad gatehouse and then an inner courtyard. The hall however was placed in the range between the two and not at the side or the far end of the inner courtyard. The outer courtyard and half the inner were pulled down in the C18. But even in its present dimensions it is on a splendid scale, and to show the lavishness of its owner it is all stone-faced, whereas the standard in Essex was brick with stone dressings, as Robert Cecil indeed did not mind using at the same time for his Hatfield mansion. The hall at Audley End is centrally placed, and to achieve external symmetry the elaborately decorated porch is duplicated behind the dais end, and the bay window is placed illogically in the middle. Immense elaboration of strapwork, caryatids, and such Flemish C16 fantasies was also lavished on the hall screen and some of the fireplaces, but the chapel still has a large window with mullions and transoms in which the individual lights are arched, as if it had been designed a hundred years earlier. In such humbler buildings as the stable range of Audley End and the remarkable Almshouses – the best in Essex, grouped round two courtyards, which is an extremely unusual arrangement – horizontal mullioned windows with arched lights also still appear. The choice for special mention amongst medium-sized Elizabethan houses must be these two: Eastbury House Barking of 1572, in which the new H-plan replaces the older plan with the courtyard, and Moyns Park of c.1575–80, which displays a symmetrical front with four gables and three polygonal bay windows of which the middle opens as a porch on the ground floor. Porters at Southend comes a little later: c.1600. Clock House, Great Dunmow, also of c.1600, has a more compact plan and shaped gables. Shaped gables also appear at about the same time at Church House Wormingford, Great Graces Danbury, and Woodham Mortimer Hall, but they survive in Essex to a surprisingly late date, as will be shown later. Another motif that seems to arrive in the county with Queen Elizabeth's reign is the pediment above a window or a door. Eastbury House has it and, probably already a little earlier, Roydon Hall Ramsey (which still has the gable with three pinnacles like Rochford Hall) and Wix Abbey. The finest Jacobean interiors are without doubt at Langleys, Great Waltham, of a 57 stupendous richness of plaster ornamentation. Finally two buildings of unusual function deserve notice: Bourne Mill, Colchester, 53 of 1591, with its fantastic shaped gables and obelisks, probably built as a fishing lodge, and Queen Elizabeth's Hunting Lodge at Chingford, built as a 'standing', that is a look-out to enjoy the sight of hunting on the edge of Epping Forest. It is timber-framed and was originally open on the sides so as to make for good views. Timber-framing remained the standard technique for farmhouses right through the C17, as is indicated by many dates on the carved bressumers or brackets.

Even in CHURCHES it can be observed that the timber technique of the Gothic style was not yet abandoned. Ramsey, Chipping Ongar, and Manningtree have roofs of the late C16 or early C17 which, though in details Jacobean, are basically Perp. Ramsey and Chipping Ongar are collar-beam roofs, Manningtree is a hammerbeam roof. At Manningtree, which is dated 1616, Perp windows can also still be seen, and other examples of this 'Gothic Survival' have been mentioned a few pages earlier. To these may here be added the wholly pre-Renaissance W tower of Waltham Abbey, dated 1556–8, and the complete little brick church of 1611–14 at Theydon Mount in the grounds of Hill Hall. The porch here has a shaped gable. The chancel at Ramsey on the other hand, dated 1597, has large transomed windows of an entirely Elizabethan domestic character. The coming of the classical style is marked – as stated already – by the introduction of arched windows in the brick N chapel of Stapleford Abbots, which is dated 1638.

While churches of between the mid C16 and the mid C17 are rare in Essex and everywhere in the country, CHURCH MONUMENTS are frequent, so frequent that selection must be arbitrary. The coming of the Renaissance has already been noted at Layer Marney (1523). The tomb-lid and effigy here is of touch, i.e. black marble. This instance was followed by monuments in the

same material to the Earl of Oxford 1539 at Castle Hedingham
35 and Lord Audley 1544 at Saffron Walden. The latter is by
Cornelius Harman, who may well have done the Castle Hedingham monument and also the tomb-chest to Prior Vyvyan at
Bodmin in Cornwall, who died in 1533. Tomb-chests remain one
of the usual types of monuments throughout the C16, see the alabaster tomb of the Earls of Sussex at Boreham, 1589, with recumbent effigies. Brasses on the other hand tend to disappear,
although there is the exceptional, large brass plate to Archbishop
Harsnett at Chigwell, which dates from as late as 1631. The most
popular new type is the hanging wall-monument with a kneeling
figure or two kneeling figures facing each other across a prayer-
desk. Of this there are examples all over the county. The only
one that will delight the eye is that of 1619 at Woodham Ferrers,
where the figure kneels against an arbour carved in relief. The
most usual expensive monument is the direct continuation of the
Perp canopy tomb. The tomb-chest is kept and the canopy has
assumed a round-arched form usually with flanking columns, and
achievements or obelisks instead of the former cresting. To this
type belong the monuments of the Smiths of Hill Hall at Theydon Mount. The finest sculptural quality is reached in *Epiphanius Evesham*'s Lord Rich monument at Felsted of *c.*1620. An
37 equally sumptuous display is that for Sir Thomas Middleton,
Lord Mayor of London, 1631, at Stansted Mountfitchet. The
figures on the tomb-chests are now more often semi-reclining
than recumbent, that is as a rule stiffly propped up on an elbow.
This is still to be found as late as 1658 at Orsett and 1668 at
Theydon Mount. Another attempt at achieving more variety than
the couples of the C15 lying side by side on a tomb-chest had
permitted is the odd custom of placing the husband on a shelf behind and above his wife. This appears at St Osyth *c.*1580, Waltham Abbey 1600, Great Waltham 1611, and Little Warley as late
as 1641. Another fashionable Elizabethan type of major funeral
monument is the six-poster. The Essex examples are at Borley
(1599) and at Arkesden (1592). The effigy of Robert Wiseman
1641 at Willingale Doe lies in a recess behind three columns – a
halved six-poster. Of special motifs or special types of the C16
little need be said. Monuments at Gosfield of 1554 and 1567 are
still entirely Gothic in detail, but at Little Sampford in 1556 (Sir
Edward Greene) the strapwork, termini pilasters, and so on of
the new Netherlandish fashion which was to replace the Italo-
French fashion of the Early Renaissance are already in command.
The Mildmay monument at Chelmsford, 1571, is of a type which

seems wholly original. It has steep triangular and rounded pediments and no effigy at all.*

New types appear about 1630, and in a few monuments of that date a freedom of composition begins to make itself felt which heralds the age after the Restoration. A popular new type in Essex is the frontal demi-figure. At Abbess Roding (1633) angels hold a curtain open behind the figure, at Walthamstow two figures are side by side in oval niches (1633). The Walthamstow 36b monument is by *Nicholas Stone*, the best English sculptor of his generation. At Writtle (1629) is another monument by him which in poetic conception and delicacy of carving is far above the current English standard. Frontal busts in niches had quite a vogue at that time, see Barking 1636, Dedham 1636, Clavering 1653, Fingringhoe 1655, Clavering 1658, and also, without niches, Leigh 1641 and Hempstead 1657. This last represents William 38 Harvey and is an excellent likeness as well as an excellent work of sculpture. Seated whole figures also appear now, although more rarely; at East Donyland 1613, and at Barking 1625, where Sir Charles Montague is placed inside a tent with an eve-of-the-battle scene by his side. Finally there is the short craze for shrouded figures, caused, it seems, by Nicholas Stone's upright figure of John Donne at St Paul's Cathedral. This is immediately reflected in the figure of Lady Deane at Great Maplestead (1634). Semi-reclining figures in shrouds are at Shenfield (1652) and Little Warley (1658).

This survey has taken us to about 1660. Contemporary internal CHURCH FURNISHINGS need no more than a sentence or two: the numerous pulpits of the earlier C17, the best being perhaps that of Great Baddow 1639 (also Stondon Massey 1630, and Bardfield Saling), the stalls and the *van Linge* glass in the chancel at Messing, and the church plate, of which there is a great deal – for instance 123 Elizabethan cups. The best pieces however are later. The secular Jacobean cups at Berden and Gosfield, the repoussé dishes of 1630 at Great Sampford and Hempstead, and the Irish chalice of 1623 at St Mary-at-Walls Colchester are the choice of the Royal Commission. Among HOUSE FURNISHINGS what needs attention are the plaster ceilings at Ford Place Stifford, Orsett Hall, etc., some coarse but impressive wall-painting of scrolls and geometrical patterns at Kelvedon, Josselyns near Little Horkesley, etc., and some staircases. The original ones at Audley End are rather cramped, that at Albyns, Stapleford Abbots of c.1620 is (soon one may have to say: was) larger and at

* But see note on p. 115.

least as sumptuously decorated, many others have the sturdy turned balusters familiar in houses of the Jacobean and Carolean periods.

The change to the style of after 1660 could not be seen more clearly than by comparing such staircases with that at Nelmes, Hornchurch, with its solid balustrade carved with panels of thick foliage scrolls and garlands. With this the classical style is reached which was to dominate England from the later C17 to the time of the accession of Queen Victoria. This PERIOD BE-TWEEN 1660 AND 1830 is extensively represented in Essex, with far more work than can here be alluded to, and of course much work of indifferent quality. SECULAR ARCHITECTURE must again have precedence. The first signs of a will to abandon Jacobean traditions can be watched at Fremnells, Downham. The plan is still of the E-type, and straight gables are still used, but the windows are now of the upright mullion-and-transom-cross kind and a general quiet regularity prevails. Straight gables occur even as late as Thorpe Hall Southchurch (Southend-on-Sea) in 1668, and as for shaped gables their longevity in Essex must be a record. Ford Place Stifford is of 1655, Beaumont Hall of c.1675, Saling Hall Great Saling of 1699, and Fingringhoe Hall and Old Riffhams Danbury seem even later than 1700. Meanwhile Quendon Hall had given an example of the grand new Baroque of London by using giant pilasters all along the façade – curiously irregularly placed though they are. The date must be about 1680. At the same time the plain, nicely proportioned brick house arrives such as Bois Hall Navestock of 1687 and Dynes Hall Great Maplestead of 1689, which has a three-bay pediment and a staircase with sturdy twisted balusters. Doorways are enriched by broad surrounds with segmental pediments, or by generously shaped shell-hoods such as can be seen at Wentworth House Bocking 1679, Sutton's South Shoebury (Southend-on-Sea) 1681, and Crown House Newport 1692. Crown House is also one of the foremost examples of that famous Essex technique of façade decoration: pargeting. This reached its zenith in the C17, but never became genteel. It is as a rule in the towns and villages that one has to look for its prettiest displays. The two best ex-amples other than Crown House are a house in East Street 52b Wivenhoe and the former Sun Inn Saffron Walden of 1676. As for town houses of the period under consideration the best are at Colchester (The Hollytrees c. 1716) and Dedham (Grammar 58b School c. 1730, Shermans c. 1730). Clarence House at Thaxted of 1715 also is of a town more than a country type.

Wren appears nowhere in Essex, but of his two greatest followers, the two paladins of English Baroque, Vanbrugh and Hawksmoor, the first worked at Audley End about 1721, and the style if not the person of the second is present in the church of Ingrave (*see* below). *Vanbrugh* built the majestic stone screen between hall and staircase at Audley End, and the new equally majestic stone staircase. It was a remarkable whim of the great architect who was the first to feel a serious sympathy with the English past to cover the staircase hall with a plaster ceiling in imitation of the Jacobean style. This Neo-Jacobean seems to have been his invention. It appears immediately afterwards in some readjustments of the two remaining Jacobean rooms at Langleys, Great Waltham. The Palladianism which was the expression of enlightened opposition against Vanbrugh's Baroque and which was to dominate English architecture of the C18 at its most representational began in Essex. Wanstead House by *Colen Campbell*, begun in 1715 and, alas, no longer in existence, antedated even Lord Burlington's own efforts. Of the scale of its layout the remains of avenues and water still tell us something. These features were made even before 1715. The full-blown Palladian type of country house must have wings or angle pavilions separated from the main block by colonnades or low connecting links. This type survives in Essex at Kelvedon Hall (1725, 1740) and, much grander, at Thorndon Hall (1764). The interior here is burnt out, but the general composition remains. Thorndon Hall is by *James Paine*, who also built the simpler Hare Hall, Romford (1768). In other cases the pavilions are a later addition. Thus Hylands, Widford was built about 1728, but the wings are the work of *William Atkinson* in 1819–25; Blake Hall, Bobbingworth is also early C18 and had wings added by *Basevi*; and Terling Place dates from 1772 with wings of 1818. The architect of the original Terling Place was *John Johnson* of Chelmsford, a man of some merit, as can be seen in his charming Bradwell 61a Lodge of 1781–6 and the Shire Hall to which I shall revert later.

The case at Boreham House is not quite the same. Here the centre is of 1728 by *James Gibbs*, executed by *Edward Shepherd*, and the wings by *Hopper* are of 1812; but they replace earlier wings. The centre was built for a member of the Hoare family and is in its restrained exterior and luxurious interior charac- 59 teristic of the best Early Georgian of Essex. Langleys, Great Waltham is the other paramount example, built *c*.1719. A third house with surprisingly exuberant interiors behind plain fronts is Over Hall, Gestingthorpe of 1735. The universally current 60 brick mansion of the period, nicely proportioned and of comfortable size, can perhaps best be seen at Shortgrove, Newport after 1712, Brizes, Kelvedon Hatch of 1720, Gilstead Hall, South Weald of 1726, Ditchleys, South Weald of 1729, Bower House, Havering-atte-Bower of 1729 (the earliest house by *Flitcroft*), and Rainham Hall of 1729. Inside such houses one usually finds some large and stately panelling and a staircase with gracefully twisted or varied balusters. C18 Gothic is rare in Essex. The only surviving example worth a word is Colne Priory, the exact date of which is not known.

61b Now for PUBLIC BUILDINGS. The Shire Hall at Chelmsford must of course have precedence, a stone-faced, urbane building in the Adam style, by *John Johnson*, 1789–91. Town Halls were built at Saffron Walden in 1761, quite plain and utilitarian, and Harwich in 1769, tall, narrow, not detached, and exactly like a wealthy merchant's house. The County Gaol at Chelmsford, in its oldest parts of 1822–8, perhaps by *Hopper*, is as forbidding, with its high walls and mighty gatehouse, as it ought to be. Much earlier the Government had provided Tilbury Fort with a more 58a ornate and jollier gatehouse. The date is 1670–83, the design very much in the style of the gatehouse to the Citadel of Plymouth. Also built by the Government is what remains of the C18 powder magazines at Purfleet. The Barracks at Little Warley of 1805 however, although now the Essex Regiment's, were originally erected by the East India Company – plain utilitarian ranges of yellow brick.

How small SCHOOLS were before the C19 can best be seen at Felsted with its humble timber-framed original schoolhouse, and at Chigwell, where Archbishop Harsnett founded the Grammar School in 1629. There are no grander early schools in Essex. ALMSHOUSES later than those of Audley End can be seen here and there. Architecturally the only noteworthy piece is the centre of Winsley's at Colchester of 1728, which has markedly Vanbrughian features. The comparison between Winncock's of 1678 and Kendall's of 1791 and 1803, both also at Colchester, is instructive. Chelmsford on the other hand is the town where one 2b should look round for MILLS. There are three with their miller's houses, the actual mill being usually weatherboarded. Other attractive mills, just two out of many, are at Wickham Bishops and Halstead.

GEORGIAN CHURCHES must take their place with these minor achievements of the age. Not one survives in Essex – at least not completely – which could be called a major work of architecture.

The reservation refers to *Robert Adam*'s church at Mistley of 12
1776, an enlargement of a plain brick preaching house of 1735.
Adam added the two spectacular towers with their domes at the
W and E ends and porticoes in the middle of the sides – an
utterly unorthodox and indeed ritually doubtful composition of
which only the two towers remain. The only other churches of
interest are Ingrave of 1735, in the Hawksmoor style, and Wan- 11b
stead of 1787–90, a noble neo-classical building by *Thomas
Hardwick* which is especially worthwhile in its interior. Otherwise there are a number of plain re-built W towers (Toppesfield
1699, Bradwell 1706, Woodford 1708, Terling 1732), a number
of pretty cupolas set up on towers (Little Waltham 1679, Chelmsford 1749, and more in the Halstead–Bardfield area),* the
delicious mid C18 interior remodelling of Lambourne, and – 24a
much more common – a number of plain unassuming brick naves
(Colchester St Peter, Kelvedon Hatch 1753, Shellow Bowells
1754). These are in no essential way different from the early
NONCONFORMIST CHAPELS of Essex, of which many remain.
The Baptists for example have C18 chapels at Saffron Walden –
that of 1744 is simply a cottage, that of 1792 a modest chapel of
the accepted type – and at Harlow (1756; distinguished by a
doorway with a big domestic-looking scrolly pediment). The
Congregational Chapel of 1811 at Saffron Walden already has the
more ambitious and worldly C19 type with a portico. The Friends
Meeting House at Great Bardfield with its secluded graveyard is
of 1804, and the larger, more urban one at Chelmsford of 1826.
The GOTHICK FASHION was as ineffectual in Essex churches
and chapels as in domestic buildings. The only instances that
must be recorded are the following four: first Dagenham 1800
with an ignorant, crazy, and very entertaining façade, and the
octagonal chancel at Debden 1793. The pattern, it is said, which
the architect, probably *Holland*'s brother *Richard*, wished to imitate was the York chapter house. The same pattern inspired
Mason of Ipswich in 1838 at East Donyland, quite an interesting
design of its date. Finally *John Johnson* restored and partly rebuilt
Chelmsford church (the present cathedral) in 1801–3 to the
original Perp design, but with piers of *Coade* stone.

Coade stone, the artificial stone made by Coade and Seely in
Lambeth in the late C18 which was so fashionable for domestic
exteriors, even entered the field of CHURCH FURNISHINGS in
Essex. Two *Coade* stone fonts survive, at Debden (1786) and

* Such cupolas were of course already a feature of English architecture at
a much earlier date, see for instance Clock House, Great Dunmow of *c.*1600.

Chelmsford (1801–3). Another Gothick font, with a miniature painting of the Baptism of Christ, is at Birdbrook (1793). Other noteworthy late C17 and C18 church furnishings are as follows: the font, font cover, and reredos from *Wren*'s All Hallows Great Thames Street in London in a chapel at Halstead, the font from St Mary-le-Bow by *Wren* at Westcliff, a number of fine pulpits of *c.*1700 with garlands down the angles, for example at Thaxted, the screen at Roxwell made from the organ case of 1684 from Durham Cathedral, and a good early C18 reredos at Hatfield Broad Oak. Communion rails with twisted balusters are a very common Essex feature. Of the late C18 the best piece by far is the 30b large and noble pulpit in Wanstead Church of *c.*1795. Several earlier pulpits have wrought-iron hour-glass stands attached to them. There are about ten of these preserved. In most other counties they are rarer. If of secular C18 work the wall paintings by *Thornhill* at Bower House, Havering-atte-Bower and the wrought-iron gates from Easton Lodge now in Little Easton church are mentioned, that is all that need be said.

CHURCH MONUMENTS of *c.*1660–*c.*1830 on the other hand deserve further treatment. If space permitted, at least two dozen would here have to be mentioned and placed. All that can be said is this. The mid C17 type with two demi-figures holding hands is still preserved in the Wyseman monument of 1684 at Great Canfield (attributed to *W. Stanton*), though the two figures are now placed beneath a big segmental pediment. Another yet later frontal demi-figure is at Barking: 1706; the attitude has an elegance all of the C18. The successor of this type is that where a life-size bust, just like those in libraries, etc., is made the centre of the composition. This appears in Essex in 1692 (monument at Arkesden by *Edward Pearce*) and reaches its acme in such monuments as those at Barking of 1737, at Writtle of 1740 by *Cheere*, at Pleshey of 1758, also by *Cheere*, and at Barking again of 1753 by *Roubiliac*. The semi-reclining figure also goes on into the C18, getting in the course of the years more and more comfortable and less and less religious. Examples are at Little Sampford (1712), 41 Steeple Bumpstead (1717 by *Thomas Stayner*), and Little Chesterford (1728).

But the new, most ambitious and clearly least religious type of *c.*1700 is that which has the figure of the deceased standing life-size in the middle, in the clothes he wore or in heroic Roman dress. The type can be called a home counties speciality, cf. for example such Hertfordshire monuments as those at Sawbridge-worth of 1689 and Knebworth of 1710. In Essex the grandest of

all is that of Sir Josiah Child at Wanstead, attributed by Mrs
Esdaile to *John van Ost* or *Nost*. The date is 1699. Earlier than
this are the standing figures on the Foot monument at West Ham
(1688), the Alibon monument at Dagenham (1688), and the
Maynard monument at Little Easton (probably by *Pearce*). The
type goes on at Leyton (*c.*1703), Walthamstow (1723), Rettendon
(1727), West Ham (1743), and Little Easton (1746, by *Charles
Stanley*). The same kind of arrogance appears in the life-size
seated figures at Colchester (Rebow 1699), Gosfield (Knight
1756 by *Rysbrack*), and Faulkbourne (Bullock 1759). Of the type
with large allegories there is only one example: the Magens
monument of 1779 at Brightlingsea. The Faulkbourne monument is by *Peter Scheemakers*, the Brightlingsea monument by
the lesser-known *Nicholas Read*. Other named monuments of
before 1770 are as follows (in alphabetical order): *Thomas Adye*
Little Dunmow 1753, *Cheere* Great Baddow 1753, *James Lovell*
Chelmsford 1756 (big, without effigy), Pearce see above, Read
see above, *Roubiliac* see above, and also Hempstead 1758 (two
profile medallions against obelisk) and Earls Colne 1761, Rysbrack see above, *H. Scheemakers* Wicken Bonhunt 1731, P.
Scheemakers see above, Stanley see above, W. Stanton see
above, Stayner see above, *Sir Robert Taylor* Woodford 1742 (a
column in the churchyard), and *W. Tyler* Finchingfield 1766
(also St Osyth 1773).

After 1770 signatures on funeral monuments become more and
more the rule. *Wilton* appears once at Lambourne in 1778,
Nollekens twice, at East Horndon in 1766 and at Chipping Ongar
in 1776, *John Bacon* twice, at Woodford in 1783 and Great Yeldham in 1799, *J. Hickey* once at Leyton in 1787, and *Flaxman*
four times, at Hornchurch in 1784, at Leyton in 1807 and 1813,
and at Hatfield Broad Oak in 1816.

The younger generation is represented by three monuments by
John Bacon Jun., two by *Chantrey*, one by *Rossi*, and five by
Westmacott. Still later, i.e. Early Victorian, the works contributed
to Essex churches by *Behnes*, *Baily*, and *J. Edwards*. As for minor
names, all the successful monumental masons of London seem to
have had Essex jobs (*Clark* of Wigmore Street, *Cooke*, *Gaffin*,
Garrard, *Hinchcliffe*, *Kendrick*, *Moore*, *Regnart*, *Rouw*), and in
addition on the one hand so distant a firm as *King* of Bath and on
the other the local masons of Braintree, Chelmsford, Colchester,
Ipswich, and Stratford.

With all this the threshold of the VICTORIAN AGE is reached.
The chief Victorian contribution to Essex is of course the growth

of London until the town filled the whole SW corner of the
county. Of that something has already been said. C19 industri-
alization and urbanization in other parts of Essex have not done
much damage. Individual architectural events in the county are
on the whole minor. The cavalcade of styles imitated one after
another takes place here as everywhere – the Neo-Norman
fashion for instance affecting church design about 1840* and the
names of the leading Victorian church architects appear here and
there. But none of their foremost works are in Essex. *Sir George
Gilbert Scott*, when he was young, designed the Neo-Jacobean
workhouses of Billericay and Great Dunmow, then in 1843 the
equally big, equally Jacobean Royal Wanstead School and also in
1843 (with his partner *Moffatt*) Holy Trinity Halstead as the
first work in Essex of the learned and anaemic archaeological revival of Gothic church architecture, and later St Nicholas Colchester (since demolished) and Christ Church Wanstead. High
Victorian at its grossest, and at the same time – an unlikely combination – at its most Ruskinesque is represented by *Clarke*'s
62a former Merchant Seamen's Orphan Asylum at Snaresbrook,
Wanstead of 1861. Just as gross is the fabulously insensitive completion of the E end of Waltham Abbey by *Burges* in 1859. *Teulon*
is another architect who revels in the masculine ugliness of which
the High Victorian style was capable, see his church of 1861 at
Silvertown. *Arthur Blomfield* also began in this vein (St John
Colchester 1862–4), but soon turned to smoother, more correct
and less robust forms (Chingford 1903; an excellent job of the
completion of an indifferent church of 1844). This sensitive and
tactful fag-end of archaeologically faithful Gothicism is also
shown in *Brooks*'s church at Southend (1889) and *Bodley &
Garner*'s at Epping (1889). The latest Victorian and Edwardian
tendency to break away from imitation and revive once again
originality is as a rule less noticeable in churches than in domestic work. But *Lee*'s church at Brentwood (1882–90) has some
curious details and treatments of surfaces which herald the wilful
things that E. S. Prior was soon to perpetrate. *Caröe*'s tower at
Stansted Mountfitchet of 1895 introduces all kinds of Arts and
Crafts or Art Nouveau motifs into his Perp, *Sir Charles Nicholson*'s early church at Westcliff (Southend-on-Sea; 1898) already
shows some of his elegance in the handling of period elements,
Temple Moore at Clacton-on-Sea combines an earnest Perp ex-

---

* St James the Less Colchester 1837 by *Scoles*, St Botolph Colchester 1837
by *Mason*, Holy Trinity Chelmsford 1843 by *J. Adie Repton*, St John
Loughton 1846 by *S. Smirke*.

terior with an interior half round-arched and half pointed-
arched, and *Townsend* at Great Warley in 1904 adopts without [24b, 32]
qualms Voysey's domestic roughcasting and other motifs for
church use.

Charles F. A. Voysey was the leading figure among the architects of private houses about 1900, and his comfortable and free
treatment of Tudor elements in roughcast with horizontal windows, low picturesque roofs, and sloping buttresses appears at
its prettiest at The Homestead, Frinton-on-Sea, of 1905. But
Voysey only continued what had been begun as early as about
1860 by *William Morris* and his friend Philip Webb on the one
hand, and by Norman Shaw on the other. Morris himself was
chiefly responsible for the reform in design. He and his friends,
chiefly Burne-Jones, worked on tiles and wallpapers, textiles and
stained glass, and so on ever since Morris had founded his firm
in 1861. *Burne-Jones* as a designer of stained glass can be seen in
Essex at his very best. His E window at Waltham Abbey of about [31]
1860 is as bold, as vigorous and unsentimental as anything
achieved in the C19. Good somewhat later Burne-Jones glass,
made by Morris's firm, exists also at Frinton-on-Sea. Of the other
leading glass artists of those years *Henry Holiday* can also be seen
at Waltham Abbey with early work of the highest quality (1867),
and early *Kempe* windows are at St John's Moulsham Street,
Chelmsford (1879).

Now to return to architecture. Webb is not represented in
Essex, but *Norman Shaw* is, with the lively Chigwell Hall of
1876. Two years later *Eden Nesfield*, who about 1860 had been
young Shaw's slightly older partner, built Loughton Hall near by, [62b]
in a very similar style. Nesfield had a good connexion in Essex,
as witnessed by his restoration of Radwinter church and the
building of a pretty row of shops there, the building of the Newport Grammar School, and a remarkably original bank at Saffron
Walden.

This 'Domestic Revival' of the seventies was a demonstration
of revolt against the presumptuous, stodgy and uncomfortable,
oversized country-houses built by the architects of the older
generation in the Gothic or the Italianate or mixed style. The
type is exemplified in Essex by the younger *Hardwick*'s Hassobury, Farnham of 1868 and the younger *Cockerell*'s Down Hall,
Hatfield Broad Oak of 1873. But while the pomposity of such designs on the whole disappeared from domestic architecture as the
C19 drew to its close, it had a glorious revival in public architecture of the Edwardian years. The imperial optimism of that

precarious phase found expression in the wild exuberance of
63a super-Loire-châteaux such as the West Ham Technical College
by *Gibson & Russell* (1896–8) or of Neo-Palladian palaces such
as *Sir John Belcher*'s highly successful town hall at Colchester
(1898–1902).

The twenty years after the death of Edward VII and the out-
break of the First World War had little to add to the achievements of architecture in Essex, though much to its bulk. For they
saw the growth of Becontree as an L. C. C. housing estate and of
innumerable housing estates elsewhere near London. The architectural style of the TWENTIETH CENTURY appeared however
early in the county, though only in one place and without immediate consequences: at Silver End, thanks to the initiative of
Lord Braintree. *Thomas Tait* began to build little white houses
with flat roofs and horizontal windows in 1926. They are in fact
only antedated in England by one house (at Northampton) designed by Peter Behrens a little earlier. Next after Silver End
came *Joseph Emberton*'s Royal Corinthian Yacht Club at Burn-
ham-on-Crouch of 1931, a remarkably mature example of the so-
called International Modern Style. Public architecture, that is
the town halls, civic centres, and so on of the prospering new
boroughs on the eastern outskirts of London, did not go so far.
Here one finds large and ambitious versions of the Neo-Georgian
or Neo-Palladian tempered by modern motifs such as porticoes
with pillars instead of columns, or tall wide staircase windows or
little lanterns and cupolas on the Swedish pattern. Examples are
the Civic Centres of Dagenham and Walthamstow, and the tamer
South-West and South-East Essex Technical Colleges. The
Second World War brought a second break, and after it at last
the style of the C20 seems to have acclimatized itself in Essex.
63b Now the excellent London Transport stations on the new eastern
extension of the Central Line went up, such as Wanstead and
Redbridge, now the great education drive brought forth such
large and pleasantly designed schools and technical colleges as
those at West Ham and East Ham and a whole chain of excellent
schools developed by the county architect, *H. Conolly*, and his
team of assistants, now estates of flats well planned and well detailed made their appearance, as at Walthamstow and Dagenham,
64 now the New Town created at Harlow began to take shape under
the skilful hands of *Frederick Gibberd*, to give the British for the
first time a taste of what a completely modern, if not a completely
urban community can provide in the way of visual pleasures.
Much of this is still in the course of development as this volume

is being got ready and only a continual perusal of the architectural papers can keep one up-to-date.

POSTSCRIPT, 1964

'As this volume is being got ready' referred to 1954. The last ten years have seen much of new estates around London, some good, some bad, some indifferent. Harlow has gone on growing most satisfactorily with its Civic Centre by *Frederick Gibberd* and housing by many architects, the best perhaps Ladyshot by *Yorke, Rosenberg & Mardall* and Northbrooks by *Powell & Moya*. Basildon New Town has also come on, and the centre now has an impressively mighty tower block by *A. B. Davis*. To choose the best recent individual buildings must always remain a matter of personal taste. Here is a recommended half-dozen or so, nearly all commercial: the seed warehouse by *Chamberlin, Powell & Bon* at Witham, the Bank of England printing works by *Easton & Robertson* at Debden, the Standard Yeast Co. by *Ove Arup & Partners* at Dovercourt, the Eastern Region stations at Barking and Harlow Town, *Erdi & Rabson's* Motel at Epping, and Keddie's store at Southend by *Yorke, Rosenberg & Mardall*.

FURTHER READING

Literature on the pre-C 20 architecture of Essex is alas only too static. Not much research work and even less work of historical ordering seems to go on. The Royal Commission on Historical Monuments published its four volumes on the county in 1916 to 1923. They must form the basis of all further investigation, at least, as far as they go – that is, to be precise, to the year 1714. For Georgian architecture there is no guide. Here, as indeed for earlier domestic architecture, the best source is the volumes of *Country Life* (and H. Avray Tipping's *English Homes* compiled in nine volumes out of articles in *Country Life*). The *Victoria County History* for Essex has in its first two volumes (1903–7) not yet proceeded beyond prehistory. Volume III on Roman Essex came out in 1963, volume IV on the Ongar Hundred in 1956. The most useful general guidebook to Essex is still the volume of the *Little Guides* written originally in 1909 by that indefatigable regional traveller and researcher, the late J. C. Cox. Of old literature two works at least are still indispensable: P. Morant's *History and Antiquities* of 1768 and T. Wright's *History and Topography* of 1836. For individual subjects such as fonts or bench ends books will of course have to be used which treat them over the whole country. Special Essex literature of this kind can only be given for medieval monuments (F. Chancellor 1890), brasses (M. Christy and others; new edition 1948), church chests (F. Roe 1929), and church plate (G. M. Benton 1926). More literature may well have been overlooked, and I can only repeat what is said in a note at the beginning of this book, namely that I shall welcome any corrections kind and unkind readers and reviewers may be ready to make.

ESSEX

*

ABBERTON

ST ANDREW. Overlooking the South Essex reservoir. C14 nave, early C16 brick tower with blue bricks in diaper pattern. Thin buttresses, two-light brick bell-openings. The chancel, also of brick, dates from the C19.

ABBESS RODING

ST EDMUND. Nave C14, chancel C15, E window from the restoration of 1867, W tower also 1867. The nave roof has tie-beams on arched braces with a little tracery in the spandrels. Inside the chancel on the N side a niche which was originally the opening into a closet recognizable on the outside. – FONT. Square, of the late C12, decorated on one side with a Norman foliage trail, on one with a trail of a rather unusual stylized shape, on the third with the sun, a whorl, and two rosettes, and on the fourth with two flowers and three small roses. – SCREEN. With two-light divisions, the mullion being carried up into the apex of the four-centred arch. Each light has an ogee arch with some panel-tracery above. – PULPIT. With an uncommonly fine, generously large tester; C18. – HOUR-GLASS STAND. Wrought iron, early C18, near the pulpit. – STAINED GLASS. In a chancel s window. Good figures of a Bishop and a female Saint surrounded by tabernacle-work not in its original state; C15. – MONUMENTS. Sir Gamaliel Capell † 1613, with the usual kneeling figures facing each other, the children kneeling in the 'predella'. – Lady Lucklyn † 1633, with frontal demi-figure, head propped on elbow and a book in front of her. Two cherubs, seated on the outer volutes, hold a curtain open. Flying little putti behind. The monument has been attributed to *Epiphanius Evesham* (J. Seymour).

(ROOKWOOD HALL, ¾ m. WSW. Barns of the early C16. The larger with two porches and a fine tie-beam roof with octagonal king-posts. R.C.)

ABBOT'S HALL *see* SHALFORD

ABRIDGE

HOLY TRINITY. Small uninteresting brick church of 1833, enlarged by *R. W. Edis* in 1877.

Quite a pretty village centre along the main road, with one half-
timbered, gabled house, and (in a good position facing the
traveller, as he approaches from the E) the Early Victorian
BLUE BOAR. It has quoins and a Tuscan porch.

ALBYNS *see* STAPLEFORD ABBOTS

ALDBOROUGH HOUSE *see* ILFORD

ALDHAM

ST MARGARET. 1855 by *Hakewill*, with the materials of the old
church, but very Victorian in the picturesque grouping, specially from the outside, and the wild overdoing of flint as the
surfacing material. Even the walls of the porch look all cobbled.
The porch otherwise, that is in its timber-work, is the only
medieval piece. It is of the C14 with ogee-traceried side panels
and a heavily bargeboarded gable. The bargeboarding also
ends in an ogee arch. – DOOR to the tower with symmetrically
arranged C13 iron scrolls.

(ALDHAM HALL, ⅔ m. S. Timber-framed, C16 and C17. The
porch with C17 bargeboarding and a pendant. On the first
floor a room with late C16 panelling and overmantel. R.C.)

FORD STREET. Several nice houses in the street, especially BOY
SCOUTS' HALL, early C16 and C17 with exposed timbers,
and some Georgian houses.

ALPHAMSTONE

CHURCH. Nave, lower chancel and belfry. All much restored by
Sir Arthur Blomfield. Norman one blocked N window, C13 the
completely plain N doorway. The rest mostly C14, windows
especially and SEDILIA. The latter of three seats, framed in
one, with the PISCINA, cusped pointed arches on detached
shafts. S arcade (also C14) of three bays with octagonal piers
and double-chamfered arches. – FONT. Of the familiar Purbeck type, square, with five shallow blank arches on each side,
C12. – FONT COVER. Handsome, if modest, C17 piece. Semi-
globe with ribs crowned by a finial of openwork scrolls carrying
a ball.

CLEES HALL, 1 m. SSE. Splendid C16 BARN, 120 ft long,
weatherboarded, with a queenpost roof.

ALRESFORD

CHURCH. Nave, lower (rebuilt) chancel, and (rebuilt) belfry. Roman brick quoins at the w end date the nave as Norman. Nice w gallery with twisted balusters, C18.

ALRESFORD HALL. Early C18 front of five-bay centre with segment-headed windows and slightly projecting pedimented wings.

THE QUARTERS (formerly Grotto Cottage). In the grounds of the hall, by a stream. A cottage of no interest converted into a pretty extravaganza by giving the windows some kind of fancy Gothic shape and adding an octagon with a Chinese concave-sided roof and a wooden verandah. It may have been used as a summer house or even for fishing from the verandah.* Modern extension, 1951–2 in the style of the original.

ROMAN VILLA, 400 yds SE of Alresford Lodge. Part of a corridor villa was excavated in the C19, when tessellated pavements and painted wall plaster were found. A modern house now covers the site.

ALTHORNE

ST ANDREW. Nave, chancel, and w tower – all Perp. The w tower is of flint and stone and has diagonal buttresses. The battlements have a trellis pattern of ashlar against the flint ground. Above the w door is an inscription which reads as follows: 'Orate pro animabus dominorum Johannis Wylson et Johannis Hyll quorum animabus propicietur deus amen.' They no doubt paid for the building of the tower. The nave is of flint, embattled, the chancel lower and of brick. – FONT. Octagonal, Perp, with fleurons on the foot, panel tracery on the stem, and on the bowl figures of angels, saints, a baptism, the martyrdom of St Andrew, etc. The figure carving is thoroughly bad. – BRASS to William Hyklott † 1508 'which paide for the werkemanship of the wall of this churche'.‡

AMBERDEN HALL see DEBDEN

AMBRESBURY BANKS see EPPING

APPLETON'S FARM see BULPHAN

* It appears in a painting by Constable, now in the National Gallery of Victoria at Melbourne. In a letter to his wife Constable refers to this 'little fishing house'.

‡ Mr H. V. Molesworth Roberts draws attention to the BLACK LION and TYLE HALL, both of the late C18 or early C19.

ARDEN HALL *see* HORNDON-ON-THE-HILL

ARDLEIGH

ST MARY. W tower of *c.*1500: brick and flint and dark brown stone with two diagonal buttresses and pinnacled battlements of flint and brick decoration. S porch of about the same date. Extremely elaborate East Anglian work, all flint inlay and stone. Decorated walls and battlements. Pinnacles with animals. Two figures of lions *couchant* as stops of the hood-mould of the doorway. In the spandrels of the doorway lively figures of St George and the Dragon. Above the doorway three niches. The inner doorway has Adam and Eve in the spandrels and also a niche above. Side-openings of three lights with Perp tracery – the pattern identical with that of the aisles at Brightlingsea. The rest of the church by *Butterfield* 1881, except for the W bay of the nave. Butterfield enjoyed the ornate medieval parts, but his forms are bigger. In the interior he is here very restrained. – SCREEN. Dado only, with pretty traceried panels. – DOOR. *c.*1500, elaborately traceried. – PLATE. Cup of 1584; Paten probably of the same date; both with bands of engraved ornament.

In the village on the S side of the street one specially good HOUSE with exposed timber. The upper storey originally projected. Some of the original windows are preserved, in particular one of five lights in the E wall. Inside, beams decorated with leaf trails.

ARKESDEN

A pretty, small village by a tiny stream.

ST MARY. Traces of a Norman round tower were found when in 1855 the present W tower was built. At the same time the church was heavily restored. It consists of a C13 nave and a C13 chancel. Roofs, clerestory, and chancel arch belong to 1855. Inside, the S arcade has circular piers, the N arcade octagonal piers. Both have arches with two slight chamfers. So they must both be C13, and not too late. – PLATE. Cup of 1562; Paten of 1567. – MONUMENTS. Brass to a Knight, mid C15, the figure 3 ft long. – Effigy of a Priest, C15; in a very low two-bay recess in the chancel N wall. The recess has three broad piers with niches for figures. – Richard Cutte † 1592 and wife. Large standing wall-monument with two recumbent effigies, and the children kneeling against arches on the front of the tomb-chest. The effigies under a heavy six-poster with odd short baluster-columns which have leaves growing up the lower thirds of their shafts. Straight top with obelisks and achievements. – John Withers † 1692 and wife. Standing wall-monument with an excellent stone relief of skulls and branches and higher up excellent busts of marble. It is a first-class work and has recently been convincingly attributed to *Edward Pearce*.

(WOOD HALL, ½ m. SSW. 1652, externally much altered. Inside an early C16 richly carved beam in the former kitchen, brought in from elsewhere. In the SE room a fireplace dated 1652 with much elaborate strapwork. R.C.)

ASHDON

ALL SAINTS. Mostly C14, but externally much renewed. The W tower has a W window of early C14 type, angle buttresses, stepped battlements, and a spire. The S chancel chapel, which is taller than the chancel, also has two early C14 windows and is, besides, separated inside from the chancel by a two-bay arcade with an early C14 circular pier and moulded arches. To the same date the Royal Commission ascribes the kingpost roof of the chapel with four-way struts. The post itself is quatrefoil with moulded capital. Again early C14 one window in the S aisle. Later the arcades between nave and aisles which have a broad polygonal shaft without capital towards the nave and finer polygonal shafts with capitals towards the (two-centred) arches. The chancel arch is similar. C15 porches, and early C16 clerestory (a will of 1527 refers to three of the clere-story windows). – STAINED GLASS. Bits in the N chapel N window; c.1400. – PLATE. Cup and Paten on foot of 1621. – MONUMENT. Big tomb-chest with three shields on intricately cusped panels; coat of arms on the back wall; early C16.

GUILDHALL, S of the church, perhaps really a Church House. Built c.1500; timber-framed and plastered.

ROSE AND CROWN INN. In one ground-floor room well pre-served early C17 painted decoration, chiefly of geometrical panel patterns, with strapwork.

WINDMILL, I m. NE. Post-mill in poor condition.

BARTLOW HILLS. There were originally eight barrows in this cemetery, only four of which survive. The largest is 45 ft high and 144 ft in diameter. The barrows covered cremation burials in glass cinerary bottles, in some cases contained in a wooden chest or tile-built chamber. Grave goods included further glass vessels, bronze flagons, and pottery. The finds suggest that the cemetery was in use in the late C1 and early C2. A few of the objects from the barrows are preserved in Saffron Walden Museum, but the majority perished in the fire at Easton Lodge in 1847.

An EARTHWORK runs between the barrows in an E–W direction and can be traced almost to the Granta, SE of Bartlow church. It may originally have served as part of the cemetery enclosure.

ROMAN VILLA, on Great Copt Hill. The foundations of a building 52 ft long and 17 ft wide were discovered in the C19. The seven rooms of the building had floors of very coarse tesserae. Half of the structure was heated by a hypocaust system, and the whole may represent the bath building of an adjacent villa. The site is now marked by a spread of rubble.

ASHDON PLACE see BARTLOW END

ASHELDHAM

ST LAWRENCE. Entirely of the first half of the C14. W tower with diagonal buttresses and later brick battlements, nave and chancel. The windows are either cusped lancets or have some little ogee detail. The chancel s window, s doorway (with head-label-stops), and SEDILE form a group. – PLATE. Cup of 1563 with band of ornament; Paten on foot of the mid C17.

CAMP. Traces of a prehistoric plateau camp, now hardly visible, 600 yds w of the church.

ASHEN

ST AUGUSTINE OF CANTERBURY. One small lancet window in the nave indicates a C13 origin. The W tower with diagonal buttresses and battlements was added about 1400, the brick stair-turret with the battlements on a trefoiled corbel-frieze about 1525. The chancel dates from 1857. – DOOR in s doorway, with damaged C13 ironwork. – BENCHES. A few fragments in the nave. Also an inscription in Roman capitals, dated 1620, which reads: 'This hath bin the churching the mearring stool and so it shall be still'. – PLATE. Cup and Paten of c.1570. – MONUMENTS. Brass to a Knight of c.1440, the figure 21 in. long (nave, E end). – Luce Tallakarne † 1610, an odd design with termini caryatids and between them decoration with panels, a shield, and the inscription plates.

(STREET FARM, NW of the church. Early C16 house, timber-framed with original hall, screens, and parlour. All these have moulded beams and joists. The hall also possesses two original doorways and doors. R.C.)

ASHINGDON

ST ANDREW. Nave and chancel with a small W tower only about half the width of the nave. The tower has diagonal buttresses and a pyramid roof. The brick S window in the nave is C18, but the brick E wall of the chancel, as shown by the black diapering, is of *c.*1500. This is also the date of the two-light brick window on the N side of the chancel, and may be the date of the timber S porch, a relatively plain specimen. The nave must be earlier, see the window on the N side which has Y-tracery. Such windows are usually of *c.*1300. The chancel must belong to the same moment. Its arch has the original N respond left (trefoiled in plan with moulded capital). C15 to C16 roofs in nave and chancel. – PLATE. Cup of 1564 with band of ornament; Cup on baluster stem of 1640; Paten of the late C17.

AUBYNS see WRITTLE

AUDLEY END

AUDLEY END was the largest newly built mansion of the Jacobean era. What remains now is only a fragment, and even that is hardly less in size than the whole of Hatfield. Audley End can be called newly built, although it is the successor of Walden Abbey which, at the Dissolution, came into the hands of Lord Chancellor Audley. His daughter married the Duke of Norfolk and the son of the marriage, Thomas Howard, made Earl of Suffolk in 1603 and Lord Treasurer in 1604, began a completely new house on a splendid scale, it is said, in 1603. His Surveyor, according to Vertue, was *Bernart Janssen*. The house had a square W forecourt slightly wider than the whole present W façade, with a broad one-storeyed gatehouse, angle pavilions of three storeys and N and S ranges of two. The façade of to-day is essentially unchanged, but whereas now to the E of this there are only two projecting wings, these were originally longer and formed the N and S sides of a big inner courtyard, extended in its turn to the E in two projecting wings similar in

form to what we see now. So one whole courtyard has disappeared and nearly half the main building.* What remains
is however big enough, and its ambitions can at once be seen
by the fact that the house appears not of brick, like Hatfield,
but faced with Chilmark and Ketton stone. In its elevation
it is of great evenness of fenestration, with many-mullioned
windows that have one or two transoms. The roofs are hidden
by a balustrade with divers, none too fantastic, strapwork
patterns. They are punctuated by square angle turrets, three
on each side to emphasize the angle block of the w front and
two bigger ones over the returning angles. There were originally more. The details of some of the surviving ones look as
though they might have been altered by *Vanbrugh* (*see* below),
and a good deal more was restored, renovated, or remodelled
in the late C18 and the C19, but all this was done surprisingly
sensitively and respectfully. The pretty, convex caps on the
turrets seem original Jacobean work. Two elements of the
elevations must be emphasized. First the *piazzas* or colonnades
on the E side towards the former inner courtyard and on the S
side. Both are now closed. Both had arched openings with
columns between the arches carrying an entablature. That on
the S side is early C17, the other represents an addition made
about 1760 for convenience's sake and provided, for the same
reason, with an upper floor almost immediately after. Such
colonnades came into fashion just in the years when Audley
End was built (Hatfield, Knole, Cranbourne, Holland House,
Neville's Court Trinity College Cambridge). Before 1600 they
had been rare (Burghley). The other remarkable motif of the
elevations is connected with the arrangement of the Great Hall.
This lies in the centre of the present w front, though one would
rather expect it to be in the (no longer surviving) far side – that
is the E side of the inner court. The Hall is still in the medieval
and Tudor tradition entered by a porch leading into a screens
passage. But in order to achieve external symmetry at all costs,
the porch is duplicated and the bay window of the Hall placed
near its centre instead of at the dais end. It is a solution less
revolutionary than say at Hardwick, where the whole hall is
placed at right angles to the façade, but also indicative of the
new tendency towards symmetry rather than utility. The two

* For the demolition of the w courtyard *Vanbrugh* is responsible (*see*
below); the demolition along the E courtyard followed c.1750. The new E
fronts of the wings with their canted bay windows are supposed to be of
c.1760–85.

porches are the show-pieces of the house, far more ornate than anything else and indeed overcrowded with columns and curly strapwork. They look like the contribution of quite another taste and hand. Especially surprising is the contrast with the completely unadorned bay window which lies between them. Inside both porches are fine original wooden doors.

The interiors of Audley End are not on the whole up to the highest decorative standards, with one exception, the Hall and Staircase. The HALL runs up the whole height of the w range. It has wooden panelling and a flat plaster ceiling with the beams of timber. The main cross-beams rest on curly brackets and have pretty pendants. The plaster panels are adorned with medallions containing heads and emblems in relief. All this is rather thin and dainty, and may be partly (or largely?) C18 repair or remodelling. It is in contrast to the obviously original two E doorways and in complete contrast to the two-storeyed SCREEN, which is thick, coarse, and massive. Its chief decoration is the pairs of terminal figures on both floors. The whole is structurally quite illogical, statically precarious-looking, and covered over everywhere by blank panels, strapwork, garlands, and so on. The fireplace is similar in style even if not quite so ornate.* Could this perhaps be *c.*1720 rather than *c.*1610? The question arises on the strength of what faces the screen.

This is a second SCREEN, of stone. It is as restrained as the other is profuse: three arches separated by coupled Tuscan pilasters on the ground floor, and the same motif repeated on the first floor with Ionic pilasters. From the two other arches starts the main STAIRCASE, in two straight parallel flights to the upper landing. The staircase also is of stone, though it has a fine wrought-iron handrail. This noble work is due no doubt to *Sir John Vanbrugh*, who was consulted about 1721. And, when he rebuilt the staircase, he must have done another job which is of considerable interest. The ceiling of the staircase seems at first sight Jacobean and is called that by the Royal Commission and Avray Tipping. The details however seem to me unlikely as C17 work. They must be a consciously Neo-Jacobean design of Vanbrugh's. The suggestion is not as surprising as it may appear at first. Only fifteen years later William Kent designed Jacobean ceilings at Hampton Court,‡

* During the third quarter of the C18 communicating corridors were added on the E side of the Hall.

‡ In addition cf. Langleys, Great Waltham.

and Vanbrugh was, we know, in other ways also a pioneer of a romantic revivalism.

As for the rest of the house, what remains after the demolitions is highly ornamented and very puzzling. Quite obviously the Neo-Jacobean taste lived on. Jacobean plasterwork was copied in the 1760s,* the early C19 (by the first Lord Braybrooke), and later. Of special features in the rooms open to the public, the following need mention (in the order in which they are seen). The SALOON has a specially ornament-incrusted fireplace, thin clustered Gothick wall-shafts of the C18, a quatrefoil frieze belonging to the same years (*Joseph Rose* was paid for it in 1763–4), and a pretty plaster ceiling with small closely spaced pendants, and whales, mermaids, sea-monsters, etc., in the panel. The ceiling as well as the fireplace is of the early C17. – An original fireplace also in the DRAWING ROOM. But the Jacobean-looking ceiling is of *c*.1830. The SOUTH LIBRARY has a chimneypiece of *c*.1770, but the rest is of *c*.1830. – In the main LIBRARY another Jacobean-looking ceiling of *c*.1820–5. Only the chimneypiece is genuine. – The DINING ROOM has a ceiling of *c*.1820–5 and chimneypieces which are baffling. Is one of them genuine, and was it copied about 1820–5 ? – The SOUTH STAIRS are visually perhaps the most attractive feature of Audley End: narrow oblong well and narrow straight flights of stairs. The well is bordered by eight wooden posts in rows of two fours, reaching right up to the ceiling in pretty little obelisks. The stair balustrade has tapering square pillars instead of balusters. The stockade of decorated uprights is most successful. The date is of course that of the house. – The NORTH STAIR is similar but less lively. One reaches it by traversing the PICTURE GALLERY, a room added *c*.1764 and provided with its thick chimneypiece *c*.1865. – In the NORTH WING, apart from some Jacobean chimneypieces the most interesting thing is the CHAPEL, completed in 1786. The original chapel lay in the SE projection from the Jacobean Inner Courtyard. The new chapel is Gothick at its prettiest. Its designer is given as *Hobcraft*. It has a thin plaster vault on thin quatrefoil shafts with a centrally placed kind of transept. The arches have gables and thin

* The most recent guidebook of the Ministry of Public Building and Works (1963) concurs with my view. Mr Gunnis refers to much mason's work in 1761–7, and also to new fireplaces during the same years. See also W. Addison: *Audley End*, 1953, pp. 115–25, especially for the share of *Robert Adam*.

tracery in them. There are a fireplace in the family pew and a fan-vaulted w gallery. The chairs also are consistently Gothick, and so is the LECTERN. – Then down the North Stair and to the LOWER GALLERY which runs to the E of the Hall. It was added for the sake of communication c.1760, and the openings were filled in c.1865. – In the SOUTH WING on the GROUND FLOOR are the bedrooms which, however, until c.1820 were living rooms. They were decorated c.1765 by *Robert Adam*. By him especially the two screens of columns of the DINING PARLOUR. The GREAT DRAWING ROOM has an Adam stucco ceiling and chimneypiece. The PAINTED DRAWING ROOM is Adam-Etruscan (i.e. Pompeian) and has a pretty alcove. *Biagio Rebecca* was paid in 1769 for work in this room.

The GROUNDS of Audley End were landscaped by *Capability Brown* (1763 etc.). As was the fashion of the day pieces of garden furnishing were scattered about, exquisitely hidden, half-concealed, or thrown into relief by planting. They are the following:

Three-arched BRIDGE to the SW, by *Robert Adam*, 1763–4.

CIRCULAR TEMPLE, also by *Robert Adam*, on the slope to the W of the house, beyond the road. It has unfluted Ionic columns and was erected to commemorate the British successes in the Seven Years' War (1756–63).

PALLADIAN BRIDGE with Summer House on it, close to the CASCADE, 1783, to the NW.

SPRINGWOOD COLUMN higher up, dedicated to Lady Portsmouth; 1774.

TEMPLE OF CONCORD, to the E of the house, 1791 by *R. F. Brettingham*, rectangular with tall unfluted Corinthian columns, grouped at the corners in clusters of three (it was built to commemorate George III's recovery from illness in 1789).

ICEHOUSE LODGE, along the footpath to Saffron Walden; 1827, by *Buckler* and *Rickman* (?).

Still later the various LODGES including that from the village. Also in the grounds, to the NW of the house the STABLES, a symmetrical E-shaped range of brick, with thin gables and dormer windows. The windows are of three lights with the lights all arched. Lantern above the centre. The building is not dated, but may well be Jacobean, though with more traditional motifs than the house.

Outside the Lion Gate AUDLEY END VILLAGE, just a few prettily grouped Georgian houses (one with Gothick windows) and, at r. angles, the village street of planned C18 cottages.

3—E.

The w side is of one consistent design. The street leads to the COLLEGE OF ST MARK (Almshouses), a Late Elizabethan brick building of uncommon completeness and plan. Two courtyards with the hall and chapel range separating them, as in such colleges as Wadham. Each courtyard had ten dwellings. Straight gables, and the only other external accent the two-transomed chapel window of brick with all individual lights arched (cf. for example the chapel at Hatfield House). The windows of the dwellings all have arched lights. The college was dissolved in 1633 and gradually fell into disrepair. It was restored about 1948–51 and the chapel rebuilt. – In the former Kitchen is a fireplace lintel of interesting C17 design, not *in situ*. – In the chapel STAINED GLASS. Many fragments of unknown provenance, some perhaps from Walden Abbey. A specially fine piece is a Virgin and Child of the late C14.

AVELEY

ST MICHAEL. Low w tower, low flat-roofed N aisle, higher N chancel chapel. All windows renewed. The building history begins with the one unsplayed early C12 window inside the nave close to the E end of the N arcade. Later in the C12 the three-bay S arcade was made with broad piers of Greek cross section. The two E bays have one-stepped arches, the w bay instead a double-chamfered arch. In the E respond a C14 niche. The N arcade with circular piers and double-chamfered arches is C13, as are the N chancel chapel of two bays and the w tower with angle buttresses and a single-chamfered tower arch. – FONT. C12, the Purbeck type often met with: square bowl decorated with shallow blank round arches; five supports. – PULPIT with tester, the Elizabethan-Jacobean type; dated 1621. – SCREEN between chancel and nave, C15, uninteresting. – PLATE. Cup and Cover of 1620; Almsdish of the late C17. – MONUMENTS. Important Brass to Ralph de Knevynton † 1370; Flemish. Rectangular plate with thin buttresses and traceried spandrels. – Brass to the Bacon children, 1588. – Epitaph to Elizabeth Bacon † 1583, brass of infant in swaddling clothes under Purbeck marble arch.

COUNTY PRIMARY SCHOOL, Stifford Road, opened 1950, and DACRE COUNTY PRIMARY SCHOOL, Shannon Way, 1957, both by the County Architect *H. Conolly*. Two of the many excellently designed new schools put up recently by the County Council.

(BRETTS, 1¼ m. NNW. Timber-framed; C14. Of the C15 the blocked square-headed E windows of the hall and the re-set doorway. Fragments of the original roof. Incomplete moat. R.C.)

(FORD PARTS DEPOT. By *E. R. Collister & Associates*, *c*.1955–6. A block of 350,000 sq. ft. The main part is 525 by 43 ft, divided into sixteen bays, steel framed. On the S side, offices, of the same length, and 54 ft wide.)

AYLMERS *see* SHEERING

AYTHORPE RODING

ST MARY. Nave and chancel, C13, but much renewed, and C15 belfry with broach spire. – BENCHES. Plain, in the nave, C16, also fragments of the C17.

WINDMILL, ½ m. ESE of the church. Post-mill in good condition.

BAILEYS *see* MASHBURY

BARDFIELD SALING (or LITTLE SALING)

ST PETER AND ST PAUL. A C14 church with the chancel probably completed last. It was shortened in the C19. Round W tower whose windows look early C14. Early to mid C14 windows in the nave and chancel, but quite a marked difference in style between the S arcade and the chancel arch. The former has strong piers consisting of four main shafts and four keeled shafts in the diagonals, with moulded arches and head-stops; the chancel arch has late-C14-looking responds. Big ogee squint. – PULPIT. Elizabethan, the usual arched panels treated in perspective. The pilasters between of termini shape. – SCREEN. Contemporary with the chancel, that is of large and relatively plain forms, ogee arches and, above in niches, quatrefoils coming down to an ogee point. Strong framing. – STRAW DECORATION for the altar made *c*.1880, chiefly extremely naturalistic vine trails with grapes.

(ELMS FARM, ⅔ m. NE. Timber-framed late C15 house. The hall had a ceiling inserted *c*.1600, but keeps two blocked doorways originally leading into the screens passage. The solar projects on the N side on curved brackets. Central chimney-stack of *c*.1600 with diagonally placed shafts. R.C.)

WINDMILL, ½ m. SE. Post-mill in a dilapidated condition.

BARKING

Barking in the Middle Ages was famous for its ABBEY. This was founded c. 666 by St Erkenwald for Benedictine nuns and remained powerful to the date of the Dissolution. The church was pulled down in 1541. The site was excavated in 1910, and much of the medieval evidence can now clearly be read inscribed in stone lines in the grass. The buildings lay just N of the parish church. The abbey church faced the parish churchyard. It was of C12 date, just under 300 ft long, and had a chancel with apse, chancel aisles with smaller apses, crossing tower, transepts with one E chapel each, nave of ten bays with aisles, and two W towers projecting slightly beyond the aisles. In the early C13 a Saint's Chapel and Lady Chapel were added at the E end. To the N of the nave lay the cloister with the monastic buildings arranged in the usual way: Chapter House off the E walk, Dormitory off the W walk and projecting N beyond the Cloister, Reredorter, that is lavatories, beyond to the W and separated by a passage, Refectory along the N walk. N of the chancel beyond the Chapter House was the Infirmary with its separate chapel. Of all the monastic buildings only one remains upright: the E gate or FIRE BELL GATE, a gate-tower with upper chapel, containing a badly worn, but originally excellent mid C12 (?) ROOD with three figures. The figures are in relief and the whole is built up of oblong blocks, like the more famous contemporary reliefs at Chichester.

ST MARGARET. A church of proper town-size, not small, like the near-by churches of East Ham and Dagenham. Nave and aisles, outer N aisle, chancel and chancel chapels, W tower. The chancel is of the early C13 – see its lancet windows (E window early C16). The octagonal piers of the N arcade of the same period. At that time the church must have had crossing and transepts, see the much wider opening of the present E bay of the arcades. Earlier still than the C13 appears the E chapel of the outer N aisle, and especially the arcade of two bays to the N chancel chapel. This has circular pier and semicircular responds, all with scalloped capitals. The ashlar masonry also is Norman. The Royal Commission suggest re-use after the Dissolution. In the C15 the W parts of the N arcade were reconstructed, then the W parts of the S arcade built, the W tower (with taller stair-turret) added, and then the E parts of the arcades renewed (arches with two hollow chamfers). The tower is of Reigate ashlar, while the rest of the church is of rag. C15 also the chan-

cel chapels. The date of the outer N aisle seems to be early C16.
The nave roof is original, that of the chancel has a prettily
stuccoed vault of 1772. All this makes a confusing picture, to
the mind as much as the eye. – FONT. Bowl on baluster stem,
with ornate scrolly ornament, just going gristly, i.e. c.1635. –
PULPIT. C18, with staircase railing of finely twisted balusters.
– ORGAN CASE. C18, by *Byfield*. – SCULPTURE. Fragment,
c.12 in. high, of Saxon cross shaft with close thin interlace ornament. Perhaps C10. – PLATE. Paten given in (16)77; Chalice
by *I.B.*, Cover Paten, and Flagon all of 1680; Almsdish of
c.1700. – MONUMENTS. Brasses of Priest c.1480, of Thomas
Broke † 1493 and wife, and of John Tedcastell and wife † 1596;
in chancel. – Brass of Richard Malet † 1485, demi-figure of
Priest, in N aisle. – Incised slab to Martin, first Vicar of Barking, † 1328, large demi-figure, an important work of its type. –
Sir Charles Montague † 1625. A beautiful and unusual design
with small seated figure in tent, musketeers l. and r. outside
the tent, and many more tents in the distance. Sir Charles
seems to muse on the next day's destinies, and there is a great
deal of suspense in the eve-of-battle atmosphere. – Francis
Fuller † 1636, with frontal bust in oval niche. – John Bennett
† 1706, a spectacular monument with a frontal demi-figure in
an elegant attitude between two columns carrying an open
segmental pediment. To the l. and r. ships in relief. – Sir
Orlando Humfreys † 1737, standing wall-monument with
detached Corinthian columns carrying a far-projecting broken
segmental pediment. Between them the bust of Sir Orlando;
outside the columns cherubs. Original iron railings. – John
Bamber † 1753, bust against obelisk, attributed by Mrs Esdaile
to *Roubiliac*. Original iron railings. – Sir Crisp Gascoyne
† 1761, Lord Mayor of London, elegant with weeping putto
against a grey obelisk.

ST PATRICK, Blake Avenue. 1940 by *A. E. Wiseman*. An odd
attempt at modern church architecture, with a circular E tower
housing the apse and ending in bell-openings of somewhat
streamlined design.

(TOWN HALL with adjacent ASSEMBLY HALL. Designed in
1936 by *Jackson & Edmonds* but not built until 1954–8.)

EASTBURY HOUSE (Cultural Centre). A very valuable example
of a medium-sized Elizabethan manor house. Dated on a rainwater-head 1572. Some details look a little earlier, e.g. the door
pediment. H-shaped with short wings projecting in the front,
larger wings framing a back courtyard closed by a wall. In the

returning angles of the courtyard were two spiral staircases. One is now demolished. In the front the symmetry is broken by a porch attached to the w wing. This led into the one-storeyed hall, which has however been subdivided. Above it the Great Chamber with some (boarded-up) wall paintings of landscapes and seascapes separated by twisted columns. Similar paintings in a room in the E wing. Otherwise the inside has not much of value. The outside is all the more impressive. It is of red brick and has regularly arranged windows of three lights with one transom. There are quite a number of gables, and groups of twisted chimneys and the staircase tower reached up yet higher. The gables have polygonal angle posts – an early C16 motif – and the porch doorway with four-centred head carries a pediment with Perp tracery motifs. That also looks rather 1550 than 1570.

(RAILWAY STATION. 1959–61, by *H. H. Powell* (Architect to the Eastern Region). One of the best of recent English stations. Also other railway structures.)

(THE LINTONS, Queens Road area. 1960–3 by *M. Maybury*, Borough Architect. Residential blocks, one of sixteen and six of seven storeys. Perhaps the first in the country to be built of totally precast factory made concrete components. Information from Borough Architect's Department.)

BARKINGSIDE

HOLY TRINITY, Mossfield Green. 1839–40 by *Blore*. Norman, in yellow brick, with starved tower on the N side close to the w end. Long Norman lancets, exceedingly long especially at the w end. The chancel added *c*.1875.

ST GEORGE, Woodford Avenue. 1931 by *Sir Charles Nicholson*. Red brick with short broad square w tower with copper-covered spire. The church, low and broad, has no clerestory and no structural division between nave and chancel. The piers are octagonal, but the E window is frankly Perp.

DR BARNARDO'S VILLAGE HOME. Opened in 1873 with about four cottages. The management of Dr Barnardo's Homes could not supply any useful architectural information, except that the CHAPEL dates from 1892 and the AUSTRALASIAN HOSPITAL from 1912 (*W. A. Pite*).

BARLING

ALL SAINTS. Stately w tower with diagonal buttresses with three set-offs, ogee-headed niches l. and r. and above the w window, a frieze of flint and stone chequer above the window, battlements, and a recessed boarded spire. Late Perp (Tudor) the N aisle with its two- and three-light windows without tracery and its concave-sided, relatively tall and slender octagonal arcade piers. Rood stairs in the N wall. – FONT. Perp, octagonal, with shields, quatrefoils, etc. – PULPIT. With big tester and back wall with a big odd-shaped panel flanked by volutes. – SCULPTURE. Two headless alabaster figures, C15, one seated, the other standing, only 12 and 15 in. long. – PLATE. Cup of 1562 with two bands of ornament; Paten of 1568.

BARNSTON

CHURCH. Nave Norman with two N windows, one S window, and a plain S doorway with one order of columns with scallop capitals. Chancel E.E. with one N lancet window and a fine DOUBLE PISCINA of the type of Jesus and St John's Colleges at Cambridge, that is with intersected round arches. The shafts have stiff-leaf capitals. The foliage runs on as a frieze behind the capitals towards the wall and fills the spandrels of the arches as well. C15 belfry with C18 cupola. – PLATE. Cup and Paten on foot of 1712.

BARRINGTON HALL see HATFIELD BROAD OAK

BARSTABLE see BASILDON

BARTLOW END*

WALTONS.‡ An interesting house with a complex building history and a fine plain Georgian front of c.1730. This seven-bay, two-storeyed front with a three-bay pediment, the Hall behind it with its carved doorways, the staircase behind the Hall and the rooms to its NW with more carved doorways and a beautiful fireplace are however the latest stage in the building history. The house began in the Elizabethan period, turned the other way, as a half-H with double-gabled projecting wings and a recessed centre. The original arched doorway still exists inside the present house and some brick corbelling above, presumably for an oriel window. Some blocked windows also indicate where the former wings extended. The visible windows are mullioned and still have arched lights. Later on, but

* Parish of Ashdon.

‡ Severely damaged by fire in 1954 and since restored without an attic storey.

still in the C17, the space between the wings was filled in, and then *c.*1730 the new S front was put on. At the same time offices were added to the SE with blank rusticated arcading and oval windows to fill the space behind the SE side of the old house, and another extension to connect the house with an Elizabethan outbuilding in line with it. This has straight mullioned windows and a fine group of central diagonal and star-shaped chimneyshafts. A second Elizabethan outbuilding further NE of the former. The 1730 front was widened by a porch and curved wings which have since disappeared.

(ASHDON PLACE, Stevington End. Handsome half-timbered C16 house on a half-H plan. Façade with exposed timbers; the plastered infilling decorated with flowers etc. R.C.)

BARTLOW HILLS, *see* Ashdon.

PLACE FARM. Timber-framed with cross-gables. The timbers are exposed. Central group of polygonal chimneystacks.

BASILDON

INTRODUCTION

Basildon, like its counterpart in NW Essex, Harlow, is one of eight New Towns established after the War in a ring round London just beyond the Metropolitan Green Belt, and intended as self-contained towns to reaccommodate in congenial surroundings the surplus population and industry from London. With an area of over 7,800 acres, making it the largest of the London New Towns, Basildon had the additional problem of an indigenous population of 25,000 at the time the Development Corporation was appointed (1949), contained in 5,000 or so substandard dwellings strung out along nearly 80 miles of unmade roads. The site is roughly rectangular, 6 miles long, to include the two loosely-knit and unrelated communities of sparse inter-war shack development around the old village nuclei of Dunton–Laindon–Langdon Hills–Lee Chapel in the W and Basildon–Nevendon–Vange–Pitsea in the E; and 3 miles wide between the London to Southend Arterial Road (A127) in the N and the A13 and Tilbury to Southend railway in the S. Although close to the Thames Estuary, the area is by no means flat, and the larger part of the built-up area of the town lies on the N slope of a ridge which runs from the highest point in Essex, Langdon Hill, just outside the New Town boundary in the SW, through Westley Heights and Vange Hills to Pitsea in the E. Subsidiary

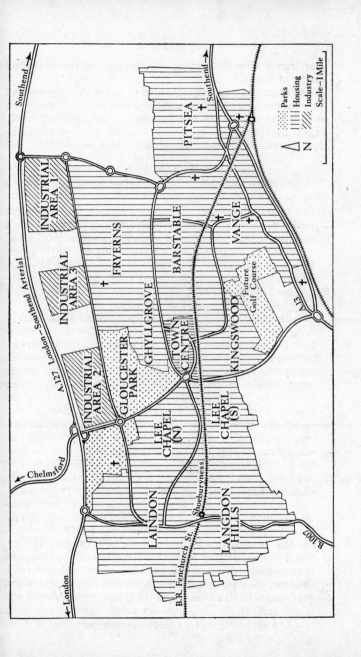

Parks

Housing

Industry

N

Scale—1 Mile

Southend

Southend

PITSEA

INDUSTRIAL AREA 1

INDUSTRIAL AREA 3

FRYERNS

BARSTABLE

VANGE

A.127 London—Southend Arterial

INDUSTRIAL AREA 2

GLOUCESTER PARK

GHYLLGROVE

TOWN CENTRE

KINGSWOOD

Future Golf Course

A13

Chelmsford

LEE CHAPEL (N)

LEE CHAPEL (S)

LAINDON

LANGDON HILLS

Shoeburyness

B.R. Fenchurch St. line

London

B.1007

spurs run N through Laindon and through the site of the old hamlet of Basildon.

The town was originally intended to house 50,000 people all told, but this figure has been increased with revised master plans in 1958 and 1963 to the present target of 106,000. So far over 11,000 dwellings have been built, housing some 35,000 additional people and bringing the population to over 60,000.

CHURCHES

The new town includes the pre-new-town churches of seven villages.

HOLY CROSS, BASILDON. Small church with unbuttressed W tower, C14 nave and chancel rebuilt in brick in 1597. S porch of timber, C15, plain. Chancel roof with embattled purlins and wind-braces. – COMMUNION RAILS with twisted balusters still quite substantial in girth; c.1700. – WEATHER-VANE dated 1702. – PLATE. Cup of 1709.

ST MARY, DUNTON. 1873 by *Bartlett*. – PLATE. Cup of 1563 with bands of ornament; Paten of 1567.

ST NICHOLAS, LAINDON. On a steep eminence above a sea of bungalows. A small church with a timber belfry, dark weather-boarded and crowned by a broach-spire. W of it an annexe, called the Priest's House, C17, much restored, two-storeyed. Inside the belfry one of the splendid sturdy Essex timber constructions. In this case (cf. Horndon-on-the-Hill, Leaden Roding, etc.) it is independently built inside the walls of the church. Nave and two-bay C14 S chapel with octagonal pier and double-chamfered arches. Chancel also C14. S porch timber, C15, mostly rebuilt. However, the oddly primitive carvings in the spandrels of the archway against the nave doorway are original, a beast pierced by a cross-shaft, a dragon, etc. C15 nave and chancel roofs. – FONT. Of the Purbeck type, with shallow blank pointed arcades on each side; C13. – PLATE. Cup on baluster stem of 1656; flower-decorated Paten (secular?) of 1672. – BRASSES. Two brasses of Priests, one 3 ft 3 in. long of c.1480, the other a little over 1 ft, c.1510.*

ST MARY THE VIRGIN AND ALL SAINTS, LANGDON HILLS. Small church, prettily placed – a surprise in these bungalow surroundings. Nave and chancel early C16, of brick with brick windows, the E window of three lights with Perp panel tracery, very similar to Horndon-on-the-Hill. A N chancel chapel was added in 1621. It has a two-bay arcade with a thick short

* LAINDON HALL has recently been destroyed by fire.

octagonal pier and round arches. The chapel itself was rebuilt in 1834. The timber belfry was rebuilt in 1842. – TYMPANUM, i.e. plastered wall between upper parts of nave and chancel, resting on a tie-beam. Painted on it the ROYAL ARMS, with the date 1660. – Painted inscription of 1666 on the N wall. – COMMUNION RAIL, dated 1686, conservative for its date – not yet of the Wren style.

ST MARY, LANGDON HILLS. 1876 by *William White*, tall and very narrow, with W tower, standing immediately along the road, with the wood behind – a romantic setting.

ST PETER, NEVENDON. Small. Nave with two C14 doorways, chancel with some renewed C13 lancets. Roofs C15. Belfry resting on tie-beams instead of posts.*

ST MICHAEL, PITSEA. On a hill with a fine view of the Holehaven Creek and towards the Thames. 1871 by *Sir Arthur Blomfield*, with much restored W tower of *c.*1500. – PLATE. Cup of 1568; Paten on foot of 1692.‡

ALL SAINTS, VANGE. A small church, on its own, on the escarpment of the Thames. Nave and chancel and small bell-turret. In the nave S wall remains of a Norman window. The church was restored in 1837, by *T. Sneezum*. He must be responsible for the E and W windows and probably also the W gallery on cast-iron columns. – FONT. Square bowl on five supports. One side of the bowl with a zigzag motif. C12–13. – PULPIT with READER'S PEW below. – COMMUNION RAIL, partly C17.

Of new churches the most noteworthy are:

ST BASIL THE GREAT (R.C.), BARSTABLE. By *Burles, Newton & Partners*, *c.*1956. Quiet, dignified, and sensible.

ST CHAD, VANGE. By *Humphrys & Hurst*.

PERAMBULATION

Owing to the extent of the existing settlements, it was decided that redevelopment should begin at the E end of the town, just W of Pitsea, and proceed westwards to form a physical link

---

* A group of nice houses near the church, e.g. FRAMPTON'S FARM, T-shaped C16 house, NEVENDON HALL (three-bay red brick, *c.*1800), and a C17 BARN NE of this. The barn is weatherboarded and thatched. (For Nevendon see also p. 305.)

‡ PITSEA HALL, ¼ m. SW, is a timber-framed and plastered house of *c.*1600. In the HIGH STREET are several timber-framed and plastered houses (WHITE HOUSE, dated 1641) and also weatherboarded houses (TELEGRAPH COTTAGE, dated 1721). 1 m. N is GREAT CHALVEDON HALL, T-shaped, of the C16, tall and narrow, timber-framed and weatherboarded. Chimney-stack with diagonal shafts. C18 windows on the S side.

between the two older centres, and to provide an early build-up around the new town centre.

It is interesting to follow the course of development as it moved from E to W from the early neighbourhoods of Fryerns (incorporating the old church of Holy Cross, Basildon) and Barstable and parts of Vange, with their conventional, open 'new town' layouts; through Kingswood and Lee Chapel South on the S side of the town centre and Ghyllgrove on the N, where the gradual adoption of the rear-access principle can be seen; and so to Lee Chapel North, NW of the centre, where can be found the first full-scale development of separate vehicle and pedestrian routes between all parts of the neighbourhood, as the need for such complete segregation was becoming ever more apparent. In the later neighbourhoods, too, can be seen the result of the increased target of population which has been planned for: the evolution of a notably more urban character derived from the use of bold and simple materials, from the sense of enclosure created by internal and external corner units to continue the line of a block or terrace unbroken, and the closing-up of distances between house fronts permitted by a segregated pedestrian circulation, and from the greater use of 'hard' landscaping and textures to balance the soft landscaping.

The new TOWN CENTRE, which is about half completed, occupies a 65-acre site in the geometric centre of the area, on the N side of the London to Shoeburyness railway line which bisects the town from W to E, and about 1¼ m. SE of the old Laindon church. It is approached from the A127 via the new underpass junction ½ m. E of the Fortune-of-War roundabout, Laindon; and from the A13 via the new roundabout at the Five Bells near Fobbing. The architects to the town centre are *A. B. Davis*, the then architect to the Development Corporation, with *Sir Basil Spence* as consultant. The shopping precinct is formed by an entirely traffic-free pedestrian concourse at two levels, approached through open arcades, and lying within an inner ring-road which gives service-vehicle access to the rear of the shops and access to peripheral car-parks. The heart of the town centre is marked at the junction of the main Town Square with the lower-level East Square by BROOKE HOUSE, a fourteen-storey tower of eighty-four flats standing on eight 27-ft-high reinforced concrete 'pilotis' or V-shaped struts. All windows project triangularly in plan. This is an exceptionally large-scale feature, such as is much needed in the New Towns, and it is a marker visible over most of the town and a large part of the surrounding country-side to both N and s.*

Three Industrial Areas are in the course of erection on the N side of the town close to the Southend Arterial Road, but separated from it by a broad strip of land which it is intended to land-scape, so improving the views and amenities of both indus-trialist and motorist. Specially notable factories are the follow-ing: The FORD TRACTOR PLANT, by *E. R. Collister & Associates*, occupies the whole of area three, that is the centre. It is an unrelieved block of about 400 by 625 ft and was built *c*.1956. The centre has two raised bays, each 80 ft wide and 27 ft high. It incorporates the town's second major landmark, a huge 600,000-gallon water tower, which is basically a large sphere balanced with elephantine circus grace on a slender tubular shaft. In area one are the YORK SHIPLEY FACTORY, by *Ove Arup & Partners, c.*1962, big and clear with interesting roofs, not at all fussy, the SHIP CARBON FACTORY, by *Shires & Redditch, c.* 1959, very sheer and impressive, and the ILFORD FACTORY, by the *Development Corporation* (architect *A. B. Davis*).

Outside the town centre the neighbourhood centre at LEE CHAPEL NORTH, NW of the centre, and now nearing com-pletion, and THE KNOWLE ought to be visited. This latter is a group of higher-income-group houses sited conspicuously on the Vange ridge about $\frac{2}{3}$ m. SE of the town centre along Clay Hill Road and developed by the Corporation for sale. The group is set informally around a landscaped cul-de-sac loop, The Knowle, connected to Clay Hill Road via Furlongs and Swan Mead. This was in fact a pilot scheme for other housing of a similar type which the Corporation is developing as part of the policy to provide a socially well-balanced population, an essential aim difficult to realize in an artificially created town.

Of individual buildings or features the following may be noted in order of neighbourhoods, starting N of the town centre and walking or driving clockwise.

GHYLLGROVE. PRIMARY SCHOOL (*The Austin-Smith, Salmon, Lord Partnership*). – Good HOUSING, well worth the explora-

---

* In the entrance hall is a statue of Homer by *McWilliam*. At the w end of the Town Square a large block of offices and shops is going up at the time of writing. It is by the same architects as the rest of the Town Square, of concrete, with exposed mullions in pairs.

tion. The population is fairly dense (22·4 dwellings per acre), the major and minor roads differ in character, there are pedestrian ways everywhere, and the street frontages are fairly coherent. The shopping groups are convincing too.

FRYERNS. SECONDARY TECHNICAL SCHOOL (*H. Conolly*, County Architect). – WHITMORE PRIMARY SCHOOL (the same). Chief accent the tank. – MANOR PRIMARY SCHOOL (*Clifford Culpin & Partners*). – Housing by the Development Corporation (*A. B. Davis*) at Orsett End.

BARSTABLE. The BARSTABLE GRAMMAR SCHOOL and the TIMBERLOG SECONDARY SCHOOL are both by *Yorke, Rosenberg & Mardall*. In the former the concrete framing is exposed with the columns detached from the glazing behind.

KINGSWOOD, s of the town centre. The WOODLANDS BOYS' and WOODLANDS GIRLS' SECONDARY SCHOOLS are by *H. Conolly*, the County Architect.

LEE CHAPEL NORTH. Good NEIGHBOURHOOD CENTRE with ten shops, a hall, a pub, and a four-storeyed block of maisonettes. – Interesting the experimental Siporex HOUSING of 1963. Siporex is a gas concrete much used in Sweden. The Basildon group has ingeniously interlocked one- and two-storey units.

LAINDON. NEIGHBOURHOOD CENTRE with forty-seven shops and HOUSING of over 1,000 units. The density is 22·7 dwellings per acre. Long terraces forming rectangular patterns. Begun 1964. – The NICHOLAS SECONDARY SCHOOL is by *H. Conolly*, the County Architect.

BAYTHORN HALL *and* PARK *see* BIRDBROOK

BAYTHORNE PARK *see* HALSTEAD

BEAUCHAMP RODING

ST EDMUND. C14 nave and C15 chancel and W tower. The tower is quite tall and has diagonal buttresses and battlements. It is at the time of writing in a dangerous state of preservation. Chancel roof with a tie-beam on arched braces. The beam rests on carved stone corbels.

LONGBARNS, ¾ m. N. Good timber-framed house with three gables and chimneystacks of the C16 and C17. The timberwork is exposed, and the N gable of the W wing has original bargeboarding.

BEAUCHAMPS *see* SHOPLAND

BEAUMONT-CUM-MOZE

St Leonard. *c.*1854 by *C. Hakewill*, with some fragments of the medieval church kept. Nave, chancel, and odd, diagonally placed bellcote, the w corner resting on a central w buttress. – COMMUNION RAIL. Late C17, with sturdy twisted balusters. – PLATE. Elizabethan Cup and Paten; Paten of 1683.

Beaumont Hall. A remarkable and characteristic example of Essex brick architecture of *c.*1675. The core of the house is a square two-storeyed block of brick with gables on the NE, NW, and SW. They are shaped and consist of a concave quadrant, then convex quadrants, and then a top pediment, segmental or triangular. Lower and quite irregular additions to the NW and SE, also gabled. Small staircase with twisted balusters. Other internal features, however, seem to prove that the house itself is earlier and was only remodelled about 1675. In the garden small bronze FOUNTAIN with three playing children: French late C18; from the Bagatelle near Paris.

BECKINGHAM HALL *see* TOLLESHUNT MAJOR

BECKTON

(GASWORKS. The buildings include a bridge of 1,150 ft span to transport coal. Also new OFFICES by *Elie Mayorcas*, 1957.)

BECONTREE*

The largest of all L.C.C. Housing Estates. It has a population of over 100,000. Administratively it belongs partly to Barking and partly to Dagenham. It was begun in 1921. In the peak years 1922–3 and 1926–9 between 2,000 and 4,000 houses per annum were built. The design is due to *G. Topham Forrest*. Valence Avenue is the central N–S spine, and here (actually in Becontree Avenue) a mansion has respectfully been kept which had existed for centuries before.

Valence, an irregular gabled Jacobean house (see the panelling in two upper rooms) with alterations of *c.*1700 (staircase with twisted balusters) and the C18. It is now partly a museum. Otherwise the estate is characterized by winding roads, cottages in terraces (neither detached nor semi-detached), pubs in a genteel Neo-Georgian taste ('not conducive to inebriety'), and a lack of accents. It is impossible to plan for such a large

* See also under Dagenham.

number of people without planning on urban principles. Even
the churches help only locally and timidly.

ST ELIZABETH, Wood Lane. 1932 by *Sir Charles Nicholson.*
Red brick, Neo-Perp, but with a tall Baroque bellcote over
the NW entrance.

ST JOHN THE DIVINE, Goresbrook Road. 1936 by *A. E. Wiseman.* Neo-Byzantine red brick with arched windows and big
square tower. Remarkable interior with big tunnel-vault, low,
narrow side passages instead of aisles, and a chancel separated
from the church by a triple arch.

ST MARTIN, Goresbrook Road. 1930-2 by *J. E. Newberry &
Fowler.* Neo-Perp, low, with big roof and *flèche.* Red brick.

HOLY FAMILY, R.C., Oxlow Lane. 1934 by *W. C. Margan.*

(ST MARY, Grafton Road. 1936 by *Welch, Cachemaille-Day &
Lander.*)

A truly urban character of housing has only recently been introduced, just S of the Dagenham Civic Centre. The estate is by
Norman & Dawbarn. It is called HEATH PARK ESTATE and
consists of cottages as well as slab-shaped blocks of flats of
three, four, and five storeys, with a great deal of variety of design. There is for example a screen of four-storeyed maisonettes at the N end, one group of five-storeyed flats in the centre,
parallel to them five blocks of three-storeyed flats, and close to
these the site of the low, spreading social centre, alas not yet
built.* Further S again one slab of five storeys at r. angles to
the others and three of three storeys. The bulk of the estate,
however, is two-storeyed.

BEELEIGH ABBEY

The architectural and the picturesque interest of Beeleigh Abbey
are equal, the one chiefly concerned with the interior, the other
with the exterior. The abbey was founded about 1180 for Premonstratensian canons. The fragment which one sees to-day is
the E and SE parts of the buildings adjoining the cloister and
chiefly the Chapter House and the undercroft of the Dormitory.
Their date is the first half of the C13, and the Chapter House is
naturally more elaborate and elegant than the undercroft,
which incidentally has a large fireplace and was probably used
as the warming house. The Chapter House has three Purbeck
marble piers of octagonal section along its centre line, dividing
it into eight bays. The ribs have a deeply undercut filleted roll-

* The first stage has now been completed (1964).

moulding. The second and the fourth pair of bays have their centres distinguished by bosses with stiff-leaf decoration. The entrance is as usual by a double door. The *trumeau* serves as a respond for the row of centre piers. It is semi-octagonal with three detached shafts and decorated with dogtooth. To the l. and r. of the entrance are two-light windows with a quatre-foil above. The only original outer window is a plain lancet. The Chapter House is separated from the undercroft by a plain rectangular room. The undercroft is also of eight bays with a row of middle supports of Purbeck marble, but these are circular, and the ribs are simply single-chamfered. The fireplace has an elaborate C15 mantelpiece perhaps made up of fragments of a tomb. In the windows are panels of stained glass of the C15. The Dormitory itself has an impressive roof made up of collar-beams and arched braces so as to form a wagon-vault of four-centred section. The E exterior has brick buttresses and between them large three-light C15 windows with one transom and Perp panel tracery. The upper windows are small. The r. hand gable corresponds to the Chapter House and the later rooms above it, the l. hand gable to the Reredorter or lavatories, which in the original state projected from the Dormitory. After the Dissolution an addition was made to this narrow block on the W side, timber-framed with narrowly placed exposed uprights and brick in-fillings. Of the former Refectory range on the S side of the cloister only the E stump stands up with a passage and the site of a staircase. All this was incorporated in the C16 house, and the corner where this irregular piece meets the timber-framed gabled addition is a picturesque delight.*

BELCHAMP OTTON

ST ETHELBERT AND ALL SAINTS. The nave is Norman, see the S doorway. It has two orders of columns with beaded spiral bands, decorated scalloped capitals, and zigzag ornament in the arch. The windows are Perp. C19 belfry on two posts with cross-beams and arched braces. Early C19 BOX PEWS and NW GALLERY. – PULPIT. Simple, with some blank arcading; c.1600. – COMMUNION RAIL with twisted balusters, c.1700 – PLATE. Cup and Paten of 1567.
WINDMILL. Tower mill; the sails missing.

* Mr Clifton-Taylor mentions Beeleigh Abbey as a characteristic example of building in puddingstone rubble.

BELCHAMP ST PAUL

St Andrew. Nave, chancel, and w tower, all c15. The w tower has diagonal buttresses with fine set-offs and battlements. Chancel with good roof with embattled wall-plates and e window of five lights with panel tracery. n arcade of two bays, with octagonal piers and double-hollow-chamfered arches. n chancel chapel of one bay with embattled capitals to the responds. – FONT. Octagonal, with sunk panels decorated by saltire crosses, shields, etc. – CHANCEL STALLS. Seats with misericords decorated by simple flower and leaf motifs – the only misericords in Essex except for Castle Hedingham. Traceried fronts and ends with poppy-heads and good carved seated figures. – PLATE. Cup and Paten on foot of 1680. – MONUMENTS. Brasses to members of the Golding family, 1587 and 1591, the figure of the man in armour, 2 ft long. – Tablet of 1811 by *J. Challis* of Braintree, a reminder of how long local craftsmen provided monuments in churches.

Paul's Hall. L-shaped, of the c16 and c17. The c16 part is of brick and has original chimneystacks and a few original windows. The other wing is timber-framed.

BELCHAMP WALTER

St Mary. Chancel, nave, and w tower. The chancel is much lower than the nave and is, judging by its (renewed) lancet window, E.E. The nave dates from *c*.1320, as indicated by the windows with intersected tracery with cusps. c15 timbers porch with pretty bargeboarding. c15 w tower with diagonal buttresses and battlements, a high stair-turret, and a very tall transomed w window of three lights. The interior of the church rather wildly painted in High Victorian days (restoration 1860), probably by the same craftsman (or firm) who worked at Foxearth. In the nave MONUMENT to Sir John Boutetort † 1324 or 1325, extremely ornate. Tomb-chest and effigy missing. A big cusped and sub-cusped arch flanked by thin buttresses. Fleurons, leaf-branches, bossy leaves, shields serve to enrich the surfaces. Ogee details in the main arch and the cusping, but rather subdued. Also of the c14 the large WALL PAINTING of the Virgin suckling the Child which was discovered in 1926, and on the s wall traces of a large Wheel of Fortune, 12 ft in diameter. – FONT. Circular, c12, the bowl damaged along the top. Decoration with beaded scrolls, leaves, etc. – MONUMENT. Sir John Raymond † 1720. With Roman pilasters, two seated cherubs, and more cherubs' heads. Good quality; signed by *Robert Taylor Sen*.

BELCHAMP HALL. Built in 1720. Façade of nine bays and two storeys with giant pilasters at the angles and again two bays from the angles. The centre bay has a pediment. Dormers with alternating triangular and segmental pediments. The material is white brick with much rubbed red brick for the dressings. The short wing to the NW angle and the canted bay window on the S side are additions of *c*.1880. Inside, original C18 panelling. In the Dining Room two fine late C18 marble columns. Stables of red and blue chequered brick, with lantern and circular windows.

(ST MARY HALL, 1¾ m. WSW. Timber-framed late C16 house on an H-plan. SE of it, almost detached, late C15 kitchen wing with heavy beams on the ground floor and original roof truss on the upper floor, consisting of tie-beam on arched braces, kingpost, and two-way struts. R.C.)

BELHUS, nr AVELEY

The house, which has been demolished, was of Early Tudor brick and called 'newly builded' in the will of John Barrett, who died in 1526. Dark red brick with blue brick diaper. The plan type is that with an inner courtyard. No symmetry in any façade. Tall porch on the S side with polygonal angle buttresses crowned by pinnacles, and a taller stair-turret. This leads into the Hall. To the W a big chamber, now the library. The main kitchen lies behind this in the NE corner. The N front is well preserved, with stepped gables and two big chimneystacks with diagonal chimneys. The whole W side is a symmetrical very early Gothick alteration. It goes back to Horace Walpole's friend Lord Dacre, who was also a close friend of Sanderson Miller. So he was right in the centre of the rising Gothic fashion. His alterations to Belhus, of which much of rather thin interior work survives, are indeed partly as early as 1745–9. The rest dates from 1751–*c*.1760. In the latter work *Sanderson Miller* had a hand. The staircase and one rich fireplace on the upper floor are Jacobean. Outbuildings to the E, C16 Stables and at right angles more Stables of *c*.1700 (chequer brick front of seven bays).

BELSTEAD'S FARM *see* LITTLE WALTHAM

BERDEN

St Nicholas. Norman nave. The only evidence of the date is
the two large blocked windows on the N and S sides close to the
w wall. The C15 w tower cuts into them. Next in time comes
the N transept with one C13 doorway. The S transept also is
C13, but later, as proved by the arch towards the nave. Thin
angle shafts and slight single chamfer in the arch. The S transept windows however are early C14, and the N transept arch
was renewed at the same time. Contemporary with the S transept the chancel with lancets as well as two-light windows with
a cusped circle above. The latter are externally renewed (and
the E window is entirely of 1868), but internally they are
original and lavishly enriched. They have shafts close to the
window surface and stronger shafts in the rear arch. Both have
stiff-leaf capitals, and stiff-leaf friezes connect the capitals
along the arch jamb. The spandrels between the cusped lights
and the circles also have stiff-leaf. All this seems to date the
chancel c.1260–70. – PULPIT. Later C17, with geometrical
patterns in the panels. – PLATE. Pear-shaped Cup of 1602 by
I. E., silver-gilt, with twisted tree-trunk stem and chased bowl;
Cover with steeple-top; silver-gilt repoussé Paten, foreign,
C17. – BRASS. William Turnor † 1473 and wife (N transept).
The figures only 12 in. long. – Also Brass of 1607.

BERDEN HALL. Elizabethan, brick, with three straight gables
to each side. Some mid C17 mullion-and-transom-cross windows (date of rainwater-head 1655). Good staircase with
square open well. The stairs are 6 ft wide. The handrail has
square openwork termini balusters and strapwork in the
interstices.

THE PRIORY. Elizabethan, timber-framed with exposed timbers. The house stands on the site of an Augustinian priory
founded in the C12.

FORTIFIED MOUND, ½ m. SE. 10 ft high, 123 ft in diameter. The
origin is uncertain.

BERECHURCH

St Michael and All Angels. A brick church of *c.*1500.
W tower with diagonal buttresses with stone dressings; battlements. E window of three lights dated C17 by the Royal Commission. E window of the N chapel of three lights, depressed
pointed with intersected tracery. The N chapel is the only
interesting part of the church, on account of its hammerbeam

roof, with decorated purlins and wind-braces, the C17 shields applied to the hammerbeam, and the C17 MONUMENT against the N wall. To Sir Henry Audley and wife, erected 1648. Stiffly semi-reclining, in armour; kneeling figures below. Big reredos background with inscription and segmental pediment. Black and white marble. – Sir Robert Smyth † 1802, large, with urn in relief. – Mrs Charlotte White † 1845. By J. *Edwards*, 1848. She lies on a couch, with two angels hovering near her. – DOOR. Early C16, of linenfold and other panels.

BERECHURCH HALL.* Broad and towering Neo-Elizabethan mansion, quite asymmetrical, with plenty of French motifs mixed in. By *Lee*, 1882.

BERECHURCH DYKE *see* COLCHESTER

BERNERS RODING

CHURCH. Nave and chancel, and weatherboarded belfry with pyramid roof. Two early C16 brick windows in the chancel. – The chancel has a tie-beam with kingpost and four-way struts. Nicely moulded wall-plates. – PLATE. Cup of 1627.

BICKNACRE PRIORY

2¼ m. NNW Woodham Ferrers

Founded *c*.1175 by Maurice Fitz-Geoffrey for Augustinian canons. All that remains is one tall, lonely arch. It was the W arch of the crossing of the church and is of mid C13 date. Piers with big semicircular shafts. The low respond at the N end is re-set.

BIGODS *see* GREAT DUNMOW

BILLERICAY

A pretty High Street with a number of good houses leads N to a triangle, where Chapel Street meets High Street, and at that point, in the angle of the two streets, stands the church.

ST MARY MAGDALENE. Brick W tower of *c*.1500, with set-back buttresses below and chamfered angles above continued in polygonal pinnacles. The battlements between these are stepped (cf. East Horndon). The battlements rest on a trefoil-arched corbel frieze. W window of two lights with Perp

* Now demolished.

brick tracery. The w ends of the aisles in the same style, probably 1880. The interior late c18 with a shallow apse at the e end and another facing the triangle of High Street and Chapel Street to the N. Three galleries on thin cast-iron columns. – FONT. Bowl with two cherubs' heads; c18. – COMMUNION RAIL. c18.

Just N of the church in Chapel Street ST AUBYNS and THE NOOK, c16–c17, timber-framed, gabled, and plastered. Adjoining them the CHEQUERS INN and Nos 38–40 HIGH STREET, 1577 and c18, weatherboarded. Opposite No. 51 High Street, lying back from the street, a three-bay, two-storey, Early Georgian house, red brick, rusticated brick quoins, the same quoining used to single out the centre bay, a pediment over this, and a Tuscan porch. N from this centre on the w side Nos 43 and 39, both also early c18 and also with rusticated quoins. Both have recessed centres too. No. 43 is the more original, only three bays wide, with the middle bay recessed and the upper window here with a rusticated frame. Opposite a little higher up No. 12, with the best exposed half-timber gable of Billericay.

Opposite the front of the church the CHANTRY HOUSE and Nos 57–59, an altered hall-house dated 1510. Here the Pilgrim Fathers assembled before embarking for America. An irregular group with exposed timberwork. Then to the s the Gas Board Offices, a c16 timber-framed house with cross-gables, and several more timber-framed and gabled (Nos 82, 108) and Georgian brick houses (Nos 69, 98–100). No. 127 is a noteworthy High Victorian atrocity, utterly unconcerned with the *genius loci*.*

BURGHSTEAD LODGE is the best house of Billericay. It lies back behind wrought-iron gates, has five bays and two-and-a-half storeys, and a doorway with pediment on Tuscan pilasters.

No. 146 is much smaller (three bays, two storeys) but especially delicate in the details of the doorway.

ST ANDREW'S HOSPITAL, just N of the railway station (former Poor Law Institution). An early *George Gilbert Scott*: 1840. He had a successful practice in workhouses at that time. Red brick, Tudor, with stone dressings, gables, and diagonal chimneys, low and long.

GATWICK HOUSE, ¾ m. SE. Handsome Georgian brick house of five bays and two storeys. Close to it some timber-framed houses.

* The N portion of the house is c18.

(OUTWOOD COMMON ESTATE. By *F.G. Southgate*, completed 1963.)

BIRCH

ST MARY. 1850 by *Teulon*, but with none of the offensive features so favoured by this architect. Quite a normal aisled interior, and an exterior ambitious, but not showy. The W front has a tall NW steeple with spire, 110 ft high. Dec tracery.

OLD ST MARY, by Birch Hall. A small Norman church now in ruins and not much looked after. w tower all in ivy. In the nave one can still recognize the plain C12 S doorway, one S window with Roman brick jambs and one much larger N window with one Roman brick jamb.

BIRCH HALL. Large and dignified Italianate villa, chaste and correct in the motifs; nothing debased yet. Ionic colonnade on one side, deep Ionic porch on the other. The architect is *Hopper*, the date *c*.1845. Menaced with demolition.*

BIRCHANGER

ST MARY. Norman nave and E.E. chancel. A round tower was demolished at some time. The bellcote on the nave is C19. N aisle by *Sir Arthur Blomfield*, 1898. The interesting thing about the church is the two Norman doorways, w (reset and no doubt originally N) and S. The S doorway was discovered only about 1930. The two doorways are similar in decoration, but there is, as usual, a little more emphasis on the S. Abaci decorated with chip-carved saltire crosses, tympana with frieze of saltire crosses at the foot. On the S side in addition foliage scrolls along the extrados of the arch and – a feature unique in Essex although quite common in many other counties – figure carving high up in the tympanum. It is a minimum of figure carving, a lamb, small and placed oddly at a slight angle. – BENCHES. Seven, plain, with buttresses; restored. – PLATE. Cup of 1567.

BIRDBROOK

ST AUGUSTINE OF CANTERBURY. Nave, chancel, and belfry. Nave and chancel have herringbone masonry in the N walls, an indication of Early Norman date. Inside the nave one blocked Norman window in the N and one in the S wall. The

* Now demolished, except for the stables.

other windows chiefly C13 lancets belonging partly to a lengthening of the chancel to the E and the nave to the W. At the E end a group of three with individual hood-moulds and two blank quatrefoils above and between them. At the W end also three lancets, the middle one being placed much higher up. In the C15 an arch was struck across the nave to carry the belfry. – FONT. Thin octagonal piece with neatly decorated stem and bowl – a Gothic imitation dating from 1793. In the E panel a circular medallion 4 in. across with a miniature painting of the Baptism of Christ said to be by *Samuel Cooper*. – COMMUNION RAIL, with twisted balusters; *c.*1700. – SCREEN. Bits of the former screen used in the front of the chancel stalls. – PLATE. Paten of 1561; Cup of 1562; Flagon and Paten given in 1722. – MONUMENTS. To Martha Blewitt and Robert Hogan. He had seven wives, she nine husbands. – James Walford † 1743 and family, put up *c.*1790. By *King* of Bath. – Thomas Walford † 1833. By *G. Lufkin* of Colchester. So as late as that the lord of the manor might use a local sculptor for a church monument.

(BAYTHORN HALL. The house has an aisled timber hall of two bays with two jettied cross-wings. Late C14. Original doorways to buttery etc. remain, also moulded crown-post roof. An elaborately moulded timber ceiling was put in the solar in the early C16. Information from Mr J.T. Smith.)

BAYTHORN PARK, 1½ m. ENE. House of seven bays and two storeys with a hipped roof and a cupola. It was built in 1668, but was altered in 1801, when the Tuscan porch was added and probably the cupola renewed. Inside several earlier C17 fireplaces and earlier C17 panelling.

BLACKMORE

ST LAWRENCE. Blackmore possesses one of the most impressive, if not the most impressive, of all timber towers of England. Outside it has on the ground floor lean-to roofs on three sides, then a square part with vertical weatherboarding, then again four lean-to roofs, the square bell-stage, which is straight, and finally a shingled broach spire. Internally it possesses ten posts, making a nave and two aisles. The tower itself stands on the centre six, three N and three S. The arched braces for the cross-beams run N–S, thrown across the second and the fourth pairs. In addition there are smaller and lower arched braces in an E–W direction between posts 2 and 3 and 3 and 4.

Above these are two tiers of cross-struts. It is a most elaborate piece of carpentry and looks very powerful.* The church itself is Norman and had aisles from the beginning. The explanation of this is that it was a priory church. The priory was founded for Augustinian canons c.1155–60 by Adam and Jordan, Chamberlains of the Queen. The W wall of the Norman church still exists behind the timber tower, with a doorway of three orders of columns with scalloped capitals. The arch is stepped and not otherwise moulded. Two large windows are above, and above these is a circular window. The first bay of the nave on the N and S has a plain pier but colonnettes placed in the angles. These also carry scalloped capitals. The arches are wholly unmoulded. A first pair of upper windows can also still be seen. The E parts of the priory church and all the monastic buildings have completely disappeared. There is no indication of a crossing. All that now tells of the monastery is two blocked pointed C13 doorways at the E end of the S aisle. One of them no doubt led into the cloister. The priory was dissolved as early as 1527, so that certain C16 alterations to the church may well be connected with the adjustments necessary when the church became parochial. The N aisle is early C14 (quatrefoil piers with many-moulded arches), but the S aisle clearly C16. The octagonal piers and the arches are of brick. Of brick also the arches and responds to the aisle E chapel (that is the parochial chancel chapel). The half-timbered W end of the S aisle and the C17 dormers on the N, and C19 dormers on the S side, add a touch of irresponsible picturesqueness. – BRASS. Civilian of c.1420; lower half lost. – Thomas Smyth † 1594 and wife. Recumbent alabaster effigies, the heads on a rolled-up mat. The tomb-chest with decorated pilasters is not original, and the tomb is not complete.

BLACKMORE HOUSE. Square brick house which deserves detailed investigation. The windows and facing bricks are early C18 (built c. 1715–20), but the plan with four square angle towers is not at all Georgian but corresponds to a few mid C16 brick houses such as Syon near London and Ince Castle in Cornwall.

BLACK NOTLEY

ST PETER AND ST PAUL. Nave, chancel and belfry. Norman windows and plain doorways. The belfry stands on eight posts

* Mr C. M. Hewett suggests a date c.1480. *Archaeological Journal*, vol. 119, 1962.

forming a nave and aisles. The 'nave' has arched braces, the aisles trellis-strutting in a N–S as well as a W–E direction. The church was restored by *A. W. Blomfield* in 1879. – DOOR. Some of the ironwork is C12. – STAINED GLASS. In a N window some C15 tabernacle work. – PLATE. Paten of 1567; Cup with ornament probably also of 1567. – MONUMENT. Floor slab in the chancel with Lombardic inscription 'Sir Walter de Wydenal iadis person de cest . . . gist ici Dieu de sa alme eyt merci amen'.

BLACK NOTLEY HALL has a big C15 BARN of five bays, weatherboarded.

BLACK NOTLEY LODGE, ½ m. N. Blue and red brick, three bays, with segment-headed windows and arched middle window, but the gables at the end developed with concave and convex forms still entirely in the C17 tradition.

(STANTON'S FARM, ¾ m. SE. Built *c.*1340* with an aisled hall, solar wing (destroyed), and office and kitchen wing. What remains of the central hall is two blocked doorways with two-centred arches and the roof truss on octagonal piers with moulded capitals. Hollow-chamfered tie-beam on arched braces. R.C.)

BLAKE HALL see BOBBINGWORTH

BLUEBRIDGE HOUSE see HALSTEAD

BOBBINGWORTH

ST GERMAIN. A disappointing church. Tower at the NW end, of white brick, 1841, containing the porch; chancel 1840; nave refaced with red brick also in the C19. The interior is more appealing. – PULPIT with attached reader's desk, and BOX PEWS. The pulpit with simple early C17 decoration. – PLATE. Cup of 1635; Paten probably of 1683. – TABLETS. 1773 by *H. Rouw*, 1820 by *P. Rouw*, 1839 by *Dorman* of Chelmsford.

BLAKE HALL. Queen Anne house of seven bays and two-and-a half storeys. Entrance Hall with a screen of two Tuscan columns towards the fine late C17 staircase which comes, it is said, from Schomberg House, London, built *c.*1698. It has balusters formed partly as slender Tuscan columns and carved tread-ends. Wings were added by *Basevi* about 1840. The fine rooms in the r. wing were a victim of occupation by British forces in the Second World War. Only two beautiful Neo-

* Or, according to Mr J. T. Smith, even a little earlier.

Greek bookcases have survived. By *Basevi* no doubt also the four-column Greek Doric porch.

BOCKING

St Mary. A large church for a prosperous village. Except for the C14 chancel, all is C15. W tower with decorated base and doorway with decorated spandrels. The buttresses are most unusual: diagonal, but so broad that they have their own little buttresses placed so that it looks at first as if the tower had angle buttresses. Battlements and stair-turret with a pretty wooden cupola of 1887. Nave and aisles parapeted, E parts embattled. S porch embattled with niches l. and r. of the doorway and two two-light windows on each side. Large three-light windows in aisles and N and S chapels. The five-light chancel E window and the very impressive chancel S window with two transoms, which looks like the bay window of a proud Tudor hall, are of 1913. Wide four-bay nave with piers of the four-shafts-and-four-hollows type, with capitals only to the shafts. Two-light clerestory windows. Chancel chapels with piers of a complicated section with polygonal shafts and wave and hollow mouldings in the diagonals. – DOOR. Four vertical battens and between them rows of six scrolls each; C13. – STAINED GLASS. Chancel, of *c*.1860, in a quite unusual style. Large figures and colours with a deep glow. – PLATE. Large Paten on foot and Plate of 1698; large Flagon and Paten on foot of 1700. – MONUMENTS. Brass to John Doreward † 1420 and wife, in the N chapel, the figures about 30 in. high. – Grisell Moore † 1624, alabaster monument with kneeling figure, a common type.

St Francis, R.C., Convent Lane. By *Bentley*, 1898. A fine and original composition. The end of the small church faces the street. It is accompanied by a polygonal SE turret and then a porch which is the public entrance into the convent church. It leads into a long aisled S transept facing a N altar – a cross axis opposed to the main axis which runs from the nuns' choir to the high altar.*

St Peter, St Peter's Road. 1897 by *Micklethwaite* (GR). Competent and sensitive.

Masonic Lodge, Bradford Street. By *Thomas Tait* and *D.G. Armstrong*, 1933–4. In the modern style which was just then entering England. Small symmetrical façade, white with some

* Nearly opposite the church a picturesque white weatherboarded mill by the river.

trim of black bricks. Obviously in its over-emphasis on many horizontals under the influence of Dudok and the Dutch style of the twenties.

The parish church lies in the village of Bocking, close to the river. This situation prompted a mill to settle just by the church, and out of that mill, on the same spot, gradually grew the large factory of Courtauld Ltd. The buildings, towering behind and alongside the church, are mostly of the C20.

Now if one tries to forget about the mills and see the village as it was before they became its centre, one would have to notice BOCKING HALL immediately NW of the church and the DEANERY across the river to its SW, both timber-framed houses of some size and value. The village centre was Bridge Place and Bridge End. The main streets were Church Street to the ENE and Church Lane to the S, towards Braintree. In CHURCH STREET nothing of special interest, until one sees on the top of the hill the WINDMILL, a white post-mill of c.1680, moved to the present place in 1830 when it received a round-base of brick. Until about twenty years ago it was in perfect working order.

Returning to the bridge, just this side of it a lane leads SE and on to DOREWARD'S HALL, an L-shaped, timber-framed house which, for reasons unknown, was provided in 1572 (date-stone) with a SE front far too grand for it, perhaps the beginning of an ambitious rebuilding scheme. The front is of brick, only one bay wide, with polygonal angle turrets of brick and generous stone dressing. Between them a three-light one-transom ground-floor window with a steep pediment, a five-light one-transom first-floor window with a broader, lower pediment, and a steep gable with a three-light one-transom window – all very typical of the 70s.

Once more back to the bridge and up CHURCH LANE. Here, amongst others, Nos 35–37, TABOR HOUSE, picturesque early and late C16, with overhang and moulded bressumer; fine chimneystacks. Also, on the opposite side, BOLEYNS, late C18, with two bays and a central Venetian window. Church Lane is continued in the long BRADFORD STREET with wealthy C19 villas, but also Nos 114–116, picturesque early C16, with overhang and carved bressumer and carriageway at the S end, No. 89 with C18 front of five bays and two storeys and pediment on attached Roman columns, and No. 87, WENT-WORTH HOUSE, with two gables and two overhangs, but a big shell-hood over the door. The house has a rainwater-head with the date 1679. Then Nos 77–83 (former Woolpack Inn), again good C16, with three gables at different levels and projecting beyond the first-floor overhang. Carved bressumer dated 1590. Near the S end No. 4, early C18, with five bays, segment-headed windows, and a pedimented doorcase on Roman pilasters, No. 25 (VICTORY HALL), Georgian, six bays with a doorway of Roman Doric pilasters, a triglyph frieze and a segmental pediment, No. 13 (BRADFORD HOUSE) also Georgian, of seven bays, and LITTLE BRADFORDS, late C16, much modernized.

Without any interruption BOCKING END follows, which is visually wholly part of Braintree and in fact, with its two best houses, leads right into the centre of the town. One is on the SE side, C18, five bays, two storeys, with a doorway with Roman pilasters and a triglyph frieze, the other is the WHITE HART, seemingly part of Bank Street, Braintree. It is large, with timbers exposed, and of the C17. Alterations of the C18 and contemporary interior features.

LYONS HALL, 1 m. E. Of c.1600 with C18 additions. The E front is very handsome, with bargeboarded gable and carved bressumer.

WINDMILL, 1 m. SE. Post-mill in good condition.

BOIS HALL see NAVESTOCK

BOLEYN CASTLE see EAST HAM

BOREHAM

ST ANDREW. The appearance from the street is most curious – more curious than beautiful. Nave and aisles, but the S aisle first narrow, and then, E of the S porch (timber, with six arched openings on the W and E sides), wider. Then the building recedes considerably so as to expose the sheer wall of the Norman tower, a central tower. The chancel follows, as narrow as the tower, but widening into the late C16 Sussex Chapel. On the N side which roughly, but far from exactly, corresponds to this chapel is the Tufnell Chapel of 1800.* The tower has a staircase in the thickness of the wall which projects into the interior, Norman windows on the ground floor to the N and S, and a complete E arch of the plainest. Of the W arch the Roman brick voussoirs remain above the C14 chancel arch. Higher up

* The Waltham Mausoleum of 1764 in the churchyard was pulled down in 1944.

are doorways to the E and W, and two-light windows to the N and S with a middle shaft with block capital. The bell-openings are similar but pointed. The battlements are brick. A pyramid roof crowns the tower. Chronologically the nave and S aisle – the narrower part – follow, see the W lancet of the S aisle, and the square chamfered arcade piers (also of the N arcade) and pointed, only slightly chamfered arches, no doubt cut out of the solid Norman nave walls. Yet there is a Roman brick arch partly revealed in the E wall of the N aisle in line with the arcade which is hard to explain, unless the Norman nave was wider than it is now. The arch probably held a side altar. The S aisle has in its wider parts early C14 windows of two cusped lights with a cinquefoil in a circle above. The chancel is contemporary, as shown by the cusped lancet windows on the N and S. The N aisle windows are C15, large and plain, with panel tracery – three lights on the N, five lights on the W side. A five-light Perp window also at the W end of the nave. – FONT. Early C14, hexagonal, no distinction of stem and bowl, each side with a gabled blank cusped arch. – SCREENS. Under the E tower arch and at the W end of the N aisle. The latter very plain, the former with each division of three lights, the centre one wider and with a crocketed cusped ogee head. The top straight. – PLATE. Cup of 1699. – MONUMENT. To three Radcliffes, Earls of Sussex, † 1542, 1567, and 1583. Alabaster. All three recumbent on one tomb-chest. By *Richard Stevens* of Southwark, completed 1589.*

54a NEW HALL. Henry VIII, shortly after 1518, erected here a large mansion, called Beaulieu, quadrangular, with gatehouse in the S range, Great Hall in the E range, and chapel in the W range. All that remains of it of architectural or decorative features is some piers and ribs in a basement of the present E wing and a magnificent large carved coat of arms (now in the Chapel), as good as (and very similar to) the carvings of Christ's and St John's College gateways at Cambridge and King's College Chapel.‡ The Earl of Sussex in 1573 modernized the N range, but that range was pulled down about 1738. In 1798 the Canonesses of the order of the Holy Sepulchre from Liège settled down in the house. What exists today is chiefly the splendid S façade of the house of 1573, with seven symmetrical bay windows, the middle one containing the entrance with Roman Doric columns and a metope frieze. The façade, which

* The monument cost £266 13s. 4d.
‡ Stained glass now at St Margaret Westminster, London.

was severely damaged in 1943, but has since been repaired, is crowned by a plain (later) parapet; no gables. The entrance led into the Great Hall, apparently from the beginning in a central, not an asymmetrical position, as was still so much more usual in the Elizabethan period. This centre was redecorated c.1740–50 and is now the chapel of the convent, altered again in 1799.

BOREHAM HOUSE. Built in 1728 for Benjamin Hoare.* An ambitious, though not a large house. Brick. Only seven bays wide and two storeys high, but with wings, originally carrying lanterns, and with a straight pond or canal in front. About 1812 the wings were altered by *Thomas Hopper* and the present grand carriageways on the l. and r. created, with their display of coupled columns. The original house has two rooms of surprising splendour, the Saloon and the Entrance Hall. They 59 have pedimented doors, a fireplace on caryatids, a kind of reredos of Venetian window shape with Victories lying in the arch, and superbly carved details. The date is clearly c.1730. The staircase, lying immediately to the l. of the Entrance Hall, has a heavy cast-iron railing, probably belonging to the 1812 alterations. The deep four-column Tuscan porch is a C19 addition.

BORLEY

CHURCH (dedication unknown). A topiary walk to the porch is the most notable feature of the church. The nave may be C11, see the SW quoin. The chancel and the W tower are Late Perp, the tower with thin diagonal buttresses and stepped battlements. – MONUMENTS. Sir Edward Waldegrave † 1561 and wife † 1599. Tomb-chest with recumbent effigies under a six-poster. The columns have shaft-rings. Straight top with big achievement. – Magdala Southcote † 1592; with big kneeling figure; not good. – Black marble floor slab to Humphrey Burrough † 1757, rector of Borley and Gainsborough's uncle.

BOURCHIER'S HALL *see* TOLLESBURY

BOURNE MILL *see* COLCHESTER

BOWERS GIFFORD

ST MARGARET. Small church, quite on its own. The charm of the church is the huge diagonal buttress propping the small W

* Designed by *James Gibbs* and executed with modifications by *Edward Shepherd* (Mr Derek Sherborn's comment, conveyed to me by J. Harris).

tower at the SW corner only, and the asymmetrically placed W windows of the tower. The tower top and broach spire weather-boarded. Inside, this wooden upper part rests on unbraced posts with trellis strutting. – CHANCEL SCREEN. 1926 by *Sir Charles Nicholson.* – FONT COVER. Polygonal pyramid; C17. – BRASS. Figure of *c.*1350, 6 ft tall, said to represent Sir John Gifford † 1348. The head not preserved. Shield with lovely fleur-de-lis and trail pattern. Legs not crossed.

BOXTED

ST PETER. Norman W tower chiefly of puddingstone with a generous use of mortar. Several exposed or blocked contemporary windows. Completed early in the C16 in brick, with diagonal buttresses, renewed top parts and battlements. The whole in its variety of textures happens to look extremely lovely. Chancel with Perp windows. The rest much pulled about in the C18. Inside more Norman evidence: blocked windows in the nave (N side) above the very rawly cut-through arcade. The S arcade identical. Chancel arch on plain imposts with one roll-moulding. Above it, and on the W side, the Norman roof-line is visible. Above this, and above the choir, two quaint little C14 E windows. W gallery on cast-iron columns, 1836. – MONUMENTS. Elizabeth, wife of Nathaniel Bacon † 1628, small epitaph with a marble panel with an angel and a skeleton, probably not in the original context. – Sir Richard Blackmore † 1729, quite a good epitaph, without figures.

BOXTED HALL. Large early C17 house. Brick, two-storeyed, with hipped roof; four bays and projecting wings of two bay-widths each.

(RIVERS HALL, ¾ m. E. Timber faced and plastered. Some stucco-work dated 1713. R.C.)

BOYLES COURT *see* GREAT WARLEY

BRADFIELD

ST LAWRENCE. C13 W tower, see the lancet openings with later diagonal buttresses. C13 chancel, see the DOUBLE PISCINA with dogtooth decoration. C13 nave, see the renewed paired lancet windows. C19 transepts. The whole exterior unfortunately cemented. – FONT. Octagonal, of Purbeck marble, C13, with two shallow blank pointed arches on each side of the bowl. – PULPIT. C18, with earlier panels of the C16 and C17, one

being a relief of the Crucifixion. – HELM. C16; in the chancel. –
PLATE. C17 Cup. – MONUMENTS. Brass to Joane Risbye
† 1598, the figure about three feet tall. – Elizabeth Agassiz, by
Chantrey, undated, with kneeling, mourning female figure.

BRADFIELD HALL. As one approaches it the house seems a normal plastered, two-storeyed farmhouse. Behind, however, that
is facing S, one impressive Early Tudor brick gable with blue
brick diapering, stepped gable with three diagonally placed
pinnacles, and two main windows, the upper of one light, but
the lower of three (mullions destroyed) with depressed pointed
head and intersected tracery.

BRADFIELD'S FARM *see* TOPPESFIELD

BRADWELL-JUXTA-COGGESHALL

HOLY TRINITY. Nave, chancel, and belfry. W quoins of the
nave, one window high up on the W side, two S windows, the S
doorway, the N windows and the N doorway, and also one recently uncovered E window in the chancel, are all Norman with
Roman brick trim. Other windows plain Dec, chancel E plain
Perp with panel tracery. S porch of timber; C14. The ogee tops
of the side openings survive, but below them are, quite a pretty
effect, C17 balusters. – SCREEN. Of single-light divisions with
ogee tops and a little tracery above; C15. – FONT COVER.
Octagonal, with panelled sides and ball top; C17. – HELM. C17;
in the chancel. – PAINTINGS. The wall paintings of Bradwell,
though not well preserved, make the church one of the essential
ones to visit in Essex. They date from about 1320 and are
aesthetically of the highest quality, not at all rustic, like so much
English church fresco-work. The most easily recognizable
ones are in the splays of a S window (Doubting Thomas and
opposite a Saint) and in a N window (the Trinity, that is the
Lord seated holding a small crucifix in his hands, and opposite
Christ rising from the tomb). On the N wall near the W end
small head, perhaps of an Infant Christ. There is no doubt
much more hidden underneath the plaster, and if it could be
recovered, it would make a worthy C14 comparison to the C12
Copford. – MONUMENTS. Incised figure of a priest, only the
lower half preserved; with inscription in Lombardic letters
and the date 1349. – Anthony Maxey † 1592 and wife, also
their son and his wife, alabaster, behind the altar. Two arched
recesses flanked by black columns carrying an entablature. In
each recess kneels one couple at a prayer-desk.

(VILLAGE HALL. By *Arthur H. Mackmurdo*, c.1932. Big, barn-
like structure, with large roof and arcading along the sides.)
GLAZENWOOD, I m. w. Plain square red brick house of c.1800;
the home of William Curtis of the *Flora Londonensis*. He
started the nurseries here.

BRADWELL-JUXTA-MARE

Bradwell is really two sites, on the one hand the Roman fort and
St Peter's by the sea-wall, on the other St Thomas, the parish
church, and Bradwell Lodge, 2 m. to the w, inland.

The ROMAN FORT now shows only by one 4 ft high fragment
of the s wall. It stands close to the church, a little to its s.
Excavations have proved the fort to have been 520 ft long. The
E walls have been destroyed by the sea. So the width cannot be
ascertained. Of the N wall 290 ft are known. At the NW corner
and in the w wall further s were horseshoe bastions. The walls
were c.12 ft thick. The fort is one of the class known as Saxon
Shore forts, constructed to guard against attacks by sea rovers.
The class is superbly represented in Kent and Sussex, and
there is a fine example just outside Great Yarmouth (Burgh
Castle). Bradwell-juxta-Mare has been tentatively identified
with the fort named OTHONA listed in the *Notitia Dignitatum*
in which case it was garrisoned by a force of irregulars known
as Fortenses. The coins from the site suggest a foundation date
in the last decade of the c3.

4b ST-PETER-ON-THE-WALL stands astride the w wall of the
fort. It is in all probability the very church built by St Cedd
c.654. It consists now of nothing but the nave, but the existence of a w porch and an apsed chancel as wide as the nave
have been ascertained. In addition there were probably *porticus*, i.e. side chambers in transeptal positions to the N and s
just as in the earliest Saxon churches of Canterbury. Bradwell
belongs in style to this Kentish group, the earliest group of
surviving Christian churches in England. The chancel was
separated from the nave by a tall arcade of three arches, just
as at Reculver and St Pancras Canterbury. In the responds of
the l. and r. arches, Roman brickwork can be recognized. The
church is almost entirely built of Roman materials – apart from
brick, also ashlar and septaria. The doorway is original except
for the lintel. Original also is the w window, of quite a generous
size. The side windows high up have original splays and jambs.
The chapel lies completely alone except for one cottage a little

distance away, exposed to the east winds of the North Sea, a moving sight.*

St Thomas. w tower of 1706, brick, with arched windows, diagonal buttresses, and battlements. Timber s porch with ogee-headed partitions on the E and w sides from St Mary, Shopland. The nave and chancel C14, much renewed by *Chancellor* in 1864. A curious detail is the remains of an early C16 brick gable at the E end of the nave. It rested on a trefoil-arched corbel-frieze. Another curious thing is the several C14 head-stops of former hood-moulds now set in the s wall of the nave, and also the hood-moulds of the C19 E window. – FONT. C14, octagonal bowl, with four big ugly heads reaching up from the stem, as if their shoulders carried the bowl. – PLATE. Cup of 1626. – BRASS to Margaret Wyott † 1526 (chancel, N wall).

Handsome village green just s of the church, with divers cottages, one six-bay Georgian brick house, and to the s Bradwell Lodge.

BRADWELL LODGE, the former Rectory. It is a Tudor house 61a (exposed moulded beams in what was the Hall) to which was added in 1781–6 a new s side, in a style clearly metropolitan. The architect was *John Johnson*, the client the newly introduced rector, the Rev. Henry Bate Dudley, a friend of Gainsborough and an extremely able journalist. The s front consists of two rooms and a circular library between. Behind this is the staircase with wrought-iron railing. It opens to the N towards what was at first a carriageway in, but was soon converted into an Entrance Hall with two doors behind each other. The second, the centre of the house, is glazed. On the roof an unusually spacious Belvedere decorated by Ionic columns. In its four corners run the chimneys of the house. The rest is glazed. All internal decorations are of the finest. There seems every reason to believe that *Robert Adam* himself had something to do with the design of the plasterwork and the fireplaces, and *Angelica Kauffmann* with some of the painting. The ceiling of the Drawing Room however is by *Robert Smirke*, father of the architect of the British Museum.

NUCLEAR POWER STATION. By *Maurice Bibb*, begun in 1957.)

BRAINTREE

St Michael the Archangel. A disappointing church, ex-

* The building of a detached vestry on the NW in about 1953 was a major visual crime.

cept for the C13 w tower with tall shingled broach spire. The exterior otherwise is almost entirely renewed or new (N aisle) – of 1864–6. The interior is decidedly spacious. It has three-bay arcades of the C13 with alternating circular and octagonal piers – alternating also across the nave. The arches have two slight quadrant hollows instead of chamfers. The N chancel chapel is only of one bay. The s chapel is of two with an early C16 pier. The section is of four main and four subsidiary shafts connected by deep hollows. Good early C16 roofs in the N and s chapels. – PLATE. Two decorated Cups of 1616. – MONUMENTS. Several by *John Challis*, all minor.

TOWN HALL. 1926–8 by *Vincent Harris*. A successful building, in spite of a lack of originality. Just right in size for a small but prosperous town. Five bays only and two storeys, red brick with stone dressings. Central open bell-turret. Inside, wall paintings by *Maurice Greiffenhagen*.

Other public buildings see below.

There is little of architectural interest in the town. The centre is now to the E of the church, where at the foot of the High Street an opening has recently been created. Here a pretty FOUNTAIN with a boy, a huge shell, and fishes; bronze, by *John Hodge*, *c*. 1938.

In the HIGH STREET No. 104 and No. 100 half-timbered, then the CORN EXCHANGE of 1839 with four-pillar portico, later filled in, and at the end HORNS HOTEL, C18, with two bay windows and a central carriageway. The continuation of the High Street is GREAT SQUARE, funnel-shaped, and opening towards the E where the CONSTITUTIONAL CLUB stands, a broad Georgian seven-bay front of three storeys, with keystones to the windows. To its r. a nice early C19 white brick house of five bays. An intricate neighbourhood of little lanes and little openings N of Great Square with LITTLE SQUARE (OLD MANOR HOUSE, late C16 with oversailing upper storeys, carved brackets and fascias and plaster decoration) and then leading into BANK STREET, which can also be reached direct from the end of the High Street. It is the best street of Braintree, and the best house is the SWAN INN, long and varied, with exposed timber-work, in the place where Bank Street widens into a kind of subsidiary market place. s of this Nos 37–39, a broad, rather clumsy C18 house of seven bays with three-bay pediment – red brick, with white brick quoins, bands, etc. N of the Swan, in the place where Braintree becomes Bocking, the White Hart (see Bocking).

BRAXTED PARK see GREAT BRAXTED

BRAYS GROVE see HARLOW

BRENTWOOD

ST THOMAS. By *E. C. Lee*, 1882–90. Large and serious, flint with a tall NW steeple; spire with four spirelets. The interior is E.E., competent but rather dull, but the outside has certain mannerisms which are reminiscent of such a younger man as E. S. Prior. The flints are of pebble size, and the buttresses as well as the stair-turret are semicircular in plan. It gives the exterior a curiously primeval flavour.

ST THOMAS'S CHAPEL, High Street. Very little left. Some W and N walling of the nave and the stump of the NW tower. C14. Prettily overgrown with ivy. Brentwood could make better use of this accent in a visually not very successful town.

ROMAN CATHOLIC CATHEDRAL, Ingrave Road. 1861. Ragstone with a polygonal SW turret, of that assertive ugliness which is characteristic of much church work of the sixties. – STAINED GLASS. E window by *Mayer* of Munich.

CONGREGATIONAL CHAPEL, New Road. 1847. Typical, with its broad stuccoed front with big pediment, square piers on the ground floor forming a loggia, and arched windows above.

BRENTWOOD SCHOOL, Shenfield Road and Ingrave Road. A complex group of buildings of various styles and dates. Of the original brick building of 1568 in Ingrave Road only the outer walls and a doorway remain. On top of it a dormitory of 1856. In the old School Room, woodwork from Weald Hall was installed as a chimneypiece in 1953. In the School Chapel are three lancet windows by *Sumner* from Great Warley church. The main, Victorian-looking, building in Ingrave Road dates from 1909–10 and is by *F. Chancellor & Sons*. The Georgian house also in Ingrave Road which belongs to the school (School House) can be dated 1773. The entrance block was added in 1926. Also in Ingrave Road, Barnards House, brick, five bays, two storeys, with parapet. The front looks *c*.1700. In Shenfield Road two houses on the S side and two on the N side* have also been taken over: Mitre House, half-timbered of *c*.1600, and Roden House, dated on a rainwater-head 1724. Opposite – the best Georgian houses of Brentwood – one of six bays, probably of *c*.1700, and another with a bow-window.

(TEACHERS' TRAINING COLLEGE by *H. Conolly*, County Architect, 1963.)

* These two no longer belong to the school.

MENTAL HOSPITAL. The extensive original buildings by *H. E. Kendall*, 1853, with additions of 1864, 1870, 1889, etc. Red brick with black diapers. Steep gables, turrets, etc.

In the HIGH STREET not much of note, and the interesting houses too far apart and too much interrupted by C20 commercial premises to be visually rewarding. No. 12 Georgian, brick, five bays, two storeys with Roman Doric porch. The WHITE HART HOTEL with a remarkably good coaching yard. The oversailing upper storey has dark weatherboarding and a row of low arched openings. They belonged to a long gallery. The date may well be before 1500. Two nice weatherboarded houses opposite.* Immediately to the w of the ruined chapel stands a small brick house of *c.*1700.

(About 2 m. NW of Brentwood on the Ongar road, PILGRIM'S HALL, probably Late Georgian with Victorian (1860?) alterations, adding up to a Regency effect. Two-storeyed, with an iron balcony between two semicircular bays. Information kindly provided by Mr F. G. Emmison)

BRETTS *see* AVELEY

BRICK HOUSE *see* BROXTED

BRICK HOUSE *see* WICKEN BONHUNT

BRICK HOUSE FARM *see* SHENFIELD

BRIDGEFOOT FARM *see* KELVEDON

BRIDGEHOUSE FARM *see* FELSTED

BRIGHTLINGSEA

ALL SAINTS. A town church, yet away from the little town, higher up and on its own. Like Dedham, a grand example of the East Anglian type on Essex soil. Yet there is ample evidence of a building earlier than the years of Perp prosperity. In the s aisle wall w of the doorway a round-headed recess with Roman brickwork, probably the remaining doorway of an Early Norman church whose nave s wall would have been here. After this follows the chancel. Here, on the N side, one blocked C13 lancet window, on the s side opposite another. The nave s doorway also C13 and simple. Moreover the E parts of the s and N arcades (octagonal piers and double-chamfered arches) be-

---

* Now threatened with demolition (1964).

long to the C13 or to *c.*1300. Then however the Perp style began its enlarging and remodelling. The w tower was completed in the 1490s. The nave was then lengthened to join it. The s vestry was added *c.*1518, the N chapel *c.*1521. The s chapel and s porch seem contemporary. Finally *c.*1530 the N aisle was reconstructed. The clerestory fell in 1814 and was not rebuilt – a great pity. The w tower is big and sturdy with a base decorated by shields in quatrefoils. Diagonal buttresses of an unusual section enriched by niches. Four-light w window, two-light window on the second stage, three-light bell-openings with one transom. Battlements pierced and decorated; crocketed pinnacles. s porch with flushwork decoration. Diagonal buttresses with niches. Flushwork base and battlements. Doorway with fleurons and crosses in the voussoirs. One niche above. Three-light side openings. s aisle plastered, with flint battlements. Three-light windows with Perp tracery. s vestry with flushwork decoration in the battlements. N chapel with flushwork decoration in the battlements and base. The N chapel tracery is like that of the s aisle, the N aisle tracery is simpler and later. The arcades inside in the w half of the nave, i.e. the work of *c.*1500, have piers of an odd section: lozenge-shaped basically with attached shafts towards the arches (with capitals), a thin polygonal shaft to the nave, and recessed parts in the diagonals (all this without capitals). Many niches scattered in the interior: in one of the C13 N piers, in the C13 s window in the chancel, in the E wall of the N chapel. – FONT. Perp, octagonal, with traceried stem and, on the bowl, quatrefoils with roses. Traces of colour found and renewed. – PLATE. Two Cups of 1620, large and scrolly with bands of ornament. – MONUMENTS. Brasses in the N chapel, which was the chapel of the Beriffe family. John Beryf † 1496 and wives. Husband, one wife, some children. – John Beriffe † 1521, wives and children. Also a merchant's mark on the plate. – William Beryff † 1525 and wife. – Alice Beriffe † 1536 and daughter. Below the figures part of an early C15 architectural surround. – William Beriff of Jacobes † 1578. Also, in the N aisle: Margaret B. † 1505 and Mary B. † 1505 with children. – In the chancel sumptuous monument to Nicholas Magens † 1764. By *N. Read*. According to Mr B. Butte the monument is described in the *Ipswich Journal*, 8 November 1766. Mr Butte also found that Magens was German by birth and grew rich in London in the insurance business. He died 'worth £100,000'. The centre of the monument is a globe. To the l. of it a winged female figure holding a large scrolled parchment with inscription. To the r. a putto on a gigantic cornucopia. On the r. also a big anchor, on the l. relief of ships. Cherubs and cherub heads on top. No effigy.

St James. In the little town. 1834–6 by *William Mason*, white brick, in the lancet style, but with none of the personal features that sometimes occur in that architect's work. (Modern chancel.)

The town is not specially attractive. The only house individually remarkable is Jacobes in the High Street, first recorded in 1315. Two gabled wings projecting towards the street. They are of about the same size. Roof with tie-beam and crown-post. One Early Tudor ceiling. The rare feature is an early C16 polygonal brick stair-turret in one of the re-entrant angles. It has battlements and a small crocketed conical roof on brick trefoil friezes (cf. Faulkbourne). Opposite a nice red Georgian house of five bays with a thick Early Victorian porch of cast-iron trellis-work.

(Bateman's Folly. A tower 25 ft high, used for a short time as a lighthouse. Barbara Jones, *Follies*.)

Roman Building. The foundations of a Roman house with tessellated pavements were found in Wells Street while laying water mains in the C19.

BRINKLEY GROVE see COLCHESTER

BRITTONS see HORNCHURCH

BRIZES see KELVEDON HATCH

BROADOAKS
2 m. SSE Wimbish

Moated brick house of *c*.1560. The house originally E-shaped, and what survives is only the upper arm of the E. Two gables to the E, one taller one to the N, at the E end. Here the ground floor has a six-light window, the first floor a six-light window with two transoms, and the gable a low four-light window. The chimneystacks are splendid, all with octagonal shafts. The tops are renewed. Fine, quite classical stone fireplace in the main room on the first floor.

BROOK STREET see SOUTH WEALD

BROOMFIELD

ST MARY. Norman round tower with much Roman brick re-
used. Low, with later shingled broach spire. Unmoulded
round-headed tower arch. Norman also both nave and chancel,
see the Roman brick quoins on the s side. The chancel was
lengthened and given its large E window in the C15. The N side
of the church belongs to 1870. – FONT. Square, of Purbeck
marble, C13 with three shallow blank pointed arches on each
side and (an exception) angle shafts. – PLATE. The old plate
has gone to St Luke, Ramsgate.

PRIORS, ¾ m. SW. An interesting C16 house, built of brick, with
original brick windows and an original canted bay window.
Next to this two timber-framed gables with exposed timbering.
Good staircase of c.1600.

BROOM HOUSE see HENHAM

BROOMWOOD see CHIGNAL

BROXTED

ST MARY. C13 nave and chancel, and C15 N aisle and belfry.
The belfry is weatherboarded and stands on four posts, two of
which rest on corbels (alteration?). The chancel has original
lancet windows, the nave no early features. The N arcade piers
have an elongated semi-polygonal shaft without capital towards the nave and normal semi-polygonal shafts towards the
arches, which are double-chamfered. W of the arcade in
the C13 wall a tall ogee-headed niche with a small vault. In
the nave S wall two early C16 brick windows. The church
was restored by *J. Clarke* in 1876. – PULPIT. With elaborate
Elizabethan arabesque ornament.

CHURCH HALL. Exceedingly picturesque façade of four gables
of different sizes and heights, late C16 with a mid C17 addition,
grouped with the C17 brewhouse and barn.

(BRICK HOUSE, 1½ m. E. Built c.1540, plus a C17 (?) N addition.
On the façade the upper storey projects on brackets, with
moulded bressumer. Part of the tie-beam roof on arched braces
is visible. Some early C17 panelling. R.C.)

BULMER

ST ANDREW. The emphasis of the church lies on its chancel,
unusually long, of early C14 style, with a band inside going all

the way and rising and falling to give way to the s doorway, the windows, the sedilia, and the piscina. The SEDILIA and the (double) PISCINA have cusped arches on detached shafts. The chancel roof is much later, *c.*1500, and has collarbeams on braces with a little tracery in the spandrels. The braces rest on angel figures. N arcade, also C14, with octagonal piers and double-chamfered arches. C15 W tower with diagonal buttresses, some flint and stone chequer-work at the base, and battlements. – FONT. Octagonal, C15; bowl with foliage and angels holding plain shields. – PULPIT. C18; panelling and a little inlay.

BULPHAN

ST MARY. The interest of the church is entirely its timberwork, the tower, the porch, the screen. The tower externally tile-hung with ornamental tiles, no doubt in Late Victorian days. It stands internally on six posts forming a nave and aisles. The aisles are divided horizontally by cross-beams with diagonal braces. Braces for the cross-beams of the centre spring from the aisles too. The centre has beams on big braces springing from the 'arcade' posts. Also of good timber construction is the s porch of *c.*1500. It has ornate bargeboarding with tracery decoration. – SCREEN. C15, uncommonly rich. Two side openings and doorway. Each side opening is of two lights under one arch with the mullion rising up into the apex of the arch and cusped tracery. All spandrels have blank tracery panelling. – PLATE. Cup of 1650.

(APPLETON'S FARM, ½ m. NE. C15 house, timber-framed and plastered. Central hall and cross-wings. The original kingpost roof of the hall survives. R.C.)

BURNHAM-ON-CROUCH

ST MARY. Not a church type of South Essex. Nave and chancel, and aisles and chancel chapels, without any structural divisions. There is thus a total of nine bays from W to E, even if the somewhat lower arches of the last three bays indicate that they belong to the chancel. Yet the church is not as big as all this sounds. The piers are not high, and the arches not wide. The main view is from the s – nine identical three-light Perp windows with four-centred arches and a variety of panel tracery a little more imaginative than the common run of South Essex. The aisle and chancel chapel are embattled, as is the s porch.

This incidentally is decorated with shields. The N side of the church is definitely the back side. But it has a pretty early C16 brick porch with a stepped gable. The N windows of the church are C14, those of the aisle earlier than those of the chancel chapel. The aisle windows go with the W tower, which must be early to mid C14, as indicated by the ogee-reticulated W window of an odd shape. The tower has angle buttresses. The upper part with the battlements was rebuilt in 1703. The odd shape of the W window is answered inside the church by the equally odd, though different shape of a niche in the N aisle wall (not *in situ*). This also is clearly C14. The interior of the church is characterized by the contrast of the long arcades with the C19 plastered vault with dormer windows. The arcade on the S side has filleted quatrefoil piers of the C14, re-used in the C15, when the bases were made to fit the length of the piers, and the capitals and moulded arches were added. The N arcade has octagonal piers with double-chamfered arches. – FONT, *c.*1200, square bowl on five supports, Purbeck marble, undecorated. – PLATE. Cup and Paten on foot of 1638.

The little town lies one mile S of the church. Its chief attraction is one terrace of low houses along THE QUAY. The centre is the White Hart Hotel, a little higher than the others, with a porch on carved brackets. The other houses are red, or yellow-washed, or white-washed, of no composition, but very pleasant, where they stand. A little further out towards the sea, a note of a very different kind, the ROYAL CORINTHIAN YACHT CLUB. This is a tall, broad, white building with long bands of windows, entirely modern, and a relatively early example of the style in England. 1931 by *Joseph Emberton*.

THE HIGH STREET is of less interest.* It runs, not straight of course, parallel with the river and widens into a kind of market square, where the Clock Tower of 1877 is the chief accent, not a lovable piece. There are no houses of special value. A nice Georgian one is No. 28. An Early Victorian attempt at a more urban scale a little to the E: two-and-a-half storeys, white brick, with a Tuscan doorway. Otherwise the usual weather-boarded cottages, an odd marbled Doric porch, and such-like minor pleasures.

(SECONDARY MODERN SCHOOL, Southminster Road. By *Johns, Slater & Haward*, completed 1962.)

CHERRY GARDEN, London Road, ½ m. W. Brick house of the

---

* Much changed for the better, I am told, since the Civic Trust High Street Improvement Scheme under *R. W. Johnson*, completed 1963.

C17 with a pedimented porch. The pediment however still rests on a curly gable. The main gables of the house are still straight. The date may be c.1670.

BUSH ELMS see HORNCHURCH

BUTTSBURY

ST MARY. Small and alone. Short nave of two bays with two aisles, that is wider than it is long. Date C14. Chancel of the C18 with C19 E window. Small W tower of timber, weatherboarded. The nave arcades are typical Late Perp, composite, with the centre parts to the nave carried on into the arches without capitals and the side parts concave-sided semi-octagonal. Two original traceried windows were found during a restoration in 1923. – DOORS. The N and S doors are both old, that on the N more interesting. Some of the metalwork is C13, some later. – PLATE. Cup of 1563 and Paten of 1567, both with bands of ornament.

CAMULODUNUM see COLCHESTER

CANEWDON

ST NICHOLAS. Considering the part of Essex where it stands, an unusually stately church. Big, massive and tall W tower of elephant-grey dressed ragstone. Built in four stages, with angle buttresses and battlements with stone and flint chequer. W doorway with decorated spandrels. Three-light W window and to its l. and r. two shields. Also recesses l. and r. of the doorway and in the W faces of the buttresses. All this must be C15. Of the same time the S front of the nave and broad three-light windows with coarse panel tracery, and the S porch with battlements of stone and flint chequer, an outer and an inner doorway with shields in the spandrels, and two-light N and S windows. The rest is mostly C14, see the three-light intersected tracery in a N aisle window and the W bays of the N arcade with octagonal piers and hood-moulds on defaced corbels. The E pier is late C15. Nave roof with tie-beams, king-posts, and four-way struts. – FONT. From St Mary, Shopland. Early C13. Square bowl on five supports. Decoration on one side with interleaved arches, on another with trefoiled arches, on the other two with fleurs-de-lis and crosses in niches. –

PULPIT. From St Christopher le Stocks in the City of London. Panels with garlands and cherubs' heads. – PLATE. Cup of 1665.

Close to the church the VICARAGE of 1758, much added to, and CANEWDON HALL of 1807, a plain white brick cube. By the E entrance to the churchyard the LOCK-UP, dated 1775, with the stocks preserved inside. It is a small weatherboarded shed.

LAMBOURNE HALL, 1 m. E. Timber-framed and plastered. Of c.1500 with a C17 SE wing including the two-storeyed porch of the SW front. Also C18 and C19 additions.

CANNING TOWN

Nowhere is London-over-the-Border more undistinguishably London than at Canning Town. Canning Town was named after the chief employer of labour in the neighbourhood and begun in 1851.

ST CEDD, Beckton Road. 1938 by *Gordon O'Neill*. Red brick with arched windows and a square battlemented tower. A satisfactory design.

ST LUKE, Jude Street. 1874–6 by *Giles & Gane*. Tall, without tower. E.E. and with geometrical tracery. Yellow brick. Flèche as in Continental friars' churches.

ST MARGARET, R.C., Barking Road. 1875–6 by *Tasker*. The star-shaped tracery of the W window is supposed to be of the same date. Can it be?

PUBLIC HALL AND PUBLIC LIBRARY, Barking Road. 1893–4 by *Lewis Angell*. Red brick. Retrograde Italianate.

SOUTH WEST HAM COUNTY TECHNICAL SCHOOL, Barking Road, Alexandra Street, and Morgan Street. 1951–2 by *T. E. North* with *R. B. Padmore* and *H. C. Macaree*. A good big asymmetrical building in the modern style. Flat roofs and a successful distribution of the various wings.

MANSFIELD HOUSE CLUB, Barking Road near Ingal Road. 1897–8 by *Troup*. Red brick and yellow artificial stone. Free Neo-Tudor.

ROYAL VICTORIA DOCK. 1855. 94 acres of water.

ROYAL ALBERT DOCK. 1880. 86 acres of water.

KING GEORGE V DOCK. 1921. 57 acres of water.

The most remarkable urban development of recent years is the conversion of the slums N of the Docks into a town of terraced cottages in the Council Estate style.

New housing also in RATHBONE STREET. Eight ten-storey blocks by *T. E. North*, 1963–4.

CANVEY ISLAND

Canvey Island was reclaimed after 1620. When the sea wall had been built and the land was secured, Dutch labourers were settled, and two cottages, both called DUTCH COTTAGE, are the earliest surviving buildings on the island. One is at the corner of the lane leading to Hole Haven, the other by the main road a little further NW. They are dated 1621 and 1618, octagonal in plan and thatched. The character of the island has completely changed during the C20. Its whole E half is now one bungalow and seaside development.

CASTLE HEDINGHAM

CASTLE. It is well understandable that the castle has found its way into the name of the little town. It dominates the town and all the country round, it was one of the mightiest and most famous of East Anglia, it was built by, and belonged to, one of the most powerful families of Norman England, the de Veres, Earls of Oxford, and it stands to this day as an ideal picture of a keep – on a mount, high above old trees, with two of its square corner turrets still rising up to nearly 100 ft. It is besides probably the best-preserved of all tower-keeps of England. In proportion, style, and detail that of Rochester is its nearest relation, and the two may well be the work of the same architect or *ingeniator*, as the designer of fortifications was called.

The KEEP stands on a mount which represents the inner bailey. Of the outer bailey the E parts are recognizable and now embrace the irregular Georgian house, of which the principal range is of seven bays and two storeys with a three-bay pediment. This dates, it is said, from 1719.* The keep was built of Barnack stone about the year 1140. Its interior has suffered from a recent fire. Attached to the keep on the W side is a forebuilding of which only rough walling remains. At ground-floor level, inaccessible from outside, were stores. The forebuilding perhaps contained the prison. The staircase to the main entrance ran up inside the forebuilding parallel with the W wall of the keep. It led to a doorway with thick columns with scalloped capitals and an arch decorated by zigzag ornament. Through this doorway the large first-floor room was reached. This had an arch across from E to W and still possesses a fire-

* Handsome, spacious contemporary staircase with wrought-iron railing.

place in the E wall with a zigzag arch. The windows are shafted inside and outside. Outside they are of course very small. In the thickness of the wall are divers narrow chambers or recesses. One of these, in the NE angle, can be identified as a garderobe or lavatory. The main staircase is in the NW angle. On the second floor lies the Hall, 38 by 31 ft in size by 27 ft in 43 height. It is surrounded by a gallery at about half its height. Across the Hall, again from E to W, a large arch is struck. It rests on responds with angle shafts and in the middle on heavy demi-columns each carrying extremely heavy two-scalloped capitals. The arch moulding is of two rolls with a small ridge between. The fireplace has again a zigzag arch, and the windows here also have zigzag decoration on their nook-shafts. The gallery openings are as large towards the hall as the window recesses. To the outside shafted twin openings correspond to them, as against the single openings below. The entrance from the staircase to the gallery is enriched by some pretty beaded spiral fluting. The third floor is lower and simpler. On it rested the roof with its paved walk behind the former battlements. Of the four much taller angle turrets only two survive, and these also are now deprived of their battlements.

Excavations have shown that the GREAT HALL stood SW of the keep and had a vaulted undercroft and a bay window. The CHAPEL was immediately to the S of the keep. Outside the curtain-wall to the S are the two bases of the octagonal angle turrets of the Perp GATEHOUSE, which was of brick. Of brick also the handsome, preserved BRIDGE across the moat E of the keep. It seems to be of c.1500.

ST NICHOLAS. The brick W tower is dated 1616, but seems to be substantially of the early C16. It is impressively high when you stand near it, but suffers from the position of the whole town centre in a dip. The tower is built entirely in the Tudor style, with diagonal buttresses, a higher stair-turret (with a small cupola), stepped battlements, and (obelisk) pinnacles. Above the five-light W window is a frieze of shields referring to the 13th Earl of Oxford, who died in 1512, e.g. a chain of state, because he was Lord Great Chamberlain. On the aisle walls the battlements are also of brick; so is the clerestory. A frieze above the clerestory windows has a de Vere emblem too, the *molet*, a star. Early C16 also the S porch. The windows of the church are mostly Perp, except for the chancel, and the chancel windows are externally all sadly renewed.

In spite of this external appearance and the dominance of the tower, the church, once it is entered, reveals itself as one of the most important and, of its period, the most ambitiously designed in Essex. A complete Late Norman parish church, 125 ft long to the E arch of a Norman tower replaced by the Tudor tower. Nave and aisles of six bays, and a long chancel. The nave arcades rest on alternatingly circular and octagonal piers with splendidly carved leaf capitals, mostly of crocket-like leaves, but in one case also of real crockets on the French Early Gothic pattern. That dates the nave as not earlier than c.1180. The complex mouldings of the arches indicate so late a date too. The clerestory has rere-arches with a flat wavy band (cf. Felsted). The same motif in the tall tower arch, which has semicircular responds. It must have led into a tower of substantial size. The triple-chamfered arch however is Tudor, if not 1616. The s as well as N doorway belong to the Late Norman building. They have columns with volute and waterleaf capitals and round arches. The chancel of Hedingham is even more of a showpiece. First externally. It has an exceptionally impressive design for the E end. This design does not seem to have been decided upon at once. The ground floor has two shallow buttresses or pilaster-strips ending at the sill level of the windows. There are three small lancet windows shafted outside and inside and above them a large wheel-window with eight columns as spokes. This is a rare motif in Norman England (Barfreston, Peterborough). On the s side is a doorway with one order of colonnettes with long thin volute-capitals and two-dimensional zigzag-work in the (round) arches. The s and N windows are shafted like those at the E end. Internally a whole order of blank arches on shafts runs round the windows, a large arch for each window and a narrower and also less high one for each interval. Here also all the arches are round, and the same flat wavy motif accompanies them which we have found in the tower arch. The chancel arch makes a special display of three-dimensional zigzag and similar motifs and very thin long nook-shafts, and besides is the only one in the church which is pointed. Can it be earlier than c.1190?

The late medieval alterations and additions are minor and have been mentioned – with one exception: the double-hammerbeam roof of the nave which, as a crowning motif, is worthy of the Norman columns. It is one of only four roofs of such type in Essex.

SCREEN. One of the most ornate in a county poor in worthwhile screens. One-light divisions, each with a heavily cusped

and crocketed ogee head and much panel tracery above. –
CHANCEL STALLS. On the S side with misericords, e.g. a wolf
carrying off a monk(?), a man's face and two leopards' heads, a
fox with a distaff, etc. – CUPBOARD (under the tower). The
front is made up of panels of C17 dates. – DOORS. In the N and
two S doorways, contemporary with the church, with long iron
battens with long thin scrolls. – SCULPTURE. (Lunette-shaped
small panel with the frontal head of a young king, c.1250.) –
Small wooden Relief of the Magdalene washing Christ's feet,
probably Flemish, early C16 (E end of S aisle). – Demi-figure
of a woman praying; small; probably C12 (S aisle S wall). –
Norman ornamental carving with a head and leaves l. and r.,
used as a stoup (S aisle). – (PAINTING. Fragment of plaster
with the head of a bishop or king, diaper background, preserved in a glass case at the W end. Early C14. E. W. Tristram,
English Wall Painting of the early C14.) – MONUMENT. John,
fifteenth Earl of Oxford, † 1539 and wife. The other de Veres
were buried at Earls Colne Priory. The monument is of black
marble. Against the foot the kneeling figures of four daughters.
On the opposite side four sons, not now visible, as the monument, which was originally placed in the middle of the choir,
now stands against the wall. On the lid the kneeling figures of
the Earl and his Lady under some drapery gathered up, and
above a large coat of arms. Only minor details are in the new
Renaissance taste. The monument is probably by *Cornelius
Harman*, to whom we owe the Audley Monument at Saffron
Walden (1544) and also perhaps the Vyvyan Monument at
Bodmin in Cornwall (1533) (cf. p. 333).

The little town is throughout pleasant to look at. What there is of
unsightly developments lies half a mile to the W along the A-
road. Close to this there was in the Middle Ages a Benedictine
Nunnery founded in 1191. The town is a triangle with Bayley
Street to the N, St James Street to the S, and Crown Street to
the W. The pattern is repeated right in the centre by the small
triangular opening E of the churchyard. Here, almost facing
each other, a C15 to C16 half-timbered inn with a projecting
upper storey on carved brackets and a Georgian brick house of
five bays. To the S of this another, seven bays wide with a parapet. This links up with St James Street and Queen Street,
where at the corner of St James Street a particularly pretty
half-timbered house, and a little further SW in Queen Street
the Vicarage, the best classical brick house: five bays, two-and-
a-half storeys, stone quoins, Ionic doorcase, Venetian window

above, and semicircular window above that. The house must
be Early Georgian.

As for the other streets, no houses need be singled out for
mention.

CHADWELL HEATH *see* ROMFORD

CHADWELL ST MARY

ST MARY. Norman nave with s doorway. Above the N doorway
tympanum with rosettes and saltire crosses. Chancel C14 with
original roof. w tower of *c.*1500 with diagonal buttresses at
the foot, w doorway and little ogee-headed niche to its r. The
difference in the Norman and the C15 flintwork is worth
noting. – CHAIR. Late C17, sumptuously carved, perhaps
French. – PAINTING. Finding of Moses, ascribed to one of the
Carracci, but closer to *Luca Giordano*.

SLEEPERS FARM, w of the church, timber-framed and gabled.

CHAFFORD SCHOOL *see* RAMSEY

CHAPPEL

CHURCH. Nave and chancel in one, and belfry with very pointed
little spire. The church was consecrated in 1352 and yet the
window tracery is still of a type usually connected with the
early C14: two lights cusped under one pointed head, with a
cusped pointed quatrefoil in the spandrel.

MILL, s of the church. Nice, Late Georgian, weatherboarded,
of three storeys.

CHELMSFORD

Chelmsford is the county-town of Essex. With its 52,000 inhabitants and its large industrial establishments (Marconi, Crompton
Parkinson, Hoffmann's Ball Bearings) and its extensive council
housing – the Boarded Barns Estate has over 1,000 houses – it is
essentially a modern town. Yet it has preserved a quiet dignified
centre near to and chiefly s of the parish church, now the
Cathedral.

CHURCHES

CATHEDRAL OF ST MARY. Chelmsford was raised to the rank
of a cathedral town in 1913. But the church will, whatever
adjustments can be made, remain the parish church of a prosperous late medieval town. Perhaps Liverpool and Guildford

and Coventry have been wiser to build new temples. The best
impression of the building is the outside from the SE, with the
commanding late C15 W tower, the spectacular S porch, the
nave, aisle, and chancel, and the new E end of *Sir Charles
Nicholson*'s, a little higher than the chancel. Its date is 1923,
but *Sir Arthur Blomfield*'s E window of 1878 was re-used. The
W tower has set-back buttresses, but the angles are chamfered.
The battlements are decorated with flushwork and carry eight
small pinnacles. The charming open lantern is of 1749, when
the leaded needle spire was also rebuilt. W doorway with ogee
gable and tracery and shields in the spandrels, three-light W
window, three-light bell-openings. The rest of the church
over-restored. The outer N aisle and N transept are an addition
of 1873. The chapter house, muniment room, and vestries,
very much more attractive in design, date from 1926 and are
also due to *Sir Charles Nicholson*. On the S side the S porch
has plenty of flushwork decoration and inside a ceiling re- 9b
using blank tracery perhaps from bench-fronts. E of it the
last two bays of the nave are alone ashlar-faced. The interior
reveals one earlier restoration, 1801–3 by *John Johnson* (see
below). He rebuilt the late C15 piers with their characteristic
lozenge shape and their mouldings and on the S side used
Coade & Seely's *Coade* stone for the purpose. The clerestory
windows were renewed by Johnson and the prettily ribbed,
coved Tudor ceiling of the nave is also by him. The aisles
embrace the tower, the chancel aisles the chancel. The N
chapel opens in an early C15 arcade of two bays which has an
unusual shape: round arch divided into two pointed arches
with openwork panel tracery in the spandrel. The thin pier
has four shafts and four hollows in the diagonals. – ALTAR by
Wykeham Chancellor, 1931. – BISHOP'S THRONE with high
Gothic canopy by *Sir Charles Nicholson*. – PROVOST'S STALL
with simpler square canopy by *Wykeham Chancellor*, 1936. –
COMMUNION RAIL with thick openwork foliage and cherubs,
*c.*1675, said to come from Holland. – PULPIT. 1872. – STAINED
GLASS. Mostly by *A. K. Nicholson* and rather prosaic with its
realistic figures on a ground of clear glass. – E window by
Clayton & Bell, 1858. – PLATE. Cup of 1620; two Flagons of
1697; Almsdish of 1700; two Patens on foot of 1707. – MONU-
MENTS. Thomas Mildmay, erected 1571, a standing wall-
monument of a curious shape, and without any major figures.★

★ Mr P. J. Oldfield convincingly suggests that major figures originally
existed.

Base with colonnettes and small figures of kneeling children. Above this zone one with two steep triangular pediments and one semicircular pediment and above that zone a big ogee top with strapwork decoration. – Matthew Rudd † 1615. Small mural incised slab. Attributed by Mrs Esdaile to *Epiphanius Evesham*. – Robert Bownd † 1696 (N aisle), with fine flower garlands. – Earl Fitzwalter (Benjamin Mildmay) † 1756. Large standing wall-monument with an oversized urn in the centre flanked by Corinthian columns, and big cherubs standing to the l. and r. Signed by *James Lovell*. – Mary Mash † 1757. Of various marbles with an urn and fine Rococo decoration.

IMMACULATE CONCEPTION (R.C.), London Road. 1847 by *Scoles* (GR). Cheaply executed. Gothic, with nave and aisles and no tower.

ST JOHN, Moulsham Street. 1841 by *Thomas Webb*. White brick, in the lancet style, with W tower facing the street. The transepts etc. added in 1851–2. No aisles. – STAINED GLASS. One N and one S window, each of one light, have single figures executed by *Kempe* as early as 1879. His style then was more flamboyant than later, but the faces and the colouring remained the same.

ST PETER, Primrose Hill. In the church the former FONT from St Mary – *Coade* stone, ordered in connexion with the *Johnson* restoration. Elaborate and crisp Perp, octagonal, with traceried stem and cusped panels. Identical with the font at Debden.

HOLY TRINITY, Trinity Road, Springfield. Neo-Norman by *J. Adie Repton*, 1843. The date corresponds to the height of the fashion for a Norman Revival, specially ill-advised where, as here, the material is white brick. Tall round-headed lancet windows. Angle turrets to the façade. Elaborate decoration. No aisles, no galleries.

(TRINITY CHURCH (Methodist), Rainsford Road. By *Cubitt-Nichols*, 1961.)

CONGREGATIONAL CHAPEL, London Road. 1840. White brick, five bays wide, with a three-bay pediment and a loggia of four Greek Doric columns on the ground floor.

FRIENDS' MEETING HOUSE,* Duke Street. Quite a big meeting house; built in 1826 of white brick. Sides of four tall arched windows, pedimented front of three. Porch on four sturdy Tuscan columns. The timber roof is supposed to have the largest span in Essex, 42 ft.

* Now part of the Mid-Essex Technical College.

PUBLIC BUILDINGS

SHIRE HALL, Tindal Square. 1789–91 by *John Johnson*, Surveyor 61b
to the County. A thoroughly civilized public building, spurred
probably by Adam's for Hertford a few years before and indeed
considerably superior. Five-bay width only, but generous
spacing and good Portland stone. The three middle bays project slightly and have arched entrances. The whole ground
floor is rusticated. Above in the middle four attached giant
columns with Adam capitals. The windows between them have
pediments. The outer windows are tripartite and segment-
arched. Then above the middle windows three relief-plaques
(by the elder *Bacon*, executed in *Coade* stone) and a pediment.
No unusual motifs or peculiarities of handwriting, but a very
refined handling of familiar material.

COUNTY HALL, Duke Street. Much bigger, but a sad anti-
climax. The height of the building ruins the skyline of the town
from many points by depriving the cathedral tower of its pre-
eminence. Classical motifs handled loosely and without distinction. Also the building has no space and is indifferently
sited. It might be a city bank in any city bigger than Chelmsford. By *J. Stuart*, 1935.

(COUNTY OFFICES. By *H. Conolly*, County Architect, begun in
1959.)

(CIVIC CENTRE. By *Jackson & Edmonds*, 1962.) This group of
buildings also incorporates the PUBLIC LIBRARY, 1933 by
Cordingley & McIntyre. Two-storeyed, symmetrical, Neo-
Georgian. Brick with the centre treated in stone.

MID-ESSEX TECHNICAL COLLEGE, Market Road. 1904–5
by *Chancellor & Son*. Symmetrical red brick block with stone
dressings. The usual Neo-Tudor mixed with Baroque motifs.
Not specially interesting. (Extensions 1960–2 by *A. R. Dannant
& Son*, in association with the County Architect.)

CORN EXCHANGE (now Casino), Tindal Square. 1857 by *F.
Chancellor*. Yellow brick. Neo-Renaissance, with arched entrances below and arched windows above. Top balustrade. In
front of the Corn Exchange STATUE of Chief Justice Tindal,
by *Baily*, 1847.

COUNTY GAOL, Springfield Road. The original buildings are
of 1822–8 by *Thomas Hopper*. Alterations on the model of
Pentonville in 1848, also by Hopper. To him is due the sombre
entrance with heavy rustication and Tuscan pilasters, and the
long brick wall with buttresses like Tuscan pilasters: 420 ft
long.

(Supply Depot, Essex County Council, Widford Industrial
    Estate. By *H. Conolly*, County Architect, 1958–9.)
(Indoor Swimming Pool, Waterloo Road. By the *Borough
    Engineer's Department*, started 1963.)
(Rivers House, Springfield Road, for the Essex River Board.
    By *E. R. Collister & Associates*, 1959–62.)

PERAMBULATION

A walk through the town does not afford much excitement. But
it is pleasant, because the centre has remained singularly un-
affected by the coarser and louder forms of commercialization.
The main streets are still architecturally quiet and in scale with
the Shire Hall and the former parish church. The centre is
Tindal Square with the Shire Hall and the Corn Exchange.
Opposite the latter the Saracen's Head, c18, five bays,
three storeys, with quoins and a later porch, and Barclays
Bank in a quiet, excellently handled Neo-Georgian, 1905 by
Sir Reginald Blomfield. From the Square to the N into New
Street. Here the white brick back of the Shire Hall and some
white brick houses of *c.*1800 form a quiet, well-suited back-
ground to the Cathedral. Nos 55–57 has a central motif of
Doric columns and two symmetrical pediments. No. 53 is of
seven bays, but the front hides features of a much earlier house.
Early c16 linenfold panelling in the Hall.

s of the Square two parallel streets, Tindal Street and High
Street. Tindal Street is quieter and more provincial. No
special houses, except perhaps the nice shop-front of No. 13.
The street continues as London Road, and here, past the
bridge, we are back at Early Victorian white brick. The biggest
unit at the beginning, Nos 44–56, a thirteen-bay terrace of
three storeys with a five-bay centre and giant pilasters. This
was built shortly after 1839. The Institute of 1841, white
brick with giant Tuscan pilasters, and opposite the Congregational Chapel, see above, and smaller and more modest white
brick terraces, gradually changing from Early to Mid-
Victorian.

Even the High Street has little in the way of individually
remarkable houses. The best is No. 26 with a centre window
with brick pilasters carrying Corinthian capitals of stone and a
brick pediment, Early Georgian probably. Opposite three
varieties of Modern: the Dutch, the quiet 1950, and the Tec-
ton-Fry-International – all three in provincial dress. At the s
end the Bridge of 1787, designed by *Johnson*, with a single

span and a boldly curved parapet with sturdy balusters. The
roadway of course was originally also curved. Just before the
Bridge Springfield Road leads to SPRINGFIELD. Nos 85–91
are a terrace of white brick cottages, dated 1814 – again typical
for the outer development of early C19 Chelmsford. Off Springfield Road to the w is SPRINGFIELD MILL, weatherboarded, 2b
with the miller's house of red and blue brick. Down Sandford
Road to the E of Springfield Road one reaches Barnes Mill Road
and Mill Vue Road, with the BARNES MILL, also weatherboarded, and its miller's house, C17 at the back, C18 in the
front. Back to the Bridge, the continuation of the High Street is
MOULSHAM STREET,* where more timber-framed cottages
survive than anywhere else. Moulsham was a separate village
in the Middle Ages. Off to the E in Baddow Road MOULSHAM
MILL with a nice C18 brick house of five bays and two-and-
a-half storeys. The mill itself is weatherboarded. Off Moulsham Street a little further s, also on the E side, in HALL
STREET at the far end a factory of 1861, built for silk weaving
but taken over by the Marchese Marconi as his first factory.
Yellow brick. Much further s, in Moulsham Street, the
MILDMAY ALMSHOUSES of 1758, red brick, twelve bays and
two storeys with a four-bay pediment and segment-headed
windows.

Finally off Tindal Square to the w, where Duke Street has felt
the impact of untidy commercialization more than any other
street of Chelmsford. Yet even here occasionally the signs of a
quiet early C19 growth can still be seen. More in BROOM-
FIELD ROAD right out to the house called Broomfield Place
(Planning Department), and in Rainsford Road. Here also – as
a final contrast – the elegant CONDUIT of 1814, moved from
the High Street to Admiral's Park in 1939, a rotunda with
Tuscan columns and a small dome, and the crude and robust
High Victorian red brick WATER TOWER of 1888.

(Recent building in Chelmsford includes:

MELBOURNE COURT, near Melbourne Park playing fields. A
fifteen-storey residential block by the *Borough Engineer's
Department*. Completed 1962.

* ROMAN SETTLEMENT. The area of the settlement is roughly defined
by Moulsham and Hall Streets and Hamlet Road. Its S E limit has not been
ascertained, but it is not thought to have extended beyond Mildmay Road.
The boundary of the settlement is marked by a scarp immediately s of Hall
Street. The total area enclosed is approximately 850 ft square. Finds from
the area span the period from the C1 to the C4.

OFFICE and FACTORY BUILDINGS for Marconi Ltd, Waterhouse Lane. By *E. R. Collister & Associates*, completed 1964.)

CHELMSHOE HOUSE *see* GREAT MAPLESTEAD

CHEQUERS *see* LITTLE BARDFIELD

CHERRY GARDEN *see* BURNHAM-ON-CROUCH

CHICKNEY

ST MARY. Saxon nave with two original double-splayed windows. Chancel with small E.E. lancets. The chancel arch is
about a hundred years later. Its imposts are exceedingly
curious; they are regarded by the Royal Commission as C19,
but are not necessarily so. Pretty two-light squint to the l. of
the arch. – FONT. C14 with buttressed stem and bowl with
deep crocketed ogee arches with shields in the spandrels. –
FONT COVER. C16, pyramidal, with embattled foot, and
crockets, but certain leaf motifs which look Elizabethan. –
PLATE. Small Cup with baluster stem, *c.*1630–40.
CHICKNEY HALL. 1935 by *A. Whittingham*. The restrained
Neo-Tudor type, say, of Sir Herbert Baker.
(SIBLEY'S FARM, 1¼ m. NNW. Timber-framed C15 house,
altered outside. But much of interest remains inside. In the
hall a C16 or earlier partition, an original doorway W of this,
original beams in several rooms, original roof constructions of
various types, and a late C16 newel staircase. R.C.)

CHIGNAL

ST JAMES. Nave, chancel, and C19 bellcote. The church was so
much restored in the C19 that little evidence of interest remains except a two-light early C16 brick window in the chancel. – PLATE. Cup of 1667.
ST NICHOLAS, Chignal Smealy. An all-brick church of the early
C16. The brick is decorated with blue brick diapers. The view
from the E is specially picturesque with three gables of different
heights. The W tower is not tall. It has diagonal buttresses,
battlements, and brick windows. Brick windows in nave and
chancel as well. The E window is renewed; the N aisle was
added in 1847. The two-bay arcade however is original and one
of the rare cases of a complete brick arcade. Octagonal pier and
four-centred arches. – FONT. Even the font is of brick (cf.
Potter Heigham, Norfolk), octagonal and quite undecorated,

except for the moulding between stem and bowl. – SCREEN. Plain, one-light divisions with ogee arches. – PULPIT. Nice plain C17. – PLATE. Secular Cup of 1617 with chased bowl.

BROOMWOOD. Built by *Fred Rowntree* for Miller Christy, the Essex antiquary, in the local Essex style, half-timbered, gabled, and with Tudor chimneys.

CHIGWELL

Dickens called Chigwell 'such an out of the way rural place'. The visitor to-day is surprised to find it still a real village, the first as one leaves London in a NE direction. I say: still; for t he new Central London Line loop will no doubt soon scatter about its housing estates?

ST MARY. A village church also, though enlarged in 1886 to more than twice its original size. The original church was Norman and still has its s doorway with one order of rat her tall columns, one-scallop capitals, a curved lintel, an arch w ith zigzag decoration, and a tympanum with carved diaper ornament, little squares, divided into two triangles. C15 N arc ade with piers of the familiar four-shafts-four-hollows profile. C15 roof with tie-beams, king-posts, and four-way struts. C15 belfry on eight posts, two against the N and two against the s wall, the remaining four forming a square in between. T he usual arched braces connect the wall-posts with the square. Beams along the N and s sides of the square, and cross-strutting. Outside, the belfry is weatherboarded, painted white, and has a copper broach-spire. The C19 chancel was decorated by *Bodley*: stencilled walls, painted ceiling, alabaster and marble REREDOS, flanked by paintings of angels on both sides. The PULPIT also by *Bodley*. – STAINED GLASS. Easternmost N window by *Kempe* 1902. – PLATE. Paten of 1559; Secular Cup with Tudor roses and sunflowers, 1605 or 1610; Cup and Paten of 1633; Paten of 1633; Flagon of 1713. – MONUMENTS. Brass to Samuel Harsnett, Archbishop of York, † 1631, bearded with cope and mitre. Frontal figure about life-size. The archbishop had been vicar of Chigwell and founded the Grammar School here. – Thomas Colshill † 1595 and wife, small, with the usual kneeling figures facing each other.

Opposite the church the KING'S HEAD, a C17 timber-framed building, much vamped up, especially by a large addition of 1901, but still with some original exposed studs and brackets –

extremely picturesque in its particular position. To the E of the church the GRAMMAR SCHOOL, founded in 1629. The large original school-room survives with its brick walls, the roof with tie-beams and queen-posts, and at least two original four-light mullioned windows. Very pretty the Head Master's house at r. angles projecting towards the street. Its front is Georgianized, and it has a late C18 doorway. To its E a taller Gothic brick addtion of 1871 by *Dollman*.

A little to the s two good Georgian houses: GRANGE COURT of 1774, yellow brick with small one-bay, one-storey wings, and BROOK HOUSE, red brick, of five bays and two-and-a-half storeys. Opposite the grounds of CHIGWELL HALL, the former manor house, which was rebuilt by *Norman Shaw* in 1876. It is his only house in Essex, and a specially good one, surprising in its freshness, and looking as if it might well be twenty-five years later. The s front has an asymmetrical bay window, a tile-hung upper floor with three windows projected slightly like those of Paycocke's House at Coggeshall, and then three gables of equal size.

Further s, towards Woodford Bridge, is the former manor house, now the CONVENT OF THE SACRED HEART. It is Georgian, of yellow brick, with a sadly altered façade, but has a fine graceful original staircase and iron railings and gateways of unusual quality. The chapel is by *Stokes*, Neo-Georgian and tunnel-vaulted, and not specially interesting.*

(OAKFIELDS, St Winifred's Close, off Manor Road. By *Stanley Keen*, 1961. According to Mr Nairn 'a very good example of the enlightened kind of small estate that has followed on Span's pioneer work'.)

NEW SCHOOLS. The Essex County Council has recently erected three specially well designed schools at Chigwell, the MANFORD WAY PRIMARY SCHOOL and the GRANGE SECONDARY SCHOOL, also in Manford Way, both by the County Architect *H. Conolly*, and the KINGSWOOD SECONDARY SCHOOL, Huntsman's Road, Hainault Forest, by *Yorke, Rosenberg & Mardall*. Also WEST HATCH TECHNICAL SCHOOL, Chigwell High Road, 1957–63 by *H. Conolly*.

CHIGWELL ROW

ALL SAINTS. 1867 by *Seddon*, 'excellent of its sort' (GR). Yellow stone with white stone dressings. NW tower, low three-bay

* Mr E. S. Phillips draws my attention to SHEPCOTES, on the road from Chigwell Row to Lambourne End, Georgian, white brick, of unusual type and very attractive.

entrance porch with wheel window above. The style of the
church is C13. Inside, arcades with thickly carved stiff-leaf
capitals. The chancel was rebuilt in 1918–19.

On the Green opposite the church HAINAULT HALL, a five-bay
brick house with three-bay pediment. Lower down, to the w,
the FREE CHURCH, former Congregational Chapel, white
brick with arched windows. It was built in 1804, but has, alas,
a Victorian front.

KINGSWOOD SECONDARY SCHOOL, see Chigwell.

CHINGFORD

Chingford is three different things. The medieval church stands
away from the present town, surrounded by C20 housing. The
principal church is in the centre, a typical near-London suburban centre, sometimes quite like a town in itself, but the London
buses remind you at once of where you are. Thirdly there is the
wooded border of Epping Forest, near the C20 centre, yet very
different in character.

ALL SAINTS. High up with a w view towards the reservoirs of
the Lea valley and the Brimsdown power station. Late C13 s
arcade with circular piers and double-chamfered arches.* The
external features Perp. The chancel was building in 1460,
when money was left in a will 'versus fabricham novi cancelli
sive chori'. Restored after a long period of unchecked decay in
1929. Nave, chancel, and w tower. The material is ragstone.
Brick porch early C16. – PLATE. Cup and Paten of 1595. –
MONUMENTS. All minor. Mary Leigh † 1602, small tablet
with reclining woman and baby behind her, in relief. – Sir
Robert Leigh † 1612, Margaret Leigh † 1624, both with
kneeling figures.

ST PETER AND ST PAUL, The Green. 1844 by *Vulliamy*. The
E parts by *Sir Arthur Blomfield*, 1903, white brick with much
flushwork decoration. An uncommonly bold way of adding.
The old church had a w tower with spire, no aisles, and a w
gallery. The new parts are aisled and three bays long, added
without any compromise, so that the old nave seems a kind of
roofed forecourt. – FONT. Purbeck marble, square, C12, with
five shallow blank arches to each side of the bowl. – PULPIT.
Good early C18. – PLATE. Paten on foot 1699; Flagon 1705.

(COUNCIL OFFICES and COURT HOUSE. 1960–1, by *H.
Conolly*, County Architect.)

* Rebuilt after the collapse of the roof in 1904. The restoration of 1929
was by *C.C. Winmill*. (Information from H. V. Molesworth Roberts.)

A systematic perambulation would hardly repay. The following buildings, etc. may be mentioned: the granite OBELISK on Pole Hill, put up in 1824 as a N mark from Greenwich Observatory; then CARBIS COTTAGE and the BULL & CROWN PUBLIC HOUSE on the Green, as an impressive sign of development, from the early C19 cottage to Edwardian pomposity, brick, with plenty of yellow terracotta decoration in the wildest Loire style; also PIMP HALL FARM* (s of King's Road) and FRIDAY HILL (Simmons Lane) for a similar contrast, the one still the C17 farmhouse, once entirely in the open country, the other a rich Early Victorian country house, white brick in a mixed Elizabethan style, by *Vulliamy*, 1839; finally Queen Elizabeth's Hunting Lodge and the FOREST HOTEL of 1933, both half-timbered, one original, the other recent imitation and consequently so much bigger and more striking that it overshadows the genuine article completely.

QUEEN ELIZABETH'S HUNTING LODGE. A very interesting survival – a timber-framed three-storeyed 'standing', that is a building from which to view the hunting. In stone such a structure exists e.g. at Chatsworth. Chambord in a way was the same. But they are rare, and Chingford is specially early, dated by the Royal Commission early C16. The two upper floors originally had no infillings between the studs where there are now windows. The building is small and L-shaped, the shorter wing being filled by the staircase, which goes up round a square open well. The first-floor room has a ceiling with moulded beams, the second-floor room an open roof with collar-beams, arched braces, queen-posts, and wind-braces.

Two schools at Chingford are amongst the best recently built in the county, the LONGSHAW ROAD PRIMARY SCHOOL and the HEATHCOTE SECONDARY SCHOOL (Whitehall Road), both by the County Architect, *H. Conolly*.

CHIPPINGHILL see WITHAM

CHIPPING ONGAR

ST MARTIN OF TOURS. Uncommonly complete Norman village church. Nave and chancel, both with characteristic masonry, Roman brick quoins, and small windows. Two plain chancel doorways also survive, and a w window high up in the gable. The E end is altered, but traces, especially inside, prove

* Now demolished. Barn and dovecote remain.

that there were originally three or four windows and two above
them in the gable, which was higher than now. The date of the
belfry is probably C15. Dormers in the roof 1752 (VCH).
The S aisle was added in 1884. Nice W gallery on two Tuscan
columns. Chancel roof with arched braces supporting collar-
beams and additional arched braces carried to a pendant hanging from the collar-beam. The Royal Commission dates the
roof early C17. The nave roof is simple, with arched braces on
head-stops and tracery between the braces and the tie-beams.
King-posts in addition. – PULPIT. Panels with diamond-cut
frames and thin strapwork, c.1600. – COMMUNION RAIL.
With twisted balusters, c.1700. – PLATE. Paten of 1705.
– MONUMENTS. Nicholas Alexander † 1714, epitaph with two
cherubs' heads at the foot. It might be by *Edward Stanton*. –
Mrs Mitford † 1776. By *Nollekens*. Epitaph with the usual
obelisk and two cherubs against it and an urn between them;
one stands, the other sits and sobs.

CASTLE, NE of the church and hidden from the High Street.
Mount of 48 ft with a 230 ft diameter at the E end, inner bailey
W of it, and fragments of an outer bailey enclosing the
medieval town yet further W.

The town is of little interest. The centre is the market-like
widening of the HIGH STREET with a timber-framed house
of 1642 at the corner of the lane which leads up to the church
(scrolly brackets supporting the overhanging upper storey),
and nearly opposite the KING'S HEAD INN, a five-bay brick
house of 1697. Not much else need be mentioned: a nice late
C18 three-bay house on the E side further S with rather a fanciful arched porch, the CONGREGATIONAL CHURCH of 1833
lying back behind a row of terraces (white brick with big pediment, by *John Sadd*); yet further S, and at the S entry into
Ongar, at MARDEN ASH a group of more rewarding houses,
chiefly a small, white weatherboarded one with pretty bits of
plastered garlands, and MARDEN ASH itself, a large nine- by
six-bay brick house of c.1700, refaced c.1750. It is of two
storeys, with parapet and pedimented doorway on Ionic
columns. Inside a handsome staircase with twisted balusters.
(About ⅓ m. ENE of Marden Ash is NEWHOUSE FARM, a timber-
framed house of c.1600 with much panelling and a good fireplace inside. R.C.)

More worthwhile houses at the N entry into Chipping Ongar.*

* A number of other minor houses at Chipping Ongar are described in
vol. IV of the VCH.

CHRISHALL

HOLY TRINITY. Quite a large church, on a hill, and on its own. The material is pebble-rubble. C13 remains are the responds of the tower arch and of an arch at the E end of the N arcade. The rest is all Perp, the diagonal buttresses and the flint and stone chequered battlements of the W tower (spire taken down in 1914), the battlements nearly all round the church (not N aisle), and most of the windows, and also the aisle arcades. These have an elongated semi-polygonal section without capitals and only towards the arches small semi-polygonal shafts with capitals. – FONT. Plain, of c.1300. – PAINTING. Large copy of *Rubens*'s Adoration of the Magi of 1624 at Antwerp. – PLATE. Cup and Paten on foot of 1686. – MONUMENTS. Effigy of a Lady in a recess with depressed segmental arch and battlements; late C14. – Brass to Sir John de la Pole and wife, c.1380. Figures, 5 ft tall, under a tripartite arch with thin side buttresses, an uncommonly important and satisfying piece. – Brass to a woman, c.1450 (12 in. long). – Brass to a man and wife, c.1480 (18 in. long; good).

(CHRISHALL GRANGE, 2½ m. NNW. Brick, of c.1700, on a rectangular symmetrical plan with shaped gables at the E and W ends. S and N sides with slightly projecting middle bays. R.C.)

CLACTON-ON-SEA

The discovery of Clacton as a seaside resort came later than that of Walton, earlier than that of Frinton. Clacton in its centre offers the unusual picture of seaside architecture chiefly in the homely bargeboarded gabled style of the Early Victorian suburb. One can study its varieties here with much profit. A specially good example is CROSSLEY HOUSE, Marine Parade East and Victoria Road. But there are plenty of whole terraces (Beach Road for example). The corresponding type of a less informal hotel architecture is equally far from showy, the ROYAL HOTEL built in 1872, plain, long, white, with a thick iron verandah on the first floor. The next style after that can be illustrated by the former GRAND HOTEL, 1897 by *Smith, Son & Gale* – like a block of Kensington flats, red brick with many white ornamented friezes of foliage, putti, etc.

A domestic curiosity must be mentioned in addition before we can go on to churches and public buildings: MOOT HALL, Albany Gardens West, a half-timbered house which looks as though it might be of the C15, purely because its timbers were taken from a barn at Hawstead near Bury St Edmunds. In the process of re-erection, the house acquired a symmetry not originally its own.

St James, Tower Road. 1913 by *Temple Moore*. The nave unfinished. The exterior looks earnest, Perp and a little grim. The interior is surprising. Nave arcade with two very large pointed arches on the plainest piers. Perp two-light clerestory windows. Chancel with galleries on both sides and clerestory. But the two sides are treated completely differently, as if two periods had been at work. The s side Early Christian, as it were, with plain round arches, the N side pointed. On both sides all the detail very severe, and only the sparsest bits of red brick to relieve the whiteness of the plastered walls.

Our Lady of Light (R.C.), Church Road. 1902 by *F. W. Tasker*. Neo-Norman with nave with low circular piers, crossing with crossing tower, transepts with E aisle, and apse with narrow ambulatory – quite an uncommon type of design about 1900. Rockfaced exterior, W front with three stepped roundheaded lancets and square angle turrets.

Town Hall, Station Road. 1931 by *Sir A. Brumwell Thomas*. In the conventional Neo-Georgian regarded as suitable for such buildings. Brick with stone dressings. Giant centre portico and pediment.

Pier (1873, altered 1897 and 1931) and Pavilion (1890–3, by *Kinipple & Jaffrey*) for the eye oddly mixed up with the surrounding switchback architecture.

Recent building at Clacton includes Reunion House, Jackson Road, a block of offices and shops by *E. Caney*, completed in 1962 (information from T. A. Baker).

Martello Towers. Three in the W half of Clacton, the first low and broad by the Palace (Tower Road), the second in the Butlin Holiday Camp, the third on the Golf Links. The Martello Towers – the name comes from a Torre della Mortella on the island of Corsica which impressed the English in the campaign of 1794 – were built, mostly of brick, in 1810–12 by the Royal Engineers as a defence against a Napoleonic invasion. The plans were provided by *Col. Twiss* and *Capt. Ford*.

CLAVERING

An attractive village with the main buildings on an island between the two main roads. The short main street connects the two and has good houses on both sides. The other street running to the church has two interesting houses. The first has a rambling brick front of c.1700 but behind it earlier C17 work. This is timber-framed and specially interesting because it contains a shop towards the street (s of the bay window) and a store-room behind it. Several wall paintings of the C17 are preserved. The other house is late C15 and has a long overhang. It is along this that one is led into the churchyard.

St Mary and St Clement. A church of pebble-rubble, all Perp and all embattled. The w tower has angle buttresses, the aisles, clerestory, and s porch three-light windows. Inside, the N and s arcades have curiously detailed tall, slim, lozenge-shaped piers. They have a thin demi-shaft on a semi-polygonal base and towards the (four-centred) arches semi-polygonal shafts. The roofs are all original, low-pitched, and have a number of original head corbels. The nave roof has tie-beams, the slightly earlier chancel has not. – FONT. Octagonal, of Purbeck marble, with two shallow blank pointed arches to each side; c.1200. – PULPIT. Elizabethan, with two tiers of the typical short, broad, flatly ornamented arches. – BENCHES. Plain in the s aisle, with traceried ends in the N aisle. – SCREEN. with broad, tall, one-light openings, cusped and crocketed ogee heads and panel tracery above. – STAINED GLASS. Much of the C15 in the N windows; probably Norwich school. – MONUMENTS. Effigy of a Knight in chain-mail with coif and mail-coat reaching nearly to the knees. Purbeck marble, early C13. – Brass to one Songar and wife, c.1480 (17-in. figures). – Brass of 1591 with kneeling figures. – Brass of 1593. – Margaret Barley † 1653 and Mary Barley † 1658, both wives of the same man, almost identical, with frontal busts in oval niches between columns. Attributed by Mrs Esdaile to one of the *Marshalls*. – Haynes Barlee † 1696, erected in 1747. Elegant frontal bust with decoration of a cool and classical style.

Clavering Castle. Remains of the site N of the church, near a handsome gabled C17 house called The Bury. The site is rectangular with a ditch 75 ft wide and 18 ft deep. There probably have been stone buildings in the castle.

(Clavering Grange, ¼ m. w of the church. In the grounds an early C16 house with exposed close-set timber-framing. Some original windows, some external carving and barge-boarding. R.C.)

Windmills, ¾ m. NW. Two tower-mills, both without sails.

CLAYBURY see WOODFORD

CLEES HALL see ALPHAMSTONE

CLOCK HOUSE *see* GREAT DUNMOW

CLOVILLE HALL *see* WEST HANNINGFIELD

COGGESHALL *see* GREAT and LITTLE COGGESHALL

COLCHESTER
See also BERECHURCH, GREENSTEAD, HYTHE,
LEXDEN

INTRODUCTION

Colchester, though not the county town, is without any doubt
the foremost town of Essex, and it is, what is more, a town richer
than most in the country in traditions and survivals of a distant
past. As Camulodunum it was the capital of Cunobelin. It became a Roman *colonia* under Claudius in A.D. 49–50. Its Roman
walls, oblong in shape, are about 3,000 by 1,500 ft long. The
Royal Commission's list of Roman buildings of which traces
have been found at one time or another runs to 92 within the
walls (1922), to which 15 outside the walls have to be added.
Over fifty tessellated and mosaic pavements have been found.
Some of them are now exhibited at the Castle Museum. Around
the castle lay, it seems, the Forum. Anglo-Saxon remains are
scarce, but with the Conquest Colchester became once again
a centre of building. The Keep built by William is the largest in
Europe, and St Botolph's Priory must once have been as grand
as any of the other great monastic churches of the C11 and C12.
To this day six medieval parish churches lie within the walls:
there were originally two more; one, in the middle of the High
Street, was pulled down in 1878, and the other in 1955. In addition there was a Benedictine Abbey, and later the Greyfriars as
well as the Crutched Friars had establishments. The Colchester
of the C16 to C18 was more modest no doubt, but of a solid
prosperity, still based on the cloth trade, as its medieval wealth
had been.* The Royal Commission lists 264 houses as wholly or
partly of before 1714. Georgian houses must be about as frequent.
The following pages cannot give more than very brief accounts
of a limited selection of them.

The population of Colchester in 1801 was 11,500, in 1851
19,000, in 1901 38,000. It is now 65,000. The old town lies on a

---

* 'The whole town is employ'd in spinning weaveing washing drying ad
dressing their Bayes [baize] . . . the town looks like a thriveing place by the
substantiall houses, well pitched streetes which are broad enough for two
coaches to go a breast . . .' Celia Fiennes, *Travels* (1698).

5—E.

hill, with the walls embracing its top and the High Street running along its brow. The chief accents are the tower of the Town Hall of 1898, and the preposterously massive Water Tower of 1882, and in addition the spire of the Congregational Church of 1884, and the big square tower of St Botolph of 1838 – a weird assortment to prepare for a town of such venerable relics.

ROMAN REMAINS

The visitor to modern Colchester at once notices the remains of the Roman city, which occupied a space of 108 acres and was oblong in shape. The fact that Camulodunum, the seat of government, enclosed within its walls an area less than that of several other Romano-British townships calls for comment. Londinium contained 330 acres, Corinium (Cirencester) 240 acres, Verulamium (St Albans) 200 acres, Uriconium (Wroxeter) 170 acres. It must be remembered, however, that the town walls served the purpose of a refuge to which citizens who lived in suburbs outside them could retire in times of trouble. The area enclosed by the town walls gives little positive indication therefore of the size of the population.

Excavations at Silchester, Caerwent, and Verulam have shown that inside the walls of these towns there were large empty spaces on which no houses had ever been erected. Attempts by the civic-minded Romans to urbanize the British peasantry were never blessed with more than moderate success. Myres has written: 'Town walls were evidently laid out on a generous scale to make room for large increases of population, and more land was included than was ever required.'

Most of the WALLS are still visible, and also the very impressive remains of the great W gate, known as the BALKERNE GATE.

WALLS. The Roman walls are nearly 9 ft thick, and constructed of concrete with cut stone faces and bonding-courses of brick. They sometimes rest on a bed of mortar spread directly on hard gravel sub-soil, but more frequently the sub-soil is sand, and then there is a heavy foundation 2 ft or more thick, of large stones in mortar. The early rampart was at least 25 ft wide, and the face of the wall covered by it is very finely finished, with every joint marked out by the trowel. Four internal rectangular towers are known, and it is pretty certain that there was one at the end of each street, and at each corner. These are Roman. There were six or seven external circular bastions, of which four remain; these are medieval.

BALKERNE GATE. This was the main gate of the *colonia* and one 4a of the largest and most impressive town gates in Roman Britain. 107 ft long, it projects 30 ft in front of the wall. There were four arched entrances, two of them 17 ft wide for wheeled traffic, and two 6 ft wide for pedestrians. The gate was flanked by towers of an unusual quadrant-shaped plan. Two of the arches still survive, and the N tower is still over 15 ft high. The date of the first gate structure falls within the second half of the C2, contemporary with the building of the town wall. Following destruction by fire, the arches of the two main carriageways were narrowed and a new central pier built. These reconstructions were carried out in the C4. The final alterations, which cannot be precisely dated but are pre-Conquest, consisted of the erection of a rough wall of coarse masonry across the passageways of the gate.

The Balkerne Gate and the position of the E gate give the main axial line of the Roman city, the *decumanus maximus*. The *cardo maximus* is thought to have skirted the W wall of the Forum and led to the N gate at the foot of Castle Hill.

In 1920 excavations were undertaken of a large Roman *insula* in CASTLE PARK. They revealed a Roman street, a seven-roomed house, and a large double building of courtyard type.

At HOLLYTREES MEADOW, close to the Castle, a massive-walled Romano-British building was excavated in 1928. It contained a room with a thick concrete floor which was 8 ft below the level of the floors of the adjoining rooms. The room contained four straight channels, to hold wooden beams. It has been suggested that the building was a Mithraeum, dedicated to the worship of Mithras, whose cult was popular in the Roman army in the C3. Some scholars, however, do not accept this interpretation. The building appears to have been demolished in the mid C4.★

In the CASTLE MUSEUM a large collection of prehistoric and Roman remains. The Museum possesses the distinction of housing the largest number of Roman relics gathered from a single site in the whole of Great Britain.

In the massive vaults, now cleared of soil, under the Norman Keep of Colchester Castle can be seen the substructure of the TEMPLE OF CLAUDIUS (see Introduction). These vaults, which are between 6 and 16 ft thick, are certainly Romano-British. They seem originally to have stood in the centre of a large quadrangular enclosure, surrounded by a double series

★ The foundations have now been earthed in.

of foundations, the inner of which may have supported a colonnade along its N front. The massive foundations of the s front of the enclosure were discovered after a fire at the premises of Messrs Kent, Blaxill & Co. They suggest some form of architectural screen separating the temple area from the street outside. The whole precinct measures approximately 535 by 425 ft. Two major building phases have been established, but further excavation will be required to reconstruct the whole history of the site.

CHURCHES

ALL SAINTS, High Street.* In an impressive position, facing the modern opening towards the castle. Little of interest, except the fine w tower of flint, with diagonal buttresses and flint and ashlar decoration of the battlements. Big three-light bell-openings. The rest mostly 1855–9. C15 the pier between chancel and N chapel – of the familiar four-shafts-and-four-hollows section. Double-chamfered arches. – STAINED GLASS. The N windows pretty, no doubt of *c*.1861, the w window by *Kempe*, 1905. – PLATE. Early C17 Cup on baluster stem; large Cup and small Paten of 1714; Flagon of 1777. – MONUMENT. Stone tablet with crocketed ogee top and indents of brasses; *c*.1500. Transferred from St Nicholas.

ST BOTOLPH. Built immediately s of the Norman ruins and therefore, with the curious assertiveness that belongs to the Victorian age, in the Norman style and yet bigger than the old priory. 1837, by *W. Mason* of Ipswich. White brick, with a massive w tower, plenty of Norman ornament, and a broad interior with coarse Norman columns in two tiers, the upper one at the level of the usual galleries of the early C19. The gallery railings by the way decorated with intersected arches. Groin-vaulted aisles and tunnel-vaulted nave. Straight E end. – MONUMENT. William Hawkins † 1843, with a life-size female allegory, standing and looking up. By *J. Edwards* of London, 1854.

ST GILES,‡ just off St John's Green. Small; nave with chancel and N chapel. The w tower of timber, weatherboarded, as well as the present interior of the nave are of 1819. Thin N and s arcade shafts and w gallery. Flat ceiling. The N windows however, with Perp tracery all straightened out, may well be the posthumous Gothic of the C17, as the Royal Commission sug-

---

* Now used as a Natural History Museum. The plate is in the Castle Museum.
‡ Now St John Ambulance depot.

gests. Of 1907 (*Sir A. Blomfield & Son*) the brick N and S chancel arcades and the S chapel. But the brick S porch is original early C16 work. In the chancel E of the S arcade a C13 lancet window has been discovered. N chapel of *c*.1500. – DOOR, N doorway. C14 with rich tracery. – PALL. Of the Lucas family, dated 1628. Purple velvet with original embroidery; square.

ST JAMES THE GREAT, East Hill. The chancel and chancel chapels of this church, high up above the rise of East Hill into High Street, are perhaps the best Perp work in Colchester. The rest of the church is of less importance. The NW angle of the nave with its Roman bricks is proof of Norman origin. The W tower may be C13 (see one upper S window) altered in the C14. Diagonal buttresses and battlements. The odd little spire does not belong to the restoration of 1871. Does it belong to the restoration of the late C17? Of 1871 the clerestory windows, and N and S aisle windows. The N and S chancel chapels and the chancel E end are faced with knapped flint. The N chapel in addition, as it faces the street, has a parapet decorated with a frieze of triangles with trefoils alternately the right and the wrong way up. Internally the chancel is splendidly tall with a five-light E window and tall N and S arcades. The piers are lozenge-shaped with four slim shafts and four long shallow diagonal hollows. The two chapels have large three-light windows and ceilings with prettily carved beams. The S chapel E window even has four lights. Both chapels have flat ceilings also with carved beams. The nave arcades are more curious but less impressive. They are of four different varieties, in chronological order SE (two bays, octagonal pier, arches with one concave and one convex moulding; *c*.1300), NE (two bays, octagonal pier, arches with two hollow chamfers; mid C14), then SW and NW differing only in minor features (C15 piers with, towards the nave, as their central motif, thin polygonal shafts without capitals). – STAINED GLASS, S chapel E and SE. Tall figures of apostles, *c*.1850, said to have been obtained from Belgium or Holland. – PLATE. Salver of 1705; two Flagons of 1752. – MONUMENTS. Brasses of 1569 and 1584 in the chancel floor. – Arthur Winsley † 1727. Standing wall-monument with semi-reclining figure in informal dress.

ST JAMES THE LESS (R.C.), Priory Street. 1837 by *J.J. Scoles* (GR), white brick, in the Norman style. Enlarged and re-decorated 1904–10. Wide interior with Norman columns, clerestory, chancel arch, and apse. Exterior without tower, but with the typical angle turrets of the (Gothic) Commissioners' Churches of the early C19. The Presbytery to the r., attached to the church, and also Neo-Norman.

ST JOHN, Ipswich Road. 1862–4 by *Arthur Blomfield* (GR) and still with the grit which he possessed in his youth. Red brick with yellow and blue bricks and stone dressings. Nave and chancel. Small and low w baptistery with timber porches l. and r., and the weirdest (and most tasteless) way to connect this with a bellcote which is circular, with a conical roof and a kind of open lantern with thick short black columns.

ST MARTIN, West Stockwell Street.* The NW angle of a C12 N aisle, narrower than the present aisle, reveals a church of that date. The w tower also Norman but a little later. It was built with much use of Roman bricks, but is now in ruins and looks very picturesque with the two fine old chestnut trees at the entrance to the churchyard. The chancel follows next; early C14, as can at once be seen from the E window, of three lights, with ogee-reticulated tracery, the s doorway, and the PISCINA inside, both with richly crocketed ogee heads. The way in which the SEDILIA are subdivided into two seats by simply bringing down the mullion of a two-light window in a double curve is also characteristic of the Dec style. But perhaps the most impressive early C14 feature is one roof truss across the chancel which possesses moulded wall posts, arched braces with elaborately foiled tracery, an embattled tie-beam, an octagonal king-post with capital, and four-way struts. Early Perp transepts with tall windows with panel tracery, and Early Perp N and S arcades with octagonal piers and double-hollow-chamfered arches. The s porch is attributed to the early or mid C17, perhaps on the strength of the amusing side windows with balusters instead of mullions. – FONT. Octagonal, C14, with recesses in the stone crowned by three-dimensional ogee arches bending forward on to the bowl. – (PULPIT with sections of C16 and C17 woodwork.) – SCREEN. Six early C15 traceried arches below the rail. – MONUMENT. Big, heavy, Neo-Greek sarcophagus to William Sparling † 1816, in the churchyard, s of the porch.

ST MARY-AT-THE-WALLS, just E of Balkerne Hill. Big Late Perp w tower with diagonal buttresses and at the base a frieze of shields. Upper parts brick, of 1729; the very top of 1911. The rest of the church 1872 by *Sir Arthur Blomfield*. Long nave with circular piers with elaborately and naturalistically

* Now a cultural centre.

carved capitals and circular clerestory windows. Straight E
end. – PLATE. Finely shaped and decorated Chalice of 1623;
Cup and Paten of 1714. – MONUMENT. John Rebow † 1699.
Whole figure, seated, very well carved.

ST MARY MAGDALENE, Magdalene Street. 1853 by *F. Barnes*
(GR). Flint with small polygonal SW turret and large transept
with arches inside open as wide as the chancel arch.

ST MICHAEL, Mile End. 1854 by *Hakewill* (GR).

ST NICHOLAS, High Street.* Essentially the work of *Sir George
Gilbert Scott*, 1875–6, and a proud work, in this prominent
position right in the centre of Colchester. Scott found a small
and humble church and made it serve his more ambitious purposes. The ground floor of the tower, a N tower, is Perp; so are
the N aisle (or chapel) W of it, and the present N aisle. Originally they formed nave and chancel. The date of these parts is
C14, see the quatrefoil piers. Scott carried on, quite tactfully,
as usual, and without much personality or grit. – REREDOS.
By *Temple Moore*, c.1925. – PULPIT and LECTERN, 1893 to
Scott's designs. – ORGAN CASE. By *Oldrid Scott*. – PAINT-
INGS. Four Evangelists, Flemish, mid C17; Abraham and
the Angels. By *G. S. Marucelli*, 1679 (?). – PLATE. Ornamented Cup 1569; Paten 1569; Elizabethan Cup with band of
ornament; large Cup on baluster stem and Paten probably of
1667; Paten on foot of 1708.

ST PETER, North Hill. Essentially C18. Square red brick W
tower of 1758. The upper part has white brick quoins and
white brick battlements. To the street on a coarse bracket a
clock, put up in 1866. The aisle windows all arched, of c.1700.
White brick battlements. Inside, a few reminders of the medieval church; the arcades with piers with demi-columns to the
aisle arches but a slim demi-polygonal shaft to the nave: C15.‡
N and S galleries on Tuscan columns behind the arcades.
Below the N vestry a BONE-HOLE of c.1520 with a brick vault
with single-chamfered arches and ribs. The clerestory is of
1895. – PULPIT. Fine piece of c.1700 with richly moulded
frames of the panels and garlands of fruit down the angles;
cherubs' heads at the top of these. – Heavy Neo-Gothic FONT,
1859 by *C. F. Hayward*. – COMMUNION RAIL with twisted
balusters, used for the tower staircase. – DOOR in S doorway
with large iron scrolls, late C13. – PLATE. Paten on foot of

---

* Demolished in 1955. The plate is now in the Castle Museum and a
tablet of c.1500 in All Saints, Colchester.

‡ In the C18 the nave arcades were extended to the E in pseudo-C15 style.

1698. – MONUMENTS. A number of rectangular plates with kneeling figures and inscriptions, ranging from 1509 to 1610. – Martin Basill † 1623 and wife, with the usual kneeling figures, quite large; the figures set against a blank arch; columns l. and r. – George Sayer † 1577 and wives, smaller and broader, also with kneeling figures, but with three columns and a straight entablature.

HOLY TRINITY, Trinity Street. The w tower is the only Anglo-Saxon (pre-Conquest) monument of Colchester. Built with plenty of Roman bricks, and crowned by a recent low pyramid roof. Small w doorway with triangular head, a wholly Saxon feature. E arch into the nave with odd capitals of the responds in three steps of brick, without any mouldings. Saxon upper windows, the bell-openings developed as twin windows but not separated by a turned shaft or colonnette as usual. On the sides below that stage traces of a blank arcade. The rest of the church is of 1886, except for the E end of the chancel with an early C14 three-light window with flowing tracery, the s arcade, which is C14 too, and the outside of the s aisle and the s porch, which are of the C15. – FONT. Perp, octagonal, with shields and nobbly foliage in the panels. – PLATE. Fine Mazer, C15.*

ST BOTOLPH'S PRIORY. The most important and impressive ecclesiastical monument of Colchester; the ruin of an Early Norman church of considerable size. St Botolph's was founded late in the C11 as the first British house of Augustinian Canons. What remains is a ruin, and the ruin only of the w front and the nave (108 ft long). Transepts and E end have completely disappeared. The church was built of rubble with plenty of Roman bricks, used in the walls as well as more consistently for dressings. The w front is broad; the two towers stand outside the aisles, not identical incidentally either in size or in shape. There are three portals; the middle one of four orders of columns, the capitals with finely intertwined scrolls or decorated scallops (badly preserved), the arches with much zigzag. Above the portals, but with the middle one cutting into it, two tiers of intersected arches without capitals. The principal w window was circular, and the earliest major round window in England. The façade must date from after the mid C12. Nothing survives of the upper parts of the towers. Inside the façade a passage, carried on a tunnel-vault, runs on the first floor from one tower to the other, open to the nave. The

* Now in the Castle Museum.

nave has mighty circular piers (5 ft 8 in. in diameter). They [14] have no proper capitals and support a gallery with unsubdivided openings as large as the arcade. The arches are single-stepped and unmoulded on both floors. Flat pilaster strips stand on the circular piers to divide the bays of the gallery from each other. The aisles were groin-vaulted. The building is immensely impressive as a ruin, but the grim severity which the absence of all surface embellishments gives may have been a quality of the church even when it was new. It would share this quality with the contemporary Benedictine St Albans and to a certain degree with all Early Norman buildings. To the s of the church, foundations of the N wall of the cloister.

ST JOHN'S ABBEY, St John's Green. Of the Benedictine abbey founded by Eudo Dapifer in 1096, nothing at all remains but the N GATEHOUSE, dating probably from the C15. It is a [48a] splendid piece of display, characteristically more ornate to the outer world than to the abbey precincts. The outer façade is of flint with a great deal of flushwork decoration, chiefly shafts and blank crocketed arches. Tall carriageway with four-centred head and tall niches above and to the l. and r. Below the r. niche the entrance for pedestrians, also with four-centred head. Two two-light upper windows and battlements. Flanking polygonal angle turrets with big crocketed pinnacles. No flushwork on the other side and only one wide gateway with a much simpler arch moulding. Inside the gateway is a star-shaped lierne-vault. The whole gatehouse was extensively restored in the C19.*

CONGREGATIONAL CHAPEL, East Stockwell Street. 1816–17, front 1834. Red brick. Three bays wide with three-bay pediment. Entrance with short Tuscan columns *in antis*.

CONGREGATIONAL CHURCH, Lion Walk. 1863, by *Frederick Barnes* of Ipswich. In the geometrical style. The very tall NW spire, a landmark, was rebuilt after the earthquake of 1884.

(BAPTIST CHURCH, Eld Lane. 1834, restored 1883. White brick front with pediment. Three arched windows, centrally grouped. Galleries supported by metal columns.)

Former BAPTIST CHAPEL, now Elim Pentecostal Church, Stanwell Street, St John's Green. 1811. Three-bay red brick chapel with arched windows.

PUBLIC BUILDINGS

TOWN HALL with VICTORIA TOWER. 1898–1902 by *Sir John*

* Just N of the gate GIMBER COTTAGE, prettily Gothick and dated 1823.

Belcher. Even those who have by now learnt to sympathize with some appreciation of Victorian buildings find as a rule no access yet to Edwardian architecture. Yet, here also, there exists the valuable side by side with the valueless, and values differ in kind as much as they always have. Belcher designed in the exuberant display style of *c.*1900–10 with more braggadocio than anyone, and the Colchester Town Hall is proof of that. But the way in which he placed his exceedingly high tower – 162 ft is the height – in exactly the spot where the High Street narrows, as one walks towards the w, is excellent according to any standard, and the scale is excellent too. The tower is slender and square, of brick, and ends in a Borrominesque flourish – two stages of stone columns, big curved pediments on the lower, concavely curved sides between the columns on the upper. Seated allegorical figures which can mean nothing to anybody are of course also present. The crowning bronze figure is St Helena with the cross. The main façade has three pairs of giant columns, gigantic giant columns, each carrying a broken pediment. These are segmental, triangular, segmental. All the details on the brackets of the main balcony swell and bulge. – PLATE. Mace, by *E. Jennings*, 1729; Mayor's Chain, beautifully simple, given 1765; Mayor's silver Theatre Ticket, 1764; Silver Oyster and Silver Oars, 1804; Silver Spoons (later presented) of *c.*1580, 1672 etc.; Loving Cup, 1670; four small Ward Maces, Jacobean; two Communion Cups dated 1715 and 1717.

42 CASTLE. Colchester Castle is the largest keep in existence. It measures 151 by 110 ft, that is considerably more than the White Tower in London. It belongs to the same type of late CII keeps as the White Tower, the type often called hall keeps, that is buildings much broader than the more usual tower keeps and not so high in proportion. Like the White Tower, Colchester had a chapel projecting with an apse, and the main rooms were subdivided, perhaps because, if undivided, they would have been too large to cover them with timber ceilings. The keep was originally faced with septaria stone and tile and in places with ashlar. But now the rubble core with many Roman bricks is showing nearly everywhere. The walls are articulated by broad flat buttresses. In the E and w walls and the s w turret traces remain of a temporary crenellation indicating a break in the building history or a sudden need of defence while building was in progress. The keep has now only a ground floor and one upper floor. It must have possessed

one, if not two floors above.* The entrance lies on the s side at ground-floor level, a remarkable exception. The doorway had two orders of columns with typical Early Norman capitals (upright leaves and little volutes) and an arch with several roll-mouldings. Traces of a large forebuilding, all part of the complex entrance to the keep, were exposed in 1932; also the foundations of an early chapel to the s. To the l. of the doorway, in the largest of the angle towers, is the main stair, a spiral stair with a rising tunnel-vault. To the r. of the doorway are the well and then two thick walls forming small chambers. The main interior area is now divided into two but was at first divided into three rooms. It is an open question as to whether the Great Hall was on the first floor extending through the floor above, or was actually on the second floor. The second floor seems more likely, since the first floor does not give access to the chapel, but only the chapel undercroft, a low tunnel-vaulted room with the very exceptional feature of two pairs of apsed side-chapels forming in their vaults groins with the main vault. The one dividing wall of the main area has much herringbone masonry with the use of Roman bricks. In the N wall is a blocked postern doorway, a very unusual feature. The NW turret starts a second smaller spiral stair on this level. It is flanked by two garderobes or latrines. A third is in the E wall of the keep, about half-way down. It has a tunnel-vaulted lobby. A tunnel-vaulted chamber lies in the NE turret. Four large fireplaces with rounded arches and flues leading to holes in the walls survive, two in each of the W and E walls. They are among the earliest known. Of the hall and chapel floor proper hardly anything remains, except for the lower courses of the chapel apse, showing that the apse had flat inner pilasters. The present top structures of the keep belong to the mid C18, the time when the keep stood in the grounds of Hollytrees and was considered a somewhat Brobdingnagian garden ornament. The outer bailey originally extended as far N as the Roman N wall, and the inner bailey made it necessary, s of the castle, for the High Street to bend a little.

ART GALLERY, see The Minories, p. 141.

MUSEUM, see Castle, p. 138, and The Hollytrees, p. 141.

PUBLIC LIBRARY. By *Marshall Sisson*, 1939.

(NORTH EAST ESSEX TECHNICAL COLLEGE, Sheepen Road. By *H. Conolly*, County Architect, and *N. R. Astins*, a large block with curtain walling. 1954–9.)

* The upper stages were taken down in 1683.

GRAMMAR SCHOOL, Lexden Road. 1853 by *Henry Hammond Hayward*. In the Tudor style, red brick with blue brick diapers. Later additions.

ESSEX COUNTY HOSPITAL, Lexden Road. The oldest parts of 1820, still Late Georgian in style, with an Ionic porch. White brick. Later buildings behind. (A good new addition, by *W. G. Plant*, was completed in 1964.)

ROYAL EASTERN COUNTIES INSTITUTION, North Station Road. Built in 1843 as a remarkably sumptuous station hotel, but not successful as such. In design the building is like a large Italianate villa. It is of white brick and has an asymmetrical tower.

WORKHOUSE, Lexden Road, see Stanway, St Albright's Hospital.

WATER TOWER. Red brick, 1882, by a *Mr Charles Clegg*. The tower is 105 ft high and lies at the w end of the vista along the High Street. In design it is, with its large and small round-headed arches, no doubt meant to be in the Roman spirit. The top part however bulges out in a way only the Victorians could have desired. Pyramid roof and little lantern to finish the painfully assertive composition.

PERAMBULATION

The spine of the town is the HIGH STREET. In a town the size of Colchester it can hardly be perfect; there is too much intrusion of C19 and C20 mixed purposes: genteel recent banks, Messrs Burton's with their own style, gabled Gothic of 1879, and so on. The skyline on both sides is jagged and untidy. The main visual accents are the Water Tower of 1882 (see above) at the w end and the Town Hall in the centre. Of other buildings one may note the following from w to e: First on the N side the offices of the ESSEX AND SUFFOLK EQUITABLE INSURANCE by *David Laing*, built as the Corn Exchange in 1820, nine bays wide with a colonnade of slender Greek Doric columns (of cast iron) across the pavement, an idea no doubt borrowed from Nash's work in London. Opposite No. 11 with a Late Georgian front of five bays and two-and-a-half storeys and a two-storeyed central bow-window. No. 21, also Late Georgian, has a pretty pedimented tripartite central window on the first floor, No. 22 a shallow bow window. A little further on, also on the s side, No. 39 with elaborate mid C17 pargeting on a wing at the back (R.C.), and then the RED LION HOTEL, a remarkable building of *c.*1470 and *c.*1500, timber-framed

with the timbers of the front (*c.*1500) exposed. The upper
storeys project. The first floor has a band of traceried panels
below the sill line between the studs. Inside the earliest part
(now the Grill Room) still possesses moulded beams, and
carved brackets. The later front part is even richer in original
detail. It was added, it seems, when the former private house
was converted into an inn. (Nos 45–47 has a mid C14 doorway
inside and at the back C17 strapwork pargeting. R.C.) On the
other side again, further down the GEORGE HOTEL, with an
C18 front and a nice cast-iron balcony. Then, also on the N
side, No. 108 noteworthy especially for a good, rich early C18
plaster ceiling in a first-floor room.*

Then there is a stretch of less interest, until All Saints Church
is reached and the recent opening towards the Castle with the
somewhat florid WAR MEMORIAL, 1923 by *H.C.Fehr*. To
open out in this place towards the castle, which, until then,
had not visually been part of the picture of the town at all, was
a good idea, but the opening should have been kept much
narrower. As it is, it breaks the continuity of the street entirely
and makes the castle appear less enormous than it could. Moreover THE HOLLYTREES, the best C18 house of Colchester, is
now much too isolated. It should be part of a general street
façade, like all the other Georgian houses. The Hollytrees was
built about 1716. It is of red brick with rubbed bricks for the
trimmings. It has three storeys and five bays of segment-
headed windows. The doorcase has Roman pilasters, a straight
entablature on lusciously carved brackets, and a frieze rising
to a point in the middle, in a fashion typical of the time of
George I. In 1748 the W wing was added with a Venetian
window to the gardens, and the main window to the street
provided with a raised brick surround and a pediment. To the
street are good iron railings. In the gardens which comprised
all the castle grounds (and the castle) stands a small Greek
temple with two Tuscan columns *in antis*. It stands quite near
the castle and forms a contrast in style and scale to it which
makes one wonder at the mentality of those who built it. To
the same period may also belong the cyclopic pedimented gateway E of the castle, built of materials of the wall or the castle.

The houses Nos 69 and so on on the other side of the street form
a suitable, quiet Georgian background to The Hollytrees.
There follow THE MINORIES, 1776, for Thomas Boggis, with
central porch and a bay window resting on it. In the garden a

---

* Now demolished. The ceiling is in the Castle Museum.

large Gothick summerhouse, *c.*1745, formerly in the grounds of East Hill House. Across from The Minories, the GATE HOUSE, an excellent house of *c.*1600, refronted, still pre-classically, as late as 1680. It is plastered, with rustication imitated by the plaster, and has four symmetrical gables with curved oriels under. In the centre an oval window. The next pair is GREY FRIARS on this same N side, 1755, brick, with two symmetrical windows and a doorcase with pediment on attached Ionic columns, and, on the S side, EAST HILL HOUSE, a specially fine early C18 house of seven bays with segmental pediment on the Tuscan doorcase. The top storey is of *c.*1742.

EAST HILL is the direct continuation of High Street, down the hill. On the S side Nos 9–10, early C18,* a double house with two doorways side by side, the l. one impressive with Roman Doric pilasters and a broad segmental pediment. On the N side No. 86, 1818, plastered and with a heavy Greek Doric porch, and No. 82, Early Georgian of seven bays, with segment-headed windows, unattractively plastered. Then No. 72, nice early C19 with a blocked doorway with recessed columns carrying Empire capitals. Further on on the N the Colchester Brewing Company, of a calibre quite different from the street houses, and on the S some good earlier half-timbered houses, chiefly Nos 16 and 17, early C16 with oversailing upper floor and no gable to the street, and Nos 35 to 39 with one gable at the far end. Nos 48–51 and opposite Nos 60–61 are a good quiet C16. (For details see the Royal Commission.) At the foot of the hill EAST BAY and a Green with no special houses.‡ To the l. by the bridge the mills of Messrs Marriage, consisting of the small Georgian miller's house, a big Victorian white brick factory, and a modern extension behind the Georgian house. East Bay is continued in EAST STREET, which has on both sides a specially pleasing row of gabled, oversailing houses: SIEGE HOUSE (much restored house of *c.*1500; the timber-framing shows the marks of the siege of Colchester in 1648), 11–12, 17–18, 29–33 (particularly good), the Rose and Crown Hotel (restored by *G.F.Roper*). Nos 21–23 is Early Georgian with a Gibbs surround to the door and a Venetian window above.

* Extended after 1775.

‡ In East Bay, the Youth Hostel, later C18, double house, brick, shallow bays and doorcases with Adamish detail. Information from Mr J. Bensusan Butt.

The other streets of Colchester can now be reviewed as they lead off the High Street, first to the N, then to the S.

In NORTH HILL opposite St Peter's church No. 60, Georgian, stately, with two symmetrical bay windows and a Tuscan doorcase, and No. 59 with a Gothick doorcase, that is composite shafts instead of columns, and a pediment decorated with tracery. The houses on both sides of the street climb down the hill in steps, always a nice effect. On the E side Nos 4, 5 (with little iron balconies to the windows, iron window-heads, and the date 1809), and 8 are Georgian. The best timber-framed houses come lower down: Nos 13–15 of the C15 and No. 24, the MARQUIS OF GRANBY, of c.1525. This is much restored, but has exceedingly good, very richly carved interior detail in the E wing. The main ceiling beam with foliage, animals, 4 dragons, etc. rests on brackets with very well characterized figures. In the passageway from the street two doors probably once leading from the screens passage to the offices – wooden surrounds with leaf carvings in the spandrels. Nos 19–20 between the two former is Georgian again with one Venetian window. Fragments of NORTHGATE WALL are visible on the corner of Northgate Street. At the foot of North Hill are MIDDLEBOROUGH and the Bridge – a pattern similar to that at the E end. No. 20 is a pretty picture, whitewashed, gabled to the street, and with oval brick panels between the windows to the S. NORTH STATION ROAD is of less interest, except perhaps for its pleasing start with the Castle Inn by the river (two gables to the street, two irregular oriels to the water).

Further E off the High Street WEST STOCKWELL STREET, perhaps the most attractive street of Colchester, narrow, not straight, and relatively unspoilt.* Near the top Nos 3–6, late C15, with exposed timbers, the upper storey oversailing on brackets with demi-figures of angels, original doorway to the screens passage. The hall lay to the r. (now shop). Original window tracery in the N window, and several original doorways inside. Then Nos 8–9, a five-bay early C18 house by the churchyard of St Martin, and, opposite, ST MARTIN'S HOUSE, 1734, and then Nos 59–60, a Georgian double house, with giant angle pilasters and as its centre, below a three-bay pediment, two doorways and between them two Venetian windows above each other. Nos 53–55 are again C15 with cross-wings (N wing C17), and opposite are Nos 13–16, C17

* Some fifty houses in this area were restored and renovated by the Town Council in the 1950s.

timber-framed,* and then the Stockwell Arms, C15 and over-
restored. Specially picturesque Nos 29–31 with three gables
and two overhangs on brackets. From West Stockwell Street
one can return to the High Street by EAST STOCKWELL
STREET, of a similar character. Here The Gables, C17, with a
garden on its W side and No. 30, two houses at different levels,
partly C14 (screens of former hall preserved) and partly *c.*
1500.

Less of note in MAIDENBURGH STREET. The former CHAPEL
OF ST HELEN, stone with bands of Roman brick and some
C13 lancet windows, and from there a nice view down to the
N, with Nos 23 and 51–52, both timber-framed C17 with pro-
jecting upper storeys.

Now off the High Street to the S, starting at the E end. Queen
Street turns off at the corner of the churchyard of All Saints.
On the other side of the churchyard it is met by CULVER
STREET. The houses in Culver Street facing the church are
Nos 69–71, both red brick and both Georgian. No. 69 is of
1743, with blue brick chequer and an oval window in the
centre of the upper storey. No. 71 is a little later. QUEEN
STREET itself has not much of importance. No. 2 is Georgian
brick, but not very remarkable. Queen Street is continued S
in St Botolph Street, and at the foot of this Magdalene Street
turns towards the Hythe (see p. 247) and MILITARY ROAD to
the SE. Here close to each other are WINNOCK'S ALMS-
HOUSES and Kendall's Almshouses. Winnock's are a range of
six, dated 1678. They are of low, broad proportions and have a
pediment and two superimposed orders of which the upper
oddly dies into the wall as if it were buttresses. KENDALL'S
ALMSHOUSES are two ranges side by side, each of four bays
and two storeys, and each with a small pediment. They are
dated 1791 and 1803. In OLD HEATH ROAD, the continuation
of Military Road, WINSLEY'S ALMSHOUSES, originally a
centre with a remarkably freely treated frontispiece. The date
is 1728. The sides of the frontispiece are polygonal shafts like
medieval turrets, the crowning motif is a pediment on two
curves as in the Dutch gables of about 1630. Two short wings
jut forward. These wings have been continued forward since,
until they formed a courtyard so deep that it seems a cul-de-
sac. The additions are of about 1800, and then 1906–7 (that
moment chose of course to break the accepted skyline by
gables), and finally 1928. To the S of Military Road Bourne

* Now demolished.

Road leads to BOURNE MILL, a delightful piece of late 53
Elizabethan playfulness, built in 1591 probably as a fishing
lodge. It is one-storeyed, of stone, with mullioned windows,
and has two wildly oversized end gables of the utmost exuberance. They go up in convex and concave curves and carry
four pairs of obelisks, each one a tall polygonal chimneyshaft.
On the side opposite the entrance in the C19, when the house
was used as a water-mill, a weatherboarded hoist loft was
added. Half a mile down stream is CANNOCK MILL, another
water-mill, still in working order.

Now back to the High Street. By the Red Lion a narrow passage
leads to Culver Street, close to the corner of TRINITY
STREET. In Trinity Street Nos 9–11, a good L-shaped C15
house, and No. 8 (Tymperleys), lying back from the street and
reached by an archway. Then No. 6, a seven-bay red C18
house. At its s end Trinity Street meets SIR ISAAC'S WALK,
where No. 11 is an interesting early C18 house, lying back with
a handsome front garden. The house is of five bays and two
storeys and the centre has a bow window of a curve more than
a semicircle and crowned by a concave roof à la chinoise. From
the s end of Trinity Street a few steps run down into SCHERE-
GATE. The steps are inside a gateway through a house. The
house and the others in this short street, mostly of the C17,
look particularly picturesque from the s. The frontages narrow
funnel-wise to the gateway.

Finally HEAD STREET, off the High Street at its w end. The
houses to be noted here are first Nos 37–39 on the w side, with
a late C18 brick front with a central bow window, then Nos
44–52 on the E side, a fine seven-bay house, c.1765, with a
three-bay pediment, then, further s on the w side, Headgate
Court, the former King's Head Inn, standing back in a courtyard, and again on the E side Nos 54 of 1767 (five bays with
eared central window) and Rebow's House (Nos 58–62), the
house of Sir Isaac Rebow, cf. Sir Isaac's Walk; basically C17.
Divided in the mid C18, with bay window.* From Head Street
CROUCH STREET turns w. It is chiefly a Late Georgian
street, with an occasional Adamish doorcase, Greek Doric
doorcases or porches. Nos 20–22 is the best house, a large

---

* Mr Bensusan Butt draws attention to three houses in lanes off Head
Street. In CHURCH STREET, No. 6, ST MARY'S, refronted 1802 with double
shallow bays, and No. 8 (late County Court Offices), five-bay stucco façade
divided by pilasters; arched windows, c.1802. In CHURCH WALK, ST
MARY'S COTTAGE, Gothick, 1823.

square brick building of 1763, five bays and two-and-a-half storeys with the middle bay slightly projected and the central window arched. The continuation of Crouch Street is LEXDEN ROAD, where THE OAKS and ST MARY'S TERRACE are of c.1830, of white brick with neo-classical trim. St Mary's Terrace, which was built by *H.H.Hayward*, is two groups, the first a range of six houses, the second five semi-detached pairs with lower connecting links. THE TURRETS follows, a plastered fantasy with battlements and turrets. By *Robert Lugar*, 1818, a surprisingly early date. The road leads to Lexden (see p. 267).*

HYTHE, *see* p. 247.

LEXDEN DYKES

Four main dykes are now visible, aligned roughly N and S, and spanning the area between the River Colne and Roman River. These earthworks form an enormous fortified enclosure some twelve square miles in area. Two systems are apparent; an earlier curvilinear work and a later and larger rectangular defence system. The outermost dyke is the most impressive. This is GRYME'S DYKE, which is 3 m. long and in fairly good condition. 'Gryme' is the Devil, to whom in Christian times many prehistoric edifices whose origin and purpose had been forgotten were attributed. The 50 ft ditch and 10 ft rampart of the Dyke can be examined.

At Stanway Green the Dyke makes two sharp right-angled turns before proceeding S to Roman River. At the spot now occupied by the great gravel pit known as 'King Coel's Kitchen' the Roman roads from Cambridge and London once converged to cross the Dyke. Part of the Roman road, which gave final form in the CI to an earlier unmetalled road, has been studied by excavation in the neighbourhood of the Grammar School. Here were found also two celebrated Roman tombstones, one of the centurion M. Favonius Facilis of the XXth Legion, and the other of the cavalryman Longinus of Sardica, *duplicarius* in the Ist Ala of Thracians. Both are of CI date. Behind Gryme's Dyke run the remnants of the TRIPLE DYKE, and also, reinforcing the portion of Gryme's Dyke S of Stanway Green, a barely traceable section of ditch running through Oliver's Thicks, crossing the Roman River and continuing through Chest Wood in the direction of Layer de la

* Among recent buildings at Colchester, one may be singled out: the OFFICES of Wood's Ltd, by *Bailey & Walker*.

Haye vicarage. In Chesthunt Field, behind this much-broken section of the defensive line, the remains of what seems to have been an important pre-Roman sanctuary later converted by the Romans into a temple-enclosure have been discerned. Behind the Triple Dyke lies a great barrow called 'The Mount', excavated in 1910, when it was found to have been rifled in antiquity, probably in Roman times. The third of the Lexden Park ditches is the LEXDEN DYKE, extending from a little S of the modern by-pass as far as Bluebottle Grove. N of the River Colne is a continuation of the Lexden Dyke, also ½ m. long, called the MOAT FARM DYKE. Many pre-Roman graves have been found in the vicinity of the Lexden Dyke. The most famous is the great barrow, lying within the ditch itself, known as the Lexden Tumulus. This was excavated in 1924, and yielded up a marvellous treasure, now displayed in the Colchester and Essex Museum. An authority has written that 'the interment displays a barbaric luxury imbued with romanizing taste, such as evidently prevailed at Cunobelin's court'. The objects of bronze included a table, a pedestal, a statuette of Cupid, and models of a boar, a griffin, and a bull. There were fragments of leather and chain mail and traces of very fine gold tissue. A notable find was a striking silver portrait-disc of the Emperor Augustus, with the head cut from a *denarius* of 17 B.C. It seems likely that the burial dates from shortly before the Roman conquest in A.D. 43, and it has been suggested that it may be the funeral-mound not of one of Cunobelin's noblemen, but of the *Britannorum rex* himself. It is interesting to note, in view of the bronze table and the fragments of chain mail that were recovered in 1924, that a tradition that the Lexden Tumulus contained the relics of 'a king with golden armour and a gold table' had always been current in the neighbourhood. 1½ m. SE of the S end of Lexden Dyke begins the relatively unexplored BERECHURCH DYKE, which runs from Monkwick for nearly 2 m. to meet the Roman River. A peculiarity of the Berechurch Dyke is that the ditch lies on the E and not on the W side of the vallum, as it does in the other dykes.

A fifth dyke, now entirely destroyed, was discovered by excavation in 1930. This is the SHEEPEN DYKE, lying within the large area of land subjected to intensive excavation by the Research Committee of the Society of Antiquaries between 1930 and 1939. On the Sheepen site were discovered two Roman temples of square Romano-Celtic type. The smaller

dated from the C3, while the larger, situated within a long
enclosure wall, belongs to the late C1. With its overall dimen-
sion of 64 ft square, the larger temple constitutes an unusually
spacious example of this class of building. The site also yielded
a series of eight C2 pottery kilns, the first manufactory of Terra
Sigillata or Samian ware to be found in Great Britain. The
manufactory was in operation between A.D. 160 and 200. A
complete mould was found, and at Sheepen were also discovered the moulds for bronze coins of Cunobelin, suggesting
the earlier presence of a British mint. The British occupation
of Sheepen appears to have been thoroughly obliterated by the
incoming Legions, whose camp with palisade and ditch was
superimposed upon the Y-shaped pre-Roman settlement.

3 m. s of Colchester are traces of an extensive lay-out of temple,
fair-ground, and theatre (?), which may represent an alternative
meeting-place provided for the native tribe of the Trinovantes
after their land had been confiscated in order to construct the
new *Colonia Victricensis*.

At BRINKLEY GROVE, 2 m. N of Colchester, is an earthwork
consisting of a rectangular site with ditch 60 ft wide and 9 ft
deep and an interior and exterior rampart.

COLD NORTON

ST STEPHEN. 1855 by *Pritchett* (GR), with a bellcote quite out
of keeping with the style of this part of Essex. But what did
the High Victorians care?* – BRASS. To a Lady, *c*.1520.

COLNE ENGAINE

ST ANDREW. The W tower with diagonal buttresses is C14
below, early C16 brick above, with battlements on a trefoiled
corbel frieze and polygonal pinnacles. Norman nave, see the W
quoins and N and S traces of windows. Much Roman brick re-
used. In the chancel a doorway and a blocked lancet window of
the early C13. The S porch is of brick, with stepped battlements and an older timber gable above. No fittings of interest.

COLNE PARK. 1775, but much enlarged about 1900. The old
part plain, of white brick, with a four-column Ionic porch.‡ In
the grounds a column with an urn, erected in 1790, to the
design of *Sir John Soane*. (Information kindly provided by
Miss Dorothy Stroud.)

* The bellcote has now been removed.
‡ Now largely demolished, but a ground-floor Venetian window remains.

COLNE PRIORY HOUSE *see* EARLS COLNE

COLVILLE HALL *see* WHITE RODING

COOPERSALE

COOPERSALE HOUSE. Mainly *c.*1700, though there are inside panelling as well as fireplaces of the C17. The façade is of nine bays and two storeys with a steep broken three-bay pediment.

COPFORD

ST MARY THE VIRGIN. The most remarkable Norman parish church in the county, chiefly because of its wall paintings, but also architecturally. The C12 building consisted of nave, chancel, and apse. Except that a S aisle was added and the S nave wall irregularly broken through, this C12 building survives. The only damage which has been done to it, and it is a very serious damage, is that the vaults of nave and chancel were removed. Norman vaults in parish churches are something exceedingly rare in England, and moreover the vaulting system of Copford was rarer still – not a ribbed cross-vault but a tunnel-vault. But for the Tower chapel in London no English tunnel-vaulted church nave exists, common as they were in France. At Copford the springers of the vault are still clearly visible, and the apse, separated by an arch on the plainest responds, has its complete semi-spherical vault. The upper windows of the nave, which also survive, cut into by the later arches on the S side, must have joined the tunnel-vault with short cross-tunnel-vaults of their own. The windows are shafted inside and out and quite large in size. Especially the lower W window recognizable inside (now C14) is surprisingly spacious. Above it is a smaller Norman window flanked by two odd blocked (or blank) circles or *oculi*. Two doorways on the N side; the one into the nave has two orders of columns with primitive capitals and in the arch two roll-mouldings. The apse is articulated by broad flat buttresses. These, and all the Norman detail, are heavily fortified with Roman bricks. The addition of the S aisle apparently proceeded gradually.* First an E bay was thrown out, as a kind of transept. This still has Transitional characteristics. The arch is pointed. The responds have angle shafts. The second bay is most interesting in its own way. The responds and the arch are triple-chamfered and entirely of brick, and only the outer order uses Roman bricks. The inner

* The bay off the chancel into the vestry is not old.

orders have home-made or imported bricks, and yet the date seems to be no later than 1300. So we have here bricks amongst the earliest medieval ones in England (cf. Little Coggeshall). The westernmost arch is of less interest. – DOOR. N doorway, original, but the ironwork of the hinges renewed. – FONT. Of the usual square Purbeck type of *c*.1200, with four shallow blank arches on each side. – CHEST. Rectangular, iron-bound, assigned to the C14. – PAINTINGS. These are by far the most important medieval wall-paintings in Essex. They date from the same time as the church, say *c*.1140–50, and are connected in style with Bury St Edmunds and St Albans. Originally no doubt the whole church, inclusive of the vault, was painted. What now remains (restored in 1872 and again by Professor Tristram) is this: Apse with Christ in circular Glory supported by angels with seated Angels in the spandrels and Apostles (almost entirely C19) below between the windows. Ornamental designs in the windows, zigzag bands, Greek key or crenellated bands, diapers of bands, etc. – all shaded. In the soffit of the chancel arch the Signs of the Zodiac. Against the N wall of the nave from E to W remains of a miracle, then The Healing of Jairus's Daughter, then the life-size mailed figure of a Virtue. On the s wall near the E end figures of two angels. On the W wall arches with architectural motifs above and a seated figure on a throne and two more Virtues. Figures also on the springers of the former vault.

COPFORD HALL. A plain, stately Georgian house – red brick, seven bays, two-and-a-half storeys, hipped roof. Porch on four Tuscan columns. The house forms an admirable picture with the church on the r. and the stables with their lantern on the l. With the lawns and trees it is almost the *beau ideal* of what to the foreigner is an English landscape scene.

STANE STREET. The parish borders to the N on Stane Street, which has here quite a number of attractive houses, among them COPFORD PLACE, white brick, of seven bays, and one red brick house further W, of three bays with white brick giant pilasters.

COPPED HALL *see* EPPING

CORBETS TEY *see* UPMINSTER

CORNISH HALL END

ST JOHN THE EVANGELIST. 1840 by *J. D. Morgan* (GR). Red brick with white brick dressings. In the lancet style with a W porch and W angle turrets. A bell-tower added in 1910.

CORRINGHAM

St Mary. The tower is one of the most important Early Norman monuments in the county, without buttresses, and with two tiers of large flat blank niches below the parapet. The middle one of the upper row on each side is pierced, has a colonnette set in, and serves as a bell-opening. Pyramid roof. The whole is in its severity and clarity extremely impressive. Inside, the tower arch facing the nave is small and has the plainest imposts. N aisle, N chancel chapel, and chancel are C14, see the two-bay aisle arcade (octagonal piers, double-chamfered arches) and several Dec windows (but the chancel E window belongs to *Gilbert Scott*'s restoration of 1843-4). – SCREEN. An early example of timber screens in the county; first half of the C14. To l. and r. of the doorway only one partition, of four lights, with thin columns with shaft-rings as mullions and intersected ogee-cusped arches. Plain straight moulded top beam. – PLATE. Paten of 1684; Cup dated 1685. – MONUMENTS. Brass to Richard de Beltoun, *c.*1340, demi-figure of a priest. – Brass to a civilian, *c.*1450. Both in the chancel floor.
Pretty GREEN N of the church with for example the BULL INN, timber-framed and gabled.
The old village is surrounded by the recent large-scale housing for the big factories to the S along the Thames.

CORYTON
2¼ m. SE of Fobbing

Mobil Oil Company Refinery. Begun in 1950. An example of how thrilling aesthetically the intricate metallic forms of industrial structures can be, when not disguised by stone, concrete, or brick. The tallest of these ingenious pieces of what seems to be abstract sculpture is the Air-Life Thermofin Catalytic Cracking Unit. A little to the S of this the twin columns of the Crude Distillation Unit. The Cracking Unit breaks up petroleum into petroleum products of different molecular structure, the Distillation Unit splits crude oil into various fractions with special interest in those used for producing lubricating oil. (TECHNICAL SERVICES LABORATORY. By *S. Greenwood*, 1957.)

CREEKSEA

All Saints. 1878 by *F.Chancellor*, who here, as at Steeple, indulges in the most curious surface effects of stone, with bits of flint, brick, and tile. – FONT. C15, octagonal, carvings of a coil (serpent ?) and a cross-saltire. – PLATE. Cup and Paten of 1699. – BRASS. Sir Arthur Harris † 1631. The inscription reads:

> If any prying man, heere after come,
> That knowes not who's the tenant of this tomb,
> Wee'l tell him freely, as our sighes giue leaue,
> One, whose religious brest to GOD did cleaue,
> One that to men iust offices discharg'd,
> And to the pinched soule his hart inlarg'd,
> One, that though laid in dust of breath bereft,
> Like dying Roses sweet distillments left
> And moulders hoping, from this stone god may
> Raise vp a child to Abraham, one day.

CREEKSEA PLACE. It is not easy now to recognize the traces of a sizeable Early Elizabethan mansion. The original approach was from the E, where the pretty gateway with a gable decorated by three diagonal pinnacles survives and the walls of an enclosed garden or outer courtyard. The house at the end of this is C19, but stands on the foundations of the E wing of the old house. Through this a narrow inner courtyard was reached. The W range of this is mostly missing, a S range perhaps never existed. But the N range is intact except for the addition of a C19 N porch and two rooms to the W of this. This N range perhaps contained the Hall. It has brick windows with mullions and transoms and smaller windows with mullions in the straight gables. There is no composition recognizable of any sort. To the W extends a much lower range with brick windows and dormers in the roof. The date of the house is known. An original rainwater-head in the main (N) range reads 1569.

(GROVE COTTAGE, ½ m. SW of Creeksea Place. Rectangular house of c.1600 with exposed timber-framing.)

CRESSING

ALL SAINTS. Nave, short chancel and stunted belfry. The nave must be Norman or replace a Norman nave – see one re-set bit of zigzag-work visible on the N wall above the N doorway. The chancel is of the early C13 and has two lancet windows in the N wall. In addition some C14 and C15 windows. Those of the C14 have a characteristic Essex motif of tracery. – HELM. Early C17, crested. – MONUMENT. Anne Smith † 1607, with the usual two kneeling figures. In the 'predella' kneeling daughter and baby in a cradle.

CRESSING TEMPLE. Cressing Temple was the earliest English settlement of the Knights Templars. They were given the manor in 1135. At the suppression of the Order it went to the Hospitallers. The date of this change is 1312. The farm was leased to a private owner in 1515. What makes it desirable to know of these facts is the survival of two exceptionally fine and interesting BARNS. Their dating has lately been a source of amazement. The weatherboarded BARLEY BARN until 47 about five years ago had been regarded as *c.*1450, the brick-built WHEAT BARN as *c.*1530. Mr J. T. Smith, now the leading 46b expert on medieval timber roofs, calls both pre-1330, and Mr C. A. Hewett has obtained a radiocarbon dating for the timbers of the Barley Barn as *c.*1000–60.* He also thinks that structural evidence points to a date no later than 1130. The timbers of the Wheat Barn he regards as late C13. Both barns are aisled and have roofs covering nave and aisles under one pitch. They are half-hipped at the ends, forming gables in their upper halves. The two barns, together with a third which is later – it is dated 1623 – and whitewashed, form an exquisite group with the farmhouse, the garden-wall, and the moat. The Wheat Barn is the largest of the three. It is 140 ft long and 40 ft high.

CRIX *see* HATFIELD PEVEREL

CUST HALL *see* TOPPESFIELD

DAGENHAM

ST PETER AND ST PAUL. A true village church, in a village street, surprising between the Becontree Estate (see p. 79) and the Ford Motor Works. Early C13 chancel with lancet windows. A group of three stepped lancets at the E end. Late C15 N chancel chapel with two-bay arcade on pier with four attached shafts and four hollows in the diagonals. The rest of the church is of 1800 but probably built with old materials.‡ Nave without aisles, chancel arch of fancy detail. This prepares for the W tower of the most ignorant and entertaining Gothick. The curly battlements are specially noteworthy. Semicircular W porch with Gothick quatrefoil shafts with shaft-rings. Restored 1878. – FONT. Bowl on baluster stem. –

* Radiocarbon testing can of course only indicate the age of the wood used, not the date of construction.
‡ The surveyor was *William Mason.*

HELMS. Two, of the C17. – PLATE. Egg-shaped Cup of 1589 (York-made), nicely decorated; large Cup and Paten on foot 1678; Almsdish 1727; Flagon 1755. – MONUMENTS. Brass to Sir Thomas Urswyck † 1479, chief Baron of the Exchequer and Recorder of London, and wife and children. The figures on a tomb-chest. They are *c.* 27 in. long. Also group of kneeling children. – Sir Richard Alibon † 1688. Standing figures in niche with urn on tall pedestal between them. Ascribed by Mrs Esdaile to *Nost.*

To the N of the church the CROSS KEYS INN, excellent timber-framed C15 house with two gables and heavy timbers. To the E of this the VICARAGE with early C17 parts and parts of 1665, much changed.

CIVIC CENTRE, at Becontree. 1936 by *Berry Webber.* Long, rather shallow symmetrical range with glazed semicircular staircase projections at the ends. The centre with a portico of four thin square pillars. The back with semicircular projection for the Council Chamber.*

(COMMUNITY CENTRE. By *E. D. Mills and Partners,* begun in 1958.)

(COLLEGE OF FURTHER EDUCATION. By *H. Conolly,* County Architect, begun 1959.)

SOUTH EAST ESSEX TECHNICAL COLLEGE, Longbridge Road, close to the Barking border. 1936 by *J. Stuart.* Symmetrical, large, with two somewhat projecting wings. The centre with a solid stone cupola. Three-storeyed, pale brick, quite an acceptable design.

(KINGSLEY HALL SCHOOL. Big extension by *E. D. Mills,* 1957–8.)

BEAM COUNTY JUNIOR SCHOOL, Oval Road. By the County Architect *H. Conolly,* an example of the pleasant and human type of school design developed in the county schools immediately after the Second World War.

CHADWELL HEATH. New SCHOOLS, see Romford, p. 329.

DANBURY

ST JOHN THE BAPTIST. The church and its churchyard lie within a roughly oval, poorly preserved earthwork. The church is remarkably roomy. Nave and aisles together are wider than they are long. Chancel, S chancel chapel, and N vestry form one straight E end. The oldest part is the N aisle

* Housing S of this see p. 80 (Becontree).

wall with cusped two-light windows with a quatrefoil in the spandrel. This must be *c.*1300. The rest is essentially C14, the arcades of three bays with the typical quatrefoil piers and double-hollow-chamfered arches (on the N side dying into a vertical continuation of the pier), and the W tower with diagonal buttresses, a W door with niches to the l. and r., a W window with two ogee lights and a quatrefoil in the spandrel, and a later recessed, rather tall, shingled spire. In the tower arch towards the nave is a pretty GALLERY of *c.*1600. The N aisle has its original early C14 trussed-rafter roof, boarded over later in the E parts with ribs resting on oak head-corbels. The S aisle and S chancel chapel were rebuilt by *Gilbert Scott* in 1866. Squint from N aisle to chancel, and small squint-like window from vestry to chancel. – BENCHES. Four in the nave with poppy-heads and various beasts on the shoulders. – PAINTING. At the E end of the N aisle remains of the original ornamental painting, a frieze of scrolls with little leaves, red, black, grey, and yellow; *c.*1300. – HELM in N aisle, late C16. – PLATE. Paten of 1667, foreign; Cup of 1771; Spoon of 1774; Paten of 1808. – MONUMENTS. In low recesses in the N and S aisles three oak effigies of Knights. All these are cross-legged, the N aisle ones earlier than that of the S aisle, late C13 and very early C14. They are all three remarkably different in attitude and mood; not at all shopwork. The earlier ones have their hand on the sword, but one of the two is bent more lyrically than the other. The younger one is in an attitude of prayer.

There are many houses of interest in and around Danbury. In the village the GRIFFIN INN, late C16, timber-framed and with gabled cross-wings, and FRETTONS, 100 yds NE of the church, a C16 house, later faced with brick. Good group of chimneystacks, early and late C16.

In Elm Green WAR MEMORIAL by *Sir Reginald Blomfield*, tall cross with inlaid metal sword, 1921.

HILL HOUSE and MILLINGTON, two five-bay Georgian brick houses. Millington is dated 1719.

DANBURY PLACE or Palace. On the site of a Mildmay mansion of 1589, but apparently built independent of it. The new house dates from 1832 and was designed by *Susan Constantia Round*, wife of the owner, and *Thomas Hopper*. They have certainly put in all the motifs of Tudor architecture that they could think of, square and polygonal towers, stepped gables with pinnacles at the apex, mullioned and transomed and Perp

windows, and arranged them entirely freely, without any
noticeable principle other than picturesqueness. The house
is large, of red brick. It was a residence of the Bishops of
Rochester from 1845 till 1892. The chapel was added by
Bishop Wigram (1860–7).

Further away from the village: NEW RIFFHAMS, ¾ m. NW, a
stately three-bay house of 1815–17 with a porch, and OLD
RIFFHAMS,* ¼ m. NE of the previous, a remarkable early C18
house with older parts. The front is symmetrical, brick, with
short projecting wings. Segment-headed windows, a broad
doorway on Tuscan pilasters, brick-rusticated quoins, yet still
small shaped gables. These also repeat on the E side. On the N
side visible parts of the older house, mid C16 brick and a
timber-framed porch with an upper oriel and a bargeboarded
gable (much early C17 panelling inside; R.C.). ½ m. W of New
Riffhams lies GREAT GRACES, a fine group of brick buildings
with a weatherboarded barn. The house is only a fragment of
a bigger house. It has a big shaped gable and, partly covered,
blocked mullioned and transomed brick windows. The date
may be c.1560. Inside is a staircase of c.1600 and a good deal
of panelling. The two outhouses, also of brick, have straight
gables. One is mid C17, the other late C17.

2 m. SE of Danbury is SLOUGH HOUSE, c.1500, timber-framed
and plastered, with central hall, gabled cross-wings, and fine
chimneys with polygonal shafts at the S and N ends.

(WOOD HILL. On the lawn in front of the house, two statues by
Samuel Carpenter. They come from Moulsham Hall. Information conveyed to me by Mr Gunnis.)

DAYMNS HALL *see* RAINHAM

DEBDEN
2¼ m. E Newport

ST MARY THE VIRGIN AND ALL SAINTS. The interest of
this church is connected with R. M. T. Chiswell, who added
the E chapel in 1793 and the font in 1786. The church itself
has C13 arcades of four bays with circular piers with moulded
capitals and moulded arches. Only on the S side the first two
capitals are enriched by upright leaves. The S aisle windows
are Dec; C14 also the S porch. The W side has no tower but a
front design which looks the idea of Gothic which the period
about 1800 had. So it no doubt also belongs to Mr Chiswell's

* Parish of Little Baddow.

time. To the same time the pinnacles must be attributed. For his E chapel Mr Chiswell got *John Carter*, the celebrated anti-quary, to provide the design. It is an octagonal structure on the pattern of such a chapter house as York, connected with the church by a broad passage. The material is white brick, and all the detail of tracery outside (E window) and inside is of papery thinness. The chapel has a ribbed plaster vault, the passage timber arches with thin pendants. Inside the chapel is the elaborate MONUMENT of R. M. T. Chiswell † 1797, a tomb-chest with foiled decoration in the style of the C15 under a sumptuous arch in the style of *c*.1300. Two other minor MONUMENTS in the current idiom of Late Georgian epitaphs are by *King* of Bath. – Large monument to William Burhill, † 1703. It is signed *Thorne* (R. Gunnis). – FONT. 1786; octagonal, of *Coade* stone, in an elaborate and crisp Neo-Perp, with foiled panels; against the stem minute figures. The design was provided by *R. Holland*. Of *Coade* stone also the two medallions with quatrefoils outside the E chapel. – STAINED GLASS. In one S window heraldic glass evidently also late C18.

The church stands all on its own in the beautifully landscaped grounds by the made lake. The Hall (by *Holland*, 1796) was demolished in 1936.

Near Debden (and partly in Widdington) a fine group of farm-houses: MOLE HALL and SWAYNES HALL close together (1 m. S), and AMBERDEN HALL, NEW AMBERDEN HALL, and THISTLEY HALL close together (1½ m. SSE). The latter two have five-bay two-storey fronts of *c*.1680.

WINDMILL, ¼ m. N. Tower-mill in a dilapidated condition.

DEBDEN
Near Chigwell

BANK OF ENGLAND PRINTING WORKS, adjoining Debden Station. By *Easton & Robertson*, 1953–6. About 800 ft long. The main printing hall is 125 ft wide and vaulted by an irregular, very effective curve to get as much N sky-lighting as possible. Hence the curve rises very slowly from the N but falls steeply to the S. The whole vault is of concrete and glass and conveys a sense of the grandest spaciousness. It may well be called Easton & Robertson's finest achievement.

DEDHAM

ST MARY THE VIRGIN. One of the most prosperous Perp churches of Essex, the visible proof of the flourishing cloth-trade of the town. The weaving industry seems to have started in the C14. The arrival of Flemish weavers under Edward III is known. Prosperity came to an end in the C17. In 1642 a petition was delivered to the King for help for the depressed condition of the town. Prosperity seems to have reached its climax in the course of the C15. The church is its principal witness. The chief donors seem to have been the Webbes and the Gurdons. Building began in 1492 and went on quickly. The N aisle was a special commemorative piece to the two leading families. On the ground floor of the tower appear the initials and merchants' marks of the Webbes. Money was left for the building of the steeple in 1494–5, 1504–5, 1505–6, and a further £20 towards finishing the steeple in 1510. In 1519 Stephen Denton left £100 'for the battlyment of the steeple'. So the tower and the whole church were probably complete by about 1520 – built it appears at one go and without change of plan. It stands large along the main street, but its S side still faces the fields. It has a long nave with clerestory, a long chancel, two tall two-storeyed porches, and a W tower about 130 ft high. The length of the church is about 170 ft. The whole building is more in a Suffolk than an Essex style.

The W tower of knapped flint has big polygonal clasping buttresses* with much stone dressing, a very large four-light W window, three-light bell-openings, battlements with flushwork decoration, and tall crocketed pinnacles. The ground floor of the tower forms a passageway from N to S. It has a depressed pointed vault entirely panelled with tracery, quatrefoils, roses and portcullis, etc. The aisles have three-light windows with depressed pointed heads, the chancel taller two-centred windows – of five lights at the E end, of three on the sides. The wall of the N side is treated as the show-side. The base for example has flushwork panels and the parapet battlements. The N porch uses flushwork for base, buttresses, and battlements. The doorway has lions *couchant* on the l. and r., tracery in the spandrels, and niches l. and r. of the upper window. The inside is airy and clear, six bays of identical slender piers with a section of thin shafts with capitals and broad shallow diagonal hollows without capitals. The roof, of low pitch, rests on shafts rising from the capitals as well as the apexes of the arches; for there are twice as many clerestory windows as arcade arches. These arches are four-centred. The chancel is not flanked by chapels.

* Cf. Great St Mary, Cambridge, and Saffron Walden.

FONT. Octagonal, with the symbols of the Evangelists and angels, the figures thoroughly defaced. – DOOR in N doorway. With tracery panelling and one band of small figures in niches. – STAINED GLASS. In the chancel by *Kempe*, E window 1902, N and S windows 1907. – PLATE. Handsome set of 1784.

MONUMENTS. The chief monument is to Thomas Webbe, erected by his son John Webbe. It is in the N aisle, built up to reach into the window space – a proud but not an imaginative piece. The decoration is copious but all too much a repetition of quatrefoil friezes, large and small, and with and without shields. The tomb-chest has two of them, in one the Webbe initials. The back of the depressed pointed recess has more, the soffit of the recess yet more. Above the recess a framed stone panel with the indents of Thomas Webbe and his family. Battlements and pinnacles above. – John Roger † 1636, frontal demi-figure in a niche, the ornament of the gristly kind fashionable in the second third of the C17.

THE TOWN. Dedham is easily the most attractive small town in Essex. It consists chiefly of the one High Street with Mill Lane branching off to the mill-stream and the river Stour. A perambulation should begin at the E end so that one gets the CONGREGATIONAL CHURCH of 1871–2 over quickly. After that one has nothing to fear. There is nothing at Dedham to hurt the eye. The manse of the minister (of 1739) still stands next to the Congregational Church. On the opposite side every house deserves a separate glance, although not one is of high individual merit: the first timber-framed with a gable at the W end, the second with an asymmetrically placed Greek Doric porch, the third of five bays and three storeys, whitewashed brick, then one also five bays but red, and so on. Meanwhile, opposite, the former GRAMMAR SCHOOL, a group of two stately Early Georgian brick houses, the one on the E a little later and dated 1732 by an inscription. This is of white brick with red brick dressings, five bays by four bays in size, and has a doorway towards the street, on pilasters with a segmental pediment, an arched niche above it, and arched ground-floor windows. The same type of doorway is the entrance to the other house, which is distinguished by giant angle pilasters. Both houses have brick parapets decorated by sunk oblong panels. The second house faces W, where in a kind of square the MEMORIAL CROSS is placed, a design by *Caröe*. N of the square MILL LANE leads down to the mill and the river Stour. In Mill Lane MILL HOUSE of *c*.1600 with an original

timber porch, and other nice houses, the best being the
MARLBOROUGH HEAD INN at the corner of the High Street.
This is the prettiest-looking half-timbered house of Dedham,
dated by the Royal Commission c.1500.

The best house in the stretch of the High Street opposite the
58b   church is SHERMAN'S of c.1730, obviously built by the same
masons as the Grammar School, but narrower in its front and
more compact; two storeys, three bays, giant angle pilasters,
a doorway with pediment on Corinthian pilasters, arched
windows in broad frames l. and r., an arched niche in an aedicule above the door pediment, and a parapet with sunk panels
curving up in the middle to allow space for a sundial – a lively,
somewhat restless composition. A little further to the W the
SUN INN, early C16, half-timbered, with a carriageway at one
end and a picturesque yard. An early C17 covered staircase
leads up to the upper floor in the yard. Next to the Sun Inn a
four-bay house with overhang, Georgianized windows, and a
big square chimneystack on the roof, and then a picturesque
four-gable front. Opposite several more timber-framed cottages. Near the W entrance to the High Street GREAT HOUSE,
in an imitation-Georgian style, of 1936 (by R. Erith), and
WESTGATE HOUSE, true Georgian, with two storeys and a
doorway with broken pediment on brackets. Opposite DED-
HAM HOUSE, a plain three-bay villa of white brick dating
from c.1830.

300 yds S of Dedham, on its own, the most important medieval
house, Southfields. It can be approached from the N or better
from the E by a lane at the E corner of which stands the former
POOR HOUSE with its big chimney-breast. SOUTHFIELDS
was built about 1500 as a rich clothier's house, including round
a courtyard his own living quarters, probably on the S side, and
the offices and warehouse. The group is timber-framed and
the timbers are exposed in parts, and plastered over in others.
At the SW angle facing S is an extremely handsome gable with
two overhangs on brackets. To the W the room on the ground
floor has an oriel window leaning against a big brick chimney.
The main feature of the N side is the carriageway with a gable
over. It lies exactly in the middle of the side. Inside the courtyard there is an original porch on the W side, and an original
doorway on the E.

DENGIE

ST JAMES. Chancel and nave of the C14 with C19 bellcote. The
Royal Commission notes in the walls the use of C14 yellow

bricks apart from Roman bricks. The variety of colour in the walls is altogether remarkable: septaria, that is a brown stone, flint, pebble, and the bricks. C14 windows, those of the nave with ogee detail, those of the chancel with a very peculiar tracery pattern. – PLATE. Cup of 1565 with two bands of ornament. – BRASS. To a Lady and Children, c.1520.

DITCHLEYS see SOUTH WEALD

DODDINGHURST

ALL SAINTS. Nave, chancel, and belfry. The bell-stage of the belfry has vertical boarding. It ends in a small, shingled spire. It stands on six posts with rather shallow arched braces and much diagonal trellis-strutting.* Uncommonly large timber porch. The sides each have ten arched openings. The chancel is C19, the nave C13, see the S doorway with one order of colonnettes and a moulded arch with dogtooth ornament. Nave roof C15, with tie-beams, king-posts, and four-way struts. – ROOD. The figures of Christ, the Virgin, and St John cannot be seen clearly from below, but seem to be German, early C16. – PLATE. Cup of 1562; Paten of 1567.

DORRINGTON HALL see SHEERING

DOVERCOURT

ALL SAINTS. Entirely plastered, with pebbledash. Norman nave with one blocked N window visible outside as well as inside. Chancel early C14, see the renewed N and S windows. A little more elaborate and slightly later N and S nave windows. The tracery here is flowing. Perp W tower with diagonal buttresses and battlements. – FONT. Octagonal, C14, with cusped panels of tracery (intersected and other), quatrefoils, etc. – POOR BOX. Plain, square, iron-bound, dated 1589. – BRASS to a Civilian, mid C15; the figure about 2 ft long.

The development of Dovercourt from a village by the high road to a resort by the sea belongs chiefly to the fifties. White's Directory calls it Dovercourt New Town and says it was built from about 1857 onwards. In fact it started earlier. The promoter was Mr John Bagshaw, M.P. for Harwich. His own house, CLIFF HOUSE, dates from 1845. It was the northern-

---

* The tower may well date from the first half of the C13. C. A. Hewett, *Archaeological Journal*, vol. 119, 1962.

most of the new seafront, the southernmost being the CLIFF HOTEL. All this is in the typical prosperous style of the fifties, the South Kensington style. To appreciate the contrast between this High Victorian and the more informal, cosier, more picturesque Late Victorian one should compare the Cliff Hotel with the ALEXANDRA HOTEL* by *Sherrin*, 1904. Mr Bagshaw built the Undercliff Walk in 1858. In 1862 the two pretty lighthouses with open steel underframes were built.

(SIR ANTHONY DEANE SECONDARY MODERN SCHOOL. By *Johns, Slater & Haward* in collaboration with *H. Conolly*, County Architect. Completed 1958.)

STANDARD YEAST COMPANY, King George's Way. Excellent extensive factory by *Ove Arup & Partners* (consultant architect *David Aberdeen*). Chiefly three blocks connected by glass-walled bridges.

DOWN HALL see HATFIELD BROAD OAK

DOWNHAM

ST MARGARET. Big sturdy brick W tower of *c.*1500. Diaper pattern of vitrified headers. Diagonal buttresses with four setoffs. Battlements. The church is of 1871 by *Street* but has a few original windows from its predecessor. – PLATE. Small Cup and Paten of 1562. – MONUMENTS. Under the tower several handsome minor epitaphs of the C18 and early C19.

DOWNHAM HALL. Near the house, octagonal C18 brick DOVECOTE with cupola.

FREMNELLS. The Royal Commission here is in error. It gives the date *c.*1670 for the whole house, no doubt on the strength of the date on one of the gate-posts of the front garden: 1676. But the gate-posts have brickwork different from the front of the house and stone volutes which are in style nowhere matched in the front. The front is the important thing about Fremnells. It must be *c.*1630–40. Symmetrical, on the E-plan, with, as its centre, not the porch but the Hall bay window. The entrance to the Hall lay further on the r., next to the r. hand projection. Broad mullion-and-transom cross windows and stone sunk panels between them. Sunk panels also in the parapet. Three straight gables for the short access of the E and the centre. The centre gable is behind the parapet. All this would be inconceivably conservative for 1670. Moreover, the room

---

* Now Alexandra House, a Methodist Home for the aged.

with the r.-hand projection has very good linenfold panelling of the mid C16 at the latest, and that also seems to be the date of the timber-framed and plastered side and back of the house and the chimneystack of the Hall. It is said that the house is to be submerged by the Hanningfield Reservoir. That would be a thousand pities, as it is the best house of its date in Essex.*

DUKES see ROXWELL

DUNTON see BASILDON

DYNES HALL see GREAT MAPLESTEAD

EARLS COLNE

ST ANDREW. A large but disappointing church. The most rewarding part is the W tower. Big, with diagonal buttresses and three-light bell-openings. Battlements with flushwork decoration dated 1534 and bearing the de Vere arms. Stair-turret, in its top parts of brick and carrying an iron openwork 'corona' for the weathervane. This latter adornment dates probably from the early C18. It is the only feature easily remembered of the church. The rest mostly 1884, except for the S aisle with C14 windows, and the S arcade with octagonal piers. The chancel inside has nice Victorian stencilled decoration on walls and ceiling panels. – PLATE. Late C15 Paten with incised figure of Christ in the middle; large late C16 Cup with bands of ornament. – MONUMENT. Richard Harlakenden † 1602 and four wives, the usual type of epitaph with kneeling figures. – John Wale † 1761, tablet by Roubiliac with relief of Mercury and Justice (R. Gunnis).

A number of good timber-framed houses to the w.

COLNE PRIORY. The house is of red brick and in the C18 Gothick style, the front with two symmetrical castellated bay windows and a tripartite central window with ogee tops – that is Georgian in disguise. The house stands partly on the site of a Benedictine priory, founded from Abingdon about 1100–5. Hardly anything survives above ground, but excavations have shown the church to have had nave and aisles of six bays, two W towers standing outside the aisle-ends as at St Botolph Colchester, crossing and transepts, and chancel with chancel chapels. There were five staggered apses (transepts, chancel

* It has now been submerged.

aisles, chancel) as at Barking. Later in the C12 the chancel and its aisles were slightly enlarged and provided with square ends. Later still, in the C15, the s chancel aisle was rebuilt on a much larger scale (as in the C14 at Little Dunmow). The Cloister and the apsed Chapter House have also been traced. The monuments of the de Veres, Earls of Oxford, which had survived were taken to St Stephen near Bures (Suffolk) in 1935.

(COLNEFORD HOUSE, Pounds Green. Richly pargeted front with date 1685, mostly big foliage scrolls. R.C.)

EAST DONYLAND

ST LAWRENCE. 1838 by *William Mason* of Ipswich. Quite remarkably original. An octagonal church of white brick, in the lancet style. Groups of five stepped lancets on three sides, entrances on two others, and three lancets above the altar. – MONUMENT. Elizabeth Marshall † 1613. Frontally seated woman, full-length, flanked by obelisks. Below in the 'predella' one kneeling daughter and two babies in cradles. Long inscription which reads as follows:

Clotho: In tender armes thy tickle rocke I beare
   Wherin consists of life this hemispher
   Frayle flyinge fadeinge fickle sliperye
   Certaine in nothing but uncertaintye

Lachesis: From of thy rocke her slender thred I pull
    When scarce begun but yt my spoole is full
    Then tyme begetts bringes forth & with her haste
    Makes after tyme tymes former workes to waste

Atropos: I with my knife have cutt that thred in twayne
    And loosde that knott not to be knitt agayne
    What two wer one my knife hath both opposd
    In heaven her soule in earth her corpes inclosd.

The verses are attributed to Gilbert Longe, then vicar of East Donyland.

EAST DONYLAND HALL. Stately seven-bay, two-storeyed block of red brick, of c.1700, with rusticated brick quoins and a parapet with vases. Facing the entrance three low pedimented ranges of outbuildings, arranged slightly fanwise. Splendid cedar-trees near the house.

ROWHEDGE QUAY is a picturesque waterside street.

EAST HAM

ST MARY MAGDALENE, High Street South. It is surprising to find a prosperous medieval village church between an East-

End suburb, a by-pass road, and the vast hump of the Northern Outfall Sewer.* The w tower of the early c16, low, of big reddish rubble. The rest of the church essentially Norman, with masonry of large coursed rubble. Norman windows, deeply splayed inside, preserved on both sides. Nave wide and aisleless, lower and narrower chancel, and yet lower and narrower apse. The apse has two pilaster buttresses outside and a corresponding pilaster inside on the SE. Its plain moulding is identical with that of the w arch of the apse. It indicates that the apse was intended to be vaulted. In 1931 however a Norman ceiling was discovered above the apse. The chancel has inside as an enrichment intersecting arches with zigzag decoration, well preserved on the N side, hardly recognizable on the s. The w doorway of the Norman church is preserved. It leads now into the w tower. It is of three orders of columns with scalloped capitals. The s side of the chancel has a three-light brick window, probably of the c17. The nave windows are from the restoration of 1844–5. In the N chancel wall the remains of an opening of the early c16 towards an anchorite's cell, in the s side of the apse a PISCINA of the c13. Double opening with trefoiled heads under pointed arch. – FONT. Bowl of 1639 on late c17 or early c18 baluster stem. – PAINTING. In the apse remains of early c13 wall-painting, imitating ashlar facing with red joints. In the arch to the apse small flowers and foliage frieze with head of Christ in the apex. – PLATE. Cup of 1563; Cover of 1573; Cup and Cover of 1623. – MONUMENTS. Brasses to Hester Neve † 1610 and Elizabeth Heigham † 1622. – Standing wall-monument to Edward Nevill, Earl of Westmorland, early c17, surrounded by the original iron railings. Two large kneeling figures facing each other, and kneeling children below. Alabaster, good quality. – William Heigham † 1620 and wife, good alabaster monument with two standing cherubs; no effigies. – Giles Breame † 1621, kneeling figures also facing each other, smaller than the Nevill tomb. – Higham Beamish † 1723, plain against obelisk, signed by *Nathaniel Hedges*. – In the churchyard William Stukeley, the antiquarian, is buried († 1765).

ST BARNABAS, Browning Road, Little Ilford. 1900–9 by *Bucknell & Comper*. Red brick. Fine quiet three-gable front with Perp windows. Interior wide with wide aisles, cool and competent. No chancel arch. Large Perp windows, four-lights even in the aisles.

* The OUTFALL SEWER was constructed by *J. W. Bazalgette* in 1864.

ST BARTHOLOMEW, Barking Road. 1901 by *Micklethwaite &*
Somers Clarke. Dignified, neo-E.E. church of red brick.
Severely damaged in the Second World War.

ST MARY, Church Road, Manor Park. The parish church of
Little Ilford. A small church and not impressive, though love-
able. Nave with bell-turret, cemented. Chancel rebuilt in 1724.
Of the same date the Lethieullier Chapel containing the fine
MONUMENTS to John Lethieullier † 1737, Smart Lethieullier
† 1760, and his wife. The two latter are slender urns, the centre
is held by the red marble sarcophagus of John. The whole is
placed against an architecture with Tuscan columns and a
pediment. The nave is of the C12, as seen in one N window. –
BRASSES. Thomas Heron † 1517, schoolboy with ink-horn
and pen-case. – William † 1614 and Ann † 1630 Hyde, the infant boy in swaddling clothes. – MONUMENT. William Waldegrave † 1610 and wife, with kneeling figures; not large.

ST MICHAEL, Romford Road and Toronto Road. 1897–8 by
Charles Spooner. Red brick, Perp, with tall, original timber
flèche. Wide interior with hammerbeam roof. The timbers here
and in the aisles demonstratively heavy – in the Arts and Crafts
spirit. The chancel narrower, tall arch of noble proportions,
with tall giant wall-arcading.

(ST MICHAEL (R.C.), Tilbury Road. By *J.Newton*, 1958–9.)

(ST STEPHEN (R.C.), Church Road. By *D. R. Burls*, 1958–9.)

METHODIST CHURCH, Katherine Road. 1905 by *G.Baines &*
Son. Red brick, in the pretty fancy Neo-Perp of the date, with
an asymmetrically placed turret.

TOWN HALL, Barking Road. 1901–3 by *Cheers & Smith*. Plum-
coloured brick and yellow artificial stone. Mixed Tudor and
Baroque, also some hints at Loire châteaux. Tall asymmetrical
tower. The best thing about the building is that it is recessed
from the street and thus given sufficient prominence to act as a
town centre. It succeeds in giving East Ham a more urban
character than any of the surrounding towns possess. Moreover, the old TECHNICAL COLLEGE building adjoins it
immediately to the E and the PUBLIC LIBRARY to the SW,
both in the same style. The library is by the town engineer
Campbell, 1908. Other large buildings close by, the METHO-
DIST CENTRAL HALL, by *Gunton & Gunton c.*1905, more
Baroque than the Town Hall and also with an asymmetrical
tower, and the POLICE STATION (1904) opposite the Library,
with a new building behind, tall, utilitarian, modern, seven
storeys high.

(The new TECHNICAL COLLEGE, High Street South, is by *J. W. Taylor*, 1959–62.)

LANGDON CRESCENT SECONDARY SCHOOLS. By *J. W. Taylor* and built 1953–64. Three secondary schools with common dining room etc. Tall, slender tower with somewhat Swedish lantern. Divers low brick buildings, freely grouped so as to avoid any institutional associations.

SECONDARY SCHOOL FOR GIRLS, Plashet Grove. By *George Whitby*, 1953–4. The school had to be built on a very confined site; hence the exceptional plan with seven upper storeys standing on a ground floor which spreads the gymnasium and the hall further out to the W and E. Concrete, with much use of precasting.

(RECTORY MANOR SECONDARY SCHOOL, Browning Road. By *J. W. Taylor*, 1955–7.)

(BRAMPTON MANOR SECONDARY SCHOOL, Roman Road. Also by *J. W. Taylor*, 1957–62.)

Of the domestic architecture of East Ham nothing need be reported, except three individual houses:

BOLEYN CASTLE.* This large, rambling mid C16 manor house of brick is an odd survival in the streets of East Ham. The hall range stands at r. angles to the street. The kitchen etc. are to the E of it, and s of them irregularly projecting rooms, including a broad three-storeyed tower. s of the hall is a long narrow range along the street and separate from it beyond its s end an irregularly polygonal tower. The upper parts of the hall and w range were rebuilt late in the C17. The whole is eminently picturesque, though – at the time of writing – very neglected.

EAST HAM BURNEL MANOR HOUSE, Gladding Road, Manor Park. Now part of the London Co-op Dairies. Five by four bays, two-and-a-half storeys. Gothick cupola. The house is mid C18. The date can no longer be verified inside (after war damage), but some vases outside clearly indicate it.

PRIORY COURT, Priory Road, just E of Green Street. Recent flats by *C. H. Doody*. Eight-storeyed, Y-shaped, an impressive design.

(The following notes on new buildings have been kindly supplied by the Borough Librarian:

DORAN COURT, Central Park Road. By *C. H. Doody*, 1957–9. An eight-storey block of flats.

OLD PERSONS' BUNGALOWS, Ascot Road. By *A. W. Walls*, 1960–1.

* Now demolished.

MIXED HOUSING DEVELOPMENT, Holloway Road. By *A. W. Walls*, 1961–3.)

For the Former Industrial Schools in GREEN STREET, see West Ham, p. 418.

EAST HANNINGFIELD

ALL SAINTS. In ruins and at the time of writing completely neglected, with bushes and weeds growing rank inside the nave and aisle. Brick chancel of the early C16, with two-light brick windows in the S wall. Nave with two-bay N arcade. The pier is of brick, octagonal and heavy. In the nave S wall is one four-light window of brick.★

WILLIS FARM and RAILS FARM, ¼ m. S. of the village. Timber-framed cottages illustrated by the R.C.

EAST HORNDON

ALL SAINTS. Brick church, all alone on a hill just N of an arterial road. Eminently picturesque short C17 W tower with thick diagonal buttresses, continued in polygonal angles and polygonal pinnacles. The battlements between these are stepped. Large arched windows as bell-openings, with raised frames. The rest of the church is C15 to early C16. It has – an unusual feature – N and S transepts. Charming group of S porch and S transept under one sloping roof leading up to a gable, and then projecting S chancel chapel. Inside, this chapel is separated from the chancel by a two-bay arcade with a pier of four demi-shafts and four diagonal hollows and moulded arches. In the N chancel wall a deep recess, brick-panelled at the back, and containing the MONUMENT of Sir Thomas Tyrell † 1476 with C19 tomb-chest on which now only the Brass to Lady Tyrell. Excellent roofs, flat-ceiled in the S chapel, pitched and ceiled with panels separated by bosses in the chancel, open with tie-beams and king-posts in the nave. Balconies or galleries divide the narrow transepts into two storeys. They date from the early C17. – FONT. Square, of *c.*1200, with flat sunk decoration of interlaced arcade on two sides, and foliated crosses on the other. – PULPIT. Plain, C17. – HELMS, GAUNT-LETS, and SWORD of the Tyrell Family. – MONUMENTS. Sir Thomas Tyrell, see above. – Lady Tyrell † 1422, large incised limestone slab with figure in horned head-dress under canopy with figures of children up to l. and r. shafts. – Unknown family, *c.*1520, in recess in S transept. Tomb-chest with quatrefoil

★ Wall paintings removed to the Victoria and Albert Museum.

decoration, brasses against the back wall; only the man survives; the indent shows that he and his wife were praying to the Trinity. – Sir John Tyrell † 1766. With two cherubs' heads at the foot, inscription, and higher up urn against an obelisk. Signed by *Nollekens*.

EASTHORPE

ST EDMUND. Nicely placed with a timber-framed house opposite and Easthorpe Hall a little to the W. Small church with nave and chancel under one roof. Belfry. Essentially Norman – see the W window high up, and several N and S windows and indications of windows as well as plain doorways. The Norman church had an apse. Of this the beginning is exposed on the S side. The chancel is an alteration of the C13. It has good SEDILIA with two pointed trefoiled arches on shafts and three widely spaced stepped lancet windows with internal dogtooth ornamentation. Some C14 windows were inserted to give more light. In addition there is a curious quatrefoil 'low side window' leading to a recess in the S wall. – PAINTING. Mid C13 figures in the jambs and splay of one S window: Resurrection and Angels. – STAINED GLASS. Christ preaching, German or Swiss, c.1530 (S window). – PLATE. Late C16 Cup and Paten, remodelled.

EASTHORPE HALL was built in the C15 with central hall and cross wings. The wing N of the hall block is C17. WELL COTTAGE, opposite the church, may well be late C15. Both houses have remains of original roofs inside (R.C.).

ST MARY'S GRANGE, ¼ m. E of the church, has a C15 W wing with cambered tie-beams inside, but the main block is C17 and C18 rebuilding (R.C.).

EAST MERSEA

ST EDMUND KING AND MARTYR. Big Perp stone W tower with diagonal buttresses, battlements, and higher stair-turret. At the base a little flushwork decoration. Of the same time most of the church – see the tracery of the windows. However, several were replaced in the C18 by big bare pointed openings. Perp N arcade of four bays with tall two-centred arches and piers of a section in which four deeply undercut attached shafts are connected by deep hollows so that a non-intermittent wavy section results. The chancel arch and the arch from the chancel to the N chapel are of the same type. – FONT.

Octagonal, C15, with uncommonly pretty blank arches. –
PULPIT. Early C17, still with its tester. – PLATE. Elizabethan
Cup with two bands of ornament.

EAST TILBURY

ST CATHERINE. On the N escarpment of the Thames, close to
the river, with the grey walls of the COAL HOUSE FORT
(1866–71) below. The most interesting feature of the church is
the N arcade of four bays with alternating circular and octagonal piers, square capitals of scallops with angle volutes, and
unmoulded pointed arches. The E respond shows waterleaf,
the aisle outer walls two lancets. All this must belong to the
later decades of the C12. Evidence of the Norman church
which was enlarged by this aisle is one blocked window
above the fourth arcade arch. The chancel is a good piece of
E. E. building; three stepped E lancets, and also N and S lancets.
On the N side one two-light window of c.1300. The nave S
side shows evidence inside and out of a former arcade. It is
said that this fell victim to the Dutch raid of 1667. The present
wall is C19, but the windows are good original C14 pieces. A
C13 W tower must also have existed – see the tower arch. A new
tower was begun S of the W end of the church in 1917, but has
not yet been completed. – PULPIT. Usual Elizabethan type.
BATA SHOE FACTORY. Several large multi-storeyed concrete
blocks with large windows and red brick walls between the
concrete stanchions, and beams which are exposed. Also a
hotel. Workers' housing in small cubic blocks, each being a
pair of semi-detached houses. The whole begun in 1932 to the
design of the company's architectural office on the pattern of
the many buildings of Bata's Czech factory town of Zlin. (The
Recreation Centre behind the hotel is by *B. Katz & Vaughan*,
1957, and, as Mr Nairn writes, 'beautifully detailed and of a
showy crispness just right for a coffee bar'.)
ROMANO-BRITISH HUTS. Remains have been examined on
the Thames foreshore. They consisted essentially of an outer
ring of stones and an inner ring of stakes. The largest was
20 ft in diameter. Pottery suggests a date in the C1 and C2. The
SOLDIERS' GRAVES, W of the churchyard, are an artificial
scarp ½ m. long. The origin of the scarp is unknown.

EASTWOOD *see* SOUTHEND-ON-SEA

EDWIN'S HALL *see* WOODHAM FERRERS

ELMDON

ST NICHOLAS. 1852 and 1879, except for the W tower, which
dates from the C15 (angle-buttresses and battlements). –
PLATE. Paten on foot of 1633; Cup of 1634. – MONUMENTS.
Tomb-chest probably of Sir Thomas Meade † 1585. Three
decorated quatrefoils and shields, under depressed arch, with
quatrefoil decoration inside, quatrefoil frieze over, and cresting.
Large coat of arms against the back-wall of the recess. –
Brass to a man and two wives, c.1530, the figures 2 ft 6 in.
long (chancel).

ELM FARM see WEST HANNINGFIELD

ELMS FARM see BARDFIELD SALING

ELMSTEAD

ST ANN AND ST LAURENCE. The N side should be examined
first. It has a display of a doorway and some windows giving a
complete chronology of the church, from the Norman doorway with Roman brick surround by way of the two-light
windows with Y-tracery (c.1300) in the chancel, to the C14
and early C15. The church is essentially C14. Tower over
the porch not higher than the nave roof; W window like those
in the chancel. The best architectural feature is the S chapel,
again early C14. It has an arcade of two bays with a quatrefoil
pier and an arch of two quadrant mouldings and in addition
wall-shafts and wall-arches against the S wall. Contemporary
PISCINA on demi-shafts. Also early C14 the SEDILIA and
PISCINA in the chancel. The cusped arches have hood-moulds
resting on heads of exceptionally fine quality and gratifyingly 20a
unrestored. The E window unfortunately has been reduced in
size, see the outside. It must originally have given the chancel
great breadth and dignity. Unusual features in the church are
the quatrefoil squint S of the chancel arch and the three 'low
side windows', one in the chancel and two in the S chapel. They
have recently been fitted with C14 bits of STAINED GLASS
from the E window. – DOOR with C12 ironwork. – COM-
MUNION RAILS with C18 balusters. – BOX PEWS early C19. –
IRON CROSS with highly scrolly decoration; it was a hat-rack
originally; the date perhaps c.1800. – PLATE. Elizabethan Cup
with bands of ornament and Paten on foot. – MONUMENTS.

Oak effigy of a cross-legged Knight. His feet rest against a female figure. – BRASS. Two hands holding a heart inscribed Credo. Dated c.1500 by Haines.

(ELMSTEAD HALL. Timber-framed and plastered; of c.1500. With bargeboarded gables. In the attic of the W wing a C16 six-light window. Several C16 and C17 doorways, and doors. Much C17 and C18 panelling. R.C.)

ELSENHAM

CHURCH. Norman windows in nave (N and S) and chancel (N). In the nave on the S side in addition a three-light mid C16 brick window and a brick porch with brick doorway and two-light side openings. But inside the porch the best piece of Norman decoration of the church, a doorway with zigzag-carved columns, oddly decorated capitals (do they mean Sun and Moon ?), a tympanum with chip-carved stars and tiers of saltire crosses, and the extrados of the arch with another two strips of saltires. Inside the church against the tympanum a re-used COFFIN LID of the same early date, with a rough cross and bands of saltires. The chancel arch also is Norman. It has, like the doorway, columns with zigzag carving and two bands of saltires in the extrados of the arch. In the chancel a C13 addition, a DOUBLE PISCINA with a shaft carrying a stiff-leaf capital and arches with dogtooth decoration. – PULPIT. Early C17 with strapwork and arabesque motifs. – PLATE. Cup of 1562; Paten of 1595; Paten on foot of c.1700; Almsdish. – BRASSES of 1615 and 1619.

ELSENHAM HALL. Largish symmetrical red brick mansion, Late Georgian, castellated, with a three-bay cemented Tudor porch between the two projecting wings.

ELSENHAM PLACE, ⅓ m. N. Timber-framed with two symmetrical wings. Some woodwork comes from The Close, High Street, Saffron Walden, a house which was demolished in 1937. On the back of a wooden overmantel an inscription was discovered stating that it was originally at Beaufort House, Chelsea.

EPPING

EPPING FOREST is now an area of under 6,000 acres. Up to the middle of the C17 it had been 60,000, stretching as far as West Ham, Barking, and Ilford. In the early Middle Ages it had of course been yet larger. The N portion was put under cultivation early in the C13, it seems. What remained after the Civil War was reduced by felling for the Navy at the time of Pepys and after, until by such means and private enclosure the area had gone down to 12,000 acres in 1777. In 1793 9,000 were left and in 1851 6,000. Since even after 1851 private enclosing continued, though on a small scale, the Forest was finally purchased for £250,000 and declared open to the public in perpetuity, in 1882. Since then three small additions have been made: Oak Hill on the Theydon side 1889, Highams Park Woodford 1891, and Yardley Hill Chingford 1899. The pride of the Forest is its hornbeams. There is no larger forest of hornbeams in England, nor perhaps in the world.

In the Forest are two earthworks: Loughton Camp and Ambresbury Banks. LOUGHTON CAMP is an Early Iron Age encampment, well sited on a spur, 1 m. NW of St Mary's Church. The camp is roughly oval in shape and covers an area of 6½ acres. There is a single rampart and a 45-ft wide ditch. The location of the original entrance is doubtful. AMBRESBURY BANKS is an Iron Age hill-fort 2¾ m. S of Epping Upland church. The fort is of roughly rectangular plan enclosing 12 acres. It is of univallate construction, the rampart still surviving to a height of 7 ft in places. The ditch is 22 ft wide and 10 ft deep. The defences are broken by entrances on the W and SE. The former is of simple type and is contemporary with the building of the fort; the SE inturned entrance is medieval.

The town of Epping itself lies outside the forest, to the NE. With the help of this *cordon sanitaire* it has never been swallowed up by London and keeps to this day its individuality as a small roadside town, with many inns and few streets other than the HIGH STREET. There are few houses of individual merit. The best perhaps are at the S end where the High Street is still called HIGH ROAD: WINCHELSEA HOUSE and EPPING PLACE, both of the C18, both of brick, the former of four bays, the latter of five, with modilion frieze and hipped roof. Documentary evidence suggests that they were originally built as one house, although they differ in height and style. Close to the N end the FRIENDS MEETING HOUSE with a tripartite front window, early C19.

(In the High Street, behind the Cock Inn, lies a new MOTEL. This is by *Erdi & Rabson* and was completed in 1962. It is excellently placed and excellently detailed.)

ST JOHN THE BAPTIST. Epping has no medieval church. But

when it came to building a parish church of sufficient size, in 1889, the authorities were wise in the choice of their architects. They went to *Bodley & Garner* and got a church of remarkable dignity if not striking originality. The outstanding feature is the tower erected only in 1908–9, also by *Bodley*. It stands at the street corner separated from nave and aisle, which face the High Street with Dec windows. The tower is broad and strong with two large bell-openings on each side and three big battlements. It is all very serious, and no light relief is permitted. The motifs inside, e.g. the arcade pier and arches, are in a correct East Anglian C14 tradition. Much trouble has also been taken over the furnishing of the church. Reredos by *Bodley* and *Hare*, 1909; Rood Screen also by *Bodley*. – Stained Glass by *Kempe* (E window 1890, S aisle E window 1902).

(By the church, Nos 5–17 ST JOHNS ROAD, unusually carefully detailed. Weatherboard cottages, *c*.1820.)

(1¾ m. WSW of the church and visible from the High Road is the shell of COPPED HALL, 1753 to designs by *John Sanderson*. It was enlarged *c*.1895 by *C. E. Kempe*, who refaced the garden front and added the N wing and the arcade walls, based on Sanderson's original designs. Information from Miss N. Briggs. Kempe probably also designed WOOD HOUSE, 1898, near Epping, although the architect named is *Walter E. Tower*. It was inspired by Sparrow's House, Ipswich. Four four-storey gabled bay windows, deep eaves, elaborate pargeting. In the drawing room a fireplace of 1607.)

EPPING UPLAND

ALL SAINTS. The mother church of Epping, which was originally the hamlet Epping Street. All Saints consists of a nave and chancel in one. Badly over-restored. There is no safe indication of a date, but the fact that the windows have all been renewed as lancets indicates a C13 origin for the church. This is corroborated by the nave PISCINA (the church was perhaps lengthened to the E later), which is original and clearly E.E. Late C16 W tower of brick with diagonal buttresses and battlements. – COMMUNION RAIL. Of Roman Doric colonnettes, probably late C18. – BENCHES. A few with poppyheads in the nave. – PLATE. Cup and Paten of 1639; Paten, Flagon and Almsdish, presented 1768. – BRASS. Thomas Palmer, Professor of Common Law at Cambridge, † 1621, the figure 2 ft 6 in. long.

(TAKELEYS, 300 yds E. Timber-framed early C17 house with an elaborately carved fireplace and floral wall-paintings in black and brown on the plaster of an upper room. R.C.)

AMBRESBURY BANKS, see Epping.

FAIRSTEAD

ST MARY. Nave, chancel, and W tower with shingled broach spire. The nave is Norman, with Roman brick quoins and small original windows, one in the N, one in the S wall, also the remains of a S doorway – all with Roman brick dressings. Norman also the plain, broad chancel arch. The tower was added in the C13, also with much use of Roman brick. Lancet windows and W doorway with one renewed order of E.E. columns. Of the C13, but later, is the chancel, with restored lancet windows. The group of three at the E end is unusual in that they are stepped not only at the top but also at the foot. SEDILIA and PISCINA are original, but not specially ornate. C15 N porch of timber. – REREDOS. Of stone, fragmentary, at the N E end of the nave. What remains is part of the ribbed soffit of *c.*1500. – BENCHES. Fourteen in the nave, straight-topped ends with linenfold decoration. – CHEST. Dug-out, heavily iron-bound, C13 or C14, in the nave. – PAINTINGS. The most valuable thing in the church is its wall-paintings above the chancel arch. They date from *c.*1275 and were restored in 1936 by the late Professor Tristram. There are four tiers rising in size as the eye moves upwards. The lowest tier has small scenes, in the second one recognizes the Crowning with Thorns, the Mocking, the Scourging, Christ before Pilate, and the Carrying of the Cross. Above this the Last Supper and the Betrayal, and in the top tier the Entry into Jerusalem. The artistic quality is not high.

FARNHAM

ST MARY THE VIRGIN. 1859 by *Joseph Clarke*.

HASSOBURY. 1868 by the younger *Hardwick*. A large grey Tudor mansion with gables, asymmetrically composed.

(WALKERS MANOR HOUSE, ½ m. WSW. Built *c.*1560, but the W front faced in brick early in the C17. This has a gabled porch and gables at both ends. Inside much panelling etc. R.C.)

FAULKBOURNE

ST GERMANS. Nave, chancel, and belfry. Nave and chancel are Norman, as can be seen from N and S windows and also the group of w windows. The upper one of these is original, with the two circular openings to the l. and r. (cf. Copford). On the s side a good Norman doorway with one order of extremely odd columns, semi-polygonal, with capitals with roughly indicated crosses, and bases made of the same sort of capitals upside down. One early C19 brick porch and vestry. The belfry rests on two thin posts. – BENCHES, a few, c.1500, in the chancel. – HELM, late C16 or early C17, in the chancel. – MONUMENTS. (Mid C13 effigy of a knight. Purbeck marble with flat-topped helm, kite-shaped shield, and long surcoat. R.C.) – Josiah Bullock † 1783. With Corinthian pilasters, an open segmental pediment, and cherub's head at the foot. – Hannah Bullock † 1759. By *Peter Scheemakers*. Excellent seated female figure in front of a black obelisk. – John Bullock † 1809 and wife. In the Neo-Greek taste. Big standing female figure and portrait medallion. Unsigned.

49a FAULKBOURNE HALL. Faulkbourne Hall is the most impressive C15 brick mansion in the county, as early in its beginnings as the more regular and more famous Herstmonceaux, Tattershall, and Caister. Faulkbourne is not regular in its plan, and it is still in its appearance half castle and half mansion. There was on the site, the Royal Commission has shown, an early C15 timber-framed house. To this the brick parts were added from 1439, when Sir John Montgomery received licence to crenellate, to probably before 1489, when the new King, Henry VII, proposed to stop at Faulkbourne on one of his progresses. The entrance (w side) is in its r. half of the C19, and the l. half also is recased and provided with a C19 porch. But the symmetry of the two angle towers, rectangular but with canted outer corners, is original. Original also is at least one of the curious brick spires with their crockets on the two towers (the one on the N tower). Between the porch and the r. tower lies the original w front of the early C15 house which extended to the E from here and appears with a N-S cross-wing at the present E front, though the wall here is also encased in brick. But in the interior on this side, in the Kitchen, the w wall and part of the s wall still show their timber studding. When Sir John Montgomery encased the E wall he also added two bay windows. On the ground floor these still have their windows with four-centred heads. Their tops have battlements on trefoiled corbel friezes, and this motif occurs also in the other C15 parts of the façades. The main show-side is the N front. It has a big square tower with corbelled-out *tourelles* and a polygonal stair-turret, rather French- than English-looking. The spiral stair in the turret is also of brick with a rising brick tunnel-vault. The main room of the N range is at its W end. It is now the Dining Room but was no doubt originally the Hall. It has moulded ceiling beams and at the dais end a bay window with a very pretty brick lierne-vault. The Hall has always been one-storeyed. The upper floor of the bay has a second brick vault, and there is in addition an oriel window to its W. The C17 added a larger staircase on the side of the Hall of the early C15 house. It has turned balusters and may date from c.1640. Later still, dated on a rainwater head 1693, is the S extension of the E range with its sash-windows. In spite of this late date it still has two straight gables to the E. The STABLES are also of brick, in an C18 imitation Gothic, with heavy battlements. Several nice cottages in the village street.

FEERING

ALL SAINTS. In a pleasant village setting. All Perp. C14 N aisle and chancel, C15 W tower, early C16 nave and S porch. The latter are of brick and the most interesting feature of the church. Three- to five-light windows, a little brick and flint decoration, battlements on trefoiled corbel-friezes. Stepped battlements on the porch. Star-like tierceron-vault in the porch (cf. Great Coggeshall). Chancel and N aisle windows simply Dec. N arcade on square piers with four demi-shafts (cf. Witham), arch with two quadrant mouldings. – STAINED GLASS. Original C14 tabernacles in situ in a N window. – MONUMENT. Recess in the N wall, shafted and with ogee head.
FEERINGBURY, 1 m. NW. Large C15 house with later alterations and additions.
(HOUCHIN'S FARM,* 2 m. N. Three-storeyed timber-framed house of c.1600, with two overhangs, partly weatherboarded. One good fireplace inside. Barn of eleven bays with aisles. R.C.)
HOUSE next to the Sun Inn. In 1928 good late C16 wall paintings were discovered. They consist of foliage and flower scrolls on quite a big scale.

FELSTED

HOLY CROSS. A sizeable, prosperous town-church, excellently placed away from the main street and separated from it by a
* Parish of Great Coggeshall.

range of low houses with a gateway through. Unbuttressed
Norman w tower with later battlements and an c18 cupola.
w doorway of two orders of columns with defaced capitals,
zigzag decoration in the arches. The rest of the church exterior appears mostly c14 and is much renewed. Exceptions
are the c15 s porch and the s chancel chapel, which dates from
the middle of the c16 and, while the rest of the church is of
pebble-rubble, is faced with clunch ashlar. Inside, the building
history appears a little more complicated, as will be seen
directly one enters the church by the s doorway. The waterleaf capitals of this take one at once to the later c12, and to that
date also belongs the s arcade. It has short sturdy circular and
octagonal piers with capitals decorated with upright leaves.
The pointed arches are single-stepped with an odd soffit
decoration which recurs in the tower arch and the N arcade
(cf. Castle Hedingham). The tower arch is round, the N arcade
of octagonal piers with double-chamfered arches, c14 work.
Of the same century are the two-light clerestory windows. –
FONT. Early c14? Circular, with human heads connecting the
circular with an upper square part. – EASTER SEPULCHRE, in
the chancel, mid c14 and much restored. Recess with embattled top and a crocketed ogee arch; buttresses and finials.*
– POOR BOX. Iron-bound and studded. – PLATE. Large silver-
gilt Cup of 1641; Paten on foot of 1641; Paten on foot of 1700.
– MONUMENTS. Brasses to Christine Bray † 1420 and to a
Knight of about the same date, both with figures c.2 ft long,
and both on the chancel floor. – Richard, first Lord Rich
† 1568 and his son † 1581, erected probably only about 1620
and attributed convincingly by Mrs Esdaile to *Epiphanius
Evesham*. Lord Rich, great-grandson of a London mercer and
born in 1496 in the City of London, had risen, by means of
ability and absence of scruples, to be made Lord Chancellor in
1548. Big standing wall-monument with the figure of Lord
Rich comfortably reclining and looking back at his son, who is
kneeling on the ground by the side facing a prayer-desk
attached by a generous scroll to the monument. Behind the
figure two coats of arms and three reliefs of groups of standing
figures, with all the lyrical intensity of which Evesham was
capable. They represent Lord Rich with Fortitude and Justice, Lord Rich with Hope and Charity, and Lord Rich with

---

* Mr D. Morgan draws my attention to the fact that this is not an Easter
Sepulchre, but a tomb-chest, and that it previously stood at the E end of the s
aisle.

Truth (?) and Wisdom. One looks in vain for Lord Rich with Intolerance and *Occasio*. The monument is flanked by two tall bronze columns carrying a pediment.

The house through which the churchyard is connected with the main street at its main corner is the OLD SCHOOL HOUSE, a timber-framed and plastered house with an overhanging upper floor. Its neighbour is the former headmaster's house. Across the street stands, with its gable at the corner of the two streets, GEORGE BOOTE'S HOUSE of 1596 (see the inscription on the bressumer). Several enjoyable houses also to the s towards the MILL at Hartford End (mill house with hoist loft, weatherboarded, late C18, centre earlier, r. side Early Victorian) and along the main street to the E. Here first of all, at the corner of the street which branches off to the N, INGRAM'S, formerly called the New School House. It was the first extension of the old school and was built in 1800 by *John Johnson*.

Then at once the Victorian SCHOOL interferes. Its grim principal building fortunately lies back. It is a tall dark brick structure with a tower and a gable asymmetrically placed, with blue bricks to make the effect gloomier – the scholastic style of the High Victorians at its least attractive. The date is 1860–8, the architect *F. Chancellor*. The headmaster's house stands to the W. Further W the apsed chapel, less rugged in style, though also Gothic – also by *Chancellor*, 1873. To the E Grignon Hall, 1931 by *J. J. Chetwood* and *T. F. W. Grant*, light brick with Tudor windows but a hipped roof and a dainty lantern. S of Grignon Hall Elwyns, 1901 by *Sir Reginald Blomfield*. The Cricket Pavilion of the school is immediately next to Elwyns, one of the old timber-framed houses of Felsted. It faces one or two more of the best timber-framed houses in the town. W of the Pavilion the nice CONGREGATIONAL CHAPEL of three bays, and a group of ALMSHOUSES around a courtyard open to the street which date from 1878 and are again by *Chancellor*.

The village street continues to the E past several impressive farms, especially CHAFFIX and more at Bannister Green (OXNEY'S FARM, C15, with several original features). No more details of houses in the parish can here be mentioned. The Royal Commission lists 108.

(One farm is given special prominence by the Royal Commission: GATE HOUSE FARM on the road to Great Saling on the l. shortly before Stane Street is reached. It does not look interesting from outside, but has inside an extremely unusual roof construction of *c.*1400 which is explained and illustrated in the Royal Commission vol. II.)

(LEIGHS LODGE, 2 m. ESE. Barn, built in the C16, 159 ft long, of eleven bays, with an aisle and three porches on one side. R.C.)

(SPARLING'S FARM, 1½ m. NE. C15 farmhouse with its hall still open to the roof, tie-beam on arched braces, king-post and two-way struts. R.C.)

(BRIDGEHOUSE FARM, Thistley Green. C15 farmhouse with its hall still open to the roof. The construction was as at Sparling's Farm. The solar wing also remains, though extended later. R.C.)

FINCHINGFIELD

ST JOHN. Norman W tower, originally unbuttressed, though the one C19 diagonal buttress no doubt adds punch and the C18 cupola grace. Doorway of three orders of columns with scalloped capitals and decorated zigzag arches. Defaced heads at the top of the inner jamb like crockets. The tympanum has been removed. The tower arch towards the nave is low and completely plain. To its l. and r., inside the tower blank arcading continued along half the N and S sides of the tower. What was its purpose ? Was it connected with former altars ? The next period can only be discovered inside, the C13, to which the chancel arch, the N chancel arcade of two bays, and the S nave arcade of five bays belong (octagonal piers, double-chamfered arches). A little later, early C14, the more handsome N arcade with four major and four minor shafts, all with fillets, and complex arch mouldings. The W bay alone is different. It has a characteristically Perp pier, similar to that of the S chancel chapel. The window tracery is mostly of the same date, say the last third of the C14, and of interesting shapes. The cross of figures of eight especially which one meets so often in Essex C14 tracery is prominent. The chancel has, an unusual and successful feature, a clerestory. Its windows are straight-headed, of intersected pointed and cusped arches. Straight-headed also the side openings of the (C19) S porch. The nave clerestory is C15. It is like all the rest of pebble rubble, the typical material of this part of Essex. Flat-pitched chancel and nave roofs on stone corbels. – FONT. Octagonal with quatre-foils and shields. – SCREENS. The S aisle screen is the earlier, of the same date as the aisle; see the Dec details inside the

Early Perp panels. The rood screen is one of the most elaborate in Essex, with tall divisions with big crocketed ogee heads and much fine panel tracery between it and the straight top. – S DOOR. C14 with much tracery, also Christ crucified, a Pelican, a Dove, etc. – MONUMENTS. John Berners and wife † 1523, tomb-chest with Purbeck marble top and brass effigies. The tomb-chest decorated with the inescapable quatrefoils. – William Kempe † 1628 and wife, erected 1652. Tablet with inscription on an oval plate and handsome scrolls and flower bunches. – Thomas Marriott † 1766. Large monument with bust in front of a medallion. Signed by *W. Tyler.* – Anne Marriott, by *R. Westmacott,* 1811. With large Greek female figure and urn.

Finchingfield village is more often illustrated in journals and calendars than any other in Essex, and rightly so. It is the picture-book village of a completeness not often found. The church lies on a hill. Its little cupola on the square tower is an accent which is lovable and a little funny. The street runs down and bends towards a bridge and a duck pond, with a triangular green beyond. The houses along this are of all kinds of heights and styles and do not all stand on the same level. Architecturally the chief effect is HILL HOUSE with its five bargeboarded gables standing on an eminence on the NW and facing at an angle a memorable row which begins by the pond with a tall Georgian house of three bays; then follows a cottage with Gothick windows, another cottage with a late C16 chimneystack with octagonal shafts, and so on to a gabled cottage with exposed timbers, the School of 1856 (red brick with Gothick windows, a front as narrow as that of a Nonconformist chapel in a village) and the CONGREGATIONAL CHURCH – rendered, with a pediment and a Tuscan porch.

By the church, as an excellent beginning of the exploration of the village, the former GUILDHALL of *c.*1500, a long white timber-framed cottage with a gateway through from the churchyard to the street.

Leaving the village towards the N one finally finds a WINDMILL (post-mill) on the r. and a little later the ROUND HOUSE, a hexagonal cottage with thatched roof lying a little higher. It was built by the squire of Spains Hall in the late C18 as a model cottage.

SPAINS HALL, see p. 361.

ROMAN BUILDING, see Spains Hall.

FINGRINGHOE

ST ANDREW.* Visually quite exceptionally successful, owing to position, the view to the E, and the little pond with oak-trees below to the W, and also to upkeep. The merit is that of not having done too much. A slight impression of neglect can be an asset. The nave is Norman, see the quoins on the N side and one complete and one fragmentary window (discovered in 1928), all with much Roman brick. Tower, S aisle, and chancel C14. The tower has bands of stone and flint, flint and stone chequerwork at the base, added brick buttresses only below, and above a parapet but not battlements. Flint S porch with battlements of stone and flint chequer. Embattled S aisle. Large red, tiled roofs. The S porch has in its spandrels St George and the Dragon. White and plain interior. The S arcade is no more than a cutting of pointed arches through the Norman S wall. – FONT COVER. Tall, octagonal, of wood, much repaired. Buttresses with pinnacles at the angles. Plain panels between ending in traceried heads. Plain second stage. Top stage with openwork ogee ribs carrying a finial. – DOOR in the S doorway, traceried, C14, badly preserved. – PAINT-INGS. Unusually much still visible, even if only faintly. The most interesting remains are of a St Christopher above the N doorway; on the piers of the S arcade Virgin, St Michael and a seated Woman, Christ as Man of Sorrows. – MONUMENTS. Brass to John Alleyn, c.1600. – George Frere † 1655. Good frontal demi-figure, hand on a skull. In an oval niche framed by a wreath. Curly segmental pediment on top. No doubt the work of a good sculptor of the day.

FINGRINGHOE HALL. Brick front crowned by three big symmetrical shaped gables, that is probably mid C17. The front itself remodelled in the Early Georgian style with segment-headed windows and a doorway the Corinthian pilasters of which carry a frieze rising to a point in the centre, and a segmental pediment.

TIDE MILL, below the church by the water. It is now used as a store, but is one of the rare survivals in the county of mills which were driven by tidal water.

ROMAN PORT. Traces of a port probably established by the Roman invaders of A.D. 43 have been found.

FITZJOHN'S FARM see GREAT WALTHAM

* Or St Ouen, see G.M.Benton 1938.

FLEMING'S FARM see RUNWELL

FOBBING

ST MICHAEL. In the N wall one blocked Late Anglo-Saxon window visible from outside and inside. In the chancel N wall one small C13 lancet. The rest is C14 and C15. C15 the big W tower with higher SE stair-turret and diagonal buttresses – looking proudly across the marshes – C14 the S aisle, as wide as the nave and separated from it by an arcade with octagonal piers and double-chamfered arches. C14 also the chancel and S chancel chapel (modern arcade pier). The timber S porch is typical C15 Essex work. Original C15 roofs inside chancel and chancel chapel, nave and aisle. – FONT. C13, Purbeck marble, octagonal, with shallow blank trefoil-arched arcades; two panels to each side. – PULPIT, plain C18. – BENCHES in the S aisle, plain, c.1500. – IMAGE. Virgin and Child, headless, only about 10 in. high, C15? (S chapel, E wall). – PLATE. Cup of 1633. – MONUMENT. Inscription tablet of c.1340: 'Pur lamur Jesu Crist priez pur sa alme ke ci gist pater noster et ave Thomas de Crawedern fur apelle'.

Just NW of the church PROSBUS HALL, with chequered brick C18 front and older parts at the back.

Several handsome timber-framed and gabled houses further N, especially WHEELERS HOUSE and one with thatched roofs like big hats yet a little further N on the other side of the road.

FORD END

ST JOHN THE EVANGELIST. 1871 by *Chancellor*; chancel added 1893 (GR). Tower with spire with an oddly broken outline, at the E end of the S aisle. It is adorned by large figures of the Evangelists at the angles. S aisle covered by the same big roof as the nave. Low one-light S aisle windows. Polygonal apse. The S porch of an unusual timber construction, not following medieval precedent. The main uprights lean towards the centre and are in fact straight braces. The brickwork inside the church is exposed.

FORDHAM

ALL SAINTS. Mostly C14. The chancel comes first, with cusped windows of two lights under one pointed arch – an early C14 form, but dated here by the Royal Commission c.1330. W tower with diagonal buttresses, the W wall early in the C19 repaired in brick. N and S aisle arcades C14 with octagonal piers and double-chamfered arches. The outer walls of the aisles and their windows rebuilt c.1500 with regular bands of brick.

CONGREGATIONAL CHAPEL (formerly of the Countess of Huntingdon's Connexion). Three bays, weatherboarded. Said to have been built in 1789. The front however with a gabled porch and hood-moulded windows looks c.1840.

FORDHAM HALL, SW of the church. Timber-framed and plastered. Mostly C17. In the front a Late Georgian, generously glazed bow window, where one might expect a porch. Big C17 weatherboarded BARN, E of the house.

FORD PLACE see STIFFORD

FOULNESS

Foulness Island at the time of writing was a prohibited area. No personal report is possible.

ST MARY THE VIRGIN. 1850 by *William Hambley*. Tower with spire, nave with aisles, and chancel, in the E.E. style. The island had been a parish since 1550. – PLATE. Cup of 1612; Cup and Paten of 1712.

FOXEARTH

ST PETER AND ST PAUL. The main effect is Victorian (1885 by *J. Clarke*): externally the rather over-ornate W tower of 1862 with unusual bell-openings (fine tall cusped lancets in a row on each side), internally the decoration everywhere by wall paintings and under the tower even by mosaics. But the chancel is of c.1340 with a three-light E window with flowing tracery, and the N arcade may be of the same date: slim octagonal piers and double-chamfered arches. The N windows are Perp, the S windows renewed or new. – SCREEN. Only the dado with over-restored painted figures of saints is original. – STAINED GLASS. Mostly of c.1860 and good of its date.

FOXEARTH HALL. Late C15 timber-framed house. On the first floor the roof construction of the Hall which went through both the present storeys can still be seen, with tie-beams and king-posts.

VICARAGE, SW of the church. Seven-bay, two-storey brick

house of 1702 with doorway adorned by fluted pilasters and pediment.

FRATING

CHURCH (dedication unknown). Nave, chancel, and w tower. The nave has a Norman window with Roman brick surround on the s side, and a Dec window which is repeated similarly on the N side. The chancel windows are of c.1300. Plain timber s porch. w tower with thin diagonal buttresses, a three-light w window, and tall brick and flint panelling in the battlements. Pyramid roof. Inside, an early C16 recess in the chancel. The depressed pointed arch is adorned with fleurons, the spandrels with big leaves. – PLATE. Cup of 1584.

FREMNELLS see DOWNHAM

FRINTON-ON-SEA

Developed as a seaside resort by Sir Richard P. Cooker about 1890–1900. Of Frinton village the only relic is the old village church.

OLD ST MARY. Nave with chancel of 1879 and bellcote. s porch brick, plain, early C16. – STAINED GLASS. In the E window four panels of *Morris* glass, designed by *Burne-Jones* and obviously still in the early style of the firm, before the peacock blues and greens began to dominate colour schemes. The window is said to come from Melchet Abbey, but was bought at a London sale by the donor to the church.

NEW ST MARY, Old Road. 1928–9 by *Sir Charles Nicholson*. Perp exterior, without tower. Flint and bands of brick. The aisle flat-roofed and embattled. Bellcote over the porch, w of the s aisle. Inside not at all Perp. Italian cruciform piers with round arches, a Renaissance effect. Prettily painted ceilings, as usual in Nicholson's churches.

FREE CHURCH, Connaught Avenue. Red brick, with a NW tower crowned by a Byzantine stone dome. 1912 by *W. Hayne*. Porch and clock tower 1935.

THE HOMESTEAD, Second Avenue, corner of Holland Road. The most remarkable of the villas of Frinton. 1905 by *Voysey*. In his unmistakable, homely, and sensitively proportioned and detailed style. The house should be looked at from the corner so that the difference of levels comes out.

(At the time of writing the first tower-block development is taking place.)

FRYERNING

11a ST MARY. Small, with early C16 brick tower, with blue brick
diapering, stepped battlements on a pointed-arched corbel
frieze, and brick pinnacles. Nave of coursed puddingstone and
Roman bricks, Early Norman, with four original windows and
plain N and S doorways. – FONT. With big square bowl decorated with large scrolls, leaves, etc.; c.1200. – STAINED GLASS.
E window by *Willement*, in the Gothic style, but not the Pugin
variety. – PLATE. Cup and Cover of 1700; Flagon and Almsdish of 1716. – BRASS in the vestry. Palimpsest. Woman of
c.1460 on one side, Mary Gedge, Elizabethan period, on the
other.

THE HYDE, see Ingatestone.

WINDMILL, ¼ m. N of the church. Post-mill in a fair condition.

FRYERNS see BASILDON

FYFIELD

ST NICHOLAS. An interesting but not an attractive exterior.
Norman nave and crossing tower, the tower partly rebuilt in
brick in the C19. Weatherboarded top with short octagonal
spire. N arcade of the C13 with circular piers and double-
chamfered arches. The capitals are neither round nor square.
S arcade, later C13, with octagonal piers and double-hollow-
chamfered arches. The chancel belongs to the Dec style of the
early C14. The E window, though externally new, has an inner
surround with alternating diaper and fleuron motifs. Hood-
mould on head-stops. SEDILIA with polygonal Purbeck marble
shafts between the seats, cusped arches, and big, rather bad
head-stops. Between two of the arches the three balls, the sym-
bol of St Nicholas. E of the sedilia, also with cusped arches,
not a double piscina, but a PISCINA and a CREDENCE. The
chancel arch is C19, the W arch of the crossing tower late C14.
Of the windows the blocked E window of the N aisle deserves
notice, because of the pretty diagonally placed niche to its l.:
C15 work. – FONT. Square, of Purbeck marble, late C12, with
the familiar motif of a row of (six) shallow blank round-headed
arches on two sides, and on the two others a row of three
fleurs-de-lis. – PLATE. Cup and Paten on foot of 1634; large
Cup of 1699.

(FYFIELD HALL. One octagonal oak pier with pyramidal stops
is a reminder of the C14 aisled hall which Fyfield Hall once
possessed. In 1954 it was discovered that most of the timbers

of the N aisle are in position, although concealed. V.C.H., vol. IV.*)

THE GABLES see HORNDON-ON-THE-HILL

GALLEYWOOD COMMON
nr Chelmsford

ST MICHAEL AND ALL ANGELS. 1873 by *St Aubyn* (GR). In the Dec style, with a stone spire. (Above the altar, tile and mosaic decoration by *Burrow*, 1874.)

GANTS HILL see ILFORD

GATWICK HOUSE see BILLERICAY

GESTINGTHORPE

ST MARY. The church is small in comparison with the tower. This was added about 1498 (when 40s. was bequeathed by William Carter to the building of the tower) to a church partly Norman, partly C14, and partly C15. The chancel has a blocked C13 N window; the other windows are early C14. The five-light E window is specially interesting. The tracery is of a rare (early) variety of reticulation, where the net pattern is arrived at by simply placing arches on top of the apexes of other arches. The SEDILIA inside the chancel have simple ogee arches. The S arcade of the nave was rebuilt in the C19. The W tower is of brick with blue brick diapering. It has angle buttresses, stepped battlements, and short pinnacles. The W doorway and the W window are also of brick. The bell-openings are of three lights with one transom and have depressed pointed heads with intersecting tracery. About the time when the tower was built, the nave received a roof uncommonly splendid for Essex. It is of the double-hammerbeam type of which there are only a few examples in the county. – FONT. Octagonal, Perp, with traceried stem and a bowl decorated by shields and the symbols of the four Evangelists. – SCREEN. With one-light

29

* Mr J. T. Smith has recently drawn attention to the fact that the tie-beam to the open truss is straight and not cambered. This, he says, is a late C13 rather than a C14 feature, and so is the system of straight braces to the open truss. In his opinion Fyfield as built was a hall and nothing more: no solar or buttery wings of even the most rudimentary sort. Mr Smith also mentions the roof at LAMPETTS, which is of the C14 with trussed rafters, four-way braces, and crown-post. The tie-beam is cambered.

divisions. The heads are quite richly decorated: crocketed ogee arches and panel tracery above them. – STAINED GLASS. Seated Virgin in a N window, much restored. – MONUMENT. John Sparrow † 1626, alabaster, with small kneeling figure.

OVER HALL. Chiefly of 1735. The front has seven bays and two storeys with a three-storeyed three-bay centre with pediment. Pedimented doorcase on Ionic demi-columns. At the far end of the Entrance Hall a two-storeyed screen with two Tuscan columns below and two plain piers above. It screens the staircase, which has very finely twisted balusters. But the showpiece of the house is the Drawing Room, splendidly decorated about 1740 with stucco ceiling, an extremely ornate fireplace, and pedimented door surrounds. Rocaille as well as naturalistic flower decoration. In other rooms early C17 panelling and also a carved overmantel (Dining Room).

GHYLLGROVE see BASILDON

GIFFORD'S FARM see RUNWELL

GILSTEAD HALL see SOUTH WEALD

GLAZENWOOD see BRADWELL-JUXTA-COGGESHALL

GOLDHANGER

ST PETER. The N side of the church shows its C11 origin: one chancel window, the nave E angle, and one nave window. Much re-use of Roman brick. C14 S aisle mostly of flint, but also incorporating Roman bricks. C15 W tower with diagonal buttresses and some flint and stone decoration. The S arcade inside is of the C19. – STAINED GLASS. S chapel S and E windows of 1858, typical of their date. – MONUMENT. Tomb-chest with black cover-plate, one brass to a woman and indents of other brasses. The monument was to Thomas Heigham † 1531.

GOOD EASTER

ST ANDREW. Nave and chancel; belfry with vertical weatherboarding and a tall thin shingled spire. The belfry rests on four posts with arched braces to the E and W as well as the N and S. The nave is of the C13, the chancel also, but a little later. The evidence is not easily understood. Early C13 W window, original internally. In the E wall two blank half arches of the same date. They must at first, in their complete form, have flanked a narrower, probably Norman chancel. Then the chancel was rebuilt and widened. That also, on the evidence of the SEDILIA and PISCINA, cannot have been later than c.1240. The piscina has typical shafts, the sedilia and some blank wall arcading on the N side of the chancel have an odd alternation of arches continued below without any capitals, and arches carried on capitals ending in (Cistercian) corbels instead of shafts. The S arcade is a little later, c.1300 or so. One circular and one octagonal shaft, moulded capitals and only slightly double-chamfered arches. The westernmost pier is the same but the arches are properly double-chamfered – perhaps a later repair. – STAINED GLASS. Bits of the C14 and C15 in two S aisle windows. – HELM. Probably late C16; chancel N wall. – BRASS of 1610.

GOSFIELD

ST KATHARINE. Entirely of the C15 and C16. The most interesting parts are the N chancel chapel and the S side of the chancel with large very domestic-looking Perp windows, straight-headed, of four lights with a transom and arched heads to all lights. These parts are as late as c.1560. The arcade to the N chapel has a pier with a lozenge-shaped chamfered section and four-centred arches.* Of the C15 the W tower with diagonal buttresses and a large transomed W window, and the chancel E window of four lights with an embattled transom and much panel tracery. In 1735–6 a remarkable addition was made, a square brick room W of the N chapel with a Venetian window to the W. It is a squire's pew and at the same time a family chapel. The squire's family, of the name of Knight, sat somewhat elevated and could look at the altar from behind a velvet-covered parapet. And the congregation could see, behind the arch of this theatre-box, against the N wall of the room, the large and magnificent MONUMENT to John Knight † 1733 and his wife †1756. It is by *Rysbrack* (Mrs Webb quotes his sale catalogue and suggests that it may have been begun by *Guelfi*). T. K. Cromwell in 1818 wrote that the monument was made by Scheemakers under the direction of Pope. The two

* The outside E wall has part of a diapered band of brick and plaster, C16, along the plinth. Above the window, C16 plasterwork, black and yellow: large central latticed device with abutting stepped lozenges in squares. The position of this decoration suggests that the chapel roof was subsequently raised. Probably c.1660–70.

white marble figures are seated, with an urn between them. The sculptural quality is high. The chapel has a handsome plaster ceiling too. In the N chapel various earlier monuments. Large tomb-chests of Purbeck marble with black marble tops to Sir Hugh Rich † 1554 and Sir John Wentworth † 1567. The one has on the chest elaborate quatrefoil, etc. panels, the other blank arcading – all the motifs still entirely Gothic. A third and earlier tomb-chest (with plain quatrefoil decoration) in a recess in the S wall of the chancel. – Thomas Rolf, 1440; in the robes of a Sergeant-at-Law. Brass on tomb-chest with quatrefoil panels. – BENCH ENDS in the chancel, with poppy-heads, probably late C16. – PANELLING with Early Renaissance decoration of a style frequently found in houses, c.1550, along the back of the chancel seats. – PLATE. An unusually fine set; all gilt. Elaborately engraved Cup of 1604; Cover with steeple top of 1604; large chased Cup of 1610; Cover with steeple top of 1613 (?); engraved Paten on foot of 1704; large Flagon of 1704.

A number of nice houses along the village street. Amongst these also the neat half-timbered houses put up by Mr S. Courtauld about 1855–60, including a village hall.

GOSFIELD HALL. The mansion started as a quadrangular design of the mid C16. In its substance this is still there, although three of the four fronts have been rebuilt or remodelled and the fourth has been much restored (by Mr S. Courtauld, who owned the house from 1854 to 1881). Yet the W front remains an exceedingly impressive Tudor façade, in spite of the C19 projections at the ends. The material is red brick with occasional blue diapering. The Tudor design was completely symmetrical, with a central entrance with four-centred arch, a six-light window with one transom above (all lights arched – just as in Gosfield church), a gable above, and a later cupola. To the l. and r. of this gable are chimneystacks with polygonal shafts. Then follow recessed bays also with six-light windows, and then again gabled bays with the same windows. Only the upper storey has these large windows. Below, the walls are closed – still with a view, it appears, to security. Behind the (renewed) upper windows lies the panelled Long Gallery. The E front was remodelled by John Knight shortly after he came into possession in 1715. It has much blue brickwork with the red and two angle projections of three bays width and three bays depth. The centre between them is of eleven bays with a splendid big doorway (segmental pediment on fluted pilasters against a rusticated background; the frieze above the pilasters rising to a point in the middle). The windows are segment-headed. The Tudorized upper storey is said to be the work of Earl Nugent who died in 1788, but it looks later. Earl Nugent remodelled the s front of seventeen bays* in a plain classical style and the N front with a seven-bay raised centre embellished by giant Corinthian pilasters. Towards the courtyard the W and N sides still have a Tudor appearance. Inside, some panelling and C17 fireplaces, but nothing outstanding. The splendid lake, nearly a mile long, was made by Earl Nugent.

GRANGE FARM see LITTLE COGGESHALL

GRANGE FARM see RADWINTER

GRAYS THURROCK (or GRAYS)

The town and the old village are on separate sites, the HIGH STREET and church to the s of the railway extending in a N–S direction, the new town to the N along the E–W highway.

ST PETER AND ST PAUL. The church is of 1846, but includes some oddly disjointed parts of a much earlier time: crossing of the C12 with almost entirely rebuilt round W and E arches; C13 N transeptal tower with double-chamfered arch and similar blank N and E arches; lancet windows; s transept shorter, with work of c.1300 towards the crossing. The s doorway may also be C13. – FONT. Perp, octagonal, with quatrefoil panels. – SCREEN. Perp, plain. – CHAIRS. Two good later C17 arm-chairs. – TILES. Some medieval tiles in the vestry. – BRASS to a woman and her family, c.1510.

GREAT BADDOW

ST MARY THE VIRGIN. A splendid exterior, thanks chiefly to the Early Tudor brick clerestory with its stepped battlements on a trefoiled corbel frieze and its brick pinnacles. The chancel is a little lower and has an odd and rather daring large C19 dormer window with a straight brick gable. W tower and aisles C14, the tower with angle buttresses only at the foot, battle-ments, and a tall leaded spire, the aisles with Dec windows (mostly renewed). s doorway also C14, see the keeled columns and keeled roll-moulding. Battlements were added in brick at

---

* Dr Guy Barr tells me that Sir Thomas Millington, c.1700, should be credited with the reconstruction of the s range. His crest is over the door of the court-yard.

the time when the clerestory was built. Addition also of the s and N chancel chapels with brick responds. The aisle arcades are of three bays and give evidence of an earlier church. They are E.E. The N arcade came first: one circular pier, the others octagonal. W respond on a head-corbel. Arches only slightly double-chamfered. The s arcade has all circular piers and normal double-chamfered arches. – PULPIT. The best early C17 pulpit in the county. Dated 1639, but in style entirely Jacobean. Complete with a big tester on a long narrow back panel up the wall. The motif of the panels of the pulpit itself is little aedicules on columns. In the centres false perspectives. Strapwork along the sides of the back panels and on top of the tester. – PLATE. Flagon of 1627; Almsdish of 1675. – MONUMENTS. Brass of Jane Lewkenor † 1614 (the figure nearly 3 ft long). – Monument to the Gwyn sisters, erected 1753. By *Sir Henry Cheere*. Big, with the usual grey obelisk, a cherub in front of it, leaning on a draped oval medallion with the portraits of the two sisters. Rocaille and foliage at the foot.

Great Baddow must already in Georgian days have been a village where wealthy Chelmsforders built houses for themselves. There are a surprising number of good Georgian brick houses about, not sufficiently recorded, e.g. the VICARAGE, s of the church, *c.*1725, five bays, two storeys, with curved parapet and Roman Doric porch, PITT PLACE, lying at the E entry to the village, which has a parapet and an Ionic porch, and THE VINEYARDS, built in 1740, altered in the 1760s and again in 1907 (by *A. Mitchell*). The Vineyards has a five-bay two-storey front and a pretty late C18 plaster ceiling in the principal bedroom. W of The Vineyards an Early Georgian house of five bays and two storeys, with segment-headed windows, giant pilasters, and parapets.

(MARCONI LABORATORY. By *Taylor & Collister*, 1957–8.)

GREAT BARDFIELD

ST MARY THE VIRGIN. Early C14 W tower without buttresses. Small lancet windows and a small, pretty, recessed lead spire of the C18. The rest is all later C14, with the surprising feature of large, straight-headed three-light windows with curiously High Gothic tracery, i.e. no specifically Dec or Perp motifs, but a development from the classic moment of Geometrical tracery. Such windows fill the walls of the N and s aisles and also appear in the chancel (many are renewed). The s porch has in addition very pretty side openings on the E side. They look earlier than the larger windows, and it is quite possible that the porch as well as the s aisle and chancel masonry are earlier than the straight-headed windows. The openings in the porch consist of one two-light Dec window flanked by small quatrefoil windows (cf. Stebbing). Four-bay arcades inside with late C14 piers of four polygonal shafts connected by deep hollows with four slim circular shafts in the diagonals. Moulded arches; head-label-stops. Flat-pitched roofs on stone corbels in nave and aisles. Also late C14 is the most prominent and famous feature of the church, the stone SCREEN between nave and chancel. It is tripartite and, with its openings and tracery, fills the chancel arch completely. The idea came to Great Bardfield from Stebbing, but how it came to Stebbing we do not know. That Bardfield is later than Stebbing is obvious. Both, it is true, share the luxuriance of design, the rich cusping and crocketing and the delight in ogee arches. But at Bardfield the two main dividing shafts or mullions run straight up into the arch, an unmistakable sign of the Perp style. Also the arch responds are decidedly first half of the century at Stebbing, second half of the century at Bardfield. The figures of the rood above the main central ogee arch are a reconstruction of 1892 and due to *Bodley*. – s DOOR. Late C14, with much tracery. – ORGAN CASE. Said to be by *Pugin*. – Two HELMS. Early C17. – STAINED GLASS. Many late C14 fragments in the N aisle windows, including complete figures. – MONUMENT. Low Purbeck tomb-chest with frieze of small quatrefoils. On it brass to the wife of William Bendlowes † 1584. The tomb-chest is no doubt older. It also served as SEDILIA.

In the picture of Great Bardfield the church has no part. It lies away at the SE end close to the timber-framed and plastered HALL (c.1600) to its S. s of the Hall a square brick dovecote with pyramid roof and a big weatherboarded C17 barn. A separate picture also the WINDMILL, a tower-mill of brick, by the Shalford road, an excellent first accent on approaching the village from that side.

The centre of the village was once no doubt a triangular Green. It is now built up along its sides, though the FRIENDS' MEETING HOUSE of 1804 keeps much of the inner space green with its humble and secluded graveyard. The principal houses of Great Bardfield are along the High Street from the triangle to the SE. The best stretch is from the police station onwards, chiefly a nice five-bay Georgian brick house with chequer brickwork and then several half-timbered cottages.

Opposite is the funny TOWN HALL of 1859, looking exactly like a Nonconformist chapel, but placed back behind four pollarded lime trees, rather like in a French town. The end of this stretch of houses is PLACE HOUSE on the other side, which combines c16 exposed timbers with brick infilling (a date on the carved bracket, perhaps 1564) and a brick window, with a Georgian doorway with Roman Doric half-columns. To its SE a small outbuilding also with a c16 brick window.

GREAT LODGE, 1½ m. SE. Early C17. A large fragment of a mansion. At the time when the Royal Commission described it, it still had a length of 225 ft, although it can hardly have been more than the outbuildings of the house proper. Recently the centre of the long range has been pulled down. However, several original brick windows and the two barns with their original timberwork remain.

GREAT BENTLEY

ST MARY THE VIRGIN. Nave, chancel, and W tower. The N side shows clearly that nave and chancel are Norman. The puddingstone is laid diagonally and bedded in excessive amounts of mortar. N doorway with responds with a scroll each. Arch extrados with trellis decoration. S doorway with one order of slightly decorated scalloped capitals, gabled lintel with two tiers of rosettes, and voussoirs with zigzag. The end of the chancel is C19, but has two charming early C14 niches inside with rosettes in the jambs, ogee tops, and leaf sprigs in the spandrels. W tower later C14, with diagonal buttresses, W doorway with fleurons, three-light W window, later battlements. – FONT. Octagonal, with trefoils and shields; simple. – TILES. Nine tiles of c.1300 in front of the altar; red, with pattern including a stag and a greyhound. – MONUMENT. P. Thompson † 1865, by *Sanders* of Euston Road, still in the traditions of 1800.

GREEN. The village green of Great Bentley is the largest in Essex, so large that it is almost a common. Whatever houses border on it seem small, seen across the green, and there are in any case hardly any larger than cottages. One tongue reaches into the green, and two islands are in it, one with a white Early Victorian villa and the dark trees of its garden, the other with the red brick METHODIST CHAPEL of 1843 (with Gothic windows) and other later red brick buildings. The best houses are on the SW side, towards the church.

GREAT BRAXTED

ALL SAINTS. A picturesque setting of the first order, with the large serpentine lake and the generous trees of the grounds of Braxted Park as a background to the little church, which is itself also picturesque.* The best view is from the w, with the C13 tower with w buttresses and a bellcote of 1883 (?), behind which appears the timber belfry stage of the tower with two-light windows. Were the recent additions designed by the Rev. *E. Geldart*, rector of Little Braxted? Of the C13 a s and a N lancet and the tower arch towards the nave without any break between jambs and voussoirs. The rest of the church principally Norman, see one N window of the nave (widened) and one of the chancel. The chancel was originally apsed. Its present E end is C13 and has lancet windows, at the E end a group of three single ones stepped. The s porch is C15 with a timber roof on carved corbels. – PANELLING. In the chancel, early C17, not originally in the church. – STAINED GLASS. Window of N transept above the Du Cane vault, 1844 by *Warrington*. – PLATE. Cup of 1562; Paten also Elizabethan; Almsdish of 1646; Flagon of 1660; Paten of 1711. – MONUMENT. Robert Aylett † 1654. Inscription tablet, and l. and r. of it two tablets with shields and two roundels with skulls, bones, and a shovel (under the tower).

BRAXTED PARK. The dates are not clear. The house was bought by the Du Cane family and rebuilt on a different site. The first part (mid-Georgian?) seems to be the NW wing with a centre bay window and three bays on each side of it. Some time later, but still Georgian, the addition of the rest, which made the earlier house one wing of the later. The completed mansion was of thirteen bays width on the N side with a seven-bay centre on the s side and two-bay wings projecting five bays forward. All very plain, red brick, without any decoration. The entrance faces an avenue of eight lines of elm trees, on the other side a lake of nearly fifteen acres, exceedingly beautifully contrived.‡

* The materials of the church are septaria, flint, freestone, Roman bricks, and clunch.

‡ Mr W. A. Gimson in *Great Braxted*, 1958, says the original house was *c*.1670. Additions were made in 1745, and in 1834 the house was finally built in its present form. Mr John Harris tells me that there is documentary evidence to suggest that the house was re-designed in 1752–5 by *Sir Robert Taylor*, and Miss Nancy Briggs draws my attention to alterations of 1804–6 to designs by *Johnson*.

GREAT BROMLEY

St George. A fine sight, proud and compact; entirely in the East Anglian style. Big w tower, tall nave with tall clerestory of closely set windows, short chancel. The w tower is the most spectacular piece. It starts at the base with a quatrefoil frieze. The buttresses are clasping but continue higher up as a combination of diagonal and angle buttresses. w doorway with fleurons in the jamb and arch mouldings, hood-mould on a griffin and an angel. Five-light w window with panel tracery, three-light bell-openings with one transom. Stepped battlements and crocketed pinnacles. The s porch is all flushwork-panelled. It has a parapet instead of the more usual battlements. Niche above the doorway, St George and the dragon in the spandrels, standing figures as stops – one now missing – and three-light side openings. The s doorway has fleurons in one order and a foliage trail in the other, both in jambs and voussoirs. Above two re-set spandrel figures: Adam and Eve. The s chapel is also singled out as something special – by flushwork panelling at the base. Three-light windows in the aisles, with Perp panel tracery, the patterns different on the s and n sides.* Two-light windows with one transom in the chancel (the e window is c19). The clerestory windows of two lights are oddly not in line with the arcades below. There are seven windows to three bays. The s arcade is c14, the n arcade c15. Both have octagonal piers, but the proportions differ characteristically. The s piers have capitals generously decorated with leaves. The westernmost instead uses figures of angels, lions, a head with tongue out, and a dragon and a frog biting him. The nave is covered by one of the most magnificent roofs of Essex, a double-hammerbeam (cf. Castle Hedingham, Gestingthorpe). – w and n doors. Both elaborately traceried; c.1500. – brass. William Bischopton † 1432, figure of a priest, about 3 ft long, under an arch and a gable with concave sides, crocketed and originally pinnacled.

GREAT BURSTEAD

St Mary Magdalen. Low c14 w tower with angle buttresses and tall timber spire. Nave and chancel without structural division, and s aisle with separate pitched roof. The nave is Norman, as witnessed by one small window on the n side. The

* n doorway minor, yet with three orders of fleurons in jambs and voussoirs.

rest C14–15. N doorway with head corbels and angels in the spandrels; N porch of heavy timber. Inside, the arcade to the S aisle has octagonal piers and double-chamfered arches. There is also an early C16 S chancel chapel, separated from the chancel by a two-bay arcade with a composite pier and hollow-chamfered arches. – REREDOS with Corinthian pilasters and a broad segmental pediment, now at the W end. From St Christopher le Stocks in the City of London. – COMMUNION RAIL, late C18, also said to come from a City church. – BENCHES, S aisle, C15. – CHEST. Dug-out type, bound with iron, C12–13. – MONUMENT. James Fishpoole † 1767, graceful tablet of various marbles, with obelisk and urn.

BARROWS. In Norsey Wood, 1 m. NW of Billericay church, are two barrows.

GREAT CANFIELD

ST MARY. Nave and chancel and belfry with recessed shingled spire. This is of the C15, as is the embattled stone S porch. Otherwise the church is essentially Norman. Norman nave and chancel N and S windows, as in many village churches. In addition a plain N doorway with columns with carved zigzag pattern and a more ornate S doorway with ornamented capitals (the l. one with a bearded face and two birds pecking at it), a tympanum with flat concentric zigzag decoration probably meaning the Sun, roll-mouldings, and a billet-moulding. The remarkable feature of the church is the Norman chancel arch (one order of columns with scalloped capitals and arch with an outer billet-moulding*) behind which, at the E end of the straight-headed chancel, appear three round arches. Those to the l. and r. contain small windows, that in the middle must always have been connected with some form of reredos. It now enshrines a WALL PAINTING of the Virgin and Child seated [27] which is one of the best C13 representations of the subject in the whole country, full of tenderness. It is drawn in red, with some yellow. Other colours have disappeared. The ornamental borders and other decoration around, also in the adjoining windows, is mostly of the stiff-leaf type. The date must be c.1250 (cf. the Matthew Paris manuscripts). – PLATE. Cup and Paten of 1577; Set of 1681. – MONUMENTS. Brass to John Wyseman and wife † 1558, both figures kneeling, and children behind (chancel, floor). – Brass to Thomas Fytche, wife † 1588, and children (chancel, floor). – Monument to Sir William

* The abacus of the S respond is a Saxon mid C11 grave slab.

Wyseman † 1684 and wife with demi-figures holding hands, below a segmental pediment. Good. – Also Floor Slab to Lady Wiseman in the chancel floor. Black marble with no words but Anne/Lady Wiseman/1662.

CASTLE. Of the motte-and-bailey type. It lies to the SE of the church. The mount is 45 ft high and at the foot 275 ft across. The bailey can be seen S of the mount, and an outer bailey S to SW of the church.

GREAT CHALVEDON HALL see BASILDON

GREAT CHESTERFORD

ALL SAINTS. W tower of the C15, rebuilt in 1792, altered in 1842. The W parts of nave and aisles also C15. The whole church is over-restored. Material: flint-rubble. In the chancel on the N side one original lancet, proof of a C13 date. Arcades with circular piers, also originally probably of the C13; but re-cut. Indications of former transepts. – BRASS. Woman, early C16, S chapel floor. – Baby in swaddling clothes (John Howard † 1600, aged 12 days), under arch into S chapel.

ROMAN TOWN. The site lies in the fields NW of the modern village, much of which lies outside its area. Following on an earlier Belgic settlement, the first Roman work on the site was a permanent fort established in the mid C1. The dimensions of this fort have not been determined. The walls of the later town were still visible in the C18 but were subsequently obliterated by quarrying for road-making material. The walled town was of roughly oval plan, 36¼ acres in area, and may be dated to the C4. It was strengthened by an external ditch which is clearly visible on aerial photographs but difficult to detect from the gound. Most of the internal buildings appear to have been of timber, but in the N part of the town the foundations of two stone-built houses were found.

GREAT CLACTON

ST JOHN THE BAPTIST. A Norman church and quite remark-able for a village, though badly ill-treated by *Hakewill* in 1865. Due to him the E front, even more painful inside than outside. Due to him also all the window detail. The Norman church must always have been very impressive in size, tall and wide, as the proportions of the chancel arch prove. The broad flat outer buttresses are also remarkable. Do they indicate an original intention to vault (cf. Copford)? The windows too seem to be correct, at least in their unusual size. s doorway with two orders of columns and two roll-mouldings in the arch; all renewed. N doorway of similar design, but two of the columns decorated with carved diaper (or star) and spiral motifs. The chancel was rebuilt in the C14, the w tower in the C15, replacing, it seems, a belfry, the tie-beams of which were kept. The w tower has angle buttresses and a three-light w window. It was not completed, and later a weatherboarded upper storey was added. On this, thin early C19 pierced parapet with battlements and a pyramid roof. – FONT. Octagonal, with three seated figures and two angels holding shields; defaced; C15.

Nice village street close to the church, with the MANSION HOUSE, red brick, Georgian, the QUEEN'S HEAD with a generous bow window, some cottages, and further s the SHIP INN, a C16 house with exposed timbers.

GREAT CODHAM HALL see WETHERSFIELD

GREAT COGGESHALL

ST PETER-AD-VINCULA. A large church (c.125 ft long) built to one plan in the C15: w tower, nave and wide aisles, chancel and equally wide chancel chapels. The chancel does not project at the E end; so the church is, except for the tower, just a parallelogram. There is however a chancel arch to separate nave from chancel, and there are short solid walls projecting from the E end to separate altar spaces from each other. Nave and tower are in ruins, due to the Second World War.* w tower with diagonal buttresses and battlements. The rest of the church also embattled, including the two-storeyed s porch. Aisle walls flint-rubble, E parts ashlar-faced. On entering the church from the s the tierceron-vault of the porch with its bosses still exists. The nave and chancel N and s arcades are of tall slender piers with four attached shafts carrying capitals and four thin polygonal diagonal shafts with concave sides and running on into the arches without capitals. Four-centred arches. Clerestory windows of three lights. Aisle windows large and also of three lights. Renewed E window of seven lights, E windows of the chancel chapels of four lights – all with Perp panel tracery. At the E end a frieze of shields at the base and

* Now rebuilt.

below the E window a cusped recess. – MONUMENTS. Brasses
of John Paycocke † 1533 and wife with indent of a brass of the
Virgin above; in the floor of the N (Paycocke) Chapel. In the
same chapel Thomas Paycocke † 1580; two women of c.1480. –
In the s chapel Mary Honywood † 1620, monument with kneeling figure. From Markshall, transferred to Coggeshall at the
demolition of Markshall church. The inscription says that Mrs
Honywood left 367 children, grandchildren, great-grand-
children, and great-great-grandchildren.

The plan of the little town is at first very simple. It lies along the
Braintree–Colchester road with Bridge Street coming in more
or less at r. angles from the bridge and Little Coggeshall and
Church Street leading off at an angle towards the church. In
fact the main crossing seems ingeniously deflected. Bridge
Street is not continued the other side towards the church.
There is a break here – good for the eye and good for traffic –
and the development of the town other than the arterial ribbon
starts a little further w. It takes the form first of a little triangular market, carefully kept away from the through-road
and acting as a collecting point towards which Stoneham Street
and Church Street converge. The plan is really the main thing
about Coggeshall. The houses themselves are of little interest –
except for one.

46a PAYCOCKE'S HOUSE is in West Street. It was built by the chief
clothier of the town, Thomas Paycocke, about 1500 and is one
of the most attractive half-timbered houses of England, regard-
less of the fact that much in its façade is restored. It is a façade
right along the street and consists of five bays. The timber
studs are narrowly placed and have brick infillings which are
not original. The façade starts on the l. with a carriageway
decorated by two little figures l. and r. Then there is a doorway
and then the first of two oriel windows, externally renewed
but apparantly correctly. The oriels are of five lights and are
followed by a three-light window. All have transoms. There
are two more doorways, the r. one with a door with linenfold
panelling, not in its original position. The upper floor hangs
over with a richly carved bressumer. In the carved frieze are
Paycocke's initials. The upper floor has five not quite evenly
spaced oriels, some of five, some of four lights. They do not
exactly correspond to the oriels below. Inside there are several
rooms with moulded and carved beams, and several original
fireplaces.

West Street is continued in EAST STREET, without much of

interest. Yet the Royal Commission lists twenty-nine houses here, and on one has twenty-two lines of description. A house not mentioned by the Commission should perhaps have a word here, CROMWELL LODGE, because its very good, Baroque pargeting motifs date from 1902. Pargeting is an art which kept traditions alive long, and one has to be careful not to be deceived. Of MARKET HILL the chief attraction is its shape. In a strategic position the small polygonal CLOCK TOWER with cupola. Its date is 1887. To the l. in STONEHAM STREET the CONGREGATIONAL CHAPEL of 1865, still of a clumsy Late Neo-Classical, four bays with four-bay pediment and a Tuscan porch. ROYAL OAK COTTAGE has a projecting two-storeyed porch and an original chimneystack of the C17. More in CHURCH STREET. Near the beginning a photographer's and a baker's shop face each other, the one mid C16 with exposed timber-framing and a gable, the other blue bricks with red trim, early C18. Then for a while nothing, until the CONSERVATIVE CLUB is reached (C17, with overhang, but much altered). Past Albert Place on the r. two houses with carved bressumers, one early C16, the other with Renaissance motifs, dated 1565. Opposite a whole row of timber-framed houses. Then again on the other side a five-bay Georgian brick house and a three-bay one with a Tuscan doorway and a belvedere on the Early Victorian roof. At the end just before reaching the church, at the very corner the WOOLPACK INN, an exceedingly picturesque house with exposed timber, two gables at different levels and between them the head of a former ground-floor oriel window like those at Paycocke's and a small oriel above. Interesting interior features, e.g. the screens and a king-post roof-truss. There were in fact halls in two storeys from the beginning.

HOUCHIN'S FARM, see Feering.

GREAT DUNMOW

ST MARY. A large town church, though it lies at Churchend, away from the town and to this day in quite rural surroundings. Pebble-rubble, and externally all of a piece, although, alas, all very restored. In fact the chancel is earlier than the rest, early C14, as the windows clearly show. Thin tracery with cusped lancet lights, foiled circles, spheric triangles, and no ogee arches: these motifs are a safe indication of date. The E window is unusually sumptuous, of five lights. Chancel arch on triple-shafted responds. Inner nook-shafts to the windows. SEDILIA

with polygonal shafts. DOUBLE PISCINA. W tower with angle
buttresses connected by a chamfer, an uncommon form, battlements and polygonal embattled pinnacles. Above the W doorway a frieze of shields. Three-light W window and large
straight-headed three-light bell-openings. The S side all embattled, with two-storeyed porch with a higher stair-turret.
Niches l. and r. of the doorway. The S chancel chapel projects
a little to the S beyond the S aisle. The N side also embattled.
The aisle windows all renewed. Only the S doorway proves
that the S aisle was in fact built as early as the chancel. It has a
handsome arch with roll-mouldings with fillets and a hood-
mould ending in big scrolls. The wide four-bay arcades inside
are C15. They have piers of the familiar four-shaft-four-hollow
moulding with no capitals over the hollows, and two-centred
arches. The fact that the W tower has E buttresses projecting
into the nave shows that it was built before the nave joined up
with it. The most attractive feature of the inside is the wooden
balcony extending from the upper storey of the porch into
the S aisle. It is of late C15 date. – STAINED GLASS. Many C15
fragments assembled in a S aisle window. – Small figures of
Saints on purple panels, C18, Dutch, also in S windows. –
PLATE. Silver-gilt Cup and Paten on foot, C17; Silver-gilt
Dish of 1709. – BRASS of 1579. – MONUMENTS. William Beaumont † 1718, by *C. Horsnaile*, and Sir George Beaumont
† 1762 and his wife † 1814, by *Rossi* (R. Gunnis).

CLOCK HOUSE, ½ m. N. Timber-framed house of the late C16
with a stately symmetrical brick front which cannot be much
later. It is only three bays wide, and the proportions of the
front form about a square to the tops of the gables. These
gables are shaped and the side-gable is larger and also shaped.
The façade windows are of three and four lights and transomed.
On the roof in the middle a clock turret which is said to be
contemporary.

BIGODS, I m. N. The house itself is visually of no great interest,
but to its SW stands an Elizabethan Summer House of two
storeys with a pilastered doorway and a shaped gable.

The town has not much to give. The High Street bends from W
to SSE. In the bend a little square where Star Hill comes in
from Doctor's Pond,* North Street, and the church. The little
square has the two inns facing each other.

WORKHOUSE. The former Workhouse on the Chelmsford Road
was built in 1840 to the design of young *George Gilbert Scott*.

* In 1785 the first Life Boat was tested here.

It is Jacobean, with a long symmetrical façade and a central cupola. Small gatehouse rather close to in front. Red brick with yellow brick dressings.

WINDMILL, ¼ m. SE of the church. Tower-mill of which only the tower remains.

GREAT EASTON

ST JOHN AND ST GILES. Nave and chancel and C19 belfry. The nave is Norman, see the S doorway with one order of columns (scalloped capitals). The E half of the nave has noticeably thicker walls, an indication that originally it carried a crossing tower. The chancel is E.E., with lancet windows. – PLATE. Cup and small Paten on foot of 1634; Paten on foot and large Stand Salver of 1686; Flagon of 1712.

In the grounds of Easton Hall are the remains of a MOUNT AND BAILEY CASTLE. The mount is 21 ft high and 130 ft across at the base. The ditch is 45 ft wide. The bailey lay to the S.

(The R.C. mentions a house 130 yds ENE of Bridgefoot Farm as a complete C15 house, with original traceried bargeboarding and several preserved interior details.)

(WARRENS FARM, Duton Hill. Early C17 staircase with Ionic pilasters as balusters. R.C.)

GREAT GRACES see DANBURY

GREAT HALLINGBURY

ST GILES. C15 W tower with thin diagonal buttresses and a tall shingled spire. The rest externally all Victorian, of 1874 by G. E. Pritchett. Internally however, to one's surprise, one finds a complete Early Norman chancel arch built up entirely of Roman bricks, with the imposts of unmoulded stepped bricks. The arcade of 1874 is of circular piers with very richly and naturalistically carved capitals. An original motif the screen-like stone arches to the l. and r. of the chancel arch. Another reminder of the Norman church is one S window close to the W end. Ecclesiologists will be interested in the extremely rare feature of a PISCINA high up, apparently to serve the rood-loft. – PLATE. Cup of 1661; Paten dated 1675.

(HALLINGBURY PLACE, ¾ m. SE. The kitchen is part of the offices wing of a brick house of the early C16. The Stables are also of C16 brick. R.C.)

WALLBURY CAMP. Early Iron Age hill-fort, well sited on a spur 1½ m. SW of the church. The fort is a pear-shaped area covering 31 acres. The ditch is 50 to 70 ft wide, and there is a double rampart 7 ft high, a most unusual feature in monuments of this class in Eastern England. There were originally two entrances.

GREAT HENNY

St Mary. Nave and chancel without division; w tower. The lower parts of the tower are Norman, the diagonal buttresses C15 or later, the broach-spire early C18. The rest of the church is C14, except for one Early Tudor brick window in the s side and the absolutely plain brick s porch. The only things calling for attention are the DOUBLE PISCINA with cusped pointed arches on detached shafts, and the nave roof with tie-beams on shallow arched braces, and queen-posts. Corbels with figures carrying musical instruments. – STAINED GLASS. E window, 1860, looks as if it might be *Hardman*'s. – BRASS to William Fyscher and wife, c.1530, with children; small figures, the parents only c.10 in.

GREAT HOLLAND

All Saints. By *Sir Arthur Blomfield*, 1866. Nave and lower chancel. The w tower of brick was preserved. It has polygonal clasping buttresses and a higher polygonal stair-turret. Tower and turret are embattled. w doorway with many mouldings in the arch. Large four-light brick w window with panel tracery. Blomfield shows himself here, in 1866, already tamed. No longer the challenging Butterfieldian crudities of his first years. He is now competently and dully E.E. with circular piers and geometrical tracery. – MONUMENT. Henry Rice † 1812, by *Hinchcliffe* of London. With a kneeling, mourning female figure.
Windmill, ½ m. w. Smock-mill, partly demolished.

GREAT HORKESLEY

All Saints. The nave has Norman sw quoins; that is all that survives of the C12. Of the C13 the w tower, unbuttressed with some small lancet windows. The rest is Perp, with big three-light windows with panel tracery of usual patterns. The battlements oddly enough are of Roman bricks. Handsome C15 s porch: timber with traceried lights to the sides and a barge-boarded gable. C15 N arcade of three bays on thin piers with a section of four main shafts and four slimmer shafts without capitals in the diagonals. The arches (and also the chancel arch) are decorated with fleurons (cf. e.g. St Peter, Sudbury, across the Suffolk border). Hood-moulds with head-stops. Roof on big head corbels. – PULPIT. Elizabethan, with arched as well as moulded panels. – FONT COVER. Of tall, pinnacled Gothic form (cf. Sudbury) but mostly C19.

CHAPEL OF ST MARY, 1 m. SSE. Converted into a cottage. It was originally a combined chapel and two-storeyed priest's house, the latter at the W end, with the upper storey projecting into the chapel. Small brick parallelogram. Decoration by blue brick diapers. Blocked large E window; small niche above. Doorway in the N wall. Very steep stepped gables at both ends. Dated by the R.C. earlier than 1500.

(BARRACK YARD, S of the chapel, is a timber-framed C15 house with an L-shaped plan, a thatched roof, and an original king-post roof-truss inside. R.C.)

PITCHBURY RAMPARTS. Early Iron Age encampment, 2 m. S of the church. Only the N end of the oval camp survives, but this N end is well preserved in a wood. There is a double rampart and a ditch, the ramparts 10 ft high and the ditch 60 yds wide. The double rampart is an unusual feature in Iron Age camps in East England (cf. Wallbury Camp, Great Hallingbury). The attempt of early antiquaries to identify Pitchbury Ramparts as an outpost of the Lexden Dykes defensive system (see Colchester) has now been definitely disproved.

GREAT ILFORD see ILFORD

GREAT LEIGHS

ST MARY. Norman round tower with small windows and spire 7 of 1882. W doorway with zigzag ornament in the arch. Nave also Norman (two N windows, one S window). Chancel with renewed two-light windows of the early C14. The E window is of four lights and has very elongated reticulated tracery. The interior of the chancel is generously decorated. A large recess in the N wall with an arch on short shafts flanked by thin buttresses. The arch is cusped and sub-cusped and gabled. In the spandrel of the gable an extremely good spray of leaves in 18b deeply undercut carving. The leaves are already bossy or nobbly, but much of the naturalism of c.1300 is still preserved. No ogee forms occur yet. But the SEDILIA and PISCINA arches opposite have ogee heads. Yet the style is otherwise very similar. The seats are separated from each other by buttresses, not by shafts. Recess and sedilia are much restored. – FONT.

Perp, octagonal. Stem with tracery, bowl with quatrefoils carrying fleurons and one shield. – BENCHES. Eight in the nave with straight-topped, traceried ends. – STAINED GLASS. A little of the C14 *in situ* in the chancel N windows. – PLATE. Cup and Paten of 1560. – BRASS to Ralph Strelley † 1414, rector of Great Leighs. Demi-figure in prayer. The head replaced from a late C14 brass.

GREAT LODGE see GREAT BARDFIELD

GREAT MAPLESTEAD

ST GILES. Sturdy, unbuttressed Norman W tower with later battlements, and Norman apse, complete with its three windows. The chancel however is E.E. (one N window with a low-side window beneath, and remains of a second N window). C14 S aisle with the typical octagonal piers continued with a vertical piece which dies into the double-chamfered arch. The W end renewed in brick early in the C16. A C14 S transept was extended to make a family chapel in the C17. The N side of the church is Victorian. – FONT. Perp, octagonal, with traceried stem, and bowl with foliage decoration. Remains of colour found in 1929. The panels were bright blue with thin yellow diapering. – MONUMENTS. Sir John Deane † 1625. Semi-reclining figure stiffly propped up on one elbow, columns left and right supporting a shallow segmental arch. Between the columns against the back wall kneel the children. – Lady Deane, erected by her son in 1634. Reclining effigy of her son rolled towards us with arms crossed. The figure is propped up on a folded-up mat. Behind him stands most impressive and ghostly the figure of the lady in her shroud. She looks up and raises one hand. In the coffered arch carved angels. The arch is broken open in the middle, and there a crown appears, and above the arch the Trinity. The monument rests on three short Ionic columns. It is the work of *William Wright* of Charing Cross, one of a series of such macabre monuments the most familiar of which is Nicholas Stone's Donne in St Paul's Cathedral. They are all of the 1630s; there was a decided fashion for them at that moment. The inscription below says:

> Her shape was rare, her beauty exquisite
> Her wytt acurate, her judgment singular
> Her entertaynment hearty, her conversation lovely
> Her heart merciful, her hand helpful

> Her courses modest, her discourses wise
> Her charity heavenly, her amity constant
> Her practice holy, her religion pure
> Her vows lawful, her meditations divine
> Her faith unfayngd, her hope stable
> Her prayers devout, her devotions diurnal
> Her days short, her life everlasting.

DYNES HALL, 1 m. s. Remains of the early C17, but mainly of 1689. Seven-bay front of two storeys with three-bay pediment, parapet, and hipped roof. Brick quoins, raised brick frames of the windows, the walls of red and blue brick chequer. Staircase with heavy twisted balusters.

(CHELMSHOE HOUSE, ½ m. NNW. Early C18 brick house with pedimented doorway. R.C.)

GREAT OAKLEY

ALL SAINTS. C18 W tower with weatherboarded upper stage and pyramid roof. Long aisleless nave of the C12 (N wall: one Norman window and traces of a second, besides a mid C16 brick window of three lights), and long, lower early C14 chancel. The chancel E window however is Early Perp – of four lights with panel tracery. The chancel arch also is late C14 in style. Inside the chancel a charming small N doorway with figures of angels in jambs and voussoirs. – FONT. Plain C12, of Purbeck marble, on five shafts.

HOUBRIDGE HALL, 1 m. WSW. A plain early C19 house of white brick, remarkable mainly because it has a Greek Doric porch and above it a re-used shell-hood.

GREAT PARNDON see HARLOW

GREAT SALING

ST JAMES THE GREAT. Late C14 W tower, narrow, with one thin diagonal buttress and battlements. The chancel is of 1857–64 (by *Withers*), and the nave too much renewed to deserve notice. – FONT. Octagonal, with tracery panels.

SALING HALL. Early C17 or earlier, with a good deal of panelling surviving, but refaced on the S façade and the W and E. Red and blue chequerwork, mullion-and-transom-cross windows of timber. On the main front two plus five plus two windows, and on the side parts two symmetrical shaped gables consisting of a double-curved piece and then a segmental top (cf. Beaumont Hall). The alteration is dated 1699, a late date for choosing shaped gables.

GREAT SAMPFORD

St Michael. The s chancel chapel is the transept of a former church. It dates from the later C13, as is proved by the two two-light E windows with a separated sexfoiled circular window above. The two pointed windows each have two pointed trefoiled lights and an unencircled quatrefoil above. The rest of the church is all of the first half of the C14, and the chancel is more lavish than usual. It can hardly be later than 1320, as ogee arches occur only very secondarily in the s side windows. The E window is very large, of five lights with a large circle as the central tracery motif. In the circle are four smaller circles with quatrefoils arranged in two tiers, and not crosswise. Buttresses with niches. Also two niches l. and r. of the E window. Inside, seats under deep cusped pointed arches run all along the sides, and all windows are shafted. The N aisle is contemporary with the chancel. The windows show that, and also the arcade of quatrefoil piers with very thin shafts in the diagonals (cf. Thaxted) and double-chamfered, two-centred arches. The s arcade is characteristically later. The piers are octagonal, and the arches start with short vertical pieces dying into them. Nice arch from the s aisle into the s chapel. The capitals have bossy leaves, and there is one horrified face among them, bitten by a dragon. In the chapel at the foot of the s wall a C14 recess with a crocketed gable and deep niches to the l. and r., also with crocketed gables. The roofs of the church are all original. The best is that of the s aisle. – FONT. Elaborately traceried stem, plain bowl; C14. – PLATE. Cup and Paten of 1562; Dish of 1630, secular, with repoussé decoration.

A village of pretty gabled houses, especially just s of the church.

GREAT STAMBRIDGE

St Mary and All Saints. Evidence of a Saxon church, though very slight evidence. In the N wall of nave and chancel indications can be found of blocked small round-headed windows, and the wall itself is too thin for Norman work. The s aisle was added to the nave c.1300, see the s arcade of three bays with octagonal piers and double-hollow-chamfered arches. – FONT. Octagonal, Perp, with concave sides and quatrefoiled panels with shields etc. – PLATE. Elizabethan Cup.

The former SHEPHERD AND DOG INN at Ballards Gore is a specially pretty piece of exposed timber-framed architecture, mainly of the C15.

TIDE MILL. In a poor condition as a mill, but a lovely picture with the contrast of weatherboarding and red brick.

GREAT TEY

ST BARNABAS. In Norman times this must have been a magnificent church, and one would like to know the reasons for this display in this particular place. The crossing tower is one of the proudest pieces of Norman architecture in the county. The nave had aisles, or at least one aisle, and there were no doubt a chancel and transepts. As it is, the chancel and transept have only C14 features and the nave was pulled down in 1829. The tower is of four stages with much Roman brick for dressings. The lowest stage must have communicated with the roofs. The second has on each side small coupled groups of three arches, the third two large windows, and the fourth the bell-openings with a colonnette and side windows. There is a circular stair-turret higher than the tower. The battlements are later. Inside, the plain E and W arches are preserved. The C14 chancel is also a fine piece of work, with a very large five-light E window with flowing tracery, and two designs of Dec motifs in the tracery of the two-light N and s windows. The N transept N and s transept s windows are of the same date. So are the (much restored) SEDILIA: three arches on shafts with nobbly foliage in the spandrels. The stump of a nave of 1829 is flanked by porches, and in the s porch one circular pier of the Norman nave is still recognizable with a low capital with angle volutes. – FONT. Octagonal, Perp, with shields in circles or quatrefoils. – PULPIT. Plain, C17, with decorated lozenge-shaped centres of the panels. – BENCH ENDS. C15, with traceried panels and poppy-heads, used in the Reader's Desk. – PLATE. Cup with band of ornament, and Paten, both of 1561.

GREAT TOMKINS see UPMINSTER

GREAT TOTHAM

ST PETER. Nave and chancel probably C14. N aisle by *J. Clarke*, 1878. C15 roofs. – PAINTINGS. Remains of figures in the NE corner of the nave and the splay of a s window; C15 to early C16. – PLATE. Cup and Paten of 1630. – BRASS to Elizabeth Coke † 1606 and daughter (chancel).

GREAT WAKERING

ST NICHOLAS. The most singular feature of this church is the
two-storeyed C15 W porch added to the Norman W tower.
This is an Early Saxon motif, and one wonders what can have
been the reason for introducing it here ? Older foundations, or
simply some obstacle in the way of a two-storeyed S porch ?
The nave of the church is Early Norman, as is shown by one
blocked N window and the more interesting blocked W window.
This proves that the W tower, though in its lower stage with
the flat broad pilaster buttresses also clearly Early Norman,
must be later than the nave. It has a tower arch into the nave
with the simplest imposts and a one-stepped arch. The upper
parts of the tower are later Norman, and the neat shingled
broach spire is C15 or later. In the chancel S wall two C13
lancets, in the nave N wall one two-light window with Y-
tracery, cusped, of a type characteristic of c.1300. Nave roof
with tie-beams, octagonal king-posts with moulded capitals
and four-way struts.
The church is reached by a pretty village street which just avoids
being absolutely straight.

GREAT WALTHAM

ST MARY AND ST LAWRENCE. Quite a large church with a
substantial W tower, originally Norman, but strengthened
with brick buttresses; nave and aisles, and chancel. In the nave
Norman quoins of Roman brick can be seen. The aisles are
outside all new. The N aisle was actually built in 1875, and the
S aisle was severely restored. In the chancel also traces of Norman work with Roman bricks, the rest mostly restored. The
nave is remarkably wide for a Norman village church. Plain
Norman tower arch. Perp S arcade of three bays with piers
having demi-shafts towards the arches and a polygonal shaft
without capital towards the nave. Good nave roof of alternating tie-beam and hammerbeam trusses. The hammerbeams
with figures of angels. – BENCHES. About thirty with traceried,
straight-headed ends. – PLATE. Silver-gilt Paten of 1521, engraved with the head of Christ; two Cups and a Paten of 1632.
– MONUMENTS. Two Brasses of 1580 and 1617. – Monument
to Sir Anthony Everard, erected in 1611 (T. K. Cromwell).
Standing wall-monument with stiffly reclining figures of husband and wife on two shelves – that of the husband higher and
behind – between pilasters carrying stone inscription tablets.

Large coffered arch above with two small arched windows in the back wall the glass of which is considered by the Royal Commission to be original. Small figures of children on small tomb-chests on the ground in front.

The village street bends round the churchyard, with a number of handsome houses and the grounds of Langleys as the background to the N.

LANGLEYS. Langleys was bought in 1711 by Samuel Tufnell, who was then aged 29. He was a City man of great business acumen as well as taste and sensibility. He sat in Parliament and he wrote poetry. The house is of brick, large and straightforward in plan, built on an H-shaped plan and incorporating in the N wing much of a preceding house of c.1620. The entrance side is thirteen bays wide, of which the two angle bays on each side belong to the wings projecting by three bays. On the garden side the rhythm is the same, but the projection of the wings is slight. There are two-and-a-half storeys, and the hipped roofs are hidden behind a parapet with sunk panels. The three centre bays on the entrance side were brought forward about 1820 to form an entrance hall. But when this was done, the trim of doorway, windows above, and top pediment were preserved and re-set. The doorway has a broad segmental pediment resting, very oddly, on Corinthian pilasters as well as two thin brackets. The curved window is connected with the pediment and has in addition the big ears typical of c.1720, i.e. volutes coming down by its side and hung with thick garlands. The central window in the second floor is again connected with the window below and has a raised surround, also typical of c.1720. On the garden-side all this is repeated almost identically. While these decorative refinements were no doubt left by Mr Tufnell to the craftsmen he employed, he seems to have been his own architect for the general plans of the house. Its date is confirmed by the 1719 on a rainwater head.

As for the INTERIOR, the most remarkable ensembles are without doubt the two of about 1620, the LIBRARY and the OLD DINING ROOM. They display plasterwork of an exuberance not exceeded anywhere in the country. The library ceiling is vaulted, the dining room ceiling flat. Both have patterns made by broad bands. The bands are adorned with fine trails of foliage, the spaces between them with strapwork cartouches and coats of arms, etc. As the rooms are not high, the effect is almost oppressively rich. The fireplaces in both

57   rooms are yet more ornate. That in the library has in the over-
     mantel the five senses, full-bosomed allegorical figures, that
     in the dining room Peace and Plenty. The mantel-shelves rest
     on elaborate termini caryatids. In addition the 'tympana' of
     the end walls of the library have a seated figure each: Doctrina
     and an angel with a coat of arms. Samuel Tufnell must have
     liked all this Jacobean splendour; for not only did he not
     destroy it, but he seems even to have restored and altered it in
     a style intended to be Neo-Jacobean. The c18 work is notice-
     able in the pieces put in to reduce the size of the fireplace
     openings, and also perhaps some other details which only de-
     tailed study could ascertain. In any case, side by side with
     Vanbrugh's Neo-Jacobean at Audley End, Mr Tufnell's must
     be of the earliest in England.

     Mr Tufnell's own period appears at its grandest in the
     SALON, the principal apartment on the garden side. It is
     two-storeyed, and decorated by heavy fluted Corinthian giant
     pilasters and a towering chimneypiece. Excellent furniture of
     the 1720s is still in the Dining Room. Other rooms were re-
     decorated about 1797–8 (White Drawing Room, Best Bed-
     room; the furniture by *Charles Elliott*) and about 1820 (En-
     trance Hall). The house is in every detail in a perfect state of
     preservation and upkeep.

     The LODGE at the entrance to the avenue which leads to-
     wards the house is to an amusing degree a miniature version of
     the house itself. Only one storey and only a door and two win-
     dows, but pilasters to flank the door, ears to the windows, and
     a top-heavy pediment across all three bays.

HOUSES. The Royal Commission lists about eighty houses in
     the parish. A few of them must here be mentioned. Imme-
     diately E of the church is an Elizabethan timber-framed
     house with a shop and four fine chimneystacks of two shafts
     each. On the S side of the churchyard are two long gabled
     houses, one of them the SIX BELLS INN. WALTHAM HOUSE
     is Georgian, of five bays and two storeys with segment-
     headed windows and lower projecting wings. Good barn close
     to the house.

In BARRACK LANE one particularly pretty early c16 house with
     exposed timber-framing.

Farther afield the GREEN MAN INN, at How Street, is of the
     c14 and has the original hall roof with a king-post and four-
     way struts. Also at How Street, SE of the Green Man, a c15
     house with two gabled cross-wings which has a doorway inside

dated 1623 and an original C15 roof truss with arched braces and a king-post.

1½ m. NE of the church is HYDE HALL of c.1600, timber-framed and plastered with projecting four-gabled front and staircases with some flat pierced balusters. A C15 (?) BARN W of the house.

FITZJOHN'S FARM,* 1¼ m. NW of the church. C15 and C16, with four-gabled front; all four gables provided with late C16 bargeboarding. Of the same date the central chimneystack. Good C15 hall roof with tie-beam and collar-beam, both on arched braces; on the tie-beam queen-posts, on the collar-beam a king-post.

GREAT WARLEY

OLD PARISH CHURCH (CHRIST CHURCH). Nothing survives but the W tower. It looks an ancient monument at first, but is in fact the remains of a yellow and red brick church of 1855, by *Teulon*. The gracelessly fanciful W window betrays him. It is an 'Art Nouveau' without any of the sophistication of 1900. High versus Late Victorian. That can best be checked at Great Warley itself.

NEW PARISH CHURCH OF ST MARY THE VIRGIN. 1904 by *Charles Harrison Townsend*, the architect of the Whitechapel Gallery and the Horniman Museum in London. Modestly pretty exterior embedded in trees, roughcast à la Voysey with buttresses à la Voysey and a bell-turret. But the inside is an orgy of the English Arts-and-Crafts variety of the international Art Nouveau. Tunnel-vaulted with broad decorated silver bands across, apse with silver decoration. Panelled walls with lilies in the design. The FONT with two standing bronze angels, the SCREEN with a wild growth of flowering fruit trees, etc. All by *William Reynolds-Stephens*. – STALLS AND PEWS: designed less excessively by *Townsend* himself. – STAINED GLASS. Apse windows designed by *Heywood Sumner*. – PLATE. Set of 1700.

N of the church, on the GREEN, WALLETS, C15 and late C16, gabled and with exposed timbers. Also some other old houses.

BOYLES COURT. 1776 by *Thomas Leverton*. Red brick. Central part of five bays with ground floor and two upper storeys, parapet, and three-bay pediment. Tuscan six-column porch. Recessed pavilions with big Venetian middle windows, con-

* Parish of Pleshey.

nected with the main block by lower communications. Fine staircase with delicate balusters of thin alternating shapes and carved tread-ends. Reconstructed to a wrong design.

GREAT WIGBOROUGH

ST STEPHEN. 1885, except for the C14 nave. The Victorian building makes use of old materials, but there is nothing of special interest, old or new. – FONT. Octagonal, Perp, bowl with panels filled by shields in quatrefoils or rosettes. – PLATE. Cup, late C16, but altered; Paten also of the late C16.

HYDE FARM, W of the church. C15, partly timber-framed and partly brick-built.*

GREAT YELDHAM

ST ANDREW. Entirely Perp. Nave, N aisle, and chancel mid C14, but the N arcade redone in 1884. For reasons not convincingly explained a huge W tower was added to the nave on its S side, near the W end. It was begun later in the C14, with angle buttresses and a big S doorway enriched by an ogee canopy and two niches l. and r. This was not continued and later given a blank stepped brick gable as a piece of decoration. Instead, late in the C15, a more normal W tower was erected, also with angle buttresses. It has bell-openings of three lights with one transom, stepped battlements with pinnacles and, between them, in the middle of each side, a smallish figure of an angel. – PULPIT. Elizabethan, with two tiers of blank arches with plaited decoration on each panel. – SCREEN. One-light divisions with ogee tops and a little tracery above them. On the r. side of the screen the dado is painted with figures of saints, in the East Anglian manner. The quality of the paintings is low. – BRASS. Plate with arched top and kneeling figures, Symonds family, 1627. – (MONUMENT. Mr Gunnis mentions Gregory Way † 1799, by *John Bacon*.)

SPENCER GRANGE. Mid C18 house, refronted, it seems, about 1820, when the Greek Doric porch *in antis* was also inserted.

(OLD RECTORY. Timber-framed C15 house. On the first floor in the SW wing an exceptionally fine ceiling with arched braces and moulded beams. R.C.)

* Mr P. Russell Walker draws my attention to MOULSHAMS MANOR, which he assigns to the early C14.

GREENSTEAD

ST ANDREW. Thin W tower of c.1600, with two- and three-light arched windows without any arches to the lights or any tracery. The W window is of the C18. Nave and chancel Norman. NW angle with Roman brick. Plain Norman N doorway. The S arcade and whole S aisle C19. – PLATE. Cup of the early C17.

GREENSTED

ST ANDREW. The church is famous all over England as the only survival – and what an unlikely survival – of a log-church. Moreover, it can with some probability be dated c.1013, the year of the passing through of St Edmund's body.* The nave is built of oak-logs split vertically in halves and set vertically in an oak sill. The present sill and the brick plinth belong to the restoration of 1848 (*Thomas Henry Wyatt*). The nave roof is of 1892. But the Tudor dormers of timber are original save for two and worth some study. The chancel of brick is early C16 (one S window and the S doorway), its E end C18. The W tower is also entirely of timber, in the Essex tradition. Its date is uncertain. It has the usual internal construction, is externally weatherboarded and painted white, and carries a shingled broach spire. – PAINTING. Small arched panel of St Edmund, c.1500. – STAINED GLASS. Head of a man; c.1500 (W window).

GREENSTED HALL. The exterior now mostly in the form given it in 1875. Inside some Elizabethan panelling and a staircase of the same period and an early C18 staircase (V.C.H.).

GROVE COTTAGE see CREEKSEA

GRYME'S DYKE see COLCHESTER

GUISNES COURT see TOLLESBURY

GUTTRIDGE HALL see WEELEY

HACTONS see UPMINSTER

HADLEIGH

ST JAMES THE LESS. A complete little Norman church, essentially unaltered, but unfortunately placed immediately S of an

* Or perhaps much earlier: Dendro-magnetic tests in 1960 have suggested a date of c.850 for several of the nave timbers. Recent excavation has also revealed the traces of two earlier chancels with timber walls.

A-road with unsightly shops and shacks near its E end. This E
5b end is apsed. A chancel precedes the apse, a nave the chancel.
At the W end a boarded belfry resting inside on a free-standing
four-post structure, the only later (C15) addition. Otherwise
only a few windows are not original: nave N one C13 lancet,
chancel S one two-light Dec window, nave S one two-light
Perp window. – FONT. Made up of various parts. The best is
the lower part of the bowl with stiff-leaf growing diagonally. –
PAINTINGS. Very remarkable fragments. In the nave NE lancet demi-figure of St Thomas of Canterbury of c.1275, in the
window W of this Angel with spread-out wings (?), C13; on the
wall further W trefoiled canopy said to be C14. – PLATE. Cup
and Paten of 1568; both with bands of ornament.

HADLEIGH CASTLE is by far the most important later medieval
castle in the county. It was built originally for Hubert de
Burgh, Chief Justiciar, c.1232, but then rebuilt by Edward
III. It was in course of erection in 1365. The chief residential
parts were to the S and have been entirely obliterated by a
landslide. What survives is the W, N, and E curtain-wall, but
not to any impressive height, the wall and one outer turret of
the barbican on the N side, and four circular towers, all open
towards the bailey. The highest, famous from Constable's
painting, is the SE tower. Here three storeys can still be recognized with windows and chimney flues. The tower to the N of
this has two storeys remaining. The broadest tower is the one
next to the barbican. The whole castle is of irregular oblong
shape, and visually a little disappointing after the high hopes
raised by Constable's interpretation.

HADSTOCK

ST BOTOLPH. The church contains rare and interesting evidence
of an C11 building, probably of before the Conquest. To this
belong the double-splayed windows of the nave and the N
doorway with one order of columns, a square abacus, an inner
roll-moulding of the arch and an outer band, quite distant
from it (cf. Strethall). The capitals, abaci, and the band around
the arch are decorated with an irregular pattern of diagonal
lines which may signify leaves. Inside the church the evidence
is even more interesting. It concerns the arches towards the
13a two transepts. That on the S side is complete to the abaci. Of
that on the N side only the bases survive. Saxon transepts are a
rarity (cf. e.g. Dover). The rest is C14. The arch on the S side

is earlier, probably C13. The Saxon jambs have one order of colonnettes at the angle towards the crossing and again a quite unskilled abacus. The capitals of the colonnettes, again decorated with the same sketchy leaf pattern, have basically a shape so similar to the Norman one-scallop that they may well be a Saxon craftsman's version of this unfamiliar motif introduced with the Conquest. The N transept has an early C14 N window with flowing tracery. The W tower was added in the C15, see its tall arch towards the nave, the flint and stone chequer decoration at the base, and the diagonal buttresses. – SCREEN (to S transept). C15, damaged, with broad single-light divisions, ogee arch inside pointed arch, with quatrefoil and other motifs between the two. – LECTERN. Good, C15, on octagonal concave-sided base. – BENCHES. Throughout the nave, C15, plain. – DOOR. In the N doorway is that unique thing, an Anglo-Saxon oak door. It is treated quite differently from the Norman way. It has plain oak boards and three long undecorated iron straps riveted through to circular wooden bars at the back.*

ROMAN VILLA, 1¼ m. NNE of the church, on the S bank of the Granta. The site was discovered and partially excavated in the C19. Part of a winged corridor villa, incorporating a bath suite, was uncovered. Several mosaic pavements were found on the site, including one which was removed and relaid at Audley End.

HAINAULT HALL see CHIGWELL ROW

HALLINGBURY PLACE see GREAT HALLINGBURY

HALSTEAD

ST ANDREW. In the centre of the little town. Of flint rubble, much renewed. The chancel pretty well deprived of medieval detail. The W tower of 1850. The rest mostly C14, porches and vestry C15. The windows not of special interest. S aisle Dec, N aisle Perp. Inside six-bay arcades of the C14, with square piers with four demi-shafts and double-chamfered arches. The chancel roof, whose exact date (1413) is known from documents, is hidden behind boarding. – FONT. Octagonal, Perp, with motifs of shields and flowers. – REREDOS. 1893 by *Sir Arthur Blomfield.* – STAINED GLASS. S window in the S aisle

---

* Miss H. M. Lake draws my attention to HILL FARM, a timber-framed house of the C16 with the original screen inside.

of 1891 (Brewster) by *Powell & Sons*, in a style showing
clearly the influence of Burne-Jones in design if not in colour.
– MONUMENTS. John Bourchier and wife (?), effigies of
Knight and Lady each under a separate canopy on thin
shafts, *c*.1300. The tomb-chest with weepers and shields and
the diapered panels behind do not belong. They seem to date
from the middle of the C14. – John, Lord Bourchier, † 1400
and wife. Tomb-chest richly decorated with quatrefoils
carrying shields. Two recumbent effigies under tall canopy of a
chaste, rather frigid design, again with frieze of shields, and
ending in a cresting with small shields. Higher angle shafts. –
Brass to Bartholomew Lord Bourchier † 1409 and wives (s
aisle floor, mostly covered by a seat).

HOLY TRINITY. By *George Gilbert Scott & Moffatt*, 1843–4.
Still in the lancet style, but already with a bold steeple with
tall broach spire standing by the side of the s aisle close to the
w end. Alternating circular and octagonal piers inside; square
capitals with early C13 decoration. – The STAINED GLASS of
the w window of the same period – typical elongated medallion shapes and glowing colours. By *Clutterbuck*.

ST JAMES, Greenstead Green. 1845 by *George Gilbert Scott*.
The upper stage of the w tower is octagonal and accompanied
by four pinnacles. Spire on top. The church is in the Dec style.

CHAPEL on the premises of Fremlin's Brewery. Built in 1883
but housing the FONT, FONT COVER, REREDOS, and some
more fragments from All Hallows, Great Thames Street, London – work of the finest Wren standards. The font is of
marble with leaves spreading up the stem and thick flutings
leading over into the bowl. The font cover is beautifully
carved. The reredos has Corinthian pilasters and an open
pediment. Also, to frame all this and to separate the consecrated from the unconsecrated part of the chapel, an arch on
two fine Corinthian columns. The names of the carvers are not
recorded. – COMMUNION RAIL with twisted balusters, from
St George's, Deal.

CONGREGATIONAL CHURCH,Parsonage Street. An ambitious,
lifeless building with fussy tracery and a big spire. By *F.
Barnes*, 1861–2.

COTTAGE HOSPITAL, Hedingham Road. 1884 by *George Sherrin* in his characteristic half-timber style. Built at the expense
of George Courtauld.

THE TOWN of Halstead is not one of the most attractive of
Essex. There are things only here and there which need picking

out. The best individual house stands just N of the parish church, now occupied by a firm of solicitors, a large C18 brick house of five bays with a two-bay projection at one end. The doorway has a pediment on Ionic pilasters. The majority of things worth mentioning are to the S. First down the HIGH STREET, a broad street down the hill. The better houses are all on the W side, especially Nos 22–24, large red brick of two plus five bays with, in the centre, a Venetian window, then a semicircular window, and then a pediment. No. 26 is known as the CHANTRY HOUSE. It was founded under the will of Bartholomew Lord Bourchier in 1412. The hammerbeam roof of the original building can still be seen in fragments. No. 32 is of about 1800, white brick with a Tuscan porch. Then the former CONGREGATIONAL CHAPEL, white brick, with an odd three-gabled front and Gothic fenestration. It was built in 1832.* At the foot of the hill BRIDGE STREET with two very minor disused public buildings, the former Corn Exchange, then Technical School, just by the station, built in 1865, and the former House of Correction, now a Flour Mill. It dates from 1782. To the E the CAUSEWAY leads from here to Messrs Courtauld's factory. The nucleus is the handsome, long, three-storeyed, white, weatherboarded mill across the stream, with impressive uninterrupted bands of windows on two floors. It was erected late in the C18. From the W end of Bridge Street by TRINITY STREET (Trinity House, C17 timber-framed, with Late Georgian white brick front) to Holy Trinity and CHAPEL HILL. In Chapel Hill the best-looking half-timbered house: Nos 9–11, C15, with cross-wings and two asymmetrical gables, rather altered.

WINDMILL, N of St Andrew's church. A partly demolished smock-mill.

BLUEBRIDGE HOUSE, 1 m. E. Front of 1714. Blue and red brick. The windows still straight-headed. The doorway is later. Staircases with twisted balusters. Other interior features are of the C17. Good wrought-iron railings and gate.

(BAYTHORNE PARK, 2 m. NE of the parish church. Nine bays, two storeys, parapet. Hipped roof. Apparently late C17.)

(OAKLANDS, ½ m. W of Halstead. *By C. F. Hayward.*)

As for new building, PARKFIELDS ESTATE, to the S of Halstead, by *A. E. Wiseman* and *N. E. G. Weston*, is still being developed (1964).‡

* Now demolished.
‡ Information from the Halstead Chief Librarian.

HARE HALL *see* ROMFORD

HARE STREET *see* HARLOW

HARLOW

(I) HARLOW OLD TOWN

ST MARY THE VIRGIN. Alas so thoroughly restored in 1878–
80 that it is virtually a Victorian church. Only the fact of a
crossing tower remains as evidence that Harlow belonged to
that type very unusual in Essex. Between the medieval church
and the present rebuilding lay another rebuilding of 1709. –
CHEST. In the S transept. Italian, C17, with scenes in shallow
relief and pokerwork. – STAINED GLASS. In the N vestry small
C14 figure of the Virgin seated, only about 12 in. long. –
PLATE. Flagons of 1618 and 1623; large Cup and Paten of
1639; two Candlesticks of 1697; Spoon of 1709. – BRASSES.
An uncommonly large number collected in the N transept.
Especially noteworthy: Knight and Lady *c*.1430 (19-in.
figures); so-called Robert Doncaster † 1490 and wife (2-ft
figures); Thomas Aylmer † 1518 and wife (10-in. figures);
Richard Bugges † 1636 and wives (3-ft figures); W. Newman
† 1602 and wife, plate with standing figures and inscription
between them: Veritas mihi dulcior vita; in the floor of the
crossing Civilian and wife, late C15 (16-in. figures, perhaps of
Robert Doncaster and wife). – MONUMENTS. Alexander Stafford † 1652 and wife, with large kneeling figures facing each
other, a type rather out of date in 1650. – John Wright † 1659,
wooden tablet with small figures of Faith, Hope, and Charity
on top.

FORMER CHAPEL, Harlowbury. Norman. Nave and chancel in
one, with a C15 king-post roof. The chapel has its original
three E windows and N doorway (with columns with waterleaf
capitals). Also two original N and one original S windows.

ST JOHN THE BAPTIST. 1839–40. Yellow brick, in the lancet
style. No aisles. With W tower and original STAINED GLASS
in all the E windows.

BAPTIST CHAPEL, Potter Street. 1756. The usual plain little
brick rectangle, but adorned by a doorway quite exceptionally
fine. Scrolly open pediment on brackets, the scrolls expressed
in lush foliage.

ST MARY'S COLLEGE. 1862 by *Withers*. Gothic, in the mixture
of yellow and red brick then popular.

The centre of Harlow is the crossroads by the George Hotel.

Opposite, THE GABLES, a C16 house with exposed timber and a pretty Georgian doorway. S of the police station the former BRITISH SCHOOL, yellow brick, symmetrical, with Tuscan porch; 1836. Into HIGH STREET with the Georgian nine-bay house part of which is now the National Provincial Bank. Doorway with broken pediment on thin pilasters. In the High Street several more Late Georgian houses, e.g. one of yellow brick, three bays, with Tuscan doorway and ground-floor windows set in arches. At the end of the High Street MULBERRY GREEN, the visually best spot of old Harlow. HILL HOUSE is a curious building, Georgian in its windows, but with square towers flanking the façade. It deserves some further study. Next to this MULBERRY GREEN HOUSE, late C18 with two bow windows. Further E a small block of ALMSHOUSES built in 1716, single-storeyed, originally with four doors. Then the corner of CHURCHGATE STREET is reached, the street close to which lies the church. At the corner of the churchyard the STAFFORD ALMSHOUSES, dated 1630, half-timbered. Several nice Georgian houses and at the foot of the street THE CHANTRY,* three-storeyed, three-gabled late C16 house with later additions, timber-framed and plastered.

ROMANO-CELTIC TEMPLE. The site lies on a small hill 250 yds W of the railway station. The base of the hill is surrounded by an earthwork which probably marks the boundary of the temple precincts. The temple was excavated in 1927 and consisted of a square shrine with sides measuring 18 ft 9 in. internally, standing within an enclosure $48\frac{1}{2}$ ft square. Access to the shrine was from the SE. The walls had been plastered internally and perhaps externally as well. The temple itself is dated to the C4, but finds beneath its floor suggest occupation of the hilltop in the second half of the C1.

A hollow 180 ft in diameter at the NW end of the hill may mark the site of a THEATRE, which is frequently associated with such temples.

(2) VILLAGES WITHIN HARLOW NEW TOWN

GREAT PARNDON

ST MARY. All C15, including the unbuttressed W tower. The only exception is the Victorian transepts. Nave and chancel without structural division. – FONT. Perp, octagonal, with traceried stem and a bowl decorated by quatrefoils carrying

* Now Churchgate Hotel and sadly altered.

roses. – BENCHES. A few old poppy-heads. – STAINED GLASS.
Nave N wall window, fragments of original glass with figures.
– BRASS. Rowland Rampston † 1598 (chancel floor).

LATTON

LATTON PRIORY, 2½ m. S of Latton church. The priory was
founded in the C12 for Augustinian Canons. All that survives
of it is the crossing of the church, now part of a barn. It is C14
work, with piers to the main sides consisting of big semicircular shafts and very thin shafts between. Moulded arches.
Of the nave, in addition, one shafted window remains, deprived of its head. There is no certainty of the extent and plan
of the monastic buildings.

ST MARY THE VIRGIN. Recent investigations have brought out
a Norman window in the S wall and the arch of the Norman S
doorway, both dressed with Roman bricks. Another brick
doorway also discovered recently must be C16 and may have
belonged to a rood-loft staircase. Late C15 N chapel of brick
with two-light stone windows. C16 W tower with diagonal
buttresses, a three-light W window, and battlements. The N
side of the church was refaced in the C18. – PAINTINGS.
Scanty remains in the N chapel of a cycle of late C15 wall
paintings. – MONUMENTS. Recess between chancel and N
chapel. Tomb-chest with three large panels with quatrefoils
and shields. On the lid brasses of Sir Peter Arderne † 1467,
Chief Baron of the Exchequer, and his wife. Figures of 3 ft
length. Heavy canopy of three arches, the middle ones damaged. Fleuron frieze and crenellations. – Other brasses to
William Harper and wife (? c.1490; chancel; 2 ft 3 in. figures)
and to Frances Frankelin † 1604, woman in boldly ornamented
dress (chancel floor). – James Altham † 1583 and wife.
Monument with the usual kneeling figures. Children kneeling
in the 'predella'. – Sir Edward Altham † 1632, erected 1640.
Monument with flanking figures of angels. – Lady Campbell
† 1818 by *G. Garrard*, R.A.; no effigy; cherubs' heads at the
foot.

NETTESWELL

ST ANDREW. Nave and chancel in one, C13, and C15 belfry. The
belfry has four arched bell-openings in a row on each side and
a short broach-spire. It stands on two posts and a tie-beam
with arched braces. The chancel has lancet windows. Other
windows are Perp insertions. It is not possible to decide to

what work the brick panel in the S wall near the W end can allude which has the arms of Abbot Rose of Waltham, who ruled the Abbey from 1497 to 1500. – PULPIT. Incorporating a frieze with a vine pattern, dated 1618. – BENCHES. Two in the nave with plain poppy-heads. – STAINED GLASS. Two small C15 figures in a N window. – PLATE. Cup and Paten of 1641; Almsdish of 1656. – BRASSES. Thomas Laurence † 1522 with wife and children. – Also a brass of 1607.

SCHOOL. At the S end of Netteswell Cross. Plain Georgian three-bay brick house with an inscription bearing the date 1777.

See also below.

(3) HARLOW NEW TOWN

Harlow was set up as a New Town in 1947, and *Frederick Gibberd* was appointed to prepare the master plan. He did this, and has since been responsible for the design of the town, an unusual case of cordiality between architect-planner and Corporation. The original plan was designed for 60,000 inhabitants but, after the first few years of building, higher than normal densities were obtained and it was possible to raise the population figure to 80,000 without departing from the original design. By 1964 the population had reached 60,000, and its original purpose of providing a balanced town for overspill population from London had succeeded – only some 5 per cent leave the town to work outside, against which some 4 per cent come in to work from the hinterland.

The site for the town is about 6,300 acres and was originally a rural area, with no small town that could form a nucleus of a town centre and no urban authority. The plan form imposed on it is semicircular, with the railway (the main Liverpool Street–Norwich line), the river Stort, and the new Norwich motorway forming the base line on which are sited the two main industrial estates, Temple Fields on the E and Pinnacles on the W, with the railway station in the centre between them. The town centre extends from the railway station to the top of a hill, to dominate the rest of the town, and beyond it, to the S, housing is grouped as four neighbourhood clusters within the semicircle.

A PERAMBULATION along the main roads gives some idea of how the topography is used to give the town individuality – a major problem in a new town. The roads run in the landscaped valleys, with the buildings grouped in masses on high ground. The route from the A11 to the town centre is typical:

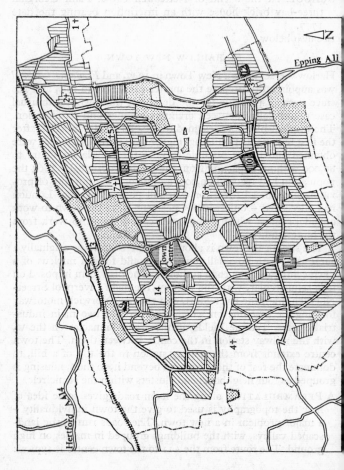

on entering the town there are prospects of dwellings set in trees well back from the road; close to the first roundabout a motel and blocks of flats; back behind playing fields a large secondary school (BRAYS GROVE SECONDARY SCHOOL, by *Yorke, Rosenberg & Mardall*); approaching the second roundabout the landscape opens up into a wide prospect with the road disappearing into a wood on the horizon (Mark Hall), flanked on the r. by a large block of research laboratories (STANDARD TELECOMMUNICATIONS, by *Waterhouse & Ripley*) and on the l. by more housing, dominated by a tower block (QUARRY SPRINGS, by *Norman & Dawbarn*). The l. fork from the roundabout (SECOND AVENUE) passes along one side of the valley, with more housing in the background, then another tower block (HUGH'S TOWER, by *Frederick Gibberd*). Then the road curves to focus on the CIVIC CENTRE, by *Frederick Gibberd* and the *Harlow Development Corporation*, with the MUNICIPAL OFFICE tower as the dominant, until the mass of the TOWN CENTRE, with its office blocks, stores, and further towers fills the scene.* The journey has taken only a few minutes, the scene is a bold one, in scale with the speed of the motorcar.

Other main town roads converge on the town centre (FIRST AVENUE, THIRD AVENUE), and other journeys reveal the same kind of scene with interesting building compositions set in the landscape, such as the large secondary schools; but, apart from the dominant mass of the town centre and large buildings like secondary schools and tower blocks, the scene is a rural rather than an urban one. It was Mr Gibberd's intention to obtain a sharp contrast between compact building masses and open landscape, but the greater part of the housing is only two storeys, which never breaks the skyline of trees.

A drive along the baseline of the town (A11–Edinburgh Way–Elizabeth Way) reveals the quite different environment of industry. A long, straight road forms the spine of TEMPLEFIELDS ESTATE; on its frontage are the largest factories (Harlow Metal, Revertex, Standard Telephones & Cables are typical *Harlow Development Corporation* designs); and, behind, rectangular blocks accommodate the smaller factories on the principle of flatted accommodation. Orderly office blocks, for the most part in glass and London stock bricks, screen the varied forms of the production areas.‡ From

---

* On the Town Centre see p. 230.
‡ The SIMPSON SHAND factory is by *Frederick Gibberd*.

Temple Fields, through the TOWN PARK, connecting the town to the Hertfordshire hills, and then the town centre on the hill to the S dominates the view. From the roundabout a branch leads to the Harlow Town RAILWAY STATION, one of the best examples of modern railway vernacular, by the *Eastern Region Architect's Department* (*H.H. Powell*).* Along ELIZABETH WAY the town's service industry flanks the railway; then across the landscape of the GOLF COURSE, designed by *Henry Cotton*, to arrive at PINNACLES, where a geometric road grid is again imposed on the landscape. Here the buildings, being designed later than Temple Fields, make greater use of prefabricated materials – the vast plant of COSSORS and the PITNEY BOWES four-storey office block (both by the *Harlow Development Corporation*) are noteworthy.‡

A good way of seeing the town is by bicycle: here a separate system of cycle tracks, under-passing the main roads, wend their way along the old tree-lined lanes and through the heart of the built-up areas; the scene is casual and intimate, in character with the speed of cycling.

The housing can only be seen by walking: the architects began with the grouping of dwellings, roads being subservient to pavings. The four clusters are made of eleven neighbourhoods and two further ones. The old villages of Harlow and Potter Street remain as appendages on the E.

A visit might begin with MARK HALL NORTH, the first neighbourhood to be built, to see how it has settled down and the landscape developed. It is the northern one of the cluster and illustrates the planning theory which has been followed for the rest of the town. In the heart the TANYS DELL PRIMARY SCHOOL (by *Richard Sheppard, Robson & Partners*), a small group of shops, a pub, and a recreation area; the cycle track links this area to the industrial area and the town centre. The housing is in three distinct groups, each by a different architect – the intention was that architectural character should give individuality to the place. The main accent on the E is 64 *Frederick Gibberd*'s tower block, THE LAWN, the first built in Britain, set amongst magnificent oak trees. W of this area on

* A low, crisp, entirely ungimmicky arrival and departure building is linked to a raised bridge across the lines. The principal accent is the three concrete lift towers rising above the bridge.

‡ Other factories at Pinnacles include COLORA INKS by *Austin Vernon & Partners* and BERK CHEMICALS by *J. Douglas Matthews & Partners*.

mixed development is TANYS DELL and THE CHANTRY, by *Maxwell Fry, J. Drew & Partners*, where the main block is a staggered composition of four-storey flats. Further to the w is a different architectural expression, at GLEBELANDS, by the *Development Corporation*. Here also a piece of sculpture by *Barbara Hepworth*, called 'Contrapuntal Forms', and a children's wild play area by *Sylvia Crowe*. The communal fronts, with their lawns and varied planting, give Mark Hall North a happy, green look, but the buildings are too widely spaced.*
At MARK HALL SOUTH can be seen the first attempts at tightening up, to produce a more urban environment. ORCHARD CROFT, by *Frederick Gibberd* and the *Development Corporation*, is an example. The street façades have become much longer and continuous and turn the corners by means of blocks of flats; there is the introduction of three-storey terrace houses, and the spaces between buildings are much smaller; a pleasant paved square and pedestrian alley lie in the centre. Contrasts in architectural design to the ESE at COOKS SPINNEY (by *H. T. Cadbury-Brown*) and CHURCHFIELD (by *Richard Sheppard, Robson & Partners*); and to the SE, LADYSHOT (by *Yorke, Rosenberg & Mardall*), the last a most successful layout of yellow brick terraces of two, three, and four storeys, charmingly grouped and detailed with discrimination and without mannerism. In the heart a pretty little COMMUNITY HALL raised on piers, with alternative access by a mound of earth – a result of the Corporation's insistence that old people must not have to climb stairs; adjacent, the SHEEP SHEARER, by *Ralph Brown*.
The southern boundary of the neighbourhood, QUARRY SPRING (by *Norman & Dawbarn*), is formed by long undulating four-storey maisonette blocks with a point block as focus from the adjacent parkway. The estate is composed round a disused quarry pit.‡
The third neighbourhood of the cluster, NETTESWELL, follows the Mark Hall South pattern. PITTMANS FIELD (*by H. T. Cadbury-Brown*), a rigid layout of small rectangular spaces; a bronze donkey by *Willi Soukop*; another group by *Richard Sheppard, Robson & Partners* (PARSONAGE LEYS), on the w

---

* Also at Mark Hall North the MARK HALL SECONDARY SCHOOL by *Richard Sheppard, Robson & Partners*, 1954. This is at the junction of First Avenue and the A11. Mr Nairn calls it the best school at Harlow.
‡ For Mark Hall South *H. T. Cadbury-Brown* designed a JUNIOR SCHOOL, a three-unit composition, all low.

HUGH'S TOWER (see above), which, with an identical block, marks the E and W entries to the town centre.*

At the focus of these neighbourhoods, at the main town cross roads (FIRST AVENUE and HOWARD WAY), is THE STOW, the first of the neighbourhood centres to be built. This is by *Frederick Gibberd*, and those who know his Market Place at Lansbury, Poplar, London, will recognize his handwriting at once. The layout is intricate and highly successful. It was designed for pedestrians only and has now been restored to them. Many different activities are associated with shopping, such as service industry, a COMMUNITY CENTRE, a Health Centre, NUFFIELD HOUSE (by *Booth & Ledeboer*), ST ANDREW'S METHODIST CHURCH (by *Paul Mauger & Partners*),‡ and a variety of different kinds of play areas.

Adjacent to the cross roads, a ten-storey block by *C. E. P. Monson*, the Roman Catholic church of OUR LADY OF FATIMA by *Gerard Goalen* with a high spike, transepts, and stained glass by the monks of *Buckfast Abbey*; and further along the First Avenue, towards the town centre, the SWIMMING BATH by the Urban District Council (*T. Hinchliffe*), behind which lies the Town Park. The Swimming Bath has a 110 ft basin and an undulating roof.

The NW quarter of the town, HARE STREET and LITTLE PARNDON, being associated with the town centre, has a comparatively small centre at HERONS WOOD, given prominence by four-storey maisonettes and a tall slab block, both by *William Crabtree & Jarosz*. Some of the housing is dull – one wearies of so much two-storey development – but there are two exceptions, both close to the town centre: on the N HORNBEAMS and RIVERMILL, a development of *Frederick Gibberd*'s early work, where the dwellings are either drawn together into a series of enclosed, rectangular spaces, each of a different colour and linked by narrow alleys, or are in exceptionally long terraces, to form street pictures. The other specially noteworthy design, on the SW, NORTHBROOKS, is characteristic of *Powell & Moya*'s style. Here, box-like terraces (flat roofs were generally barred by the Corporation) in parallel series, with narrow footpath access,

* Two secondary schools have been built at Netteswell, the NETTESWELL SECONDARY SCHOOL by *Hening & Chitty*, 1955 (The Hides, E of the Town Centre) and the BURNT MILL SECONDARY SCHOOL by *H. Conolly*, the County Architect, 1963 (N of First Avenue).

‡ By the side of the church is a courtyard with classrooms and halls on three sides and cloister walks on two.

climb the hill to four-storey blocks set at right angles: a compact, geometric building mass superbly set in the landscape; in the heart, one of the first examples in England of middle-class patio houses.*

The SE quarter of the town, BRAYS GROVE, TYE GREEN, and LATTON, again has a major centre at the cross roads, BUSH FAIR – a design advance on The Stow, as the architects, the *Development Corporation*, were allowed to design a pedestrian precinct: adjacent, a lively octagonal LIBRARY AND COMMUNITY CENTRE (by the *Development Corporation*) and a small factory estate – the industrial pattern is a dispersed one. The individual neighbourhoods follow the previous pattern. At BRAYS GROVE is work of *Ralph Tubbs* and *David Aberdeen* (Little Brays and Highfield), and in the w neighbourhood, TYE GREEN, a distinguished design by *Sir John Burnet, Tait & Partners* (WESTFIELD, Bushey Croft). The old village of Tye Green incorporates detached modern houses by various architects. At LATTON an interesting design – 416 houses all grouped in small squares – by the *Architects' Co-Partnership* (Spinning Wheel Mead and Upper Mealines) and, on the southern boundary of the town, RADBURN CLOSE (by the *Development Corporation*), which, as its name implies, has complete segregation of vehicles from pedestrians.‡

The SW cluster of four neighbourhoods – Passmores, and Great Parndon (N of Southern Way) and Stewards and Kingsmoor (on the S) – is the last area to be built and marks a further stage in design development, due to an increase in densities (seventy people to the acre) and the raising of housing standards as an outcome of the Parker Morris Report. The neighbourhood centre, STAPLE TYE, under construction at the time of writing, takes the form of one single building rather than an assembly of buildings as in the others, with the pedestrians on a shopping deck above car parking and servicing.

The areas N of Southern Way are now largely built. At PASSMORES, the *Development Corporation* have two very individual designs, WATERHOUSE MOOR and HOOK FIELD: but

---

* Also in this neighbourhood the HARLOW HOSPITAL, see p. 231.

‡ At Tye Green are the BRAYS GROVE SECONDARY SCHOOL by *Yorke, Rosenberg & Mardall*, 1956 (Tracyes Road, by the junction of the A11 and Southern Way) and the LATTON BUSH SECONDARY SCHOOL by *R. Shepbard, Robson & Partners*, 1959 (S of Southern Way).

when built the most original will probably be two competition winners, OLD ORCHARD (*Clifford Culpin & Partners*) for speculative middle-class housing and *Michael Neylan*'s scheme at BISHOPSFIELD MAIN, won in an open housing competition – the latter has fingers of single-storey patio houses radiating from a tightly-built multi-level nucleus of flats over garages, like a kind of citadel. At GREAT PARNDON is a typical example of *Eric Lyons*'s familiar modest style in black brick and white paint (SHAWBRIDGE); and further N, at HILLY FIELD, will be work of *James Cubitt & Partners*.*

s of Southern Way the housing promises to be even more interesting as the architects, *Clifford Culpin & Partners*, *Leonard Manasseh & Partners*, and *Associated Architects and Consultants*, have been given greater freedom.‡

POTTER STREET, E of Brays Grove and Latton, is an old village, but one of little distinction. In consequence there has been built a new Shopping Centre, PRENTICE PLACE (*Development Corporation*), and large areas of housing, including flats and maisonettes, all by *Hening & Chitty*, 1962 etc.

Whatever doubts one may have about lack of urbanity in the housing, there can be none about the TOWN CENTRE: whichever way one approaches it, it dominates the environment as a large-scale mass, much bigger in scale than any old town of comparable size would possess, and the more impressive because it is contrasted with open landscape. Arriving, one is confronted with belts of car parking and from them short cuts lead to the pedestrian core – Harlow was the first of the new towns with a pedestrian town centre.

The plan, a rectangle running N to S, has market and other squares on the N connected by two parallel shopping streets to the civic spaces on the S which overlook the landscape. Beginning with the MARKET SQUARE, the first part to be completed, there are lively and varied buildings (by the *Development Corporation*) on three sides, with the POST OFFICE in the corner (by the *Ministry of Public Building & Works*), and two rather dull shopping blocks on the other. An

* Also at Great Parndon the CREMATORIUM by *T. Hinchliffe* (Urban District Council).

‡ At Great Parndon the PASSMORES SECONDARY SCHOOL is by *Yorke, Rosenberg & Mardall*, 1961 (Tendring Road), the STEWARDS SECONDARY SCHOOL by *H. Conolly*, the County Architect, 1964 (S of Staple Tye Neighbourhood Centre).

advance on Lansbury is an upper terrace on one side, the W, with bridges to a café and adjacent buildings giving exciting views down on to the market scene and accommodating service shops and buildings like halls. In the square, 'Meat Porters', by *Ralph Brown* and 'Portrait Figure' by *McWilliam*.

Leading from the Market Square, BROAD WALK, the main shopping street, flanked by 'multiples', fortunately contained within one architectural framework, and terminated by a large CO-OP store (*Development Corporation*), and the town's LIBRARY (*H. Conolly*, County Architect), which face the civic precincts. The CIVIC BUILDINGS, all by *Frederick Gibberd*, form the southern boundary of the centre; being by the same designer and utilizing the same materials – reinforced concrete, stone, and glass – they form a cohesive S wall to the town centre. From E to W the CROWN OFFICES, POLICE STATION and COURT HOUSE, and the tower of the TOWN HALL form one square; adjacent is the Civic Square, not completed at the time of writing; and beyond a further square formed by the COLLEGE OF FURTHER EDUCATION and the church of ST PAUL (by *Humphrys & Hurst*).* Along the S lies a terraced garden in which water in a long canal, with seven fountains, is discharged through seven lions' heads (by *William Mitchell*), into a second canal and then into lower pools, linking the civic spaces to the landscape: sculpture by *Rodin, Henry Moore* (Family), and *Karel Vogel*.

Between the town centre and the railway, to the N, associated activities are located: in the service area, the FIRE STATION (*H. Conolly*, County Architect) and GILBEYS' large distillery (by *Alexander Gibson*); the SPORTS CENTRE, with Sports Hall and public house, both by *Frederick Gibberd*; to the E the Town Park and, on the W, the HARLOW HOSPITAL (by *Easton & Robertson, Cusdin, Preston & Smith*).‡

* The COURT HOUSE is low, strictly symmetrical, and decidedly elegant. The TOWN HALL is cross-shaped, with the N arm the circular Council Chamber, the E and W arms also low, and the S arm a tower block. The top storeys are recessed and crowned by the somewhat modish motif of four arches. The COLLEGE OF FURTHER EDUCATION is a successful group of one-, three-, and seven-storey parts. ST PAUL has a heavy, short bell-tower to the r. of the façade. The church itself has transepts, a flèche, and against the E wall a mosaic by *John Piper*.

‡ The first part, 1958–60 is cross-shaped with a five- to six-storey E–W block for wards, and outpatients, operating theatres, etc., in the low S and N arms.

HAROLD HILL
1½ m. NE Romford

HAROLD HILL ESTATE. One of the largest L.C.C. housing enterprises after the Second World War. It is now (1964) virtually complete, with a total of 7,631 houses with space for over 25,000 people. They are grouped in two neighbourhoods. Architecturally not much of special interest can be discovered.

(GOOSHAYS FARM, in the middle of the estate, a plain red brick C18 building, now used as a Community Centre.)

(HAROLD HILL GRAMMAR SCHOOL, Noak Hill Road. By *H. Conolly*, County Architect, 1958–60. ' Friendly and naturally decorative ', as Mr Nairn writes.)

(HARROWFIELD SECONDARY BOYS' SCHOOL, Sheffield Drive. By *Richard Sheppard & Partners* in collaboration with *H. Conolly*, County Architect, 1952–4.)

(WAREHOUSE for Taylor Bros, by *J. M. Austin-Smith & Partners*, 1960–1.)

HARWICH

Although present-day Harwich might well be called the poor relation of Dovercourt, it is pleasant to look at and to wander in, whereas Dovercourt is not. The key to the architectural character and development of Harwich is the N tip : three inns, if that word can be applied to the former GREAT EASTERN HOTEL, 1864 by *Thomas Allom*, a white elephant, if ever there was one. It is now the town hall. It is built of white brick, in five storeys, and exhibits what the time called the 'free Italian or mixed style'. Immediately to the E of it the PIER HOTEL, lower, and with considerably lower ceiling heights to the rooms. The architectural style is also debased, but it is not showy but jolly. Painted white with a first-floor balcony painted blue, and a belvedere on top. Immediately E of the Pier Hotel the ANGEL INN, a two-storeyed pub with a weatherboarded gable on the l., and an oriel window on the r. The three buildings are the history of the borough in a nutshell.

We shall now examine the little town by walking along its main streets from N to S. They are all more or less parallel – a planned medieval town. WEST STREET is the West End, broader and straighter than the others and mainly Georgian : No. 39, early C18, originally of five bays, then, opposite, Almshouses dated 1785, then No. 32, and opposite No. 63 and Bridewell House.

CHURCH STREET starts with a quiet Georgian group on both sides. The best is No. 42 (doorway with Ionic pilasters, fretwork frieze and pediment). The Wesleyan Chapel (METHODIST CHURCH) is dated 1829, a domestic front of white brick, for the pediment. Then just N of the church on the E side the THREE CUPS HOTEL, early C16, with an L-shaped plan. Late C16 plaster ceiling on the first floor. Staircase of c.1700 with twisted balusters. Opposite the GUILDHALL, built in 1769, entirely like an ambitious merchant's house: red brick, three storeys, with tall canted bay windows l. and r. of the one-bay centre. This has to one's surprise a Gothick doorpiece with three-shafted supports (with shaft-rings) carrying an ogee arch inside a broken Georgian triangular pediment. Above it a normal Georgian window with a segmental pediment. Above that a coat of arms under the Rococo triple-curved pediment.

In KING'S HEAD STREET No. 16 is Georgian of five bays, No. 21 is C17 with oversailing upper floor and two gables.* KING'S QUAY STREET is probably the most rewarding street, although it has fewer houses of individual interest. Near its s end it crosses the churchyard, passes the CORPORATION SCHOOL with an 1840 Tudor-looking nucleus, and then arrives at some wealthier early C19 houses, facing the Green and the sea: No. 29 has absurdly big ironwork trim outside, No. 31 two bow windows. On the GREEN the old CRANE from the disbanded Naval Yard.‡ Later C17, operated by tread-wheels worked by men. The crane house is weatherboarded.

At the s end of West Street the HIGH LIGHTHOUSE, c.90 ft high, polygonal, of white brick. Designed by *Asher Alexander* and built in 1818.

ST NICHOLAS, Church Street. 1821 by *M. G. Thompson*. Gothic of the lean Commissioners' type. Yellow brick, tall w tower with spire, castellated porches l. and r. Interior of nave and aisles with three galleries, two-storeyed windows, and very thin piers carrying a sham groined vault. The chancel is effective – as tall as the nave but polygonal and with only one tier of large windows. – The STAINED GLASS is original: borders and shields. – FONT. Octagonal, of Purbeck marble, of the usual type with two shallow blank pointed arches to each side, early C13. – PAINTING. Moses giving the Law. Said to be by *William Paris*, 1700. – PLATE. Paten of 1683.

HARWOOD HALL *see* UPMINSTER

* It was the house of the master of the 'Mayflower'.
‡ A new jetty is to be built on this site (1964).

HASSENBROOK HALL *see* STANFORD-LE-HOPE

HASSOBURY *see* FARNHAM

HATCHES FARM *see* LITTLE BURSTEAD

HATFIELD BROAD OAK

ST MARY THE VIRGIN. The second Aubrey de Vere about 1135 founded here a Benedictine priory. The present church is the parts of the priory church w of the crossing. Of the parts further E nothing remains but the two w crossing piers, with demi-shafts and one waterleaf capital of *c.*1175. The N wall of the present church also is C12, but the only ornamental feature surviving on the outside, two arches of a blank arcade, is a C15 enrichment. The fact that the aisle windows are placed so high is connected with the existence of the cloister on that side. In 1378, in a quarrel between the priory and the village, the cloister and part of the walls were damaged, and afterwards the nave and aisles must have been rebuilt. It is this state that we now see inside, arcades of five bays with piers of the common four-shaft-four-hollow section with no capitals above the hollows. Two-centred arches and extremely good small head-stops for the hood-moulds. The nave roof is of 1843, and very handsome with tie-beams and panelling to cover the rafters. Externally it is rather the C15 that dominates. To this belong most of the windows, the s porch, which has a doorway with tracery spandrels, battlements, pinnacles, and three-light side openings with panel-tracery, the s turret to the former rood loft, the s chapel with a very large four-light window with panel tracery, and the big w tower with angle buttresses, stepped battlements, a higher stair-turret, a w doorway with tracery spandrels, a three-light w window, and three-light transomed straight-headed bell-openings. The clerestory windows are, it seems, original late C14 work. The whole exterior of the church is of pebble-rubble, except for two later additions, the N vestry of late C17 chequer brick, and the Library to the E of the s chapel, which was built in 1708. It contains 300 volumes of the C15 to C17. — REREDOS and CHANCEL PANELLING, early C18 and quite sumptuous. Ascribed to *John Woodward,** who, *c.*1725, worked in Trinity College Chapel, Cambridge. — SEAT (w end of s aisle). Of the same date and the same courtly style, with openwork foliage scrolls

20b

* One panel can be folded back and reveals a window into a watching chamber secured by a C15 IRON GRILLE.

– COMMUNION RAIL with sturdy twisted balusters, the bulbous foot surrounded by growing-up leaves. Again belonging to the same set of woodwork. – SCULPTURE. The four Symbols of the Evangelists, probably from chancel stalls, also very good, and also early C18. – Kneeling figure of a worshipper, c.30 in. tall, of c.1400. It was originally part of a hammerbeam truss in the chancel. – SCREEN, N chapel. C15, of simply traceried one-light divisions. – CANDELABRA. Gorgeous C18 piece, of brass, in the nave. – STAINED GLASS. One s window (Christ on the waves) by *Hardman* 1893. – MONUMENTS. Effigy said to be Robert de Vere, third Earl of Oxford, c.1300, cross-legged, very defaced (chancel). – Sir John Barrington † 1691. Standing wall-monument with two rather coarsely carved putti and an urn between them. – Sarah Chamberlayne † 1742 and Richard Chamberlayne † 1758, identical monuments with profiles in oval medallions in front of the usual obelisks. – Stanes Chamberlayne † 1782, characteristically more classical in all the ornamental details; the portrait medallion here is at the foot, standing putti higher up. – Sir Charles Barrington † 1788 by *J. F. Moore* of London, of marbles of various colours, with oval relief of mourning female figure, an urn, and a weeping willow. – Lady Ibbetson † 1816 by *Flaxman*, with two almost horizontally floating angels above the inscription plate.

Pretty village, consisting of two streets meeting at r. angles. In the street starting along the churchyard (ALMSHOUSES of 1708, a few plain brick cottages) several nice Georgian houses (one with two bows and Gothick windows), in the other called Cage End several gabled timber-framed houses (especially the former TOWN FARM with divers gables, C15, early C16, and 1630; and the house facing the other street which has a gable above a carriageway. The upper-floor room below the gable has disappeared and the timber posts are now like a screen).

BARRINGTON HALL, 1 m. N. 1735 with Neo-Jacobean alterations of 1863. According to Mr G. Spain, the alterations are by *Edward Browning* of Stamford. Some original plasterwork remains.

DOWN HALL, 3 m. SW. 1871–3 by the younger *Cockerell*, in a sumptuous Italian style with a colonnade and much sgraffito decoration. The walls are of concrete. In the grounds a famous avenue of hornbeams, planted by Matthew Prior. The house preceding the present one was the Earl of Oxford's, and he gave it to Prior.

MOUNT, 2½ m. NW. Low and square, 100 ft diameter, 5 ft high. Perhaps the remains of a barrow.

HATFIELD PEVEREL

ST ANDREW. Hatfield Peverel possessed a Benedictine priory, a cell of St Albans Abbey. The whole present parish church is the nave of the priory church, with a C15 N aisle and a S aisle of 1873 added. The nave was followed by a central tower and transepts. Of the priory chancel nothing exists now, of the S transept the E wall of the vestry, of the central tower the W arch, plain and clearly of the early C12, and some wall stumps of the N and S walls. Of the nave the W wall survives, with a doorway with one order of columns with scalloped capitals and zigzag in the arch voussoirs. The S wall of the nave is also original (C13 lancet) to the point where the S aisle adjoins. Of the N wall of the nave one upper window, now above one of the N arcade arches, bears witness. The N arcade of octagonal piers with double-chamfered arches is ascribed to the C15. In the N wall one early C14 and one C15 window, the others are C19. The brick battlements and stair-turret are of c.1500. – SCREEN (N arcade, E bay). Perp, with panel tracery. – BENCH ENDS. Three in the chancel, poppy-heads and heads of a King, a Queen, etc. – STAINED GLASS. Small fragments of the C14 and C15 in N windows, larger pieces of the C16 to C18, largely foreign, in S windows. – W window by *Kempe*, 1895. – HELM, GAUNTLETS, SWORD, and SPUR, mid C17. – MONUMENTS. In the chancel a tomb-chest of blue marble with very fine, elaborate quatrefoil decoration. – On the sill of a N window effigy of a man in civilian clothes holding his heart in his hands, c.1300, badly preserved. – Various C18 and early C19 tablets, e.g. Arthur Dabbs † 1750, with Rococo cartouche surrounded by flower and putti-heads. Also tablets by *Thompson* (1817) and *Coulman* (1818).

HATFIELD PLACE. By *John Johnson*. 1791–5, of three bays, with rusticated ground floor and coupled pilasters on the upper floor.

CRIX. Built c.1775. Red brick, six bays, with a broad Adamish doorway.

HAVERING ATTE BOWER

ST JOHN THE EVANGELIST. By *Basil Champneys*, 1875–8, that is an early work of his. Flint, with Dec windows and an arcade in the Essex tradition. A little freer only the S tower with an open E–W passage through, a higher stair-turret, and openwork battlements. – FONT. C12, of Purbeck marble, octagonal, with two shallow blank arches on each side.

On the Green, outside the church, to the SE, the STOCKS, quite a rarity in Essex. Of houses worth mentioning not many are left. The best by far is BOWER HOUSE, built in 1729 by *Flitcroft*, his first building. Red brick. The wings were added about 1800. They are single-storeyed and have canted ends towards the S. The house itself is of five bays and two storeys with a three-bay pediment and a doorway with pediment on alternatingly rusticated pilasters. Entrance Hall with a fine fireplace. Staircase with dark wall-paintings by *Thornhill*, one of his last works, as he died in 1734. In the house a stone corbel with the arms of Edward III is preserved. This comes from the royal manor of Havering. The stables have on the l. and r. large alternatingly rusticated archways, now blocked, and a lantern in the centre.

ROUND HOUSE, E of church and Green. An oval building of *c.*1800, three storeys, plastered, with eight windows on each storey. Four pairs of giant Tuscan pilasters. Porch of two pillars and two Ionic columns.

HAWKWELL

ST MARY. Small, of nave and chancel (C14) with a belfry (C15). The low-side window on the S side of the chancel is original. The belfry rests on four oak posts with cross-beams supported by arched braces. – PLATE. Cup of 1662.

RECTORY. Built 1831, enlarged 1858.

HEATH PARK ESTATE *see* BECONTREE

HELION BUMPSTEAD

ST ANDREW. Brick W tower of 1812, with pointed windows and battlements. C13 chancel with some renewed lancet windows. S aisle arcade mid C14 with massive octagonal piers and double-chamfered arches. The outer wall of the S aisle is largely of *c.*1812. – FONT. Perp, octagonal, with traceried stem and the usual quatrefoils along the bowl. – BENCHES. Panels of bench ends, also re-used in chancel stalls, pulpit, etc. – PLATE. Cup of *c.*1600; Paten on foot of 1699. – MONUMENT. Devereux Tallakarne † 1627 and wife, epitaph of unusual design. No figures. Inscription and ornamental panels between termini caryatids. Tall obelisks and shield on top. The monument is a copy of that to Luce Tallakarne at Ashen.

HEMPSTEAD

ST ANDREW. An all Perp church. Nave and aisles C14 (consecration 1365), chancel probably C15, W tower C15, but rebuilt recently (begun 1933), E end of brick, early C16, N additions of brick C17. The outer aisle walls were rebuilt in 1887–8 by *S. Knight*. The arcades have quatrefoil piers with slight sharp hollows in the diagonals and two-centred arches with a two-quadrant moulding. – HELM. C17; with the Harvey crest (N arcade, E end). – PLATE. Cup of 1561; Bowl of 1630, a secular piece with two handles and repoussé decoration. – MONUMENTS. Brasses to a Knight and Lady, *c*.1500 (the figures 27 in. high; N chapel); to a Civilian and wife *c*.1475; a Civilian of *c*.1480; a Civilian of *c*.1518 (3 ft long); a Civilian and wife of *c*.1530 – all in the nave. – William Harvey † 1657, chief physician to Charles I, the discoverer of the circulation of the blood. Frontal bust of outstanding workmanship, and said to be a striking likeness. By *Edward Marshall*. The bust is in a restrained Baroque surround. – Sir William Harvey † 1719. Standing wall-monument with a big arched niche inside which a low broad urn on a fat column. Baroque scrolls, flower garlands, etc. No figure. – William Harvey † 1742 and wife, erected 1758. The sculptor according to Wright is *Roubiliac*. Standing wall-monument with the usual grey obelisk, and in front of it two profile medallions with drapery arranged around them.

HENHAM

ST MARY THE VIRGIN. C13 chancel with some lancet windows and a plain S doorway. The rest mostly C14 (except for the embattled C15 S porch). C14 W tower with diagonal buttresses (also into the nave, where a squinch is necessary to under-pin the buttress). Later brick battlements, and recessed lead 'spike' of Herts type. C14 arcades of four bays inside, with quatrefoil piers, moulded capitals, and double-chamfered arches. The S arcade is earlier. It has sturdier piers. At its E end an irregularity explained by the Royal Commission as follows. The original nave, about 1300, was enlarged by a S transept. To this belong the two semi-octagonal responds. The S aisle was added later and incorporates the earlier transept.

The N arcade has a similar irregularity. A piece of the C13 nave was left standing at its E end. The capital of the middle pier has a delightful enrichment, a tiny carved demi-figure of 21a the Virgin, very simply dressed with rather baroque folds and two censing angels l. and r. of her. Their style seems to me to be c.1500. – SCREEN. Specially sumptuous, as Essex screens go, single-light divisions with ogee heads and elaborate panel tracery above. – PULPIT. C15 with two panels to each side of the hexagon and a buttress between them. – DESK with C17 plaited ornament and an acorn knob l. and r. of the desk top. – MONUMENT. Samuel Feake, 1790, by *W. Vere* of Stratford. Very purely neo-classical, with an urn against an obelisk. The urn on a base projecting triangularly – a design quite out of the ordinary run.

Specially pretty village green.

PLEDGDON HALL, ¾ m. SE. Good timber-framed C17 house with gables and barn.

(BROOM HOUSE, 1½ m. SW. Handsome late C16 timber-framed house. Symmetrical front with two gables; the timbers exposed. R.C.)

HEYBRIDGE

ST ANDREW. A church almost completely Norman, with an impressive W tower, nave, and chancel. The E end of the chancel alone (with its five-light window) is Perp. The W tower, a little later than nave and chancel, is impressive for accidental reasons. It was laid out very broad, but stopped when it was hardly higher than the nave, and later covered with a big pyramid roof. Moreover, in the early C16 one very massive diagonal brick buttress was put up to prop it. Original NW stair-turret, and original, though blocked, W doorway. In nave and chancel there are on the N side three original windows and one doorway, on the S side two doorways and two blocked but still noticeable windows. Inside the nave the splays of the Norman clerestory windows also still exist, not in line with the lower windows. The chancel roof has at the E end a hammer-beam truss, sign of its Perp origin, W of that tie-beams, with king-posts and four-way struts. The nave roof is similar, but one tie-beam carries queen-posts. – FONT. Square, of Purbeck marble with the usual blank arcading motif and some other motifs, almost entirely re-cut. – COMMUNION RAIL with twisted balusters, c.1700. – DOOR with C12 ornamental iron hinges. – STAINED GLASS. Female Saint, late C13, N chancel window. – PLATE. Paten of 1617; Cup probably of 1705. – MONUMENT. Thomas Freshwater † 1638 and wife. Big, with kneeling figures opposite each other. Corinthian columns l. and r.

Two noteworthy houses, HEYBRIDGE HALL, SE of the church, timber-framed and plastered, on an L-plan, C17, and THE TOWERS, ENE of the church, Italianate of 1873. The garden is embellished by two castellated towers. House and garden walls are, it is said, of concrete. This seems to mean blocks of pressed sand and gravel. The house was built for Mr E. H. Bentall, M.P., head of the Heybridge Iron Works. In 1863 he built the biggish warehouse by the canal, of yellow brick, three-storeyed, seventeen bays long, and still classical in its mood (with a pediment).

HEYBRIDGE MILL, W of the church, forms a pretty picture of small Georgian red brick miller's house and weatherboarded mill-house.

HIGHAMS see WALTHAMSTOW

HIGH BEECH

HOLY INNOCENTS. 1873 by *Sir Arthur Blomfield*. Right in Epping Forest, surrounded by old trees everywhere. Grey stone with a NW spire, transepts, and an apse.*

HIGH EASTER

ST MARY THE VIRGIN. Wide and large Norman nave and Norman chancel. The quoins of Roman brick are unmistakable, also some Roman bricks used herringbone fashion in the walling. Remains of the chancel arch. Plain Norman S doorway. The nave was heightened early in the C16 and given three-light clerestory windows and battlements. There is also an E window above the chancel arch. The roof is unusually impressive, of flat pitch, with tie-beams on braces with tracery, and with numerous carved bosses. The N aisle was added in the C14. It has two-light windows with an octofoiled circle over two ogee heads. The arcade of four bays has octagonal piers and double-hollow-chamfered arches. The W tower of C15 date has diagonal buttresses, a little chequer flushwork

* Mrs Barbara Jones in her book on Follies mentions the CATACOMBS made from stones of Chelmsford gaol.

along the base, and a doorway with the demi-figure of an angel in the apex and big leaves in the spandrels. Three-light w window, two-light, transomed bell-openings, battlements, and taller, embattled, stair-turret. Early c16 embattled brick porch. – FONT. Octagonal, Perp, with the symbols of the Evangelists and four shields. – SCREENS. Two Parclose Screens at the E end of the N aisle, c15. – PLATE. Paten and Cup of 1562, with chased swags, fruit and flowers, satyr-heads, etc. – TOMB-STONE in the churchyard to Thomas Witham † 1772 with decoration in the style of local pargeting (F. Burgess).

The approach to the church from the village is charming, a narrow passage between two c15 timber-framed and gabled houses. Others opposite.

WINDMILL. A partly demolished post-mill.

HIGH LAVER

ALL SAINTS. Norman nave with E quoins of Roman brick and one original N window, E.E. chancel with renewed lancets, at the E end a group of three. C14 w tower with Dec two-light window, but much renewed in brick in the c18. Battlements and short recessed spire. C14 also the chancel arch, a broad four-centred arch on responds which run on into the arch without any capitals. – FONT. Octagonal, Perp, with traceried stem; bowl with quatrefoils carrying shields. – BRASS. Edward Sulyard and wife, c.1500, the figures 18 in. long. – MONUMENT. John Locke, the philosopher, lies buried at High Laver. The tablet with Latin inscription composed by him is no longer outside the church. It is now on the inner s wall.

HIGH ONGAR

ST MARY. s tower of white brick with porch, 1858 (by *E. Swans-borough*). The nave is Norman and has one of the most ornate doorways in Essex, with one order of columns, a curved lintel with zigzag, a tympanum with three strips of rosettes, also curved, an arch with zigzag, and a hood-mould with saltire crosses, etc. Norman also the N doorway and several windows. The chancel belongs to the E.E. period, see some lancet windows. The three tall s lancets are c19 externally, but their internal aspect with detached shafts is original. Good nave roof with tie-beams, octagonal king-posts with capitals and four-way struts. – FAMILY PEW. c18. –

PULPIT. Plain, early C17, with some little strapwork decoration. – COMMUNION RAIL. With few heavy balusters, mid C17. – BENCH ENDS. With two flat poppy-heads like small cartouches. One is dated 1680 and yet has no indication of classical elements. – MONUMENTS. Brass to a Civilian, c.1510. – Two minor tablets with urns, but without figures, by the younger *John Bacon*, 1801 and 1806.

A little to the w a nice five-bay, two-and-a-half storeyed Late Georgian brick house with pedimented Tuscan porch.

HIGH RODING

ALL SAINTS. C13 nave and chancel, and C19 bellcote. Stone s porch of c.1400. – FONT. Octagonal, Perp, with quatrefoils with shields. – N DOOR with C13 ironwork. – PULPIT with traceried panels of c.1500. – STAINED GLASS. Small bits in several windows, mostly C14. – PLATE. Paten of 1562; Cup of 1562 with chased band; Dish probably of 1697.

BARN, at New Hall, ¾ m. w. The house has disappeared, but the large early C16, partly weatherboarded and partly timber-framed barn survives. The infilling between the timber posts is of brick. It is of seven bays, with a king-post roof and two entrances.

HILL HALL see THEYDON MOUNT

HOCKLEY

ST PETER AND ST PAUL. Away from the village. A short, unusual w tower with big bulky angle buttresses at the foot and then changing from the square into an irregular octagon. Battlements and recessed spire. The big cusped, ogee-headed w doorway is said to date from the restoration of 1842. The rest of the church is C13. Nave and low, narrow N aisle separated by a four-bay arcade on round piers with stiff-leaf capitals (upright leaves) and one-stepped, slightly single-chamfered arches. Original aisle windows small. The nave roof is ascribed to the C14. It has tie-beams and king-posts with moulded capitals. – FONT. Uncommonly big, octagonal, C13, of the Purbeck type, with shallow blank pointed arcades. – (STAINED GLASS. Some old pieces in the N aisle E window.) – PLATE. Cup of 1562 with band of ornament.

In 1838 a salubrious spring was discovered at Hockley, and so in 1842 in Spa Road a PUMP ROOM was built. It was designed by *James Lockyer*. It is a modest building as Pump Rooms go, but of course of quite a different order from what the village knew until then. Tall arched windows, Tuscan pilasters, and a heavy somewhat restless pediment. It is typical 1840s, in a chaste yet formal mood. A little later the SPA HOTEL was built at the fork of Spa Road and the main road. Two-storeyed with quoins and upper arched windows. It is of no special architectural interest.

PLUMBEROW MOUNT, 1 m. E of the church. The mound is 76 ft in diameter and 14 ft high. Excavation in 1914 revealed a core of clay covered by a capping of gravelly earth. Roman and Early Saxon pottery was found on top of the clay core. The function of the mound is uncertain, but it is probably of post-Roman date. The ten or more mounts 1½ m. NE of the church across the river Crouch are probably the remains of medieval salt workings.

(VICARAGE. The front rooms were added about 1820 to an existing farmhouse. Information from Mr D. Morgan.)

HORHAM HALL
2 m. SW of Thaxted

Horham Hall is one of the two or three finest brick mansions [49b] of pre-Reformation date in Essex. The house was built by Sir John Cutte, Treasurer of the Household of Henry VIII. He had acquired the manor in 1502, acquired the manor of Thaxted in 1514, and he died in 1520, leaving the house unfinished. It consists now of one range facing E with a N wing at right angles to it. This formerly extended further to the E, where probably lay the chapel, and also to the W, where it touched the moat. In addition there is a S wing including parts of a timber-framed mid C15 house. The moulded timber roof of the solar of that house is preserved. The brickwork of the S wing, however, including the ornate chimneystack, dates from *c*.1575 and the present kitchen was rebuilt *c*.1660. Of the moat the N and W sides are still in existence. The E side is filled in, and it was here that a Gatehouse introduced the visitor to the mansion. Its façade indeed faces E. It is entirely irregular and eminently picturesque, with its variety of shades of colour in the brickwork and its busy stone dressings. The Hall lies in the traditional place and is approached, as usual, by a porch leading into the screens passage. The porch is two-storeyed and has a doorway with a four-centred arch. The

windows of the hall lie high up except for the magnificent large
canted bay window which extends with three transoms and a
front of six lights right to the parapet and its (renewed) battlements. It is the showpiece of the house. The individual lights
are arched and cusped, and along the top runs a glazed frieze of
quatrefoils. Inside, the hall has a plinth with an ogee frieze
which runs right into and along the bay window. The bay
window (as well as the other hall windows) has tracery-
panelled reveals. The hall has a ceiling hiding the timber roof,
but in its middle a louvre opening communicating with the
charming lantern on the roof which the Royal Commission
seems to regard as original, but which more probably belongs
to the work of *c.*1580. To return to the exterior, to the r. of
the bay window the façade is continued by an odd skew two-
storeyed passage of later Tudor date. This leads to a straight
passage along the front of the N wing and so to the staircase
tower. The tower dates from *c.*1580 (top part *c.*1610–20) and
has a solid square newel surrounded by the stair rising in
three flights from storey to storey (cf. St Osyth). The E and W
fronts of the N wing (between hall and tower) are provided
with stepped gables. Of interiors nothing else need here be
discussed. The house was restored in 1841.

HORNCHURCH

ST ANDREW. A large, townish church, although Hornchurch
was a village until London got hold of it and made it into a
dormitory with more than 100,000 inhabitants. The church
has a C13 chancel and a C13 arcade between nave and aisles
(circular piers with moulded capitals; double-chamfered
arches). Perp N and S aisles, clerestory, N and S chancel chapels,
N porch, and W tower. The church is light, thanks to three-
light aisle and clerestory windows (the E window is new). The
chancel chapels have octagonal piers and double-hollow-
chamfered arches. The W tower is big and prominent, with
diagonal buttresses, higher SW stair-turret, and recessed spire.
– SEDILIA. Tall late C13 arches, five-cusped on slim shafts.
A squint in the back wall of the westernmost seat. – DOORS.
N and W doorways, C15 or early C16. – STAINED GLASS. Bits
(e.g. Crucifixus, headless) in the E window of the N chapel;
C15. – PLATE. Cup and Paten of 1563; Paten of *c.*1690, Flagon
of 1690; Almsdish of 1716; Paten of 1719; Cup and Paten of
1733; all good pieces. – MONUMENTS. Several Brasses in

chancel and N chapel, e.g. five boys of c.1500. – Tomb-chest with quatrefoil decoration, to William Ayloffe † 1517. – Francis Rame † 1617, monument with kneeling figures; alabaster. – Richard Blakstone † 1638, with two kneelers and two standing angels pulling away a curtain; alabaster. – Richard Spencer † 1784, by *Flaxman*. Two standing angels and medallion with double portrait. – Outside the churchyard gate the WAR MEMORIAL by *Sir Charles Nicholson*, 1921.

Opposite the church the OLD CHAPLAINCY with C17 parts. W of the church in the High Street WYKEHAM COTTAGE, Gothick with thin exposed timbers. Numerous cottages, weatherboarded and otherwise, further W. More in NORTH STREET, where – lying a good deal back – is LANGTONS, now Council Offices, probably of 1760. Seven bays, two storeys, red brick. On in the High Street the APPLETON ALMSHOUSES of 1838, small humble imitation-Tudor composition in yellow brick, then the former PENNANT ALMSHOUSES of 1597, but rebuilt in the C18, then the gargantuan embattled lodge of GREY TOWERS, a mansion of 1876 now demolished.

(SWIMMING BATHS. By *V. Williams*, Council Surveyor, and *D. Pearcy*, Council Architect. 1957–8.)

SW of Hornchurch off the Rainham Road BRITTONS, C18 farmhouse with older bits and a fine C16 brick BARN.

N of the centre of Hornchurch in Nelmes Way NELMES, now called Manor House, a complex house with a C16 E wing containing the one-storeyed original Hall, a S front of c.1720 (rusticated yellow brick; Venetian windows), and an excellent late C17 staircase in the angle between the two. The staircase parapet has richly carved pierced panels.

(BUSH ELMS, 1¼ m. NW of the church. A C15 house, much altered but still preserving the original screen inside between screens passage and former hall. R.C.)

HORNDON-ON-THE-HILL

ST PETER AND ST PAUL. Primarily an E.E. church, as is evidenced by both nave arcades and the remains of a clerestory above and the N chancel chapel arcade. The N nave arcade seems to have come first: four bays, alternatingly circular and octagonal piers and capitals with crockets and flat stiff-leaf. The voussoirs of one of the arches are decorated by rosettes, a most uncommon motif. The S arcade is nearly identical, except that the capitals are undecorated. The E responds however have upright leaves which look as if they might have been re-tooled in the C15. The arcade to the chancel chapel has an octagonal pier with moulded capitals. The arches are double-chamfered, whereas most of the arches of the nave arcade are of one step with one chamfer. The C13 clerestory windows were quatrefoil. C13 also the S doorway with two orders of colonnettes, of which one is keeled, and many-moulded voussoirs. At the W end a timber bell-turret was erected inside the first nave bay from the W, an independent construction on four sturdy posts with crossbeams and carved braces. An interesting feature is that the N and S beams cantilever out to the E and support struts for the superstructure. Trellis-strutting above the crossbeams. Broach-spire. The roofs of chancel and nave are partly original. One alteration is that dormer-windows have been set into the nave roof on both sides. The timber S porch does not contain much of the C15. Not much of interest in the windows. The E window of four lights is Perp; in the S aisle two C14 windows.* – FONT. C14, square bowl with some panelling; on square stem. – LECTERN. 1898. Good Arts-and-Crafts job, straight in all its timber-work but with some turquoise enamel inlay and some copper. Whom by? – PLATE. Cup of 1567; Flagon of 1700. – MONUMENT. Daniel Caldwell † 1634 and wife. With inscription and two black columns; figures of prophets with scrolls stand outside these.

Horndon is a nice village with several good houses, e.g. the HIGH HOUSE, dated 1728 (five bays, two storeys, segment-headed windows), the BELL INN (C15, half-timbered with gables), the OLD MARKET HALL (C16; originally open on the ground floor), THE GABLES (½ m. S), ARDEN HALL (½ m. NE, five-bay Georgian), and SAFFRON GARDENS (⅔ m. SSW, with a good C17 stone fireplace inside; R.C.).

HOUBRIDGE HALL see GREAT OAKLEY

HOUCHIN'S FARM see FEERING

HUTTON

ALL SAINTS. Rebuilt by *G. E. Street* in 1873. A small church and not one of Street's masterpieces. Of the medieval church

---

* Mr Alan Reed kindly tells me that the chancel was restored in 1890 by *W. D. Caröe*, and the nave in 1898 by *C. R. Ashbee*. Mr Reed is of the opinion that the pretty CUPBOARDS etc. in the church and the STAINED GLASS in the vestry were designed by Ashbee.

the nave arcades with quatrefoil piers, moulded capitals, and arches of one wave and one hollow-chamfer mouldings survive – typical C14 work. The chancel arch and the nave roof belong to the same date. The bell-turret is also medieval, but probably of the C15. It stands on six posts, the distance between the first being much wider than between the others. Tall braces from N and S and trellis strutting from W to E. – LECTERN etc., metalwork in the typical *Street* style. – PLATE. Cover of 1567; Paten on Foot probably of 1648. – BRASS. Knight and Lady of *c*.1525.

HUTTON HALL. The house is not mentioned by the Royal Commission, and most of it seems indeed to belong to *c*.1730. Seven-bay front, long wings to the back. Segment-pedimented porch on fine fluted Ionic columns. Entrance Hall panelled and with a central Ionic column of wood. Staircase with twisted balusters of varying shapes. In one room a marble fireplace, in another thin Gothick panelling similar to the work of 1745 at Belhus. But the front has three symmetrical straight gables and there are similar gables at the back, and their brickwork and shapes look decidedly of the C17. Inside is one C17 fireplace which may however not originally belong to the house.

(The following list of new housing estates at Hutton was kindly supplied by the Brentwood Library:

THE LONDON COUNTY COUNCIL ESTATE, completed in 1955.

THE BRENTWOOD URBAN DISTRICT COUNCIL ESTATE, completed in 1963.

THE COMBINED AUTHORITIES ESTATE, by *The East Ham Borough Council*, completed in 1963.)

THE HYDE *see* INGATESTONE

HYDE HALL *see* GREAT WALTHAM

HYLANDS *see* WIDFORD

HYTHE

Hythe is really part of Colchester and is known locally as The Hythe.

ST LEONARD. Close to the street. Impressive but much restored. The battlements and pinnacles of the C14 W tower (angle buttresses) e.g. are new. The S porch is rebuilt, the (embattled) S aisle has new windows. The N side is more rewarding.

N aisle of *c.*1330, N chancel chapel of *c.*1500. The N arcades show these dates clearly too. The piers of the Dec style are quatrefoil, as usual, the C15 piers are of four shafts and four hollows in the diagonals. The arch mouldings differ too. The C15 type appears in the s arcade, the w bay of the N arcade, and both chancel chapels. Modest hammerbeam roof in the nave. – FONT. Octagonal, Perp, with shields in quatrefoils and big leaves. – PLATE. Fine Mazer with gilt rim, 1521; large Elizabethan Cup; large Cup probably of 1624; Paten of 1713. The best houses of Hythe lie immediately by the church. w of the churchyard No. 133 HYTHE HILL,* timber-framed, white, and crooked, with a gabled overhang just at the church-yard corner. Opposite, No. 62, Georgian brick, with a pedi-ment on pilasters with fancy decoration, and a Venetian win-dow above. A little further w No. 143, Georgian brick, of three bays with two Venetian windows on the ground floor. A little further E HYTHE QUAY, a picturesque waterside street with warehouses, and HARBOUR HOUSE, a fine five-bay house of vitrified bricks with red brick dressings. The date is Early Georgian.

ILFORD‡

ST MARY THE VIRGIN, High Road. The old parish church, 1829–31 by *Savage*. The Commissioners' type of church. Yellow brick with thin w tower. Lancet windows, with pre-archeological tracery. Chancel 1920.

ST ANDREW, The Drive. 1924 by *Sir Herbert Baker*. In com-parison with Lutyens Baker may be one of the smaller fry. In a between-the-wars-suburban area a church such as St Andrew will at once be noticed as remarkable. Tall, red brick, with tall, slim w bell-turret and a copper-roofed baptistery apse between two round-arched entrances below. The interior has a low round-arched arcade with no capitals at the springing of the arches, a tall clerestory, and a tall apse with two-light windows. That is: a frank mixture of Gothic and classical motifs.

ST LUKE, Uphall Road. 1941 by *E. T. Dunn*. Mr Goodhart-Rendel called the church uncommonly fine, though entirely traditional.

ST PETER, Aldborough Road. 1862 by *Ashpitel*. Small, very crude church of ragstone with a little N turret at the E end of

---

* Recently unsympathetically treated.
‡ See also under Barkingside and Newbury Park.

the nave in the returning angle to the chancel. – PLATE. Cup, Flagon, and Almsdish from the chapel of Aldborough Hall, 1771.

TOWN HALL, High Road. 1901 by *B. Woolland*. 'In a free classic style' (Tasker). Additions 1927 and 1933. Nothing special.

(LIBRARY and SWIMMING BATHS. By *F. Gibberd*, begun in 1960.)

ILFORD HOSPITAL, High Road. A very charming sight behind its high brick wall, so detached from the surburban bustle of Ilford. The hospital was founded about 1140. It now consists of a C14 and C19 chapel and two short projecting wings of the early C18. They are one-storeyed with hipped roofs and each with a central gable. The windows have heavy wooden casements. The chapel has an early C14 nave and chancel and an aisle of 1889 (by *J. M. Burns*). The two-light windows, though much restored, are of the original early C14 shape. – STAINED GLASS. In the chancel two lozenge-shaped panels with the arms of John Gresham, later C16. – W window of aisle and W rose-window of nave by *Morris & Co.* (designed by *Burne-Jones*, *c*.1891). – MONUMENT. John Smythe † 1475, master of the hospital, all C19, except the very finely ornamented pilasters (near the W end of the aisle), and these must be some fifty to sixty years later than Smythe's death.

GANTS HILL STATION, London Transport, Eastern Avenue. Designed by *Charles Holden* 1937–8, built 1947–8. In the middle of the roundabout, to be reached by subways, an original and successful arrangement.

REDBRIDGE STATION, London Transport, Eastern Avenue. Designed by *Charles Holden* in 1937–8, built 1947–8.

The only private or formerly private houses worth recording are the following:

VALENTINES, in Valentines Park. Plain big yellow brick mansion with red brick dressings. Rainwater head 1769, much altered 1811.

ALDBOROUGH HOUSE, Aldborough Road. Derelict at the time of writing.* Five-bay, two-storey house with cupola with concave roof. Many Victorian alterations. Said to be part of a larger mansion (probably centre) which was built *c*.1730.

CAR SERVICE STATION, 543 High Road. 1934 by *Cameron Kirby*. An early example for England of the modern style in architecture.

* Now demolished.

(Of recent commercial buildings the following deserve mention: MOULTON'S STORE, by *Katz & Vaughan*, HARRISON GIBSON'S STORE, by *D. Forrest*, both completed in 1960, and ILFORD'S OFFICES, by *E. H. Willison*, completed 1958.)

UPHALL CAMP. Early Iron Age or Roman rectangular camp, on low-lying ground near the River Roding. Lavender Mount, a mound at the N end of the rampart, is 21 ft high and 85 ft in diameter. The camp is now completely obliterated.

INGATESTONE

A large village with quite a prosperous High Street and, further out, far more prosperous Late Victorian houses of Londoners.

ST EDMUND AND ST MARY. A truly magnificent W tower of red brick with black diapers. Tall, with angle buttresses, a three-light brick W window with Perp panel tracery, and two-light windows in two tiers above it. Stepped battlements on a corbel frieze. Behind the tower the small and shortish N wall of the nave, obviously Norman, with walls of puddingstone and Roman brick. The projecting N chancel chapel is C17 brick. S aisle and S chancel chapel C15 to early C16. The S chapel is of brick and was built by the Petre family in 1556. Three-light E window with a transom and two- and three-light S windows. Inside, the impression is somewhat disappointing after the glory of the tower. Three-bay S arcade with short piers of the well-known Perp four-shaft-four-hollow section, and double-chamfered arches. Three-bay brick arcade to the Petre Chapel, with octagonal piers and triple-chamfered arches. Nave roof with tie-beams, octagonal king-posts with capitals and four-way struts. – FONT. Perp, octagonal with quatrefoil panels bordered by friezes of small quatrefoil panels. – HOUR GLASS of iron, early C18, fixed to the wall. – PLATE. Cup of 1675; Paten and two Flagons of 1725; two Cups and covers of 1728. – Three HELMS of *c.*1570. – MONUMENTS. Between chancel and S chapel the alabaster tomb-chest of Sir William Petre, Secretary of State to Henry VIII, and Privy Councillor to him, Edward VI, Mary, and Elizabeth I, † 1572, and wife, with recumbent effigies on rolled-up mats. Very fine quality. The tomb-chest with shell-headed panels separated by columns. It is perhaps by *Cornelius Cure*, Crown Mason.* – In the chapel itself Robert Petre † 1593, monument with the usual kneeling figure; between columns of touch. – Also John

33b

* Essex Record Office, *Essex Churches*, 1956.

Troughton † 1621, with an outstandingly good portrait bust 36a
in an oval niche. Relief, in an informal demi-profile. Attributed to *Epiphanius Evesham*.* – In the N chapel John, Lord
Petre † 1613 and wife. Standing wall-monument of triptych
composition with two kneeling figures in the wings, and two
kneeling figures on a higher step in the centre. These are under
a coffered arch. The parts are separated by black columns. The
whole is straight-topped with obelisks and achievements. On
the base in relief nice figures of kneeling children.

INGATESTONE HALL. Ingatestone was a manor of the nunnery
of Barking. In 1539 it came into the hands of Sir William Petre,
son of a wealthy tanner in Devon, protégé of Cromwell, busy
in the commissions for the dissolution of the monasteries,
Secretary of State (cf. above) and Chancellor of the Order of
the Garter. The house is of brick and was externally complete
by 1548, though interior work seems to have gone on to
c.1560. It consisted originally of a base court, a middle court,
and an inner court. What remains is chiefly the inner court,
though shorn of its W range, which contained the Great Hall.
This lay between middle court and inner court and was
pulled down c.1790–1800. One enters the former base court
by a GATEWAY remodelled and provided with its pretty bell-
turret in the C18. The remaining three ranges of the main
structure are still entirely lacking in the systematization which
is characteristic of the Elizabethan style and exists in some of
the leading buildings already before her time. On the other
hand the mullioned and transomed windows already have
the Elizabethan form without arches to the tops of the lights.‡
The most striking external feature is the stepped gables. A big
BARN also has stepped gables. Some of the pretty chimneystacks of the house are original. The main apartment is the
LONG GALLERY in the E range with its chimneypiece. Its
continuation into what remains of the chapel, rebuilt in 1860,
may indicate a former family pew. A true PRIEST HOLE is in
the (Elizabethan ?) S projection in the middle of the S range,
and some good mid C16 panelling in an upper room in the N
range. Two of the panels have the profiles in medallions
typical of the mid C16. They are probably re-set.

The HIGH STREET has no house of independent value, but in
the aggregate its Georgian brick and its fewer C16 and C17

* Essex Record Office, *Essex Churches*, 1956.

‡ Some are original on the W side of the E range. The others belong to the
good restoration of the 1920s.

timber-framed houses form a happy picture. The doorway of one four-bay Early Georgian house on the W side, the keystone heads of one three-bay Georgian house on the E side, and the Early Victorian lettering of the Spread Eagle Hotel should be specially noted. The church lies a good deal back from the street. In the S part of the street the CONGREGATIONAL CHURCH of 1840 with a broad white brick front with plenty of lancets. Further S yet the PETRE ALMSHOUSES of 1840, Neo-Tudor, brick, one-storeyed, with three ranges round a court.

In the last decades of the C19 the architect *George Sherrin* had a house at Ingatestone, and he built here quite a number of prosperous houses, in a picturesque sham Tudor style, of brick with half-timbered gables and plentiful ornamental tiles, e.g. GATE HOUSE, near the station (Sherrin's own house), THE TILES close to this (*c.*1870), and LIGHTOAKS (*c.*1882) and MILLHURST on the road to Mill Green.

INGATESTONE STATION is of 1846, in a friendly Neo-Tudor.

THE HYDE, ½ m. N. Built in 1719. Plain two-and-a-half storeyed block of nine by six bays. Blue bricks with red rubbed brick dressings. Segment-headed windows, parapet, no light relief. The Entrance Hall was created out of five rooms by *Sir William Chambers* in 1761. It has a two-storeyed screen-wall at the back, where the staircase runs up. The columns are Tuscan below and Ionic above. The staircase makes use of the typical balusters and carved tread-ends of the 1720 style, but runs in the Later Georgian fashion first in one arm and then splitting up into two at r. angles.

INGRAVE

ST NICHOLAS. The most remarkable C18 church in the county. Erected in 1735 by Lord Petre of Thorndon Hall. The architect is unknown. He cannot have been far from *Hawksmoor*.
11b Red brick. Massive W tower widened by recessed polygonal turrets, which rise above the parapet of the tower. This rests on an arched corbel frieze. Big inscription plate. The interior much plainer. Nave with central entrances from N and S; arched windows. Narrower chancel with arch on very thick imposts. – FONT. Perp, octagonal, with quatrefoil panels. – PULPIT. Panelled, probably *c.*1735. – BRASSES. Margaret Wake † 1466, wearing a butterfly headdress. – Sir Richard Fitzlewes † 1528 and his four wives.

THORNDON HALL, see p. 388.

INWORTH

ALL SAINTS. Ambitious red brick w tower and w porch, competently if not sensitively done. The date is 1876, the architect *Joseph Clarke*. The rest is Early Norman with the chancel E end of the later C14. The two C11 windows in the N and S chancel walls are memorable. They have the equal outside and inside splays typical of their date. The masonry – stone, flint, puddingstone, and Roman brick – should also be studied. C11 also the low and narrow chancel arch inside. To its sides and in the adjoining nave N and S walls C13 blank arches (cf. South Shoebury, Southend-on-Sea). The ones by the side of the chancel arch are pierced by large squints. Above the chancel arch remains of late C13 WALL PAINTINGS, not easily recognized. In the lower tier a bishop next to a tower and also a boat with a sail and a man by its side. – SCREEN under the chancel arch, three bays. – BENCH in the nave with uncommonly carved back panels, early C16. – STAINED GLASS. C14–C15 fragments in a S window. – PLATE. Cup with incised ornament and Paten, both of 1571.

JENKIN'S FARM *see* WORMINGFORD

JOSSELYNS *see* LITTLE HORKESLEY

KELVEDON

The church lies at the w end of Church Street, that is at one end of the little town.

ST MARY THE VIRGIN. The NW angle of the nave is evidently Norman. Nothing else of the period is visible. Nave and aisles belong to the C13, see especially the arcades. They have circular piers, except for one N pier with a four-shaft-four-hollow section. The capitals are partly moulded, partly with some stiff-leaf and crocket decoration. The arches are of many mouldings. C14 w tower with diagonal buttresses, battlements, and a recessed spire. Also embattled the two aisles. The C14 chancel has an E window with reticulated tracery put in by *Sir Arthur Blomfield* in 1876. The N aisle chapel is an early C16 brick addition with a stepped gable and a four-light window with intersected tracery applied to a depressed four-centred head. Between chancel and vestry a C14 window and a C14 doorway made out of the head of a two-light window. –

STAINED GLASS. E window by *Burlison & Grylls*; s chapel, second s window from E by *Clayton & Bell*, 1859; w window by *Lavers & Westlake*, 1896; s chapel E window by *Powell* (belated pre-Raphaelite; designed by *L. Davis*). – SCULPTURE. Small wooden panel in the vestry, probably Flemish, early C17. – PLATE. Cup of 1562; Paten also Early Elizabethan. – MONUMENTS. To the Abdy family, especially Sir Thomas † 1679 with inscription on a draped stone curtain (by *W. Stanton* ?), and Sir Anthony † 1704 (by *Edward Stanton*).

CHURCH STREET starts by the church with the Georgian VICARAGE, lying far back, then on the opposite side two detached Georgian cottages and a five-bay red brick house with white brick giant pilasters and a three-bay pediment, and an Ionic doorway. The corner to the High Street is a long range of timber-framed cottages. The way in which the HIGH STREET does not start in line with the Roman road from the s but only after quite noticeable a kink is worth pondering over. It closes the s view out of the town and breaks the through-traffic. Plenty of old houses in the High Street. The Royal Commission lists twenty-five prior to 1714. The general impression is of a great variety of skyline and more of gables than of Georgian brick-cubes. A noteworthy group the FRIENDS' EVANGELISTIC BAND (five bays, early C18) and the two timber-framed houses s and N of it. Opposite MONTROSE with two Georgian shop-windows and MASON'S the Butcher's with a good broad doorway of *c.*1700. Then BRIMPTON HOUSE, early C19, white brick. After that a stretch with less of interest.* A workshop (BRADDY'S) should be noted, weatherboarded and pedimented with the front windows running from corner to corner – very modern-looking. Then ORMONDE HOUSE and ORMONDE LODGE, the one early C17, refaced early in the C18, the other a little later, a nice group, as the Lodge lies further back than the House. A little further N, and also lying a little back, a former CHAPEL, red brick of four bays with arched windows and hipped roof. Again a few good Georgian buildings besides the earlier ones listed by the Royal Commission. Past the bridge some more nice houses, especially one with a cast-iron verandah.

(BRIDGEFOOT FARM, ½ m. SE of the church. Timber-framed

---

* The CONGREGATIONAL CHAPEL of 1853 lies back and is not part of the street frontage. It is of red brick with white brick trim, classical, with a big pediment across the whole four-bay width.

house of *c.*1500 with the original screen remaining inside.
R.C.)

(FELIX HALL, ¾ m. N of the church. Originally built *c.*1760.
Only the shell of the centre block remains, with alterations by
Lord Weston made after 1795. These include a noble Ionic
tetrastyle portico, probably by *Thomas Hopper.*)

ROMAN SETTLEMENT. Although no structures are now visible, the modern village probably lies on the site of the Roman
town of CANONIUM. Finds suggest an earlier Belgic settlement in the first half of the C1 and later Roman occupation
until the late C4. The areas which have been most prolific in
finds include that to the E of the Freemasons' Hall, where
large numbers of rubbish pits have been located, and S and E
of the main road. Excavations between 1956 and 1960 in the
latter area have produced Belgic ditches and rubbish pits, a
Roman kiln, pottery, and coins.

KELVEDON HATCH

ST NICHOLAS. 1895 by *J. T. Newman.* Red brick with oddly
stunted apse and dormers in the roof. – PLATE. Cup and Paten
of 1674. – This church replaced an older one, close to Kelvedon Hall.

ST NICHOLAS. The old church is disused and at the time of
writing neglected. It was built in 1753, but in general shape
kept to the Essex tradition. Nave and lower chancel, and
belfry. Red brick. The chancel has a Venetian E window, the
nave arched windows. Also circular windows in both nave and
chancel. Inside still some elegant tablets, etc. of the later C18.

KELVEDON HALL. The house has rainwater-heads of 1725 and
1740. It is of red brick, seven bays wide, and has in addition on
the entrance-side quarter-circle connecting passages to pavilions of three-bay length, and on the garden side three-bay
pavilions in line with the façade. The façades are both very
plain. The main doorway alone is distinguished by a pediment
on attached Tuscan columns. Inside, the Entrance Hall and
the Staircase are in the state of *c.*1740–5, with pediments over
the doors. The staircase walls are stuccoed with hanging garlands, trophies, etc. and the stair-railing is of wrought iron.
The other best rooms were redecorated *c.*1775, especially the
Dining Room and Drawing Room. In one of the pavilions towards the garden is the former Oratory with a segmental
vault, attached columns on the slightly apsed altar side, and

pilasters on the side opposite. In the study a painted ceiling, probably by Italian workmen.

BRIZES. Nine-bay, two-and-a-half-storey Early Georgian house with a four-column porch and a three-bay pediment over. The house is supposed to have been begun in 1720. Entrance Hall with a Venetian triple-arch to separate the room from the staircase, which is of the grand type starting with one flight and then, at the intermediate landing, turning by 180 degrees and continuing in two flights.

KILLIGREWS see MARGARETTING

KINGSMOOR see HARLOW

KINGSWOOD see BASILDON

KIRBY-LE-SOKEN

ST MICHAEL. Surprisingly big and important looking w tower. Knapped flint with a quatrefoil frieze at the base, massive diagonal buttresses with four set-offs, tall two-light bell-openings with one transom, and battlements with flint and stone chequer decoration. The rest of the church looks almost entirely Victorian. Nothing of the rebuilding of 1833 remained visible under the treatment of *Henry Stone*, the restorer of 1870.

LAINDON see BASILDON

LAMARSH

HOLY INNOCENTS. Round tower, plastered, with Norman windows. The roof with dormers belongs to the restoration of 1869, and looks it. Nave and chancel in one, mostly with early C14 windows. The chancel E lancets are not original. s porch early C16 brick, plain. – SCREEN. Two traceried panels to each division; C15. – PLATE. Cup and Paten of 1691.

LAMBOURNE

ST MARY AND ALL SAINTS. A church of quite exceptional charm and historical range. It consists of C12 nave and chancel and C15 belfry, but the exterior and interior were re-modelled boldly, naively, and very successfully in the Early Georgian age. Norman windows on both sides, a plain Norman s doorway, and a more elaborate N doorway, with one order of

(a) *Scenery:* Wivenhoe

(b) *Scenery:* Finchingfield

(a) *Scenery:* Dedham (*Copyright Country Life*)

(b) *Scenery:* An Essex Watermill: Chelmsford

An Essex Windmill: Stansted Mountfitchet. Looking up through
the brake-wheel

(a) *Roman:* Colchester, Balkerne Gate

(b) *Church Exteriors, Saxon:* Bradwell-juxta-Mare, St Peter, *c.* 654

4

(a) *Church Exteriors, Saxon:* Colchester, Holy Trinity

(b) *Church Exteriors, Norman:* Hadleigh, the Apse

5

Church Exteriors, Norman: High Ongar, Doorway

Church Exteriors, Norman: Great Leighs, Round Tower

Church Exteriors, Decorated: Tilty

(a) *Church Exteriors, Perpendicular:* Saffron Walden, c. 1450-1525

(b) *Church Exteriors, Perpendicular:* Chelmsford
Cathedral, Porch with flushwork

(b) *Church Exteriors, Perpendicular*: Pebmarsh, Porch of Brick, early sixteenth century

(a) *Church Exteriors, Perpendicular*: Margaretting, Timber Porch, fifteenth century

(a) *Church Exteriors, Perpendicular:* Fryerning, Tower, early sixteenth century

(b) *Church Exteriors, Georgian:* Ingrave, Tower, 1735

Church Exteriors, Georgian: Mistley, by Robert Adam, only partly preserved, 1776

(a) *Church Interiors, Saxon:* Hadstock

(b) *Church Interiors, Norman:* Waltham Abbey, early twelfth century

13

Church Interiors, Norman: Colchester, St Botolph's Priory, c. 1100

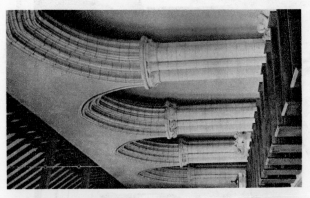
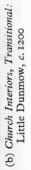

(b) *Church Interiors, Transitional:*
Little Dunmow, *c.* 1200

(a) *Church Interiors, Transitional:*
Castle Hedingham, *c.* 1190

15

(a) *Church Interiors, Early English: Berden, Chancel, c. 1260–70*

(b) *Church Interiors, Decorated: Maldon, South Aisle, c. 1340*

Church Interiors, Decorated: Lawford, Chancel, c. 1330

17

(b) (*above*) *Church Interiors, Decorated:* Great Leighs, Gable of Recess, early fourteenth century

(a) (*left*) *Church Interiors, Decorated:* Lawford, Detail of a Window Jamb

Church Interiors, Decorated and Perpendicular: Thaxted, Arcade,
c. 1340, Clerestory, *c.* 1510

(a) Elmstead, Head Corbel, early fourteenth century

(b) Hatfield Broad Oak, Head Corbel, late fourteenth century

20

(a) Henham, Virgin and Child, above a capital, early sixteenth century

(b) Stambourne, Macwilliam Arms, above a capital, early sixteenth century

Church Interiors, Perpendicular: St Osyth, early sixteenth century

Church Interiors: Blackmore, the Tower

(a) *Church Interiors, Georgian:* Lambourne, King-Post, decorated in the eighteenth century

(b) *Church Interiors, Art Nouveau:* Great Warley, by Harrison Townsend and William Reynolds-Stephens, 1904

24

Church Painting, Norman: Copford, c. 1140–50

Stained Glass, French: Rivenhall, *c.* 1200

Church Painting, Early English: Great Canfield, *c.* 1250

Church Furnishings: Stebbing, Chancel Screen, stone, *c.* 1340–50

Church Furnishings: Gestingthorpe, Double Hammerbeam Roof,
c. 1500

(a) *Church Furnishings:*
Takeley, Font Cover, *c.* 1500

(b) *Church Furnishings:*
Wanstead, Pulpit, *c.* 1790

Stained Glass, Pre-Raphaelite: Waltham Abbey, East Window,
by Edward Burne-Jones, 1861

Metalwork, Art Nouveau: Great Warley, Chancel Screen, detail,
by William Reynolds-Stephens, *c.* 1904

(a) *Church Monuments:* Little Dunmow, Walter Fitzwalter,
†1432 and wife

(b) *Church Monuments:* Ingatestone, Sir William Petre,
†1572 and wife

Church Monuments: Dedham, Thomas Webbe, *c.* 1500

Church Monuments: Saffron Walden, Lord Audley, †1544, by Cornelius Harman

(a) *Church Monuments*: Ingatestone,
John Troughton, †1621

(b) *Church Monuments*: Walthamstow,
Sir Thomas Merry, †1633, by Nicholas Stone

36

Church Monuments: Stansted Mountfitchet,
Sir Thomas Middleton, †1631

Church Monuments: Hempstead, William Harvey, †1657,
by Edward Marshall

(a) *Church Monuments:* West Ham,
Thomas Foot, †1688, and wife

(b) *Church Monuments:* West Ham,
James Cooper, †1743, and wife

39

Church Monuments: Wanstead, Sir Josiah Child, †1699

HERE LYETH BURYED THE BODY OF
Sʳ HENRY BENDYSHE BARᵀ
WHO DEPARTED THIS/LIFE THE THIRD DAY OF SEPTEMBER MDCCXVII
IN THE XLIII YEAR OF HIS AGE.
HE WAS SON OF Sʳ JOHN, AND GREAT GRANDSON OF Sʳ THᵒ BENDYSHE
WHO WAS CREATED BARᵀ THE NINTH OF KING IAMES THE FIRST, WHO
ALSO LY HERE INTERRED TOGETHER WITH MANY OF THEIR ANCESTORS.
HE MARRYED KATHARINE GOSTLIN, DAUGHTER OF Sʳ WILLIAM GOSTLIN
KNIGHT LATE SHIRIFFE OF THE CITY OF LONDON. BY WHOM HE HAD
ISSUE ONE SON HENRY BENDYSHE WHO DYED AN INFANT OF FIVE
MONTHS OLD. AND LYES BURYED HERE.

Church Monuments: Steeple Bumpstead, Sir Henry Bendyshe, †1717,
by Thomas Stayner

Secular Architecture: Colchester, the Keep, late eleventh century

Secular Architecture: Castle Hedingham, the Keep, *c.* 1140 *(Copyright Country Life)*

Secular Architecture: Thaxted, the Guildhall, fifteenth century

Secular Architecture: Colchester, carved beam in the Marquis of
Granby Inn, *c.* 1525 (*Copyright Country Life*)

(a) *Secular Architecture:* Great Coggeshall, Paycocke's House, *c.* 1500

(b) *Secular Architecture:* Cressing Temple, Wheat Barn, *c.* 1530
or considerably earlier

Secular Architecture: Cressing Temple, Barley Barn, interior, *c.* 1450
or considerably earlier

(a) *Secular Architecture:* Colchester, Gatehouse of St John's Abbey, fifteenth century

(b) *Secular Architecture:* St Osyth's Priory, Gatehouse, fifteenth century

(a) *Secular Architecture:* Faulkbourne Hall, fifteenth century

(b) *Secular Architecture:* Horham Hall, early sixteenth century

Secular Architecture: Layer Marney Towers, *c.* 1520–3

Hill Hall, Wall Painting of *c.* 1570

(a) West Hanningfield, Cloville Hall, Wall Paintings of 1615

(b) Wivenhoe, Pargetting of house in East Street, *c.* 1630–50

Colchester, Bourne Mill, 1591

(a) Boreham New Hall, 1573

(b) Audley End, Engraving showing the original extent of the
house of 1603-16

Audley End, Porch, *c.* 1603

Audley End, Hall Screen, *c.* 1615 (*Copyright Country Life*)

Great Waltham, Langleys, Fireplace and Ceiling of *c.* 1620

(a) Tilbury Fort, Gatehouse, 1670–83

(b) Dedham, Sherman's, c.1730
(*Copyright Country Life*)

Boreham House, c. 1730 (*Copyright Country Life*)

Gestingthorpe, Over Hall, *c.* 1740

(a) Bradwell-juxta-Mare, Bradwell Lodge, by John Johnson, 1781–6

(b) Chelmsford, Shire Hall, by John Johnson, 1789–91

(a) Wanstead Hospital (former Merchant Seamen's Orphan Asylum), by G. C. Clarke, 1861

(b) Loughton Hall, by Eden Nesfield, 1878

(a) West Ham College, Library and Museum, by Gibson & Russell, 1896–8

(b) Loughton, Railway Station, by Murray Easton, 1940

Harlow New Town, The Lawn, by Frederick Gibberd, 1951

columns, an arch decorated by zigzag, and a fragmentary tympanum diapered with carved stars. The other windows are C18, pointed in the nave, arched in the chancel. The W doorway with a canopy on carved brackets is dated 1726, the W gallery inside 1704 (the gift of an ironmonger of London). This hides much of the substructure of the belfry, which outside is crowned by a leaded broach-spire. But more unusual and ingenious is the way in which the C15 roof construction was hidden. The tie-beams are plastered and have Greek-key friezes along their undersides, and one king-post with its four-way struts is clothed in rich acanthus leaves. The chancel arch is low and broad, of segmental form, and rests on thick coupled brackets. – FONT. C18, with baluster stem. – REREDOS with Corinthian pilasters and a Gothick ogee arch round the E window. – CHANCEL STALLS with fine openwork foliage carving. – PULPIT. Jacobean. – WALL PAINTING. Upper half of a large figure of St Christopher; c.1400, of high quality. – STAINED GLASS. Fine small panels of C17 Swiss glass. – PLATE. Cup of 1559, a rare date. – MONUMENTS. Brass to Robert Barfott † 1546 and wife, with children below; 18 in. figures; chancel floor. – Many C18 and C19 monuments to the Lockwood family, mostly unsigned, the most ambitious that of John Lockwood, erected in 1778. Largish figure of Hope with an anchor and an urn. By *Joseph Wilton*.*

LAMBOURNE PLACE (Old Rectory). Fine seven-bay, two-storey house of c.1740. Brick quoins also for the slightly projecting pedimented three-bay centre. Doorway with pediment on corbels, arched window above. Good, graceful contemporary staircase, from the demolished Lockwood mansion, Dews Hall.

LAMBOURNE HALL see CANEWDON

LANGDON HILLS see BASILDON

LANGENHOE

ST MARY. 1886, of old materials. Of the W tower especially much must have stood the earthquake of 1884. Diagonal buttresses, battlements, and higher stair-turret. The church also has some of the original C15 windows. – FONT. Perp, octagonal, with panels with flowers in quatrefoils.

* Mr Gunnis also quotes a MONUMENT by *Flaxman* to Matilda Maydwell † 1801. It is on the splay of one of the S windows.

LANGFORD

ST GILES. From the outside the church looks at first entirely
C19 or the date of its restoration: 1880–2 by *Edward Browning*.
It is only when one walks round that one sees a Norman apse,
complete with three small windows. The impression is confusing, because an apse in England is only expected at the E
end, and the apse at Langford is undoubtedly a W apse – indeed the only one surviving, although it is known that Abingdon about the year 680 had a church with apses at both ends.
Langford also originally had an E apse as well. The type is in
all probability to be derived from Carolingian and Ottonian
Germany, where apses at both ends were quite frequent,
though, it is true, not for village churches. Thus, even inter-
nationally speaking, Langford was a great exception, and it is
much to be regretted that the E apse did not survive the late
Middle Ages. Apart from the apse the only Norman evidence
is the plain S doorway.

LANGFORD MILL. The buildings of the mill adjoin the church
and form a welcome background, partly Georgian and partly
Victorian.

LANGFORD GROVE. 1782 by *John Johnson*, a very handsome
building of white brick, but at the time of writing derelict.
Five bays, two-and-a-half storeys, with a tripartite doorway of
Coade stone exactly like those of Bedford Square in London.
Single-storeyed connecting passages and then three-bay pedimented outer pavilions. On the garden side the centre is a
tripartite window, a Venetian window above it, and a three-bay
pediment.

Between Langford and Langford Grove first an L-shaped timber-
framed house, then LANGFORD HALL, red brick, of *c.*1700
with an addition of 1748.

LANGHAM

ST MARY. The church lies right in a wood with only Church
Farm (timber-framed, C17) near by and Langham Hall (plain,
*c.*1740) at a distance. Norman nave, now only recognizable by
the NE quoins of Roman bricks. The one small N window looks
all new but may be renewed correctly. Later C13 W tower with
later diagonal buttresses, battlements with crocketed pinnacles, but cusped lancet windows. C14 S aisle with low six-bay
arcade of octagonal piers and double-chamfered arches. The
windows of the aisle are also of the C14, the E window of an

unusual variety: straight-headed, of five lights with slender
ogee heads. In the S wall a recess with three heads, two as label-
stops, one as keystone in the apex. The chancel is C14 too, see
for example the reticulated tracery of the E window. – BENCH
ENDS. With poppy-heads, two with angel figures. – INSCRIP-
TION in the porch, mid C19, cast iron, no doubt not *in situ*:

> The Dumb Animals Humble Petition.
> Rest Drivers rest on this steep hill,
> Dumb Beasts pray use with all good will.
> Goad not, scourge not, with thonged whips,
> Let not one curse escape your lips.
> God sees and hears.

MONUMENT. Margaret Maud † 1853, with sarcophagus and
soul soaring up. By *Manning* of London.

VALLEY HOUSE, I m. NW. C16 house, timber-framed and
plastered. Early C17 porch on thick scrolly brackets. Early C17
also the chimneystacks with octagonal shafts, and the added
staircase wing of brick at the back, with mullioned and transomed windows. The staircase itself uncommonly ornate for
its small scale. Three flights round a small square open well,
through two storeys. Symmetrical balusters, newel-posts with
strapwork ornament and tall terms, one decorated with a
demi-figure.

LANGLEY

ST JOHN THE EVANGELIST. Nave, chancel, and unbuttressed
W tower with pyramid roof. The nave is E.E., see the S doorway, restored, with, in the arch, one roll-moulding and one
keeled roll-moulding. The chancel is of brick, mid C16. –
PLATE. Cup of 1563; Paten on three feet of 1708.

RUMBERRY HILL. Large round barrow, 120 ft in diameter and
8 ft high. The site was excavated in the C19, when fragments
of Roman brick, glass, and Samian ware were found.

LANGLEYS see GREAT WALTHAM

LATCHINGDON

ST MICHAEL. Just the nave and a S porch. In the N wall a four-
light brick window of 1618, still with the lights ending in four-
centred arches. At the W end a four-post structure for a belfry
which has disappeared.

CHRIST CHURCH. 1857 by *St Aubyn* (GR).

LATCHLEYS *see* STEEPLE BUMPSTEAD

LATTON *see* HARLOW

LAWFORD

17 ST MARY. The early C14 chancel is one of the most splendid
monuments of its date in the county. It is four bays long,
divided by buttresses into two pairs of two. The buttresses
between and the diagonal buttresses at the E end have niches,
no doubt for statuettes, a preparation for the show to come.
The large N and S windows of three lights have eight different
tracery patterns of which at least five are quite unusual and
must probably be credited to the imagination of this particular
master mason. The E window is unfortunately renewed, and
the reredos underneath it (by *C. F. Hayward*, 1884) by trying
to outdo the magnificence of the medieval stonework in
alabaster and naturalistic carving is another blemish. It needed
all the Victorian self-confidence not to restrain oneself in the
presence of so much ornamental carving as the interior of the
chancel displays. The windows are shafted and up the voussoirs run thick bands of bossy foliage. Between the pairs is a
buttress outside, and inside a narrow blank arch with a tall
concave-sided gable flanked by thin buttresses. In the third
window from the W on the N side one detects owls in the leaves,
on the S side squirrels. Moreover the easternmost N window
18a has instead of foliage two chains of little men. They dance,
wrestle, play musical instruments, hold each other by their
feet. It is all full of indomitable exuberance. On the S side the
priest's door, SEDILIA, and PISCINA make a similar display,
five ogee arches separated by triple shafts, the front part of
which is square and diapered, while the side parts are the
usual demi-shafts. The spandrels again are full of figures, their
heads broken off by vandals. Some are angels making music on
the portable organ, psaltery, gittern, organistrum (hurdy-
gurdy), and harp.

As for the rest of the church, nave, S porch, and W tower are also
C14, but seem in their details (especially the nave S windows)
later than the chancel. The S porch has on the sides the remains
of tracery. The W tower is much repaired in brick. The tower
arch is early C16 brick. The N arcade dates from 1826, the
chancel arch from 1853. In the N aisle an early C19 wooden
gallery, on cast-iron shafts. – FONT. C18 on baluster stem. –
STAINED GLASS. Minor fragments of tabernacles and leaves

in the chancel windows, *in situ*. The glass in the E window must be *c*.1850, and if the REREDOS (see above) errs on the side of showiness, this glass errs on the side of humility. – MONU-MENT. Edward Waldegrave † 1584, and wife, with the usual kneeling figures facing each other.

LAWFORD HALL. A large E-shaped mansion of 1583, timber-framed and plastered. The main show-front does not reveal that; for it was faced with brick and entirely Georgianized about the year 1756. The new front has a five-bay centre and two-bay wings projecting a little. In the middle a three-bay pediment. Parapet with balls, and hipped roof. The entrance hall belongs to that date too. But behind, where the wings project considerably more, the Elizabethan character is almost unchanged. The wings are gabled, and their upper storeys project with moulded bressumers. There are in the re-entrant angles two stair-turrets. Some original windows are also pre-served, that at the end of the W wing of five lights with one transom. Two original chimneystacks with octagonal shafts.

LAWFORD PLACE. Early C19 with a Tuscan colonnade of six sturdy columns now hidden in modern bay windows.

THE LAWNS, STROUD GREEN *see* ROCHFORD

LAYER BRETON

ST MARY OR ST NICHOLAS. 1923. In it an interesting piece of SCULPTURE: Tondo of the Virgin seated on the ground and playing with the Child; Italian Mannerist.

LAYER DE LA HAYE

CHURCH. Overlooking the South Essex Company's reservoir. Norman SE angle of the nave. The remaining parts mostly C14. Good S porch of timber with C14 gable – see the bargeboards. S side and S arcade C19. W tower with diagonal buttresses and battlements. In the chancel a C15 MONUMENT, combined with Easter Sepulchre. The recess is straight-headed with curves down to the jambs. Quatrefoils in the coving, quatre-foil frieze above, and cresting. No effigy or brass on the tomb-chest. – PLATE. Late C16 Cup with band of ornament, on later stem; late C16 Paten.

LAYER MARNEY

The Marneys had held Layer Marney from the C12. But they did not reach prominence until the time of Sir Henry, who was born

about the middle of the C15 and by and by became a Privy Councillor of Henry VII and Henry VIII, Captain of the King's Body-
guard, and Sheriff of Essex, and finally, shortly before his death
in 1523, Keeper of the Privy Seal. His son succeeded him, but
died two years later, in 1525. The line was then extinct.

We do not know when the first Lord Marney began to re-
build the church and when the house. It may have been about
1505 or 1510. But the most lavish parts of the house can, for
reasons to be given later, hardly be earlier than c.1520.

ST MARY THE VIRGIN. Rebuilt to the W of the house, of brick
with blue diapering throughout. W tower of a type frequent in
Essex (cf. Ingatestone, Rochford, St Osyth, etc.) with diagonal
stone-dressed buttresses, battlements, and polygonal stair-
turret. The W window of three lights with a depressed head
and an odd variety of intersected tracery as favoured 200
years before. The two-light bell-openings with a transom.
Embattled S aisle. S porch and S chancel porch (a rare addition)
with stepped battlements. The windows all with four-centred
heads, and all of brick. The E window is of five lights with
Perp panel tracery. At the W end of the N aisle a priest's chamber with a chimney which adds to the W view of the church
an element of surprise. The arcade piers inside as well
as the tower arch have semi-octagonal shafts and hollows in
the diagonals. The roof has tie-beams, but at the rood-place
the tie-beam is enriched by braces and braces up to the collar-
beam – a hammerbeam effect without hammerbeam. –
PULPIT. Made up of various bits. The tester is c. mid C17. –
SCREENS. The rood screen has one-light sections with ogee
arches and a little panel tracery above. – The screen to the
Marney Chapel is severely plain, only straight lines. The sections of two lights separated by iron mullions. – BENCHES in
the nave with some linenfold and early C17 panelling. – CHEST.
Very long, iron-bound, C14 or C15. – PAINTING. Large C15
figure of St Christopher, curiously rustic for a place so
intimately connected with the taste of the court. It helps to
date the church. – STAINED GLASS. Figure of St Peter, early
C16, and several heraldic medallions, N chapel, E window. –
MONUMENTS. Sir William Marney † 1414, alabaster, on a
tomb-chest with elaborately cusped quatrefoils and shields.
The knight wears bascinet, camail, and hip-belt, as was
the fashion. Round the tomb six original oak posts with zigzag carving. – Henry Lord Marney † 1523. Between chancel
and Marney chapel. The composition of tomb-chest, recum-

bent effigy, and canopy above is in the Perp taste, but the detail is all of the Early Renaissance. What is more, it is executed in terracotta, a material favoured by the Italians at the Court (cf. below). The tomb-chest has panels with shields separated by balusters, the lid and the beautifully carved effigy are of black marble. The canopy has balusters and Renaissance foliage, but they are not used in a Renaissance spirit. The angle pilasters e.g. clearly suffer from a Gothic hangover, and the canopy has pendants for which the designer does not mind using Ionic capitals. On the canopy four semicircular pediments or gables or acroteria – a predominantly Venetian motif. – John Lord Marney † 1525, clearly by the same hands. The effigy of the young man has all the characteristics of that of his father. The tomb-chest is simpler, but also terracotta and also with balusters. The monument is organically connected to the w with a chantry altar placed at r. angles to it. The decoration is again the same. – Robert Cammocke † 1585, chancel s wall, tomb-chest on which stand two short Tuscan columns supporting an entablature. Brasses (without figures) against the back wall. – (Nicolaus Corsellis the Belgian typographer, † 1674, very elegant. Information from Mr Ian Lowe.)

LAYER MARNEY TOWERS. It can well be understood that the house became known as Layer Marney Towers; for Lord Marney's showpiece is a gatehouse with four towers, higher than any of other Tudor mansions that had preceded his. These gatehouses were the ambition of the age. They were no longer needed for fortification and reached fantastic heights of display, especially in the brick counties of the E. Tattershall of the 1440s may still have had some military considerations, even if they were secondary. At Oxburgh in 1482 they can hardly have played a part any longer. And the gatehouses of St James's Palace and Hampton Court, of Christ's and St John's Colleges and then of Trinity College at Cambridge, or Lupton's Tower at Eton are all for the purpose of a chivalric display only. But not one of all these reached Layer Marney. From the size of the gatehouse one can presume that the house itself was intended to be on a grand scale. It was to be to the s of the gatehouse, but was never even begun. There probably was no time left for it to be built. The date when Lord Marney started is not preserved. But because of the use of terracotta in Italian forms (see below) it can hardly have been before 1520, and in 1523 and 1525 the first and second Lords

Marney died. Quite evidently the gatehouse was hurried up
at once and then a beginning made on the ranges to the w and
E of it. That to the w remains, that to the E is rebuilt and now
links up with a range of outbuildings in line with it. In addition, to the s of this, there is another range of outbuildings on
their own.

50   The GATEHOUSE is flanked by turrets which are square to
the outside and polygonal to the inside, that is the future inner
courtyard of the mansion. The outer turrets have seven windows above each other, the inner eight. The top is decorated
in the accepted way by a trefoiled corbel frieze. But above this
are instead of battlements little semicircular shell-gables with
dolphins on them – an Italian Quattrocento motif, executed
in the newly fashionable Italian material, terracotta. This had
been introduced into England by the Italian Torrigiani a little
before 1510. Behind the Italian frieze appear the Tudor chimneys of pre-Italian twisted shapes. Between the turrets is the
gateway and above on the first and second floor are two large
rooms with wide windows to E and w. The windows appear
at first to be straightforward five-light Perp windows with
ogee-arched heads and one transom. But in looking at them
carefully one discovers that the mullions and transoms are of
terracotta decorated with the typical candelabra forms of the
Italian Early Renaissance, and the ogee tops consist of Renaissance scrolls and counter-scrolls. The same windows repeat
on the upper floor of the w wing. They must have been meant
to be the beginning of a type of fenestration, large, wide, and
regular, as it was then still very unusual, but not unique, since
during exactly the same year windows of a similar general
shape were put in at Sutton Place in Surrey. But at Layer
Marney any regularity which must have been intended was
defeated by the short time available before the death of Lord
Marney. So the wing was completed with a fenestration wholly
without a system. The gable to the s is in fact different in the
brickwork and probably somewhat later. The wing finishes on
the w side with a stepped gable. The E wing also has ends with
stepped gables. Its windows are simple, of the straight-headed
medieval type with the individual lights arched and cusped.

    Of internal features no more than this need be said. In two
rooms on the first floor of the w wing are ceilings of interest.
One of them must be one of the earliest in the country with
polygonal panels of various sizes made into a pattern (cf. Wolsey's rooms at Hampton Court). Also in the w wing, in the

modern N room is a most interesting early C16 fireplace. It has
ornamented pilasters, brackets, and an ornamental frieze, all
of a purity extremely rare in England. Again in the W wing is
an early C17 timber fireplace with overmantel flanked by
caryatids. In another room of the same wing a C17 marble
fireplace, no doubt the work of a Fleming. It has demi-cary-
atids, carrying capitals. They are white against black terms.

The so-called GALLERY range S of the main buildings was
only converted into a gallery and ante-room in the C20. It
must originally have had a much humbler purpose, as is witnessed by the coarse, though impressive roof. The tie-beams
each carry thirteen queen-posts and the collar-beams above
them four. The rafters are strengthened by wind-braces. The
exterior has at the end stepped gables.

LEADEN RODING

ST MICHAEL. Nave, chancel, and belfry. The belfry is weatherboarded with a shingled broach-spire. It rests on posts with
thin, low braces and cross-strutting to the l. and r. Nave and
chancel Norman, the windows much renewed. S doorway with
odd capitals of four thin stone slabs on top of each other. The
nave roof simple, of trussed rafters, with low tie-beams. –
PULPIT. C15 with traceried panels and quatrefoils at their
foot. – COMMUNION RAIL. C17, with sparsely placed heavy
balusters. – PLATE. Cup and Paten of 1662.

LEE CHAPEL see BASILDON

LEEZ PRIORY
1¾ m. NW Little Leighs

The priory was founded for Augustinian Canons probably early
in the C13. Excavations of which much is exposed have revealed the plan. The house was dissolved and in 1536 went to
Lord Rich. He pulled down most of it and built himself a
mansion in its place. Of this certain fragments remain upright, but the greater part was razed in 1753. The foundations
of the C16 house are also visible and can easily be confused
with those of the medieval buildings. The Great Gatehouse
(see below) stands somewhere in the W range of the monastic
buildings. The foundations of this range were used by Lord
Rich. The cloister to the E became his inner courtyard. To the
N of this lay the Refectory, to the E several chambers including

the Chapter House which projected eastward, and to the s was
the church with transepts with E aisles, a chancel, and a much
longer Lady Chapel instead of a N chancel aisle. The only
medieval features of some eloquence are bases of the piers of
the crossing tower, trefoiled in section and filleted. Many Purbeck shafts have been excavated, and also some early C13
capitals, etc. The E parts of the church can be dated by them;
the Lady Chapel was added about 1300 or a little later (cf.
Waltham, Little Dunmow).

Lord Rich's house was built entirely of red brick ornamented with blue brick diapers and other patterns, including
chequer-work. It consisted of an outer and an inner quadrangle, just like Hampton Court, except that the main gateway
into the outer courtyard was at r. angles to, instead of in axis
with, the inner gateway. The main living quarters lay round
the inner courtyard. The great hall was in the nave space.
There were two spiral stair-turrets at the NE and SE corners of
the quadrangle, and to the outer world polygonal turrets at
the corners and buttresses, chimneys, and bays breaking the
frontages irregularly.

The surviving parts are the Inner Gatehouse and parts of
the s and w ranges of the outer courtyard. The OUTER GATE-
HOUSE is flanked by polygonal turrets with angle pilaster-
strips and two trefoiled corbel friezes. The top is all embattled.
The main window is of three lights with a transom. The adjoining quarters are two-storeyed, the w range a little lower
than the s range. The windows are mullioned or mullioned and
transomed, of two and more lights, mostly renewed. The
individual lights are still arched. In the w wing, but again not
in line with the Inner Gatehouse, is a cross-gable, and there
was a subsidiary gateway here. It led into the walled Kitchen
Garden, which contains the lowest of a series of fishponds.

The INNER GATEHOUSE is considerably more ornate than
the Outer. It is one storey higher and has two main rooms between the turrets, both with four-light, transomed windows
and both with original fireplaces. The original decorated chimneystacks also still exist. The doorway has the Tudor rose and
the French fleur-de-lis in the spandrels.

In the Cloister now stands a Gothic CONDUIT, no doubt
made and placed here late in the C18 or early in the C19. The
Privy Garden lay to the N of the N range. Two C16 BARNS
remain to the s of the outer s range (with brick walls and
queen-post roofs), and a tall rectangular structure, called the

FISHING HUT, also of C16 brickwork, stands to the NW of the outer quadrangle.

LEIGH-ON-SEA see SOUTHEND-ON-SEA

LEIGHS LODGE see FELSTED

LEDXEN

ST LEONARD. 1820–1. Cemented, Neo-E.E., but the window tracery Neo-Perp. W tower with funny spire. Chancel 1894 by *J. C. Traylen* (GR). – STAINED GLASS. E window by *Heaton, Butler & Bayne*. – S aisle E and S by *Kempe*. The E is earlier. It has Kempe's signature, the wheat-sheaf, repeated three times in a shield. The S window is of 1910. The sheaf is combined with a tower, the sign of Kempe's partnership with *Tower*. – (WALL HANGING by *Morris & Co*. GR) – MONUMENT. Richard Hewitt † 1771. An exceedingly good standing wall-monument, without effigy. Also without signature. Big plinth with rich neo-classical ornamentation. Inscription plate held by two genii. Large urn high up with a scene in relief. – GARDEN OF REST in the churchyard. Brick walls, a trim garden, an altar and a chapel. 1950 by *Bailey & Walker*.

To the E of the church LEXDEN PARK, a large Italianate residence with a tower. It is said to have a nucleus of 1825–6 (by *D. Laing*), but must essentially be of *c*.1850–60. There are plenty of other wealthy Victorian villas in and around Lexden. Nice cottages of the earlier village W of the church.

LEXDEN DYKES see COLCHESTER

LEYTON

ST MARY THE VIRGIN. Red brick W tower with diagonal buttresses of 1658. C18 clock turret on the top. Part of the N aisle wall surely also 1658; W end of the chancel, 1693; S aisle and vestry, 1822; baptistery, 1884. The church was much altered and enlarged at the E end in 1932. The octagonal shape of the piers e.g. is 1932. – HOURGLASS. Four in one. C18, from the Augustinian Church at Munich. – ALMSBOX. In the SE porch. Dated 1626. Small and with a pretty figure of a lame man. – PLATE. Cup of 1775; fine set of 1794. – MONUMENTS. Ursula Gasper † 1493, small brass (N arcade W end). – Sir Michael Hicks † 1612 and wife, two semi-reclining effigies, propped up on their elbows, lying in opposite directions.

The monument is probably not in its original state. – Sir
William Hicks † 1680 and his son Sir William † 1703, large
standing wall-monument with standing figures of man and
woman and between them, semi-reclining, the father.
Ascribed by Mrs Esdaile to *B. Adye*. – Newdigate Owsley
† 1714, small tablet signed by *S. Tufnell*. – John Story by
J. Hickey, 1787. Good standing figure of Fame against large
grey obelisk. – Hillesdon children, 1807 by *John Flaxman*.
Monument with allegory of woman seated on the ground and
reading. – William Bosanquet † 1813. With fine scene of the
Good Samaritan in relief. Also by *Flaxman*. – E. Brewster
† 1898. Still with the mourning allegorical female bent over
an urn, just like a hundred years before. Signed by *Gaffin* of
Regent Street, a firm which also goes back a long way. – In the
Churchyard MONUMENT to Samuel Bosanquet, 1806 by *Sir
John Soane*, of typically Soanian Neo-Greek detail. W of the
church tower.

ALL SAINTS, Capworth Street. The church of 1865 by *Wiggin-
ton*. Behind it the SCHOOL with additions of 1909 by *Frere*, of
a very delicate and original style.

EMMANUEL CHURCH, Lea Bridge Road. By *Martin Travers*
and *T. F. W. Grant*, 1934–5. Interior very Baroque in style.

TOWN HALL (1896 by *John Johnson*) and LIBRARY (1893 by
J. M. Knight), High Road. Both rather depressingly debased.
Much prettier, in the usual mixed municipal style of *c*.1900,
the CARNEGIE LIBRARY in Lea Bridge Road, 1905 by *W.
Jacques*.

Leyton was a village until well into the C19. Close to the church
was Leyton Grange, engraved in *Vitruvius Britannicus* and
demolished in 1860.* The chief development took place from
1860 onwards. There were plenty of other C17 and C18 houses,
but most of them have disappeared. All that remains now is
ETLOE HOUSE, Church Road, of *c*.1760–70, with long low
Tudorized front, the CONSERVATIVE CLUB in High Road at
the corner of Dawlish Road, GROVE HOUSE in High Road
(with Victorian bays added), and LIVINGSTONE COLLEGE,‡
Knotts Green, a large, rather plain, C18 mansion of yellow
brick, built apparently in 1733–45 with the bow-windowed
part added in 1791.

* In the grounds of Leyton Grange considerable ROMAN REMAINS were
found in 1718.

‡ Demolished 1961. The site is now occupied by the block of flats
LIVINGSTONE COLLEGE TOWERS. By the *Leyton Borough Council*.

LONDON MASTER BAKERS' BENEVOLENT INSTITUTION, Lea Bridge Road. By *T. Knightley*, 1857. Large court, open to the street. The style is a debased Italianate with numerous chalet gables and two towers in the re-entrant angles. Stuccoed, two-storeyed.

LEYTONSTONE

ST JOHN THE BAPTIST, High Road. 1832–3 by *Blore*. Yellow brick, Neo-E.E. Altered in 1893 and again in 1902 etc. Wide airy interior with quatrefoil piers. No furnishings or monuments worth mentioning. – PLATE. Set of 1778–9.

ST COLUMBA, Janson Road. 1894 by *E.P. Warren*, now a shell.* A good red brick Neo-Perp church with W baptistery and a small SE turret.

(WELSH PRESBYTERIAN CHURCH, High Road. By *T. & H. Llewelyn Daniel*, 1958.)

JEWS CEMETERY, Buckingham Road, see West Ham.

HIGH SCHOOL FOR GIRLS, Forest Road and Colworth Road. 1911 by *W. Jacques*. Very pretty red brick building with two asymmetrical projecting wings and one asymmetrical turret in one of the two re-entrant angles. Several gables with black and white chequer pattern.

(HARROW GREEN BRANCH LIBRARY, Cathall Road. By *John H. Jacques*. Begun in 1938, but completed only in 1959.)

A few houses remain which are worth inspection. Off the High Road in Davies Lane THE PASTURES, dated 1697 on a cistern, five bays and two storeys, with doorway with pediment on unfluted Ionic columns; derelict at the time of writing. Also off the High Road further N in AYLMER ROAD, a terrace of Georgian houses originally facing the High Road. Their front gardens are now built over. The terrace is of fifteen bays with Tuscan porches. Still further N on the W side SYCAMORE HOUSE, red brick, neglected at the time of writing,‡ and then (part of the Hospital) LEYTONSTONE HOUSE of five bays and two-and-a-half storeys with lower wings to l. and r., and a Tuscan porch.

FOREST HOUSE, James Lane, part of the Whipps Cross Hospital. An eleven-bay, two-and-a-half storeyed stuccoed mansion with four-column porch on Tuscan columns. This external appearance hides a house of *c.*1700 whose panelled

---

* Since demolished.
‡ Demolished, 1958.

Entrance Hall and staircase with thick twisted balusters remain. At r. angles the pedimented Stables, also c.1700, and
still with its original exterior. Red brick, with brick quoins.*

LILYSTONE HALL see STOCK

LINDSELL

ST MARY THE VIRGIN. A charming approach through the
yard of Lindsell Hall, a house with two symmetrical gables to
the E, both with oversailing upper storeys. The church is small
and compact, and of an unusual colour, because it is of pebble
rubble with red brick dressings. The tower moreover is in an
unusual position, at the SW end. It is of the late C16, stone,
with a diagonal buttress and battlements. The nave reveals a
Norman building. The arch towards the chancel is round-
headed on the simplest imposts. Large pointed squinch-arch
S of it. S aisle of two bays, E of the tower, with a quatrefoil pier
and two quadrant mouldings in the arches, i.e. early C14. The
later tower cuts into the arcade. In 1927 traces of an ANCHOR-
AGE were discovered N of the chancel N wall with a small hatch
into the chancel as its only opening. – FONT. C15, octagonal,
with quatrefoils and shields. – STAINED GLASS. In the E
window well arranged fragments of the C13 to C16; specially
noteworthy two small C13 figures of Saints. – PLATE. Cup and
small Paten on foot of 1632. – BRASS. Thomas Fytche † 1514
and wife; the length of the figures is 16 in.

LISTON

CHURCH. Nave and chancel Norman, see the masonry at the E
end, and the plain, blocked N doorway. The chancel was
widened in the C13, but the windows are all renewed. W tower,
not too big, early C16, of brick with blue brick diapers, diagonal buttresses, a three-light brick W window, and stepped
battlements on a trefoiled corbel frieze. The stair-turret reaches
higher than the tower. The S chancel chapel was added in
1867. – FONT. Octagonal, Perp, traceried stem, and bowl with
cusped panels and shields. – BENCH ENDS with two poppy-
heads. – STAINED GLASS. N window, in the tracery, several
small C15 figures. – PLATE. Large Plate of 1683; Paten on foot
probably of 1683; Flagon of 1702; Cup probably of 1702.
LISTON HALL has been demolished.

* Dorothy Stroud in her book on *Soane* mentions minor repairs and
alterations in 1786 and 1801.

LITTLE BADDOW

St Mary the Virgin. w tower of the c14 with angle buttresses on one side, a diagonal buttress on the other, w door with two niches, two-light Early Dec w window and battlements. Very wide nave which seems somewhat lop-sided, because it consists of a Norman nave of which the N wall with a plain doorway remains, and an early c14 s wall pushed so far to the s as if an aisle had been intended. This s part has a Dec two-light E window and in the s wall two low recesses, designed to form one group with the PISCINA. It is typical Dec, with richly crocketed ogee arches. In them stand two very low tomb-chests with quatrefoil decoration. On the tomb-chest are two EFFIGIES of oak, a man and a woman, of c.1320. The man lies straight, the woman slightly and very tenderly bent. The figure of the woman especially is of uncommonly fine quality. The architect of the church also appreciated sculpture. There are small heads used as label-stops and otherwise. – FONT. Circular trough with four handles, resting on a mill-wheel. – PAINTING. St Christopher, large, on the N wall, c15. – STAINED GLASS. St Michael and the Dragon; also several fragments; all c.1400 (E window). – PLATE. Large Cup of 1700, with bands of ornament. – MONUMENT. Henry Mildmay † 1639. Standing wall-monument with reclining figure, propped on elbow, between black columns which carry an open segmental pediment. Large kneeling figures of two wives below, on the ground trophies and oval inscription plate as background.

INDEPENDENT (now CONGREGATIONAL) CHAPEL. 1708. Plain gabled parallelogram, with arched windows with a mullion-and-transom cross and a second transom at the foot of the arch.

(VILLAGE HALL. By *Graham & Baldwin*, 1961.)

LITTLE BADDOW HALL, opposite the church. Lovely timber-framed house of the c14 or c15 with extensions.

OLD RIFFHAMS, see Danbury.

LITTLE BARDFIELD

St Katherine. Late Anglo-Saxon w tower, unbuttressed, with arched openings on three floors. Later recessed pyramid roof. The nave masonry is of the same character as that of the tower. One Saxon s and one N window, double-splayed. –

ORGAN. Said to be by *Renatus Harris*, c.1700, and to come from Jesus College Chapel, Cambridge. The case with open-work foliage scrolls and a cherub's head.

In the village ALMSHOUSES of 1774, row of six dwellings, each consisting of door and two windows.

Next to the church LITTLE BARDFIELD HALL, with a sym-metrical gabled front with central porch, delightfully par-geted. A rainwater-head says 1634. In the Hall a fireplace dated 1580. Fine C18 iron gate. Good late C16 staircase. But a recent owner has introduced into the house much that did not originally belong. So the antiquarian has to be careful.

CHEQUERS, ¾ m. ENE. Handsome timber-framed house with a date 1609, but certain older details.

LITTLE BELHUS *see* SOUTH OCKENDON

LITTLE BENTLEY

ST MARY THE VIRGIN. Chancel C13; see the three stepped E lancets and one each in the N and S walls. The N aisle Early Perp, but heightened and lengthened in brick early in the C16, when much other renewing and adding also went on. The W tower, e.g., of an attractive mixture of stone, flint, and odd bricks (early C15, with W door with shields in the spandrels and large three-light W window), was heightened in brick and embattled. The S wall is entirely of brick with blue brick diapers and parapet. One (renewed) three-light brick window. The S porch also brick, with diagonal buttresses and battle-ments. Three-light side openings. Inside, to one's surprise, one sees that the nave must be Norman; for it has a N arcade cut roughly through the wall early in the C13. Arches with one slight chamfer on circular piers with minimum capitals. Fine hammerbeam roof. – FONT. Octagonal, plain, only one shield on the E front (Pyrton arms). – BENCH ENDS. Some few with poppy-heads. – CHEST. Very impressive, large C15 piece, iron-bound and closely studded, with semi-cylindrical lid. – HELM. C16, in the chancel. – PLATE. Cup and Flagon of 1623, both with the original leather-covered wooden cases. – BRASS. Sir William Pyrton † 1490, wife and children (vestry floor).

S of the church a pretty octagonal thatched LODGE of Little Bentley Hall. (In the grounds square Elizabethan brick summerhouse. R.C.)

LITTLE BRAXTED

St Nicholas. Norman nave and apsed chancel. Of the windows original only one – in the apse. It is tiny. Two c13 lancet windows in the w wall. Another re-used in the n aisle, which was added in 1884. c19 also the pretty half-timbered w gable and the renewal of the belfry. c15 roof starting very low above one's head. Decoration by the *Rev. E. Geldart, c.*1884. – PLATE. Cup and Paten of 1567; Almsdish of 1683. – BRASS to William Roberts † 1518, and two wives, with small kneeling children below; as usual.

Little Braxted Hall. c16 with additions. Original chimney-stack with diagonal shafts, and a square barn. Just below a MILL with the adjoining Late Georgian miller's house.

LITTLE BROMFORDS *see* NEVENDON

LITTLE BROMLEY

St Mary the Virgin. Nave and chancel in one, and w tower. The nave is Norman, see one n and two s windows. The chancel belongs to c.1300, e window of three lights with intersected tracery, n and s cusped lancet windows. Plain c16 s porch. Of the same time the completion in brick of the c15 w tower. Diagonal buttresses, three-light w window. – FONT. Octagonal, stem with buttresses, bowl with the four Symbols of the Evangelists and four rosettes. The figure carving is very primitive. – COMMUNION RAILS, c.1700, with twisted balusters. – PLATE. Paten, perhaps Elizabethan.

LITTLE BURSTEAD

St Mary. In a nice position overlooking rolling country. Wooden belfry, c15, resting on six posts with beams on braces, and crowned by a shingled broach-spire. Norman nave – see one n window. Also in the n wall of the nave a small c13 lancet. Chancel with early c16 brick windows, three-light with Perp panel tracery at the e end, two-light on the s side. The nave roof is of the c15 and has tie-beams on braces and king-posts. The braces rest on angel corbels. The chancel roof, a little later, has braces connected with the tie-beams by tracery. – PLATE. Cup and Paten of 1629.

Stockwell Hall. c18 front with older parts behind. The main rooms immediately behind the front have indeed Jacobean panelling and fireplaces. At the s end of the house a large clock in the gable and a bellcote above.

HATCHES FARM. Later c16 farm containing two doors of c.1545, each with six panels with heads in roundels, cupids, and foliage, rustically carved.

LITTLEBURY

HOLY TRINITY. The E parts of 1870–5 by *Edward Barr*. At the same time much restoration of the other parts went on. All windows for example look new, except that in the w tower, which has flowing tracery. That dates the tower. It has half-angle buttresses, because both aisles extend nearly as far w as the tower, a feature very uncommon in Essex. The s doorway must be re-set. With its waterleaf capitals on two orders of columns and its two roll-mouldings of which the outer is keeled, it cannot be later than the late c12. Here we may well have the date too of what originally was a s transept – see the E bay of the s arcade – and it is most probably that of the N arcade as well, with circular piers and one-step arches with one slihtg chamfer. The s arcade in its w parts is later. The details here tally with the tower arch, i.e. correspond in date to the Dec style. The most ambitious pieces, at least in their conception, are however the two porches. For when they were rebuilt (or built) early in the c16, they were given entrance arches much taller than usual, two-centred, with large two-light openings in the sides. What is more, the porches were fan-vaulted, as at Saffron Walden, or were meant to have fan-vaults. Fragments remain. – FONT CASE. Square, with linen-fold panelling and a pyramidal canopy with niches, gables, buttresses, crockets, and finial – early c16 (cf. Saffron Walden). – LECTERN. On a concave hexagonal base, with buttressed stem, c15, the bookrest not original. – SCREEN to the N chapel. With much pretty inlay work and other ornamental details in the Neo-Early-Renaissance taste; 1911, designed and carved by the *Rev. H. J. Burrell*. – DOOR (N doorway). Late c15. On one horizontal batten two shears as the only decoration, referring no doubt to the source of income of the donor. – PAINTING. Kneeling Angel, 1879; signed F.S. Is it by *Frederick Shields*? – PLATE. Cup of 1626. – BRASSES. Civilian, c.1480, and Priest, c.1510 (N aisle E end); Civilian and wife, c.1510 (figures 2 ft long); Civilian, c.1520; and two others, of 1578 and 1624 (s aisle s wall).

LITTLEBURY CAMP. Early Iron Age encampment, well sited on Ring Hill, ¾ m. s of the church. The camp, which covers 16½ acres, is in fairly good condition. There is a wide ditch and an internal rampart. The original entrance is unidentified.

LITTLE CANFIELD

ALL SAINTS. The general impression and much of the detail are due to the *Rev. C. L. Smith*, an amateur architect. He designed the N tower and restored and remodelled much outside and inside. The chancel especially, though built in the C14, was never as ornate as it is now. It also contains several unexpected motifs without period precedent, notably the canopy over the priest's door. The STAINED GLASS incidentally is contemporary with the restoration. The nave on the other hand still keeps one piece of evidence of its Norman origin, a s doorway with one order of columns (one-scallop capitals). Interesting are the straight-headed ogee-reticulated C14 windows on the N as well as the s side. – CHEST. C13. Broad boards as feet. In the front of the feet semicircles are cut out and little colonnettes put in instead, as an attempt at decorative enrichment. – SCREEN. With four-light sections ending in interlaced cusped arches, C15. – PLATE. Rich secular Dish of 1634; also rich Cup of 1675. – BRASSES of 1578 and 1593.

LITTLE CHESTERFORD

ST MARY THE VIRGIN. Long nave and long chancel of the C13 under one roof. C19 bellcote. Lancet windows on the N and s sides and a PISCINA which is over-restored. – SCREEN. Plain, C15, with two-light divisions. – MONUMENTS. Brass to the wife of George Langham † 1462. The figure is 28 in. long. – James Welsingham † 1728, in a recess added to the s wall of the chancel. At the time of writing it looked sadly bedraggled. Yet it is no doubt the work of a leading London sculptor. Standing wall-monument with comfortably semi-reclining figure in Roman toga. Unsigned, it seems.

MANOR FARM, W of the church. That rare survival, an early C13 manor house. To that time belongs the stone wing on the E side. The walls are very thick. Two surviving doorways with moulded two-centred arches which originally led from the offices to the hall screen or the hall. Two surviving small straight-headed windows as if from an original cellar. Their rere-arches are round. On the upper floor remains of keeled shafts to a window. But the main window here was inserted in the Elizabethan period: four lights and one transom.* The timber-framed hall in the middle of the present building is attributed to the early C14.‡ It must have been subdivided horizontally in the C16. Originally it went through to the roof, and it still has – again a rare survival – the two posts of an aisle. The posts are quatrefoil with fillets. Curved braces spring from them towards the opposite wall, forming two-centred arches. There are in addition braces in the direction from post to post.

The roof-truss over the screen, a spere-truss, has a tie-beam and crown-post with two struts. The roof construction also remains but is now hidden. The solar wing on the W is attributed to the C15. It has floorboards from 1 to 3 ft wide.

LITTLE CLACTON

ST JAMES. Nave and chancel plastered; belfry. In the chancel a Norman N window, in the nave a plain Norman doorway. Timber S porch, sturdy and unadorned, probably of the C14, together with the windows and N and S doors. The belfry stands on four posts with tie-beams and curved braces. – FONT. Of the square Purbeck type; with four blank shallow round-headed arches on each side, late C12.

LITTLE COGGESHALL

ABBEY. The Abbey was founded by King Stephen about 1140 and made Cistercian in 1148. Of the C12 church no traces remain above ground. Of the cloister S of it a little has recently been excavated: typical mid C12 stone capitals and bases and a slender shaft with spiral grooves and nail-head projections. As regards the monastic buildings there are indications of the dormitory undercroft. This must date from c.1180, but the vaulting is an early C13 addition. A fine C13 doorway leads from the dormitory into a completely preserved corridor. This is two-storeyed and has single-chamfered ribs and arches to the E. The details of the vaulting are again early

---

* Recent alterations in the E wing have revealed two external doorways in the larger first-floor room, which was probably the hall of the original manor house. One doorway is Tudor, the other may be the original entrance reached by an external stairway.

‡ Mr J. T. Smith argues in favour of a date c.1320–30.

C13. S of the corridor and of the dormitory range the Abbot's Lodging. It has lancet windows with round heads inside. The same windows also in a detached building SE of the former. This is not aligned with the dormitory and cloister. From its style and from documentary evidence Mr J. Gardner attributes these two buildings to c.1185–90. Finally, completely detached from all the rest the chapel of St Nicholas, the gate chapel or *capella extra portas* of the abbey – a plain rectangle with lancet windows, on the N side quite regularly arranged. The date must be about 1225. In this and all the other buildings the most remarkable feature is the extensive use of brick dressings – and brick which is definitely not Roman. It is very early, as medieval brickwork goes in England.

After the Dissolution a house was built into the abbey premises. It lies N of the corridor and has a porch, an original hall, and a fine N chimneystack. A date 1581 was on the porch. Inside a good screen with Doric pilasters, C17 panelling, etc. In one room is a circular C12 pier.

The picture at the back of the house with the C16 and the medieval buildings, the fast-flowing mill stream, and a weatherboarded mill is of great charm.

GRANGE FARM, ⅓ m. W of the chapel, has a BARN of c.1500, about 130 ft long, with king-post roof. It has six bays, aisles, two porches, and a huge tiled roof.

LITTLE DUNMOW

ST MARY. Little Dunmow Priory was a priory of Augustinian Canons founded in 1106 by Geoffrey Baynard. It possessed a church of nave and N (and perhaps S) aisle, crossing tower, transepts, chancel, and two chancel aisles or chancel chapels. The plan has been ascertained by excavation, but all that is now above ground is the S chancel chapel or Lady Chapel, used as the parish church of Little Dunmow and for the purpose provided in 1872 with a silly NW turret.* Its splendid windows look down on neat new council houses. It is altogether a curiously unbalanced building, but one of interest wherever one looks, and in addition of great architectural beauty in parts. For a parish church it is long and narrow. Its N wall, that is the chancel S arcade of the priory church, has five bays of magnificent thick-set solid piers of about 1200. They[15b] consist of four major and four minor shafts, alternatingly

* This is by *James Brown*, a Braintree builder (GS).

keeled. The capitals are crocketed or have stylized upright leaves, not yet of the stiff-leaf type. The arches are richly moulded. To the E of them, visible from outside, is a shafted, blocked C13 window with shaft-rings and below it blank intersected arcading. That of course belonged to the priory chancel. In the W wall of the church is the joint of the opening from the former S transept into the chapel, and in addition three niches. These are part of the extremely opulent remodelling of the chapel which took place about 1360. Its chief glory is the five windows, that at the E end of five lights and the four S windows of three and four in alternation. Here lies the first wilfulness of the composition, and there are several more. The S wall thus has a rhythm of large, yet larger, large, yet larger, and at the same time of two-centred, four-centred, two-centred, four-centred arches. In addition, also without doubt a conscious device, the E window and three of the S windows have tracery of the flowing type, but the remaining S window is entirely Perp – a concession to a coming fashion, or a deliberate proof of proficiency. Inside below the windows is a charming blank arcade with leaves and animals – a ram, a pig, a squirrel, a cow – and below the E window also with human figures. – CHAIR in the chancel (the Dunmow Flitch Chair). Made up of part of a C13 stall with tracery on one side, a trefoil frieze on the back, and shafts in front of the arms. – MONUMENTS. Walter Fitzwalter † 1432 and wife † 1464. Alabaster effigies on a tomb-chest decorated with shields, and also a figure. The two effigies are of the highest quality available, faces which in their remote dignity have a direct appeal rare in English C15 funeral sculpture. The same cannot be said of the other effigy, an unknown woman, on a tomb-chest. The effigy is early, the tomb-chest late, C15. – Sir James Halley † 1753, by *Thomas Adye*. Obelisk with seated female figure holding a portrait medallion.

(PRIORY PLACE. Within the precinct of the priory. It may have been the guesthouse. Timber-framed. Remains of an aisled hall, probably of the later C14. J. T. Smith)

LITTLE EASTON

ST MARY. The Norman origin of the nave visible only in scanty fragments of two N windows. The rest, as it appears to the eye, is essentially Perp and C15 (except for the N vestry, etc., which dates from 1881). The W tower has diagonal buttresses and a W doorway with shields in the spandrels. The

chancel has a four-light window with panel tracery. In the s
chancel chapel (Maynard Chapel), which is as wide as the
nave, are large windows, those on the s side having apparently
been converted first in the c18 into plain arched shapes and
then some time about 1840 into their present preposterous
Neo-Norman shape. The pier of the two-bay arcade towards
the chancel has semi-polygonal main shafts and circular shafts
in the diagonals. The chapel, according to T. K. Cromwell,
was built in 1621. – SCREEN. Early c18 screen of wrought iron
to the Maynard Chapel. It was originally a gate of Easton
Lodge. – PAINTINGS. Splendid figure of a seated Prophet,
c.1175; the black underpaint for the flesh has been compared
by Tristram to St Albans, the style to the Bible of Bury St Edmunds. – Stories from the Passion of Christ in two tiers, early
c15. The scenes represented are Last Supper, Agony in the
Garden, Betrayal, Christ before Pilate, Christ crowned with
Thorns, Christ carrying the cross, Crucifixion, Deposition,
Entombment. The iconography is not Flemish but North
Italian, and c14. – STAINED GLASS. S windows, six c17
panels of South German glass, put in in 1857. – PLATE.
Silver-gilt Cup of 1618; Paten on foot of 1618; Paten on foot
of 1634; large Flagon of 1641. – MONUMENTS. Brass to
Robert Fyn, priest, praying; c.1420; the figure 18 in. long. –
Monument to Lady Bourchier, c.1400. Tomb-chest with three
cusped panels carrying shields. Tall cusped ogee arch between
thin buttresses with finials. Six shields in the spandrels. On
the tomb-chest a small effigy of a c13 Knight, only 2 ft long. –
Viscount Bourchier, Earl of Essex † 1483 and wife. Tomb-
chest, panelled and traceried, with brasses on top, the figures
4 ft long. Large heavy straight-topped canopy, tripartite, with
richly cusped vault. – Sir Henry Maynard † 1610 and wife.
Alabaster monument with two reclining effigies on a tomb-
chest with large kneeling figures of children. The sculptural
value high. – Lady Maynard † 1613, reclining figure. – Sir
William Maynard and wife, late c17, large standing wall-
monument with life-size standing figures in Roman costume,
an urn between them. The type is one familiar from Grinling
Gibbons, but according to Dr Whinney the style is not his.
The monument said by R. L. Gwynne to be by *Pearce*. –
Lord Maynard and family, erected in 1746; by *Charles
Stanley*. Also a large standing wall-monument. Lord Maynard in the middle in a musing attitude leaning against an urn,
with the portrait of his wife. Other members of the family as

busts or relief-medallions. Big relief below with figures of
Justice (blindfold), Charity, Fortitude, etc. – Frances, Countess of Warwick † 1938, bust in very Edwardian costume and
attitude. – In the churchyard wooden TOMBSTONE with a
rough head carved on and elaborate decoration (F. Burgess).

MANOR HOUSE. A lovely group of C17 timber-framed houses
(dated 1624) with attached plain and nicely proportioned C18
wing, a detached C18 five-bay house, and the barn round the
corner.

LITTLE HALLINGBURY

ST MARY THE VIRGIN. Norman s doorway with Roman bricks,
C13 chancel with renewed lancet windows. Belfry half-timbered with recessed shingled spire. Interesting s porch of
timber with unusual tracery of squashed ogee arches and
squashed circles with ogee tops and bottoms – C14.

Pretty group NW of the church of timber-framed house with
symmetrical outer gables, weatherboarded barn, and brick
maltings behind a little pond.

LITTLE HORKESLEY

(ST PETER AND ST PAUL. Completely destroyed by a bomb in
September 1940. Rebuilt 1958. – MONUMENTS include: Oak
effigy of a Knight, c.1250, with knee cops and long surcoat, the
feet resting on a lion. – Oak effigy, c.1270, with the remains of
a shield on the left arm, and hands of figures which formerly
supported the head. – Late C13 oak effigy of a Lady in long
gown, wimple, and veil. Her head rests on two cushions supported by angels. – Sir Robert Swynborne † 1391 with son
† 1412, low tomb-chest with brasses of two men in armour
under elaborate triple-arched canopies. – Part of the side
of a tomb-chest, late C15, Purbeck marble with cusped
panelling enclosing shields with rivets of former brasses.
– Brass to Katherine Leventhorp † 1502, in a shroud. –
Brygete, wife of Thos. Fynedorne and John, Lord Marney,
† 1549. Tomb-chest with brasses of lady in pedimental head-
dress and two husbands in armour.)

JOSSELYNS, I m. NE. A delightfully large timber-framed house
of c.1500 with all the timberwork exposed. Well restored in
the C20. Three gables on the front, irregular in size and spacing: one each on the two projecting wings, which also project
to a different depth, the third not symmetrical either. Nor are

the gables aligned with the entrance windows. These are of four and five lights with one transom and are placed in projecting frames almost like oriels (cf. e.g. Paycocke's House at Great Coggeshall). Moulded and carved bressumers. The back with two big chimneystacks is equally attractive. A room on the first floor has Late Elizabethan stencilled decoration.

LOWER DAIRY FARM, 500 yds NE of Josselyns. Timber-framed with exposed timbers. Cross-wing ending in a fine gable with carved bressumers, dated 1601.

LITTLE ILFORD see EAST HAM

LITTLE LAVER

ST MARY THE VIRGIN. Mostly of 1872 (by *J. Goldicutt Turner*). – FONT. Square, *c.* 1200. The four sides have decoration with a trail of stylized foliage of the usual Norman type, three fleurs-de-lis, sun, moon, a whorl, two roses, and two rosettes, and two four-petalled flowers or rather quatrefoils with rose centres. This latter detail especially makes it likely that the sculptural representations have been re-cut. – PLATE. Fragmentary Cup of 1562 and Cup of 1563; undated contemporary Paten.

WINDMILL, ½ m. SSE of the church. The rare type known as a composite mill.*

LITTLE LEIGHS

ST JOHN THE EVANGELIST. Nave and chancel of flint rubble. The nave is of the C12, the chancel of the C13; it can be observed that the C12 laid the stones coursed, the C13 did not. One Norman window each in the N and S walls. No original windows in the chancel, but an original C13 doorway in the nave, with one order of columns and a roll-moulding with fillet. In the chancel N wall is an early C14 recess with ogee arch, cusped and subcusped, thin buttresses by the sides, and a big finial. In the spandrels oak, roses, etc. – the leaves already bossy. Over the W end of the church a belfry with a shingled broach-spire. – FONT. Octagonal, with tracery panels, C14. – PULPIT. With some old panels, e.g. linenfold. – BENCHES. Ten in the nave of a plain design, with a kind of vertical reeding on the ends. – SOUTH DOOR. C13, with two scrolled iron

* Now demolished.

hinges. – PLATE. Cup and Paten of 1706 in a stamped leather case. – EFFIGY of a Priest, oak, c.1300.

LITTLE LEIGHS PRIORY, see Leez Priory.

LITTLE MAPLESTEAD

ST JOHN THE BAPTIST. Those who believe in texture and the handiwork of the medieval mason will not be pleased by Little Maplestead. Most of what they see is from the restoration of 1851–7 started under *Carpenter*. But those who are looking for design and composition can still enjoy the noble rotunda which takes the place of the nave. Little Maplestead was the church of a Commandery of the Knights Hospitallers and as such was built (as the Templars had done before) on the pattern of the church of the Holy Sepulchre at Jerusalem, that is as a circular building. There are only five circular churches left in England, the late C12 church of the Temple in London being the most famous. The others are at Ludlow Castle, Northampton, and Cambridge, all three Norman. Little Maplestead was built as late as c.1335. The piers of the rotunda are trefoil with sharply V-shaped shafts separating the columns. The arches have two quadrant mouldings. The windows are of two lights and also of a typical early C14 form. But the rich corbels of the arches along the walls are entirely Carpenter's. So is probably the W doorway with its rich fleuron decoration.* The timber porch is a replacement of a previous porch. The chancel is contemporary with the rotunda and has an apse. – FONT. Square with chamfered angles. Very raw decoration – a saltire cross, two arches, a composition of two volutes – it may well be C11.

LITTLE OAKLEY

ST MARY. The nave is Norman, see N windows. The W tower was begun c.1500: brick, with diagonal buttresses. But it was not completed and does not reach above the nave roof. It was conceived quite ambitiously. The W doorway has shields in the spandrels, a hood-mould resting on two lions couchant, fleurons in jambs and voussoirs, a frieze of small shields above, and then the three-light W window. However, the chancel of c.1330 is what really matters at Little Oakley. It has a three-light window with reticulated tracery and inside two niches l.

* Mr P. G. M. Dickinson suggests that this is in fact original C14 work; also that the corbels inside the church are of C14 design 'renewed' by Carpenter.

and r., with very steep canopies with crockets and finials. The PISCINA is of the same character. Its steep gable is flanked by thin tall decorative buttresses. The N and S windows are of two lights of three different simple kinds of Dec tracery. The priest's door on the S side is placed in the middle of a buttress which widens porch-wise to take it.

LITTLE PARNDON see HARLOW

LITTLE SALING see BARDFIELD SALING

LITTLE SAMPFORD

ST MARY THE VIRGIN. W tower of the type exemplified by Great Dunmow, that is with set-back buttress, but the angles between them chamfered, carried on polygonally towards the top and provided with polygonal flat-topped pinnacles (later spirelets added). Battlements and later lead spike. All this is C14, as is also the nave with clerestory (quatrefoil windows) and the N aisle. The arcade has piers of an exceptional form: lozenge with four attached shafts. No capitals at all. The tower arch is of a similar design. The chancel is later, probably C15, see its broad five-light E window. Early C16 window near the W end of the S side, and brick S porch of the C17. – SCREEN with broad single-light divisions with segmental arches and a little panel tracery above. – BENCHES. Quite plain, in the nave. – STAINED GLASS. Fragments of tabernacles in the E window. – MONUMENTS. Sir Edward Grene † 1556 and wife. Large cartouche on the N side of the chancel with term pilasters and strapwork. Inscription of modest size and position; no figures. – Opposite, on the S side the monument is repeated, entirely without inscriptions. – William Twedy † 1605 and wife. Small epitaph with the usual kneeling figures. – Bridget Peck † 1712. Standing wall-monument with the lady comfortably reclining. She holds a book in her hand which she has just laid down. Pilasters to the l. and r.; a piece of drapery and three cherubs' heads above the figure. In and around the top pediment flower and fruit garlands.

LITTLE SAMPFORD HALL. Rebuilt in 1936; it is said, with old materials, especially the shaped gables. These are of white brick, which is surprising if the house were really Elizabethan. But *P. F. Robinson* in 1832 built a house called Sampford House. Could this not have been a remodelling of something older, in white brick and in the Neo-Tudor taste just then coming to the fore?

(Tewes, 1 m. w. Small manor house of the late C15. Mullioned windows to the front. Porch and sw bay C20. In two ground-floor rooms finely carved beams and wall-plates. Small C17 wing to the NW.)

LITTLE STAMBRIDGE

Little Stambridge Hall. Five-bay Georgian front hiding Tudor work at the back, e.g. the hall fireplace of red brick with black diapers.

LITTLE TEY

St James the Less. Nave and chancel without a break, and belfry with a pyramid roof. Several small Norman windows. s doorway with a tympanum decorated with Norman lozenge diapering.

LITTLE THURROCK

St Mary the Virgin. Norman nave and chancel arch (rebuilt except for the slightly decorated abaci of the responds). Plain Norman s doorway. C14 chancel. w front with bell-turret and inside a pretty triple arch separating the tower part from the nave. All this seems to belong to the restoration of 1878, but looks rather c.1840. – SEDILIA. Three seats separated by shafts with moulded capitals; pointed arches, hood-moulds; the whole framed. – PULPIT. 1700; plain panels; the Jacobean tradition at last completely gone.

LITTLE TOTHAM

All Saints. A good Late Norman s doorway is the most rewarding piece of the church. It is of two orders of columns and decorated with certain unusual motifs. The columns for instance have square blocks with rosettes round their waists – rather a low waist-line, that is about one third up. The voussoirs combine roll-mouldings with a kind of three-dimensional double-saltire frieze. One frieze runs parallel, one at r. angles to the door opening. An earlier Norman N doorway, quite plain. C13 lancets in the nave on the N and s and also the chancel N and s. Handsome E end with three stepped single lancets. Early in the C16 a big W tower was added, of squared flints. But the enterprise was stopped and the tower later finished in timber, weatherboarded, with a pyramid roof. Inside, original roofs with low tie-beams. – FONT. Perp, octagonal, the bowl decorated with tracery. The font is quite unusually interesting, because the carver used apparently what were to him eight current tracery motifs. They are indeed such as one sees frequently in church windows. But although the date is no doubt C15, the Dec motifs of cusped intersection and of ogee reticulation are still there. Otherwise the motifs are those of three- and four-light panel tracery and the Perp type with straightened reticulation, both with and without transom. – PULPIT. Incorporating bits of the C17. – DOOR in N doorway. With iron hinges with large and small scrolls; *c.*1200. – ORGAN. Early C19 Gothic. – MONUMENT. Sir John Samms and wife, mid C17, but still in the Jacobean tradition. Standing wall-monument with two large kneeling figures opposite each other by a prayer desk. Each figure against an arched niche. Below a deep arched recess with the equally large kneeling figure of the son.

LITTLE TOTHAM HALL, NW of the church. Timber-framed and plastered, C15 and later. At the NE end a late C16 addition partly of brick, with angle pilasters and a blocked doorway with a four-centred arch.

LITTLE WAKERING

ST MARY THE VIRGIN. The proud W tower was contributed by Bishop Wakering of Norwich (1416–25). It has big diagonal buttresses, a W doorway with the arms of the Bishop and the Countess of Stafford, a three-light window with panel tracery, niches to the l. and r., battlements with stone and flint chequerwork, and a rather tall recessed spire. Nave and chancel are much earlier, see their tiny Norman N windows. Inside, in the nave N wall a fine early C13 recess with one order of colonnettes and an arch with a keeled roll-moulding. The rood-stair doorways and the stairs themselves are preserved. – PLATE. Cup of 1566.

LITTLE WAKERING HALL. C15 house, altered in 1599, when the Hall was horizontally subdivided (date on the bracket of a beam) and new panelling put into several rooms. In the Hall a sumptuous fireplace of *c.*1730 with caryatids in profile carrying baskets.

LITTLE WALDEN

(CINDER HALL. 'Extraordinary modern house of "Gothic"
design, of flints and brick, having battlements, turrets and
pointed lancet-like windows – but the style is really its own.'
P. G. M. Dickinson, *Saffron Walden Guide*, 1960.)

LITTLE WALTHAM

St MARTIN. Norman nave with s doorway (one order of
columns, one-scallop capitals, roll-moulding) and one s window. Chancel Perp, w tower also Perp but much repaired in
brick in the C16 or C17. Behind the battlements appears a
minute cupola with a weathervane dated 1679. – CHEST. 'Dug-
out', 7 ft long, heavily bound with iron; C13 or C14; nave w
end. – PLATE. Cup with Elizabethan stem and bowl of 1619;
Paten on foot of 1712. – BRASS to John Maltouse (?)† 1447,
in armour, the figure 3 ft long.

(BELSTEAD'S FARM, 1 m. SE. Late C15, largely rebuilt in 1678 –
the date is on the central chimneystack. Of the same date
probably the staircase with moulded balusters. R.C.)

LITTLE WARLEY

St PETER. A small church. Brick w tower of 1718 with chequer
pattern, diagonal buttresses and parapet. C15 stone nave with
some windows with Perp tracery. Early C16 brick chancel,
heavily buttressed (later) on the N side. The E wall is early C19.
s porch of timber *c.*1500. Nave roof with tie-beams and king-
posts. – BOX PEWS. C17. – PLATE. Cup of 1564 with band of
ornament. – MONUMENTS. Brass with demi-figure of Anne
Terrell † 1592. – Sir Denner Strutt and his wife † 1641. Standing wall-monument. Recumbent effigies on shelves, the wife
behind and above the husband. Big baldacchino and coarsely
carved putti lifting up the curtains. – Lady Strutt † 1658.
Standing wall-monument. Semi-reclining figure in a shroud;
cheek propped on elbow. – Father Time, early C17 alabaster
figure, reclining, from a lost monument.

LITTLE WARLEY HALL. Immediately s of the church. Quite
small now, but originally longer at the w end. A lovely early
C16 brick house with a stepped gable over the porch, next to it
the three-light Hall window (one-storeyed Hall with moulded
beams and simple fireplace), and then the massive Hall chimneystack, broad below and ending in two twisted shafts. The
bricks are red, in English bond, with vitrified headers in

diaper pattern. Inside, a staircase of c.1600 with flat balusters.
WARLEY BARRACKS (Essex Regiment). Built for the East India
Company in 1805. The style is that of such early C19 military
establishments (cf. especially Woolwich). Yellow brick, with a
minimum of adornment, but dignified in composition. The
main front is to the E: seven-bay centre of two-and-a-half
storeys, one-storeyed stretch of wall l. and r., and then two-
storeyed nine-bay wings with three-bay pediments. Regular
row of buildings behind. A little further W *Sir Matthew Digby
Wyatt* in 1857 built a chapel in that Early Christian style
which his brother Thomas Henry had made famous (Wilton,
Woolwich). Yellow and a little red brick with coupled round-
arched windows. The interior is much more dignified.
Columns with imitation Early Christian capitals. The campanile was added about 1955 as a memorial to the Second
World War. In the last twenty years or so much furnishing
has been done to *Sir Charles Nicholson*'s designs: screen,
chancel seats, pews, pulpit, W gallery.
(FORD MOTOR COMPANY, CENTRAL OFFICES, Eagle Way.
By *T. P. Bennett & Son*, to be completed in 1964. Information from Brentwood U.D.C.)

LITTLE WIGBOROUGH

ST NICHOLAS. Late C15 nave, chancel, and narrower W tower
heightened insufficiently in 1886-8. The S side lies open towards
the estuary of the Blackwater. Inside a nice display of Victorian church ironwork; Communion Rail, Lectern, Font
Cover support – all scrolly and artistic. The work of 1888
was done by *Joseph Clarke*.

LITTLE YELDHAM

ST JOHN THE BAPTIST. Nave of unknown date, but probably
earlier than the C15 chancel, which is exceptionally out of line
with the nave. Belfry of the C15 resting inside the nave on four
posts with cross-beams on arched braces. – FONT. Octagonal,
Perp, with quatrefoils etc. and shields.

LONGBARNS *see* BEAUCHAMP RODING

LOUGHTON

ST JOHN THE BAPTIST, Church Lane. 1846 by *Sydney
Smirke*. It is a surprise here to find him using the fashionable

Neo-Norman. Yellow brick is the material, which does not help the Norman spirit. The plan is without aisles, but with transept, crossing, and crossing tower. The vaults used throughout are no doubt plaster. Enlarged 1877.

ST MARY THE VIRGIN, High Street. 1871–2 by *Thomas Henry Watson*. This is the church in the present shopping-centre of Loughton. St John the Baptist and St Nicholas are both in more marginal (and leafier) positions. Nave with bellcote at the E end and apse. Yellow and red brick. Nave and aisles, the arcades with circular piers ending in capitals of the most riotous naturalism, a quite exceptionally large variety of native flowers and leaves; for the High Victorian fan very useful to study. The clerestory has trefoil windows outside, but the rere-arches are of two low lights with a separate circle above.

ST NICHOLAS, Rectory Lane. The old village church of Loughton, or rather near the site of the old village church. For the present church was entirely rebuilt in 1877. It is very small, with nave and bellcote and a short chancel. – STAINED GLASS. Two kneeling figures of *c.*1500 in N and S windows. – BRASSES of 1541, 1558, 1594, and 1637. – E of the church a very Gothic churchyard monument of 1860, in the shape of a shrine with a steep-pitched roof.

(ST EDMUND (R.C.), Traps Hill. By *Tooley & Foster*, 1958.)

62b LOUGHTON HALL (now a school), by St Nicholas. 1878 by *Eden Nesfield*, an excellent building, every bit as good as Norman Shaw's at the same time (cf. Chigwell) and very similar in style to Shaw. Nesfield and Shaw had been partners in the 60s. Brick and plastering. Symmetrical S front with three bay windows, the outer straight-sided, the middle canted, two entrances with remarkably classical details and three gables. The symmetry is however broken by a cupola which is off-centre. The other frontages also deserve attention, especially the fine, bold chimneystacks.

LOUGHTON HIGH SCHOOL FOR GIRLS, Alderton Hill, also in a good Norman Shaw style. It is by *H. Tooley*, 1908.

Of older houses very little survives, one or two in the HIGH ROAD, the (much altered) White House* in CHURCH HILL, a few cottages in BALDWIN'S HILL W of Church Hill, and so on. Otherwise the main artery is mostly c20 London Suburban, and towards Epping Forest there are well-do-do Late Victorian and Edwardian private houses. Noteworthy as a piece of ingenious and imaginative design ASHFIELDS,

* Since demolished.

Baldwin's Hill, 1914 by *Turner Powell*, similar in style to
E. S. Prior's work.

The style of the last twenty years is well represented by LOUGH- 63b
TON STATION, 1940 by *Murray Easton*, with its boldly
cantilevered concrete roofs and the new BUS GARAGE at
Goldings Hill by *Yorke, Rosenberg & Mardall*.

ST NICHOLAS PRIMARY SCHOOL, Borders Lane, and LUC-
TONS SECONDARY SCHOOL in the same street are two
specially good examples of the new type of county schools
evolved after the Second World War by *H. Conolly*, the
County Architect, and his staff.

(Recent building includes a new SHOPPING CENTRE, The
Broadway, Debden Estate, by the *London County Council*,
completed in 1958. Information from Mr B. Tuck)

LOUGHTON CAMP *see* EPPING

LUNTS *see* PAGLESHAM

LYONS HALL *see* BOCKING

MAGDALEN LAVER

ST MARY MAGDALEN. Nave with blocked Norman window in
the N wall and two blocked circular windows in the W wall. W
doorway with Roman brick dressings, chancel with remains of
C14-looking windows. Most of them belong to the restoration
of 1875. W tower of timber, weatherboarded. It is probably
C16 and in any case replaces a small C15 one for which the
tie-beams with queen-posts still survive in the W part of the
nave. The tower has a centre with four posts carrying beams
with queen-posts. The posts are cross-strutted. There are narrower N, S, and W aisles outside the square formed by the four
posts. The tower aisles have pent-roofs, and above the bell-
chamber is a pyramid roof. – FONT. Octagonal, Perp, with
traceried stem and quatrefoils carrying shields. – SCREEN.
Interesting because of its relatively early date, probably not
later than *c.*1350. On each side of the door six openings,
separated by slender circular shafts with shaft-rings, and carrying an ogee arch. Circles with quatrefoils in the spandrels.
Straight top. – HELM. C16, in the nave. – PLATE. Cup, small
Paten, and large Flagon of 1665.

(WYNTERS. Mid C14, much altered in the late C16 by horizontal subdivision of the hall and alterations to the wings.

10—E.

The hall had a single-span open truss (with corner-post), which has short principal rafters and big curved braces supporting the collar-beam. For Essex this is an early date to clear the posts from the hall, in which aisled construction now remains only in the end walls. Information kindly given by Mr J. T. Smith.)

MALDON

The little town lies on a hill by the river Blackwater, in the place where the river widens into a shallow estuary. The chief parish church lies at the top. Market Hill descends steeply to the bridge, while the High Street runs down the brow of the hill gently, passes the (disused) second parish church, and in the end reaches the third, placed close to the water.

ALL SAINTS. Long s side without a break between s aisle and s chancel chapel. The w tower lies back a little. It is unique in England in that it is triangular. It dates from the C13 and has lancet windows (also towards the nave), a hexagonal shingled spire, and three spirelets. The rest is externally somewhat confusing; the nave of 1728, of brick, but gothicized, the N chancel chapel late C15, and the chancel and s chapel earlier C15. The architectural interest of the church lies in its s aisle, exceptionally lavishly executed inside. The exterior does not betray that. Of its windows all but one are C19. The easternmost is C14, but clearly later than the interior. It is of three lights, with ogee reticulation above, i.e. a Dec motif, but a band of Perp panelling below this. Inside it cuts into the arcading which distinguishes the aisle. This arcading is in two tiers. On the s wall there is first a tier of blank ogee arches with renewed capitals and renewed head label-stops and above this a rich framing of the windows by arches alternating with blank arches to fill the wall between the windows. The jambs and voussoirs of all these arches are decorated by trails of roses. On the w side of the aisle the lower tier of arches is higher, but the style is the same. The later C14 window mentioned above cuts into the SEDILIA, which are another unusual feature of this unusual aisle. A third is the crypt below it, reached by a spiral stair in the outer wall. It is vaulted and has depressed-pointed transverse arches – also C14. Nothing is known that would explain the splendour of this aisle, reminiscent, though with a good many reductions, of the Ely Lady Chapel. The date of this is c.1340, and that seems a convincing date for the s aisle

of All Saints as well. Additional proof is the arcade towards
the nave with its filleted quatrefoil piers of Purbeck marble
and its finely moulded arches. The nave is wide and bare and
has little atmosphere. A N arcade must have been ripped out in
1728, as the two C18 arches into the chancel and the N chapel
now stand incongruously side by side. The s chapel has a
three-bay arcade to the chancel with piers of the not unusual
four-shafts-four-hollows section and moulded arches, the N
arcade, also of three bays, has simply octagonal piers and
double-hollow-chamfered arches. – MONUMENTS. Thomas
Cammocke † 1602, two wives and children; with kneeling
figures, the man frontal, the wives in profile, the children
in the 'predella'. – Mary Vernon † 1647, with cherubs on an
urn between columns, a conceit unusual before the C18.

ST PETER (cf. below, Plume Library). Only the W tower remains,
with angle buttresses, battlements, and a higher stair-turret.

ST MARY THE VIRGIN. The E end quite near the Blackwater.
Big, heavy W tower with uncommonly massive buttresses. Top
brick with stepped battlements. Shingled spire on an octagonal
weatherboarded base. The nave N wall revealed as Early
Norman by a small window close to the porch. The s aisle all
of 1886. The interior shows that the Norman nave was as wide
as the present nave, quite a remarkable fact, proved by the
responds of the Norman chancel arch, which are wider than
the present chancel arch, restored with C14 bits. – FONT.
Perp stem with bowl of *c*.1700. – COMMUNION RAIL. With
twisted balusters, *c*.1700.

CONGREGATIONAL CHAPEL, Market Hill. 1801, re-fronted
c.1860, but still with classical reminiscences. Ground-floor
entrance loggia with arched windows above and a pediment.

FRIENDS' MEETING HOUSE, Butt Lane. Nice, quiet red brick
house of five by three bays, with arched windows and a hipped
roof. The old trees of the graveyard help to give it a feeling of
peace and seclusion.

MOOT HALL, High Street. Originally a plain brick tower of
c.1435 with a higher stair-turret at the back. On the ground
floor ceiling-beams of that time still exist. The porch must
have been added about 1830. It is placed astride the pavement
and has four Tuscan columns. The upper windows are
relatively recent.

PLUME LIBRARY, founded by Dr Plume before he died in 1704.
He made use of the site of the ruined church of St Peter, just
E of the tower still standing, and built there a two-storey house

of red brick with quoins and keystones to the windows. The windows are of wood, of the mullion-and-transom-cross type. The library started with 6,000 volumes; on the ground floor is now a branch of the Essex County Library. Some of the original fittings are still inside. That an archdeacon of Rochester should have felt a library to be of more use to his native town than the rebuilding of a parish church is a noteworthy sign of the period about 1700.

ST GILES HOSPITAL. A leper hospital founded, it is said, by Henry II. All that survives is part of the transepts and of the chancel of a chapel on quite an ambitious scale. The scanty details point to the end of the C12: shafts attached to the angles of the crossing piers and a W window in the N transept. Both transepts seem originally to have had E chapels. The three lancets of the S transept S wall are an E.E. alteration. In about 1922, within the space of the crossing, an apse was found, and immediately S of it the beginning of something which looked like a second apse of the same size. These foundations are in all probability pre-Norman. (Thanks for this information are due to Dr H. M. Taylor and the Ministry of Public Building and Works.)

HOSPITAL, Spital Road. Built as a workhouse in 1873 to the designs of *F. Peck*. Red brick, Tudor, symmetrical and unattractive.

RAILWAY STATION. 1846, red brick, in a pretty Jacobean style, with shaped gables and an arcade of nine bays in front. Typical of the stations all along the Maldon branch line.

A perambulation should start at the beginning of the High Street, where a pretty Georgian house at the end of GATE STREET faces it. It is of five bays, but has as a distinguishing feature an odd fat shell decoration in the arches of the two ground-floor windows. In the HIGH STREET itself the first house of note is No. 3, on the S side, C18, of three bays with a doorway with rusticated frame and a pediment. Then follow cottages on both sides, until the place is reached where the street bends and assumes its chief direction. The bend is marked by No. 15, a three-bay late C18 house, and opposite No. 22 (Stonecroft), of five bays, with quoins, and the centre bays singled out by rusticated pilasters. Broad doorway with pilasters against a rusticated background. The date must be early C18. Then All Saints appears on the l., set back only just enough to reveal some cottages at the E end of the churchyard. Opposite the church the KING'S HEAD, with a nice little late c18 porch. Meanwhile, by the church tower SILVER STREET starts, and here the church is faced by the BLUE BOAR HOTEL, which hides behind a white brick front of c.1800 some impressive c15 stabling with oversailing upper floor. There is nothing else of individual note in Silver Street, but from it one reaches, behind the church and in a completely different atmosphere, the VICARAGE, an extremely attractive c15 house with exposed timber-framing and two symmetrical gables to the l. and r. of what was the Hall.*

As one returns to the High Street the most concentrated stretch of interesting buildings follows, the MOOT HALL‡ with a wide porch breaking the continuity of the flow of traffic, and opposite Nos 40–42, of five bays and three storeys with a central Venetian window and a semicircular window above, No. 50 (white brick, early c19) of three-and a-half storeys with giant pilasters and two bowed oriels on the first floor, No. 52 (c.1700) with superimposed angle pilasters, the upper ones in the form of terms, and with a pedimented doorway with attached Tuscan columns against a rusticated background, and finally Nos 54–56, an ambitious nine-bay front of three storeys in chequered brickwork, with curly decoration over the tops of the first- and second-floor windows.

After that St Peter's churchyard is reached, whose old dark trees once again break the evenness of the street fronts. But there is no wide open space here either, as indeed the visual character of Maldon is characterized quite specially by the absence of open spaces. No Market Place, no Church Square. The Plume Library has already been mentioned.

Here MARKET HILL turns off to the N, bending and running steeply down the hill towards the bridge. There are plenty of nice houses on the E side (the best No. 34), but nothing special. What is special is the contrast of the solid E side with a W side with large front gardens and the houses much higher up (e.g. the Municipal Offices with a long staircase up to the ground floor, and a pretty c19 glazed belvedere on the roof). At the foot of the hill, across the river FULLBRIDGE starts with a few worth-while houses on the l., a flour mill on the r., and FULLBRIDGE HOUSE facing the bridge with its front, i.e. standing at r. angles to the street, a good effect.

Back once again to the High Street, where Nos 69–71 are an

* Some painted wall decoration survives.
‡ Probably second half of the c15. Known as Darcy's Tower until it became the Moot Hall in 1576.

example of the c16 timber-framed, plastered and gabled town-house. The SWAN HOTEL is another, but its front is prettified out of all recognition. The rest of the street is of less interest, except perhaps for KING GEORGE'S PLACE, a long three-storeyed modern house with a cinema at the far end, not specially well-designed in itself, but useful to show that the c20 can blend with the c15. The house is of brick, with the typical horizontal windows.

BEELEIGH ABBEY. See p. 80.

MANNINGTREE

ST MICHAEL AND ALL ANGELS. The W wall and the N aisle with its Late Perp windows date from 1616. To the same time belong the first of the N piers – of oak and with a section which is roughly circular with four attached shafts in the diagonals. Also of 1616 the braces and the curious roof, a hammerbeam variety. The rest is essentially 1839. The chancel was then added, in white brick, with round-arched windows. – REREDOS. Apparently early c18. – PLATE. Cup, Cover, and two Patens, all given in 1633 by Laud, who was then Bishop of London.

The old parts of Manningtree are chiefly the cross formed by the High Street and South Street. In the HIGH STREET mainly Georgian houses, several with Greek Doric doorways or porches. The biggest is No. 50, of seven bays, c18. More in SOUTH STREET, which runs up the hill, especially at the two corners of the lane crossing South Street. Higher up on the l. the METHODIST CHURCH of 1807, quite a big elaborate composition, white brick with a cupola. N of it the previous building, much humbler, with pediment and three arched windows. The smaller and simpler former INDEPENDENTS' CHAPEL of 1818 lies hidden at the W end of a little triangular green into which South Street widens.

At the W exit a pretty timber-framed L-shaped house; but that belongs to the parish of Lawford.

MANOR PARK see EAST HAM

MANUDEN

ST MARY. Quite a big building, all of 1864 except for the N transept and N wall. – SCREEN. Sumptuous for Essex, with large one-light divisions. Dado panels with quatrefoil frieze at the foot, blank tracery, and two top friezes. Cusped and crocketed ogee arches are the main motif above, surmounted by panel tracery. Broad straight cornice. – PLATE. Elizabethan Cup and Paten.

MANUDEN HALL, ENE of the church. Much altered, but of the original mid C16 brick house there remain the two s gables of the w front, stepped and with pinnacles on the apexes. The windows below may also be original, on the ground floor mullioned and transomed, on the upper floor only mullioned. All the individual lights are arched.

Manuden has a specially pretty, short village street with timber-framed cottages with oversailing upper floors near the church and a small assortment of Georgian houses a little further w.

MARDEN ASH see CHIPPING ONGAR

MARGARET RODING

ST MARGARET. Nave and chancel, and C19 bellcote. In the w wall of the nave an odd two-light window which may be of the C17 and above it a small Norman window. In the s wall restored Norman doorway with two orders of columns. The capitals are scalloped, one column is zigzag-carved. The lintel is curved, the tympanum has a diaper pattern. Zigzag arches and a billet hood-mould. Norman windows on the N and s sides of the nave. The chancel windows are late C14. Inside the chancel a low ogee-arched recess and damaged SEDILIA and PISCINA, also a corbel s of the (C19) E window with a caryatid demi-figure. – FONT. Octagonal, Perp, with traceried stem and quatrefoils with shields on the panels. – DOORS in chancel and nave with some ironwork of c.1200. – PLATE. Cup of 1562; Paten probably of 1562.

MARGARETTING

ST MARGARET. The church should be visited by all for its splendid C15 timber w tower, on ten posts (like Blackmore). The free-standing posts are connected from N and s by three pairs of arched braces. From E to w between posts two and three and posts three and four on both sides there are also arched braces, but lower and smaller. Cross-strutting above these. Outside, the tower has a vertically weatherboarded ground floor, the roof is hipped on N, s, and w, but straight on the E and higher than the nave roof. The bell-stage is straight again and on it sits a broach-spire. Bell-stage and broach-spire are shingled. The two-light W window with a little tracery is original, the N and S windows renewed. The N porch also is of timber and contemporary. Four-centred doorway with traceried spandrels, cusped bargeboarding and one-light side openings. The rest of the church is also essentially C15 and early C16, but all windows are renewed. The S arcade has first one bay, then a piece of wall, and then another three. The piers are quatrefoil, and the arches four-centred with double-hollow-chamfered moulding. – FONT. Octagonal, Perp, with quatrefoils carrying flowers, a crown, a mitre, a head with tongue put out. – SCREEN. Only the dado remains, with elaborate blank tracery. – STAINED GLASS. In the three-light E window the Tree of Jesse, much restored, yet impressive as a complete C15 composition: four medallions with two figures each in the side lights, Jesse, three medallions, and the seated Virgin in the centre light. – PLATE. Large Cup and Paten of 1563. – BRASS. Knight and Lady, mid C16, the figures c.22 in. long.

KILLIGREWS. Tudor house surrounded by a moat. The house received a new E front early in the C18 and a new W wing was added fairly recently. Immediately adjoining the moat the lower courses of an early C16 brick wall, and at the angles two ornamented turrets of the same date: octagonal with battlements and crocketed brick pyramid roofs or spires.

(PEACOCKS. Charming, stuccoed Regency house, like a Cheltenham villa.*)

MARK HALL NORTH *and* SOUTH *see* HARLOW

MARKSHALL

The church was demolished in 1932, the house in 1951. Monument, see Great Coggeshall, p. 200.

MARKS TEY

ST ANDREW. Base of a brick W tower with diagonal buttresses and stair-turret. Continued with vertical weatherboarding. Even the battlements are of vertical boards. Nave and chancel. In the S side one small Norman window, in the S and N sides plain Norman doorways. These and the window have surrounds of Roman bricks. Chancel C14. S porch C15, of timber,

* This entry was supplied by Mr I. Nairn.

plain. – FONT. C15, octagonal. The remarkable thing is that it is of oak. Stem with tracery panels with roses in the centres, bowl with tracery panels formerly with seated figures. – PLATE. Elizabethan Cup and Paten of 1567.

MASHBURY

CHURCH. Nave, chancel, and tiny C19 bell-lantern. On the N side a Norman window and a plain Norman doorway, on the S side also a Norman window and a doorway with two orders of columns with one-scallop capitals, decorated abaci, and zigzag arches. The belfry rests on four C15 posts with two arched braces. – PULPIT. Plain C17. – DOOR. C12 ironwork on the N door. – STAINED GLASS. Figure of a Saint, C14, N window. – PLATE. Cup and Paten of 1639.
(BAILEYS, 1 m. NNW. Timber-framed early C16 house with gabled cross-wings. In 1614 a central gable was added. Central chimneystack with four octagonal shafts. R.C.)

MATCHING

ST MARY THE VIRGIN. The church makes an extremely pleasing picture with MATCHING HALL, its barn and dovecote, the pond with a brick fishing hut, and the Rectory on the other side. C15 W tower, late C14 S aisle wall, and C13 N and S aisle arcades (W parts only, with circular piers and double-chamfered arches. The rest 1875 by *Sir Arthur Blomfield*). – FONT. Octagonal, Perp, with quatrefoils with shields and flowers. – PULPIT. A good Jacobean piece with strapwork decoration, given in 1624. – BENCHES. Four, C16, plain. – PLATE. Large Cup of 1685, with trumpet-shaped stem; Paten of 1685. – MONUMENTS. Brass of 1638. – Epitaph to Nicholas Ashton † 1716, with putti, skulls, and leaf sprays, excellently carved.
MARRIAGE FEAST ROOM, W of the church. Timber-framed and plastered, with oversailing upper storey. C15, and not specially interesting visually. Its purpose however gives it a claim to attention.

MAYLAND

ST BARNABAS. 1867 by the younger *Hardwick* (GR). Nave and chancel only. E.E. with cusped lancets and a bellcote on the E gable of the nave, an unusual motif. Tall S porch. – (STAINED

GLASS by *Powell & Sons*, 1868: E window with medallions from designs by *Holiday*; W window with the two medallions by *Casolani*; chancel window with medallions by *Holiday*.) – PLATE. Paten of 1568; Cup with two bands of ornament, probably of the same date.

MESSING

ALL SAINTS. Mostly 1840, i.e. the W tower of red brick, not at all Essex in style, and the long S transept. Medieval are part of the nave and most of the chancel. In the chancel is what makes the church worth a visit, the PANELLING and CHANCEL STALLS of 1640. No classical features yet, the stall fronts with rusticated oval frames, the backs with rusticated blank arches separated by Corinthian pilasters. The ornament entirely Jacobean, but hardly any strapwork. – STAINED GLASS. In the E window, contemporary with the panelling and attributed to *van Linge* (Abraham who worked at Peterhouse, Cambridge, rather than Bernhard). The Works of Mercy and figures of Faith, Hope, and Charity. – CHEST. Iron-bound, probably C13. – PLATE. Whole set of 1634, given by Captain Chibborne, whose arms also appear on the reverse side of the carved Royal Arms in the S transept. – BRASS to a Lady, *c*.1540 (chancel).

MESSING PARK. The back a Queen Anne farmhouse, the front georgianized about 1815. Centre of the façade with porch and Venetian window above.

TUMULUS (?) in Conyfield Wood. 6 ft high, 75 ft in diameter. It may be a mill mound, not a burial mound.

MICHAELSTOW HALL *see* RAMSEY

MIDDLETON

ALL SAINTS. Nave, chancel, and belfry. The church is of some importance, especially for its Norman features. The S doorway has colonnettes with scalloped capitals and two orders of zigzag. The chancel arch has columns also. The inner order is of a remarkable design. Polygonal shafts decorated down each side by a chain of triangles. Another such column is now (re-used ?) in a C13 recess at the E end of the S aisle. The capitals are scalloped or with volutes and slight leaf decoration. The chancel arch above the columns has decorated abaci. The arches are provided with a zigzag moulding and another with zigzags and a kind of stylized tongues lapping into them. In the nave N and S walls two identical C14 recesses on short triple shafts. Porch Early Tudor. – DOOR with traceried panels. – STAINED GLASS. E window, in the style of *Warrington*. – PAINTING. Annunciation. By a follower of *Veronese* (?). – MONUMENT. Incised slab to James Samson, a priest † 1349, 7 ft long. The style is Flemish rather than English, with an elaborate architectural surround, but the slab is of Purbeck marble, and we know too little of such pieces to decide against English authorship. The head of the figure unfortunately is renewed.

MILL FARM *see* RAMSEY

MISTLEY

ST MARY. Of the medieval church only the porch survives, with a two-centred arch to the doorway, shields in the spandrels, and flushwork decoration of the walls (a frieze at the foot, panelling above).

THE VILLAGE. The church was replaced by a new one when Mr Richard Rigby, M.P., had decided to convert Mistley into a spa. He was the grandson of a draper, the son of a factor who had made much money at the time of the South Sea speculation, and himself a man of social gifts. In 1768 George III made him Paymaster General of the Forces, one of the most lucrative jobs in the country. In the time of his father a new village had been built near the river. Morant in 1768 speaks of thirty brick houses, granaries, warehouses, a large malting office, and quays. Much of this remains by the little square with its fountain, the chief ornament of which is a swan standing in the circular basin. The malting office is below the fountain, nine bays wide with a semicircular porch on Tuscan columns, a semicircular window above it, and a three-bay pediment. To the N of the village a new church was built.

ST MARY. This new church was consecrated in 1735. It was a plain parallelogram of brick and would not be worth special attention here, if it had not been radically changed by Richard Rigby in connexion with his grander plans. He began by altering Mistley Hall, which had been built by his father, made the grounds picturesque in the fashionable landscape style, built Gothic and Chinese temples, bridges, and so on, and then called in *Robert Adam*, apparently in 1774. He was to design

a *bagno*, that is a saltwater bath by the river, the other side of
the malting office. Drawings for this exist, but it was never
carried out. Next came the church. This was taken in hand in
1776. What Robert Adam did, was to add a square tower at
the N end and another at the S (ritual E) end, and porticoes with
two pairs of Tuscan columns each at the two long sides. The
result was extremely original and far from religious-looking.
The towers were adorned with free-standing Tuscan columns,
each with a piece of projecting entablature on top, as if
they were angle buttresses gone classical. Above the entablature was a square storey with four pediments, and then a
slim circular drum with attached Ionic columns and a crowning dome. The duplication of the towers so far distant from
each other was not aesthetically wholly successful. The inter-
vening nave prevented them from being seen as one, and
today that is even more difficult, since the two towers alone
survive. The nave has been pulled down, and the portico
columns have been re-used to continue the motif of the
buttressing by columns on the sides where formerly the nave
stood. This buttressing motif, even if derived from Roman
precedent, is handled very daringly and no doubt impressed
Sir John Soane a great deal. The pulling down of the nave was
connected with the building of yet another church.

ST MARY. 1870–1, by *Wadmore & Baker* (GR). The style is
dependent on Scott. SW steeple with spire; apse; geometrical
tracery. – PLATE. C17 Cup.

The Hall does not exist any longer, but two LODGES built by
Robert Adam in 1782 remain, at the crossing of the Colchester–
Mistley and the Manningtree–Clacton roads.

MOAT FARM DYKE *see* COLCHESTER

MOLE HALL *see* DEBDEN

MOOR HALL *see* WRITTLE

MORETON

ST MARY THE VIRGIN. Nave and chancel early C13 with
lancet windows. The W tower of brick with diagonal buttresses and battlements was built in 1787. The church was
much restored in 1868–9. – FONT. Square, of Purbeck marble,
c.1200. It has on one side the familiar row of shallow blank
round arches, four in number, on two sides fleurs-de-lis, and

on the fourth sun, moon, and a whorl. – PLATE. Almsdish of
1648; Cup and Paten of 1663.
(GUILDHALL, ¼ m. WSW. Timber-framed C15 cottage with a
hall (later horizontally subdivided) which still has two openings into the former screens passage and a roof truss with tie-
beam on arched braces and moulded king-post. R.C.)
WINDMILL, ¾ m. N. A post-mill in good condition and of interesting design. It has three (instead of two) cross-trees and
six (instead of four) quarter bars, which are at present in poor
repair (V.C.H.).

MOUNT BURES

On a hill overlooking Bures and the river Stour. The Normans
built a CASTLE here, of which the mound survives, 200 ft across
and 35 ft high. The bailey lay to the SW, that is W of the church.

ST JOHN. The unusual shape of this village church is no doubt
to be explained by the connexion with the castle. Nave and
chancel, crossing tower and transepts. All Norman, but crossing tower and transepts rebuilt in 1875. The Roman quoins of
the old part can easily be distinguished from the new bricks.
Norman windows (with Roman brick dressings) in the W wall,
high up (a reticulated C14 window below), in the S wall,
blocked, and in the N wall, where there is also a plain Norman
doorway. S porch Perp with three-light windows and a doorway with decorated spandrels. – PLATE. Cup and Paten of
1641.
In the village of Bures by the river one house on the Essex side
deserves mention. Georgian red brick front with pedimented
doorway and a Venetian window above.
WINDMILL, 1 m. SE of the church. Post-mill in a dilapidated
state.
BELGIC TOMB. The tomb was found in the C19 ¼ m. SE of the
Mount, close to the railway line. It consisted of a triangular
vault, each side 7 ft long, containing a pair of iron firedogs,
amphorae, and a glass bottle. The finds are dated to c. A.D. 43.

MOUNTNESSING

ST GILES. The church makes a handsome picture with the neat
Georgian MOUNTNESSING HALL, a seven-bay brick building, with older parts at the back. The main interest of the
church is its belfry standing as an independent timber structure in the W bay of the nave. It has six posts, cross-beams

supported by impressively tall arched braces, and trellis-
strutting higher up. The E pair of braces rest on polygonal
responds with concave sides. Big buttressing struts in the
aisles of the church. The church itself is C13 except for the S
aisle, which is C19, the chancel, which is C18 (of brick), and
the brick W front with a date-plate of 1653 and heavy S-
cramps for the securing of the belfry timbers. The N and S
arcades have circular piers and double-chamfered arches. The
capitals are moulded except for one and one respond on the N
side which are enriched by stiff-leaf. Lancet windows in the N
wall. – REREDOS. Probably c.1730. Wood, with paintings of
Moses and Aaron to the l. and r. – COMMUNION RAIL. Of the
same time, with fine twisted balusters. – CHEST. Of dug-out
type; perhaps C13. – PLATE. Cup of 1564 with band of
ornament; Paten on foot of 1704.

THOBY PRIORY. What remains of this house of Augustinian
Canons founded in the early C12 is picturesque but far from
eloquent. Two ivy-covered arches of the chancel of the
church (C14 or C15) and within a house, partly early C19
castellated and partly of c.1894, scanty remains of the hall and
an adjoining room.

WINDMILL. Post-mill in good condition.

MOYNS PARK

Of an Early Tudor house the delightful SW wing of the present
building remains, half-timbered with brick infillings, an overhanging upper storey, and three gables of which the l. one is
higher and broader than the others. About 1575–80 Thomas
Gent, a Baron of the Exchequer and Steward of the lands of
the Earl of Oxford, must have begun rebuilding the old house.
He only completed the NW façade and died in 1593. The façade
is of brick with stone dressings and represents an unusual
type, with two big gables near the ends, two small ones in
between, and three bay windows between the gables instead
of below them. The two outer bays are polygonal, the centre
one starts rectangular to hold the porch and entrance to the
house but is also continued polygonal above. The ground floor
has two-transomed windows throughout, the bay windows
continue these on the upper floor as well. At the back of the
façade and dominating its appearance from a distance are tall
chimneystacks with polygonal shafts. That on the l. unfortunately has been replaced by a more recent successor. The NE

wing also half-timbered but probably not older than the façade. Inside the house much was altered early in the C18.

MUCKING

ST JOHN THE BAPTIST. 1849–52 except for the chancel (Perp three-light E window) with a blocked C13 arcade to a former N chapel, whose lancet windows, when it was pulled down, were re-used. The S chapel is C19, but its arch is C15. The S aisle has a C13 arcade of two bays with treble-chamfered arches. The pier is circular and has a big stiff-leaf capital, with two faces between the leaves. One is a so-called Green Man, that is a face with leaves sprouting out of his mouth. The W tower is mostly C19, but the S doorway which serves as a porch has recognizable C15 parts. Plain SEDILIA in the chancel. – PLATE. C17 Cup. – MONUMENT. Graceful little alabaster monument of Elizabeth Downes † 1607, with kneeling figure between ornamented pilasters.

MUNDON

ST MARY.* Nave and chancel and a timber tower, remarkable in design though hardly higher than the nave roof. Square centre with N, S, and W aisles, the W aisle connected by triangular pieces to N and S aisles (cf. Navestock). The aisle roofs are tiled and start about 8 ft from the ground. The square upper part is boarded. The nave has an early C14 N window with Y-tracery. A brick window and a blocked archway into a chapel on the S side must be early C16. The chancel is early C18. Of brick with original E and N windows. Timber N porch with pendants hanging from the lower eaves ends of the gable. Humble interior with box pews and candleholders on them. – PLATE. Jacobean Cup on a stem for which the Royal Commission suggests a pre-Reformation date.

WHITE HOUSE, ¾ m. NNW. Timber-framed C16 house, prettily restored. Moulded beams inside.

NAVESTOCK

ST THOMAS THE APOSTLE. Nave N wall with plain Norman doorway; S aisle, S chancel chapel, and S arcade E.E. Circular piers and double-chamfered arches. The pier at the E end of the arcade and the W end of the S chancel chapel is of

* Now abandoned.

oak and polygonal, almost like fluted. It is probably C16 (Rev. N. C. S. Motley). The fourth and fifth arches of the arcade are also of wood. One blocked lancet in the s chapel, one long lancet in the s aisle. Early C14 chancel with Dec windows – the E window of three lights with reticulated tracery. In the nave N wall at its E end a wide recess, E.E., with a shaft on the l. carrying a stiff-leaf capital. Probably in the C15 a s porch was added and also – a more ambitious enterprise – a timber tower. This stands to the w not of the nave but the aisle. It is oblong and had N and s aisles and in addition a w aisle connected with the others by triangular pieces – a rare arrangement. The tower is carried on four heavy posts, each with an octagonal shaft attached diagonally towards the centre. These shafts carry rib-like arched braces meeting in the middle in a foliage boss.* – DOORS. Three with ornamental hinges; one (N doorway) is C12, the other two C13. – ORGAN. Early C18, bought from Lord Southwood's house at Highgate, London. – PLATE. Cup and Paten of 1624; two Flagons, inscribed 1626 and 1630. – MONUMENTS. Mainly to the Waldegrave family, and singularly modest. Edward W., by *Bacon Jun.*, 1812, with a weeping female allegorical figure bent over military objects, and a triumphant cherub higher up. – Seventh Earl Waldegrave † 1846, with bust by *Behnes*. Also John Greene † 1653, with frontal demi-figure. – Anne Snelling † 1625, tiny reclining marble figure with tinier baby in her arms.

BOIS HALL, 1½ m. NE. Five- by five-bay block of 1687. Two-storeyed with parapet. Tuscan porch.

NAZEING

ALL SAINTS. Norman nave with rere-arch of one window. C15 N aisle with arcade piers of the familiar four-shaft-four-hollow type where capitals are introduced only for the shafts. The arches are wave-moulded. The timber s porch is also of the C15. The floor is made of tiles set closely on end. W tower of red brick with blue diapers, diagonal buttresses, battlements, and a higher stair-turret; early C16. – FONT. Perp, octagonal, with quatrefoils carrying shields. – FONT COVER. Plain, ogee-shaped with a finial; C17. – CHEST. Oblong, with flat lid, heavily iron-bound; ascribed to the C14. – PLATE. Paten of

---

* Recent radiocarbon tests on the timbers of the tower suggest that the wood used dates from the C12 or C13. On structural evidence Mr C. A. Hewett thinks that the tower might be *c.*1250 (*Archaeological Journal*, vol 119, 1962).

1817; Almsdish given in 1818. – MONUMENT of 1823, by *T. Harling* (the usual female figure by an urn).

NAZEING PARK. Built *c.*1814. On the l. and r. of the front two-storeyed bay windows, the four-bay centre three-storeyed, with a two-storeyed Ionic colonnade.

NELMES *see* HORNCHURCH

NETHER HALL *see* ROYDON

NETTESWELL *see* HARLOW

NEVENDON

ST PETER, FRAMPTON'S FARM, and NEVENDON HALL, see Basildon, p. 75.

LITTLE BROMFORDS, ¾ m. N. Timber-framed, plastered, and gabled. Probably late C16. Chimneystack with diagonal shafts. Moat partly filled in.

Housing for Basildon New Town has been erected near Nevendon.

NEW AMBERDEN HALL *see* DEBDEN

NEWBURY PARK

BUS STATION, Eastern Avenue. By *Oliver Hill*, 1949–50. Part of a future scheme comprising the Underground Station as well. The bus station is of hangar type, with semicircular concrete arches and a tunnel-vault of 60 ft span.

NEW HALL *see* BOREHAM *and* HIGH RODING

NEWHOUSE FARM *see* CHIPPING ONGAR

NEWPORT

ST MARY THE VIRGIN. Big church, formerly collegiate. It lies back, away from the main road. W tower of 1858 (by *G. E. Pritchett*) with embattled polygonal pinnacles, the chief accent of the church. It has a crossing and transepts, dating from the C13, as is shown by the forms of the arches separating them (responds with nailhead ornament) and the two N and one S lancet windows. The chancel is wide and not too high and in its masonry also C13. S arcade early C14 with octagonal piers and double-chamfered two-centred arches. To the same time belongs the s aisle w window. N arcade Early Perp with sturdy quatrefoil piers with hollows in the diagonals, slightly decorated capitals, and double-wave-moulded arches. – C15 s porch and nave clerestory, later C16 brick clerestory over the chancel. – FONT. Octagonal, with heavy gabled trefoil arches, an unusual design, probably early C13. – COMMUNION TABLE, with three Flemish early C17 reliefs. – SCREEN. Fragments of a C15 screen with six-light divisions with broad panel tracery. – LECTERN. Oak, with octagonal base and stem, tracery panels on it, and tracery in the triangle between the top book-rests. – CHEST. An extremely interesting later C13 piece. The front has three friezes of ornament, circles, lozenges,* and shields. Paintings inside the lid (Crucifixion, the Virgin, St John, St Peter, St Paul), coloured chiefly in red and green. – BENCHES. Some poppy-heads survive. – STAINED GLASS. N transept, with several whole figures (St Katherine, St Michael), early C14, bought about fifty years ago. – BRASSES of 1515 (Thomas Brond and wife, s aisle floor, 18-in. figures) and 1608.

GRAMMAR SCHOOL. The older parts, especially the Head Master's House with a double overhang, and the gabled buildings behind it, were designed in 1878 by *Eden Nesfield*. Many more recent additions.

SHORTGROVE, ¾ m. NE. H-shaped house said to be of 1684, but apparently earlier C17 (see e.g. the secondary staircase). It was given its present shape shortly after 1712. W front of thirteen bays stepping backwards in two steps towards the centre. Ground floor and first floor have straight windows, the second the typical segment-headed windows of the early C18. Original glazing-bars. Brick quoins and a (later) four-column Tuscan porch. Entrance Hall and in axis with it the Saloon with giant pilasters. Fine staircase with delicate wrought-iron scrolls.

VILLAGE. The village street is of uncommon charm and possesses two of the best Essex cottages, one of the C15, the other of 1692. The first is MONKS BARN, two-storeyed, with exposed timbers and brick-nogging, and on the l. an upper (renewed) oriel the coving of which is carved (badly) with a demi-figure of the Virgin and two ministering angels. The roof is treated in the so-called Wealden way. Near Monks Barn are several nice three-bay and five-bay Georgian houses. The house of 1692 stands further N, in the Green now cut off by the railway. It is CROWN HOUSE, actually a late C16 or

* The delicate tracery is copied.

early C17 house, but pargeted with garlands, swags, and large leafy branches in 1692, when also the inviting big shell-hood was added above the door. In the Green also other worthwhile houses, especially MARTIN'S FARM with an exposed C15 timber front. Inside several plaster fireplaces.

NEW RIFFHAMS see DANBURY

NOAK HILL

ST THOMAS. 1841–2 by *G. Smith*. Red brick, with transepts. Octagonal SW turret. The main windows with transoms. Not in a style usual in the 40s. – (STAINED GLASS. Some Flemish pre-Reformation glass in the E window.)

NORTH BENFLEET

ALL SAINTS. Away from the village but close to the moated site of North Benfleet Hall, which was recently pulled down. The church is small and of little interest outside, except for one early C16 brick window of two lights with panel tracery. The brick tower of 1903 does not betray the timber construction of the belfry inside, with braces between the posts from E to W as well as from N to S. Trellis-struts higher up. And this heavy timbering in its turn does not betray a window of *c.*1200 hidden in the Norman W wall of the nave. – FONT. Of the C13 Purbeck type, square bowl, each side with six shallow blank pointed arches. – PLATE. Cup of 1506 with a band of ornament; Cover of 1564.

NORTH END

BLACK CHAPEL. The rare case of a surviving entirely timber-framed ecclesiastical building, and also the rare case of a medieval chapel with attached priest's house. The chapel was of nave and chancel in one, the house is set to the W at r. angles and projects to the N. In the house are two original windows and remains of the roof. The chapel inside looks lovely – not in the original but in an early C19 way. Gothick window casements; on the S side the windows rise into dormers in the roof. Box pews, and a W gallery, with a tiny organ on it. – SCREEN. Humble C15 work. – BENCHES. A complete set of simple design.

NORTH FAMBRIDGE

HOLY TRINITY. Close to the mud-flats of the estuary of the river Crouch. C18, brick, with arched windows and a bell-turret. The w side altered with half-timbering and pebble-dash in 1890.

NORTH OCKENDON

ST MARY MAGDALENE. Away from the village and close to Ockendon Hall, which was destroyed during the Second World War. Norman church with E.E. N aisle and N chancel chapel, and low C15 w tower with diagonal buttresses. Norman work, besides the masonry, the s doorway of three orders with zig-zag-decorated arches survives. Its columns have one scalloped and one very stylized fleur-de-lis capital. A little later the pointed w arch of the N arcade with one chamfer. The next two bays of the N arcade of the early C13 with circular pier and double-chamfered arch. The easternmost arch is C15 with hollow mouldings in the arch, similar to the chancel arch. The N chancel chapel is connected with the chancel by an arcade of two bays with a quatrefoil pier with Perp foliage capital. Fine nave roof with tie-beams, and king-posts with four-way struts. – PULPIT. Elizabethan type, though no doubt C17. – STAIRS in the tower, steep and elementarily constructed, C15 or perhaps earlier. – STAINED GLASS. Female Saint, late C13, and much tabernacle work perhaps a little later. – PLATE. Cup and Cover of 1561; Cup and Paten on foot of 1646. – MONUMENTS. Brass to Thomasine Badby † 1532. – Brasses to William Poyntz and wife † 1502; their children below. – Eight small monuments of members of the Poyntz family, kneeling couples under arches. All eight put up in 1606. – Two large monuments with kneelers, early C17 and 1643. – Large alabaster tomb-chest with the recumbent effigies of Sir Gabriel Poyntz †1607 and wife. The unusual feature is a tester unsupported by columns. – Sir Thomas Poyntz † 1709, standing wall-monument with bust high up, one hand elegantly on his breast. Corinthian columns l. and r., supporting a broken segmental pediment with two reclining putti seated on it. – John Russell of Stubbers † 1825, bust by *Behnes*.

STUBBERS, 1 m. w. Late C18 seven-bay front of three storeys. Porch on Tuscan columns. Staircase of between 1689 and 1705, with twisted balusters. In the grounds, in 1604, the first Yucca flowered in England. The house then belonged to the botanist William Coys.

NORTH SHOEBURY *see* SOUTHEND-ON-SEA

NORTH WEALD BASSETT

St Andrew.* A church mainly in the Dec style, see the arcade
of octagonal piers with double-chamfered arches and the flowing tracery of the s chapel windows. The E window has the
unmistakable hall-mark of ogee reticulation. The w tower is
Early Tudor, of brick, with diagonal buttresses and battlements and w window of brick with Perp panel tracery. The N
windows are C19. – SCREEN. The dado has linenfold panelling,
an uncommon motif. The tracery was altered in the late C17
or the C18. The coving of the loft with rib-panelled underside
is preserved – the only case in Essex. The screen is inscribed:
'Orate pro bono statu Thome Wyher, diacon'. – STAINED
GLASS. In the s chapel SE window C14 tabernacles. – In the s
chapel E window glass by *Tower*, 1909. – PLATE. Cup of 1563;
Plate of 1682. – BRASS. W. Larder † 1606, wife and children
(N wall).

NORTON MANDEVILLE

All Saints. Small C12 fragments re-used in the walls and a
small fragment of a spiral-carved Norman column with projecting moulding, considered by the Royal Commission to be
part of a PILLAR PISCINA, tell of an earlier church on the site.
The present nave and chancel seem C14. The belfry of the C15
(?) rests on a tie-beam with king-posts inside. – FONT, Square,
with attached angle columns, of Barnack stone, late C12. –
PULPIT. Plain, C18. – SCREEN with plain one-light, ogee-
headed divisions. – BENCH ENDS. With coarsely carved
poppy-heads, C16, probably late. – PLATE. Early C17 Cup;
Paten and Almsdish given in 1703.

OAKLANDS *see* HALSTEAD

OLD RIFFHAMS *see* DANBURY

OLIVERS *see* STANWAY

ORFORD HOUSE *see* UGLEY

ORSETT

St Giles and All Saints. Norman nave – see the s doorway
with primitive volute capitals, arch with zigzag, hood-mould

* Severely damaged by fire in 1964. Information from H. V. Molesworth
Roberts.

with billet, a curved lintel, and a tympanum with diapers divided into triangles.* Evidence of a C13 N aisle the first two bays from the W – the first now blocked by the W tower. They have circular piers and one-stepped, single-chamfered arches. In the C14 the chancel was built and the N aisle widened. The chancel E window is of four lights with cusping and a quatrefoil in a circle on top. The S window and those of the C19 S organ chamber are of two lights in the same style. The chancel SEDILIA have detached shafts and moulded capitals. Of the C14 also the E part of the N arcade with piers with four demishafts and four hollows in the diagonals and moulded arches. Next in time comes the tower, placed at the W end of the aisle and occupying its first C13 bay. It is partly of stone and partly of C17 brick and has big diagonal buttresses, a thick NW stair-turret, brick battlements, and a spire. – FONT. Perp, octagonal, with buttressed stem and panels with rosettes and shields. – SCREEN. 1911 by *Comper*. – STAINED GLASS. S chapel W and organ chamber E by *Wailes* c.1845, with glaringly coloured roundels. – SCULPTURE. Five Italian C18 panels: Annunciation, Holy Family, Mourning of the Dead Christ, Ascension, Pentecost. – PLATE. Cup and Cover of 1575; Flagon of 1677; Salver of 1688. – MONUMENTS. Brasses to Thomas Latham †1485 and wife and children, minute figures. – Sir John Hart † 1658. Broad standing wall-monument with black columns, entablature with narrower segmental pediment, and semi-reclining figure with cheek propped up on elbow. – Elizabeth Baker † 1796, monument with small female with urn, above inscription plate; by *Regnart*. – Charlotte Baker † 1808, figure of faith standing; by *Westmacott*. – Dame Jane Trafford Southwell † 1809. Mourning female, urn, and standing angel, also by *Westmacott*. – Again by *Westmacott* Richard Baker † 1827, standing wall-monument with two angels, one on the floor, the other just taking off. – In the churchyard Captain Samuel Bonham † 1745, pyramid on bulgy sarcophagus.

ORSETT HALL, E of the church. Georgian front of yellow brick, not very regular façades, with several Venetian windows. The house is however older, and it contains one good mid-C17 fireplace with caryatids and seated figures of Hope and Charity and a contemporary plaster ceiling with ribs and stylized leaf and flower motifs between.

The village is rich in worth-while timber-framed and gabled

* A small window, possibly Norman, was recently discovered in the S wall near the porch.

houses, e.g. BIRCH TERRACE E of the church and a whole group s of the church. A little further W: ORSETT HOUSE of 1740 (five bays, two-and-a-half storeys, red brick, with door pediment on pilasters). Yet further W the WINDMILL, a very dilapidated smock-mill. To the NW is HALL FARM with an early C16 half-timbered gable and original four-light windows on two floors. Behind this BISHOP BONNER'S PALACE, or rather the earthwork where the bishop's palace is said to have stood. The earthwork consists of a circular enclosure of 200 ft internal diameter with a rectangular bailey to the N. Some parts are surrounded by ditches.

OVER HALL see GESTINGTHORPE

OVINGTON

ST MARY. Nave, chancel, and belfry, the latter resting on four rough posts inside the nave. Cross-beam on the two E posts. The windows indicate the C14 as the date for nave and chancel. – No furnishings of interest.

PAGLESHAM

ST PETER. Nave and chancel are Norman. On the N side three original windows remain, though they are much restored. The W tower was added in the C15, with diagonal buttresses, a three-light W window with Perp panel tracery, and battlements. – CHAIRS. Two, late C17, thickly carved. – PLATE. Cup with bands of ornament, and Cover, both of 1568.

CHURCH HALL, to the E of the church. Georgian, brick, of three bays, with tripartite windows and a doorway on attached Tuscan columns.

Between the cottages of the little High Street the PUNCH BOWL INN, weatherboarded, with its two-and-a-half storeys introduces a somewhat more townish scale.

LUNTS, ½ m. ESE. Five bays, three storeys, with porch on Tuscan piers (not columns). Red brick, built in 1803–4.

PANFIELD

ST MARY. Nave, chancel, and belfry. All C15. The belfry on timber posts, the s porch also of timber with pretty side openings. Tomb recess in the nave N wall with depressed pointed arch. – PULPIT with re-used early C16 tracery panels similar to several used in furniture at Panfield Hall. – STAINED GLASS.

Two whole c15 figures of saints (N window, nave). – PLATE. Late c16 Paten; late c17 Cup.

PANFIELD HALL. Small but exceedingly interesting. The W part c.1500, the E part Elizabethan. All brick. Of the Early Tudor Hall several windows (including one in the gable towards the Elizabethan part) survive and much of an excellent hammerbeam roof with carved brackets and tracery above the arched braces. When the Elizabethan owner added his new wing, he blocked the gable window and filled the space with the Royal Arms in plasterwork. The Elizabethan windows are mullioned and transomed, a porch tower stands at the E end.

PASSMORES see HARLOW

PATTISWICK

ST MARY. Nave and chancel of the same height, and belfry. The nave is c13 (one re-set lancet in the N vestry), the chancel c14 (two S windows each of two lights under one pointed head). Tie-beam between nave and chancel and above it a plastered half-timbered 'tympanum' like a gable. The roof of the nave has a tie-beam with an octagonal king-post, the belfry rests on a tie-beam also with a king-post. – BENCHES in the nave, c.1500, absolutely plain. – PLATE. Cup and Cover of 1702, repurchased for the church in 1922.

PAUL'S HALL see BELCHAMP ST PAUL

PEACOCKS see MARGARETTING

PEBMARSH

ST JOHN THE BAPTIST. A c14 church. The W tower came first, see its lower windows. Nave, aisles, and chancel followed, all with Dec windows, the most fanciful being the N aisle E window. The arcades have piers with semicircular shafts to the arches and semi-polygonal ones to the nave (cf. e.g. St Peter, Colchester, and St Gregory, Sudbury, across the Suffolk border). The arches are double-chamfered. The SEDILIA are the most ornate piece, of two seats only, but meant to be carried on; with crockets, finials, and head-label-stops. In the early c16 the W tower was completed in red brick, with blue diapers, battlements, and stunted pinnacles. An c18 cupola on top. Of the c16 and also in brick the embattling of the church and the unusually elaborate brick S porch, with a blank stepped gable over the entrance and another stepped gable above. In a niche a statuette of St John by *Alec Miller*. – PULPIT. Re-used traceried panels, perhaps from bench ends. – STAINED GLASS. C14 bits in chancel and N aisle windows. E window by *Clayton & Bell*, 1879. N aisle E window by *Hugh Easton*, 1934. So much is said (and done) nowadays against Victorian glass that one should consider seriously whether Clayton & Bell's is not more legitimately stained glass than Mr Easton's, which is always reminiscent of line drawings daintily water coloured. – PLATE. Cup of 1567; Paten on foot of 1697. – MONUMENT. Sir William Fitzralph † *c.*1323; The earliest and one of the most important brasses in the county. Large figure, cross-legged, with a hood of mail.

MILL HOUSE. A pretty timber-framed and plastered house. It once belonged to the silk mill which was the beginning of Messrs Courtauld's. The silk mill was started here about 1798, and pulled down about 1900.

PELDON

ST MARY THE VIRGIN. Big w tower with angle buttresses, battlements, and a higher embattled stair-turret. Stone nave with early C16 brick buttresses and brick clerestory. The clerestory windows of two lights. The nave roof is of hammer-beam type. The braces up to the collar-beams form four-centred arches. The chancel was rebuilt in 1859 in an all too familiar style not usual for additions to old churches; stone with much white brick and a little flint – in the lancet style. Now boarded off from inside. – FONT. Plain, octagonal, C13, on nine supports.*

PENNETT'S FARM *see* WHITE NOTLEY

PENTLOW

ST GEORGE. Nave and chancel are Norman. The apse is completely preserved, with its three windows. As for the nave the w doorway survives. It now leads into the tower, one of the round towers of Essex, probably C12, though with C14 windows. The tower must be later than the nave; for when the nave was built, there obviously was no tower yet at the w, or else the doorway would not have been enriched by columns

---

* Mr P. Russell Walker draws my attention to HARVEYS, a timber-framed C15 or C16 farmhouse, and to THE PELDON ROSE, also of the C15.

(one order with decorated scalloped capitals) and the little animal's head above the arch. The N chapel was added to the chancel in the C16. It has stepped brick gables to the W and E and Late Perp windows. The E window seems C15 and may be re-used. The chapel has a charming panelled tunnel-vault. It houses the MONUMENT to George Kempe † 1606, John Kempe † 1609, and his wife, three recumbent effigies on a tomb-chest with kneeling children against the front of the chest. The Royal Commission assumes that the chapel was built for this monument. But can that really be the case? Another MONUMENT in the chancel. Edmund Felton † 1542 and wife. Tomb-chest with shields on cusped panels; no figures. – FONT. Square, with angle colonnettes, Norman. The sides decorated with a cross and interlace and leaves, a star, branches, etc. – all very stylized. – FONT COVER. Square with canted front. Niches with nodding ogee arches. The canopy with buttresses, canopies, etc., crocketed and ending in a finial. – PLATE. Cup and Cover of 1724; Paten also of 1724; Flagon of 1722.

PENTLOW HALL. An uncommonly fine manor house of c.1500 with alterations of the late C16 (e.g. the hall was horizontally divided). The timber work is exposed. On the S front, facing the church, on the upper floor is a broad oriel window of twelve lights. The Hall has linenfold panelling, a fireplace decorated with heads and heraldry, and at the back the carved brackets which were originally outside and probably supported an oriel window.

RECTORY TOWER, or Bull's Tower. Tall, polygonal, thin, built in 1858 by a rector to commemorate his parents.

PILGRIM'S HALL see BRENTWOOD

PINNACLES see HARLOW

PITCHBURY RAMPARTS see GREAT HORKESLEY

PITSEA see BASILDON

PLACE FARM see BARTLOW END

PLAISTOW

ST MARY, St Mary's Road. 1890–4 by *Sir A. Blomfield*. The W front with polygonal baptistery and tall bellcote a little in the Butterfield tradition. The aisles with cross gables. Wide interior with circular piers. The walls exposed red brick.

St Andrew, Barking Road and St Andrew's Road. 1870 by *Brooks*. Vicarage 1871. Neo-E.E. with crossing tower (unfinished), vaulted inside, and large apse. Short circular piers with four attached shafts with shaft-rings and foliated capitals. Clerestory with shafted arcade. To the N and S of the crossing side chapels screened off by double arches with outsize tracery *à la* Butterfield.

West Ham (Baptist) Central Mission, Barking Road. 1921 by *W. Hayne*. Ambitious Byzantine style with two short domed towers. Red brick and white cast stone slabs.

Mansfield House Club, see Canning Town, p. 109.

One modern factory: Curwen Press, just S of the parish church. Low, of yellow brick, attractively designed by *G. A. Jellicoe* (1947).

S of the church in Greengate Street as a lodge to the Recreation Ground Essex Lodge, a gabled cottage in the typical Tudor style of *c.*1840 with hood-moulds. It incorporates fragments of Essex House, which was demolished in 1836, notably the richly carved early C18 shell-hood and the outer iron gates. Opposite the Red Triangle Club, tall and with Art Nouveau details.

PLEDGDON HALL *see* HENHAM

PLESHEY

Holy Trinity. 1868 by *Chancellor*. The only remains of the medieval church are the crossing arches to the N, S, and W. They are of *c.*1400. The unusual plan is due to the foundation of a college of priests at Pleshey in 1393. Chancellor gave his church a picturesque and restless S show front. The distinguishing feature is the stair-turret at the E end of the crossing tower. – Monuments. Sir William Joliffe † 1749. Epitaph with big urn, rocaille ornament, and three cherubs' heads at the foot. Safely attributed to *Cheere* by Mrs Webb. – She also suggests that the monument to Joliffe's nephew, Samuel Tufnell of Langleys, Great Waltham, † 1758, is by *Cheere*. This is a standing wall-monument with excellent portrait on top of a straight-sided sarcophagus and in front of a grey obelisk.

Pleshey Castle. A motte and bailey castle probably of the C12. It lies NE of the church. The mount is 50 ft high and 295 ft across at the foot. The moat is crossed by a single-span C14 or C15 bridge. The kidney-shaped bailey is situated to the

s. The site of the chapel, c.1300 with c15 alterations, was recently discovered at the w end of the bailey. The outer bailey encloses the whole village.

FITZJOHN'S FARM see Great Waltham.

PLUMBEROW MOUNT see HOCKLEY

PORTERS see SOUTHEND-ON-SEA

POTTER STREET see HARLOW

PRIORS see BROOMFIELD

PRITTLEWELL see SOUTHEND-ON-SEA

PRITTLEWELL CAMP

Early Iron age encampment, 1 m. NE of Prittlewell church. The camp is roughly elliptical, measuring 800 ft from N to S and 650 ft from E to W. The remains of a rampart and ditch are discernible.

PROUD'S FARM see THAXTED

PURFLEET

GOVERNMENT POWDER MAGAZINE. Removed to Purfleet from Greenwich from 1760 onwards. In 1771 the 'strongly arched' buildings, the quay and house for the storekeeper are mentioned. The latter is a handsome yellow brick house with side pavilions. In the garden wall a clock turret. The buildings deserve further study.

An impressive octagonal brick DOVECOTE with coved eaves cornice, c.1709, at High House at the E end of Purfleet.

ROYAL HOTEL (formerly Bricklayers Arms). A delightful white early c19 hotel by the riverside. Seven bays with a ground-floor colonnade of square piers and a cast-iron verandah on the first floor. An ilex tree by the side.

(THAMES BOARD MILLS. New building with shell concrete roof. Published 1957.)

TUNNEL ASBESTOS CEMENT COMPANY, E of Purfleet, on the A126. Laboratory by *Sir Owen Williams*, long, one-storey glass block.

PURLEIGH

ALL SAINTS. Ambitious embattled w tower with angle buttresses with three set-offs, bands of flint and stone, and also

some flint and stone chequerwork. The windows indicate a C14 date. Restored in 1892 with American money, in memory of Lawrence Washington, rector from 1632 to 1643. Brick s porch with a four-centred doorhead and two-light w and e windows. Early C14 chancel, see the intersected and cusped three-light e window and the similar two-light N and S windows, also the SEDILIA and PISCINA, where however ogee arches occur at the tops of the cusping. Nave arcades with thick short octagonal piers and double-chamfered arches. Those of the S arcade die against the vertical continuation of the piers. – PULPIT. Elegant piece of c.1700; staircase with twisted balusters, nicely framed panels, and garlands hanging down the angles. – COMMUNION RAIL. Early C18? The balusters not twisted, but no longer of C17 forms. – REREDOS. 1758. Now dismantled. The large paintings of Moses and Aaron by one *I. Fairchild.* – CHANDELIER. Brass; given in 1758. – STAINED GLASS. Early C14 tabernacles in the heads of the chancel N and S windows. Later C14 tabernacles in a S aisle window. – PLATE. Fine set of c.1760 with gadroon ornament.
MOATED MOUND, 350 yds SW. Diameter 250 ft.

QUENDON

CHURCH (dedication unknown). The exterior looks all 1881, the date of the restoration and the rebuilding of the S side. Inside, arcade of three bays, with circular piers and arches with two slight chamfers. i.e. early C13, but also over-restored. – LECTERN. A large standing alabaster angel, 1906. – PLATE. Cup of 1638(?).

QUENDON HALL. A large C19 brick house with several additions, especially the SW wing. The date must be c.1680, and the design is quite out of the ordinary. The house was in fact a half-H of the C16, and only remodelled after the Restoration. The chief addition then was to fill in the space between the two arms of the H. So it has now a flat front with two gabled one-bay side-parts, and a centre of eight much more narrowly spaced bays. The centre is divided – irregularly, one is surprised to see – by giant Tuscan pilasters. The rhythm is 1, 2, 1, 2, 2, 1. The fourth bay is wider and has the doorway with a fine straight top on richly carved brackets. The roof has dormer windows, with segmental pediments in the side parts, triangular pediments in the centre. Two rooms inside are subdivided by Tuscan columns. One has an excellently carved

mantelpiece with fruit and flower garlands. The main staircase is not large, probably on the site of a Jacobean staircase,
and has sturdy twisted balusters. Some of the glazing-bars of
the windows are original too. – Fine octagonal brick DOVE-
COTE to the W.

In the village along the main road QUENDON COURT, nice
five-bay, two-storeyed Georgian house of c.1750 with a C19
S wing.

RADWINTER

ST MARY THE VIRGIN. The church was all but rebuilt by
Eden Nesfield in 1869–70. He used some old materials and left
the remarkable porch as he found it. It has very heavy timbers
and brackets to carry an oversailing upper storey – quite different from any other of the Essex timber porches. The date is
C14 and probably not too late. Nesfield added the pretty, pargeted, domestic upper storey, very much in his Essex style.
As for the church, the material is flint with bands of tiles of
irregular length and spacing. The tracery of the windows is
geometrical and of no interest. The good embattled W tower
with a spire was added by *Temple Moore* in 1887. Inside, Nesfield kept to the surviving arcade piers which are on the S side
of the late C13 type, quatrefoil with thin round shafts in the
diagonals – all shafts carrying fillets. Moulded arches. On the
N side the arcade is mid C14: octagonal piers and moulded
arches. The chancel arch also is old; it goes with the S arcade.
The nave roof is C14 too; tie-beams, curved braces with
traceried spandrels, octagonal king-posts with capitals and
four-way struts. The chancel roof is panelled and painted and
belongs to Nesfield's time. – REREDOS. A Flemish early
C16 altar with six scenes with small free-standing figures
against shallow carved backgrounds. – CHANCEL SCREEN of
metal. Very pretty scroll-work. Made c.1880–5. – PAINT-
ING. Triptych in the N aisle. C15, Italian, perhaps Sienese.
Demi-figure of Virgin and Child in the centre, two Saints
on the wings. – PLATE. Silver-gilt Chalice of the late C15,
foreign. The base, with a crucifix, and the stem are original.
The bowl is modern.

Nesfield also did much to the immediate neighbourhood of the
church: shops and cottages dated 1873 to the E, the enlargement of the school, with Baroque pargeting, to the NE (1877),
and the almshouses to the N, dated 1887.

(GRANGE FARM, ⅔ m. ssw. Timber-framed, later C16 house with a fine brick chimneystack at the back. The diapered base is original, the shafts are modern. R.C.).

RAILS FARM see EAST HANNINGFIELD

RAINHAM

ST HELEN AND ST GILES. A complete Late Norman church with aisles and W tower – a rarity in the county.* The diagonal buttresses of the tower are a Perp addition. The tower itself is short and broad. Small Norman windows, even as bell-openings. Original small Norman N aisle N and W windows, and plain N doorway. Inside arcades of three bays with big square piers with shafts at the four angles. These have shaft-rings – a sign of late date. Many-scalloped capitals. From the W responds these run on as a frieze to connect with the tower arch. This and the arcade arches are unmoulded. The chancel on the S side has a small Norman doorway with decorated waterleaf capitals. The upper windows of the E wall – one round flanked by two of arched shape – are also original. The chancel arch has three-dimensional zigzag decoration. The chancel S wall had lancet windows inserted in the C13. Late in the C13 two blank arches were made in the NE corner of the nave, perhaps for secondary altars; one faces S, the other W. The curiously shaped clerestory windows are probably an C18 alteration. The chancel roof is C15 work with tie-beams, king-posts, and four-way struts. – Remains of the ROOD SCREEN of c.1500. – PAINTING. Ornamental C13 and C14 remains in the chancel, and on the nave N, S, and especially W walls. – PLATE. Paten of 1563; Cup on baluster stem of 1653; Paten on foot of 1713. – BRASS, to a Civilian c.1500; to a Lady with butterfly headdress c.1489.

RAINHAM HALL. Sumptuous, though small house of 1729, close to the church. Red brick with stone quoins and segment-headed windows. Five by three bays with parapet. Splendid doorway with scrolly pediment carved with deeply undercut flowers; far-projecting porch on Corinthian columns; broken segmental pediment. Outbuildings on the S side. Fine iron gates E and W of the house. Inside no room of real size, but a handsome staircase with twisted balusters.

(DAYMNS HALL, 2½ m. ENE. C17 brick house on an L-shaped plan with straight gables. R.C.)

* Restored by the *Rev. E. Geldart*, 1897–1910.

RAMSDEN BELLHOUSE

St Mary. 1880, except for the s porch and the belfry. The porch may be as early as the C14, with coarse timbers. Braces from the doorway. The belfry stands on four posts with heavy braces from N to S. Weatherboarded aisles on N, S, and W. Original C15 timber doorway. The spire is hipped. The roofs of chancel and nave are also C15 or early C16. – FONT COVER, c.1700. – CHEST. Heavily iron-bound, 7 ft long. – CHAIRS. Three in chancel, thickly carved, early C18. – PLATE. Cup with bands of ornament, 1562, and Paten of the same period.

RAMSDEN CRAYS

St Mary.* 1871 except for the belfry, with broach-spire. It stands on four posts with heavy braces from N to S. The building of 1871 makes use of some C15 windows.

RAMSEY

St Michael. All cemented. The nave with a variety of styles, entertaining to follow. In the N wall one C12 window, a C12 doorway with decorated abaci, a C13 lancet, a simple C14 two-light window. Other early C14 types of two-lights in the S wall, where the arrangement of the windows is completely haphazard. The S doorway is a handsome C15 piece, decorated in one order with fleurons, in the other with figures of a king and a queen and small suspended shields. The chancel is just as varied. It has a SEDILE of the C13 with a curiously wilful arch on short shafts and a late C14 chancel arch with small demi-figures of angels in the capitals, but E, N, and S windows and ceiling are of 1597. The windows very domestic, with straight tops and transoms. The roof has collar-beams on scrolly braces more like brackets, and is ceiled. C15 brick W tower with diagonal buttresses. – PULPIT. Elizabethan with panelling, moulded below, blank-arched above in the way familiar in Elizabethan furniture, and yet another tier of small foliage panels above these (as at Great Horkesley). – PAINTING. One C15 head high up above the second S window from the E in the nave. – PLATE. Cup of 1576 (base modern); another Elizabethan Cup; secular Dish of 1707.

CHAFFORD SCHOOL (Michaelstow Hall). 1902, in the comfortably Neo-Georgian style of the day, similar to houses by Ernest Newton.

* Disused and ruinous.

ROYDON HALL, $1\frac{3}{4}$ m. w. The interesting feature is the w gable
of *c.*1560. Straight, not stepped, flanked by polygonal turrets
with pinnacles, one pinnacle also corbelled out on the apex of
the gable, and below it two pedimented windows above each
other.

(MILL FARM, $\frac{1}{2}$ m. sw. Late c16 brick house. Front with two
gables and a porch. R.C.)

WINDMILL, $\frac{1}{2}$ m. w of the church. Post-mill in a fair state of
preservation; with a fan on the roof.

RAWRETH

ST NICHOLAS. Except for the c15 tower, the s arcade, and the
w wall of the N aisle, all of 1882 to the design of the *Rev.
Ernest Geldart,* rector of Little Braxted. A rather gaudy design
with flushwork and, in the porch, even some flint, stone, and
red tile-work. Chancel higher than nave. – MONUMENT.
Brass to Edmund Tyrell † 1576 and wife. Kneeling figures
on stone tablet with side-columns and a round arch. In the
decoration still Gothic motifs.

RAYLEIGH

A little town with a market place which is a widening of the High
Street and with three visual and historical accents: the church,
the motte-and-bailey castle, and the windmill.

HOLY TRINITY. Big, tall c15 w tower with diagonal buttresses
and higher stair-turret. w doorway and three-light w window.
c15 and early c16 is indeed the date of the whole church. Its
show front is the s side with the embattled s aisle, the embattled s chancel chapel built by William Alleyn in 1517, and
the delightful brick porch, with two-light brick side windows
and stepped battlements on a trefoil-arched corbel frieze. Inside the porch, the s doorway of the church is clearly c13 and
probably re-used. The aisle windows are all large, of three
lights, Late Perp. The N chapel has a four-light E window with
Perp panel tracery. The interior is spacious and light, thanks
to the aisle windows. Four-bay arcades on thin piers of the
four-shaft-four-hollow type, two-centred arches. Tall tower
arch, broad chancel arch. The s chapel opens into the chancel
with one broad Perp arch on responds with concave sides.
Rood stairs on the N side complete with the cusped upper

exit. Original roofs, much restored. – SCREEN between N aisle and N chapel with cusped single-light partitions and castellated top beam. – CHEST. Dug-out type, under the tower. – PLATE. Large Cup and Paten of 1681. – MONUMENTS. Brass to John Barrington † 1418 and wife, the figures only 19 in. long (N aisle). – The S chapel houses the most important piece in the church, the Alleyn Monument of c.1517. Recess with flat niches in the back wall, cambered and panelled ceiling, and tomb-chest with three large, richly cusped quatrefoil panels.

CASTLE. Motte-and-bailey castle, probably built by Sweyn, son of Robert Fitz-Wymarc, in the late C11. The motte or mound is 50 ft high above the ditch and stands at the E end. The Inner Bailey follows to the E, and the Outer Bailey lay further E immediately behind the houses of the street adjoining to the E. The earthworks were originally fortified by stockades.

To the E of the Bailey stands the OLD WINDMILL, a tower-mill without sails, and now incongruously embattled, a visually successful landmark.

The HIGH STREET has more than one nice, but no important house. At the N end, S of the church, house of five bays, white brick, with Ionic porch, no doubt early C19.* Then KINGS-LEIGH HOUSE and Nos 31, 33, 35 and opposite 40, 42. In the wider market place one more urban house, LLOYDS BANK, Early Victorian, three storeys, with Tuscan pilasters and a one-bay pediment, and opposite a whole row of humble, timber-framed cottages, some weatherboarded. In CROWN HILL off the High Street the DUTCH COTTAGE, circular and thatched, probably C18 (cf. Canvey Island).‡ Back into the High Street a little further S Nos 136 and 138.

RAYNE

ALL SAINTS. 1840 and dull, But an unusually fine Tudor brick tower with blue brick diapering, a quatrefoil frieze at the foot, a blank stepped gable above the W window with a finial on the apex, a castellated frieze below the bell-openings, and an embattled top with pinnacles and a curious stepped pinnacle as a roof to the stair-turret. – WOODWORK. c.1500. Tracery panels and also a later C16 figure relief, said to be Flemish. – PLATE. Early Elizabethan Cup with embossed stem and foot.

RAYNE HALL, NW of the church. Timber-framed and plastered,

---

* Since extended.

‡ Mr D. Morgan tells me that the Dutch Cottage has a date 1615.

probably early C16, and originally larger than it is now. Good re-used early C16 linenfold panelling in the Hall. Several good houses along Stane Street.

REDDINGS see TILLINGHAM

REDFERN'S FARM see SHALFORD

RED HOUSE see SOUTH SHOEBURY, SOUTHEND-ON-SEA

RETTENDON

ALL SAINTS. The surprise of the church is the MONUMENT to Edmund Humphrey † 1727, signed, according to Mrs Esdaile, by *Samuel Chandler*. It is a large marble affair with four standing figures and one semi-reclining. The four are arranged triptych-wise with two single figures in niches in the wings and a couple higher up together in one niche. Open segmental pediment above them. – The church still has its plain Late Norman S doorway and its C13 chancel (see the shafted splays of the new E window, inside a small N lancet, and the trefoiled SEDILIA and PISCINA). The rest is mostly Perp. Quite a big W tower with diagonal buttresses, SE stair-turret, large W window (with tracery that may be C17), battlements, and a low pyramid roof. N aisle arcade with short octagonal piers with concave sides and double-hollow-chamfered arches, N chancel chapel of one bay of the same characteristics, and N vestry, two-storeyed with a chimneystack. – STALLS in the chancel with pretty poppy-heads, decorated e.g. with a dog, a lion, a bear, a monkey. Also some traceried panels perhaps re-used. – PLATE. Cup of 1562 with two bands of ornament; Paten on foot, 1641. – BRASSES. Civilian and two wives, c.1535, with children below. On a stone slab of c.1200 with an adorned rim with leaves; also birds.

RICKLING

ALL SAINTS. The nave is E.E., as witnessed by one blocked lancet window on the W side. W tower and S aisle were added in the early C14. At the same time the chancel was rebuilt. The W tower has low diagonal buttresses. The top stage is later, with brick quoins and battlements. The chancel windows are typical of their date. So is the arcade of two bays, with a quatrefoil pier and arches of one quadrant and one hollow-chamfered moulding. – N recess in the chancel with very low tomb-chest, like a seat, and a big ogee arch. S recess with a tomb-chest with six quatrefoils with shields. – SCREEN. Typical of the C14. The divisions are broad, of four lights separated by shafts with shaft-rings, and the tracery is of squashed circles with ogee ending at top and bottom. Finer tracery within these. – PULPIT. C15 with panels with two quatrefoils at the foot (or a wheel of three mouchettes) and blank panel tracery above. – BRASS. Indent under the E arch of the arcade, mostly hidden by the seating. It must have been a very interesting piece: kneeling figure holding a model of a church, early C14.

RICKLING HALL, ¾ m. S. The remains of an extremely interesting brick house of c.1500. It was quadrangular, and the courtyard and buildings on all four sides survive. Only the Great Hall (E side of S range) has gone, and the offices and kitchen to its W are now a barn. The best preserved part is the gateway into the courtyard from the N, i.e. opposite the Hall. Also still in existence a few cusped and pointed windows, apparently not *in situ*.

RIDGEWELL

ST LAURENCE. All Perp except for an unexplained, probably re-used piece of C13 blank arcading in the N wall of the vestry. W tower with angle buttresses, some flint decoration at the foot, battlements, and a higher stair-turret. Embattled S porch. Windows with Perp tracery. N arcade with piers with semi-polygonal shafts, small to the arches, and large, without capitals, to the nave; two-centred arches. Clerestory with embattled sill. N chancel chapel with octagonal pier and semi-octagonal responds carrying embattled capitals. Delicately detailed nave roof with collar-beams on arched braces, every second resting on shafts which stand on corbels. All beams and rafters moulded. – SCREEN. Four divisions of the dado remain, with elaborate tracery including mouchette-wheels. – PULPIT. C17, plain. – LECTERN. Octagonal with a heavy foot decorated with fleurons. Book-rest new. – PLATE. Cup of 1564.

(RIDGEWELL HILL FARM, ⅓ m. ENE. Timber-framed house of 1589. Front with three projecting gables and continuous carved and moulded bressumer on carved brackets. Projecting gables also at the ends of the cross-wings, one of them with carved bargeboards. R.C.)

RINGER'S FARM *see* TERLING

RIVENHALL

ST MARY AND ALL SAINTS. 1838–9. Brick, with the use of original walls. Narrow, tall w tower with polygonal buttresses and battlements. The nave has the same feature at the angles. Intersected window tracery as was popular in the early C19. Plain white interior with coved ceiling with thin narrow transverse ribs. – COMMUNION RAILS. With twisted balusters, c.1700. – STAINED GLASS. The best in the county; assembled 26 in the E window. Two large frontal figures of the C12 (from St Martin at La Chenu N of Tours). – Four roundels of c.1200; of exceedingly good quality and of unknown but no doubt also French origin. – Horseman with helm, inscribed 'Robert Lemaire'. – Demi-figure of a Bishop c.1500. – Two HELMS of the late C16 and the C17. – MONUMENTS. Raphe Wyseman † 1608 and wife. Standing wall-monument of alabaster and marble, with tomb-chest, recumbent effigies on a rolled-up mat; the children kneel in the 'predella'. – Thomas Western † 1699, good monument with segmental pediment, scrolls, flowers, and cherubs' heads. – William Western † 1729. Big black sarcophagus in front of a big black obelisk; no effigy. – Baron Western of Rivenhall † 1844. By *Clark* of Wigmore Street. In the Gothic taste.

RIVENHALL PLACE. Large square early C18 house of white brick, hiding late C16 parts. The front is of seven bays, with quoins and segment-headed windows. Later Tuscan porch. The principal staircase has three flights of steps round a square open well. Twisted balusters. Much C17 panelling also behind the C18 façades. The grounds were landscaped by *Repton*.

RIVERS HALL *see* BOXTED

ROCHETTS *see* SOUTH WEALD

ROCHFORD

The town is quite separate from the church and the great house, and the separation became specially obvious when the railway arrived and cut off the town completely.

ST ANDREW. The *pièce de résistance* is the big tall w tower of brick, with diapers of vitrified headers, angle buttresses, a higher SE stair-turret, a big three-light Perp brick window, and battlements. The N side of the church has behind the tower

Victorian N aisle and clerestory windows, and then the chancel chapel also of red brick, but with two surprising and charming half-timbered gables. The s side was the show side. It has on the aisle and the porch battlements faced with stone and flint chequerwork. The E view is dominated by the five-light chancel and the three-light aisle and N chapel windows. The interior has three-bay arcades on octagonal piers with double-chamfered arches. The tower arch is uncommonly tall. The whole is of the late C15 to early C16. – PLATE. Cup and Paten of 1705. – BRASS to Mary Dilcok † 1514; small figure.

ROCHFORD HALL. Sadly mutilated and altered remains of a building which must once have been of great size and some architectural importance. It was a brick mansion of c.1545, with two, if not four, irregular courtyards behind a nearly symmetrical N front of 120 ft length. Of this the l. half is moderately well recognizable. Of the rest only the ground floor exists. The façade had polygonal angle towers and a big broad projecting centre block with stone walls. The NE and NW courtyards had a newel staircase in the NE and NW corners respectively. Windows are of brick and mostly small, of one to three lights with arched heads to the lights and hood-moulds, but the upper-floor windows of the remaining E half of the N block were large and oblong and must have had a transom and four lights – similar perhaps to Sutton Place, Surrey. The N gables are straight, four in the remaining E half of the façade, and carry each a polygonal chimney-shaft on a shaft which rises up the centre of the gable. The E front is a Late Georgian conversion but has also still its four original gables.

The centre of the little town is the crossing of East, West, North, and South Streets, an ingeniously managed crossing – from the visual if not the traffic point of view – in which no two roads run straight on. South Street comes to a dead end, with North Street continuing much narrower, and East Street starting in a NE direction and then bending round. Moreover, the MARKET PLACE or SQUARE lies along West Street and separated from North Street by a thin partition of houses, i.e. almost as closed as an Italian piazza. Individual houses are of less interest. In the Square the best: CONNAUGHT HOUSE on the w side, Georgian, with a fine doorway on attached Tuscan columns. At the entrance into West Street the former CORN EXCHANGE by *F.Chancellor*, 1866, modest in size and ugly in looks. Off West Street to the N the extensive low yellow brick

buildings erected in 1834 as the WORKHOUSE. Then, near the
railway, the RICH ALMSHOUSES, founded in 1567, one-
storeyed with two gabled accents. In North Street plenty of
weatherboarded cottages. CHAPEL COTTAGES off the W side
in the place where the sect of the Peculiar People, created at
Rochford by Joseph Banyard, first met. Nearly opposite the
CONGREGATIONAL CHURCH, with big pediment, said to be
of 1740, but probably a renewal of the early C19. EAST
STREET has little to offer. More in SOUTH STREET, the
stateliest street of the town. A few timber-framed, plastered
and gabled houses (Nos 17, 21–23)* and a greater number
Georgian (Nos 3, 4, 7, 15).

At Stroud Green, 1 m. W, THE LAWNS, handsome whitewashed five-bay, two-storeyed Late Georgian house with
Ionic porch. Enlarged by *Johnson*, and with Victorian additions.

ROMFORD

ST EDWARD THE CONFESSOR, Market Place. 1849–50 by
John Johnson. Part of the stone came from the colonnade of the
Regent Street Quadrant, pulled down a year before. Big, with
tall spire on the S side facing the Market. Fussy enough to
impress. – PLATE. Cup and Paten on foot, probably 1623;
two Flagons 1653; Salver 1654; large Cup 1661. – MONU-
MENTS. Sir Anthony Cooke † 1576, and family. Broad triptych
composition with Corinthian columns. Pediment over the
centre. Kneelers in all three parts. – Less good Sir George
Hervey † 1605, and wife. Also Corinthian columns and also
kneelers. – Ann Carew † 1605, semi-reclining effigy, head
propped up on elbow.

(SALEM CHAPEL, London Road. 1847, two shades of stock
brick and stucco. Good proportions.)

TOWN HALL, Main Road. 1937 by *H. R. Collins* and *A. E. O.
Geens*. Plain square modern building with entrance projection
asymmetrically placed. Flat roof, unmoulded window frames.
Not very distinguished.

(CENTRAL LIBRARY, Laurie Square. By *H. Conolly*, County
Architect, completed 1964.)

(The NORTH ROMFORD COMPREHENSIVE SCHOOL in Lodge
Lane is by *Clifford Culpin & Partners*, built in three stages,
1956–64.)

* In one of these the R.C. notes that the tie-beam roof of the hall on arched
braces is still visible on the upper floor.

The characteristic feature of Romford is its spacious MARKET PLACE, with the church on the N side and at the E end, projecting and separating it from Laurie Square, the so-called LAURIE HALL* erected by a Mr Laurie in 1840. He also built LAURIE SQUARE, with the laudable intention of developing the E end of the town. The Laurie Hall has a portico on the upper floor and debased classical detail. In the Market Square the only individual houses of distinction are CHURCH HOUSE (late C15, built with jutting upper floor; inside original beams exposed), No. 33 (early C18, five bays, segment-headed windows, doorway with pediment on carved brackets), and the BRANCH LIBRARY (early C18, formerly two houses).

Just over one mile ESE of the Town Hall, in Brentwood Road, is HARE HALL (part of the Royal Liberty School), the most ambitious surviving mansion of Romford. By *Paine*, 1768. Ashlar-faced, five-bay, two-and-a-half storey centre connected by originally one-storeyed short colonnades to two low two-storey pavilions. The house has a rusticated ground floor (with semicircular Tuscan porch) and above this, as Paine liked it, a giant attached portico of Adamish columns and a pediment decorated with coats of arms. At the angles of the house coupled giant pilasters. Behind the low entrance hall an oval staircase. No decorative embellishments preserved.

W of the Market Place in HIGH STREET a narrow house with a pretty Gothick oriel filling the width of the upper floor. (On the S side, IND COOPE'S BREWERIES, basically early C19 stock brick.) At the corner of High Street and NORTH STREET the GOLDEN LION, an Early Victorian block with original lettering hiding the C16 house of which the back wing in North Street survives, with jutting upper storey. Off North Street in THE CHASE a house called MARSHALLS,‡ with stuccoed Georgian five-bay front (Tuscan porch) and earlier gabled back parts. The continuation of North Street is COLLIER ROW LANE. Here (by Low Shoe Lane) two worthwhile cottages.

To the S, beyond the railway, as part of Oldchurch Hospital the former WORKHOUSE, built in 1838 by *Francis Edwards*, a long façade of twenty-five bays; nine bays at the centre of which three form a central bow, eight-bay wings. Yellow

---

* Scheduled for demolition at the time of writing (1964). Much rebuilding is likely in the Market Square area in the next few years.

‡ Now demolished.

brick, two-storeyed.* Also WATERWORKS, early C19, with restrained moulded arches of several orders.

At Chadwell Heath, Dagenham, one of the excellently designed new county schools should be noted: THE FURZE INFANTS' SCHOOL in Bennett Road. By *H. Conolly*, the county architect. He was also responsible for the GOBIONS PRIMARY SCHOOL in Havering Road, Romford Chase Cross.

ROOKWOOD HALL *see* ABBESS RODING

ROTCHFORDS *see* WORMINGFORD

ROWHEDGE *see* EAST DONYLAND

ROXWELL

ST MICHAEL AND ALL ANGELS. C14 nave and chancel, restored out of recognition. The N aisle was added in 1854, the belfry in 1891. – SCREEN. The screen consists of parts of the organ case of Durham Cathedral, built in 1684, and given to Roxwell by a former Precentor of the cathedral. The pieces exhibit that characteristic mixture of Baroque and Gothic which had been made fashionable at Durham by Bishop Cosin in the second third of the C17. The cornice has Baroque leaves, but the posts are decorated with bits of Gothic tracery. – STAINED GLASS. Two panels of 1600, with various biblical stories and a text in German. Each panel only the size of a page in a book of hours. – PLATE. Cup of 1695; Paten of 1698. – MONUMENT. Mrs Mary Byng † 1744. Stone obelisk and in front of it a cherub leaning on an oval portrait medallion. The monument is placed across the SW corner of the chancel and seems to be unsigned.

SCHOOL. 1834. Small brick house with two-storeyed centre and symmetrical one-storeyed l. and r. wings.

DUKES. Tall timber-framed house with two exposed timber gables to the E and six of various sizes to the W. The taller ones represent the original C16 house, the lower ones a C17 addition.

ROYDON

ST PETER. C13 nave, see one renewed lancet window on the S side. Next to it one of Dec and one of Perp style. The N aisle dates from *c.*1330, see the windows (E and W of three lights with ogee-reticulated tracery) and the arcade (short octagonal

* Information received from Mr I. Nairn.

piers and double-chamfered arches). w tower with angle buttresses and battlements. – FONT. An interesting piece of
c.1300. Octagonal with, in the four diagonals, four heads, men
who are neither saints nor clerics, but look like workmen. They
wear hats with rolled-up brims. – SCREEN. The side parts of
five lights each with plain broad ogee arches and no tracery
above them – C14, no doubt. – PLATE. Cup and Paten of 1564.
– BRASSES. Thomas Colte † 1471 and wife, the figures 3 ft long.
– John Colte † 1521 and two wives, smaller figures (2 ft 3 in.). –
Richard Swifte † 1520, 2½-ft figure, engraved 1601. – In the
churchyard a fine TOMBSTONE for R. Crowe † 1779, with
Rococo decoration (F. Burgess).

NETHER HALL, 1½ m. SW. Gatehouse and part of the curtain
wall of an Early Tudor manor house. Brick with blue brick
diaper. Of the two towers flanking the single gateway one
stands upright, polygonal, three storeys high and decorated
with trefoiled corbel friezes. The other has collapsed, and one
now looks into the guardroom which was behind it. Another
group of rooms by the side of the guardroom faces outside
with a chamfered angle. At the back some of the wall of these
rooms towards the inner courtyard remains as high as the
gatehouse.

ROYDON HALL see RAMSEY

RUMBERRY HILL see LANGLEY

RUNWELL

ST MARY. The best thing about the church is the two porches,
timber structures of the C15. The side openings are arched and
cusped. Over the gateway is a king-post. The main difference
between N and S is that the one has quatrefoils, the other trefoils in the spandrels of the arches. w tower with diagonal buttresses, battlements, and a recessed spire. Higher stair-turret.
Nave and chancel (lengthened in 1907) in one. Double Hagioscope. S arcade of four bays with short circular piers and
double-chamfered arches – the only reminder of the C13 in a
church otherwise entirely Perp. – SCREEN. By *W. F. Uns-
worth*, 1909. – POOR-BOX. Oak, hollowed-out, iron-bound. –
PLATE. Cup with band of ornament, and Paten, both of 1562. –
MONUMENT. Brasses of Eustace Sulyard † 1547 and wife
† 1587. Kneeling figures between pilasters carrying a pediment.
– Mr Gunnis also mentions a signed tablet to Edward Sulyard,
1692, by *Thomas Cartwright Jun.*

FLEMING'S FARM. Fragment of a larger house of *c*.1600. Red brick. The show piece is a two-storeyed bay window on the N side with five-light windows, on the ground floor with one transom, on the upper floor with two. The room formed a corner of the house, as on the upper floor there is another large window towards the W. The N bay has a gable with obelisks. The chimneystack with diagonal shafts on the W front is renewed, but correctly.

GIFFORD'S FARM. C16 house on a T-plan, timber-framed, plastered, and gabled. The E front is particularly handsome.

SAFFRON GARDENS *see* HORNDON-ON-THE-HILL

SAFFRON WALDEN

ST MARY THE VIRGIN. With a total length of nearly 200 ft Saffron Walden is one of the largest parish churches of Essex. It is also one of the most lavishly designed – in a style entirely from across the border, East Anglian of the Suffolk and even more the Cambridge brand. There are indeed certain features which make connexions with King's College Chapel and Great St Mary more than likely. The whole church was rebuilt between *c*.1450 and *c*.1525, with the exception of a crypt partly below the S aisle and partly below the S porch, and the arcades from the chancel into the N and S chapels, and from these chapels into the aisles. These parts are of the C13 and indicate a church with crossing and transept, narrower aisles, and a S porch, corresponding to the crypt. The CRYPT is divided into four bays and has single-chamfered arches and ribs springing from semi-octagonal responds. The chancel arcades have quatrefoil piers and moulded capitals and arches. The rebuilding started with the chancel and ended with the chancel arch, the nave clerestory, alterations to the chancel chapels, and the completion of the tower. A contract of 1485 exists with *Simon Clerk* and *John Wastell*. Clerk was master mason at Eton *c*.1460 and at King's College Chapel *c*.1480; Wastell succeeded Clerk at King's College Chapel and was one of the most distinguished English masons of his generation.

The exterior of the church is as follows. The material is 9a largely clunch. The W tower has setback buttresses, decorated battlements, and at the corners big panelled polygonal pinnacles like turrets. The tall octagonal stone spire with crockets and two tiers of dormers, the lower one of two lights

with a transom, was added in 1831 to the designs of *Rickman &*
Hutchinson, the architects, at the same time, of New Court, St
John's College Cambridge. The total height of the tower is
193 ft. The aisles, clerestories, and chancel chapels of the
church are all embattled and have pinnacles. There are large,
wide five-light windows in both aisles with elaborate but not
very interesting panel tracery, equally large windows of different, somewhat closer panel tracery in the chancel chapels, a
C19 five-light E window dating from the restoration by *Butter-*
field in 1876, and three-plus-three-light clerestory windows
of the early C16. At the E end of the nave clerestory are two
polygonal turrets with crocketed stone roofs clearly dependent
on King's College Chapel as completed in 1515. The S porch
is of two storeys, also embattled and pinnacled. It has an
upper window of four lights. The N porch has only one storey.
That is the only external difference between the two sides.*
The church lies indeed in such a commanding position, on a
hill, higher than the surrounding streets, that it can be seen
as prominently from the N as the S.

Now for the interior. The arcades of seven bays are very
tall with lozenge-shaped piers enriched by four attached shafts
and with hollows and finer connecting mouldings in the diagonals. Only the shafts towards the arches have capitals. The
shafts to the nave run on unbroken (except for a thickening at
the main horizontal course) to the springers of the roof and
only there have capitals. The diagonal members have no
capitals at all. The spandrels of the arches are closely decorated
with tracery as at Great St Mary's Cambridge and of course
also at Lavenham and other Suffolk churches. The horizontal
course has fleurons, the clerestory mullions are carried down
in panels to the string course. The roofs are original everywhere, low-pitched and adorned variously with bosses, tracery,
badges, etc. As for other enrichments, the three bays of the N
aisle have blank wall-arcades with different intricately carved
heads. Especially the easternmost bay is worth studying. The
figures in the spandrels represent King David, St John,
Doubting Thomas, the Virgin, the Scourging of Christ, the
Agony in the Garden. They are clearly earlier than the aisle
and must for some reason be re-used material – FONT.
Octagonal, C15 to early C16, with quatrefoils and shields. –

---

* Internally the S porch vault is more elaborate than that of the N: a two-
bay fan-vault with two bosses (cf. Cambridge customs of the early C16 as
against a simple one-bay tierceron-vault of star shape.

SCREEN. 1924 by *Sir Charles Nicholson*. – ORGAN CASE. The one side still in the pretty Gothick state of 1825, the other redone by *Bodley* in 1885. – PAINTING. Copy of Correggio's 'The Day' by the Rev. *W. Peters*. – SCULPTURE. Small piece of a C15 alabaster altar in the s porch, N wall. – STAINED GLASS. Good Shepherd, Samaritan, etc. s aisle, 1858, whom by ? – Four Evangelists s aisle by *Lavers & Barraud*, 1859. – N aisle windows (East Anglian Saints, Four Musicians) by *Powell*. – N chapel E window by *Burlison & Grylls*, 1904. – PLATE. Silver-gilt Cup, Paten, and Flagon of 1685; silver-gilt Cup and Paten given 1792.

MONUMENTS. All the brasses with figures are collected against the N wall of the N aisle: three Women of *c*.1480–90; Priest, perhaps Richard Wild † 1484; Civilian of *c*.1500; Civilian and wife of *c*.1510; Woman of *c*.1530; Civilian of *c*.1530; Thomas Turner † 1610 and wife. – Monument to Thomas Lord Audley, Lord Chancellor, † 1544 by *Cornelius* 35 *Harman*. Black marble tomb-chest decorated with wreaths round medallions and ornamented pilasters in the taste of the tomb of Henry VII in Westminster Abbey; back-plate with splendidly carved coat of arms between pilasters (s chapel). Harman may well have done also the Vyvyan Monument at Bodmin, Cornwall, and the Oxford Monument at Castle Hedingham. – Tomb-chest for John Leche † 1521, with lid and inscription but no figures (N chapel). – One side of a tomb-chest, N wall, N aisle.

BAPTIST CHAPEL, see Perambulation.

CONGREGATIONAL CHURCH, see Perambulation.

TOWN HALL, Market Place. A properly townish red brick house of 1761–2, provided in 1879 with an ostentatious and coarse half-timbered gable.

CORN EXCHANGE, Market Place. 1847–8 by *R. Tress*. In a tasteless and jolly Italianate style, with coupled giant columns, clock and cupola on big scrolls etc. (*Illustrated London News*: 'an elegant pile of an Italian character'.)

CASTLE. Large fragments of the flint-rubble walling of the C12 keep. The keep had a fore-building to the W which was ascended from the s along the W wall of the keep by a staircase.

MUSEUM, W of the Castle. Small symmetrical Neo-Tudor building of brick, erected in 1834.

TRAINING COLLEGE, South Road. 1884 by *E. Burgess* of London and Leicester. Additions of 1912 and 1938, the latter by *R. Robertson*.

GRAMMAR SCHOOL, Ashdon Road, now occupied by the
Dame Bradbury School. 1881 by *E. Burgess*.

FRIENDS' SCHOOL, Mount Pleasant Road. 1879 by *E. Burgess*.
Art room and classrooms block by *Fred Rowntree*, 1922. – The
three educational buildings of Burgess are of red brick, in a
Tudor style, and have little to recommend them architecturally.*

SECONDARY MODERN SCHOOL, Audley End Road. By
Richard Sheppard, 1952–3. Excellently planned and uncommonly extensive.

HOSPITAL, London Road. 1863–6 by *William Beck*. Gothic,
symmetrical red brick. Later alterations to the façade and
otherwise.

PERAMBULATION

Saffron Walden with its present population of 7,000 is a small
town, compared with others in the county. In the Middle
Ages it was busy and prosperous.‡ Its wealth was the wool
trade like that of the other East Anglian towns. But in addition
there was saffron, to which plant the town owes its name.
Saffron was used for dyeing and as a medicine.

The town has two centres, the Market Place and the High Street.
They are quite separate from each other, and the church is
separate from both. That has to be remembered first of all to
get the right picture of the visual qualities of the town. The
Market Place is not a widening of the main street, and the
steeple appears always framed narrowly.

The MARKET PLACE is on the whole C19 in its chief accents:
the Town Hall gable on the S and the Corn Exchange on the
W side. In addition there is on the E side BARCLAYS BANK,
1874 by *Eden Nesfield*, an original, self-certain Neo-Tudor
design that looks a good deal later than it is. Two bold, very long
four-light transomed windows close together on the ground
floor. Next to them a tall and deep two-centred arch up which
the stairs lead from the street level to that of the banking hall,
and a small, as it were, pedestrian entrance to the r. of that,
with Franco-Flemish early C16 detail. The building is higher
than those surrounding it and ends in a parapet decorated
with rosettes. To its r. the ROSE AND CROWN HOTEL of
c.1600 but with a front of *c*.1700. Handsome shell-hood on
carved brackets. This inn must have been the most con-

---

* Recent additions by *K. Bayes* (published 1961).
‡ The Royal Commission lists about 120 houses of before 1714.

spicuous building before the C19.* The old town hall was very
restrained, and opposite it, on the N side, there still is a quiet
early C19 frontage with an upper iron verandah.

The High Street will be examined from its S end towards the N.
It is approached from early C19 streets, especially LONDON
ROAD with a former Chapel of 1822 and contemporary villas.
The HIGH STREET itself in its S part also is essentially Late
Georgian, see e.g. Nos 75 and 73, stuccoed with typical ornamental motifs. On the other side No. 74, five-bay, two-storey
house with Tuscan doorcase, and No. 72, also five bays, also
two storeys, but an earlier house, with brick quoins and a
doorway with rusticated brick pilasters. No. 67 opposite has a
specially elegant early C18 doorway. No. 65 also is early C18:
Ionic pilasters to the doorway on a rusticated background and
decorated window-frames above. No. 55 must be c.1830, with
its heavy Tuscan porch. No. 53 has a Greek Doric porch and
two bow windows of the same date, but the house itself may
be earlier. After that, by the GREYHOUND INN, the street narrows and we enter a different period. It is heralded by the inn,
a mid C16 house with a gable and a carved bressumer. There
follows the POST OFFICE on the other side, a fine seven-bay
brick house with a three-bay pediment and a doorway with
carved brackets – an early C18 façade. Then the CROSS KEYS
HOTEL of the C16, with a corner overhang, and finally Nos
4–12, mostly C16, a gap showing the church spire, and THE
CLOSE, a detached timber-framed house with exposed timbers
and a gable on one side.

BRIDGE STREET continues the High Street. Here, right at the
beginning, at the corner of Myddelton Place, stands the
YOUTH HOSTEL. It is without doubt the best medieval
house of Saffron Walden, low and long, with exposed timbers
and a courtyard. In MYDDELTON PLACE two charming upper
oriel windows, at the corner a diagonally set carved bracket on
a carved post. Inside, the most interesting feature is the original screen with a wide arch in the middle and smaller and
lower doorways l. and r. The spandrels of the centre arch have
leaf carving. The house seems to date from c.1500.‡ Nos 5–7
are also of the C15 and also have a screened passage, Nos 13–17

---

* Exterior alterations and redecoration by *Nesfield*, in 1874.
‡ Myddelton Place leads to MYDDELTON HOUSE (with an early C16
fireplace framed by heavily carved timbers. R.C.) and then to WALDEN
PLACE, large red brick, five bays, two-and-a-half storeys, with a doorcase
with Roman Doric columns. It lies in its own grounds.

are a large C18 house with quoins and a plain doorway with
segmental pediment. At the NW end is a good (earlier)
chimneystack with octagonal shafts. The N end of Bridge
Street is a very pretty row of cottages with overhanging upper
storeys on the l. and the EIGHT BELLS INN, also C16, on the
r. It has a bressumer carved with leaves and four original upper
windows with plastered coving underneath. Carved dolphins
below the centre window downstairs.

The side streets off the High Street must now be looked up,
again starting from the S. In GOLD STREET Nos 23–27, C18,
brick, with a large two-storeyed carriageway and extensive
former maltings at the back. Then Nos 34–38, early C16 with
remains of two original doorways, and No. 6 with a charming
plaster frieze with a dolphin – c.1700. Then George Street,
continued in HILL STREET, where No. 5 is of the early C18,
see the carved brackets of the doorway with the characteristic
upcurved frieze, and the red and blue-black brick chequer-
work. At the end of Hill Street the former BAPTIST CHAPEL
of 1744, a plain cottage and behind, a detached parallelogram,
the BAPTIST CHAPEL of 1792, three windows wide, with a
porch. From Hill Street into EAST STREET with the former
BRITISH SCHOOL, dated 1838, a nice, neat yellow brick
building, nine bays wide and low, with a three-bay centre of
Tuscan columns which no doubt was originally open. It carries
a pediment. Instead of going into East Street, one can turn
from the end of Hill Street towards the COMMON. On its W
side THE PRIORY, with an Elizabethan S half and a N half of
the C17. Fine chimneystack with diagonally placed shafts.
Two-storeyed porch with an upper window made Venetian in
the C18. On the E side of the Common THE GROVE, built in
1804, and other Late Georgian villas.

The next crossing of High Street is ABBEY LANE on the W.
Here the Almshouses of 1834, red brick, Tudor style, with
bargeboarded gables to the detached wings. These are of 1840
and 1881. Then the CONGREGATIONAL CHURCH of 1811,
cemented front, with big pediment and Ionic four-column
porch. To the E from the same crossing up KING STREET to
the Market Place. In King Street Nos 20–22, late C15 with a
tall carriageway, Nos 17–21, also C15, with the heads of four
original shop windows on the W side. The same feature on the
S side of the Hoop Inn. The Market Place has already been
described. So now up MARKET HILL to Church Street. At
the corner of Market Hill and CHURCH STREET is a group of

houses amongst the most precious of Saffron Walden. There are four of them, dating from the C14 and C15, with oversailing gables of many sizes, curved brackets, moulded bressumers, and the most lively C17 enrichments in plaster, geometrical patterns, foliage, birds, and also figures. On one of the houses appears the date 1676. This is the one (formerly the Sun Inn) which also exhibits the two figures of Thomas Hickathrift and the Wisbech giant. Returning to the High Street by way of Church Street, on the r., CHURCH PATH with a row of pretty late C16 cottages, once one building, and the church steeple behind it, and then No. 6 and No. 4 both with Georgian brick fronts.

Finally CASTLE STREET, long and quiet, with plenty of cottages, with oversailing upper storeys and gables, but nothing individually important, except perhaps a freak, the former RAILWAY MISSION, three bays with castellated gable and pointed windows.

(According to information kindly supplied by the Saffron Walden Library, recent building includes an Old People's Estate built by the *Borough Council*, FOUR ACRES, E of South Road; FARMADINE ESTATE, and HARVEY WAY and SHEPHERD'S WAY, off the Ashdon Road, 1960–2.

Also THE ACROW CORONATION WORKS, Shire Hill Industrial Estate, by *Acrow Engineers*, 1953–6.)

BATTLE DITCHES. At the W end of the town, immediately s of the line of Abbey Lane, a bank and ditch runs s for 484 ft and then turns sharply to the E for a further 495 ft. In the W part of the earthwork were found over two hundred Late Roman graves, although sections cut across the bank and ditch in 1959 indicated that the earthwork was constructed in the C13 as part of the town extension at that period.

RING HILL, 1½ m. w of the town. Iron Age hill-fort. The defences consist of a bank, ditch, and slight counterscarp bank enclosing a roughly oval area of 16½ acres. The earthwork is now broken by several entrance gaps, some of which are probably modern.

ST AYLOTTS

2 m. NE Saffron Walden

Rectangular house of *c.*1500, with a brick ground floor and a timber-framed upper floor, with the timbers exposed. On the ground floor a stone doorway and a stone window, both straight-headed, and further s, beyond a new outhouse, a stair-turret and a stone oriel window with arched lights. The upper storey projects, on diagonal angle-brackets, and the bressumer is in parts decorated with scrolls. Inside, the Great Hall can still be recognized, and the jambs of the bay windows survive. There are also a good brick fireplace with a decorated oak lintel, several doorways, and the roof with tie-beams on arched braces, collar-beams, and two rows of wind-braces.

ST CLAIR'S HALL see ST OSYTH

ST CLERE'S HALL see STANFORD-LE-HOPE

ST LAWRENCE (NEWLAND)

ST LAWRENCE. 1877–8 by *Robert Wheeler* of Tunbridge Wells, Nave and chancel and belfry.

ST MARY HALL see BELCHAMP WALTER

ST OSYTH

ST OSYTH PRIORY. St Osyth was the daughter of the first Christian king of the East Angles. She was martyred in 653 near the place of the present Priory, where she had founded a nunnery. The priory (later abbey) was established for Augustinian canons by Richard de Belmeis, Bishop of London, shortly before 1127. A few fragments remain, and a few more from the C13. The state of the buildings at that time will first be examined. The priory church lay NE of the surviving (later) Gatehouse. The cloister was to the N of the church, surrounded as usual by domestic ranges on the w, N, and E sides. On the ground floor of the w range were the cellars, or rather storerooms, because they were not below ground. Two of these with single-chamfered ribs across, dating from the C13, exist in the range sw of the so-called Bishop's Lodging. Opposite, in the E range, in direct communication with the N transept of the church, to make access easy at night, was the Dormitory. Of this several chambers of the undercroft can still be seen. They are of the earliest period, roughly groin-vaulted. In the N range was the Refectory. All that exists of this is a piece of cusped blank arcading at its E end, fine C13 work. Of equally high quality is the passage the other side of that E wall, now converted into a chapel. This is the best piece of the earlier Middle Ages at St Osyth, with two slender Purbeck shafts dividing it into six bays and with tripartite elegantly filleted ribs. In addition N of the site of the Refectory, close to the C19 Kitchen wing, is a corner of a C13 building with two semi-circular responds. The capitals can no longer be recognized in their details.

We have no means of ascertaining C14 and early C15 alterations or additions of any size. But in the late C15 the GATE-HOUSE was built, the most splendid survival of the abbey. It 48b vies with the gatehouse of St John's Abbey at Colchester for first place amongst monastic buildings in Essex. Like the gatehouse of St John's the façade to the outer world is of much more magnificence than that to the monastery. It has a wall covered all over with flushwork panelling, from the quatrefoil frieze at the base to the chequer-pattern of the battlements. The tall carriageway has a two-centred arch with lively carvings of St Michael and the Dragon in the spandrels. To its l. and r. are two pedestrian entrances. There are tall slender niches above all three entrances, the higher middle one with a canopy reaching right up to the two-light upper windows. To the l. and r. of this centre are very broad polygonal towers of three storeys. Inside the gatehouse is an elaborate lierne-vault of two bays with carved bosses. It springs from slim wall-shafts, the middle one on each side carrying thirteen ribs. The outer side towards the monastery has no flushwork panel tracery, only chequer and diaper patterns. It has only one wide gateway but four square turrets. The spandrels of the gateway are decorated with angels in quatrefoils holding shields. The gatehouse has two-storeyed embattled ranges to its l. and r. The r. one must be much older; for, invisible from outside, its E bay contained originally a C13 gateway of two orders. The rest C15, like the gatehouse. However, at r. angles to the l. range, projecting to the S, are the remains of another range. There is no more left of it than its E wall, with a round-headed gateway apparently of the C14. So here was yet one more building connecting the priory with the outer world.

The next to enrich the architecture of St Osyth's Abbey was Abbot John Vintoner. A date 1527 is carved on one of his works. He built (like e.g. the abbots of Forde in Dorset and Muchelney in Somerset at the same time) a mansion for himself which, though attached to the abbey, could compete with that of any nobleman. It is of brick, which had by then become the fashionable building material, and extends N of the C13 cellarer's range (i.e. W of the refectory) and then turns W to

face the great gatehouse. Here Abbot Vintoner built a triple
gateway not quite in line with the older gatehouse and above
it his own hall with a magnificent tall oriel window of six
lights. The window itself is new, but the corbelling, base, and
head are original, as well as the stone panelling of the jambs
and arch of the oriel inside. It is all of the richest, though the
motifs are not fanciful nor indeed imaginative – mostly cusped
panelling, quatrefoils, and shields. Only at the head does the
new Italian style make an appearance – one of the earliest in
Essex. There are small naked figures and Renaissance leaves.
The range behind this gateway and oriel was entirely remodelled in 1865. It is known as the Bishop's Lodging. The
range to the SE of it is much plainer with straight gables and
straight-headed windows of several lights, each light with an
arched head. No attempt is made to match the oriel front nor
to show symmetry in any other way. Inside this building on
the ground floor there is much good panelling, not *in situ*, ex-
hibiting vine ornament (for Vintoner), initials, dolphins, etc.

The abbey was dissolved in 1539. It belonged for a time to
Thomas Cromwell, then to the Princess Mary, and finally in
1558 came into the hands of Lord Darcy. His additions certainly resulted in a vast and splendid mansion, but what it was
like, when he and his son lived there, it is difficult to evoke.
The church and much around the cloister had been pulled
down. The refectory perhaps was the Great Hall. Above the
dormitory undercroft, instead of the dormitory, were several
rooms of some size. A proud tower was built at the SE end of
this range to lead up to these. It has a square newel stair with
solid newel. The exterior has square turrets, windows still
similar to those of Abbot Vintoner, and is faced with chequer-
work of limestone and septaria (as is also the new upper dormitory storey). S of the Abbot's s range Lord Darcy also added,
with septaria chequer and also with forms still entirely
Perp, polygonal angle turrets or buttresses. Here another
tower was built too. This now carries a pretty C18 lantern
with a clock. Moreover a completely new detached range was
put up N of the old dormitory. Of this only one angle with a
polygonal turret stands upright. Into what kind of pattern can
all this have formed itself? The answer probably is: none. No
symmetry was attempted, just as no Renaissance decoration
was used.

The rest of the story is brief. About 1600 a brick range was
built connecting the clock tower part with the old dormitory

parts. Then decay set in. Nothing was kept up carefully, and
when in the mid C18 convenient accommodation was wanted,
an addition was made for Lord Rochford to the w of the abbot's
hall – no more than a red brick villa with a bow window. Was
it at that time also that the lawns were made and the trees
planted to convert the whole into a picturesque landscape
garden with ruins?

One more word on the outbuildings – a large BARN continuing the range w of the great gatehouse. It is of the C16, of
stone on the N side, timber-framed on the others, and has tie-
beams with arched braces inside. To the N of this and to the
sw of the C18 'villa' is a detached C16 building of unknown
purpose.

ST PETER AND ST PAUL. The parish church lies just outside
the abbey precinct, SE of the priory church. It is in one way a
most remarkable church – in that its large nave has brick 22
piers and brick arches. The impression on entering is of a
North German more than an English church. This nave with
its aisles dates from the early C16. It has a hammerbeam roof,
and the aisles have flat roofs with moulded (N) and richly
foliated (s) beams. A new chancel was also contemplated, as
the responds of a wide and tall chancel arch prove. It was not
built, and much lower and narrower arches, perhaps originally meant to be temporary, connect the ambitious Tudor nave
with the older church. The older church, at first hardly
noticed, was however also quite ambitious. It dates from the
C13 and had a chancel and long transepts with E chapels or
rather an E aisle. These were shortened in the C16, because the
Perp style did not like side excrescences. However, the chancel
is still that of the C13 (one blocked s window), and the transepts still have thin E piers carrying triple-chamfered arches.
The piers are circular, the N with four, the s with eight
attached shafts. There is indeed, though almost unnoticeable,
some evidence of a yet earlier age. The w wall contains the s
respond of a Norman arcade, plain with the simplest capital.

Now the exterior. Two C13 chancel windows, with their
mullions and tracery lost, survive. The E window is Perp of an
unusual tracery pattern. In the E wall of the s transept aisle are
two early C14 windows. The s transept s window goes with
the chancel E end. N and s aisle windows are latest Perp, of
four lights with depressed heads and the simplest panel tracery.
But the s aisle is red brick (as is also the s porch), whereas the
N aisle is faced with flint and septaria and the window orders

are of flint and red brick. This aisle looks as if it might well be of post-Reformation date. The w tower was in existence when nave and aisle were built. It was probably attached in the C14 to the Norman nave. It has big angle buttresses with three set-offs, and battlements. A curious connexion, including a squinch, was made in the C16 between the s aisle and the stair-turret. – FONT. Octagonal with panels containing a head of St John, an angel holding a shield, etc. – PLATE. Large Cup and Paten of 1574. – MONUMENTS. In the chancel two large standing wall-monuments facing each other. They are almost identical in design and commemorate the first and second Lord Darcy and their wives. They date from c.1580. Alabaster and marble tomb-chest with recumbent effigies, the husband behind and a little higher than the wife. Restrained background; no columns, no strapwork. – John Darcy † 1638, signed by *Fr. Grigs* (s chapel), recess containing the tomb-chest with recumbent alabaster effigy. Against the back wall brass plate with inscription. – Lucy Countess of Rochford † 1773. Standing wall-monument with a straight-sided sarcophagus, and on it two urns. No effigy. Signed by *William Tyler*.

ST CLAIR'S HALL, ½ m. SSE. Here is the extremely rare case of a surviving aisled hall. It is in the centre of a C14 house with cross wings, i.e. of H-shape. There is one pair of sturdy octagonal piers, and they carry, just like the posts in barns, braces along as well as across. The roof runs straight down over the aisles, again as in barns. The N front has two gables, one with overhang, the other formerly with an overhang too. The space in the latter can be seen where a projecting window frame once sat similar to those of Paycocke's House at Coggeshall. The l. gable has below the overhang a pretty C18 bow window. Much C16 alteration in the cross-wings. To this belong the brick parts in the E wing. The staircase in its present form seems to be Jacobean.

(PARK FARM. Late C14 timber building, refronted in the late C18.)

MARTELLO TOWERS. 1810–12. Three of these towers survive at St Osyth: one on Beacon Hill, one on the beach; the third is now a café. On the Martello Towers see Clacton-on-Sea.

SALCOTT

ST MARY. w tower with some flint and stone decoration, much renewed – like the rest of the church – after the earthquake of

1884. – PULPIT. C18 with elegant stairs in inlay in the centre
of the oak panels. – PLATE. Cup with band of ornament and
Paten, both of 1574.
Several good half-timbered houses in the village.

SALING HALL see GREAT SALING

SANDON

ST ANDREW. Nave and chancel Norman, see the remains of
Roman brick quoins, also W of the chancel E end which is a
Perp addition. The N aisle was built in the C14, as is shown by
the three-bay arcade. This has semi-polygonal shafts to the
nave and semicircular ones to the arches – all with capitals.
The arches have two quadrant mouldings. Early in the C16, in
the favourite Essex fashion, the W tower and S porch were
erected in brick, red with diaperwork of blue bricks. The tower
has a much higher polygonal stair-turret. Both are crowned
by battlements. The tower in addition has a little brick dome.
The brick W window is of three lights. The porch is distinguished by a rib-vault and stepped battlements on a
trefoiled corbel frieze. – PULPIT. A fine, not at all showy, C15
piece. Its foot and stem are preserved, which is rare. The stem
is a polygonal pier and the connexion to the pulpit proper is
trumpet-shaped. Simply traceried panels. – PAX. The church
possesses a C15 Pax, that is a small board for the Kiss of Peace
to be given at services. On one side is a painted Crucifixion.
The Pax, one of very few surviving, is on loan at the Victoria
and Albert Museum. – PLATE. Flagon of 1624; Cup and Paten
of 1628. – BRASS to Patrick Fearne † 1588, with kneeling
figures.*
RECTORY, S of the church. Five-bay, two-storey house with
three-bay broken pediment and a doorway with attached
Tuscan columns connected with a window which has volutes
at the bottom. Built in 1765 (rainwater head).

SEWARDS END
2 m. E of Saffron Walden

(Among the more important houses are CAMPIONS, c.1580,
built on an L-shaped plan, with C16 wall paintings on the first

* According to the *Essex Arch. Soc. Trans.* vol. 22, p. 67, the late Mrs
Esdaile has recognized *Epiphanius Evesham* as the sculptor of a MONUMENT
in the church. I cannot see what monument she can have meant.

floor, and POUNCES HALL, which is of the C17 and has a fireplace with an iron crane. Information from Mr P. G. M. Dickinson.)

SHALFORD

ST ANDREW. An early C14 church. But the most unusual motif is the straight-headed two- and three-light windows with a kind of reticulated tracery straightened out, and these are Early Perp. i.e. later C14. In the chancel and the N aisle some earlier C14 windows. The SEDILIA with cusped arches on polygonal shafts and no ogee forms also are early C14. W tower with clasping buttresses and a three-light W window. The arcades to the N and S aisles rest on piers with four major and four keeled minor shafts. The arches are two-centred and have head-stops. The most remarkable feature of the church however is its three large and almost identical tomb recesses, one in the N aisle, one in the S wall of the chancel, and one in the S aisle. There is no effigy or record on any of them to tell us who had them erected. Two hold tomb-chests with indents for brass figures. All three have canopies with thin buttresses and large cusped arches and ogee gables with crockets and finials. In the gables of two is a quatrefoil in a circle. The third has the quatrefoil cusped. The one in the chancel moreover has to the l. and r. of the gable large shields. The S aisle recess seems the earliest, the chancel recess the latest: but all three must be C14. – FONT. Octagonal. Traceried stem, bowl with two small quatrefoils with shields in each panel. – SCREEN with simply traceried lights. – S DOOR with much tracery; C14. – STALLS (W end of nave). Two with poppy-heads. – COMMUNION RAIL. c.1700, with twisted balusters. – STAINED GLASS. Many bits, especially in the E window – the arms of the Norwood family and its alliances; C14. – STRAW DECORATION for the altar, premiated at an 1872 exhibition in London. – PLATE. Small Cup and Paten of 1562.

SHALFORD HALL. Plain, comfortable, late C17 building of two storeys with mullion-and-transom-cross windows of timber and a hipped roof.

ABBOT'S HALL, 1 m. SE. 1823, of white brick.

REDFERN'S FARM, ¾ m. NW. Specially fine C16 manor house with an E part of diapered brick with brick windows, and a timber-framed and plastered W part with a porch with oversailing upper storey.

SHEEPEN DYKE *see* COLCHESTER

SHEERING

ST MARY THE VIRGIN. Norman nave, see the NW quoin
strengthened with Roman bricks and some fragments of
diapering loose inside the church. Unbuttressed W tower of the
C13, completed or restored and embattled in the C16 in brick.
The rest Early Perp, including the five-light E window. –
STAINED GLASS. In the head of this window a complete
Coronation of the Virgin with two censing angels and eight
orders of angels, late C14 and well preserved. – PLATE. Cup
with band of ornament, 1561; Paten probably also 1561.

AYLMERS, 1¼ m. WSW. Good timber-framed early C17 house
with three gables on the E front, the middle one a little larger
and probably originally containing the porch. The timbering
is exposed.

DORRINGTON HALL, opposite Aylmers. Built *c*.1770. Five-
bay front perhaps altered and originally of seven bays. Centre
with pediment and Corinthian porch. Bay windows to the l.
and r. and above them Venetian windows.

SHELLEY

ST PETER. 1888 by *Habershon & Fawckner*. With NW tower and
broach spire. Windows in the C13 style. – PLATE. Jacobean
Cup.

SHELL HAVEN
1 m. SE of Corringham

(ADMINISTRATION OFFICES for the Shell Refining Company
by *Howard V. Lobb & Partners*, 1955–6.)

SHELLOW BOWELLS

ST PETER AND ST PAUL. The whole church is of 1754, and
C18 churches are a rarity in Essex. Nave and short chancel
separated by a heavy, rather low chancel arch. Two arched N
and two S windows. Front with gable and gothicized window.

SHENFIELD

ST MARY THE VIRGIN. The most interesting part of the
church is its timber N arcade of six bays, with slim piers (four
attached shafts and four hollows in the diagonals) and four-

centred arches. Timber also, but heavier timber, the sub-structure of the bell-turret. Eight posts grouped in pairs from w to E, big braces to hold the cross-beams, trellis-strutting along the N and S walls above. The shingled spire is specially tall and thin. – PEWS. Under the tower, c.1600, plain. – PLATE. Cup and Cover of 1663; Salver probably of 1709. – STAINED GLASS by *Kempe*. E window 1883, Annunciation in S window 1896. – MONUMENT. Elizabeth Robinson † 1652. Semi-reclining and shrouded, with infant in swaddling clothes in her arms. Alabaster. No superstructure.

S of the church SHENFIELD PLACE, a brick house of 1689, by *Robert Hooke*, with hipped roof and much original panelling, and the SCHOOLHOUSE of 1865, a specially revolting brick and stone building with a turret, but very typical of minor High Victorian work.

(BRICK HOUSE FARM, 1 m. NW. Early C17 brick house with bargeboarded gables and two-storeyed gabled porch. R.C.)

(Of recent building, the SHENFIELD BRANCH LIBRARY, 1961, and the TECHNICAL SCHOOL, 1963, are both by the County Architect, *H. Conolly*.)

SHOPLAND

ST MARY.* Norman nave and chancel, and weatherboarded belfry. Of the Norman time two windows (one blocked) survive. The chancel was built early in the C14, as shown by the small ogee-lancet on the S side. Original nave and chancel roofs. The belfry rests on four posts with cross-beams and curved braces.

BEAUCHAMPS, ½ m. E. Timber-framed and plastered. E front of 1688. A room has a good plaster ceiling with two oval wreaths.

SHORTGROVE see NEWPORT

SIBLE HEDINGHAM

ST PETER. Except for the W tower a church dating from about 1330–40. The window tracery is typical and not of special interest.‡ The W window of the tower also belongs to that period, although the tower itself with its angle buttresses car-

---

* Recently demolished. The porch went to Bradwell-juxta-Mare; the font is now at St Nicholas, Canewdon, the brass at Sutton.

‡ But the chancel E window was made during the C19 restoration of the church.

ried up in four set-offs and its stepped battlements is of the early C16. Buttresses are also carried down into the inside of the church. The quatrefoil clerestory windows are not original, but the back-splays may indicate that the form is correct (cf. Little Sampford). The arcades between nave and aisles and the chancel arch have octagonal or semi-octagonal supports and double-chamfered arches. The most interesting feature of the church is the MONUMENT in the S aisle, a low tomb-chest like a seat, decorated with six cusped panels holding shields. Big ogee arch flanked by buttresses. The spandrels have Perp panelling. The monument is considered to be a cenotaph for Sir John Hawkwood † 1394, who, the son of a tanner at Sible Hedingham, rose to be a *condottiere* of the Florentine army and the son-in-law of a Duke of Milan. He is buried in Florence Cathedral, where a fresco by Paolo Uccello commemorates him.

In the village round the church two noteworthy houses, the WHITE HORSE INN of the C15, with exposed timber-work and a gable on curved brackets, and the C18 RECTORY with a seven-bay two-storeyed front, parapet, Ionic porch, and a staircase with turned balusters.*

More good houses at SWAN STREET along the main (Roman) s–N road. One of them, with a remodelled front of c.1700, is called Hawkwoods. But it is not older than the Early Tudor age.

SIBLEY'S FARM *see* CHICKNEY

SILVER END

The village was started by Lord Braintree (then Mr Crittall) in 1926 in conjunction with a subsidiary factory for disabled men. The interest of the housing is in the flat-roofed houses by *Sir Thomas Tait*, which are amongst the earliest in England in the International Modern Style. They were designed under immediate continental influence and especially that of New Ways, built by Peter Behrens in 1925 for Mr Bassett Lowke at Northampton. Some details look very dated now, especially the little triangular oriels, but on the whole the estate has aged well. The main development starts from a kind of circus (with a large house called Le Château) and goes along Silver Street

---

* Miss M. Blomfield draws my attention to GREYS HALL, a short distance E of the church, which may have been the former Rectory, 1714, by *Moses Cooke*.

and further on. Other houses at Silver End, e.g. Lord Braintree's by *C. H. B. Quennell*.

The church of St Francis, weatherboarded with a thatched
roof, was designed by *Mr G. C. Holme*, the editor of *The Studio*,
in 1929.

SILVERTOWN

Reached from West Ham and Canning Town by Silvertown
Way, an elevated fast-traffic road built in 1933–4. Silvertown,
in spite, and partly because, of its heavy war damage, has much
poetry. The mixture of the vast ships in the docks, the vaster
factories and mills (C.W.S. Warehouses, 1938–44 by *L. G.
Ekins*; Messrs Spiller's Millennium Mills; Tate & Lyle's
premises), the small, mean, huddled and not uncomfortable
houses, the scrubby vegetation of the bombed sites, and the
church cannot fail to impress.

St Mark. 1861–2 by *S. S. Teulon*. As horrid as only he can be,
and yet of a pathetic self-assertion in its surroundings. No
lived-in house seems anywhere near.* Yellow brick with bits
of red and black brick. Nave with three tall dormers as clerestory windows. Low aisles. Crossing tower with pyramid
roof and circular stair-turret. Apse. Tracery partly of a harsh
version of the plate variety, partly (bell-openings) fancy.

SLOUGH HOUSE *see* DANBURY

SNARESBROOK *see* WANSTEAD p. 413n

SOUTH BENFLEET

St Mary. A biggish church, as churches in this part of the
county go. Big w tower with angle buttresses at the foot, and a
recessed spire. The original windows indicate an early c14
date. Nave with Perp clerestory, s and n aisles, both Perp, but
the (embattled) s aisle probably a little earlier. The chancel
also is Perp. The most rewarding part of the church is the
timber s porch, c15, unusually ornate, with panel tracery in
the spandrels of the doorway, an embattled beam, tracery
panels in the gable, cusped bargeboarding, and a fine two-
bay hammerbeam roof inside. On entering the church
one becomes aware of the much earlier origin of the nave.

* There has since been large-scale housing development in the Andrew
Street area.

The W wall has a plain Norman doorway (into the later
tower) and high above two unusually large blocked Norman
windows. Was a higher middle window or a circular window
between them? The nave is impressive by its height. Its roof
was raised in 1902. The carved stone corbels lower down tell
of the earlier roof. The height of the present roof allows for
two small windows above the chancel arch. As for the arcades
between nave and aisles, the S arcade has octagonal piers, the
later N arcade piers with four attached shafts and four hollows
in the diagonals. The arches on both sides are double-chamfered. The chancel roof has tie-beams with king-posts and four-
way struts. – SCREEN (1931) and WEST GALLERY by *Sir
Charles Nicholson* – the Nicholsons were a Benfleet family. –
PLATE. Cup with band of ornament and Paten, both of 1576.
PARISH HALL, School Lane. By *Sir Charles Nicholson*, 1932.
Nothing special.

SOUTHCHURCH *see* SOUTHEND-ON-SEA

SOUTHEND-ON-SEA

Southend-on-Sea has now 166,000 inhabitants. It is a town of
recent growth and has gradually covered the area of six parishes
with their village centres lying quite distant from each other:
Eastwood to the NW, Leigh to the W, Prittlewell in the centre,
Southchurch and North and South Shoebury to the E. In
addition Westcliff, between Leigh and Southend proper, has
grown as a seaside resort concurrently with Southend. Southend
proper will here be described first, the adjoining parishes after.

SOUTHEND

ALL SAINTS, Southchurch Road. 1889 by *Brooks* (GR). The
two W bays 1934. Long, towerless building of even red bricks.
Inside, square chamfered piers without capitals, decorated by
broad alternating bands of brick and stone. The roof very
high up, of a semicircular wagon type. The chancel arch has a
large triple arch above, as the chancel is not lower than the
nave. The E end is straight and has two tiers of lancets, the
upper tier stepped. – WAR MEMORIAL by *Sir Charles
Nicholson*.
(ST JOHN THE BAPTIST, Church Road. By *Thomas Hopper*,
1841. N and S aisles added 1869; new chancel 1873; alterations
and side chapel 1912.)

(CLIFFTOWN CONGREGATIONAL CHURCH, Nelson Street. Nave and S aisle 1865. N aisle 1889. Balconies early C20.)

(CIVIC CENTRE, Victoria Avenue. By *P.F.Burridge*, Borough Architect. Begun in 1960.)

CENTRAL PUBLIC LIBRARY, Victoria Avenue. 1906 by *H.T.Hare.*

MUSEUM see PRITTLEWELL PRIORY, p. 354.

TECHNICAL COLLEGE, Victoria Circus. Placed diagonally so as to emphasize the circus. Eleven bays, two storeys, with giant pilasters and heavy segmental pediments at the ends. Brick and stone dressings. Quite decorative and successful as a show-piece. By *H. T. Hare*, 1900. (The Technical College buildings in London Road are by the Borough Architect, *P.F.Burridge*, 1958.)

The name 'Sowthende' first appears in a will of 1481 to denote the S end of Prittlewell. Until the C18 there were no buildings along this part of the shore. Then after about 1700 oyster cultivation was begun. Within twenty years the whole of the foreshore from Southchurch to Leigh was leased as oyster feeding grounds, and huts for the oystermen were built in the neighbourhood of the present Kursaal (see Southchurch, p. 356). In 1767 a very humble terrace of a few red brick cottages of two storeys was built near the oystermen's huts. This was PLEASANT ROW (now demolished). The house which became the SHIP HOTEL in Marine Parade dates, it is said, from the same period. Visitors in small numbers were coming to Southend to bathe in the sea, but it was not until 1791 that a syndicate was formed to develop a resort at 'New Southend'. The Terrace, renamed ROYAL TERRACE in 1804 after the Princess of Wales stayed in Nos 7, 8, and 9, was built then. The ROYAL HOTEL (formerly Grand Hotel) dates from the same time, but was enlarged in 1824. The Venetian window above the semicircular porch belonged to the Assembly Room. The Royal Terrace now looks a little bedraggled; too much more up-to-date building has taken place around it; and as a period piece it does not seem to have been discovered yet. The centre is distinguished by five pilasters. The houses have balconies or verandahs of cast-iron. Similar in style a few houses in MARINE PARADE, e.g. the Hope Hotel. Towards the E end of Marine Parade by the corner of Pleasant Road RAYLEIGH HOUSE of 1824. The OYSTER BAR opposite the Royal Hotel was Rennison's Library, started before 1794. It had Gothick trim originally.

Things remained that humble until the development of CLIFF TOWN began in 1859. The houses were built of white brick. The moving spirits were Sir Morton Peto, Brassey, and Lucas Brothers. They were also responsible for the London, Tilbury & Southend Railway. Separate from the houses up Cliff Town, looking rather like Bayswater, PALACE COURT of *c.*1901, six-storeyed, with a round tower and tourelles, proud, tasteless, and rather grim-looking. It now forms a group with the RITZ CINEMA, a sound modern building of 1934, and the GRAND HOTEL.

The PIER in its present form dates from 1889–95, 1923, and 1929. It is said to be the longest in the world.

On the other side, opposite the Cliff Town houses, the BAND-STAND, very gay and flimsy Edwardian Rococo, and then – in a different mood – *Sir Edwin Lutyens*'s WAR MEMORIAL, an obelisk, with its base and pedestal remarkably subtly proportioned.

PORTERS, Southchurch Road. This manor house, once standing quite on its own, is now the Mayor's Parlour of Southend. It is a symmetrical brick building of *c.*1600, but contains traces of an earlier date. The plan is H-shaped, with the Hall in the middle and gabled cross-wings on the sides. The symmetry is broken by the porch attached on the N side to the W wing. The windows are mullioned and transomed, of four and five lights, and of three in the gables. Small polygonal shafts rise on the gable-tops. Inside, the Hall has early C16 linenfold-panelling, moulded ceiling-beams, an early C17 screen, an Elizabethan fireplace, and in the panelling some, probably French, panels, of demi-figures, very Mannerist, of *c.*1535. Elizabethan fireplaces in several other rooms. The early C17 stair balusters have been re-used later. The staircases were originally of the newel type. The Parlour has early C18 panelling.

(Recent building at Southend includes:

BOWLING CENTRE, Pier. *By Silverton & Weston*, 1960–1. Steel frame construction. The roof consists of a large number of inverted pyramids.

CROWN OFFICE BUILDING, Victoria Avenue. By *E. H. Banks* (Ministry of Works), 1961–2.

KEDDIE'S STORE, Warrior Square. By *Yorke, Rosenberg & Mardall*, 1961–3. The addition to the store occupies base-ment, ground floor, and first floor. Second and third floors are for car parking. The fourth to eleventh floors are offices. The contrast between the various functions is clearly brought out in the fenestration.

VICTORIA HOUSE, Victoria Avenue. By *H. G. Huckle & Partners*, 1962.

CARBY HOUSE, Victoria Avenue. By *D. Francis Lumley*, 1963.)

EASTWOOD

ST LAURENCE AND ALL SAINTS. The Norman church is recognizable only inside. The N wall above the arcade shows three Norman outer windows. The wall below was pierced in the C14 by two broad arches with much wall left standing between. The chancel is C13, as its lancet windows indicate. The W tower, added to the S of the nave, can be ascribed to the same century on the strength of a W lancet. Its upper part is of timber, weatherboarded, and ends in a hipped and then needle-thin spire. The S arcade of three bays with octagonal piers and double-chamfered arches may be of *c.*1300. The tower arch is of the same design. The exterior of the S aisle is remarkable for its pretty brick porch (early C16) and the two plastered gables on the S aisle wall (C16 or C17?). Timber priest's chamber in the N aisle. – FONT. Norman, circular, with intersected arches. – DOORS. Its two surviving C13 doors are what the church will be visited for. The earlier one is now inside and unhinged. It is of the early C13 with ironwork in two-and-a-half tiers of large curves and small tendrils between. The other is now the S door, mostly late C13 work with a few of the large early C13 C-curves left. The late C13 added the smaller curves with realistic three-lobed leaves. – PLATE. Cup with band of ornament, and Cover of 1562. – BRASS to Thomas Burrough † 1600.

(MORMON CHAPEL, Arterial Road. By the Church Architectural Department of Salt Lake City, modified to British requirements by *Graham & Baldwin*, 1963.)

(EASTWOOD HIGH SCHOOL FOR GIRLS, Rayleigh Road. By *P. F. Burridge*, Borough Architect, 1960.)

LEIGH-ON-SEA

ST CLEMENT. High above the sea with steps down to the village High Street by the shore. C15 W tower with diagonal buttresses, W door with shields in the spandrels, three-light W window, battlements and higher stair-turret. C15 N aisle with four-light W window (Perp panel tracery) and three-light N windows, chancel and S side C19. S porch of brick, with thick brick doorway and two-light W and E windows. N arcade of four low bays with octagonal piers and double-hollow-chamfered arches. – STAINED GLASS. C18 Crucifixion, very pictorial, with sinister grey clouds; E window. – Chancel S window of two lights with replicas of two of *Reynolds*'s figures for New College Oxford, with incongruous Gothick canopies added. By *Eginton* (?). – MONUMENTS. Brass to Richard Haddok † 1453, two wives and son, also small kneeling children below, the larger figures *c.* 16 in. – Also two C17 brasses. – Robert Salmon † 1641, Master of Trinity House, with frontal demi-figure between pilasters.

ST MARGARET, Lime Avenue. 1931 by *Sir Charles Nicholson*. A remarkably restful interior with an arcade of Tuscan columns, or rather circular piers without entasis. An apse at the E end; open timber roof, lightly painted. The exterior also points to Early Christian inspiration.

(OUR LADY OF LOURDES AND ST JOSEPH, Leigh Road. 1924–5, designed by *Fr. Gilbert*.)

(ST MICHAEL AND ALL ANGELS, Leigh Road, by *Sir Charles Nicholson*. Begun 1926, N and S aisles dedicated 1957. Work on the completion of the church, which is to include a tower, began in 1965.)

At Leigh the only survival of a pre-Victorian age is the HIGH STREET, the street of a fishing village, separated now from the rest of Leigh by the railway. There is no individual house of special interest, except perhaps the CROOKED BILLET INN described by the Royal Commission.

NORTH SHOEBURY

ST MARY THE VIRGIN. Wide and rather low chancel of the early C13 with lancet windows. Also C13, but later, the S aisle, later demolished. The arcade piers and arches are still recognizable, octagonal piers with moulded capitals. In the nave N wall one window of *c.*1300: Y-tracery, cusped. The W tower is in its lower parts also C13, see the W windows. Later, big diagonal buttresses were added and the top parts with a pyramid roof in two steps, the upper with broaches. – FONT. Square bowl on five supports. The sides undecorated, but on the top in the four corners fleurs-le-lis. – STAINED GLASS. E window by *Powell & Sons*, 1866, with medallion of Ascension by *Poynter*. – PLATE. Cup and Paten of 1568. – MONU-

MENT. Fragment of a coffin lid with an exceptionally richly adorned foliated cross and some letters; early C13.

PRITTLEWELL

PRITTLEWELL PRIORY, Priory Park. The priory was founded from Lewes, the chief Cluniac Benedictine house in England, c.1110. Of the buildings little survives. What is most prominent now is the Refectory on the S side of the former cloister and the W range of the cloister, containing the Prior's quarters with a C15 roof. The church adjoined the cloister on the N, but only part of the core of the S wall remains. However, as the result of excavations in 1954 it has now been possible to mark the foundations with concrete strips laid out on turf. The excavations revealed three building periods: the original small Oratory of c.1100, choir and apse of 1170, and nave aisle and N transept of 1280. The REFECTORY, which is contemporary with the choir and apse, has its original, though much restored, doorway with two orders of columns with crocket capitals and a pointed arch with zigzag and dog-tooth decoration. Inside the Refectory there is no more of original work left than one lancet window with keeled shafts and dog-tooth decoration, and the splay at the foot going up so steeply that the exterior form is a pointed trefoil. Against the same wall a fragment of an arch with nailhead ornament, re-set. C15 roof with tie-beams, king-posts, and four-way struts. The WEST RANGE is two-storeyed. It contains of original work a roof similar to that of the Refectory and one fireplace. The S front of this range is Georgian, of four bays and cemented. The building now houses the Southend Museum.

To the W of the Priory the CROWSTONE has been re-erected, the stone which stood on the foreshore at Chalkwell and marked the E end of the jurisdiction of the City of London over the Thames. It is an obelisk and dates from the mid C18. Its successor of 1836 is still *in situ*.

ANNUNCIATION OF THE BLESSED VIRGIN MARY. Large church, standing, with quite a lot of space all round, in a position which during recent years has lost much of its character. The church has a large W tower of the Tudor period, with diagonal buttresses in three set-offs, a W door with shields in the spandrels, a three-light W window with niches to the l. and r., three-light bell-openings, and battlements with flint and stone chequer decoration. The same decoration on the battlements of the nave N wall, chancel and S aisle walls, and the two-storeyed s porch. The N wall of the nave and the N and E walls of the chancel are Norman, although to the E of the pulpit in the N wall of the chancel is a C7 Saxon doorway arch with Roman brick voussoirs. It is also visible inside. The s aisle windows are big, of three lights; Late Perp. On the N side the nave clerestory is visible. Other Norman evidence is the two small blocked windows which now appear above the arcade in the s aisle. They were once the nave s windows. On entering the building the surprising thing is that so prosperous a church should have no N aisle. This lop-sidedness remains a little disturbing. The s aisle arcade of eight bays consists of a w portion of three bays, with heavy octagonal piers without proper capitals – the Norman wall just pierced – then three bays of the late C15 with slimmer octagonal piers with concave sides and arches with one wavy and one hollow-chamfered moulding, and then the two bays of the s chancel chapel, of similar design and date. – FONT. Perp, octagonal, with concave sides with roses, crossed spears, etc. – DOOR. Early C16, with panels with blank crocketed ogee arches. – COFFER. Remains of an ornately traceried C14 front of a coffer. – STAINED GLASS. s aisle, E window. C16; stories, German or Swiss. – PLATE. Large Cup of 1668.

(ST LUKE, Bournemouth Park Road. 1959–60 by *H. T. Rushton*.)

SOUTHCHURCH

HOLY TRINITY. In 1906 a new church was built N of the Norman one, reducing this to an aisle. The architect of this addition was *Sir Ninian Comper*. In 1932 a new chancel was added to the church of 1906. This was designed by *F. C. Eden*. The old church was small and entirely Norman. Its s doorway is in position, with one order of colonnettes with one- and two-scallop capitals, and zigzag and roll-moulding in the arch. The N doorway was re-erected as the w doorway of the new church. It has also one order of colonnettes, also one-scallop capitals, also zigzag in the arch, but in addition a billet-decorated hood-mould. In the old s side is one C13 lancet window and one C14 window with segmental head. In the chancel are on the s as well as the N side C13 lancets. In the new church, re-used, one lancet and one small original Norman window. At the w end of the old church is a C15 belfry resting on eight posts, forming, as it were, a nave and aisles. – The most interesting part of the church is the two RECESSES in the chancel walls, that in the s wall early C14,

ogee-headed on short shafts, that in the N wall a combined
funeral monument and Easter Sepulchre. It consists of a low
segmental arch under which stands a low tomb-chest with
cusped arch-head decoration, and above, the more spacious
four-centred, cusped arch of the Easter Sepulchre itself. –
STAINED GLASS. Typical of the date of the restoration of
the old church: 1856. – PLATE. Cup and Paten of 1682.

ST ERKENWALD, Southchurch Avenue. Very tall, yellow brick
in the E.E. lancet style. SW tower not yet built. By *Sir
Walter Tapper*, designed in 1905.

SOUTHCHURCH HALL, Southchurch Hall Close (now Public
Library). Moated mid C14 manor house. One-storeyed with
exposed timbers. The N gable of the W wing on an oversailing
upper storey. Chimneystacks with diagonal shafts. The s
side altered and now tile-hung. The interior has the rare
survival of a hall, still open to the roof. The central truss is
original, with tie-beam, octagonal king-post with capital, and
four-way struts. Some fragments of C14 timberwork: a
doorway and some tracery.

KURSAAL. The Wrenian dome stands out oddly against the
maze of the super-switchback behind. Brick and stone, low
except for the dome. 1902 by *Sherrin*.

At THORPE BAY, a residential area between Southchurch and
North Shoebury:

(ST AUGUSTINE, St Augustine's Avenue. By *W. H. Allardyce*
1935.)

THORPE HALL, Thorpe Hall Boulevard. Dated 1668. Ye
still gabled. But the doorway has a brick pediment with three
balls.

SOUTH SHOEBURY

ST ANDREW. Norman nave and chancel with original simple
N doorway, slightly more elaborate s doorway (one order of
colonnettes, roll-moulding in the arch, and billet decoration
of the hood-mould) and an original chancel N window. In
addition some C13 lancets, a Perp nave s and a Perp chancel
window. Early C14 W tower with diagonal buttresses. C17
brick battlements. C15 timber porch. Inside the church the
chancel arch is Norman, with one order of columns (scallop
capitals), and in the arch a roll-moulding and a double
zigzag. To the N and s of the arch curious recesses, more
clearly recognizable on the s side. They consist of a blank
arch in the wall next to the chancel arch and, at right angles,

second blank arch in the N and S walls of the nave respectively. The S recess has shafts at the outer sides of the two arches and one corbel for the two inner sides. What was all this provided for? Side altars? Nave roof with tie-beams on curved braces (tracery in the spandrels) and polygonal king-posts with capitals. – PLATE. Cup on short stem, with band of ornament, probably Elizabethan; Paten of 1630.

SUTTONS (Manor House), 1¼ m. NE and now in a War Department prohibited area. Dated 1681. Red brick, symmetrical front with shell-hood over the doorway. Hipped roof with dormers with triangular and segmental pediments and central cupola – a well-known type of the second third of the C17.

RED HOUSE, 1 m. NE. Dated 1673. Still with a gable, but the panel with initials and date has an architrave and a small pediment.

ENCAMPMENT. Very fragmentary remains, now mostly obliterated by barracks building. The camp is ascribed to the Danish chieftain Hasten and has been dated c. 894.

WESTCLIFF-ON-SEA

ST ALBAN, St John's Road. An early and extremely interesting work of Sir Charles Nicholson, or rather at that time *Nicholson & Corlette*: 1898–1908. Flint and rubble with red brick dressings. SE lady chapel visible outside by two gables and large Dec windows below. The altar is in a special narrower extension which lies at the foot of the SE tower of the church. The nave has a spacious six-light W window and arcades with chamfered square piers. The roof is prettily painted. Rood screen and rich reredos. – FONT. From St Mary-le-Bow in London; found there in the crypt by Sir Charles Nicholson and bought by him. Octagonal stem with large leaves going up its lower part. Bowl with thick flutings.

(ST PETER, Eastbourne Grove. By *Humphrys & Hurst*, 1963. Square plan, wide nave and low aisles. The roof supported by precast concrete frames.)

(ST SAVIOUR, King's Road. By *Hoare & Wheeler*, 1911. Stone, in the Decorated style.)

METHODIST CHURCH, Park Road. 1872 by *E. Hoole*. Called by a local writer of the later C19 'one of the greatest ornaments of Southend'. Ragstone, laid like crazy paving. W window with bare plate tracery. No tower, only frontal angle turrets.

(CROWSTONE CONGREGATIONAL CHURCH, Crowstone

Road. By *Burles & Harris*, 1910. Kentish ragstone, stone dressings, traceried windows.)

(WESTCLIFF BRANCH LIBRARY, London Road. By *P. F. Burridge*, Borough Architect, 1960.)

(WESTCLIFF HIGH SCHOOL FOR BOYS. The Science block in Eastwood Lane is by *P. F. Burridge*, 1957.)

Westcliff-on-Sea also had a village, or rather hamlet centre. It was called Milton Hamlet. In 1899 a writer noted that it was 'fast becoming a High Street'. It is that now, with not a single house worth mentioning here. E of it, in Milton Road, attached to a convent and the R. C. Church of Our Lady and St Helen is a range added by *Leonard Stokes*. It has a gable decorated by a Baroque niche and mullioned-and-transomed windows – a typical Stokes mixture.

SOUTH FAMBRIDGE

ALL SAINTS. Just a chapel. Nave and chancel only. Yellow brick with lancets. Bellcote. Built in 1846.

SOUTHFIELDS see DEDHAM

SOUTH HANNINGFIELD

ST PETER. Nave, chancel, and belfry with broach-spire. The nave is of the C12. It has a small and another lengthened original window in the N wall, and one in the S wall. In the S wall in addition a two-light C15 window. The belfry was added probably in the C15. It rests on four posts with big curved braces. The chancel is C19. – DOOR with iron hinges. Dated by the Royal Commission *c*.1400. – PAINTING. The jambs of the C15 s window have very pretty foliage scrolls. – PLATE. Cup of 1562 with bands of ornament.

SOUTHMINSTER

ST LEONARD. A largish, odd, and aesthetically unsatisfactory church. The aesthetic failings are chiefly due to what was done about 1750 and in 1819. It is not quite clear which period did what. The result anyway is an extremely wide nave, the shape of an early C19 Methodist chapel with a yet wider crossing, transepts, and a polygonal chancel. All this is covered by plaster rib-vaults of entirely unconvincing weight, a regrettable mistake in a church which possesses that rare thing in the county, a stone-vaulted s porch with a star-shaped tierceron-vault and bosses. It dates from the C15. The porch has two-light side windows and above the entrance three richly canopied and crocketed niches. The transepts and each of the three sides of the polygonal chancel carry a gable. An examination of the nave shows that it is of stone, and was heightened in flint and yet more heightened in brick. The brick is C18 or C19, the flint with the clerestory windows C15; so the stone must be older. And indeed the s doorway turns out to be Norman. Norman also is the w window above the triple-chamfered C14 tower arch. The whole w tower is C14. It has one big diagonal buttress and flint-and-stone-ornamented battlements. – FONT. Perp, octagonal, with decorated foot, stem, and bowl. The ornament is chiefly the usual quatrefoils. – BENCH ENDS. Two, of the C15, with poppy-heads, in the chancel. – PLATE. Cup of 1568 with band of ornament. – BRASSES. Man and wife c.1560; J. King † 1634 (both chancel floor).

SOUTH OCKENDON

ST NICHOLAS. Not much old, but a splendid Late Norman N doorway with three orders of supports, the middle colonnettes spiral-fluted and enriched by shaft-rings. The three orders of voussoirs of three-dimensional varieties of the zigzag motif. The date, say, c.1180. Of the C13 the fine circular flint tower. Perp N chancel chapel, two-and-a-half-bay N arcade (octagonal piers and double-hollow-chamfered arches), and rood-stair-turret on the s side. The rest of 1866. – HOURGLASS STAND. Wrought iron, C17. – MONUMENTS. Brass to Sir Ingram Bruyn † 1400 (headless). The figure 4 ft long, surrounding of thin architecture fragmentary. – Brass to Margaret Baker † 1602. – Sir Richard Saltonstall † 1601, Lord Mayor of London; standing wall-monument of alabaster. The usual kneeling figures, the six sons and nine daughters in the 'predella'.

Nice Green by the church with e.g. the ROYAL OAK INN, C17, H-plan, symmetrical gables. About 400 yds s of the Green the RECTORY, timber-framed and gabled C17, and QUINCE TREE FARM just s of this.

To the E of the Green lying back is SOUTH OCKENDON HALL of c.1870, with the big moat of the previous Hall adjoining, and a WINDMILL of c.1830. It is a smock-mill and was originally driven by water.

OCKENDON COURTS SECONDARY SCHOOL. By *Denis Clarke Hall*. Close to much L.C.C. housing. In the architectural idiom of today – loosely planned and sunny. Central spine-block of two storeys with four classroom blocks leading off it at an angle. The gymnasia are isolated blocks reached by covered ways. Light steel-frame construction essentially on a 3 ft 4 in. module. Much colour inside. The character of the work is quite different from that of the schools built by the county architect's office. It is wise policy to employ private architects side by side with official architects.

LITTLE BELHUS, 1 m. SW. Largish weatherboarded late C16 house with much panelling inside. The most handsome feature is the gateway into the walled garden with a steep curly gable.

BARROWS nr South Ockendon Hall. Two; the larger 150 ft in diameter and 17 ft high, the smaller 130 ft in diameter and 10 ft high.

SOUTH SHOEBURY *see* SOUTHEND-ON-SEA

SOUTH WEALD

ST PETER. A large church in a fine position and with a surprisingly big W tower of *c*.1500, ashlar-faced, with angle buttresses, battlements, and a higher stair-turret. The medieval church behind it consisted of nave, chancel, and N aisle. Its S and E walls survive, but heavily over-restored, when they were reduced to being the S aisle of a new church with its own large chancel which took the place of the former N aisle. The arcade is reconstructed but, it is said, correctly. With its circular piers and double-hollow-chamfered arches it represents a C13 model. Older still and fortunately preserved is the Norman S doorway. It has one order of columns with zigzag-carved shafts, a carved lintel, an arch with zigzag decoration, and a tympanum with diaper ornament, little squares divided into two triangles. The new church is of 1868, designed by *Teulon*. – FONT. 1662, polygonal, with thick leaves sprouting up the stem. – CHANCEL RAILS. Of iron, designed by *Scott*. – STAINED GLASS. Two late C15 panels in the W window, probably Flemish; W window by *Powell & Sons*, 1868. – E window and S aisle E window by *Kempe*; 1886 and 1888. – PLATE. Cup of 1564; large Cup of 1635; Paten of 1686. – MONUMENTS. Set of Brasses at the W end; returned to the church in 1933. All small. Civilian of *c*.1450; Woman and Children of *c*.1450 (originally husband, three wives, and three groups of children); Civilian of c.1480; kneeling Children of c.1500; A. Crafford † 1606; Robert Picakis and Allen Talbott, two kneeling Children, † 1634. – Hugh Smith † 1757. Standing wall-monument with sarcophagus and grey obelisk. Against it large roundel with two profiles facing one another. Unsigned.

Pretty group of houses near the church, especially the TOWER ARMS, early C18, with red and blue chequer brick front, the BELVEDERE TOWER just NE in the grounds of Weald Hall,* a polygonal castellated structure, the SCHOOL by *Teulon*, 1860, and, round the corner the ALMSHOUSES, by *Teulon*, 1858, a picturesque, long, low group of brick, asymmetrically composed, though with the chapel in the centre. The houses are gradually stepped down the hill.

(At Brook Street the GOLDEN FLEECE INN, of the C15 with remains of original hammerbeam roofs of the hall, and an early C17 staircase with heavily turned balusters. SW of the Inn BROOK HOUSE, brick of c.1700 with a hooded doorway. R.C.)

Further away a number of good Georgian houses.

GILSTEAD HALL, 1¾ m. NW. Dated 1726. Fine nine-bay house with parapet, porch covered by a broad segmental pediment, and staircase with thin twisted balusters.

DITCHLEYS, 1¾ m. NW. Dated 1729. Seven-bay house of two-and-a-half storeys with a three-bay pediment and a Tuscan porch.

ROCHETTS, ½ m. NW. Plain late C18 brick house with pediment and lower three-bay wings. The wings have been much altered externally.

SOUTH WEALD CAMP. Early Iron Age encampment, now in very poor condition. Approximately circular in shape. Originally it covered about 7 acres. Remains of the rampart are visible. Entrance doubtful.

PILGRIM'S HALL, see Brentwood, p. 102.

SPAINS HALL
1 m. NW Finchingfield

Built of red brick with stone dressings towards the end of the C16. The plan from the beginning seems to have been quite irregular. The front has six gables all of convex-concave outline, but not all identical in detail. They are of different sizes and arranged apparently in no system. The windows are mullioned or mullioned and transomed and again quite casually

* Weald Hall was demolished in 1950.

placed. The porch with two upper storeys is near the centre. It leads into the Hall, which is only one-storeyed and has a nine-light window with two transoms. This main front of the house is turned to the SW. The NW side has a more irregular and modest appearance, with timber-framed and plastered walls and gables. The N end of this side is early C17. Against the back of this range and facing SW, the frontage was rebuilt about 1768, regular and symmetrical with a central cupola. The SW end of the main wing occupied by the Drawing Room has two bay windows. Alterations here are dated 1637 by rain-water heads. The fireplace in the Drawing Room indeed goes well with that date. The main staircase is of c.1600, with turned balusters. In a first-floor room another elaborately carved fireplace.

The Lake to the SE of the house was originally two of eight rectangular ponds. In the garden is a square two-storeyed Summer House of brick with battlements and angle pinnacles.

ROMAN BUILDING. The site lies in the field known as Further Brixted, ¾ m. W. Excavations in 1931–2 revealed a rectangular building measuring 67 ft by 47 ft, with stone footings supporting a timber and daub superstructure. The central room had a hypocaust and produced fragments of painted wall plaster and window glass. Pottery suggests an occupation beginning in the mid C2.

SPARLING'S FARM see FELSTED

SPRINGFIELD*

HOLY TRINITY, see Chelmsford.

COUNTY GAOL, see Chelmsford.

ALL SAINTS. Norman nave, as proved by one N window with Roman brick surround. Early C14 chancel. The renewed windows are shafted inside and have hood-moulds with head-stops. Head-stops also above the PISCINA. The C14 W tower with set-back buttresses was repaired and partly rebuilt in brick in 1586. – FONT. Mid C13, and the best of the date in Essex, especially the E side with big, lush stiff-leaf scrolls. Two large rosettes each on the other sides. – SCREEN. Tall, with one-light divisions with cusped arches. Dado with various blank tracery motifs. – PANELLING. Early C17, in the chancel. – PAINTINGS. Moses and Aaron, probably late C17. – PLATE.

---

* Administratively in the Municipal Borough of Chelmsford.

Large Cup of 1658; Paten on foot, perhaps also 1658. – BRASS
to Thomas Coggeshall † 1421; in armour.
The church stands close to the Green on the E and surrounded
by the old trees of Springfield Place and other houses.
SPRINGFIELD PLACE is a large early C18 house. The s front
has nine bays with two-bay projecting wings. It is two-
storeyed with an attic. Segment-headed windows, Ionic doorcase and pedimented window above. – To the s of the church
SPRINGFIELD DUKES, a seven-bay, two-storey Early Georgian brick house with a one-bay segmental pediment and a
projecting frame round the central window. The RECTORY
s w of the church is also Georgian and also of brick. The rainwater-heads are dated 1752. Brick quoins and a one-bay
pediment.

STAMBOURNE

ST PETER AND ST THOMAS. Impressive broad and powerful
C11 W tower, unbuttressed, with two large windows fairly
high up on the W, N, and s sides, an arch to the nave with
decoration on the N abacus, and later battlements. The rest
C15 to early C16 (early C16 the plain brick s porch), and
apparently largely due to the generosity of the Macwilliam
family. All windows Late Perp, several of three lights with depressed heads and intersecting tracery. One s window in the
nave has four lights, and the E jamb inside is decorated by two
niches with elaborate canopies. The N arcade of three bays has
slim octagonal piers with partly wave-moulded arches. The N
aisle roof is specially good. The N chancel chapel is only one
bay long, but the E respond has a quite exceptional enrichment: a niche for a figure and above it a shield with the Mac- 21b
william arms, a beautifully carved helmet and as a background
a spray of leaf-work. Early C16. – STAINED GLASS. In the E
window the kneeling figures of Henry Macwilliam and his
first wife, who died in 1530; also small fragments in the
tracery. – FONT. Octagonal, with traceried stem and the usual
quatrefoils and shields on the bowl. – SCREEN. One-light
divisions with ogee tops and simple panel-tracery above. The
dado on the l. side painted with figures of saints – an East
Anglian rather than an Essex tradition. The quality of the
paintings is low.

STANESGATE PRIORY *see* **STEEPLE**

STANFORD-LE-HOPE

St Margaret of Antioch. The village has recently grown
into a little town, and the church bears out that development.
It is dominated by its big tower at the E end of the N aisle
which dates from 1883 and is designed on the pattern of that
of Prittlewell church, Southend-on-Sea. The w front also is
C19. These two hide a building which at least rudimentarily
can be traced back to the C12 – see the two windows visible
inside in the N and S walls of the nave close to the chancel. The
N arcade is clearly E.E. with alternating octagonal and circular
supports and one-stepped arches with two slight hollow chamfers. The S arcade – a usual change – has octagonal piers only
and double-chamfered arches, i.e. belongs to the C14. C14 also
is the chancel, see the SEDILIA and the low ogee-headed recess
in the N wall. In it stands a tomb-chest of c.1500. – FONT.
Octofoil plan, C13, on nine supports. – SCREEN at W end of S
chancel chapel, of one-light divisions, simple and graceful,
c.1400. – PLATE. Cup on baluster stem, and Paten of 1709. –
MONUMENTS. Sir Heneage Fetherstone † 1711 with two
weeping cherubs and between them a relief of ill-assorted
bones. – In the churchyard a more gruesome display of bones:
monument to James Adams † 1765. Big tomb-chest with
rounded lid and on this crudely carved cherubs, bible, and
masses of bones. At the back against the churchyard wall
baldacchino with curtains raised, which, in less rustic monuments, is a C17, not a C18 motif.
St Clere's Hall, ½ m. w. Early C18 five-bay, two-storey
house. Doorway altered, with three vases. The front was later
castellated.
(Hassenbrook Hall, ½ m. N. Early C17 brick house, altered.
The Royal Commission mentions an original chimneystack
and illustrates the brick gateway into the garden.)
Hassenbrook Secondary School. By *Gerald Lacoste*,
1951–3. For 600 children. A spreading plan, as most modern
schools have. A clock-tower as a vertical accent away from
the main entrance, Hall, and gymnasium. These parts en-
livened by odd brickwork patterns.
(Water Tower. For Fison's by *Brian Colquhoun & Partners*,
c.1958.)

STANFORD RIVERS

St Margaret. C12 nave with original w window high up, two
N and two s windows. The w window is blocked by an in-

triguing slab with a primitive figure carving. The chancel is
Dec, see the windows (but the E window is C19). Good N porch
of timber; late C15, now blocked. Belfry on four posts as usual
and with leaded broach-spire. Nave roof with tie-beams on
braces and king-posts. – FONT. Of the usual Purbeck type of
c.1200, but of Barnack stone. Octagonal with two shallow
pointed arches to each side. – SCREEN. Bits of tracery have
been re-used in the W gallery. – BENCHES. Eighteen oak
benches; plain ends with two buttresses each. – COMMUNION
RAIL. With turned balusters, mid C17. – (PAINTING. In the
splays of the easternmost window in the S wall, traces of two
figures, each in a painted niche; above shields. Early C14.
E. W. Tristram, *English Wall Painting of the C14.*) – PLATE.
Set of c.1780 in silver on copper. – BRASSES. Hidden below
the altar (see Royal Commission).

STANSTEAD HALL
1 m. SE Halstead

One range of a larger C16 brick building. The range has its main
elevation to the N, flat and symmetrical, of two storeys and
with three large shaped gables. The windows are of 2, 3 – 3, 3 –
3, 3 – 3, 2 lights and transomed on the upper floor. All window
lights are still arched. The doorway is small with four-centred
head, no display of columns or pediment. On the S side big
chimneystacks with polygonal shafts. On the E a central bay
window flanked by polygonal turrets. Their tops and the gable
are C19. N of the range fragmentary foundations of another,
originally no doubt across an enclosed courtyard. Inside some
fireplaces, ceiling beams, and panelling.

STANSTED MOUNTFITCHET

ST MARY THE VIRGIN. With its 'spike' on the W tower (brick,
embattled, of 1692) and its wealth of monuments more a Hertfordshire than an Essex church, and indeed close to the border.
Nave and N aisle of 1888;* chancel much renewed at the same
time. But the chancel arch is remaining proof of the Norman
church. Capitals with incised zigzag decoration, arch with zigzag and an outer Norman 'bell-flower' motif. The S doorway
is Norman too, with three orders of columns carrying scalloped
capitals, arch with zigzag and saltire-cross decoration, and a
tympanum on a curved lintel, with diaperwork. On the N side

* By *Francis T. Dollman* (GS).

of the N aisle another (of course re-used) Norman doorway. It has three orders of columns, with scalloped capitals, and the rest also very similar to the S doorway. The chancel dates from the C13 and has inside tall blank shafted arcades embracing the windows. The renewed E end was similar, as is shown by the angle-shafts (with shaft-rings). On the N side an E.E. arch into a side chapel and a plain C14 arch. The E.E. arch has responds with capitals decorated with volutes at the angles and between them stiff-leaf in the E, upright three-lobed leaves in the W respond. – FONT. A big heavy circular piece with coarse angle volutes, c.1300. – FONT COVER. Plain, ogee in outline, with foliage finial; early C17. – COMMUNION RAIL. Graceful; C18. – CANDLESTICKS. Wood, gilt, tall, with foliage decoration; C18. – SCULPTURE. Cartouche of the early C17 at the E end of the N aisle. It is surrounded by the thirty pieces of silver, a shield with the Instruments of the Passion and the crown of thorns as a crest, etc. – STAINED GLASS. N chapel E end. Good Samaritan; three lights, signed by *Warrington*, 1859. – PLATE. Paten on foot of 1676. – MONUMENTS. Cross-legged Knight of c.1300 (N chapel). – Hester Salusbury † 1614, coloured recumbent effigy wearing the fashionable high hat. Alabaster sarcophagus with two big shields surrounded by gristly ornament. The tomb is not in its original state. Mrs Esdaile has pointed out that the escutcheon with the Instruments of the Passion indicated *Epiphanius Evesham* as the author. – Sir Thomas Middleton, late Lord Mayor of London † 1631. Uncommonly sumptuous standing wall-monument with bulgy sarcophagus-like base decorated with skulls, recumbent effigy, between coupled black marble columns carrying a shallow coffered arch. Straight top with achievement. Outside the columns two standing angels and inside also two, of specially good quality, holding the large inscription plate. – William Harcourt Torriano † 1828, with mourning female figure leaning over an altar. By *E. Gaffin*.

ST JOHN THE EVANGELIST. 1889 by *Caröe*, an early work of his, but already with the touches of wilfulness which characterize his style. The tower a little later; 1895, and consequently more original. The interior in fact, with exposed brick, is still quite conventional. Nave and S aisle. The only distinguishing detail is the canted W balcony. The tower, also very red, as is the whole church, treats the Perp of the church freely. Tower top with gargoyles, pinnacles, stepped battlements, and a lantern-shaped upper ending of the stair-turret.

CASTLE. Less than ¼ m. E of St John. Small circular inner bailey having once probably possessed a stone keep, and small bailey to its E.

STANSTED HALL. Large symmetrical Neo-Jacobean house of 1871. Brick with stone dressings. By *Robert Armstrong*.

MARY MACARTHUR HOLIDAY HOME. Neo-Jacobean, with shaped gables. By *C. R. Pritchett*, 1875. With additions of c.1880 and 1898.

WINDMILL, ¼ m. W of Station. Tower-mill in good condition. 3

VILLAGE. Chiefly two parallel streets. The one further E runs down a hill and has a few specially nice houses on the W side, one in particular with exposed timber, just N of the Queen's Head. The other follows the line of the Roman road. The centre here is an elaborate cast-iron fountain of 1871. Just N of it a good five-bay two-storey Georgian brick house with pedimented doorway. Nice cottages further N.

STANTON'S FARM see BLACK NOTLEY

STANWAY

ST ALBRIGHT. The nave is C12, see the S doorway and one S window, two N windows, and the restored W window (all with much Roman brick). The rest is of 1880, designed by *Sir George Gilbert Scott*: chancel, S aisle, S chancel chapel, and belfry. The S arcade however is original work of c.1500, brought to Stanway from the church of St Runwald at Colchester. – FONT. Octagonal, Perp, with panels with shields and with the chalice and the host surrounded by rays. – GLASS. E window and one S window by *Kempe*, 1892, with his characteristic faces and the pale green general tone.

ALL SAINTS. In the grounds of Stanway Hall. In ruins. An interesting building, consisting now only of tower and nave. The late C14 tower is of bands of flint and brick, the brick not being Roman any longer. Early in the C17 the N aisle was removed and replaced by brick windows, the N porch was added, and the chancel arch blocked and provided with a three-light brick window.

ST ALBRIGHT'S HOSPITAL, formerly Colchester Workhouse. 1837, red brick, still Late Georgian in the details. The grouping of the buildings is radial with a taller central block.

(HOUSE at Stanway Green. One-storeyed, by *J. E. C. Brand*, 1957–8.)

OLIVERS, 1 m. ESE of the old church. C18, but with one C15

roof-truss. Dovecote octagonal of brick and higher up weatherboarding.

STAPLEFORD ABBOTS

St Mary. Yellow brick w tower of 1815 and hideous church of 1862, by *T. Jekyll* of Norwich. The walls faced with a crazy-paving pattern. The windows with geometrical tracery. Nice small N chapel of brick, built in 1638. The windows, a remarkable fact, are round-arched and no longer Perp. – PULPIT. Nice late C16 piece with blank arches in the panels. – HELM in the N chapel, late C16. – STAINED GLASS. Very fine, small early C14 figure of Edward the Confessor (N vestry). – PLATE. Cup, Paten, larger Paten, and Flagon, all of 1687; Almsdish of 1692. – MONUMENT. Sir John Abdy † 1758. Standing wall-monument with large putto standing by an oval medallion with frontal, rather vacant, portrait. Broken pediment on brackets at the top.

ALBYNS. Of the house of *c.*1620 described in so much detail by the Royal Commission only a fragmentary shell remains after the Second World War. The Hall range and the S range are gone. The courtyard still exists, though in a dilapidated state, and the excellent staircase with flat openwork strap decoration but apparently without the figures on the newel posts. The stables are undamaged, with straight gables and mullioned windows.

STAPLEFORD TAWNEY

St Mary. Nave and chancel assigned to the C13, on the strength of renewed lancet windows and the blocked N doorway. Belfry on four posts; low E–W braces, higher N–S braces. Above the beams carried by the braces is cross-strutting in all four directions. – COMMUNION RAILS, C17 with square tapering openwork balusters. – PLATE. Almsdish of 1685; Large Cup and Paten inscribed 1698.

OLD RECTORY. Good C18 brick building.

STEBBING

St Mary the Virgin. Entirely a C14 church, and perhaps rather earlier than *c.*1360, the date suggested by the Royal Commission. The tracery of all the windows has Dec forms, the SEDILIA and PISCINA don't look later either, and no Perp

feature appears yet anywhere. The w tower (with angle buttresses, battlements, and a recessed lead spire) has a w window
with (renewed) reticulated tracery. The s porch is given one
original feature: the side openings are small and of quatrefoil
shapes (cf. Great Bardfield), one on the l., two on the r. The
N and s arcades of the large nave inside have piers of an
uncommon section, four slim polygonal shafts and in the diagonals four round ones. Complex arch mouldings in the two-
centred arches. Head and leaf stops. It is important to come
to some conclusion about the date of all this, because of the
one distinguishing, and at the same time most effective, feature
of the church: the stone rood screen, filling with a bold tripar- 28
tite openwork design the whole of the tall chancel arch. This
motif exists in only one other Essex church, at Great Bardfield,* and there we have every reason to assume that it is later.
The Stebbing Screen has basically three stepped lancet arches
and then many ogee arches, some quatrefoils and some ball-
flowers in the decoration. That should not be later than c.1350
and may well be a little earlier. In the middle part an embattled
transom runs through the arch at the point of its springing to
hold, on three plinths, the three figures of the Rood. – The
chancel roof is of flat pitch with arched braces carrying tracery
in the spandrels, and collar-beams. Wall-plates with foliage
trails and battlements; embattled purlins. The nave roof is also
flat-pitched. The principals rest on brackets, the sub-princi-
pals start with figures of angels. Two bosses on each sub-
principal. – REREDOS at the E end of the N aisle. Very defaced. Traces of a rib pattern in the soffit. – COMMUNION
RAIL. C18, with alternating slim balusters. – BRASS to a widow,
c.1390, large (nave).

FRIENDS' MEETING HOUSE. The date plate 1674 cannot refer
to the house in its present form, with segment-headed windows and a small porch. Mostly red and blue chequer, but
also diaper. Probably the house was remodelled early in the
C18.

A group of nice houses just s of the church, especially PAR-
SONAGE FARM (exposed timbers) and CHURCH FARM facing
down the main street. In the main street the Royal Commission lists sixteen more houses. Off to the w, down Mill Lane,
TAN OFFICE FARM and then the TOWN MILL.

North of this by Stebbing Park the MOUNT of a former castle,
44 ft high.

* And besides at Trondheim in Norway.

STEEPLE

ST LAURENCE. 1884. Nave and chancel, belfry. In the late E.E. style with cusped lancets. The remarkable thing is that the architect, *F. Chancellor*, who built the church, using materials of the preceding medieval church, has indulged in an orgy of mixing into his brown stone walls bricks entirely at random and in all directions. Even the window dressings are not completely of brick, but use the brick intermittently without any principle but that of variety. Inside, the w end is divided off by a circular pier into two bays.

STANESGATE PRIORY. The priory was Cluniac, founded probably early in the C12. Of all that the Royal Commission could still describe in 1923, only one wall now remains visible.

STEEPLE BUMPSTEAD

ST MARY. There was here a remarkably large C11 church. The w tower (see its lower windows, open and blocked) belonged to it, and the chancel (see its quoins). The diagonal buttresses, and also the buttresses into the present nave, were added later. The top is all brick. Brick also the tops of the aisles, the s porch, and the whole clerestory. Most of the exterior features are due to the restoration of 1880. But in the N aisle are still two fairly reliable windows. They look late C14 or early C15. The N arcade and the identical s arcade may well belong to the same date. They have piers with semi-polygonal shafts without capitals to the nave and semicircular shafts with capitals to the arches. The aisle roofs deserve some notice too. – FONT. Octagonal, Perp, with quatrefoils carrying shields. – BENCHES. Two in the nave with panelling dated 1568. Also some poppyheads and some more panelling. – POOR BOX. Iron-bound, on panelled stem, *c*.1500. – HELM. Late C16, N aisle, E end. – PLATE. Two large Flagons of 1639: two Cups, two Patens, and a Paten on foot of 1712. – MONUMENTS. Sir Henry Bendyshe † 1717. Standing wall-monument by *Thomas Stayner*. Sir Henry is shown elegantly reclining with his elbow on a cushion, like a French prelate. By his side a tiny baby. Twisted columns l. and r. and a rich pediment with seated putti. A first-rate work. – Sir John and Lady Bendyshe, erected *c*.1740. Large monument with the usual obelisk and in front of it a big putto and an oval medallion with two profile portraits. By *Joseph Pickford*.

The village street runs from a ford past the church to the GUILD-HALL (?), a miniature edition of the Thaxted Guildhall.

Formerly open ground floor with small four-centred arches. The timbering of the upper floor exposed. The building originally housed the school, which was founded in 1592, but it is unlikely that it was built as a school exclusively.

LATCHLEYS, 1 m. SW. Timber-framed and plastered manor house of which the SE wing is of Early Tudor date. In it one room with foliage-decorated beams. The staircase is of the early C17 with a square well and heavy turned balusters. S of the house a C16 brick bridge of two arches leads across the unusually wide moat.

(BRICK HOUSE. Two-storeyed, timber-framed, with brick-nogging. The date 1571 on the chimneystack. *The Times*, 12 October 1964.)*

STEWARDS see HARLOW

STIFFORD

ST MARY. Square, short C13 W tower with hipped spire. Steep primitive stair inside. Nave with two-bay S arcade also C13 (circular pier, double-chamfered broad, depressed pointed arches). The responds more remarkable than the pier, especially the E respond with a head corbel, and original colouring; fine mouldings. Late C13 the S chancel chapel with lancet windows with cusped rere-arches inside. Sign of an earlier Norman past the plain N doorway. – PULPIT. 1611, of the type then usual. – HOURGLASS STAND, C17, wrought iron, fixed to the pulpit. – DOOR, on the N side with some C13 ironwork. – (STAINED GLASS. By *Powell & Sons*, E window, 1863, and one window in the S aisle with medallions by *Holiday*, 1868.) – PLATE. Cup and Cover of 1627; Flagon of 1665; Paten on foot of 1683. – Many BRASSES, e.g. Ralph Perchehay, rector of Stifford, large demi-figure of *c*.1380; shroud brass of a priest, *c*.1480; John Ardalle † 1504, and wife.

FORD PLACE, ½ m. W. An excellent house dated 1655. To this date belong the Dutch gables at the back and the plaster ceiling of one room. Later in the C17 the W front was renewed. It is of yellow brick with red brick trim connecting the windows vertically. The front has nine bays and two storeys with dormer windows with alternating triangular and segmental pediments. The central first-floor window has a characteristic

* Mr D. M. Palliser told me about this.

brick surround. Extremely rich late C17 plaster ceiling of one front room, with thick garlands and figures of the four seasons. The staircase has three slim columns to each tread and scrolly decoration of the tread-ends.

STISTED

ALL SAINTS. A church of odd external shape; but it must be remembered that the tower, standing at the E end of the S aisle, was built only in 1844. Chronologically the history of the church began with the N arcade of five bays, or rather three with odd narrower arches at the W and E ends. The arcade is of c.1180–90 and has short circular piers with very good square foliage capitals. The E capital is a little later: round with heads at the corners. The S arcade has in the corresponding place a capital of the same type. The others are without carving. The N and S arches have only one slight chamfer. The chancel belongs to the same time as the E capitals. It possessed a fine group of five (renewed) stepped single lancets; lancets also on the N and S sides. Finally there are the N and S aisle walls with C14 Dec windows of no special interest. – PULPIT with panelled sides, one with a coat of arms, early C18. – PAINTING. Adoration of the Magi, by *Gaspar de Crayer*. – STAINED GLASS. A whole collection of fragments in the chancel windows, mostly Flemish and mostly C16. In a S window some C14 tabernacle work. – MONUMENTS. Charles Savill-Onley † 1843 with profile portrait in a medallion; by *Gaffin*. – Caroline Savill-Onley † 1845 with a soul in long garments rising to heaven; by *Baily*.

STISTED HALL. 1823 by *Hakewill*. Five bays with slightly projecting angle bays and a big purely Greek Ionic tetrastyle porch with pediment.

STOCK

ALL SAINTS. The most interesting part of the church is the belfry.* Square ground floor with four posts set so as to form a Greek cross with four small corner spaces. The W arm serves as the entrance to the church. It has a doorway with three tracery panels over. The N and S arms have one three-light traceried wooden window each. The tracery differs slightly. The centre is braced from N to S as well as E to W. The arms

* Mr C. M. Hewett considers it to be of the late C13. *Archaeological Journal*, vol. 119, 1962.

have N–S braces. Trellis-strutting above from E to W and N to S. The upper part of the belfry has a hump on the E side. Tall bell-stage and tall thin broach-spire. The weatherboarding is dark and vertical below, white and horizontal above. Of timber also the S porch, with six ogee-arched openings on the W and E sides. The doorway has blank panel tracery above. The church itself is of less architectural interest. The E chapel of the aisle and the chancel are of 1848. The front of the S aisle is heavily renewed. N arcade inside of three bays with octagonal piers and double-hollow-chamfered arches, that is C15. The chancel roof has recently been prettily painted, somewhat in the taste of Sir Charles Nicholson. – CHAIRS. In the chancel two richly carved late C17 chairs. – BRASS to Richard Twedye † 1574, in armour.

Nice High Street with long Green. The church lies outside the village, and close to it are the ALMSHOUSES, late C17 brick, of one storey.

WINDMILL, ½ m. E of the church. A well-preserved tower-mill.

LILYSTONE HALL. Three bays, two storeys, with giant pilasters and a Greek Doric porch. Built in 1847. A private chapel was added to the house in 1879. It is a simple apsed structure by *Buckler*.

BARROW, 600 yds SW. Diameter 55 ft.

STOCKWELL HALL see LITTLE BURSTEAD

STONDON MASSEY

At Stondon Massey William Byrd, the composer, spent the last thirty years of his life. His house, Stondon Place, has since been rebuilt twice.

ST PETER AND ST PAUL. Nave and chancel are Early Norman. Two original windows remain on the N side and two on the S; also both doorways, though that on the N is blocked. They are completely plain and unmoulded. The only later medieval addition of importance is the belfry, which is placed a little further E than the W end. It rests on four posts carrying two tie-beams and connected with them by arched braces. There are also beams in the E–W direction forming a square with the others. – FONT. Perp, octagonal. Bowl with quatrefoils carrying fleurons. – SCREEN. Plain one-light divisions with ogee arches and a minimum of panel tracery above them. – PULPIT and READER'S DESK. Dated 1630. Good work with strap decoration and bands of diamonds. – BRASSES of 1570 and 1573.

STONDON HOUSE, the former Rectory, was built about 1800.

STOW MARIES

ST MARY AND ST MARGARET. Chancel taller than the nave. The nave is C15 (see the N window of three lights with panel tracery) but was heightened in brick early in the C16, to which the trefoil-arched corbel frieze and the stepped E gable belong. – BRASS. Mary Browne † 1602, nothing special.

MOUNDS, 1½ m. SW. These are not prehistoric burial mounds but the remains of medieval salt workings.

STRATFORD

ST JOHN THE EVANGELIST, Broadway. 1832–4 by *Blore*. E.E. with lancets; yellow brick. Tall and ornate SW spire. Thin many-moulded piers with depressed arches. Clerestory and thin tie-beams with tracery. The chancel was added in 1882. – MARTYRS' MEMORIAL in the churchyard, 1879 by *J. T. Newman*. Polygonal with angle-shafts and top-heavy spire.

ST AIDAN, Ward Road. Tiny E.E. brick church, yellow and red. The style is combined with a few minimum Baroque features. The only remarkable fact is that the architect is *Sir Banister Fletcher*. The date is 1895–9 (chancel 1908).

ST FRANCIS (R.C.), Grove Crescent Road. 1868. The altar has a painting by *Bartolommeo Carducci*, a pupil of Federigo Zuccari.

CONGREGATIONAL CHURCH, The Grove.* 1868 by *Roland Plumbe*. A big monstrosity with attached portico and two façade towers of which only one was built. It has a spire. All the detail is very debased classical and ornate. The façade columns for instance have various bands.

TOWN HALL, Broadway. 1867–8 by *Giles Angell*. Enlarged 1886. The style is debased arched Cinquecento. The main accent an asymmetrical tower with a domed top. Opposite it the GURNEY MEMORIAL, a plain tall obelisk of granite, by *J. Bell*. Behind the Municipal Offices the COURT HOUSE by *Angell*, in the latest classical style usual for court houses. The material is yellow brick, the windows are arched.

WEST HAM MUNICIPAL COLLEGE, see West Ham.

Stratford, now entirely part of the East End of London, is often

* Since demolished.

mentioned under the medieval name of Stratford-atte-Bow, but that is not correct. Stratford-atte-Bow was on the London side of Bow Bridge, the bridge originally built E of Bow church early in the C12, and renewed late in the same century. The present bridge dates from 1905. It is the main gateway from London into Essex.

After crossing Bow Bridge the traveller was in the marshes of the river Lea and the river Channelsea. Here, s of the present High Street, near Abbey Road and Abbey Lane lay the Cistercian Abbey of Stratford Langthorne. Nothing at all remains now on the site. One or two fragments which were found are now in West Ham Church (see p. 416).

But a little to the w, at the end of Bisson Road, lies what is now visually the most rewarding bit of Stratford, the THREE MILLS. The area is reached by footpath along the Channelsea river with a view across it towards nothing but factories, yet owing to the foreground of water, decidedly picturesque. The mills go back to those of Stratford Langthorne Abbey. They got into the hands of a distillery in 1730, and now belong to Messrs Nicholson's Distillery. They consist of the following: The mill proper with four waterwheels, eight pairs of grinding stones, and a date plate DSB 1776. It is a tall-roofed building of two-and-a-half storeys with segment-headed windows, and the water rushing underneath. Secondly there is the former master's house of five bays,* and thirdly, opposite, the polygonal clock tower with Gothick windows. This is attached to the so-called Clock Mill. The clock tower is of 1753, the clock mill is dated 1817. The clock mill has three water wheels, fourteen pairs of grinding stones, and two drying kilns. To the NE in Abbey Lane is the ABBEY MILLS SEWAGE PUMPING STATION, 1868 by *Bazalgette* and *E. Cooper*, a building in a vaguely Italian Gothic style, but with a central lantern that adds a Russian flavour. Interior with much florid cast-iron work. The original beam engines have been removed.

The rest is quickly described. Up the High Street on the NE side YARDLEY'S BOX FACTORY, quite good, straightforward Modern, 1937 by *Higgins & Thomerson*. Nothing else here or in Broadway or in The Grove, except a few odd Late Georgian terrace houses in THE GROVE.

NW of The Grove across the railway is STRATFORD NEW TOWN, built in 1847–8. It was originally called Hudson

* Now demolished.

Town, after the railway king, and housed mainly workmen of the Eastern Counties Railway Engine Works.

A few Late Georgian houses in ROMFORD ROAD, e.g. No. 2, and more into West Ham.

STRETHALL

ST MARY. C11 chancel arch, Saxon in most details, but with a few which indicate a post-Conquest date (decoration of the capitals). The arch is similar in composition to that of St Benet's at Cambridge, that is with three strips of different sections running up the sides and round the arch, but though they look like pilaster and arch mouldings, they are quite illogically kept away from the imposts and the arch proper – a sign of lacking appreciation of what mouldings really mean. The nave is also Saxon; see the long-and-short work at the w quoins. C15 chancel and w tower. – PLATE. Cup of 1561; Paten of 1567. – MONUMENTS. Brass to a Priest, C15, the figure over 2 ft long. – Tomb-chest with quatrefoil decoration in a recess in the chancel N wall, four-centred arch and cresting.

STUBBERS see NORTH OCKENDON

STURMER

ST MARY. Away from the village, amid trees, with Sturmer Hall to the w. An C11 nave, the only evidence of which is the un-rebated N doorway with a lintel decorated with a chequer pattern. C12 S doorway with one order of columns carrying scalloped capitals, zigzag in the arch, two heads like projecting knobs at the top of the door jambs, and a tympanum decorated with two ornamental crosses and two rosettes. The latter may mean sun and moon, but why two crosses ? And why this completely unplanned arrangement ? It looks like nothing but incompetence, and it seems an odd incompetence that cannot put two almost identical shapes on the same level. The chancel is Norman too, as shown by one small N window. It was altered in the E.E. style, when three smallish separate lancet windows were inserted at the E end. C14 W tower with diagonal buttresses and pyramid roof. Early C16 S porch of brick with stepped gable. The nave roof has double hammerbeams, but they are small and the spandrels are all decorated with rather thin tracery. – PLATE. Small secular goblet of 1776.

SUTTON

ALL SAINTS. Nave and chancel with weatherboarded belfry with pyramid roof. It rests inside on eight posts, or rather on four, each of which has as a reinforcement an additional post along the N and S wall of the nave. Thus a kind of nave with aisles is created. But the curved braces start from the wall-posts and meet in the middle, while the trellis-strutting connects the nave posts from E to W. All this is C15. The rest is Norman, see the good chancel arch with one order of columns with scalloped capitals and a corresponding roll-moulding in the arch. Ornamental painting, renewed. Norman windows in the nave, and remains in the chancel. Also in the chancel a C13 lancet window. Also C13 the nave S door. Doorway with three orders of columns and manifold moulding of the arches. The S porch has a round-headed doorway dated 1633. – FONT. C13, of the Purbeck type, with five pointed shallow arcades on each side. – COMMUNION RAIL. Later C17. – PANELLING. Early C17, in the porch, probably from somewhere else. – PLATE. Cup on baluster stem of 1601. – BRASS. From the demolished church at Shopland, Thomas Stapel † 1371. In armour, but the figure mutilated.

SUTTON HALL. Early C18 front with C16 and C17 work behind.

SUTTONS see SOUTH SHOEBURY, SOUTHEND-ON-SEA

SWAN STREET see SIBLE HEDINGHAM

SWAYNES HALL see DEBDEN

TAKELEY

HOLY TRINITY. Quite a large church, and quite on its own. Norman quoins and windows in the nave, with some Roman bricks. Chancel E.E. with much renewed lancet windows. The E window is of 1874. The windows are shafted inside. C14 S aisle with characteristic (restored) window* and arcade of octagonal piers and double-chamfered arches. The easternmost respond and arch however are a little earlier, say c.1300; and evidence of a S transept preceding the S aisle. The C15 contributed the S porch and W tower. The latter has diagonal buttresses, a doorway with shields in the spandrels, a three-light W window and a niche above it. – FONT COVER. Very tall, with a lavish display of crocketed nodding ogee 30a

* The window further W in the nave must be re-used.

arches and buttresses and flying buttresses with crocketed pinnacles, tier above tier. C15 but much restored. – BENCHES. Eleven; plain, with buttresses and a little tracery. – PAINTING. Tall and narrow oil-painting of the Nativity; copy of *Romanino*'s altarpiece in S. Alessandro at Brescia.

TAKELEYS *see* EPPING UPLAND

TANHOUSE FARM *see* ULTING

TEMPLEFIELDS *see* HARLOW

TENDRING

ST EDMUND KING AND MARTYR. The interest of the church is wholly the one extremely unusual hammerbeam roof-truss close to the w end. It stands just above the N and S doorways, and so the ingenious carpenter framed these by posts, then connected them by a gable, and from these gables started his braces for the hammerbeam. The tracery detail of the gables is clearly of the C14, and not too late in the century either, and thus this truss, as far as one can say, is earlier than the hammerbeam roof of Westminster Hall, in the textbooks still called the earliest in existence. The circles with wheel figures of mouchettes might be mistaken for the Late Flamboyant sometimes found in England in the early C16 under Flemish or French influence, but the pointed trefoils etc. cannot be so late. C14 timber porch, C13 nave and chancel, see two N windows. The W tower of 1876. – FONT. Octagonal, with elaborate foliage and shields in the panels. – PLATE. Cup of 1567. – MONUMENT. Edmund Saunder † 1615, small, alabaster, with kneeling figure.

TERLING

ALL SAINTS. The best piece is the W tower of 1732 with arched doorway and arched windows, their surrounds consisting of rustication of alternating sizes. The rest not impressive from outside. C19 N aisle, completely renewed S aisle. The chancel seems to be of the C13. It has one small lancet window on the N side, and otherwise windows of c.1300. Nice C15 timber porch. Inside, three-bay C15 S arcade with octagonal piers with concave sides and wave-moulded arches. The low many-moulded tower arch is proof of the existence of a previous C13 tower. – FONT. C13, octagonal, of Purbeck marble, with

two shallow blank pointed arches on each side. – COM-
MUNION RAIL. Early C18, with slim twisted balusters. –
BRASSES. Two large early C16 kneeling figures (3 ft 11 in. and
3 ft 10 in.), and two groups of kneeling figures of 1558 and
1584.

The village is specially attractive. Immediately N of the church
the delightful small MANOR HOUSE with exposed timbers,
two cross-gables, and a large W chimneystack decorated with
a blank stepped gable. Octagonal chimney-shafts. The house
dates from the C15 and still has the original king-post truss of
the central hall. Late C16 panelling in another room. N of the
church also the CONGREGATIONAL CHURCH, a modest
rectangular building, 1753, of three bays with mullion-and-
transom-cross windows. Inside is a brass candelabrum of the
C17.

TERLING PLACE. Large Georgian house of white brick. The
centre is by *John Johnson* and was built in 1772–*c.*1780. It had
its original entrance on the garden side, and here therefore is
now blank arcading on the ground floor. On the upper floor
a display of attached columns. In 1818 wings were added at an
odd angle, ending in little temple fronts *in antis* with pediments. It all does not hang together very well. At the same
time the entrance was turned the other way, a porch with
Tuscan columns built, and short projecting blocks, to its l. and
r. One of these houses the new staircase. The area of the
old staircase was made into a proud Neo-Greek Saloon going
through two storeys. It is a perfect room of its date. Its chief
decoration is a frieze by *J. Henning Sen.*, based on that of the
Parthenon, a very recent British acquisition at the time. A gallery runs round the room above the frieze with a beautiful
cast-iron railing and Ionic columns of yellow marble. The
ceiling is made into a shallow saucer-dome. The Library also
dates from the same time, whereas the Drawing Room has
the delicate plasterwork of Johnson's time. Much re-decorat-
ing was done in 1850, and the conservatory was then added.

WINDMILL, ½ m. NW of the church. A smock-mill in a good
state of preservation.

(RINGER'S FARM, 1 m. SW. Timber-framed house of *c.*1400.
The original doorway to the screens passage is preserved. It
has a two-centred arch and tracery decoration in the spandrels.
R.C.)

TEWES *see* LITTLE SAMPFORD

THAXTED

Thaxted in the C14 and C15 was one of the most prosperous towns of Essex. Its present population of about 1,800 makes one forget that it vied in business importance with Saffron Walden and indeed many towns now ten and twenty times as populous. Yet only by remembering that can the size of the church be understood.

ST JOHN THE BAPTIST. The church, as we see it now, appears at first all of one piece, proud, spacious, clear and a little frigid inside, and outside dominated by its splendid tall steeple. The spire reaches 181 ft up; the church is 183 ft long. The material is pebble rubble. Ashlar is not used; but otherwise, in innumerable details, it is obvious that much money was spent on the building. It is embattled all round, pinnacles are used in addition to battlements, decorative friezes of ornament or figures appear here and there, and so on. The church has often been restored, but care has always been taken and, except for the C18 windows of the transept fronts, not much has been changed. The spire, it is true, was struck by lightning in 1814 and had to be rebuilt, but the reconstruction was accurate. The tower has setback buttresses, but the angles are not of 90 degrees. They form two sides of a polygon. At the top of the tower battlements and panelled pinnacles connected by flying buttresses to the spire. This is of Northamptonshire type, with crockets and three tiers of dormer windows. Niches to the l. and r. of the W door and the W window. The aisle windows are identical on the N and S sides, with depressed heads and panel tracery – mostly four lights; five at the W end. The chancel chapels have long, straight-headed windows, again identical on the N and S sides and again with panel tracery. The E window is huge, of five lights, and has an odd mixture of Perp detail and intersections. Both porches are two-storeyed, but that on the S side (the earlier – built between 1362 and 1368) is slightly less sumptuous. Even so it has a main S doorway and subsidiary doorways from the E and W, three-light side openings, and a star-shaped tierceron-vault. The N porch vault has liernes as well and many bosses. This porch is taller than the other, in fact almost as high as the transept, which is most effective when one looks at the church from the NW. The doorway has large shields in the spandrels, two upper windows side by side, with fleuron surrounds, a turret at the NW angle which is higher than the porch, and a figure-frieze below the battle-

ments. There are even head-stops to the gables of the first
set-offs of the buttresses. A similar figure frieze below the
battlements can also be noticed in the N transept, and there
are many more minor enrichments, gargoyles, etc.

The interior in its present form is white and bared of all
major furnishings, though there are plenty of smaller objects
of devotion about, mostly brought in recently. The surprising
lightness is largely due to the fact that clear glass is used everywhere. The arcades are the earliest element of the church. [19]
They date from c.1340. The piers are quatrefoil with very
thin shafts in the diagonals. The two-centred arches have
mouldings with two quadrants. The hood-moulds rest on comparatively big head-stops. The crossing arch belongs to the
same C14 church.

The C15 rebuilding proceeded as follows: S transept late
C14, N transept c.1400, N aisle widened and N porch added
c.1445; steeple probably late C15, chancel and chancel chapels,
crossing arches to N, S, and E, and clerestory c.1510. The date
of the S transept can be deduced from the fine blank arcading
below the S window, with alternating pointed and coupled ogee
arches, all crocketed richly. The date of the N transept appears
in the corresponding arcading on the N side and the fine RERE-
DOS on the E wall with ogee-headed niches and a frieze above
in which Christ appears between censing angels. The tall
tower arch and the vault inside the tower must be C15. The
chancel arcades of c.1510 have an interesting, very complex
pier section: semicircular shafts to the arches, but to the chancel a combination of thin shafts and thin hollows not having a
capital but turning round to the l. and r. above the arches to
form frames. In the arch spandrels is broad simple openwork
tracery. The roofs of all parts of the church are original, and all
are flat-pitched. Tie-beams are used only in the chancel. The
figures of the brackets and the bosses will repay some attention.

FONT CASE AND COVER. Case with two tiers of traceried
panels hiding the font completely. Top with buttresses,
canopies, finial, etc., a little broader and heavier than at Littlebury. – PULPIT. A fine late C17 piece with garlands hanging
down the angles between the panels. The staircase with twisted
balusters does not belong. – COMMUNION RAIL. With twisted
balusters; c.1700. – SCREENS to the N and S chapels late C17,
with a frieze of thick openwork foliage scrolls. – DOOR. In the
N doorway, with traceried panels, C15. – ORGAN. Said to have

been made by *John Harris* for St John's Chapel, Bedford Row, London in 1703. – BENCHES. A number of French (?) benches of the mid C17 with tall ends. – STAINED GLASS. Many figures and other fragments have been distributed over N and s windows. The most notable are the early C16 figures of Saints in the N windows, the late C14 figure in the s transept s window, and the stories from Genesis, with small figures, of *c.*1450, in a s aisle window. – E window and N chapel E window by *Kempe*, the former 1900, the latter 1907. – PLATE. Cup of 1562; large Cup of 1622; Paten on foot of 1632; Almsdish of 1795. – MONUMENT. Brass to a Priest (chancel), *c.*1450. The dearth of monuments more than anything tends to give Thaxted church that curious atmosphere of remoteness which one cannot help feeling directly one enters.

PERAMBULATION. The church lies high up, at the N end of the town, visible as a climax from everywhere. The other climax in the landscape, curiously enough, is the WINDMILL, not far to the s, a tower-mill of compact form, as it has lost its sails, in complete contrast to the articulate, manifold form of the church. The streets approaching the church from the N and W have little of individual merit, and it may as well be said at once that Thaxted is not rich in houses of special qualities. Except for the Guildhall there is nothing that will be remembered singly, like Paycocke's House at Great Cogges-hall or the Monk's Barn at Newport, or Cromwell House at Saffron Walden. Yet the town as a whole is very perfect, chiefly because there is truly not one house in it that would appear violently out of place. All is in scale, nothing too high or too ostentatious, mostly white, cream, pink plastering or exposed timber-framing. The walk will start at the exit from the church, and here, on the s side, are two rows of white ALMSHOUSES, one thatched, the other with a bargeboarded N gable. Opposite the N porch lies the Swan Hotel with a Late Georgian nine-bay front, which was originally of eleven bays and went right to the corner of Newbiggen Street – an excellent quiet start. Then some cottages, and then CLARENCE HOUSE, the only ambitious C18 house at Thaxted, early C18 without doubt. It has a seven-bay front of two storeys with segment-headed windows and a doorway with a segmental pediment carried on Corinthian pilasters. The frieze below the pediment rises characteristically in the middle. The rain-water heads indeed give the date 1715. After that modest cottages climbing down the hill.

So the hub of Thaxted is reached, the GUILDHALL, free-stand- 44
ing on three sides, three-storeyed with two overhangs, the
ground floor open with arched posts, the first floor also arched
between the studs (this however was done during a C20 restoration), the second with two pairs of diagonals indicating a division into two which is carried on by the hipped
roofs. The Guildhall is in the best position of the town, at the
top end of Town Street, where it forks. Between the two main
prongs, immediately l. of the Guildhall, a narrow lane leads up
to the churchyard. In it, just behind the Guildhall, an impressive, very picturesque group of three more timber-framed and
overhanging houses.* They date from the C15, as does the
Guildhall also. TOWN STREET is a much quieter sight. The
best houses are close to the Guildhall on the s side, first one
(C15?) with the upper overhang supported by three canted
oriel windows. The doorway has Tuscan columns and a pediment. Then, after a few more, the RECORDER'S HOUSE,
whose C15 overhangs are supported on the ground floor as
well as the first floor by two canted oriel windows each, a
remarkable sight. Opposite, next to the Cock Inn THE
PRIORY with a nice Neo-Georgian front of 1938 with two
bow windows on the ground floor and an iron balcony above,
but inside the remains of a late medieval hall with a wagon
roof, an unusual feature in Essex, and decorative wall paintings of the late C16, geometrical as well as of big leaves.

Near the foot of Town Street, on the N side a house, formerly
the Duke's Head Inn, which preserves the original C14 timber
ceiling of what was the carriageway in.

At the foot of Town Street, roads branch off in various directions.
Down Park Street lies PARK FARM, of the early C16 with a
probably original chimneystack and some original ceilings.
Down MILL END two houses which now form part of a
factory. One is of brick and dates from the early C16. It has an
original queen-post roof with wind-braces.

(PROUD'S FARM, 1¼ m. NNW. Timber-framed C15 house with
later alterations and additions, but original moulded beams
and doorheads and part of the original roofs. R.C.)

HORHAM HALL, see p. 243.

THEYDON BOIS

ST MARY. By *Sydney Smirke*, 1850. A small, rather ugly brick

* In one of these late C16 wall-paintings of foliage and birds have recently
been found.

church, with an unconventional s w tower with spire. The roof goes low down on the s side and has dormer windows. – PULPIT. Nice piece in the C18 style with back panels and a small canopy. By *Paul Waterhouse*.

THEYDON HALL. Yellow brick; Late Georgian.

THEYDON GARNON

ALL SAINTS. The historical interest of the church lies in the fact that the brick w tower is dated by an inscription (s side) 1520 and the brick N aisle (E gable) 1644. In the tower blue bricks are used as well but apparently without system. w doorway and w window are in all probability of the C18. The original bell-openings have two lights, and there are battlements. The N aisle is also of red brick; the difference between Early Tudor and C17 bricks can be studied. The windows unfortunately are renewed. Of 1644 also is the aisle arcade inside. It is of five bays, entirely of timber, with octagonal piers and round arches. Of the other parts of the church the chancel seems to be C13, see one restored s lancet window. The E window is quite ambitious C15 work. As for the nave, the prettiest feature, the two dormers, look Victorian now (restoration 1885), but appear in an illustration in the *Gentleman's Magazine* of 1810.* – PULPIT, with large finely detailed tester, staircase with elegant twisted balusters, and attached Reader's Desk, *c.*1710. – COMMUNION RAIL. With twisted balusters, 1683–4.* – PLATE. Cup of 1562, with bands of ornament; Paten C17; two Flagons of 1650; Plate and Paten on foot probably of 1701. – MONUMENTS. Brass to William Kirkeby, rector, † 1458, the figure *c.* 3 ft long, with engraved orphreys. – Recess in the chancel N wall, containing a tomb-chest with two cusped lozenges on the front. The arch is depressed, a straight horizontal on quadrant curves, and has a quatrefoil frieze above. Kneeling figure of brass of *c.*1520 against the back wall. – Similar recess in the chancel s wall, without figures. – Ellen Branch † 1567, small grey stone tablet with ogee arch. Inside the arch brass plate with kneeling figure. – Several monuments to members of the Archer family. The most spectacular is to William Eyre Archer † 1739, a standing wall-monument with a grey sarcophagus, and a grey obelisk. Two seated cherubs l. and r. of the sarcophagus. Against the obelisk hovers another cherub just above the portrait medallion of the deceased. Unsigned.

* Information kindly provided by Mr A. A. Dibben.

THEYDON MOUNT

ST MICHAEL. Small brick church of 1611–14,* built in the grounds of Hill Hall by the Smith family, owners of the mansion. The w tower is not high. It has diagonal buttresses and battlements and a (later?) recessed shingled spire. The w window has intersected tracery. So has the E window. The other windows are of two lights under straight hood-moulds. The details do not seem to differ between w parts and chancel. Yet the bricks and the building are too different to allow for the same date. The stair-turret adjoins the tower on the s and ends in a segmental gable. The windows are double slits of very odd forms. The s porch has a more elaborately shaped gable and a four-centred doorway and above it an uneasily balanced aedicule of Tuscan pilasters with pediment. The nave roof has collar-beams on arched braces which form semicircles. – FONT. Unusually small, of stone, attached to the wall like a stoup; it stands on a pillar, and the bowl is as elegant as a hand-washing fountain in a Hall. – REREDOS. Late C17, with coupled Corinthian pilasters l. and r. of the E window. – BENCHES. Plain, late C16. – HELMS. One, C17, in the chancel, probably belonging to the monument of 1631. – PLATE. Cup and Paten of 1587; Cup with bands of ornament and Paten of 1614; large Dish on foot inscribed 1698. – MONUMENTS. All to the Smith family, an impressive series, crowding the small chancel. Sir Thomas, † 1577 (on his career see below). Standing wall-monument. Figure stiffly reclining, head propped up on elbow. Shallow coffered arch behind the figure, flanked by two black Ionic columns with an entablature carrying two obelisks and a large achievement. Fine inscription plate with bold strapwork and fruit surround under the arch. – Sir William † 1626 and wife. Standing wall-monument with two effigies both stiffly reclining with head on elbow; he a little higher and behind her. The background more or less as before and very little stylistic change. Kneeling figures of children against the front of the tomb-chest. – Sir William † 1631 and two wives. Standing wall-monument with recumbent effigy. Three big kneeling figures behind and above. – Sir Thomas † 1668. Standing wall-monument, of black and white marble, with no superstructure. The effigy again semi-reclining, head propped up on elbow. Thick angle volutes ending in cherubs' heads. – Sir Edward † 1713, simple white marble tablet, with a cherub's

* The date was found by Mr A. A. Dibben in the church registers.

head at the foot. By *Edward Stanton*. – The Rev. Sir Edward
Bowyer Smith † 1850. Large Perp Gothic tablet by '*Osmond,
Sarum*'.

HILL HALL. Hill Hall is, in spite of its moderate size, one of the
most important earlier Elizabethan houses in the country. This
fact is on the whole too little appreciated. One or two of its
features are quite exceptional and of high architectural sig-
nificance. It is true that much has later been altered, but the
Royal Commission has exaggerated the extent of these alterations. For instance the Commission says 'All the ornamental
work of the courtyard is modern'. That is hardly right, and it
is indeed the decoration of the courtyard which more than
anything else deserves special attention. To understand its
meaning one has to realize that Hill Hall was built by Sir
Thomas Smith, who died in 1578 and is buried in the church
of Theydon Mount. He was unquestionably a remarkable man.
He graduated and lectured at Cambridge, went to Paris, Or-
leans, and Padua in 1540–2, took a D.C.L. at Padua, got
interested in the minutiae of Greek pronunciation, became
Vice-Chancellor of Cambridge University, and then went into
politics to serve Protector Somerset. Somerset, as is witnessed
by all that is recorded of Old Somerset House of *c*.1546–9,
was the leader of an architectural group believing in the
Renaissance as a style rather than as a fashion of decoration.
Their work – Sharington of Lacock Abbey and Thynne of
Longleat were the other chief members – has more affinities
with France than with Italy. Smith later on was for a time
Provost of Eton, and then became M.P. and in 1562 Ambas-
sador to France. While there he must have taken an interest
in architecture; for Lord Burghley in a letter of 1568 refers to
a French book on architecture which he had seen at Smith's
house. In France Smith travelled with the Court, for instance
to Toulouse. In 1566 he was back in England. After that he
spent three years in retirement in Essex, and it was in 1568–9★
that the courtyard of Hill Hall was given its present form.
The building of the house itself had already been started in
1557.

What the house was like externally it is difficult now to
assess. The brickwork is original, but most of the windows are
sashed, and many have their shapes altered. The N front still
has original windows with mullion-and-transom crosses,
but the porch of four Tuscan columns, the pediment, and the

★ Mrs Dewar's recent research makes 1575 a more likely date than 1568–9.

lantern are all C18. The E front of seven bays, the show side
of the house, seems indeed entirely Queen Anne in style, with
stone quoins and big stone dressings of the windows, segmental arches to the windows, and a three-bay, slightly projecting centre with a big pediment decorated by a coat of arms
and garlands. The only surprising features are four giant Tuscan columns, two and two, on tall bases not carrying more
than fragments of entablature. They stand just inside the outer
quoins and at the angles of the middle projection. One might
accept them with hesitation as of the late C17, when, it is
known, the house underwent alterations, but the S front has
the same motif again in an even less usual form. This front is
irregular with three Elizabethan gabled dormer windows and
two big projecting blocks at the corners, three storeys high
instead of the two storeys of the rest of the house. Against each
of these blocks again stand, widely spaced, two Tuscan giant
columns. Could they be Elizabethan? It would be a unique
occurrence in England and indeed in Europe.

The clue lies perhaps in the courtyard. Here the windows
are of the mullion-and-transom-cross type, and they are separated by two orders of short attached columns, Tuscan below,
with an incorrectly spaced metope frieze, and Ionic above.
Now that is a very classical motif, even if awkwardly handled
by Smith's architect. The name of the architect is incidentally
known from Smith's will. He left 'to his architect *Richard
Kirby*' £20 to be paid out on completion of the house. That
the columns belong to his work and not the C18, as the Royal
Commission says, seems to me evident from the total lack of
classical experience in their proportions and detailing. Their
precedent is not Palladio but the French C16, a house especially such as Bournazel (Aveyron) of 1545, which Smith may
well have seen from Toulouse.

Of the interiors, an early C17 fireplace and staircase in the
N wing, an Elizabethan fireplace and the colonnades of *c.*1912
in the Hall in the S wing, and also the elegant early C18 staircase projecting from the S wing, deserve special notice. The
most interesting interior feature by far is, however, a cycle of
C16 wall paintings of which considerable remains survive. [51]
They are done in the style of tapestry hangings with thick
fruit and foliage borders and show scenes from the story of
Cupid and Psyche after engravings made by the so-called
Master of the Die from Raphael designs. The most spectacular
scene is a battle with a weird jumble of intertwined figures in

the Mannerist style. The house is now administered by the Prison Commissioners.

THISTLEY HALL *see* DEBDEN

THORNDON HALL*

Built by *James Paine* for Lord Petre. Begun in 1764. Big rectangular block, eleven bays wide, connected by nine-bay quarter-circle colonnades to lower three-bay pavilions. White brick on a rusticated ground floor. This has right in the middle of the entrance front a plain, rather insignificant Tuscan porch. The three main windows above this have aedicule surrounds; the central one is arched. The outer windows l. and r. are of the Venetian variety. Top balustrade, above which the three-bay centre pediment does not rise. The colonnades are arched on the ground floor and provided with attached Ionic columns above. The pavilions also have centre pediments. The show piece of the house is the six-column giant portico (Corinthian columns) towards the garden. It stands, as usual with Paine, above the rusticated ground floor. The house was burnt out in 1878, and the only remaining room of consequence is the CHAPEL in the E wing. It reaches through two storeys and has two orders of columns on the short sides. The upper one at the N (ritual E) end screens off a shallow apse. (Hidden in the grounds, MAUSOLEUM AND CHANTRY CHAPEL for the Petre family by *A. W. N. Pugin*. FARMHOUSE, on the hill, by *Paine*, built before 1777. Four red brick towers form a square closed on three sides by colonnades. The grounds were laid out in 1766–72 by *Capability Brown* at a cost of £5,000. Near the pond, the Octagon Plantation by *Bourginion* remains from an earlier scheme planned under the eighth Lord Petre.)

THORPE HALL *see* SOUTHCHURCH, SOUTHEND-ON-SEA

THORPE-LE-SOKEN

ST MICHAEL. 1876 by *W. White*. The early C16 brick W tower was allowed to remain. Blue brick diapers, diagonal buttresses. The bell-openings of two lights with a circle as

* Recent excavations on the site of Old Thorndon Hall have shown three main periods of construction and alteration, from 1414 to 1570–90. Most of the ground plan has been recovered.

tracery – all in brick. A pretty weather-vane of 1902 on a kind of needle spirelet. – FONT. Octagonal, Perp; the sides have star-shaped panels with shields. – SCREEN. S chapel, C15. The tracery of each division is of two intersected ogee arches, cusped and crocketed. – PLATE. Paten on foot, 1695. – MONUMENT. Effigy in chain-mail of a knight, his legs crossed; c.1300. The effigy lies under a canopy with thin diapered angle buttresses and a cusped and sub-cusped ogee arch. Thick band of crocketing with large bossy leaves.

Nice village street. At its W end, on the S side, COMARQUES, largish Georgian red brick house, once the home of Arnold Bennett. On the other side just E of the church the ABBEY HOUSE, which, cemented as its surfaces are, looks rather Neo-Tudor of 1840 now, but is in fact original, with diagonally set chimney-shafts, two-stepped end gables, and a two-storeyed embattled porch. Over the porch an odd crocketed pinnacle. The material is brick, the date can hardly be later than 1550. S of the Abbey House is THORPE HALL in its own grounds, built of white brick in 1823. A wing was added in 1926.

THORRINGTON

ST MARY MAGDALEN. Fine East Anglian W tower, specially interesting because dated. In the floor of the tower a BRASS inscription to John Deth † 1477 and Margery, his wife, † 1483, 'specialis benefactor istius ecclesie et campanile ejusdem'. The tower is of knapped flint with diagonal buttresses, a three-light W window, two-light bell-openings, and battlements with flushwork panels – all in the style of the Brightlingsea tower (which can be seen across the fields to the W) but a little more modest. The church itself is of pebbles – the N aisle looks as though it were a cobble pavement put up vertically. C14 S porch with quoins of tiles on the pattern of the Norman use of Roman bricks. N aisle arcade of 1866, ornate and lifeless. – FONT. Octagonal, Perp. Stem with buttresses and tracery panels, bowl with leaves and shields. – BRASS. John Clare † 1564 and family. Only one wife and some children remain.

At the head of Alresford Creek a derelict TIDE MILL (cf. Fingringhoe) with a date stone 1831.

THUNDERSLEY

ST PETER. On a hill with wide views around. Small. Nave and aisles under one big steep roof. The eaves no more than nine feet from the ground. Chancel of 1885. Belfry, shingled, with broach-spire. Immediately behind the large three-light Perp w window with panel tracery the timber substructure of the bell-turret, not one of the more impressive ones. The arcades of N and S aisles are of the first half of the C13. Circular piers with stiff-leaf capitals of upright leaves and slightly double-hollow-chamfered arches. – FONT. Small, octagonal, Perp with quatrefoil panels. – HELM and SWORD, probably funerary. – PLATE. Cup with band of ornament and Paten, both of 1569.

RECTORY. 1830.

Thundersley is now mostly part of the dormitory miles of Rayleigh and Southend.

TILBURY DOCKS and TILBURY FORT

The DOCKS were built in the 1880s and opened in 1886. The plans are by *A. Manning*. – New Landing Stage, Baggage Halls, and Offices 1925–30 by *Sir Edwin Cooper*, brick and stone, in that architect's formal Neo-Georgian, with symmetrically placed cupolas, big stone surrounds of arches à la Somerset House, etc. *

It is rewarding to compare these large commercial installations of the C19 and C20 with TILBURY FORT a little lower down the river, built in 1670–83 against the Dutch and French, a much more modest job, also primarily utilitarian, but also consciously for display. The fort was designed by the Dutchman *Sir Bernard de Gomme*, a military engineer under Charles II. In plan it is a pentagon, though one of the five bastions was never built. Another enclosed a blockhouse of the time of Henry VIII. Much of the fort was remodelled in 1868. Emplacements of *c.*1913 mask those of 1868. The GATEWAY, 58a similar to that of the Plymouth Citadel, has a ground floor of the triumphal arch type, with four Ionic demi-columns, an archway with depressed head and trophies in the spandrels, and an upper storey only as wide as the centre part below. Two Corinthian columns carry a segmental pediment. To the l. and r. above the side parts below thickly carved trophies. The type of gateway derives from C17 France; the style is more robust and a little fussier than that of Sir Christopher Wren. The view from the Fort across the wide river towards Gravesend is impressive.

* Good new SIGNAL BOX by British Railways, Eastern Region (Regional Architect, *H. H. Powell*).

TILBURY-JUXTA-CLARE

St Margaret. In the fields under a few large trees. c15 nave and chancel and early c16 brick tower with blue brick diapering, diagonal buttresses, battlements, and a higher stair-turret. Perp windows in nave and chancel. – PULPIT with two tiers of arches with plaited ornament in each panel; Elizabethan. – PAINTINGS. Fragments of wall paintings of the late c15, with late c16 overpainting, on N and S walls. Chiefly ornamental, but also a scene with a man holding a white horse and standing in front of a half-timbered house which exhibits clearly its brick-nogging between the timber studs. In the chancel, in imitation of the ornamental parts of the old work, very rustic wall decoration. – PLATE. Cup and Paten c.1600.

TILLINGHAM

St Nicholas. The nave N doorway is Norman. Fine E.E. chancel with three stepped E lancets and a quatrefoil above and single lancets on the N and S sides – all renewed outside. The plain SEDILIA and PISCINA also belong to the c13. c14 S arcade of four bays with octagonal piers and double-chamfered arches, renewed probably when the S aisle was rebuilt in 1866. The chancel arch of the same style. The W tower also is c14, with angle buttresses and W window of two cusped lights with pointed quatrefoil in the spandrel. The battlements are later. – FONT. Late Norman, with plain square bowl on quatrefoil foot with attached angle shafts. Carved foliage. – PLATE. Large Cup of 1616. – BRASS to Edward Wiot † 1584, kneeling figure (chancel S wall, behind a door in the panelling).

Nice village street widening just S of the church into a Green. Many weatherboarded cottages. A number of these were erected as late as 1881 by the Dean and Chapter of St Paul's, who are lords of the manor.

REDDINGS, 1 m. SW. c16 house with gabled cross-wings on the l. and r. Timber-framed and plastered.

TILTY

Foundation of a Cistercian ABBEY in 1153. It was laid out as usual with the church S of the cloister, the refectory N, the chapter house and dormitory E, and the cellarer's quarters W of it. All that survives is a few fragments of the E wall of the cellarer's range with springers of a vault. But much further S is the parish church of Tilty, ST MARY THE VIRGIN, and this was once the *cappella ante portas* of the monastery (cf. Little Coggeshall). The nave is E.E. with lancet windows, and very similar to the chapel of Little Coggeshall. The three W lancets are particularly handsome. The two plain doorways on the N and S sides are also original. The chapel was, as at Coggeshall, originally nave and chancel in one, see the E window on the S side, with a higher sill than the others to leave space for the PISCINA. The S porch is pargeted and probably C17. The belfry and cupola on the nave seem to be of the C18. Early in the C14 a chancel was added, taller, wider, and much more ambitious, the gift of a rich man, or a beginning of a larger rebuilding scheme. It is in the sumptuous style of the moment, with a five-light E window the tracery of which is of a very personal style, niches outside to the l. and r. of the window, placed at an angle and cutting halfway into the buttresses, a three-light N window of more usual character, and a two-light S window with a higher sill to allow for the SEDILIA and PISCINA below. These have cusped arches, the cusping being also of quite a personal pattern. The windows are shafted inside and have hood-moulds with head-stops. Head-stops also to the l. and r. of the sedilia-piscina group. – PLATE. Cup of 1665; Paten on foot probably also of 1665; Paten on foot of 1689. – BRASSES to Gerard Danet, Councillor to Henry VIII, † 1520 and wife, the figures 3 ft long; to George Medeley † 1562 and wife, with 2 ft figures; to Margaret Tuke † 1590, with kneeling figures.

TIPTOFTS
1½ m. WSW Wimbish

Tiptofts Manor House is one of the most valuable survivals of medieval domestic architecture in Essex, although from outside that is hardly visible. It is a house of *c.*1350 with its hall complete, and what is more, an aisled hall, and what is yet more, a hall not horizontally subdivided. So, standing in it, one sees one slim detached quatrefoil pier with fillets to the shafts and a moulded capital just as in a church, and the pier opposite now partly in a later wall so that the existence of the second aisle can only be deduced from the existence of the mortice of a former horizontal strut. The piers carry traceried curved braces with the very simple motif of a large pointed trefoil. On the tie-beam stands an octagonal crown-post with capital which in its turn carries four-way struts, again exactly as in Essex churches. There were originally three roof trusses in the hall, the middle pair not resting on shafts but on hammerbeams to gain more space in the centre of the hall. The third pair is not visible. What is however clearly visible is to the l. of the piers one two-centred arch with decorated spandrels and indications of a second. There were no doubt three and they led into buttery, kitchen, and pantry in the way familiar from larger houses and university colleges.*

TIPTREE

ST LUKE. 1855 by *Ewan Christian*, small, apsed, red brick, no tower.

WINDMILL. A tower-mill kept in a very satisfactory state.

TIPTREE PRIORY, 2 m. SW. Fragment of an Elizabethan brick mansion. What remains looks now excessively tall and rather gaunt. It was the l. half of the frontage of a house which in addition had one or perhaps two lower wings coming forward. The chief features are a doorway with a four-centred head and a big steep pediment above and a number of transomed four- and five-light windows, some of them (especially those in the E wall) re-used.

TOLLESBURY

A little town rather like a village, with a real square by the church. At the NW corner of the churchyard, in the square, the LOCKUP, a small weatherboarded shed with an iron grille in the door.‡

ST MARY. Nave and W tower CII, see the nave N and S windows and the rere-arch of the S doorway. The tower was heightened in brick about 1600. It has stepped battlements. The chancel was rebuilt in 1872 (by *E. Habershon & Brock*). – FONT. Octagonal, C18, with an inscription: 'Good people all I pray take care, That in ye church you do not sware. As this man did'. – STAINED GLASS. E window by *Kempe*, 1902. – PLATE. Cup of 1562 with three bands of ornament. – MONUMENTS. Brasses to Thomas Freshwater † 1517 and wife, figures of

---

* It is Mr J. T. Smith's opinion that about 1350 the whole house was a single range comprising a hall in the middle with the two ends compartmented off. He tells me the present buttery wing is clearly a rebuilding of something earlier which continued the line of the hall roof, and this may well also be true of the cross-wing at the upper end.

‡ Since reconstructed.

17 in. length. – Jane Gardiner † 1654. Handsome tablet with oval inscription plate surrounded by fanciful scrolls and crowned by an open scrolly pediment.

TOLLESBURY HALL, s of the church. C15, timber-framed, with cross-wings.

BOURCHIER'S HALL, 1 m. NW. According to the Royal Commission the house still contains, inside the loft, the C14 roof of the hall, with tie-beams, curved braces forming a two-centred arch, octagonal king-post with capital and four-way struts.

GUISNES COURT, w of Bourchier's Hall. In a room panelling and a fine fireplace of c.1600 from Bourchier's Hall.

TOLLESHUNT D'ARCY

ST NICHOLAS. All Perp with embattled w tower with diagonal buttresses, and embattled s side. In the N chancel chapel a brick window. The most attractive feature is the coved ceiling inside the nave with bands of stylized flower and leaf decoration, designed by the *Rev. E. Geldart* of Little Braxted at the time of the restoration of 1897. – FONT. Octagonal, Perp, with shields and rosettes in the panels. – MONUMENTS. Brass panels, convincingly explained as the bottom strip of the border of a large Flemish brass panel of c.1390 (cf. Wensley Yorkshire). In the corners the lion of St Mark and the ox of St Luke, in the middle the Virgin and Child with, to the l. and r., St Bartholomew and St Philip. – Brasses to a man and woman of c.1425, to Anthony Darcy † 1540 (very curious; it is either a copy of a C14 figure or such a figure re-used; the figure is c.4 ft long), to a woman of c.1540, to Philippa Darcy † 1559. The two brasses of 1540 are palimpsests of older brasses. – Monument to an unknown person; in the chancel s wall. Recess with depressed segmental top and a quatrefoil frieze above. Indents of brasses in the back wall. Perhaps also used as an Easter Sepulchre. Converted into SEDILIA. – Thomas d'Arcy † 1593 and wife, with the usual kneeling figures.

TOLLESHUNT D'ARCY HALL. Fine MOAT with an Elizabethan BRIDGE of four round arches as the only approach to the house. The bridge is dated 1585 and built of bands of brick and stone. The main block of the house is of c.1500 and still possesses the tie-beams, king-posts, and four-way struts of the original hall roof, two wooden doorways from the screens passage to the offices, and the large hall chimney. In the w wing, which was remodelled in the late C17, is a room on the ground floor which contains good panelling of the first half of the C16, partly linenfold, partly with Early Renaissance foliage, vases, medallions with heads, etc. The beams of this room must be original; they are handsomely carved yet without any Renaissance interference. To the NE a late C16 square brick DOVECOTE with the usual square nesting niches in all four walls.

(D'ARCY HOUSE. The house has a fine Georgian front. Mr P. Russell Walker)

TOLLESHUNT KNIGHTS

ALL SAINTS. No village is anywhere near the church. Nor did the church at the time of writing give the impression of being much cared for.* Nave (with a bellcote probably of c.1880) and chancel. The details not of special interest. – FONT. Late C14, square with traceried panels. – MONUMENT. Knight of c.1380, holding his heart in his hands. Much defaced.

TOLLESHUNT MAJOR

ST NICHOLAS. A humble church of nave and chancel, with a nice s porch added in 1888 to the designs of the *Rev. E. Geldart*, rector of Little Braxted. In front of this small church, probably about 1540–5, Stephen Beckingham of Beckingham Hall decided to place a brick w tower, much too big for the older building. It is patterned with diapers of blue brick and has diagonal buttresses with four set-offs and very low battlements. The w windows are of three and two lights, the bell-openings of three with a depressed pointed head. Original roofs. – FONT. Placed against the s wall. Half an octagon, Perp, with rosettes and shields. – PAINTING. On the s wall remains of a C15 figure. – PLATE. C17 Cup.

BECKINGHAM HALL. A partly timber-framed and partly brick-built house of the C16, as there are many. To this however was added, probably as a beginning for an ambitious rebuilding of the whole, a brick gatehouse to the N which forms the centre of a long brick wall with angle turrets. The E turret is as thin as a pinnacle, the w turret is one gatepost, as it were, of a gateway of which the other post is also a turret. The main gatehouse has two circular turrets to the outside and two to the

* This is no longer so.

inside. The doorways have four-centred heads, and above them are two-light windows. The date of all this can be deduced from the facts that Stephen Beckingham obtained the manor from Henry VIII in 1540 and that a piece of ornamental panelling from the farmhouse itself at the Victoria and Albert Museum is dated 1546. It has fine Early Renaissance decoration, rather in the style of the stalls and screen of the chapel of King's College Cambridge. Especially the central bearded demi-figure in a medallion is comparable.

TOPPESFIELD

St Margaret of Antioch. w tower of 1699, built of red brick. On the w side together with other names that of the bricklayer, *Daniel Hill*, is recorded. The tower has arched windows and battlements with obelisk pinnacles. The distinguishing feature is the semicircular troughs between the battlements. The church is of the c14. It has a s aisle with an arcade on octagonal piers, carrying double-chamfered arches. The chancel on its s side has a group of cusped arches, first a low broad recess, then two single SEDILIA seats and then the PISCINA. In the recess a low tomb-chest with quatrefoil decoration. The windows are all Perp. – STAINED GLASS. In the s aisle E window small figure of the c15: Coronation of the Virgin and one censing angel. – MONUMENTS. Knight of *c.*1260, cross-legged with flat-topped pot-helmet, Purbeck marble (below the organ). – Brass to John Cracherod † 1534 and wife (also below the organ). – Dorcas Smyth † 1633. By *John Colt*, son of the more famous Maximilian Colt. The monument is a display of emblems, without effigy: beehive for Industria Dulcis, heart for Spes, hand pointing upward for Caritas. Originally there was also a dove for Fides. On the sides open books with their titles now alas mostly illegible.

Windmill, Gainford End. A dilapidated tower-mill.

(Toppesfield Hall, ½ m. se. Early c17, much altered, but with some original panelling and an early c17 fireplace from Oliver's Farm. r.c.)

(Cust Hall, ¾ m. ssw. Originally built *c.*1500. Of that date the E front with oversailing upper storey; carved bressumer. Original chimneystack on the w side. Richly moulded beams inside. r.c.)

(Bradfield's Farm, 1 m. sw. Inside some c16 wall painting with flower and leaf designs. r.c.)

TRIPLE DYKE see COLCHESTER

TWINSTEAD

ST JOHN THE EVANGELIST. 1860. Nave, chancel, and bellcote. Red brick with a wild admixture of black and yellow brick decoration outside and with bands and trellis inside. It is all very much in the style of Butterfield. The large, low, pointed window in the chancel, almost like a triangle, is also an oddity. – STAINED GLASS. In the chancel Crucifixion etc. by *Hardman*. Remarkably good. – BRASS to Marie Wyncoll † 1610 and husband, also five daughters (nave N wall).

TYE GREEN see HARLOW

UGLEY

ST PETER. Early C16 brick tower with low diagonal buttresses and battlements, and start of the S wall of the nave in brick. The rest dates from 1866 and is of no interest.

ORFORD HOUSE, 1½ m. S. Built by the newly created Earl of Orford, c.1700. Seven bays, two storeys, red brick, with a central bay and segment-headed windows. Later asymmetrically placed doorway on Tuscan columns. Fine contemporary iron gate now at the back.

ULTING

ALL SAINTS. By the river, with no village near. Essentially C13, see the lancet windows in chancel and nave and the S doorway. The W windows are of 1873, as is the Perp E window, and the belfry. – FONT. Of Purbeck marble; not square but octagonal with only one of the usual blank arches per side. The angles of the octagon are chamfered. – BENCH ENDS. Two with poppyheads, re-used. – PLATE. Cup of 1570; Paten of 1571.

(TANHOUSE FARM, 1 m. E. With fine late C16 projecting chimneystack. The lower part has a blank stepped gable; the two shafts are set diagonally. R.C.)

UPHALL CAMP see ILFORD

UPMINSTER

ST LAURENCE. A remarkable C13 W tower, four-square and sturdy, with clasping buttresses only at the foot. Short spire. Inside, the first floor is carried on two massive posts standing against the middles of the N and S sides and a big beam. Arched braces connect posts and beam. Braces on corbels carry the beams along the W and E walls. A fine piece of C13 construction. The rest of the church is mostly of 1863 (by *W. G. Bartlett*) and undistinguished. The Victorian work may well make one overlook the early C14 N arcade (short quatrefoil piers, moulded capitals, double-chamfered arches). – SCREEN to N chancel chapel. Incorporating C15 fragments. – STALL. (N chapel) with moulded rail and one poppy-head. – FONT. C15; octagonal bowl with quatrefoil panelling. – (STAINED GLASS. Armorial. N aisle, dated 1630.) – PLATE. Cup probably of 1608; Almsdish of 1686; Paten on foot of 1704. – MONUMENTS. Several brasses in the N aisle, e.g. Elizabeth Dencourt † 1455, Man in civil dress of *c.*1530, Nicholas Wayte † 1542 and wife, etc. – Andrew Branfill † 1709, monument with demi-figure on top. – James Esdaile † 1812, very plain, no figures; by *Sir Richard Westmacott*.

UPMINSTER CHAPEL. With Tuscan porch and pediment with semicircular window. 1803; enlarged 1827; refronted 1847.

(PUBLIC LIBRARY, Corbets Tey Road. By *H. Conolly*, County Architect, 1962–3.)

Upminster is mainly one long E–W street. A walk should begin by the church, which lies back from the street. Immediately W of it the PARSONAGE of 1765, H-shaped, with segment-headed windows. Opposite an early C19 three-bay house with nice cast-iron verandah, then, standing back, the WINDMILL of 1802–3, a smock-mill complete with sails and fan, a beacon for miles around. Opposite HILL PLACE, by *Bartlett*, 1871–3, with many additions for a convent. Lower down near the railway station on the N side INGREBOURNE COTTAGES, plain, two-storeyed row, built as a poorhouse in 1750 and extended in 1787.

To the E of the church CLOCK HOUSE, red brick, plain W front with pediment. Formerly the stables of New Place, built by Sir James Esdaile, *c.*1775. The clock cupola from the stables quadrangle now faces N. (The clock comes from Woolwich Arsenal.)

To the N outside the old village UPMINSTER HALL (Golf Club House), timber-framed Elizabethan, with divers gables, one-storeyed Hall with moulded beams. Opposite UPMINSTER COURT (Education Offices), a handsome Neo-Georgian villa with two straight gables and, on the ground floor along the centre, connecting them, a colonnade. By *Sir Charles Reilly*,

1906–8. Yet further N GREAT TOMKINS, good C15 yeoman's house, with exposed timber framing. The hall goes up the whole height of the building. The wings to its W and E are two-storeyed. Weatherboarded C17 Barn S of the house.

S of Upminster at CORBETS TEY is HARWOOD HALL, castellated front with raised bow-fronted centre. Built in 1782 by Sir James Esdaile. Near by red brick Dovecote with quatrefoil openings. A little to the E HIGH HOUSE, c.1700, three bays, two storeys, with shell-hood over the door and a rich fireplace inside.

NW of Harwood Hall in Hacton Lane HACTONS, built c.1770. At the time of writing partly ruined.* Red brick. Five bays and two one-storey side pavilions, three-bay projecting centre; this and the angles of the house are quoined. Three-bay pediment with semicircular window. Porch and Venetian window above. The pavilions also have porticoes. Staircase with iron railing.

UPSHIRE
nr Waltham Holy Cross

ST THOMAS. 1902 by *Freeman & Ogilvy*. – PLATE. Cup and Cover of 1782; Paten bought in Armenia; Almsdish with repoussé representation of Adam and Eve, probably Flemish.

VALENTINES *see* ILFORD

VALLEY HOUSE *see* LANGHAM

VANGE *see* BASILDON

VIRLEY

ST MARY. A ruin, but a ruin kept visually attractive. The remaining walls all in ivy, herbaceous borders inside the nave. The only feature of strictly architectural interest is the chancel arch. Transitional style, i.e. round arch with two slight chamfers, resting on semi-octagonal responds.

WAKES COLNE

ALL SAINTS. Nave, lower chancel, and belfry. Norman windows in the N and S walls, plain Norman S doorway, Norman N doorway with one order of one-scallop capitals and a rollmoulding. The chancel walls are partly so thick that they must

* Since, according to information received, over-restored.

have carried a crossing tower. In the N and S walls one Dec
window each, in the S wall in addition one early C16 three-
light brick window. The belfry rests on four posts in a row
from N to S with cross-beam and arched braces and a tie-beam
a little further E, also with arched braces. Between the four
posts a SCREEN was put up in 1920 as a war memorial, an
unusual and very successful design. – FONT. Octagonal, late
C12, with three shallow blank arches on each side of the bowl.
– PLATE. Good Cup of 1702.

WAKES HALL. Brick, c.1840 (before 1848). White brick, three
bays, with Greek Doric porch.

Just E of Wakes Colne and the background to the picture of the
village is a RAILWAY VIADUCT of 1066 ft length. It is of
brick, thirty arches, and was begun in 1847.

WALKERS MANOR HOUSE *see* FARNHAM

WALLBURY CAMP *see* GREAT HALLINGBURY

WALTHAM HOLY CROSS

WALTHAM ABBEY is no more than a fragment of what it was:
a Norman nave, a C14 chapel, a C14 W wall, and a C16 W tower.
At the E end at least two thirds of the building have gone, and
nearly all the monastic buildings have gone. The abbey was
founded in 1030 as a collegiate church of secular canons. It
was built or rebuilt with some pomp by Harold and consecrated in 1060. We have no date after that, until we come to
1177, the re-foundation as an abbey of Augustinian Canons.
In 1184 it was given the dignity of a 'mitred abbey', and it
soon became one of the most prosperous and important abbeys
in the country. It is teasing for the historian that for the main
part of the surviving building no dates exist to guide him. In
addition, until 1938, no guidance existed either as to the extent
and character of the work which followed the re-foundation
of 1177. The extent is now known, though not yet the character. The one is due to excavations carried out in 1938–9,
the other to their limited scope. The E.E. abbey meant the
addition to the Norman nave and crossing of a whole church,
that is a choir longer than the Norman nave, an E transept bigger than the Norman transept, and a long and large retrochoir.
It must have dwarfed the Norman parts completely, and may
have looked something like Canterbury Cathedral, before the

nave was rebuilt in the C14. But we do not know the style of 1177 etc. at Waltham. The E parts of the abbey were pulled down after the Dissolution.

The Norman crossing which had been left standing in 1177 was then also pulled down. So all that survives of Norman architecture is nave and aisles, a nave no more than seven bays long. It seems, except for C14 adjustments at the W end and C19 adjustments at the E end, to be all of a piece, but reveals to the attentive observer many puzzling irregularities. The present E wall is an infilling of the C19 across the W arch of the crossing and the aisle arches into the transepts. This is clearly visible from the outside, where also one S transept W window can be noticed, which now leads into the C14 chapel (see below). Below it is exposed coarse rubble masonry, laid herringbone-wise.

The exterior of the nave is simple: aisle windows with nook-shafts, circular gallery windows, and clerestory windows with nook-shafts and some zigzag decoration – all much renewed. The Norman S doorway of two orders, with an upcurved lintel and zigzag in the arches, is in its surface, it seems, wholly C19.

The inside is much more impressive. It has something of the sturdy force of Durham Cathedral, though neither its size nor its proportions. The system of elevation which applies throughout is that of nearly all major Anglo-Norman churches: arcade-gallery-clerestory. It is baffling, though only for a moment, that the gallery is deprived of its floor, so that the aisles are now much higher than they were meant to appear. The arcades have supports alternating between superordinate composite piers, and subordinate round ones. The gallery openings are large and unsubdivided. The clerestory has the usual English arrangement of a wall-passage and, towards the nave, an arcade of three arches for each bay, with the middle arch wider and taller.

In detail the most striking of all features of Waltham is the deeply grooved circular piers – a detail familiar from Durham, and also from Norwich, nearer Waltham. These piers are spiral-grooved in the first circular pair from the E, zigzag-grooved in the second, and left plain in the third. The composite piers have a buttress-like broad flat projection to the nave with a demi-shaft attached, and this projection with its shaft runs up to the ceiling without any break. The capitals are big and heavy, single- or double-scalloped. Above the first circular pier from the E they project a little more boldly than above the others. These first circular piers also have different bases, and the E respond (as also the E arch of the S aisle) is different in one detail from the W responds. Of the four capitals of the three respond shafts, the middle one is a little deeper on the E side. In the arches a difference of a similar nature can be detected. The arches have all zigzag ornamentation on the faces, but in the E ones the inner zigzag goes fairly deeply into the soffits as well – again a sign of a bolder, more three-dimensional treatment. It finds its parallel in the W crossing arch high up.* Again, looking at the arcade from the aisles, it will be noticed that in the W parts each pier, including the subordinate circular ones, has attached demi-shafts, introduced no doubt to carry transverse arches on which to support groined vaults or simply the gallery floors. Only the easternmost circular pier has no such attachment. Finally, looking at the same pier once more from the nave, a small corbel-head will be noticed, on the N as well as the S side, immediately above the column, as if to support a wall-shaft, never built. The wall-shafts start only at gallery level, as they do in the W parts as well.

Now for the gallery. Here the E bay piers have three shafts towards the arch openings, the W bays only two. The existence of these shafts incidentally indicates that the gallery openings were originally subdivided or meant to be subdivided. In the W the arches themselves have billet-decorated hood-moulds; in the E these are absent. Another distinction on the level of the gallery refers to S as against N. The corbels on which the wall-shafts between the arches rest are carved into heads on the N side, but plain (except for the easternmost) on the S. Perhaps that shows no more than that carving of such details, where it was done, was done *après la pose*.

In the clerestory there are even more differences. The W bays on the N side have round piers between the arches and a plain moulding of the stilted centre arches in each group of three. The capitals are scalloped with a little decoration between the scallops. On the S side the piers are quatrefoil in plan, and the middle arches stand on a short second tier of shafts. The arches themselves have roll-mouldings. The N and SE bays however have an alternation of circular and octagonal

---

* Another parallel is in the exterior in the clerestory windows, where the E bays have windows starting lower down, and zigzag etc. going into the arch soffits.

piers and on both sides the subsidiary shafts and roll-mouldings.

Now what does all this minor evidence indicate of the building history of the Norman nave? Taken together it can mean only one thing: that the E double bay was built later than the bays further W. That is surprising, because of the familiar fact that medieval churches were built from the E to the W. It is however quite conceivable that Harold's chancel of 1060 was allowed to remain when a new nave was begun, and that only in the course of building the decision was taken to renew the E parts as well. As for dates, the earliest grooved columns seem to be those at Durham of *c.*1095–1100. Those at Norwich are datable before 1119. The plain, heavy ground-floor capitals at Waltham Abbey look more C11 than C12. But the arches have zigzag decoration from the beginning, and zigzag does not occur anywhere in England before *c.*1105–10. So that date may mark the beginning of the W parts, including their gallery. The clerestory was then erected on the N side, then that on the S, and then finally the E bays were tackled and erected, including their clerestory and the arches to the cross-ing and transept. They may well belong to the mid C12 or even a little later.

Of the C13 – this has been said with regret before – nothing can be seen and little said, before excavations have been re-sumed and concluded.

The early C14 added a S chapel, W of the S transept. It is now the Lady Chapel. Externally it has flint and stone bands, a very unusual W window, of three times two lights, with a straight head and Dec tracery,* four fine three-light S win-dows, also with Dec tracery, and buttresses between them en-riched with recesses. The chapel itself stands on a vaulted undercroft of two bays with chamfered ribs and small win-dows decorated by head-stops. The chapel is not vaulted. In-side the W window is a delightful detached three-light arcade with pierced spandrels. Also early in the C14 the W end of the church was rebuilt. To this rebuilding belong the western-most windows of the aisles with the pretty niches against the W buttresses, the arches replacing the arches of the Norman gal-lery inside towards the W end, the last bay on the S side of the clerestory, and the W front. The remains of this are now only

---

* A watercolour of *c.*1820 by Varley, now in the Victoria and Albert Museum, shows this S chapel W window blocked up and pierced in the centre by a pointed window.

visible inside the tower. The portal is single. It is deep enough to allow for a very shallow vault, which is carried on four columns. The outer columns are a normal order of portal columns, the inner are placed on diagonal seats which form the sides of the little vaulted portal niche. The jambs and arch of the doorway are decorated with fleurons. Above the doorway is a gable and in the spandrel a circle with a quatrefoil is placed. To the l. and r. of the doorway are the beginnings of blank shafted niches as they were so usual in English church fronts. The outer w portal of the tower is of the same date and apparently re-used. It has three orders of columns with foliated capitals and fleurons in the arches, all very defaced. In date all this work seems a little earlier than the s chapel, as ogee arches do not appear anywhere.

The w tower was added after the Dissolution in 1556–8, as a characteristic sign of the change-over from monastic to parochial.* It has irregular flint and stone chequer-work below, and ashlar facing in the often restored upper parts. The stones were taken, it is said, from the crossing tower, which had collapsed in 1552. The buttresses are placed diagonally and carry square pinnacles also in a diagonal position. Each side has two two-light bell-openings.

The E wall was remodelled by *W. Burges* in 1859–60 with all the robust ugliness which that architect liked. Extremely short columns with thick shaft-rings and thick crocket capitals, plenty of carved figure work, and a big wheel window above – astoundingly loud after the silent severity of the nave.

FONT. Of Purbeck marble, octagonal, C12 or C13, absolutely plain. – PULPIT. Good, mid C17. At the angles tapering pilasters, in the panels elaborate frames crowned by open segmental pediments. This pulpit is now kept in the s chapel. The new pulpit was designed by *Burges* and made in 1876. – SCREEN, at the E end of the N aisle. The heavy construction and the simple tracery indicate a C14 date. – REREDOS. With four big carved reliefs. Designed by *Burges*. – SCULPTURE. Exceedingly fine small early C14 figures from a former reredos, at the E end of the s aisle. – PAINTING. On the E wall of the Lady Chapel. Doom; C14, very faded. – Ceiling of the nave, in the style of the original work at Peterborough; by *Sir Edward Poynter*. – STAINED GLASS. The E window by *Burne-*

31

---

* Another parochial feature introduced at an unknown date is the rood-beam, the sawn-off ends of which can still be seen above the second piers from the E.

Jones, 1861, and made by *Powell's*, in its vigorously stylized composition and figure design and its glow of colour is amongst the best glass done in the C19, much bolder than most Morris & Co. glass and much richer in the scale of colours used. Almost as remarkable and as daring the E window of the S aisle by *Henry Holiday*, 1867.* – The recent glass by *A. K. Nicholson* looks very anaemic in comparison. – PILLORY and WHIPPING POST now kept in the S chapel. – PLATE. Paten on foot of 1561, with bands of ornament; large Cup of 1633; large Paten on foot of 1674.

MONUMENTS. Brasses with wood and stone surrounds of 1555 and 1576 (S aisle). – Sir Edward Denny † 1600 and wife. Standing wall-monument. Two semi-reclining effigies, the man behind and a little above the woman. Shallow coffered arch and flanking columns.‡ In the spandrels figures of Fame and Time. Strapwork cartouche against the back wall. By *Isaac James* and *Bartholomew Adye* (Mrs Esdaile). – Lady Greville † 1619. The stiff figure only is preserved. – Capt. Robert Smith † 1697. Tomb-chest with a relief of trophies and a ship, called Industria. To the l. and r. arms and cherub's head used instead of volutes. – James and Hester Spilman † 1763 and 1761. Fine monument with the usual cherub standing by a sarcophagus against a grey obelisk. Two portrait heads in profile at the foot. – Caroline Chinnery † 1812. Plain, elegantly shaped urn on a pillar. On the urn in good lettering the one word Caroline. – Thomas Leverton (the architect) † 1824. By *Kendrick*. The usual design with a woman weeping over an urn.

The Cloister of the monastery lay N of the long E.E. choir. All that remains of it is a PASSAGE which led N from the NE angle of the cloister. It is of two bays, rib-vaulted on shafts with waterleaf capitals, and must belong to the late C12. In addition the Abbey GATEHOUSE survives, N of the W front of the church. This is of the later C14 and has to the outside a wide entrance for carriages and a small one for pedestrians. The large one has angels as label-stops. Of the angle turrets only one is preserved. The S wall should be examined with care, as it seems to have brickwork contemporary with the building, that is of exceptionally early date. The BRIDGE leading to the gatehouse is also attributed to the C14.

---

* Also by *Holiday*, 1861, the panel in the blind window above the entrance to the crypt.

‡ Mr D. M. Palliser tells me that the columns have been destroyed.

Waltham is still a little town, not a suburb of London. There are few special houses to be noted, but the general scale is a blessing for the abbey church. The best houses are the VICARAGE just N of the W end of the church, and the WELSH HARP INN in the market place, both timber-framed, but the former plastered, the latter with the timbers exposed. PARADISE ROAD and PARADISE ROW are a pleasant quiet backwater SW of the church. The houses are small, of yellow brick. The centre is the BAPTIST CHAPEL of 1836 with four-centred Gothick windows. Next to it THE MANSE, still with a date plate of 1729, but altered.

WARLIES PARK, see p. 414.

(CEMETERY. New buildings by *Lewis Solomon, Kaye & Partners, c.*1960.)

WALTHAMSTOW

When William Morris was a boy, the land round Walthamstow was 'all flat pasture, except for a few gardens . . . the wide green sea of the Essex marshland, with the great domed line of the sky and the sun shining down in one flood of peaceful light over the long distance'. That was in the 1840s. It all changed immediately after, and London engulfed Walthamstow. Population figures are characteristic. 1801 3,000, 1851 5,000, 1871, 11,000, 1961 109,000.

ST MARY. Hardly anything left of before the Reformation. W tower, aisles, and chancel chapels built *c.*1535. Altered and enlarged 1818 and again 1843.* Present galleries and roof 1876. – FONT. Fluted bowl on baluster stem, white marble, 1714. – PLATE. Set of *c.*1680; Beadle's Staff 1779. – MONUMENTS. Sir George Monox † 1543 and wife; brass with small kneeling figures. – Lady Stanley, *c.*1630, standing wall-monument with big kneeling figure. – Sir Thomas and Lady Merry, 1633 by *Nicholas Stone*; she and her husband as demi-figures in oval niches, busts of four children in flat relief below, open pediment above; of very fine sculptural quality, especially the modelling of the hands. – Sigismund Trafford † 1723 and wife and daughter, ambitious standing wall-monument with husband in Roman costume and wife, both standing, and the child kneeling between them; the artistic quality not as high as e.g. at Wanstead. – Many more monuments (Bonnell Family

36b

* In 1784 unspecified work costing £1,250 was done by *Sir John Soane* (Miss Dorothy Stroud).

*c.*1690, with big sarcophagus and no effigies; Elizabeth Morley
† 1837 by *Nicholl*, etc.). – In the CHURCHYARD more monuments, closely placed to the W of the church, and mostly early
C19.

ST BARNABAS, St Barnabas Road. 1902 by *Caröe*, relatively conventional for him. Red brick, exposed inside as well. Large,
wide interior. Exterior with a NW turret, the only fanciful
motif.

ST PETER, Woodford New Road. 1840 by *John Shaw Jun*. Much
renewed recently. In the vaguely Early Christian-Italian
Rundbogenstil. Alterations in 1854 were designed by *Charles
Ainslie*.

ST SAVIOUR, Markhouse Road. 1874 by *T. F. Dolman*. Rock-
faced, with polygonal apse and SW spire outside the S aisle.
Rather dull.

CONGREGATIONAL CHURCH see below.

CIVIC CENTRE, Forest Road. By *P. D. Hepworth*, 1937–42.
Stone-faced, in the Swedish style of *c.*1925 which became so
popular in England amongst those who were not satisfied to
be imitatively Neo-Georgian nor wanted to go modern in
earnest. Symmetrical building with projecting wings and in
the centre a tall slim portico of unmoulded square piers. Above
a tall, very slim lantern. To the r. of the building a separate
Assembly Hall intended to be matched later on the l. by a
building for the Law Courts. Inside, the Assembly Hall has
an entrance hall with wall panels and a central box office very
typical of the dainty Swedish taste alluded to before.

SOUTH WEST ESSEX TECHNICAL COLLEGE, Forest Road,
next to the Civic Centre. By *J. Stuart*, 1938. Brick with stone
dressings, thirty-five bays wide and sadly dull. The six-column
giant portico with pediment in the middle is far too much an
architectural *cliché* to relieve the monotony of the big utilitarian block.

PUBLIC LIBRARY (1907–9 by *J. W. Dunford*) and PUBLIC
HALL AND BATHS (1900 by *Spalding & Cross*), High Street.
In the pretty, somewhat ornate mixed style of the day which
was so often and successfully used for small municipal buildings. The two buildings with the ugly CONGREGATIONAL
CHURCH of 1871 by *J. Tarring & Son* (rockfaced, and originally with spire) make a plucky effort at something like a
minor civic centre.

FOREST SCHOOL, see below.

MUSEUM, see below.

WILLIAM MORRIS GALLERY, see below.

LEA VALLEY VIADUCT. 1927 by *Maxwell Ayrton* and *Sir Owen Williams*. The architect's chief contribution the two pairs of pylon-shaped towers with their vertical fins.

The Walthamstow of William Morris's youth does not visually succeed in penetrating the Walthamstow of today. Nowhere is enough left to form a picture, except perhaps in the immediate neighbourhood of the church. Here lie the MONOUX ALMSHOUSES (N of the church), of *c*.1760, one-storeyed with a raised gable in the centre.* s of the church a Late Georgian house and next to it a Late Tudor cottage, timber-framed and gabled. To the w of the churchyard the ST MARY'S IN-FANTS' SCHOOL, yellow brick, built 1828, restored 1928, and to its SW the VESTRY HOUSE and Old Armoury, now Museum. This was built as the Workhouse in 1730 and enlarged in 1756. The doorway comes from Church Hill House, an overmantel on the ground floor from Essex Hall.‡ One Georgian house not far from the church in ORFORD ROAD. A little more near the s end of HOE STREET, mostly in a neglected, damaged, or derelict condition. This incidentally applied at the time of writing to many of the pre-Victorian houses of Walthamstow. In Hoe Street No. 398, THE CHEST-NUTS (well kept), of yellow brick with red brick dressings, seven bays wide with three-bay pediment. No. 317 COURT HOUSE, *c*.1700, red brick, derelict,§ on the opposite side GROSVENOR HOUSE, Georgian, large, with four-column porch, badly damaged,§ and a little further N CLEVELAND HOUSE (Clark's College), with altered front. In HIGH STREET near the corner of Hoe Street a few more worthwhile houses, Nos 273–275 *c*.1700 behind their shop fronts, and w of these a neo-classical house.§ (Further w in High Street, NORTHCOTT HOUSE (No. 115), *c*.1750. Three storeys, yellow brick, red brick dressings.)

N of Hoe Street in FOREST ROAD a number of single houses,¶ the best WATER HOUSE, built 1762. Front of nine bays with two symmetrical three-bay bow windows. Yellow brick, with handsome entrance hall and staircase behind it. William Mor-

---

* The w end rebuilt in 1955 to the design of *Braddell & Laurence* to conform with the earlier style.

‡ Miss M. E. Weaver also draws my attention to the SQUIRES ALMS-HOUSES, adjoining the Infants' School. They are of 1795, one storey, yellow brick with red brick dressings.

§ Now demolished.

¶ At the extreme w end, by the River Lea, the C18 FERRY BOAT INN.

ris spent his childhood here, and the house is now a William Morris Gallery. In addition *Sir Frank Brangwyn* has left his collection to the museum and *Arthur H. Mackmurdo* many relics of his Century Guild, which flourished in the 80s and 90s. Further E, opposite the Civic Centre, is BROOKSCROFT (five bays, two storeys, three-bay pediment) and then THORPE COMBE (five bays, two-and-a-half storeys, three-bay pediment). Just S of this in SHERNHALL STREET lies WALTHAMSTOW HOUSE, now a convent, large, late C18, with two canted bay windows.

At the S end of Shernhall Street at the corner of LEA BRIDGE ROAD another isolated Georgian house in bad repair.* In WOOD STREET further E, off Lea Bridge Road, CLOCK HOUSE, mostly early C19 (two-and-a-half storeys, three-bay pediment).‡

The most pleasant nucleus of old Walthamstow is by the FOREST SCHOOL. This incorporates a row of handsome Georgian houses, with well-preserved interiors.§ At r. angles to the W more Georgian building, but on a more modest scale. The whole group is embodied in the Common and the remains of EPPING FOREST. In addition three individual houses further out: to the N, beyond the N end of Woodford New Road HIGHAMS, now part of the County School for Girls, and once the mansion to which the large gardens of Highams Park belonged, laid out by *Repton*. The house itself was built in 1768 by *William Newton*. It is tall and stuccoed, and has giant pilasters on the entrance side. The school has added wings on the N and more on the S side (1928 and 1938).

SW of this in HALE ROAD at Hale End BEECH HALL, nine bays, two storeys, three-bay pediment, stuccoed.

Finally at the W entry to Walthamstow in COPPERMILL LANE THE ELMS (London Playing Fields Association), red brick with four-column porch, once a fine house, now desolate. (The MHLG mentions also the old copper mill itself, now Water Board Stores. The date is *c*.1800. Yellow brick, two storeys. Centre of three bays with pilasters. Returning end to the left of seven bays; projecting wing to the r. of five bays; picturesque later tower a little behind.)

After the war the Borough, through its Borough Architect,

---

* Now demolished.

‡ Now with new flats as wings on either side.

§ In the School Chapel some *William Morris* STAINED GLASS of 1875–80; in the Library some C14–C15 glass from Howden in Yorkshire.

F. G. Southgate, erected some unusually good blocks of flats, especially the large group called PRIORY COURT (Countess Road), twenty straight six-storeyed blocks, so well grouped that they make an impressive whole of true C20 character, urban yet not inhuman. The neighbourhood has in addition one two-storeyed block for old people and a community centre in the middle of the N half. Infilling since 1953 has included a number of bungalows and shops, a two-storeyed block with Estate Office, 1954, and a four-storeyed block of flats and single-storey Health Services Clinic, both of 1959. The whole is one of the most impressive pieces of recent urban development in Essex. Another new scheme is OAK HILL COURT, Oak Hill, completed 1950. Thirty-six flats in three three-storey blocks.

(The following notes on major new building have been kindly supplied by the Borough Architect:

HOE STREET REDEVELOPMENT AREA, comprising: Central Parade, a four-storey block of shops and flats with Lecture Hall, completed 1958; No. 6 Church Hill, a four-storey office block completed in 1963; another four-storey block of maisonettes and offices with a shopping arcade, completed in 1964. All are by *F G. Southgate*.

THE DRIVE REDEVELOPMENT AREA, including Prospect Hill and part of Church Hill Road. Blocks of flats from two to five storeys. By *F. G. Southgate*, 1955–64.

PARK COURT, Grosvenor Park Road. A terrace of twelve houses and one five-storey block of framed construction. By *F. G. Southgate*, completed 1962.

ELLEN MILLER HOUSE, TOM SMITH HOUSE and ELLIS HOUSE, at the junction of Raglan Road, Shernhall Street and Barclay Road. Three five-storey blocks, again by *F. G. Southgate*, completed in 1963.)

WALTON-ON-THE-NAZE

Not mentioned in the volume of the Royal Commission – that means: no building prior to 1714. The development of Walton indeed did not start until about 1825. In a lithograph of 1829 a hotel designed by *Mr Penrice* of Colchester appears as just completed. This is now BAKER'S MARINE HOTEL, but has changed its appearance considerably. In 1832 the Crescent, now MARINE PARADE, was built. It did not become a crescent as good as its patterns at Buxton or Brighton. Today it is left straggling and unkempt. A grander attempt was made immediately after, about 1835, on the Cliff a little further N than the old village. It was financed by Mr John Warner, bell-founder of Hoddesdon. The southernmost house of the new terrace was his own, later the CLIFF HOTEL. It is distinguished by a Greek Doric porch. S of it, as the preamble to the new-town-to-be, is the WHITE LODGE, a lodge, one-storeyed and with two Tuscan columns *in antis*. To the N of the terrace Mr Warner built for his mother East Cliff Cottage, now the GOTHIC COTTAGE, in the then popular style with bargeboarded gables.

ALL SAINTS. 1873–82 by *H. Stone* (GR).

PIER. The pavilion buildings at the time of writing are nice, fresh and modern, a little like exhibition structures, merely, alas, because licences forbid more ornate entertainment architecture.

NAZE TOWER. Tall and slim, polygonal, embattled. Built in 1720 by the Corporation of Trinity House as a beacon.*

MARTELLO TOWER, in a field just N of the church. Built in 1810–12 as part of the chain of inadequate defences against Napoleon's intended invasion. Broad and not high. On the Martello Towers, see Clacton-on-Sea.

WALTONS *see* BARTLOW END

WANSTEAD

The architectural fame of Wanstead was WANSTEAD HOUSE, a large classical mansion built by *Colen Campbell* for Sir Richard Child. It was begun in 1715 and was thus the earliest major building in England in the revived pure Palladian style. It is illustrated in the first volume of *Vitruvius Britannicus*, but nothing of it remains now *in situ*. It was 260 ft long and lay due E from The Basin, a pond on Wanstead golf course, and SE of the present Golf Club Headquarters, formerly the old stables of Wanstead House. Sir Richard was the son of Sir Josiah Child (see St Mary), a 'suddenly monied man', as John Evelyn said in 1683. Sir Josiah was indeed chairman of the East India Company. Walpole told Richard Bentley that the house had cost £100,000 and the gardens as much again. Of these more can still be seen: first of all The Basin

---

* Mr P. Topham tells me that an earlier tower appears on Norden's map of 1594.

itself, once w of the house, and the broad avenue through
Wanstead Park leading straight to the E. It once led to the
canal, and this is still in existence as a straight branch of the
winding river Roding. Of garden furnishings one can look up
the two gate piers at the entrance to Overton Drive, a Grecian
Temple, and the façade of the Grotto near the canal.

ST MARY. A church worthy in its appearance of the noble
aspiration of the mansion. Built in 1787–90 by *Thomas Hardwick*, in a classical style, clearly of Gibbs derivation. Ashlar-
faced throughout. Tall porch of two pairs of Tuscan columns.
Pediment and fine circular bell-turret with pairs of columns

Wanstead House by Colen Campbell, begun 1715

in the diagonals. Windows in two storeys corresponding to the
wooden galleries inside. Interior of five bays of tall Corinthian
columns on high pedestals. The columns carry arches, the
ceiling is coved. Narrower chancel. – PULPIT. Lovely, with
sounding board carried on two palmtree columns. – High
BOX PEWS. – CHANCEL RAILS and COMMUNION RAILS of
wrought iron. – PLATE. Set of Queen Anne date converted to
its present appearance in 1790. – MONUMENTS. The monument to Sir Josiah Child † 1699 is one of the show pieces of
the period. Attributed by Mrs Esdaile to *John van Ost* or *Nost*.
Large reredos back. On the pedestal the reclining figure of a
son of Sir Josiah and two allegories. Higher up stands Sir
Josiah in Roman vestments and wig. Corinthian columns l.
and r. and open, broken segmental pediment with Fames
reclining on it. All the ornamental carving very fine. – George
Bowles † 1817, by *Chantrey* (on the gallery). Large seated
female and next to her on a high pedestal bust in profile.

CHRIST CHURCH, High Street. 1861 by *Sir George Gilbert
Scott*. Spire, s aisle, etc. a little later. The church stands in the

30b

40

Recreation Ground, unconcerned with any houses around, like a model in an exhibition. The Victorians liked that. Ragstone with N tower with spire. The windows have plate tracery. Low quatrefoil piers. Three separate roofs for nave and aisles.

ST GABRIEL, Aldersbrook Road. 1914 by *Charles Spooner*. Red brick. Good Neo-Perp with pretty *flèche*.

HOLY TRINITY, Hermon Hill. 1887–90 by *J. Fowler*. Neo-Norman, an unusual thing at that time, with NW tower standing outside the aisle.

ROYAL WANSTEAD SCHOOL, Holly Bush Hill. Built as the HACKNEY INFANT ORPHAN ASYLUM. An early work of *Gilbert Scott*'s (*Scott & Moffatt*). The date is 1843. It was illustrated in *The Builder*, volume I. Jacobean style, grey stone with buff stone dressings. Front with wings projecting symmetrically and central gatehouse motif. The motif repeated on the N front as well. Mullioned windows, strapwork decoration.

WANSTEAD HOSPITAL, Hermon Hill. Built as the MERCHANT 62a SEAMEN'S ORPHAN ASYLUM. 1861 by *G. C. Clarke* in what the *Illustrated London News* called a 'lovely Venetian Gothic'. It is that; thanks to Ruskin's enthusiasm, as far as red Victorian brick can look Venetian. But the stone parts, windows, gargoyles, etc. are all as they should be. The *ensemble* of course is more like St Pancras Station than like the Doge's Palace, chiefly owing to a tall, asymmetrically placed tower. Both main fronts are altogether quite freely assembled.

WANSTEAD STATION, London Transport, The Green. By *Charles Holden*. A good design of 1937–8, completed with the original intentions. Faced with grey tiles.

In the HIGH STREET two good C18 brick houses are all that remain from a group of five or more which were standing until a few years ago. From S to N: first a three-bay house, then the MANOR HOUSE (Conservative Club) early C18, seven bays with segment-headed windows, shell-hood over the door, and staircase with twisted balusters.

In the former GEORGE LANE* two adjoining houses: REYDON HALL, with giant Ionic pilasters at the angles and segment-headed windows, early C18, and ELM HALL, a plainer seven-bay house of two-and-a-half storeys, somewhat later.‡

* Now part of Eastern Avenue and Nutter Lane.

‡ Mr J. E. Tuffs and Mr E. S. Phillips also draw attention to THE APPLEGARTH in Nutter Lane, early C18. At SNARESBROOK is the EAGLE INN, Early Georgian with added C19 bays.

WARLIES PARK

1½ m. ENE Waltham Holy Cross

Indifferent Georgian house enlarged by *Teulon* in his unmistakable style: heavily picturesque, e.g. with elephantine brackets carrying a gabled overhanging upper storey. In the grounds a handsome Late Georgian Rotunda.

WARRENS FARM *see* GREAT EASTON

WEELEY

ST ANDREW. Early C16 tower of brick, with diagonal buttresses and battlements. Brick W doorway. The rest by *E. C. Robins* (GR), 1881. Also of red brick, in a Neo-Late-Perp. – FONT. Octagonal with rosettes and shields in the panels. – PLATE. Small Cup with band of ornament, and Paten, both Late Elizabethan.

GUTTRIDGE HALL, 1 m. WSW. C15 (?) BARN of five bays with aisles and king-post roof. Weatherboarded and thatched.

WENDENS AMBO

ST MARY THE VIRGIN. Nice, stepped exterior. The tower not too high (with a Hertfordshire spike), the nave short and not much lower, the chancel again lower. The tower is Norman. It has a W doorway with Roman bricks, remains of small windows high up, and bell-openings with colonnettes. The tower arch towards the nave also is Norman, unmoulded on simple imposts. The battlements of the tower evidently later. E.E. S arcade of circular piers with one-stepped pointed arches. The S doorway (with colonnettes) and the W lancet window belong to the same period. The N arcade is later. It has octagonal piers and double-chamfered arches. The N aisle itself was rebuilt in 1898. The date of the chancel, c.1300, is indicated by two cusped lancet windows. – FONT COVER. C16, domed, with a ball finial. – PULPIT. Good C15 piece with blank arches in the panels under exaggeratedly high crocketed gables. – SCREEN. With one-light divisions with crocketed ogee arches and panel tracery, broad and not very refined. – BENCHES. Seven in the nave, plain, with buttresses at the ends. On one end a carved beast holding one paw on a mirror. – PAINTINGS. Remains of an interesting cycle of c.1330 have come to light in 1934. They are episodes from the life of St Margaret: Instruction of St Margaret, St Margaret approached by Provost

Olybrius, Incarceration of St Margaret, The Provost Olybrius.
– PLATE. Paten of 1569; Cup of 1589, by *R.W.*, an especially
beautiful little piece. – BRASS. Knight, the figure 3 ft 6 in.
long; *c.*1415.
(WENDENS HALL. Mr J. T. Smith suggests that the hall had a
hammerbeam roof, though it is not impossible that it is an
aisled hall, with all the posts cut off.)

WENNINGTON

ST MARY AND ST PETER. The Norman s doorway with an
arch of three bands of saltire-crosses is not *in situ*. The nave,
chancel, and s aisle are C13, as is proved by the chancel N lancet, the s arcade of two bays with circular pier and double-
chamfered arches, and the remarkable W lancet now looking
into the tower. This shows that the tower is later. Its details,
e.g. the windows, are indeed C14-looking (as is the N arcade
with octagonal pier and double-chamfered arches). But the
tower has still the low, broad, unbuttressed appearance of the
earlier Middle Ages. Perp chancel arch and chancel roof (tie-
beams, king-posts with four-way struts). The date of the steep
TOWER STAIRS of primitive construction is hard to assess. –
FONT LID. Jacobean. – PULPIT. Typically Jacobean. –
CHEST. C13, of hutch-type. – HOURGLASS STAND. C17,
wrought iron, attached to the pulpit. – No monuments.

WEST BERGHOLT

ST MARY. Nave, lower chancel, belfry, and early C14 s aisle
with Dec windows and low arcade of octagonal piers and
double-chamfered arches. Early C18 w gallery on Tuscan
columns with triglyph frieze.
WEST BERGHOLT HALL. A Georgian town house, not at all
in harmony with its rural surroundings. Seven bays, three
storeys, red brick, doorway with broken pediment, Venetian
window above, tripartite semicircular window above that, and
three-bay pediment on top.
PITCHBURY RAMPARTS, see Great Horkesley.

WESTCLIFF-ON-SEA *see* SOUTHEND-ON-SEA

WEST HAM*

ALL SAINTS, Church Street. A complicated building history,
given as follows by the Royal Commission: nave walls with

* See also under Canning Town, Plaistow, Silvertown, Stratford.

blocked clerestory windows Norman. Arcades to the aisles mid C13, only five bays long. Nave lengthened to the E c.1400. Circular piers, heavy moulded capitals, double-chamfered arches. s chancel chapel late C15 (octagonal piers). N chancel chapel, the most handsome piece of architecture of the church, c.1550, of red brick with blue brick diapering and windows of three and four lights with brick mullions and depressed-arched lights. Early C19 refacing of the s side of the church with yellow brick. The commanding w tower of ragstone with taller SE stair-turret is of c.1400. The nave roof has late C15 tie-beams; the chancel roof is of c.1500. – REREDOS. 1866 by *Sir G. G. Scott*. – ARCHITECTURAL FRAGMENTS from Stratford Langthorne Abbey (see p. 375): one two-light window, late medieval, near s porch, one stone sculptured with skull, on inner N wall of tower. – PLATE. Set of 1693; Cup, Cover, and Almsdish of 1718; three Almsdishes of 1737. – MONUMENTS. Thomas Staples † 1592, brass with kneeling figures (E end of s arcade). – John Faldo † 1613 and Francis Faldo † 1632, two similar small monuments with kneeling figures (chancel s wall). – William Fawcit † 1631 and wife, and her second husband. Large monument with two kneeling figures, facing each other as usual and the first husband semi-reclining below (N chancel chapel). – Thomas Foot, Lord Mayor of London, † 1688 and wife. Two life-size standing figures in niches with black inscription plate between, the whole under a pediment (N chancel chapel). – Buckeridge Children † between 1698 and 1710. Kneeling figures of the parents, one kneeling daughter above. The other children small busts on pedestals. By *Edward Stanton*. – James Cooper † 1743 and wife. Two life-size standing figures together in one niche under a pediment. The quality of the figures is excellent, and it is a great pity that they are not signed.

ST ANTONY (R. C.), St Antony's Road. By *Pugin & Pugin*, 1887. Big, E.E., no tower.

EMMANUEL, Upton Lane and Romford Road. 1850–2 by *Sir George Gilbert Scott*.

FOREST GATE CONGREGATIONAL CHURCH, Sebert Road. 1884 by *F. J. Sturdy*. In a flabby Italianate style with two orders of pilasters and two octagonal towers of which only one was carried out. Yellow and red brick.

BAPTIST CENTRAL MISSION, Barking Road, see Plaistow.

JEWISH CEMETERY, Buckingham Road. The Rothschild Mausoleum a domed building on a circular plan with Baroquizing Renaissance details ('mixed style') by *Sir Matthew Digby Wyatt*, 1866.

WEST HAM COLLEGE OF TECHNOLOGY, LIBRARY AND 3a MUSEUM, Romford Road. 1896–8 by *Gibson & Russell*. Every conceivable motif is used which was available at that peculiar moment in the history of English architecture when the allegiance to forms of the past was at last thrown to the winds. Giant columns and Gibbs surrounds of windows are still permitted, but the turret and cupola shapes for instance are without any period precedent. Besides, the grouping of masses is completely free. The College front is towards Romford Road, a symmetrical composition with two flanking turrets. The Museum projects on the r., a lower domed block, and towards Water Lane the Library recedes, ending in a turret of odd and playful shape. Altogether the architects have certainly enjoyed being fanciful and have not minded being a little vulgar. But the whole is of a robust vitality which seems enviable today, enviable even in the light of the very well designed recent WEST HAM TRADE SCHOOL FOR GIRLS,* right opposite, in Water Lane, an honest, also freely grouped, yellow brick structure. The old Municipal College is of red brick with plenty of stone work. The exterior sculpture by *W. Binnie Rhind*. The plentiful long trailing-out tendrils and scrolls are specially characteristic of the 90s. Inside, the principal rooms are the Great Hall, now housing the College Library (80 by 40 ft, with a fibrous plaster ceiling), and the Public Lending Library.

SOUTH WEST HAM COUNTY TECHNICAL SCHOOL, see Canning Town.

(SECONDARY SCHOOL, Forest Street, Forest Gate. By *Colquhoun & Miller*. Begun 1963.)

Of architecture earlier than *c*.1850 there is very little, and of picturesque values less. In PORTWAY, E of the church THE CEDARS‡ (Essex Regiment) of yellow brick, two-storeyed, with three-bay pediment. The house was for a long time the residence of Elizabeth Fry, the prison reformer. In UPTON LANE, which turns N from the E end of Portway, UPTON HOUSE of 1731 with good interiors, e.g. a staircase with twisted balusters. (A beam in the kitchen seems to be C15 or C16. MHLG) The exterior stuccoed and generally early-C19-looking. Porch with piers. Further N the SPOTTED DOG, a

---

* Now part of Deanery High School.
‡ Now demolished.

c16 cottage partly weatherboarded, and then further E a terrace of eight bays. Yellow brick; c18. Upton Lane leads into ROMFORD ROAD (for W parts see Stratford) with scanty remains of early c19 terraces, a minor version of what can be found along the Mile End Road etc. on the E arterial roads of London. Further E villas in pairs, mid c19. To the S into GREEN STREET, where, on the E side (administratively in East Ham), lie the former Industrial Schools, a long tripartite block of utilitarian character, built in 1851 for pauper children.

New housing includes:

(CLAREMONT ESTATE. With eleven-storey blocks of flats, by *Thomas E. North*, Borough Architect.)

(KILDARE ROAD and BECKTON ROAD. Thirty-nine new houses of six types, two to three storeys, brick and timber-framing. Uncommonly interesting stepped layout. Roofs on the Parker Morris system. By *Cleeve Barr* and *Oliver Cox* (MHLG). Begun in 1963.)

(CARPENTERS ROAD, off Stratford High Street. Housing for about 2,500 people on 21 acres, houses and flats, the blocks of flats including three twenty-two-storey towers. By *Thomas E. North*, the Borough Architect. Begun in 1964.)

WEST HANNINGFIELD

ST MARY AND ST EDWARD. The timber W tower is built on a Greek cross plan with the square upper part provided with an odd W oriel. Broach-spire. On the ground floor to the S two Gothick windows. The construction inside is specially interesting, with arched braces in all four directions, buttressing struts in the arms of the cross, and on the upper floor of the centre arched braces diagonally across like ribs and meeting in a centre key-block with a grotesque face.* The church itself has a Norman nave, as witnessed by the rere-arch of a N window, the remains of a c13 chancel (see the traces of E windows),‡ a c14 S arcade and S aisle, a c15 timber porch, and an early c16 chancel. Most of the windows are probably of *c.*1800: Gothick. The S arcade of five bays stands on octagonal piers and has double-chamfered arches. The chancel has two- and three-light N windows of brick, probably c17. – FONT. Perp, octagonal, small. – COMMUNION RAIL. Late c17 with alternatingly heavily twisted and turned balusters. – CHEST. Of the

* The tower is c13 according to C. A. Hewett, *Archaeological Journal*, vol. 119, 1962.

‡ Information kindly supplied by the Rev. C. E. Middleton.

dug-out type, 8 ft long, heavily iron-bound. – PLATE. Cup of 1709; Paten on foot of 1709. – BRASS to Isabell Clouvill † 1361, demi-figure.

CLOVILLE HALL, 1¼ m. WNW. Also known as Fullers or the Meeting House. Timber-framed and plastered C16 house. In the attic floor in two rooms remarkably good and well pre-served paintings of arabesques, with centaurs, putti, fishes, etc. 52a Symmetrical compositions. In one room red and white, in the other grey and white. In the latter the date 1615.

(ELM FARM, 1 m. WNW. Timber-framed and plastered; mostly early C17, with two symmetrical gables, two bay windows be-neath them, and carved brackets supporting the eaves and gables. R.C.)

WEST MERSEA

ST PETER AND ST PAUL. The church lies in the small original village area of what is now an extensive, but not yet badly spoiled seaside resort. The W tower in its lower parts is Early Norman. One N and one S window belong to that style. There were then no buttresses. Later, probably in the C14, buttresses were added, and the upper parts of the tower with handsome two-light transomed bell-openings and battlements. The rest of the church is also late medieval. Brick N porch, brick chan-cel, and brick E window of the S aisle. The nave was heightened in brick in 1833. Inside the church the severely plain tower arch clearly belongs to the Early Norman period, the S arcade of four bays with its octagonal piers and triple-chamfered arches to the C14. – FONT. Of the Purbeck type, C13, octa-gonal, with two of the usual shallow blank pointed arches to each side. – PAINTING. Pretty cartouches with biblical inscriptions on the upper nave walls. The date is no doubt that of the heightening of the nave. – SCULPTURE. Lunette by *Giovanni della Robbia* (?), Christ and three Angels. Clearly no earlier than the mid C16. – ROYAL ARMS. C18, carved, on the W wall.

WEST MERSEA HALL, E of the church. Four bays wide, timber-framed, but with a big hipped roof – early C18.

YEW TREE HOUSE, SW of the church at the corner of The Coast. A good early C18 brick house, two-storeyed, of five bays, with segment-headed windows and top parapet. The brick is red and blue chequerwork. The doorway with Roman Doric pilasters and no pediment.

(A new house in THE LANE by *R. Finch* was published in 1955.)

MERSEA MOUNT, 1½ m. NE of the church. Romano-British burial mound, 100 ft in diameter and 22 ft 6 in. high. Its contents were remarkable. The excavators found a small chamber, 18 in. square and 21 in. high, constructed of Roman tiles. Inside the chamber was a small square lead casket containing a glass bowl 11½ in. high. In the glass bowl were the cremated remains of a grown-up person. Sherds in the body of the mound suggest a date in the C1.

WHEEL TOMB, in a garden in Beach Road, 200 yds E of the church. The tomb consists of a small hexagonal room from which radiate six walls to an encircling wall 65 ft in diameter, the whole resembling a spoked wheel in plan. Similar tombs are to be found elsewhere within the Roman Empire.

WEST THURROCK

ST CLEMENT.* The most remarkable thing about the church is its position, lovely and rather forlorn in the marshes, cut off by the railway from the village and now overtowered by a modern factory just E of it. The church has a handsome C15 w tower with diagonal buttresses and stripes of flint and stonework. The top brick. This tower replaced a former circular tower. The oldest features of the church are the tiny C12 N aisle w windows and the plain N doorway. Then follows the N arcade of two bays (circular pier and double-chamfered arches), the s arcade (octagonal pier and double-chamfered arches), N transept (now N chapel), and the chancel. Their windows are cusped lancets (chancel N and S), and two cusped lancet lights and a quatrefoil above (N chapel E, with two blank lancets to the l. and r. Was this originally a stepped-lancet-group?). The N chapel N windows are C14. So are the octagonal piers to the N and S chapels. – FONT. Perp, octagonal, with quatrefoil panels. – COMMUNION RAIL. Early C17. – STAINED GLASS. Various small bits, especially E window. – TILES. In N chapel, re-set, early C14 fleurs-de-lis, foliage, eagle, etc. – PLATE. Cup of 1564. – MONUMENTS. Coffin lid of Purbeck marble with foliated cross, C13. – Brass to Humphrey Heies † 1584 and son (hidden by chancel seats). – Sir Christopher Helford † 1608 and Lady Helford, two stiff semi-reclining alabaster figures, not in their original context.

* Foundations of a circular church with a square chancel and timber w porch have been found. The circular portion was beneath the present tower. As the church never belonged to the Templars nor ever was dedicated to St Sepulchre, it remains puzzling why it should have been given this form.

(TECHNICAL COLLEGE. By the County Architect, *H.Conolly*, *c*.1954–5.)

HEDLEY'S SOAP FACTORY. 1939–40 by *E.N.Horton* and *S. Burn*, good straightforward modern blocks without imposed symmetry.

WEST TILBURY

ST JAMES. Well placed on the edge of the escarpment looking to the s towards the river. The Royal Commission mentions an Early Norman window partly preserved in the N wall. This cannot now be seen. On the s side near the w end one deeply splayed lancet. Otherwise C14 windows. w tower of 1883. – PLATE. Chalices given in 1772 and 1797.

TILBURY FORT, see Tilbury Docks.

WETHERSFIELD

ST MARY MAGDALENE AND ST MARY THE VIRGIN. Low, massive early C13 w tower without buttresses. Small lancet windows, bell-openings of two lights separated by a polygonal shaft. Their existence in the place where they are proves that the tower was not meant to be taller. Short shingled spire of a rare, rather German than English shape. Early C14 chancel, see the E window with reticulated tracery (also the re-set E window in the C19 vestry) and the blank arcading, low N recess, and PISCINA inside the chancel. The N and (renewed) s aisle windows are late C14 – straight-headed with the Early Perp version of reticulation (cf. Shalford). The interior confirms the date of the tower: low, unmoulded, but pointed arch towards the nave. It also introduces a new period. The s arcade is clearly C13, but probably later than the tower. Circular piers and double-chamfered arches, and the E respond with stiff-leaf on a defaced head-corbel. The N arcade is yet later: octagonal piers and double-chamfered arches, but a short vertical piece first, rising from the capitals and dying into the arch. That goes with the date of the aisles. C15 clerestory and nave roof. – SCREEN. Quite tall, of one-light divisions, each with an ogee arch and panel tracery above. – STAINED GLASS. Many fragments, in various windows, mostly C14, though also C15. – PLATE. Paten of 1561; Cup of 1561 (?); both richly chased. – MONUMENTS. Possibly Henry Wentworth † 1482 and wife. Tomb-chest with alabaster effigies, not of high quality. – Mott Family, *c*.1760, one of the many, often very fine, and hardly ever signed Rococo tablets of various marbles which occur in Home County churches. Urn above, as usual, and cherub's head below. – Joseph Clarke † 1790, by *E. Tomson*, large tablet, also of various marbles.

The village of Wethersfield, though less celebrated than Finchingfield, is in its way visually just as satisfying. Whereas Finchingfield is very concentrated, Wethersfield is spread out and runs up and down divers hills. The centre is the triangular Green at the apex of which lies the churchyard. As to individual houses, the Royal Commission describes about sixty in the parish. The nicest looking are along the street to the N of the Green and the church. An equally rewarding branch goes off to the S. They are all timber-framed and mostly plastered. No specially notable Georgian house except the Rectory, 1758–9.

(GREAT CODHAM HALL, 2¾ m. SE. The original late C14 hall remains, though divided into two storeys in the C16. But one C14 roof-truss can still be seen. It has a heavily moulded tie-beam, octagonal king-post, and two-way struts. C16 and C17 wings, front C18. N of the house a cottage which was formerly a chapel. R.C.)

WHITE COLNE

ST ANDREW. So thoroughly restored in 1869 by *C. J. Moxon* that nothing of interest remains outside. Inside behind the pulpit three odd niches, the taller central one pointed, the outer two round. – The PULPIT is an unusually enriched usual C17 piece. Hexagonal, with, at the angles, term pilasters with ornament in the Jacobean style. But on three of the panels, in relief, well carved figures of the Virgin, St James the Great, and St Augustine of Hippo. The style is not English. Can it be Flemish? – PLATE. Small Cup with band of ornament of 1563; Paten probably also 1563.

WHITE HOUSE see MUNDON

WHITE NOTLEY

CHURCH (dedication unknown). Nave and aisles under one big roof. Narrower chancel. The chancel arch is the only at once visible feature of the Norman age. It is dressed with Roman bricks. To its l. and r. two round-headed niches. Traces of a Norman doorway in the S wall of the chancel can also be detected. The chancel was remodelled in the C13, see the lancet windows so far as original. The S aisle and S arcade are of c.1250. Circular piers and double-chamfered arches. The N aisle and N arcade a little later, with the same arches but octagonal piers. C14 S porch with plainly cusped bargeboarding. C15 belfry on four posts, with cusped arched braces on polygonal shafts high up. – FONT. Octagonal, Perp, traceried stem, bowl with quatrefoils with leaves or grotesque heads. – DOOR. C14, traceried. – SCREENS, N and S aisles, E end. Both of no special interest. – CHEST. Big dug-out, with bevelled lid, C13? – STAINED GLASS. Upper half of the figure of a King (?), C13.

WHITE NOTLEY HALL. C16 house, quite large, with the centre hall well preserved. This central portion of the house is timber-framed and dates from c.1530. The brick W wing is about fifty years later.

LOCKUP. Brick with curved brick roof, by the Cross Keys Inn, dated 1828.

(PENNETT'S FARM, 1 m. NW. At the N end of the house the C15 hall survives, still open to the roof. The roof has one original truss, with tie-beam on arched braces, king-post, and four-way struts. R.C.)

WHITE RODING

ST MARTIN. Norman nave with Roman brick quoins, two plain doorways, some original windows, and a plain one-stepped chancel arch. Chancel E.E. with a simple recess in the N wall. W tower c.1500 with diagonal buttresses, battlements, and recessed lead spire. – SOUTH DOOR with some C13 iron work. – FONT. Norman, square, of Purbeck marble with zigzag decoration and incised concentric circles in the spandrels on the top.

COLVILLE HALL, ½ m. W. Good C15 house with C16 and C17 additions, timber-framed and plastered, with various gables. Much original panelling inside and several mullioned timber windows. To the S Early Tudor gateway into the walled garden. To the W stables, with exposed timber and largely original brick-nogging – an exquisite piece of its type.

WINDMILL, ¼ m. SE of the church. Tower-mill in a poor condition.

WICKEN BONHUNT

ST MARGARET. Chancel C13, see some windows, especially the one high up in the E gable and the S window, which is shafted inside. The rest of the church was built in 1858–9 and designed by *John Hanson Sperling*.* – PLATE. Small Cup of

* Who may well be responsible also for the gruesome RECTORY of 1856, red and yellow brick bands and several sharp gables.

1571. – MONUMENT. J. S. Bradbury † 1731, signed by *H. Scheemakers*. Relief scene flanked by volutes on the l. and r. showing Mr Bradbury rising up with open arms and cherubs above and beside him.

CHAPEL OF ST HELEN, Bonhunt Farm, ¾ m. E. A complete Norman chapel of nave and chancel with a number of plain original windows.

BRICK HOUSE, less than ¼ m. SW. Small compact C17 brick building with one shaped and one altered gable. Transomed four-light windows. Later doorcase with segmental pediment. Above it a circular niche with the bust of a Roman emperor. The house belonged to the Bradbury family.

WICKFORD

(CHURCH (dedication unknown). Rebuilt in 1876 by *Henry Stone*; some materials from the old church were re-used, including the roof of *c*.1500. – The FONT is C15.)

WICKHAM BISHOPS

ST BARTHOLOMEW. 1850 by *Ewan Christian*. Quite ambitious, of freestone with a tall steeple with spire. With the erection of this church the old church became superfluous.

ST BARTHOLOMEW. The old church stands 1 m. SW of the new. It consists of nave and chancel with a small belfry. The only remaining feature of special interest is the SE quoin of Roman bricks, evidence of the Early Norman origin of the church.

A little N of the church WICKHAM MILLS, a very charming picture of a broad Early Georgian brick façade – blue brick with red dressings – with three-bay pediment (with an oval window in it), wings attached on the l. and r., and then on the r. the Mill itself.

Higher up in the village the house which *Arthur H. Mackmurdo* built for himself in 1904. It is surprisingly Italianate, considering that remarkable architect's earlier style. It has a big middle tower with octagonal lantern and symmetrical side lanterns on the façade l. and r. Mackmurdo never lived in the house. He had in the end to be content with a cottage near-by which is now called 'Mackmurdo's'. Opposite this another house by him, also with a central lantern.

(BEACONS. Also by *Mackmurdo*, *c*.1920, with a square turret and a good Gardener's Lodge.)

WICKHAM ST PAUL

ALL SAINTS. In 1505 in a will £20 was left for the building of the tower. It is indeed a fine specimen, though not high. Red brick with blue brick diapers, diagonal buttresses, high stair-turret, battlements, and brick pinnacles. Brick w doorway and brick w window of three lights with depressed pointed head and intersecting tracery. The rest of the church indifferent. – CHEST. Heavily iron-bound; C13. – SCREEN. With one-light divisions, ogee heads and some panel tracery above.

WIDDINGTON

ST MARY. Nave and chancel, and w tower of 1771, rebuilt in 1872. Of the same time the large imitation Perp windows on the N and S sides. The E window however and the chancel S window are original early C14 work. Inside one notices an earlier history of the chancel. There is one Norman N window and there is the surround of the Dec S window, which is of c.1260, with shafts, much dogtooth decoration, and good stiff-leaf capitals. – SCREEN. By *Sir Guy Dawber*, 1907. – By the same the WAR MEMORIAL, a simple oval tablet with good lettering. – STAINED GLASS. Sundial dated 1664 in a N window. – PLATE. Cup of 1562 with two bands of ornament; Paten and Almsdish, probably late C17. – BRASS to a Civilian, feet missing, c.1460.

PRIOR'S HALL, W of the church. One part of the house is a C13 stone structure. An outbuilding of the C15 has a wing with a five-bay timber roof: tie-beams on arched braces, and king-posts. Also a magnificent C15 barn, eight bays, aisles, tie-beams and king-posts.

RECTORY, W of the church. Timber-framed and now brick-faced. Fine S side with two slightly projecting wings, C18.

(WIDDINGTON HALL. The hall must either have been aisled or partly aisled, i.e. with an unaisled span in the middle. J. T. Smith)

SWAYNE'S HALL, see Debden.

WIDFORD,*

ST MARY. 1862 by *St Aubyn*. With a tall stone spire. – (In the churchyard MONUMENT to Viscountess Falkland, 1778, by *Edward Pearce*, designed by *G. Gibson*. See R. Gunnis.)

* Administratively in the Municipal Borough of Chelmsford.

HYLANDS.* Built for Sir John Comyns (see Writtle) about 1728. His house was seven bays wide and two-and-a-half storeys high and presumably very restrained in its exterior. In 1819–25 *William Atkinson* added a giant four-column Ionic portico and one-storeyed wings, also with Ionic centre pieces. These were heightened in 1842 by *J. B. Papworth*. Of *c*.1825 the lovely Neo-Greek decoration of the Entrance Hall and the Staircase and the Library bookcases. Of 1842 probably also the rather louder Neo-Baroque Dining Room in the l. wing and the redecoration of the other rooms in the wings.

THE WILLINGALES

WILLINGALE DOE and WILLINGALE SPAIN are two adjoining parishes. Their churches are so placed as to adjoin also. They share the same churchyard, St Christopher Willingale Doe lying on its N, St Andrew Willingale Spain on its s side. St Christopher is the larger church. It has a W tower (with diagonal buttresses and battlements), whereas St Andrew has only a belfry.

ST ANDREW is the older church. The nave has in the N wall two Norman windows and a plain Norman doorway, in the s wall one window and a doorway. These and the quoins make much use of Roman bricks. The chancel is C15, as is the belfry resting on a tie-beam carried by two posts with arched braces. – FONT. Octagonal, C14, with traceried stem and quatrefoils carrying roses and heads. – DOOR in N doorway, with uncommonly extensive C12 ironwork, divers long stems with leaves besides the usual scrolled strap-hinges. – PLATE. Cup, Paten, and Flagon of 1766.

ST CHRISTOPHER is terribly restored. The exterior has no untouched features, and the whole N aisle with its arcade also belongs to the restoration of 1853. – FONT. Octagonal, Perp, with traceried stem and quatrefoils carrying shields. – HELM (chancel, N wall). C16. – MONUMENTS. Brass to Thomas Torrell † 1442, Knight in armour, the figure 3 ft long. – Two Brasses of 1582 and 1613 in the N aisle and nave. – Robert Wiseman † 1641 and Richard Wiseman † 1618 and his wife † 1635. Large monument with semi-reclining figure flanked by two and behind a third column. Above the entablature carried by these, two kneeling figures facing each other. They kneel under two arches. Achievement on a third arch standing on the other two.

* Parish of Writtle.

WARDEN'S HALL. Built *c.*1740. Brick, of five bays and two storeys, with a doorcase with alternatingly rusticated jambs and segment-headed windows.

(TORRELL'S HALL. Front block with Doric porch designed by *John Johnson* for John Crabbe. Information from Miss N. Briggs.)

WILLIS FARM *see* EAST HANNINGFIELD

Wimbish, Brass to Sir John de Wantone † 1347 and wife
in its original state

WIMBISH

ALL SAINTS. Norman nave (see one s window and the s doorway, with two orders of columns, one of them spiral-carved and with volute capitals, the other smooth and with one-scallop capitals; both have plaited rings below the capitals). The C13 made alterations to this Norman nave, but it is not easy to understand them. The only evidence is a blank pointed arcade outside, just above the Norman window. What was its purpose? Inside, the N arcade is also C13. It has quatrefoil piers and double-hollow-chamfered arches. N aisle and s porch C15. Chancel 1868, w tower taken down in 1883 and not yet rebuilt. The N aisle roof is dated 1534 in one of the graceful tracery spandrels of the braces. – SCREEN to the N chapel; one-light divisions with ogee heads and mouchettes above; C15. – MONUMENT. Sir John de Wantone † 1347 and wife. An unusual and delightful piece. Two small brasses, only 18 in. long, both in the elegant, swaying attitudes of that age. The style is very similar to that of the most accomplished of English brasses, that of Sir Hugh Hastings at Elsing in Norfolk († 1347). Fragments of a cross-head in the form of an ogee quatrefoil around the figures.

WITHAM

The Witham which has to be looked at consists of two parts, the long High Street with the streets continuing it, and the groups of houses at Chippinghill by the church.

ST NICHOLAS. A large flint church, almost entirely of the C14. C14 is the w tower with diagonal buttresses, a w window with Dec tracery and battlements, C14 the nave and both aisles, C14 the embattled s porch, C14 the chancel and the embattled N vestry. Only the N and s chancel chapels are C15, and the s doorway is the one surviving piece of evidence of an earlier church: c.1200 with three orders of columns and voussoirs partly with three-dimensional zigzag and partly with keeled roll-mouldings. The s and N aisle windows are of the same pattern of tracery as the w window of the tower, the porch windows are different but of the same character. One s aisle window is different, but also Dec. The chancel E window (renewed) has ogee reticulation. The arcades of four bays have curious piers consisting of a square with big attached demi-shafts, and arches with a double wave moulding. Tall steep tower arch on semicircular responds. The C15 s chapel opens in two bays into the chancel. The pier has an odd section as if re-used or re-tooled. It consists of four shafts connected by deeply undercut hollows. The roofs are all original, of divers varieties but not of special note. – PULPIT. By *G. F. Bodley*.* – SCREEN. Of tall lights arched and cusped at the top and with cusped ogee arches a little lower down. – ROYAL ARMS of William III, finely carved (s chapel). – SCULPTURE. Small wooden relief of the Nativity (s chapel). Mannerist and not English. – FUNERAL HELMS (Lady Chapel). Late C15, late C16, C17. – PLATE. Alms-Basin elaborately engraved, probably a Dessert Dish; given in 1617. – MONUMENTS. Mary Smith † 1592, the usual design with kneeling couple. – John Southcotte † 1585. Plain tomb-chest with recumbent effigies; he in judge's robes. Good quality; alabaster. – William East † 1726. Large monument with excellent bust above a big inscription tablet. Columns l. and r. supporting a broken segmental pediment. Cherubs standing l. and r. and reclining on the pediment. (Signed by *C. Horsnaile*, see R. Gunnis.)

ALL SAINTS. 1842 by *J. Brown* of Norwich. Flint and white brick. Large, in the lancet style. W end with very big bellcote. Nave without aisles, but transepts and, oddly enough, a tripartite chancel, that is a chancel with aisles of two bays – all this vaulted.

BAPTIST CHAPEL, Maldon Road. 1828, enlarged 1857. Nice simple white pedimented brick front.

CONGREGATIONAL CHURCH, High Street. 1840. White brick, of five bays with five-bay pediment.

The High Street extends in a SW–NE direction along the Roman road, a long ribbon. It is continued without noticeable break in Bridge Street to the s, Newland Street to the N. We start from the s end. In BRIDGE STREET chiefly Nos 23–27, C16–C17 timber-framed, with the timbering partly exposed. Yet further s the former WORKHOUSE, 1839 with a polygonal centre block and an arched gateway. HIGH STREET is remarkable in that it widens in the middle and then contracts again before Newland Street is reached. Near the s end No. 126, five bays, early C18, blue brick with ample red brick dressings; two windows with little curly brick decoration of the lintels; the centre window arched. This motif recurs in other Witham houses (74, 85, 87). On the opposite side Nos

* Information from H. V. Molesworth Roberts.

117–119, a double house of five plus five bays and two-and-a-half storeys, also early C18, also of blue brick with red dressings; each house with its central pedimented doorway. Again opposite No. 100, C18 of seven bays. Nearer the centre the following deserve special notice: Nos 57 and 55 both C18 red brick, Nos 74 and 72 again blue with red dressings, No. 66 with a broad doorway and a window with rusticated surround above, then the SPREAD EAGLE, timber-framed, but in its façade now of Early Victorian picturesqueness.

NEWLAND STREET starts with some flourish, with Nos 2 and 4, of c.1700, refronted 1757, seven windows wide, with shell-hooded doorcase and three-bay addition. Then Nos 6–12, a pretty, if humble Georgian terrace. This is followed by ROSS-LYN HOUSE, white brick, of nine bays and two storeys with a pedimented Tuscan doorway. Opposite are the RED LION and FREEBOURNE'S HOUSE (No. 3), both timber-framed and gabled, and between them the HIGH HOUSE (No. 5), Later Georgian brick, of two storeys. Again opposite Nos 22–26, Georgian, of white brick. Then on the side of Freebourne's House the gardens of THE GROVE, a house once larger than it is now.

That is the end of that side. Now at CHIPPINGHILL, around the church, a very satisfying group of timber-framed houses lining the little triangular Green just SW of the church. They are on the church and churchyard side, all detached: Nos 18–22, then No. 24, then Nos 26–30. Opposite first Bernardiston House, with Georgian seven-bay front, then Moat Farm lying back, then No. 31 and Nos 37–41, partly pargeted.

Further out the following: One large C18 brick house in GUITHAVON VALLEY. – Following the continuation of Church Street, Chippinghill to the W: POWERS HALL, C16 house, refaced in the C18 in white brick. Fine seven-bay Barn to the SE. – S of Witham HOWBRIDGE HALL, largish timber-framed C16 house with sashed front. – SE by the river Blackwater BLUE MILLS, a very charming group with bridge, weatherboarded mill, and red brick miller's house and the adjoining five-bay brick front of a house called MATHYNS.

(SEED WAREHOUSE. For Messrs Couper, Taber & Co., Ltd, by *Chamberlin, Powell & Bon*, 1954–5. One of their best buildings, still entirely unmannered.)

EARTHWORK. On Chippinghill. Two concentric lines of oval entrenchment, now practically destroyed. Supposedly the site of a burg built by King Edward the Elder.

WIVENHOE

ST MARY THE VIRGIN. W tower of *c*.1500 with diagonal buttresses. On top a wooden cupola, C18? The rest is 1860 (by *Hakewill*) and of no interest. – FONT. Octagonal, Perp, with quatrefoils and shields. – STAINED GLASS. A good deal that is evidently of *c*.1860. – CHEST. Foreign, C16, with elaborate arabesque decoration and ornamental handles. – PLATE. Cup of 1562; C17 Paten; Flagon of 1709. – BRASSES. William Viscount Beaumont † 1507, figure of *c*.4 ft length but with a triple canopy with crocketed gables etc. which makes the whole plate 9 ft long. Same length the plate for Elizabeth, widow of Viscount Beaumont and wife of the Earl of Oxford † 1537. The figure is larger, also in an architectural surround. – Thomas Westeley † 1535, chaplain to the Countess of Oxford; in mass garments.

UNIVERSITY OF ESSEX. The University started its activities in October 1964. It began with 122 students, but it is intended to grow to 3,000 in the first ten years. The site is that of WIVENHOE PARK and its grounds, a total of 200 acres. Wivenhoe Park was built in 1758–61 but extensively altered and enlarged in the neo-Tudor style by *Hopper* in 1846–53. Red brick and stone dressings. Very elaborate and showy strapwork, termini, etc. The University, according to *Kenneth Capon*'s plans of 1962–3, will have its buildings W of Wivenhoe Park, except for the Vice-Chancellor's house, which will be built between the two picturesque C18 lakes N of the house, and the playing fields etc., which will be to the S. The main buildings consist of teaching and living quarters; the former S of the latter. Living quarters are intended to be in sixteen identical tower-blocks with study-bedrooms as well as studies for students not living in. The teaching premises are to be one very large building developed in an irregular zigzag across a spine-road. This access-road is at the bottom of the existing valley, which leads to the river Colne. Above it is a platform without any access for vehicles, and this is grouped in five close squares.

(WIVENHOE NEW PARK, N of the main Clacton Road, opposite Wivenhoe Park. A Palladian villa by *Raymond Erith*, 1964.)

The QUAY is pretty as such quays are, if the houses are well 1a looked after. But there are no houses of individual interest, in spite of nice bow and bay windows. The only house of merit is in EAST STREET just S of the church. It has a gorgeous

52b display of mid C17 pargeting, as good as any in the county. Large scrolls arranged round basic cross-shapes.

WIX

ST MARY. Nave and lower chancel with polygonal apse. They now look mostly C18 and undistinguished. But in the nave wall, on the N side, is a blocked former N arcade of the C13, with octagonal piers.

WIX ABBEY. Wix in the Middle Ages had a Benedictine nunnery founded in the C12 by Walther, Alexander, and Edith Mascherell. Of this only foundations have been found and are not now exposed. The present house has chiefly one feature which requires mention, the porch of *c*.1570 with an entrance with round arch and steep pediment, above this a former three-light one-transom window of which only the pediment (lower and broader) remains, and on the second floor another such window, completely preserved, with an identical pediment. A stepped gable crowns the porch.

WOODFORD

ST MARY THE VIRGIN, High Road. Solid w tower of red brick, built in 1708. Arched and circular windows, short, polygonal pinnacles. The body of the church is by *Charles Bacon*. Built in 1817, also red brick, with lancet windows. Nave and aisles. Thin piers and thin arcades. Recessed N and s galleries. Minor monuments, e.g. Rowland Elvington † 1595 and wife, small, with the usual two kneelers. Also Charles Foulis of 1783, by *J. Bacon*. Urn on pedestal on which in relief a seated woman holding an oil lamp. In the churchyard tall Corinthian COLUMN with entablature, a memorial to Peter Godfrey † 1742, designed by *Sir Robert Taylor*, whose early benefactor Peter Godfrey was. – RAIKES MAUSOLEUM. First interment Mrs William Raikes † 1797. Heavy neo-classical. – Edward Keeble † 1782 by *S. Robinson*, made of Coade stone; sarcophagus with angels at the corner; damaged (R. Gunnis).

(PUBLIC LIBRARY, The Broadway, Woodford Green. By *H. Conolly*, County Architect, opened 1961.)

(HAWKEY HALL, Woodford Green. By the *Borough Engineer*, 1955.)

BANCROFT'S SCHOOL. Big, symmetrical red brick building in the Tudor style with central gatehouse flanked by turrets. By *Sir Arthur Blomfield*, 1887–9. New Hall and Laboratories 1937 by *E. N. Clifton*.

(STUDENTS' HOSTEL, Queen Mary College. By *Playne & Lacey*, 1962–4.)

The remaining buildings of interest were all built as private residences. Woodford and its neighbourhood in their heyday must have been studded with Georgian houses of comfortable size. None are as spectacular as was Wanstead House near by, but several have features of luxury. Two are now no longer private houses.

CLAYBURY L.C.C. ASYLUM,* Manor Road. The asylum was built in 1890–3 to the designs of *G. T. Hine*. The tender was for £337,945 (GS). It now accommodates over 2,000 patients. In the grounds CLAYBURY HALL of c.1790. White brick brought from Woolpit in Suffolk. Garden front with bow window surrounded by a colonnade of Adamish Roman Doric columns. On another side well detailed Venetian window. The grounds were laid out by *Repton*, who in his Red Book praises the 'profusely beautiful situation'. Thatched, circular Summer House, called GROTTO; of tree trunks outside, shells, minerals, and spars inside.

DR BARNARDO'S HOMES, Manor Road. A site of 60 acres, built over by *W. A. Pite*. All houses smallish so as to create the impression of a garden city. The CHAPEL 1929 by *Walter Godfrey*. Outside very odd closely set flying buttresses forming tall lancet-like arches. In the grounds GWYNNE HOUSE, 1816 by *J. B. Papworth*, plain seven-by-five-bay, two-storeyed mansion.

A walk through Woodford may start from the church. Here and less than half a mile to S and N are the chief Georgian houses that survive. Right by the church a quite uncommonly complete stretch of houses, some in generous gardens. S of the church the COUNCIL OFFICES, plain seven-bay, two-and-a-half storey house. Opposite a group of smaller houses, followed to the S by three in gardens. The best is ELMHURST, the one furthest S, of five bays, with three-bay pediment. Yellow brick, doorway with rusticated Gibbs surround, and the window above connected with it. From here to the S, towards Wanstead, on the W side GROVE HALL‡ of nine bays and two storeys with broad doorway decorated by a segmental pediment on Corinthian pilasters (early C18) and then some more minor houses, e.g. No. 25.

To the N, at Woodford Green, on Salway Hill HURST HOUSE of

* Administratively in the Borough of Ilford.
‡ Now demolished.

*c.*1714, the best house of Woodford. It was built for a brewer. Six bays, with giant Corinthian pilasters and a parapet with vases. The doorway has Corinthian pilasters and an entablature rising to a point in the centre – a typical early C18 motif – and a big segmental pediment. Inside a staircase with daintily twisted balusters. Wrought-iron garden railings and gate.* At the N end of Salway Hill THE GREEN with several nice houses and two of more consequence: HIGHAMS on the w side (*see* Walthamstow) and HARTS on the E side. This dates from *c.*1800 and has on the entrance side two somewhat projecting side-pieces and a six-column Ionic colonnade between, and towards the garden seven bays with a three-bay pediment. Ample grounds with a sham ABBEY, built as a ruin and now more ruined.‡

WOOD HALL *see* ARKESDEN

WOODHAM FERRERS

ST MARY THE VIRGIN. Nave and aisle, chancel, belfry. With the exception of the latter essentially built between *c.*1250 and *c.*1330. The N and S arcades come first, three bays with alternating circular and octagonal piers, alternating also in a N–S direction across the nave. Moulded capitals and double-chamfered arches. Niches in the last pier and E respond on the S side. Clerestory C19, but with C13 splays. The chancel arch is of the same style, but the chancel is in one way noticeably later: the windows have bar-tracery with quatrefoils in circles. That can hardly be earlier than *c.*1275. The aisle windows have usual two-light Dec tracery. There was originally an early C16 W tower, but it has been demolished, and the tower arch bricked up. Patches of flint and stone flushwork on the l. and r. remain to indicate the character of the tower. The S porch is of timber, with six cusped arched openings on each side and a pargeted gable. The belfry rests on a big tie-beam, not on posts, as usual. – FONT COVER. Ogee-shaped, of thin ribs. – PAINTING. Doom above the chancel arch, C15, with Christ seated in the centre, angels on the l. and r., souls below, and the mouth of Hell in the r. corner. Hardly recognizable. – PLATE. Large Cup and Paten of 1668. – MONUMENTS.

* Much of the house was rebuilt after a fire in 1935.
‡ Mr J. E. Tuffs draws attention to LITTLE MONKHAMS in MONKHAMS LANE, Woodford Wells, a timber-framed house probably datable to *c.*1500.

Cecilie Sandys, wife of the Archbishop of York, † 1610, erected 1619. The usual alabaster design with a kneeling figure in profile, but in addition Father Time on the l., a missing figure on the r., and Victories on the semicircular pediment. What will be remembered as exceptional and enchanting is the background behind the figure and the whole area of the pediment, all carved into an arbour of roses.

EDWIN'S HALL, 1 m. E. Fragment of a larger house, said to have been built by Edwin Sandys, Archbishop of York. Red brick with black diapers. What now stands has a front to the s of irregular shape. The l. part has a new bay window and the porch. The r. part is recessed and has an original bay window. This part ends in a later parapet. Originally it may have possessed gables. The house went on to the E, then returned s and again w. It seems to have been a courtyard house with the Hall in the remaining wing behind porch and bay window. The windows are of stone with mullions and transoms. At the back of the remaining part brick windows and big original chimneystacks. The house is surrounded by a moat.

MOUNDS, 1¾ m. SE. They are not prehistoric burial mounds, but the remains of medieval salt workings.

BICKNACRE PRIORY, see p. 85.

WOODHAM MORTIMER

ST MARGARET. C19, except for the s wall of the nave with one small Norman window and the rere-arch of the doorway. – PLATE. Cup on Elizabethan stem. – BRASS. Dorothy Alleine † 1584, nothing special.

WOODHAM MORTIMER HALL. C17 brick front with four shaped gables. The rectangular projection was probably the original porch. Mullioned and transomed windows replaced by sash windows. On the w side one two-light brick window. Original chimneystacks.

OBELISK, opposite the Hall. To commemorate Mr Alexander, Lord of the Manor; 1825.

WOODHAM WALTER

ST MICHAEL. A red brick church entirely, small, but historically interesting, in that it was built in 1563–4, and yet is essentially still Gothic.* It has, it is true, stepped gables at the w and the E end, where that of the N vestry together with that

* The bell-turret and the E window are of the C19.

of the nave form a pretty E view, but otherwise the windows are Perp, straight-headed, with each light arched and cusped, the walls have buttresses, the arcade to the N aisle has piers superficially similar to the familiar four-shaft-four-hollow type (but the hollows are straightened out) and double-hollow-chamfered arches. The roofs also are of usual Perp types. – FONT. Large, octagonal, Perp, the stem decorated with tracery, the bowl with quatrefoils. – STAINED GLASS. In a S aisle window two heads and some scenes; C15. – PLATE. Cup of 1646; Paten on foot of 1706.

BELL INN, a little to the N, timber-framed, plastered, and with one gable. Later C16 to C17.

WOOD HOUSE see EPPING

WORMINGFORD

ST ANDREW. Norman W tower with original windows and bell-openings. Norman nave with one blocked S window. The N aisle and N windows early C14. Arcade of four bays with smallish octagonal piers and arches with two quadrant mouldings. – STAINED GLASS. C14 bits in chancel windows. – PLATE. Elizabethan Cup with band of ornament. – BRASSES. Civilian c.1450; Civilian and two wives, early C17; both in the floor under the tower.

Opposite the church CHURCH HOUSE, C16 with a later C16 S wing of brick. This has five-light transomed windows in the front and a shaped gable of very unusual form. CHURCH HALL lies to the N of the church, early C16, timber-framed and plastered.

JENKIN'S FARM, 1 m. S, was built about 1583. The date is on one of the carved brackets supporting the first floor of the porch. The gable projects beyond this first floor. The house is timber-framed with exposed timbers and specially attractive.

ROTCHFORDS, ¼ m. S of Jenkin's Farm. C15 and C16, timber-framed and plastered, but with a plain C18 front.

WRABNESS

ALL SAINTS. The point to observe is the bell-tower, if such it can be called. It is a one-storeyed weatherboarded little shed like a village lock-up, quite independent of the church. The date may be C17 or C18. The church consists of nave and lower chancel. N doorway Norman. S doorway C15, pretty,

with fleurons and hung-up shields in the voussoirs. The nave
has a hammerbeam roof, not a frequent feature in Essex. –
FONT. Octagonal, Perp, with deliberately defaced figures of
the Evangelists and their symbols.

WRITTLE

ALL SAINTS. Big and not very high W tower rebuilt in 1802.
Brick battlements and stone pinnacles. Nave and two aisles,
all embattled. The nave arcades and the clerestory 1879, with
the exception of two original piers, both circular. These belong
to the C13. The nave roof of low pitch rests on wooden demi-
figures of angels. The exterior walls of the aisles have some
Dec windows, indicating their age. The chancel chapels are
later C14. – CHANCEL STALLS with C15 poppy-heads and
fronts with open-work foliage scrolls of the early C18. –
BENCHES (N chapel) with poppy-heads, one with a bird, one
with a seated dog. – Very fragmentary WALL PAINTINGS, e.g.
St George above the N door. – STAINED GLASS. S aisle chapel
by *Clayton & Bell*, 1870. – S chancel chapel S by *C.P. Bacon*,
designed by the architect *Fellowes Prynne*. – S aisle (Queen
Victoria) by *Powell* 1902. – N aisle (1906) and chancel E (1914)
by *H. W. Bryans*. – MONUMENTS. An uncommonly large
number of Brasses. In the chancel floor Civilian and four
wives, *c.*1570 (17 in. figures), also a brass of 1609. Beneath the
entrance to the screen Knight, Lady, and children, *c.*1500
(2 ft 6 in.). In the S chapel: Two Knights and their wives,
*c.*1510 (2 ft 2 in.), Constance Berners † 1524, and another probably of 1592. – Monument to (?) Richard Weston † 1572,
tomb-chest with shields in three cusped lozenges; no effigies. –
Edward Elliott † 1595, and wife, small, with kneeling figures. –
Sir Edward Pinchon, made in 1629 by *Nicholas Stone* for
£66/13/4. Monument with an angel standing on a rock with
a wheatsheaf in front of it. The figure reaches up above a
segmental pediment behind. To the l. and the r. of the
pilasters elaborately decorated with harvest tools are two har-
vesting girls with large straw hats, asleep. The inscription is
from the parable of the Sower. The monument is a slightly
modified version of that to Joyce Austin (Lady Clarke) of
1633 in Southwark Cathedral. – Sir St John Comyns, Lord
Chief Baron of the Court of Exchequer, † 1740. Bulgy sarcophagus with life-size bust above. Urns to the l. and r. The
ornament is Rococo. Signed *H. Cheere*. Erected 1759.

ESSEX INSTITUTE OF AGRICULTURE. Mildly Neo-Georgian building of light brick with two symmetrically projecting wings and a centre lantern of the Swedish variety. 1938–9 by *J. Stuart*. (The Hostel, 1958, and Recreation Centre, 1964, are by *H. Conolly*, County Architect.)

Writtle possesses one of the most attractive village greens of Essex. The best view is to the s, with the church in the distance framed by AUBYNS, half-timbered house of *c*.1500, much restored and rebuilt recently, with two symmetrical gables,★ and MUNDAYS, a plastered C17 house with a shell-hooded entrance.

MOOR HALL. Gabled timber-framed C15 house with C16 additions. On the N front two tall gabled bay windows and a gabled porch. The gables have decorated bargeboards and the bay windows pendants and ornamented bressumers. Inside the house the Hall Screen survives partly, with one two-centred arch and another with a broad ogee head and quatre-foil tracery above.

('KING JOHN'S PALACE'. Recent excavations have proved the existence of C13–15 buildings.)

HYLANDS, see Widford.

★ The ground floor towards Church Lane was originally open in three bays with four-centred heads. What for ? As a rule such blocked openings indicate a shop.

GLOSSARY

ABACUS: flat slab on the top of a capital (q.v.).

ABUTMENT: solid masonry placed to resist the lateral pressure of a vault.

ACANTHUS: plant with thick fleshy and scalloped leaves used as part of the decoration of a Corinthian capital (q.v.) and in some types of leaf carving.

ACHIEVEMENT OF ARMS: in heraldry, a complete display of armorial bearings.

ACROTERION: foliage-carved block on the end or top of a classical pediment.

ADDORSED: two human figures, animals, or birds, etc., placed symmetrically so that they turn their backs to each other.

AEDICULE, AEDICULA: framing of a window or door by columns and a pediment (q.v.).

AFFRONTED: two human figures, animals, or birds, etc., placed symmetrically so that they face each other.

AGGER: Latin term for the built-up foundations of Roman roads; also sometimes applied to the banks of hill-forts or other earthworks.

AMBULATORY: semicircular or polygonal aisle enclosing an apse (q.v.).

ANNULET: see Shaft-ring.

ANSE DE PANIER: see Arch, Basket.

ANTEPENDIUM: covering of the front of an altar, usually by textiles or metalwork.

ANTIS, IN: see Portico.

APSE: vaulted semicircular or polygonal end of a chancel or a chapel.

ARABESQUE: light and fanciful surface decoration using combinations of flowing lines, tendrils, etc., interspersed with vases, animals, etc.

ARCADE: range of arches supported on piers or columns, free-standing; or, BLIND ARCADE, the same attached to a wall.

ARCH: round-headed, i.e. semicircular; pointed, i.e. consisting of two curves, each drawn from one centre, and meeting in a point at the top; segmental, i.e. in the form of a segment; pointed; four-centred (a Late Medieval form), see Fig. 1(a); Tudor (also a Late Medieval form), see Fig. 1(b); Ogee (introduced c. 1300 and specially popular in the C14), see Fig.

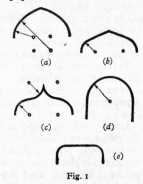

Fig. 1

1(*c*); Stilted, *see* Fig. 1(*d*); Basket, with lintel connected to the jambs by concave quadrant curves, *see* Fig. 1(*e*).

ARCHITRAVE: lowest of the three main parts of the entablature (q.v.) of an order (q.v.) (*see* Fig. 12).

ARCHIVOLT: under-surface of an arch (also called Soffit).

ARRIS: sharp edge at the meeting of two surfaces.

ASHLAR: masonry of large blocks wrought to even faces and square edges.

ATLANTES: male counterparts of caryatids (q.v.).

ATRIUM: inner court of a Roman house, also open court in front of a church.

ATTACHED: *see* Engaged.

ATTIC: topmost storey of a house, if distance from floor to ceiling is less than in the others.

AUMBRY: recess or cupboard to hold sacred vessels for Mass and Communion.

B

BAILEY: open space or court of a stone-built castle; *see* also Motte-and-Bailey.

BALDACCHINO: canopy supported on columns.

BALLFLOWER: globular flower of three petals enclosing a small ball. A decoration used in the first quarter of the C14.

BALUSTER: small pillar or column of fanciful outline.

BALUSTRADE: series of balusters supporting a handrail or coping (q.v.).

BARBICAN: outwork defending the entrance to a castle.

BARGEBOARDS: projecting decorated boards placed against the incline of the gable of a building and hiding the horizontal roof timbers.

BARROW: *see* Bell, Bowl, Disc, Long, *and* Pond Barrow.

BASILICA: in medieval architecture an aisled church with a clerestory.

BASKET ARCH: *see* Arch (Fig. 1e).

BASTION: projection at the angle of a fortification.

BATTER: inclined face of a wall.

BATTLEMENT: parapet with a series of indentations or embrasures with raised portions or merlons between (also called Crenellation).

BAYS: internal compartments of a building; each divided from the other not by solid walls but by divisions only marked in the side walls (columns, pilasters, etc.) or the ceiling (beams, etc.). Also external divisions of a building by fenestration.

BAY-WINDOW: angular or curved projection of a house front with ample fenestration. If curved, also called bow-window; if on an upper floor only, also called oriel or oriel window.

BEAKER FOLK: Late New Stone Age warrior invaders from the Continent who buried their dead in round barrows and introduced the first metal tools and weapons to Britain.

BEAKHEAD: Norman ornamental motif consisting of a row of bird or beast heads with beaks biting usually into a roll moulding.

BELFRY: turret on a roof to hang bells in.

BELGAE: Aristocratic warrior bands who settled in Britain in two main waves in the C1 B.C. In Britain their culture is termed Iron Age C.

BELL BARROW: Early Bronze Age round barrow in which the mound is separated from its encircling ditch by a flat platform or berm (q.v.).

BELLCOTE: framework on a roof to hang bells from.

BERM: level area separating ditch from bank on a hill-fort or barrow.

BILLET FRIEZE: Norman ornamental motif made up of short raised rectangles placed at regular intervals.

BIVALLATE: Of a hill-fort: defended by two concentric banks and ditches.

BLOCK CAPITAL: Romanesque capital cut from a cube by having the lower angles rounded off to the circular shaft below (also called Cushion Capital) (Fig. 2).

Fig. 2

BOND, ENGLISH or FLEMISH: see Brickwork.

BOSS: knob or projection usually placed to cover the intersection of ribs in a vault.

BOW-WINDOW: see Bay-Window.

BOX: A small country house, e.g. a shooting box. A convenient term to describe a compact minor dwelling, e.g. a rectory.

BOX PEW: pew with a high wooden enclosure.

BOWL BARROW: round barrow surrounded by a quarry ditch. Introduced in Late Neolithic

times, the form continued until the Saxon period.

BRACES: see Roof.

BRACKET: small supporting piece of stone, etc., to carry a projecting horizontal.

BRESSUMER: beam in a timber-framed building to support the, usually projecting, superstructure.

BRICKWORK: *Header:* brick laid so that the end only appears on the face of the wall. *Stretcher:* brick laid so that the side only appears on the face of the wall. *English Bond:* method of laying bricks so that alternate courses or layers on the face of the wall are composed of headers or stretchers only (Fig. 3*a*). *Flemish Bond:* method of laying bricks so that alternate headers and stretchers appear in each course on the face of the wall (Fig. 3*b*).

(a)

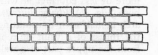

(b)

Fig. 3

BROACH: see Spire.

BROKEN PEDIMENT: see Pediment.

BRONZE AGE: In Britain, the period from c. 1600 to 600 B.C.

BUCRANIUM: ox skull.

BUTTRESS: mass of brickwork or masonry projecting from or built against a wall to give

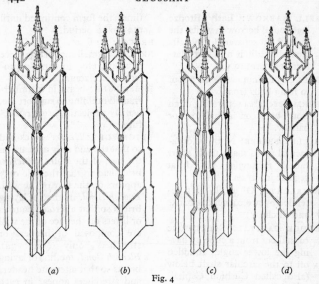

(a)   (b)   (c)   (d)
Fig. 4

additional strength. *Angle But-*
tresses: two meeting at an angle
of 90° at the angle of a building
(Fig. 4a). *Clasping Buttress:*
one which encases the angle
(Fig. 4d). *Diagonal Buttress:*
one placed against the right
angle formed by two walls, and
more or less equiangular with
both (Fig. 4b). *Flying Buttress:*
arch or half arch transmitting
the thrust of a vault or roof
from the upper part of a wall
to an outer support or buttress.
Setback Buttress: angle buttress set slightly back from the
angle (Fig. 4c).

CABLE MOULDING: Norman
moulding imitating a twisted
cord.

CAIRN: a mound of stones usually
covering a burial.

CAMBER: slight rise or upward
curve of an otherwise horizontal structure.

CAMPANILE: isolated bell tower.

CANOPY: projection or hood
over an altar, pulpit, niche,
statue, etc.

CAP: in a windmill the crowning
feature.

CAPITAL: head or top part of a
column (q.v.).

CARTOUCHE: tablet with an
ornate frame, usually enclosing
an inscription.

CARYATID: whole female figure
supporting an entablature or
other similar member. *Termini*
Caryatids: female busts or
demi-figures or three-quarter
figures supporting an entablature or other similar member
and placed at the top of termini
pilasters (q.v.). Cf. Atlantes.

CASTELLATED: decorated with
battlements.

CELURE: panelled and adorned part of a wagon-roof above the rood or the altar.

CENSER: vessel for the burning of incense.

CENTERING: wooden framework used in arch and vault construction and removed when the mortar has set.

CHALICE: cup used in the Communion service or at Mass.

CHAMBERED TOMB: burial mound of the New Stone Age having a stone-built chamber and entrance passage covered by an earthen barrow or stone cairn. The form was introduced to Britain from the Mediterranean.

CHAMFER: surface made by cutting across the square angle of a stone block, piece of wood, etc., at an angle of 45° to the other two surfaces.

CHANCEL: that part of the E end of a church in which the altar is placed, usually applied to the whole continuation of the nave E of the crossing.

CHANCEL ARCH: arch at the W end of the chancel.

CHANTRY CHAPEL: chapel attached to, or inside, a church, endowed for the saying of Masses for the soul of the founder or some other individual.

CHEVET: French term for the E end of a church (chancel, ambulatory, and radiating chapels).

CHEVRON: Norman moulding forming a zigzag.

CHOIR: that part of the church where divine service is sung.

CIBORIUM: a baldacchino.

CINQUEFOIL: see Foil.

CIST: stone-lined or slab-built grave. First appears in Late Neolithic times. It continued to be used in the Early Christian period.

CLAPPER BRIDGE: bridge made of large slabs of stone, some built up to make rough piers and other longer ones laid on top to make the roadway.

CLASSIC: here used to mean the moment of highest achievement of a style.

CLASSICAL: here used as the term for Greek and Roman architecture and any subsequent styles inspired by it.

CLERESTORY: upper storey of the nave walls of a church, pierced by windows.

COADE STONE: artificial (cast) stone made in the late C18 and the early C19 by Coade and Sealy in London.

COB: walling material made of mixed clay and straw.

COFFERING: decorating a ceiling with sunk square or polygonal ornamental panels.

COLLAR-BEAM: see Roof.

COLONNADE: range of columns.

COLONNETTE: small column.

COLUMNA ROSTRATA: column decorated with carved prows of ships to celebrate a naval victory.

COMPOSITE: see Order.

CONSOLE: bracket (q.v.) with a compound curved outline.

COPING: capping or covering to a wall.

CORBEL: block of stone projecting from a wall, supporting some horizontal feature.

CORBEL TABLE: series of corbels, occurring just below the roof eaves externally or internally, often seen in Norman buildings.

CORINTHIAN: see Orders.

CORNICE: in classical architecture the top section of the entablature (q.v.). Also for a projecting decorative feature along the top of a wall, arch, etc.

CORRIDOR VILLA: *see* Villa.

COUNTERSCARP BANK: small bank on the down-hill or outer side of a hill-fort ditch.

COURTYARD VILLA: *see* Villa.

COVE, COVING: concave under-surface in the nature of a hollow moulding but on a larger scale.

COVER PATEN: cover to a Communion cup, suitable for use as a paten or plate for the consecrated bread.

CRADLE ROOF: *see* Wagon roof.

CRENELLATION: *see* Battlement.

CREST, CRESTING: ornamental finish along the top of a screen, etc.

CROCKET, CROCKETING: decorative features placed on the sloping sides of spires, pinnacles, gables, etc., in Gothic architecture, carved in various leaf shapes and placed at regular intervals.

CROCKET CAPITAL: *see* Fig. 5. An Early Gothic form.

Fig. 5

CROMLECH: word of Celtic origin still occasionally used of single free-standing stones ascribed to the Neolithic or Bronze Age periods.

CROSSING: space at the inter-section of nave, chancel, and transepts.

CROSS-WINDOWS: windows with one mullion and one transom.

CRUCK: big curved beam supporting both walls and roof of a cottage.

CRYPT: underground room usually below the E end of a church.

CUPOLA: small polygonal or circular domed turret crowning a roof.

CURTAIN WALL: connecting wall between the towers of a castle.

CUSHION CAPITAL: *see* Block Capital.

CUSP: projecting point between the foils in a foiled Gothic arch.

D ADO: decorative covering of the lower part of a wall.

DAGGER: tracery motif of the Dec style. It is a lancet shape rounded or pointed at the head, pointed at the foot, and cusped inside (*see* Fig. 6).

Fig. 6

DAIS: raised platform at one end of a room.

DEC ('DECORATED'): historical division of English Gothic architecture covering the period from c.1290 to c.1350.

DEMI-COLUMNS: columns half sunk into a wall.

DIAPER WORK: surface decoration composed of square or lozenge shapes.

DISC BARROW: Bronze Age round barrow with inconspicuous central mound surrounded by bank and ditch.

DOGTOOTH: typical E.E. ornament consisting of a series of four-cornered stars placed diagonally and raised pyramidally (Fig. 7).

Fig. 7

DOMICAL VAULT: *see* Vault.

DONJON: *see* Keep.

DORIC: *see* Order.

DORMER (WINDOW): window placed vertically in the sloping plane of a roof.

DRIPSTONE: *see* Hood-mould.

DRUM: circular or polygonal vertical wall of a dome or cupola.

E.E. ('EARLY ENGLISH'): historical division of English Gothic architecture roughly covering the C13.

EASTER SEPULCHRE: recess with tomb-chest usually in the wall of a chancel, the tomb-chest to receive an effigy of Christ for Easter celebrations.

EAVES: underpart of a sloping roof overhanging a wall.

EAVES CORNICE: cornice below the eaves of a roof.

ECHINUS: convex or projecting moulding supporting the abacus of a Greek Doric capital, sometimes bearing an egg and dart pattern.

EMBATTLED: *see* Battlement.

EMBRASURE: small opening in the wall or parapet of a fortified building, usually splayed on the inside.

ENCAUSTIC TILES: earthenware glazed and decorated tiles used for paving.

ENGAGED COLUMNS: columns attached to, or partly sunk into, a wall.

ENGLISH BOND: *see* Brickwork.

ENTABLATURE: in classical architecture the whole of the horizontal members above a column (that is architrave, frieze, and cornice) (*see* Fig. 12).

ENTASIS: very slight convex deviation from a straight line; used on Greek columns and sometimes on spires to prevent an optical illusion of concavity.

ENTRESOL: *see* Mezzanine.

EPITAPH: hanging wall monument.

ESCUTCHEON: shield for armorial bearings.

EXEDRA: the apsidal end of a room. *See* Apse.

FAN-VAULT: *see* Vault.

FERETORY: place behind the High Altar where the chief shrine of a church is kept.

FESTOON: carved garland of flowers and fruit suspended at both ends.

FILLET: narrow flat band running down a shaft or along a roll moulding.

FINIAL: top of a canopy, gable, pinnacle.

FLAGON: vessel for the wine used in the Communion service.

FLAMBOYANT: properly the latest phase of French Gothic architecture where the window tracery takes on wavy undulating lines.

FLÈCHE: slender wooden spire on the centre of a roof (also called Spirelet).

FLEMISH BOND: *see* Brickwork.

FLEURON: decorative carved flower or leaf.

FLUSHWORK: decorative use of flint in conjunction with dressed stone so as to form patterns: tracery, initials, etc.

FLUTING: vertical channelling in the shaft of a column.

FLYING BUTTRESS: *see* Buttress.

FOIL: lobe formed by the cusping (q.v.) of a circle or an arch. Trefoil, quatrefoil, cinquefoil, multifoil, express the number of leaf shapes to be seen.

FOLIATED: carved with leaf shapes.

FOSSE: ditch.

FOUR-CENTRED ARCH: *see* Arch.

FRATER: refectory or dining hall of a monastery.

FRESCO: wall painting on wet plaster.

FRIEZE: middle division of a classical entablature (q.v.) (*see* Fig. 12).

FRONTAL: covering for the front of an altar.

GABLE: *Dutch gable:* A gable with curved sides crowned by a

Fig. 8(a)

pediment, characteristic of c. 1630–50 (Fig. 8a). *Shaped gable:* A gable with multi-curved sides characteristic of c. 1600–50 (Fig. 8b).

Fig. 8(b)

GADROONED: enriched with a series of convex ridges, the opposite of fluting.

GALILEE: chapel or vestibule usually at the W end of a church enclosing the porch. Also called Narthex (q.v.).

GALLERY: in church architecture upper storey above an aisle, opened in arches to the nave. Also called Tribune and often erroneously Triforium (q.v.).

GALLERY GRAVE: chambered tomb (q.v.) in which there is little or no differentiation between the entrance passage and the actual burial chamber(s).

GARDEROBE: lavatory or privy in a medieval building.

GARGOYLE: water spout projecting from the parapet of a wall or tower; carved into a human or animal shape.

GAZEBO: lookout tower or raised summer house in a picturesque garden.

'GEOMETRICAL': *see* Tracery.

'GIBBS SURROUND': of a doorway or window. An C18 motif consisting of a surround with alternating larger and smaller blocks of stone, quoin-wise, or intermittent large blocks, sometimes with a narrow raised band connecting them up the

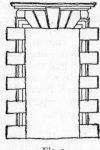

Fig. 9

verticals and along the face of the arch (Fig. 9).

GROIN: sharp edge at the meeting of two cells of a cross-vault.

GROIN-VAULT: *see* Vault.

GROTESQUE: fanciful ornamental decoration: *see* also Arabesque.

HAGIOSCOPE: *see* Squint.

HALF-TIMBERING: *see* Timber-Framing.

HALL CHURCH: church in which nave and aisles are of equal height or approximately so.

HAMMERBEAM: *see* Roof.

HANAP: large metal cup, generally made for domestic use, standing on an elaborate base and stem; with a very ornate cover frequently crowned with a little steeple.

HEADERS: *see* Brickwork.

HERRINGBONE WORK: brick, stone, or tile construction where the component blocks are laid diagonally instead of flat. Alternate courses lie in opposing directions to make a zigzag pattern up the face of the wall.

HEXASTYLE: having six detached columns.

HILL-FORT: Iron Age earthwork enclosed by a ditch and bank system; in the later part of the period the defences multiplied in size and complexity. They vary from about an acre to over 30 acres in area, and are usually built with careful regard to natural elevations or promontories.

HIPPED ROOF: *see* Roof.

HOOD-MOULD: projecting moulding above an arch or a lintel to throw off water (also called Dripstone or Label).

ICONOGRAPHY: the science of the subject matter of works of the visual arts.

IMPOST: bracket in a wall, usually formed of mouldings, on which the end of an arch rests.

INDENT: shape chiselled out in a stone slab to receive a brass.

INGLENOOK: bench or seat built in beside a fireplace, sometimes covered by the chimneybreast, occasionally lit by small windows on each side of the fire.

INTERCOLUMNIATION: the space between columns.

IONIC: *see* Orders (Fig. 12).

IRON AGE: in Britain the period from *c.* 600 B.C. to the coming of the Romans. The term is also used for those un-Romanized native communities which survived until the Saxon incursions.

JAMB: straight side of an archway, doorway, or window.

KEEL MOULDING: moulding whose outline is in section like that of the keel of a ship.

KEEP: massive tower of a Norman castle.

KEYSTONE: middle stone in an arch or a rib-vault.

KING-POST: see Roof (Fig. 14).

LABEL: see Hood-mould.

LABEL STOP: ornamental boss at the end of a hood-mould (q.v.).

LANCET WINDOW: slender pointed-arched window.

LANTERN: in architecture, a small circular or polygonal turret with windows all round crowning a roof (see Cupola) or a dome.

LANTERN CROSS: churchyard cross with lantern-shaped top usually with sculptured representations on the sides of the top.

LEAN-TO ROOF: roof with one slope only, built against a higher wall.

LESENE or PILASTER STRIP: pilaster without base or capital.

LIERNE: see Vault (Fig. 21).

LINENFOLD: Tudor panelling ornamented with a conventional representation of a piece of linen laid in vertical folds. The piece is repeated in each panel.

LINTEL: horizontal beam or stone bridging an opening.

LOGGIA: recessed colonnade (q.v.).

LONG AND SHORT WORK: Saxon quoins (q.v.) consisting of stones placed with the long sides alternately upright and horizontal.

LONG BARROW: unchambered Neolithic communal burial mound, wedge-shaped in plan, with the burial and occasional other structures massed at the broader end, from which the mound itself tapers in height; quarry ditches flank the mound.

LOUVRE: opening, often with lantern (q.v.) over, in the roof of a room to let the smoke from a central hearth escape.

LOWER PALAEOLITHIC: see Palaeolithic.

LOZENGE: diamond shape.

LUCARNE: small opening to let light in.

LUNETTE: tympanum (q.v.) or semicircular opening.

LYCH GATE: wooden gate structure with a roof and open sides placed at the entrance to a churchyard to provide space for the reception of a coffin. The word lych is Saxon and means a corpse.

LYNCHET: long terraced strip of soil accumulating on the downward side of prehistoric and medieval fields due to soil creep from continuous ploughing along the contours.

MACHICOLATION: projecting gallery on brackets constructed on the outside of castle towers or walls. The gallery has holes in the floor to drop missiles through.

MAJOLICA: ornamented glazed earthenware.

MANSARD: see Roof.

MATHEMATICAL TILES: small facing tiles the size of brick

headers, applied to timber-framed walls to make them appear brick-built.

MEGALITHIC TOMB: stone-built burial chamber of the New Stone Age covered by an earth or stone mound. The form was introduced to Britain from the Mediterranean area.

MERLON: *see* Battlement.

MESOLITHIC: 'Middle Stone' Age; the post-glacial period of hunting and fishing communities dating in Britain from *c.* 8000 B.C. to the arrival of Neolithic communities, with which they must have considerably overlapped.

METOPE: in classical architecture of the Doric order (q.v.) the space in the frieze between the triglyphs (Fig. 12).

MEZZANINE: low storey placed between two higher ones.

MISERERE: *see* Misericord.

MISERICORD: bracket placed on the underside of a hinged choir stall seat which, when turned up, provided the occupant of the seat with a support during long periods of standing (also called Miserere).

MODILLION: small bracket of which large numbers (modillion frieze) are often placed below a cornice (q.v.) in classical architecture.

MOTTE: steep mound forming the main feature of C11 and C12 castles.

MOTTE-AND-BAILEY: post-Roman and Norman defence system consisting of an earthen mound (the motte) topped with a wooden tower eccentrically placed within a bailey (q.v.), with enclosure ditch and 15—E.

palisade, and with the rare addition of an internal bank.

MOUCHETTE: tracery motif in curvilinear tracery, a curved dagger (q.v.), specially popular in the early C14 (Fig. 10).

Fig. 10

MULLION: vertical post or upright dividing a window into two or more 'lights'.

MULTIVALLATE: Of a hill-fort: defended by three or more concentric banks and ditches.

MUNTIN: post as a rule moulded and part of a screen.

NAIL-HEAD: E.E. ornamental motif, consisting of small pyramids regularly repeated (Fig. 11).

Fig. 11

NARTHEX: enclosed vestibule or covered porch at the main entrance to a church (*see* Galilee).

NEOLITHIC: 'New Stone' Age, dating in Britain from the appearance from the Continent of the first settled farming communities *c.* 3500 B.C. until the introduction of the Bronze Age.

NEWEL: central post in a circular or winding staircase; also the principal post when a flight of stairs meets a landing.

NOOK-SHAFT: shaft set in the

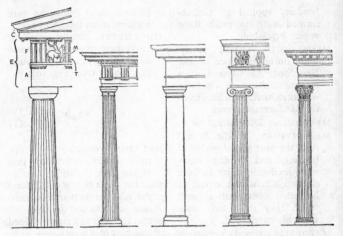

Fig. 12 – Orders of Columns (Greek Doric, Roman Doric, Tuscan Doric, Ionic, Corinthian) E, Entablature; C, Cornice; F, Frieze; A, Architrave; M, Metope; T, Triglyph.

angle of a pier or respond or wall, or the angle of the jamb of a window or doorway.

OBELISK: lofty pillar of square section tapering at the top and ending pyramidally.

OGEE: *see* Arch (Fig. 1c).

ORATORY: small private chapel in a house.

ORDER: (1) *of a doorway or window:* series of concentric steps receding towards the opening; (2) *in classical architecture:* column with base, shaft, capital, and entablature (q.v.) according to one of the following styles: Greek Doric, Roman Doric, Tuscan Doric, Ionic, Corinthian, Composite. The established details are very elaborate, and some specialist architectural work should be consulted for further guidance (*see* Fig. 12).

ORIEL: *see* Bay-Window.

OVERHANG: projection of the upper storey of a house.

OVERSAILING COURSES: series of stone or brick courses, each one projecting beyond the one below it.

PALAEOLITHIC: 'Old Stone' Age; the first period of human culture, commencing in the Ice Age and immediately prior to the Mesolithic; the Lower Palaeolithic is the older phase, the Upper Palaeolithic the later.

PALIMPSEST: (1) *of a brass:* where a metal plate has been re-used by turning over and engraving on the back; (2) *of a wall painting:* where one overlaps and partly obscures an earlier one.

PALLADIAN: architecture following the ideas and principles of Andrea Palladio, 1518–80.

PANTILE: tile of curved S-shaped section.

PARAPET: low wall placed to protect any spot where there is a sudden drop, for example on a bridge, quay, hillside, housetop, etc.

PARGETTING: plaster work with patterns and ornaments either in relief or engraved on it.

PARVIS: term wrongly applied to a room over a church porch. These rooms were often used as a schoolroom or as a store room.

PATEN: plate to hold the bread at Communion or Mass.

PATERA: small flat circular or oval ornament in classical architecture.

PEDIMENT: low-pitched gable used in classical, Renaissance, and neo-classical architecture above a portico and above doors, windows, etc. It may be straight-sided or curved segmentally. *Broken Pediment:* one where the centre portion of the base is left open. *Open Pediment:* one where the centre portion of the sloping sides is left out.

PENDANT: boss (q.v.) elongated so that it seems to hang down.

PENDENTIF: concave triangular spandrel used to lead from the angle of two walls to the base of a circular dome. It is constructed as part of the hemisphere over a diameter the size of the diagonal of the basic square (Fig. 13).

PERP (PERPENDICULAR): historical division of English Gothic architecture covering the period from *c.*1335–50 to *c.*1530.

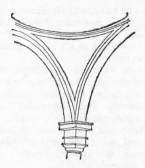

Fig. 13

PIANO NOBILE: principal storey of a house with the reception rooms; usually the first floor.

PIAZZA: open space surrounded by buildings; in C17 and C18 England sometimes used to mean a long colonnade or loggia.

PIER: strong, solid support, frequently square in section or of composite section (compound pier).

PIETRA DURA: ornamental or scenic inlay by means of thin slabs of stone.

PILASTER: shallow pier attached to a wall. *Termini Pilasters:* pilasters with sides tapering downwards.

PILLAR PISCINA: free-standing piscina on a pillar.

PINNACLE: ornamental form crowning a spire, tower, buttress, etc., usually of steep pyramidal, conical, or some similar shape.

PISCINA: basin for washing the Communion or Mass vessels, provided with a drain. Generally set in or against the wall to the S of an altar.

PLAISANCE: summer-house, pleasure house near a mansion.

PLATE TRACERY: *see* Tracery.

PLINTH: projecting base of a wall or column, generally chamfered (q.v.) or moulded at the top.

POND BARROW: rare type of Bronze Age barrow consisting of a circular depression, usually paved, and containing a number of cremation burials.

POPPYHEAD: ornament of leaf and flower type used to decorate the tops of bench- or stall-ends.

PORTCULLIS: gate constructed to rise and fall in vertical grooves; used in gateways of castles.

PORTE COCHÈRE: porch large enough to admit wheeled vehicles.

PORTICO: centre-piece of a house or a church with classical detached or attached columns and a pediment. A portico is called *prostyle* or *in antis* according to whether it projects from or recedes into a building. In a portico *in antis* the columns range with the side walls.

POSTERN: small gateway at the back of a building.

PREDELLA: in an altar-piece the horizontal strip below the main representation, often used for a number of subsidiary representations in a row.

PRESBYTERY: the part of the church lying E of the choir. It is the part where the altar is placed.

PRINCIPAL: *see* Roof (Fig. 14).

PRIORY: monastic house whose head is a prior or prioress, not an abbot or abbess.

PROSTYLE: with free-standing columns in a row.

PULPITUM: stone screen in a major church provided to shut off the choir from the nave and also as a backing for the return choir stalls.

PULVINATED FRIEZE: frieze with a bold convex moulding.

PURLIN: *see* Roof (Figs. 14, 15).

PUTTO: small naked boy.

QUADRANGLE: inner courtyard in a large building.

QUARRY: in stained-glass work, a small diamond or square-shaped piece of glass set diagonally.

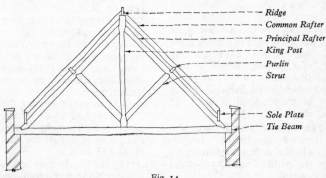

Ridge
Common Rafter
Principal Rafter
King Post
Purlin
Strut
Sole Plate
Tie Beam

Fig. 14

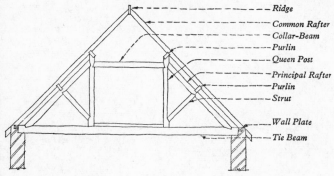

Fig. 15

QUATREFOIL: *see* Foil.

QUEEN-POSTS: *see* Roof (Fig. 15).

QUOINS: dressed stones at the angles of a building. Sometimes all the stones are of the same size; more often they are alternately large and small.

RADIATING CHAPELS: chapels projecting radially from an ambulatory or an apse.

RAFTER: *see* Roof.

RAMPART: stone wall or wall of earth surrounding a castle, fortress, or fortified city.

RAMPART-WALK: path along the inner face of a rampart.

REBATE: continuous rectangular notch cut on an edge.

REBUS: pun, a play on words. The literal translation and illustration of a name for artistic and heraldic purposes (Belton = bell, tun).

REEDING: decoration with parallel convex mouldings touching one another.

REFECTORY: dining hall; *see* Frater.

RENDERING: plastering of an outer wall.

REPOUSSÉ: decoration of metal work by relief designs, formed by beating the metal from the back.

REREDOS: structure behind and above an altar.

RESPOND: half-pier bonded into a wall and carrying one end of an arch.

RETABLE: altar-piece, a picture or piece of carving, standing behind and attached to an altar.

RETICULATION: *see* Tracery (Fig. 20).

REVEAL: that part of a jamb (q.v.) which lies between the glass or door and the outer surface of the wall.

RIB-VAULT: *see* Vault.

ROCOCO: latest phase of the Baroque style, current in most Continental countries between *c.*1720 and *c.* 1760.

ROLL MOULDING: moulding of semicircular or more than semicircular section.

ROMANESQUE: that style in architecture which was current in the CII and CI2 and pre-

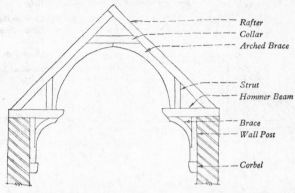

Fig. 16

ROOD SCREEN: *see* Screen.

ceded the Gothic style (in England often called Norman). (Some scholars extend the use of the term Romanesque back to the C10 or C9.)

ROMANO-BRITISH: A somewhat vague term applied to the period and cultural features of Britain affected by the Roman occupation of the C1–5 A.D.

ROOD: cross or crucifix.

ROOD LOFT: singing gallery on the top of the rood screen, often supported by a coving.

ROOD SCREEN: *see* Screen.

ROOD STAIRS: stairs to give access to the rood loft.

ROOF: *Single-framed:* if consisting entirely of transverse members (such as rafters with or without braces, collars, tie-beams, king-posts or queen-posts, etc.) not tied together longitudinally. *Double-framed:* if longitudinal members (such as a ridge beam and purlins) are employed. As a rule in such cases the rafters are divided into stronger principals and weaker subsidiary rafters.

Hipped: roof with sloped instead of vertical ends. *Mansard:* roof with a double slope, the lower slope being larger and steeper than the upper. *Saddleback:* tower roof shaped like an ordinary gabled timber roof. The following members have special names: *Rafter:* roof-timber sloping up from the wall plate to the ridge. *Principal:* principal rafter, usually corresponding to the main bay divisions of the nave or chancel below. *Wall Plate:* timber laid longitudinally on the top of a wall. *Purlin:* longitudinal member laid parallel with wall plate and ridge beam some way up the slope of the roof. *Tie-beam:* beam connecting the two slopes of a roof across at its foot, usually at the height of the wall plate, to prevent the roof from spreading. *Collar-beam:* tie-beam applied higher up the slope of the roof. *Strut:* upright timber connecting the tie-beam with the rafter above it. *King-post:* upright timber connecting a tie-beam and collar-beam with the ridge beam. *Queen-posts:* two struts placed symmetrically on a tie-beam or collar-beam. *Braces:* inclined timbers inserted to strengthen others. Usually braces connect a collar-beam with the rafters below or a tie-beam with the wall below. Braces can be straight or curved (also called arched). *Hammer-beam:* beam projecting at right angles, usually from the top of a wall, to carry arched braces or struts and arched braces (*see* Figs. 14, 15, 16).

ROSE WINDOW (or WHEEL WINDOW): circular window with patterned tracery arranged to radiate from the centre.

ROTUNDA: building circular in plan.

RUBBLE: building stones, not square or hewn, nor laid in regular courses.

RUSTICATION: *rock-faced* if the surfaces of large blocks of ashlar stone are left rough like rock; *smooth* if the ashlar blocks are smooth and separated by V-joints; *banded* if the separation by V-joints applies only to the horizontals.

S ADDLEBACK: *see* Roof.

SALTIRE CROSS: equal-limbed cross placed diagonally.

SANCTUARY: (1) area around the main altar of a church (*see* Presbytery); (2) sacred site consisting of wood or stone uprights enclosed by a circular bank and ditch. Beginning in the Neolithic, they were elaborated in the succeeding Bronze Age. The best known examples are Stonehenge and Avebury.

SARCOPHAGUS: elaborately carved coffin.

SCAGLIOLA: material composed of cement and colouring matter to imitate marble.

SCALLOPED CAPITAL: development of the block capital (q.v.) in which the single semi-circular surface is elaborated into a series of truncated cones (Fig. 17).

Fig. 17

SCARP: artificial cutting away of the ground to form a steep slope.

SCREEN: *Parclose screen:* screen separating a chapel from the rest of a church. *Rood screen:* screen below the rood (q.v.), usually at the W end of a chancel.

SCREENS PASSAGE: passage between the entrances to kitchen, buttery, etc., and the screen behind which lies the hall of a medieval house.

SEDILIA: seats for the priests (usually three) on the S side of the chancel of a church.

SEGMENTAL ARCH: *see* Arch.

SET-OFF: *see* Weathering.

SEXPARTITE: *see* Vaulting.

SGRAFFITO: pattern incised into plaster so as to expose a dark surface underneath.

SHAFT-RING: motif of the C12 and C13 consisting of a ring

round a circular pier or a shaft
attached to a pier.

SHEILA-NA-GIG: fertility figure,
usually with legs wide open.

SILL: lower horizontal part of the
frame of a window.

SLATEHANGING: the covering
of walls by overlapping rows
of slates, on a timber substructure.

SOFFIT: underside of an arch,
lintel, etc.

SOLAR: upper living-room of a
medieval house.

SOPRAPORTE: painting above
the door of a room, usual in the
C17 and C18.

SOUNDING BOARD: horizontal
board or canopy over a pulpit.
Also called Tester.

SPANDREL: triangular surface
between one side of an arch,
the horizontal drawn from its
apex, and the vertical drawn
from its springer; also the
surface between two arches.

SPERE-TRUSS: roof truss on two
free-standing posts to mask the
division between screens passage and hall. The screen itself,
where a spere-truss exists, was
originally movable.

SPIRE: tall pyramidal or conical
pointed erection often built on
top of a tower, turret, etc.
Broach Spire: spire which is
generally octagonal in plan
rising from the top or parapet
of a square tower. A small
inclined piece of masonry
covers the vacant triangular
space at each of the four angles
of the square and is carried up
to a point along the diagonal
sides of the octagon. *Needle
Spire:* thin spire rising from
the centre of a tower roof, well
inside the parapet.

SPIRELET: *see* Flèche.

SPLAY: chamfer, usually of the
jamb of a window.

SPRINGING: level at which an
arch rises from its supports.

SQUINCH: arch or system of concentric arches thrown across
the angle between two walls to
support a superstructure, for
example a dome (Fig. 18).

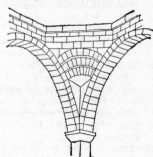

Fig. 18

SQUINT: hole cut in a wall or
through a pier to allow a view
of the main altar of a church
from places whence it could
not otherwise be seen (also
called Hagioscope).

STALL: carved seat, one of a row,
made of wood or stone.

STAUNCHION: upright iron or
steel member.

STEEPLE: the tower of a church
together with a spire, cupola,
etc.

STIFF-LEAF: E.E. type of foliage
of many-lobed shapes (Fig. 19).

Fig. 19

STILTED: *see* Arch.

STOREY-POSTS: the principal posts of a timber-framed wall.

STOUP: vessel for the reception of holy water, usually placed near a door.

STRAINER ARCH: arch inserted across a room to prevent the walls from leaning.

STRAPWORK: C16 decoration consisting of interlaced bands, and forms similar to fretwork or cut and bent leather.

STRETCHER: *see* Brickwork.

STRING COURSE: projecting horizontal band or moulding set in the surface of a wall.

STRUT: *see* Roof.

STUCCO: plaster work.

STUDS: the subsidiary vertical timber members of a timber-framed wall.

SWAG: festoon formed by a carved piece of cloth suspended from both ends.

TABERNACLE: richly ornamented niche (q.v.) or free-standing canopy. Usually contains the Holy Sacrament.

TARSIA: inlay in various woods.

TAZZA: shallow bowl on a foot.

TERMINAL FIGURES (TERMS, TERMINI): upper part of a human figure growing out of a pier, pilaster, etc., which tapers towards the base. *See also* Caryatids, Pilasters.

TERRACOTTA: burnt clay, unglazed.

TESSELLATED PAVEMENT: mosaic flooring, particularly Roman, consisting of small 'tesserae' or cubes of glass, stone, or brick.

TESSERAE: *see* Tessellated Pavement.

TESTER: *see* Sounding Board.

TETRASTYLE: having four detached columns.

THREE-DECKER PULPIT: pulpit with Clerk's Stall below and Reading Desk below the Clerk's Stall.

TIE-BEAM: *see* Roof (Figs. 14, 15).

TIERCERON: *see* Vault (Fig. 21).

TILEHANGING: *see* Slatehanging.

TIMBER-FRAMING: method of construction where walls are built of timber framework with the spaces filled in by plaster or brickwork. Sometimes the timber is covered over with plaster or boarding laid horizontally.

TOMB-CHEST: chest-shaped stone coffin, the most usual medieval form of funeral monument.

TOUCH: soft black marble quarried near Tournai.

TOURELLE: turret corbelled out from the wall.

TRACERY: intersecting ribwork in the upper part of a window,

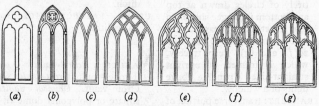

(a)　　*(b)*　　*(c)*　　*(d)*　　*(e)*　　*(f)*　　*(g)*

Fig. 20

or used decoratively in blank arches, on vaults, etc. *Plate tracery: see* Fig. 20(*a*). Early form of tracery where decoratively shaped openings are cut through the solid stone infilling in a window head. *Bar tracery:* a form introduced into England *c.*1250. Intersecting ribwork made up of slender shafts, continuing the lines of the mullions of windows up to a decorative mesh in the head of the window. *Geometrical tracery: see* Fig. 20(*b*). Tracery characteristic of *c.*1250–1310 consisting chiefly of circles or foiled circles. *Y-tracery: see* Fig. 20(*c*). Tracery consisting of a mullion which branches into two forming a Y shape; typical of *c.* 1300. *Intersected tracery: see* Fig. 20(*d*). Tracery in which each mullion of a window branches out into two curved bars in such a way that every one of them is drawn with the same radius from a different centre. The result is that every light of the window is a lancet and every two, three, four, etc., lights together form a pointed arch. This treatment also is typical of *c.*1300. *Reticulated tracery: see* Fig. 20(*e*). Tracery typical of the early C14 consisting entirely of circles drawn at top and bottom into ogee shapes so that a net-like appearance results. *Panel tracery: see* Fig. 20(*f*) and (*g*). Perp tracery, which is formed of upright straight-sided panels above lights of a window.

TRANSEPT: transverse portion of a cross-shaped church.

TRANSOM: horizontal bar across the openings of a window.

TRANSVERSE ARCH: *see* Vault.

TRIBUNE: *see* Gallery.

TRICIPUT, SIGNUM TRICIPUT: sign of the Trinity expressed by three faces belonging to one head.

TRIFORIUM: arcaded wall passage or blank arcading facing the nave at the height of the aisle roof and below the clerestory (q.v.) windows. (*See* Gallery.)

TRIGLYPHS: blocks with vertical grooves separating the metopes (q.v.) in the Doric frieze (Fig. 12).

TROPHY: sculptured group of arms or armour, used as a memorial of victory.

TRUMEAU: stone mullion (q.v.) supporting the tympanum (q.v.) of a wide doorway.

TUMULUS: *see* Barrow.

TURRET: very small tower, round or polygonal in plan.

TUSCAN: *see* Order.

TYMPANUM: space between the lintel of a doorway and the arch above it.

UNDERCROFT: vaulted room, sometimes underground, below a church or chapel.

UNIVALLATE: of a hill-fort: defended by a single bank and ditch.

UPPER PALAEOLITHIC: *see* Palaeolithic.

VAULT: *Barrel-vault: see* Tunnel-vault. *Cross-vault: see* Groin-vault. *Domical vault:* square or polygonal dome rising direct on a square or poly-

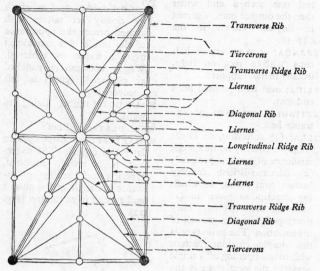

Transverse Rib

Tiercerons

Transverse Ridge Rib

Liernes

Diagonal Rib

Liernes

Longitudinal Ridge Rib

Liernes

Liernes

Transverse Ridge Rib

Diagonal Rib

Tiercerons

Fig. 21

gonal bay, the curved surfaces separated by groins (q.v.). *Fan-vault:* Late Medieval vault where all ribs springing from one springer are of the same length, the same distance from the next, and the same curvature. *Groin-vault* or *Cross-vault:* vault of two tunnel-vaults of identical shape intersecting each other at r. angles. Chiefly Norman and Renaissance. *Lierne:* tertiary rib, that is, rib which does not spring either from one of the main springers or from the central boss. Introduced in the C14, continues to the C16. *Quadripartite vault:* one wherein one bay of vaulting is divided into four parts. *Rib-vault:* vault with diagonal ribs projecting along the groins. *Ridge-rib:* rib along the longitudinal or transverse ridge of a vault. Introduced in the early C13. *Sexpartite vault:* one wherein one bay of quadripartite vaulting is divided into two parts transversely so that each bay of vaulting has six parts. *Tierceron:* secondary rib, that is, rib which issues from one of the main springers or the central boss and leads to a place on a ridge-rib. Introduced in the early C13. *Transverse arch:* arch separating one bay of a vault from the next. *Tunnel-vault* or *Barrel-vault:* vault of semicircular or pointed section. Chiefly Norman and Renaissance. (*See* Fig. 21.)

VAULTING SHAFT: vertical member leading to the springer of a vault.

VENETIAN WINDOW: window with three openings, the central one arched and wider than the outside ones. Current in England chiefly in the C17–18.

VERANDA: open gallery or balcony with a roof on light, usually metal, supports.

VESICA: oval with pointed head and foot.

VESTIBULE: anteroom or entrance hall.

VILLA: (1) according to Gwilt (1842) 'a country house for the residence of opulent persons'; (2) Romano-British country houses cum farms, to which the description given in (1) more or less applies. They developed with the growth of urbanization. The basic type is the simple corridor pattern with rooms opening off a single passage; the next stage is the addition of wings, while the courtyard villa fills a square plan with subsidiary buildings and an enclosure wall with a gate facing the main corridor block.

VITRIFIED: made similar to glass.

VITRUVIAN OPENING: A door or window which diminishes towards the top, as advocated by Vitruvius, book IV, chapter VI.

VOLUTE: spiral scroll, one of the component parts of an Ionic column (*see* Order).

VOUSSOIR: wedge-shaped stone used in arch construction.

WAGON ROOF: roof in which by closely set rafters with arched braces the appearance of the inside of a canvas tilt over a wagon is achieved. Wagon roofs can be panelled or plastered (ceiled) or left uncovered.

WAINSCOT: timber lining to walls.

WALL PLATE: *see* Roof.

WATERLEAF: leaf shape used in later C12 capitals. The waterleaf is a broad, unribbed, tapering leaf curving up towards the angle of the abacus and turned in at the top (Fig. 22).

Fig. 22

WEATHERBOARDING: overlapping horizontal boards, covering a timber-framed wall.

WEATHERING: sloped horizontal surface on sills, buttresses, etc., to throw off water.

WEEPERS: small figures placed in niches along the sides of some medieval tombs (also called Mourners).

WHEEL WINDOW: *see* Rose Window.

INDEX OF PLATES

INDEX OF ARTISTS

INDEX OF PLACES

*The references in brackets indicate the square in which the
place will be found on the map preceding the title-page.*

NOTES

NOTES

NOTES

NOTES

NOTES

NOTES